# Fundamental Equations of Dynamics

## KINEMATICS

### Particle Rectilinear Motion

**Variable a**

$$a = \frac{dv}{dt}$$

$$v = \frac{ds}{dt}$$

$$a\,ds = v\,dv$$

**Constant $a = a_c$**

$$v = v_0 + a_c t$$

$$s = s_0 + v_0 t + \tfrac{1}{2} a_c t^2$$

$$v^2 = v_0^2 + 2a_c(s - s_0)$$

### Particle Curvilinear Motion

**x, y, z Coordinates**

$$v_x = \dot{x} \quad a_x = \ddot{x}$$
$$v_y = \dot{y} \quad a_y = \ddot{y}$$
$$v_z = \dot{z} \quad a_z = \ddot{z}$$

**r, θ, z Coordinates**

$$v_r = \dot{r} \quad a_r = \ddot{r} - r\dot{\theta}^2$$
$$v_\theta = r\dot{\theta} \quad a_\theta = r\ddot{\theta} + 2\dot{r}\dot{\theta}$$
$$v_z = \dot{z} \quad a_z = \ddot{z}$$

**n, t, b Coordinates**

$$v = \dot{s} \quad \Big| \quad a_t = \dot{v} = v\frac{dv}{ds}$$

$$a_n = \frac{v^2}{\rho} \quad \rho = \frac{[1 + (dy/dx)^2]^{3/2}}{|d^2y/dx^2|}$$

**Relative Motion**

$$\mathbf{v}_B = \mathbf{v}_A + \mathbf{v}_{B/A} \quad \mathbf{a}_B = \mathbf{a}_A + \mathbf{a}_{B/A}$$

### Rigid Body Motion About a Fixed Axis

**Variable $\alpha$**

$$\alpha = \frac{d\omega}{dt}$$

$$\omega = \frac{d\theta}{dt}$$

$$\omega\,d\omega = \alpha\,d\theta$$

**Constant $\alpha = \alpha_c$**

$$\omega = \omega_0 + \alpha_c t$$

$$\theta = \theta_0 + \omega_0 t + \tfrac{1}{2}\alpha_c t^2$$

$$\omega^2 = \omega_0^2 + 2\alpha_c(\theta - \theta_0)$$

**For Point P**

$$s = \theta r \quad v = \omega r \quad a_t = \alpha r \quad a_n = \omega^2 r$$

### Relative General Plane Motion—Translating Axes

$$\mathbf{v}_B = \mathbf{v}_A + \mathbf{v}_{B/A(\text{pin})} \quad \mathbf{a}_B = \mathbf{a}_A + \mathbf{a}_{B/A(\text{pin})}$$

### Relative General Plane Motion—Trans. and Rot. Axis

$$\mathbf{v}_B = \mathbf{v}_A + \Omega \times \mathbf{r}_{B/A} \times (\mathbf{v}_{B/A})_{xyz}$$

$$\mathbf{a}_B = \mathbf{a}_A + \Omega \times \mathbf{r}_{B/A} + \Omega \times (\Omega \times \mathbf{r}_{B/A}) +$$
$$2\Omega \times (\mathbf{v}_{B/A})_{xyz} \times (\mathbf{a}_{B/A})_{xyz}$$

## KINETICS

**Mass Moment of Inertia** $\quad I = \int r^2\,dm$

**Parallel-Axis Theorem** $\quad I = I_G + md^2$

**Radius of Gyration** $\quad k = \sqrt{\dfrac{I}{m}}$

### Equations of Motion

| | |
|---|---|
| *Particle* | $\Sigma \mathbf{F} = m\mathbf{a}$ |
| *Rigid Body* (Plane Motion) | $\Sigma F_x = m(a_G)_x$ $\Sigma F_y = m(a_G)_y$ $\Sigma M_G = I_G\alpha$ or $\Sigma M_P = \Sigma(\mathcal{M}_k)_P$ |

### Principle of Work and Energy

$$T_1 + U_{1-2} = T_2$$

### Kinetic Energy

| | |
|---|---|
| *Particle* | $T = \tfrac{1}{2}mv^2$ |
| *Rigid Body* (Plane Motion) | $T = \tfrac{1}{2}mv_G^2 + \tfrac{1}{2}I_G\omega^2$ |

### Work

| | |
|---|---|
| Variable force | $U_F = \int F \cos\theta\,ds$ |
| Constant force | $U_F = (F_c \cos\theta)\,\Delta s$ |
| Weight | $U_W = -W\,\Delta y$ |
| Spring | $U_s = -(\tfrac{1}{2}ks_2^2 - \tfrac{1}{2}ks_1^2)$ |
| Couple moment | $U_M = M\,\Delta\theta$ |

### Power and Efficiency

$$P = \frac{dU}{dt} = \mathbf{F}_\wp\mathbf{v} \quad \epsilon = \frac{P_{\text{out}}}{P_{\text{in}}} = \frac{U_{\text{out}}}{U_{\text{in}}}$$

### Conservation of Energy Theorem

$$T_1 + V_1 = T_2 + V_2$$

### Potential Energy

$$V = V_g + V_e, \text{ where } V_g = \pm Wy, \; V_e = +\tfrac{1}{2}ks^2$$

### Principle of Linear Impulse and Momentum

| | |
|---|---|
| Particle | $m\mathbf{v}_1 + \Sigma\int \mathbf{F}\,dt = m\mathbf{v}_2$ |
| Rigid Body | $m(\mathbf{v}_G)_1 + \Sigma\int \mathbf{F}\,dt = m(\mathbf{v}_G)_2$ |

### Conservation of Linear Momentum

$$\Sigma(\text{syst. } m\mathbf{v})_1 = \Sigma(\text{syst. } m\mathbf{v})_2$$

**Coefficient of Restitution** $\quad e = \dfrac{(v_B)_2 - (v_A)_2}{(v_A)_1 - (v_B)_1}$

### Principle of Angular Impulse and Momentum

| | |
|---|---|
| Particle | $(\mathbf{H}_O)_1 + \Sigma\int \mathbf{M}_O\,dt = (\mathbf{H}_O)_2$ where $H_O = (d)(mv)$ |
| Rigid Body (Plane motion) | $(\mathbf{H}_G)_1 + \Sigma\int \mathbf{M}_G\,dt = (\mathbf{H}_G)_2$ where $H_G = I_G\omega$ $(\mathbf{H}_O)_1 + \Sigma\int \mathbf{M}_O\,dt = (\mathbf{H}_O)_2$ where $H_O = I_O\omega$ |

### Conservation of Angular Momentum

$$\Sigma(\text{syst. } \mathbf{H})_1 = \Sigma(\text{syst. } \mathbf{H})_2$$

## SI Prefixes

| Multiple | Exponential Form | Prefix | SI Symbol |
|---|---|---|---|
| 1 000 000 000 | $10^9$ | giga | G |
| 1 000 000 | $10^6$ | mega | M |
| 1 000 | $10^3$ | kilo | k |

| Submultiple | | | |
|---|---|---|---|
| 0.001 | $10^{-3}$ | milli | m |
| 0.000 001 | $10^{-6}$ | micro | $\mu$ |
| 0.000 000 001 | $10^{-9}$ | nano | n |

# DYNAMICS

# ENGINEERING MECHANICS
## Dynamics
### SI EDITION

**Third Edition**

**R. C. Hibbeler**

**SI conversion by S. C. Fan**

Singapore  London  New York  Toronto  Sydney  Tokyo  Madrid
Mexico City  Munich  Paris  Capetown  Hong Kong  Montreal

Published in 2004 by
Prentice Hall
Pearson Education South Asia Pte Ltd
23/25 First Lok Yang Road
Jurong
Singapore 629733

Pearson Education offices in Asia: *Bangkok, Beijing, Hong Kong, Jakarta, Kuala Lumpur, Manila, New Delhi, Seoul, Shanghai, Singapore, Taipei, Tokyo*

Original edition published by:
Prentice-Hall, Inc.
Copyright © 2004 by R. C. Hibbeler

Printed in Singapore

5  4  3

08  07  06  05

ISBN 013-124-845-6 (pbk)
ISBN 013-127-843-6 (hbk)

PEARSON
Prentice
Hall

## TO THE STUDENT

With the hope that this work will stimulate an interest in Engineering Mechanics and provide an acceptable guide to its understanding.

The main purpose of this book is to provide the student with a clear and thorough presentation of the theory and applications of engineering mechanics. To achieve this objective, the author has by no means worked alone; to a large extent, this book has been shaped by the comments and suggestions of hundreds of reviewers in the teaching profession as well as many of the author's students.

## New Features

Some unique features used throughout this third edition include the following:

- **Illustrations.** Throughout the book, new photorealistic illustrations have been added that provide a strong connection to the 3-D nature of engineering. In addition, particular attention has been placed on providing a view of any physical object, its dimensions, and the vectors applied to it in a manner that can be easily understood.

- **Problems.** The problems sets have been revised so that instructors can select both design and analysis problems having a wide range of difficulty. Apart from the author, two other professionals have checked all the problems for clarity and accuracy of the solutions. At the end of some chapters, design projects are included.

- **Review Material.** New end-of-chapter review sections have been added to help students recall and study key chapter points.

Of course, the hallmarks of the book remain the same: Where necessary, a strong emphasis is placed on drawing a free-body diagram, and the importance of selecting an appropriate coordinate system, and associated sign convention for vector components is stressed when the equations of mechanics are applied.

## Contents

The book is divided into eleven chapters, in which the principles introduced are first applied to simple, then to more complicated situations. The kinematics of a particle is discussed in Chapter 12, followed by a discussion of particle kinetics in Chapter 13 (equation of motion), Chapter 14 (work and energy), and Chapter 15 (impulse and momentum). The concepts of particle dynamics contained in these four chapters are then summarized in a "review" section, and the student is given the chance to identify and solve a variety of problems. A similar sequence of presentation is given for the planar motion of a rigid body: Chapter 16 (planar kinematics), Chapter 17 (equations of motion), Chapter 18 (work and energy), and Chapter 19 (impulse and momentum), followed by a summary and review set of problems for these chapters.

If time permits, some of the material involving three-dimensional rigid-body motion may be included in the course. The kinematics and kinetics of this motion are discussed in Chapters 20 and 21, respectively. Chapter 22 (vibrations) may be included if the student has the necessary mathematical background. Sections of the book which are considered to be beyond the scope of the basic dynamics course are indicated by a star ($\star$) and may be omitted. Note that this material also provides a suitable reference for basic principles when it is discussed in more advanced courses.

**Alternative Coverage.** At the discretion of the instructor, it is possible to cover Chapter 12 through 19 in the following order with no loss in continuity: Chapers 12 and 16 (kinematics), Chapters 13 and 17 (equations of motion), Chapters 14 and 18 (work and energy), and Chapters 15 and 19 (impulse and momentum).

---

## Special Features

**Organization and Approach.** The contents of each chapter are organized into well-defined sections that contain an explanation of specific topics, illustrative example problems, and a set of homework problems. The topics within each section are placed into subgroups defined by boldface titles. The purpose of this is to present a structured method for introducing each new definition or concept and to make the book convenient for later reference and review.

**Chapter Contents.** Each chapter begins with an illustration demonstrating a broad-range application of the material within the chapter. A bulleted list of the chapter contents is provided to give a general overview of the material that will be covered.

**Free-Body Diagrams.** The first step to solving most mechanics problems requires drawing a diagram. By doing so, the student forms the habit of tabulating the necessary data while focusing on the physical aspects of the problem and its associated geometry. If this step is performed correctly, applying the relevant equations of mechanics becomes somewhat methodical since the data can be taken directly from the diagram. This step is particularly important when solving equilibrium problems, and for this reason drawing free-body diagrams is strongly emphasized throughout the book. In particular, special sections and examples are devoted to show

how to draw free-body diagrams, and specific homework problems in many sections of the book have been added to develop this practice.

**Procedures for Analysis.**   Found after many of the sections of the book, this unique feature provides the student with a logical and orderly method to follow when applying the theory. The example problems are solved using this outlined method in order to clarify its numerical application. It is to be understood, however, that once the relevant principles have been mastered and enough confidence and judgment have been obtained, the student can then develop his or her own procedures for solving problems.

**Photographs.**   Many photographs are used throughout the book to explain how the principles of mechanics apply to real-world situations. In some sections, photographs have been used to show how engineers must first make an idealized model for analysis and then proceed to draw a free-body diagram of this model in order to apply the theory.

**Important Points.**   This feature provides a review or summary of the most important concepts in a section and highlights the most significant points that should be realized when applying the theory to solve problems.

**Conceptual Understanding.**   Through the use of photographs placed throughout the book, theory is applied in a simplified way in order to illustrate some of its more important conceptual features and instill the physical meaning of many of the terms used in the equations. These simplified applications increase interest in the subject matter and better prepare the student to understand the examples and solve problems.

**Example Problems.**   All the example problems are presented in a concise manner and in a style that is easy to understand.

**Homework Problems**

- **Free-Body Diagram Problems.** Many sections of the book contain introductory problems that only require drawing the free-body diagram for the specific problems within a problem set. These assignments will impress upon the student the importance of mastering this skill as a requirement for a complete solution of any equilibrium problem.
- **General Analysis and Design Problems.** The majority of problems in the book depict realistic situations encountered in engineering practice. Some of these problems come from actual products used in industry and are stated as such. It is hoped that this realism will both stimulate the student's interest in engineering mechanics and provide a means for developing the skill to reduce any such problem from its physical description to a model or symbolic representation to which the principles of mechanics may be applied.
- Throughout the book, all problems use SI units. Furthermore, in any set, an attempt has been made to arrange the problems in order of increasing difficulty. (Review problems at the end of each chapter are presented in random order.) The answers to all but every fourth problem are listed in the back of the book. To alert the user to a problem without a reported answer, an asterisk (*) is placed before the problem number.

- **Computer Problems.** An effort has been made to include some problems that may be solved using a numerical procedure executed on either a desktop computer or a programmable pocket calculator. Suitable numerical techniques along with associated computer programs are given in Appendix B. The intent here is to broaden the student's capacity for using other forms of mathematical analysis without sacrificing the time needed to focus on the application of the principles of mechanics. Problems of this type, which either can or must be solved using numerical procedures, are identified by a "square" symbol (■) preceding the problem number.

- **Design Projects.** At the end of some of the chapters, design projects have been included. It is felt that this type of assignment should be given only after the student has developed a basic understanding of the subject matter. These projects focus on solving a problem by specifying the geometry of a structure or mechanical object needed for a specific purpose. A force analysis is required and, in many cases, safety and cost issues must be addressed

**Chapter Reviews.** New chapter review sections summarize key points of the chapter, often in bulleted lists.

**Appendices.** The appendices provide a source of mathematical formula and numerical analysis needed to solve the problems in the book. Appendix C provides a set of problems typically found on the Fundamentals of Engineering Examination. By providing a partial solution to all the problems, the student is given a chance to further practice his or her skills.

# Supplements

Hibbeler's robust supplements package supports students and instructors. The third edition features:

**Instructor's Resource CD-ROM and Instructor Access Code** This supplement includes Microsoft PowerPoint, .pdf, and .jpg files of text figures, PowerPoint slides of examples, as well as special "active learning" PowerPoint slides, student handouts, and teacher handouts created by Sudhir Mehta of North Dakota State University and Scott Danielson of Arizona State University.

The supplement also contains an instructor access code for www.prenhall.com/hibbeler. This codes lets professors download animations and pdf files of solutions, and provides instructor access to PH Grade Assist— Prentice Hall's on-line algorithmic homework and testing system.

**Instructor's Solutions Manual** *Statics*; *Dynamics*
Provides complete solutions supported by problem statements and problem figures.

*Dynamics* **Study Pack** Improved for the third edition, this supplement now contains chapter-by-chapter study materials, a Free-Body Diagram Workbook and access to the Problems Website, containing practice problems with full solutions. All materials are organized in a chapter-by-chapter format.

- **Student Study Materials:** New chapter-by-chapter review includes key points, equations, and check up questions.
- **Free-Body Diagram Workbook:** 75-page workbooks that step students through numerous free-body diagram problems. Full explanations and solutions are provided.

**Student Practice Problems Workbook**   *Statics*; *Dynamics*

Students may purchase a further Practice Problems Workbook containing more worked problems. Problems are partially solved and designed to help guide students through difficult topics.

**Companion Website**   www.prenhall.com/hibbeler. This password-protected website provides 1000 statics/dynamics problems with solutions. Problems and solutions are supplemented and do not appear in the third edition. Solutions contain both math and associated free-body diagrams. Students can use these for practice before quizzes and tests, as well as self-drill. For instructors: Downloadable version of the powerpoint slides and Instructor's Solutions Manual are available.

## Acknowledgments

The author has endeavored to write this book so that it will appeal to both the student and instructor. Through the years, many people have helped in its development, and I will always be grateful for their valued suggestions and comments. Specifically, I wish to personally thank the following individuals who have contributed their comments to the *Statics* and *Dynamics* series:

Paul Heyliger, *Colorado State University*
Kenneth Sawyers, *Lehigh University*
John Oyler, *University of Pittsburgh*
Glenn Beltz, *University of California—Santa Barbara*
Johannes Gessler, *Colorado State University*
Wilfred Nixon, *University of Iowa*
Jonathan Russell, *U.S. Coast Guard Academy*
Robert Hinks, *Arizona State University*
Cap. Mark Orwat, *U.S. Military Academy, West Point*
Cetin Cetinyaka, *Clarkson University*
Jack Xin, *Kansas State University*
Pierre Julien, *Colorado State University*
Stephen Bechtel, *Ohio State University*
W. A. Curtain, *Brown University*
Robert Oakberg, *Montana State University*
Richard Bennett, *University of Tennessee*

A particular note of thanks is also given to Professors Will Liddell, Jr. and Henry Kuhlman for their specific help. A special note of thanks is given to the accuracy checkers, Scott Hendricks of VPI and Karim Nohra of the University of South Florida, who diligently checked all of the text and problems. I should also like to acknowledge the proofreading assistance of my wife, Conny (Cornelie), during the time it has taken to prepare this manuscript for publication.

Lastly, many thanks are extended to all my students and to members of the teaching profession who have freely taken the time to send me their suggestions and comments. Since this list is too long to mention, it is hoped that those who have given help in this manner will accept this anonymous recognition.

I would greatly appreciate hearing from you if at any time you have any comments, suggestions, or problems related to any matters regarding this edition.

*Russell Charles Hibbeler*
hibbeler@bellsouth.net

# Dynamics

## 12

## Kinematics of a Particle   3

## 13

## Kinetics of a Particle: Force and Acceleration   97

## 14

## Kinetics of a Particle: Work and Energy   159

## 15

## Kinetics of a Particle: Impulse and Momentum   207

# 16

## Planar Kinematics of a Rigid Body   293

# 17

## Planar Kinetics of a Rigid Body: Force and Acceleration   377

# 18

## Planar Kinetics of a Rigid Body: Work and Energy   437

# 19

## Planar Kinetics of a Rigid Body: Impulse and Momentum   471

# DYNAMICS

Although each of these planes is rather large, from a distance their motion can be modeled as if each plane were a particle.

# Kinematics of a Particle

**CHAPTER OBJECTIVES**

- To introduce the concepts of position, displacement, velocity, and acceleration.
- To study particle motion along a straight line and represent this motion graphically.
- To investigate particle motion along a curved path using different coordinate systems.
- To present an analysis of dependent motion of two particles.
- To examine the principles of relative motion of two particles using translating axes.

## 12.1   Introduction

*Mechanics* is a branch of the physical sciences that is concerned with the state of rest or motion of bodies subjected to the action of forces. The mechanics of rigid bodies is divided into two areas: statics and dynamics. *Statics* is concerned with the equilibrium of a body that is either at rest or moves with constant velocity. The foregoing treatment is concerned with *dynamics* which deals with the accelerated motion of a body. Here the subject of dynamics will be presented in two parts: *kinematics*, which treats only the geometric aspects of the motion, and *kinetics*, which is the analysis of the forces causing the motion. To develop these principles, the dynamics of a particle will be discussed first, followed by topics in rigid-body dynamics in two and then three dimensions.

Historically, the principles of dynamics developed when it was possible to make an accurate measurement of time. Galileo Galilei (1564–1642) was one of the first major contributors to this field. His work consisted of experiments using pendulums and falling bodies. The most significant contributions in dynamics, however, were made by Isaac Newton (1642–1727), who is noted for his formulation of the three fundamental laws of motion and the law of universal gravitational attraction. Shortly after these laws were postulated, important techniques for their application were developed by Euler, D'Alembert, Lagrange, and others.

There are many problems in engineering whose solutions require application of the principles of dynamics. Typically the structural design of any vehicle, such as an automobile or airplane, requires consideration of the motion to which it is subjected. This is also true for many mechanical devices, such as motors, pumps, movable tools, industrial manipulators, and machinery. Furthermore, predictions of the motions of artificial satellites, projectiles, and spacecraft are based on the theory of dynamics. With further advances in technology, there will be an even greater need for knowing how to apply the principles of this subject.

**Problem Solving.** Dynamics is considered to be more involved than statics since both the forces applied to a body and its motion must be taken into account. Also, many applications require using calculus, rather than just algebra and trigonometry. In any case, the most effective way of learning the principles of dynamics is *to solve problems*. To be successful at this, it is necessary to present the work in a logical and orderly manner as suggested by the following sequence of steps:

1. Read the problem carefully and try to correlate the actual physical situation with the theory studied.

2. Draw any necessary diagrams and tabulate the problem data.

3. Establish a coordinate system and apply the relevant principles, generally in mathematical form.

4. Solve the necessary equations algebraically as far as practical; then, use a consistent set of units and complete the solution numerically. Report the answer with no more significant figures than the accuracy of the given data.

5. Study the answer using technical judgment and common sense to determine whether or not it seems reasonable.

6. Once the solution has been completed, review the problem. Try to think of other ways of obtaining the same solution.

In applying this general procedure, do the work as neatly as possible. Being neat generally stimulates clear and orderly thinking, and vice versa.

## 12.2 Rectilinear Kinematics: Continuous Motion

We will begin our study of dynamics by discussing the kinematics of a particle that moves along a rectilinear or straight line path. Recall that a *particle* has a mass but negligible size and shape. Therefore we must limit application to those objects that have dimensions that are of no consequence in the analysis of the motion. In most problems, one is interested in bodies of finite size, such as rockets, projectiles, or vehicles. Such objects may be considered as particles, provided motion of the body is characterized by motion of its mass center and any rotation of the body is neglected.

**Rectilinear Kinematics.**  The kinematics of a particle is characterized by specifying, at any given instant, the particle's position, velocity, and acceleration.

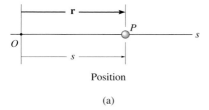

Position

(a)

**Position.**  The straight-line path of a particle will be defined using a single coordinate axis *s*, Fig. 12–1*a*. The origin *O* on the path is a fixed point, and from this point the *position vector* **r** is used to specify the location of the particle *P* at any given instant. Notice that **r** is *always* along the *s* axis, and so its direction never changes. What will change is its magnitude and its sense or arrowhead direction. For analytical work it is therefore convenient to represent **r** by an *algebraic scalar s*, representing the *position coordinate* of the particle, Fig. 12–1*a*. The magnitude of *s* (and **r**) is the distance from *O* to *P*, usually measured in meters (m), and the sense (or arrowhead direction of **r**) is defined by the algebraic sign on *s*. Although the choice is arbitrary, in this case *s* is positive since the coordinate axis is positive to the right of the origin. Likewise, it is negative if the particle is located to the left of *O*.

**Displacement.**  The *displacement* of the particle is defined as the *change* in its *position*. For example, if the particle moves from *P* to *P'*, Fig. 12–1*b*, the displacement is $\Delta \mathbf{r} = \mathbf{r}' - \mathbf{r}$. Using algebraic scalars to represent $\Delta \mathbf{r}$, we also have

$$\Delta s = s' - s$$

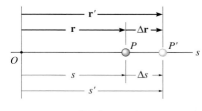

Displacement

(b)

**Fig. 12–1**

Here $\Delta s$ is *positive* since the particle's final position is to the *right* of its initial position, i.e., $s' > s$. Likewise, if the final position were to the *left* of its initial position, $\Delta s$ would be *negative*.

Since the displacement of a particle is a *vector quantity*, it should be distinguished from the distance the particle travels. Specifically, the *distance traveled* is a *positive scalar* which represents the total length of path over which the particle travels.

**Velocity.**   If the particle moves through a displacement $\Delta \mathbf{r}$ from $P$ to $P'$ during the time interval $\Delta t$, Fig. 12–1b, the *average velocity* of the particle during this time interval is

$$\mathbf{v}_{\text{avg}} = \frac{\Delta \mathbf{r}}{\Delta t}$$

If we take smaller and smaller values of $\Delta t$, the magnitude of $\Delta \mathbf{r}$ becomes smaller and smaller. Consequently, the *instantaneous velocity* is defined as $\mathbf{v} = \lim_{\Delta t \to 0} (\Delta \mathbf{r} / \Delta t)$, or

$$\mathbf{v} = \frac{d\mathbf{r}}{dt}$$

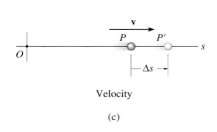

Velocity

(c)

Representing $\mathbf{v}$ as an algebraic scalar, Fig. 12–1c, we can also write

$$(\overset{+}{\to}) \qquad \boxed{v = \frac{ds}{dt}} \qquad (12\text{–}1)$$

Since $\Delta t$ or $dt$ is always positive, the sign used to define the *sense* of the velocity is the same as that of $\Delta s$ or $ds$. For example, if the particle is moving to the *right*, Fig. 12–1c, the velocity is *positive;* whereas if it is moving to the *left*, the velocity is *negative*. (This is emphasized here by the arrow written at the left of Eq. 12–1.) The *magnitude* of the velocity is known as the *speed*, and it is generally expressed in units of m/s.

Occasionally, the term "average speed" is used. The *average speed* is always a positive scalar and is defined as the total distance traveled by a particle, $s_T$, divided by the elapsed time $\Delta t$; i.e.,

$$(v_{\text{sp}})_{\text{avg}} = \frac{s_T}{\Delta t}$$

For example the particle in Fig. 12–1d travels along the path of length $s_T$ in time $\Delta t$, so its average speed is $(v_{\text{sp}})_{\text{avg}} = s_T / \Delta t$, but its average velocity is $v_{\text{avg}} = -\Delta s / \Delta t$.

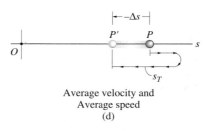

Average velocity and
Average speed
(d)

**Fig. 12–1**

**Acceleration.** Provided the velocity of the particle is known at the two points $P$ and $P'$, the *average acceleration* of the particle during the time interval $\Delta t$ is defined as

$$\mathbf{a}_{avg} = \frac{\Delta \mathbf{v}}{\Delta t}$$

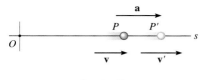

Acceleration

(e)

Here $\Delta \mathbf{v}$ represents the difference in the velocity during the time interval $\Delta t$, i.e., $\Delta \mathbf{v} = \mathbf{v}' - \mathbf{v}$, Fig. 12–1e.

The *instantaneous acceleration* at time $t$ is found by taking smaller and smaller values of $\Delta t$ and corresponding smaller and smaller values of $\Delta \mathbf{v}$, so that $\mathbf{a} = \lim\limits_{\Delta t \to 0} (\Delta \mathbf{v}/\Delta t)$ or, using algebraic scalars,

Deceleration

(f)

$(\stackrel{+}{\rightarrow})$ 
$$a = \frac{dv}{dt}$$
(12–2)

Substituting Eq. 12–1 into this result, we can also write

$(\stackrel{+}{\rightarrow})$ 
$$a = \frac{d^2 s}{dt^2}$$

Both the average and instantaneous acceleration can be either positive or negative. In particular, when the particle is *slowing down*, or its speed is decreasing, it is said to be *decelerating*. In this case, $v'$ in Fig. 12–1f is *less* than $v$, and so $\Delta v = v' - v$ will be negative. Consequently, $a$ will also be negative, and therefore it will act to the *left*, in the opposite *sense* to $v$. Also, note that when the *velocity* is *constant*, the *acceleration is zero* since $\Delta v = v - v = 0$. Units commonly used to express the magnitude of acceleration are m/s². 
A differential relation involving the displacement, velocity, and acceleration along the path may be obtained by eliminating the time differential $dt$ between Eqs. 12–1 and 12–2. Realize that although we can then establish another equation, by doing so it will *not* be independent of Eqs. 12–1 and 12–2. Show that

$(\stackrel{+}{\rightarrow})$ 
$$a \, ds = v \, dv$$
(12–3)

**Constant Acceleration, $a = a_c$.** When the acceleration is constant, each of the three kinematic equations $a_c = dv/dt$, $v = ds/dt$, and $a_c\, ds = v\, dv$ may be integrated to obtain formulas that relate $a_c$, $v$, $s$, and $t$.

**Velocity as a Function of Time.** Integrate $a_c = dv/dt$, assuming that initially $v = v_0$ when $t = 0$.

$$\int_{v_0}^{v} dv = \int_{0}^{t} a_c\, dt$$

$(\overset{+}{\rightarrow})$

$$\boxed{v = v_0 + a_c t}$$
Constant Acceleration

(12–4)

**Position as a Function of Time.** Integrate $v = ds/dt = v_0 + a_c t$, assuming that initially $s = s_0$ when $t = 0$.

$$\int_{s_0}^{s} ds = \int_{0}^{t} (v_0 + a_c t)\, dt$$

$(\overset{+}{\rightarrow})$

$$\boxed{s = s_0 + v_0 t + \tfrac{1}{2} a_c t^2}$$
Constant Acceleration

(12–5)

**Velocity as a Function of Position.** Either solve for $t$ in Eq. 12–4 and substitute into Eq. 12–5, or integrate $v\, dv = a_c\, ds$, assuming that initially $v = v_0$ at $s = s_0$.

$$\int_{v_0}^{v} v\, dv = \int_{s_0}^{s} a_c\, ds$$

$(\overset{+}{\rightarrow})$

$$\boxed{v^2 = v_0^2 + 2a_c(s - s_0)}$$
Constant Acceleration

(12–6)

This equation is not independent of Eqs. 12–4 and 12–5 since it can be obtained by eliminating $t$ between these equations.

The magnitudes and signs of $s_0$, $v_0$, and $a_c$, used in the above three equations are determined from the chosen origin and positive direction of the $s$ axis as indicated by the arrow written at the left of each equation. Also, it is important to remember that these equations are useful *only when the acceleration is constant and when $t = 0$, $s = s_0$, $v = v_0$.* A common example of constant accelerated motion occurs when a body falls freely toward the earth. If air resistance is neglected and the distance of fall is short, then the *downward* acceleration of the body when it is close to the earth is constant and approximately 9.81 m/s². The proof of this is given in Example 13.2.

## IMPORTANT POINTS

- Dynamics is concerned with bodies that have accelerated motion.
- Kinematics is a study of the geometry of the motion.
- Kinetics is a study of the forces that cause the motion.
- Rectilinear kinematics refers to straight-line motion.
- Speed refers to the magnitude of velocity.
- Average speed is the total distance traveled divided by the total time. This is different from the average velocity which is the displacement divided by the time.
- The acceleration, $a = dv/dt$, is negative when the particle is slowing down or decelerating.
- A particle can have an acceleration and yet have zero velocity.
- The relationship $a\,ds = v\,dv$ is derived from $a = dv/dt$ and $v = ds/dt$, by eliminating $dt$.

## PROCEDURE FOR ANALYSIS

The equations of rectilinear kinematics should be applied using the following procedure.

### Coordinate System

- Establish a position coordinate $s$ along the path and specify its *fixed origin* and positive direction.
- Since motion is along a straight line, the particle's position, velocity, and acceleration can be represented as algebraic scalars. For analytical work the sense of $s$, $v$, and $a$ is then determined from their *algebraic signs*.
- The positive sense for each scalar can be indicated by an arrow shown alongside each kinematic equation as it is applied.

### Kinematic Equations

- If a relationship is known between any *two* of the four variables $a$, $v$, $s$ and $t$, then a third variable can be obtained by using one of the kinematic equations, $a = dv/dt$, $v = ds/dt$ or $a\,ds = v\,dv$, which relates all three variables.*
- Whenever integration is performed, it is important that the position and velocity be known at a given instant in order to evaluate either the constant of integration if an indefinite integral is used, or the limits of integration if a definite integral is used.
- Remember that Eqs. 12–4 through 12–6 have only a limited use. Never apply these equations unless it is absolutely certain that the *acceleration is constant*.

*Some standard differentiation and integration formulas are given in Appendix A.

During the time this rocket undergoes rectilinear motion, its altitude as a function of time can be measured and expressed as $s = s(t)$. Its velocity can then be found using $v = ds/dt$, and its acceleration can be determined from $a = dv/dt$.

## EXAMPLE 12.1

The car in Fig. 12–2 moves in a straight line such that for a short time its velocity is defined by $v = (0.9t^2 + 0.6t)$ m/s, where $t$ is in seconds. Determine its position and acceleration when $t = 3$ s. When $t = 0$, $s = 0$.

**Fig. 12–2**

**Solution**

*Coordinate System.* The position coordinate extends from the fixed origin $O$ to the car, positive to the right.

*Position.* Since $v = f(t)$, the car's position can be determined from $v = ds/dt$, since this equation relates $v$, $s$, and $t$. Noting that $s = 0$ when $t = 0$, we have*

$$(\overset{+}{\rightarrow}) \qquad v = \frac{ds}{dt} = (0.9t^2 + 0.6t)$$

$$\int_0^s ds = \int_0^t (0.9t^2 + 0.6t)\, dt$$

$$s\Big|_0^s = (0.3t^3 + 0.3t^2)\Big|_0^t$$

$$s = 0.3t^3 + 0.3t^2$$

When $t = 3$ s,

$$s = 0.3(3^3) + 0.3(3^2) = 10.8 \text{ m} \qquad\qquad Ans.$$

*Acceleration.* Knowing $v = f(t)$, the acceleration is determined from $a = dv/dt$, since this equation relates $a$, $v$, and $t$.

$$(\overset{+}{\rightarrow}) \qquad a = \frac{dv}{dt} = \frac{d}{dt}(0.9t^2 + 0.6t)$$

$$= 1.8t + 0.6$$

When $t = 3$ s,

$$a = 1.8(3) + 0.6 = 6 \text{ m/s}^2 \rightarrow \qquad\qquad Ans.$$

The formulas for constant acceleration *cannot* be used to solve this problem. Why?

*The *same result* can be obtained by evaluating a constant of integration $C$ rather than using definite limits on the integral. For example, integrating $ds = (0.9t^2 + 0.6t)\, dt$ yields $s = 0.3t^3 + 0.3t^2 + C$. Using the condition that at $t = 0$, $s = 0$, then $C = 0$.

# EXAMPLE 12.2

A small projectile is fired vertically *downward* into a fluid medium with an initial velocity of 60 m/s. Due to the resistance of the fluid the projectile experiences a deceleration equal to $a = (-0.4v^3)$ m/s$^2$, where $v$ is in m/s. *Determine the projectile's velocity and position 4 s after it is fired.

**Solution**

*Coordinate System.* Since the motion is downward, the position coordinate is positive downward, with origin located at $O$, Fig. 12–3.

*Velocity.* Here $a = f(v)$ and so we must determine the velocity as a function of time using $a = dv/dt$, since this equation relates $v$, $a$, and $t$. (Why not use $v = v_0 + a_c t$?) Separating the variables and integrating, with $v_0 = 60$ m/s when $t = 0$, yields

$(+\downarrow)$
$$a = \frac{dv}{dt} = -0.4v^3$$

$$\int_{60 \text{ m/s}}^{v} \frac{dv}{-0.4v^3} = \int_{0}^{t} dt$$

$$\frac{1}{-0.4}\left(\frac{1}{-2}\right)\frac{1}{v^2}\bigg|_{60}^{v} = t - 0$$

$$\frac{1}{0.8}\left[\frac{1}{v^2} - \frac{1}{(60)^2}\right] = t$$

$$v = \left\{\left[\frac{1}{(60)^2} + 0.8t\right]^{-1/2}\right\} \text{ m/s}$$

Here the positive root is taken, since the projectile is moving downward. When $t = 4$ s,

$$v = 0.559 \text{ m/s} \downarrow \qquad \qquad Ans.$$

*Position.* Knowing $v = f(t)$, we can obtain the projectile's position from $v = ds/dt$, since this equation relates $s$, $v$, and $t$. Using the initial condition $s = 0$, when $t = 0$, we have

$(+\downarrow)$
$$v = \frac{ds}{dt} = \left[\frac{1}{(60)^2} + 0.8t\right]^{-1/2}$$

$$\int_{0}^{s} ds = \int_{0}^{t}\left[\frac{1}{(60)^2} + 0.8t\right]^{-1/2} dt$$

$$s = \frac{2}{0.8}\left[\frac{1}{(60)^2} + 0.8t\right]^{1/2}\bigg|_{0}^{t}$$

$$s = \frac{1}{0.4}\left\{\left[\frac{1}{(60)^2} + 0.8t\right]^{1/2} - \frac{1}{60}\right\} \text{ m}$$

When $t = 4$ s,

$$s = 4.43 \text{ m} \qquad \qquad Ans.$$

*Note that to be dimensionally homogeneous, the constant 0.4 has units of s/m$^2$.

**Fig. 12–3**

EXAMPLE 12.3

$v_B = 0$

$B$

$s_B$

$v_A = 75$ m/s

$A$

$s_A = 40$ m

$C$   $s$   $O$

**Fig. 12–4**

During a test a rocket is traveling upward at 75 m/s, and when it is 40 m from the ground its engine fails. Determine the maximum height $s_B$ reached by the rocket and its speed just before it hits the ground. While in motion the rocket is subjected to a constant downward acceleration of 9.81 m/s² due to gravity. Neglect the effect of air resistance.

**Solution**

*Coordinate System.*   The origin $O$ for the position coordinate $s$ is taken at ground level with positive upward, Fig. 12–4.

*Maximum Height.*   Since the rocket is traveling *upward*, $v_A = +75$ m/s when $t = 0$. At the maximum height $s = s_B$ the velocity $v_B = 0$. For the entire motion, the acceleration is $a_c = -9.81$ m/s² (negative since it acts in the *opposite* sense to positive velocity or positive displacement). Since $a_c$ is *constant* the rocket's position may be related to its velocity at the two points $A$ and $B$ on the path by using Eq. 12–6, namely,

$$(+\uparrow) \qquad v_B^2 = v_A^2 + 2a_c(s_B - s_A)$$
$$0 = (75 \text{ m/s})^2 + 2(-9.81 \text{ m/s}^2)(s_B - 40 \text{ m})$$
$$s_B = 327 \text{ m} \qquad\qquad\qquad Ans.$$

*Velocity.*   To obtain the velocity of the rocket just before it hits the ground, we can apply Eq. 12–6 between points $B$ and $C$, Fig. 12–4.

$$(+\uparrow) \qquad v_C^2 = v_B^2 + 2a_c(s_C - s_B)$$
$$= 0 + 2(-9.81 \text{ m/s}^2)(0 - 327 \text{ m})$$
$$v_C = -80.1 \text{ m/s} = 80.1 \text{ m/s} \downarrow \qquad Ans.$$

The negative root was chosen since the rocket is moving downward.
    Similarly, Eq. 12–6 may also be applied between points A and C, i.e.,

$$(+\uparrow) \qquad v_C^2 = v_A^2 + 2a_c(s_C - s_A)$$
$$= (75 \text{ m/s})^2 + 2(-9.81 \text{ m/s}^2)(0 - 40 \text{ m})$$
$$v_C = -80.1 \text{ m/s} = 80.1 \text{ m/s} \downarrow$$

*Note:* It should be realized that the rocket is subjected to a *deceleration* from $A$ to $B$ of 9.81 m/s², and then from $B$ to $C$ it is *accelerated* at this rate. Furthermore, even though the rocket momentarily comes to *rest* at $B$ ($v_B = 0$) the acceleration at $B$ is 9.81 m/s² downward!

# E X A M P L E   12.4

A metallic particle is subjected to the influence of a magnetic field as it travels downward through a fluid that extends from plate $A$ to plate $B$, Fig. 12–5. If the particle is released from rest at the midpoint $C$, $s = 100$ mm, and the acceleration is $a = (4s)$ m/s$^2$, where $s$ is in meters, determine the velocity of the particle when it reaches plate $B$, $s = 200$ mm, and the time it needs to travel from $C$ to $B$.

## Solution

*Coordinate System.*   As shown in Fig. 12–5, $s$ is taken positive downward, measured from plate $A$.

*Velocity.*   Since $a = f(s)$, the velocity as a function of position can be obtained by using $v\,dv = a\,ds$. Why not use the formulas for constant acceleration? Realizing that $v = 0$ at $s = 100$ mm $= 0.1$ m, we have

$(+\downarrow)$ 
$$v\,dv = a\,ds$$

$$\int_0^v v\,dv = \int_{0.1}^s 4s\,ds$$

$$\left.\tfrac{1}{2}v^2\right|_0^v = \left.\frac{4}{2}s^2\right|_{0.1}^s$$

$$v = 2(s^2 - 0.01)^{1/2} \qquad (1)$$

At $s = 200$ mm $= 0.2$ m,

$$v_B = 0.346 \text{ m/s} = 346 \text{ mm/s} \downarrow \qquad\qquad \textit{Ans.}$$

The positive root is chosen since the particle is traveling downward, i.e., in the $+s$ direction.

*Time.*   The time for the particle to travel from $C$ to $B$ can be obtained using $v = ds/dt$ and Eq. 1, where $s = 0.1$ m when $t = 0$. From Appendix A,

$(+\downarrow)$ 
$$ds = v\,dt$$

$$= 2(s^2 - 0.01)^{1/2}\,dt$$

$$\int_{0.1}^s \frac{ds}{(s^2 - 0.01)^{1/2}} = \int_0^t 2\,dt$$

$$\left. \ln(\sqrt{s^2 - 0.01} + s)\right|_{0.1}^s = \left. 2t \right|_0^t$$

$$\ln(\sqrt{s^2 - 0.01} + s) + 2.33 = 2t$$

At $s = 200$ mm $= 0.2$ m,

$$t = \frac{\ln(\sqrt{(0.2)^2 - 0.01} + 0.2) + 2.33}{2} = 0.658 \text{ s} \qquad \textit{Ans.}$$

100 mm

200 mm

**Fig. 12–5**

# E X A M P L E 12.5

A particle moves along a horizontal path with a velocity of $v = (3t^2 - 6t)$ m/s, where $t$ is the time in seconds. If it is initially located at the origin $O$, determine the distance traveled in 3.5 s, and the particle's average velocity and average speed during the time interval.

**Solution**

*Coordinate System.* Here we will assume positive motion to the right, measured from the origin $O$, Fig. 12–6a.

Fig. 12–6

*Distance Traveled.* Since $v = f(t)$, the position as a function of time may be found by integrating $v = ds/dt$ with $t = 0$, $s = 0$.

$$(\xrightarrow{\pm})$$
$$ds = v\,dt$$
$$= (3t^2 - 6t)\,dt$$
$$\int_0^s ds = 3\int_0^t t^2\,dt - 6\int_0^t t\,dt$$
$$s = (t^3 - 3t^2) \text{ m} \qquad (1)$$

In order to determine the distance traveled in 3.5 s, it is necessary to investigate the path of motion. The graph of the velocity function, Fig. 12–6b, reveals that for $0 \le t < 2$ s the velocity is *negative*, which means the particle is traveling to the *left*, and for $t > 2$ s the velocity is *positive*, and hence the particle is traveling to the *right*. Also, $v = 0$ at $t = 2$ s. The particle's position when $t = 0$, $t = 2$ s, and $t = 3.5$ s can be determined from Eq. 1. This yields

$$s|_{t=0} = 0 \qquad s|_{t=2\,s} = -4.0 \text{ m} \qquad s|_{t=3.5\,s} = 6.125 \text{ m}$$

(b)

Fig. 12–6

The path is shown in Fig. 12–6a. Hence, the distance traveled in 3.5 s is

$$s_T = 4.0 + 4.0 + 6.125 = 14.125 \text{ m} = 14.1 \text{ m} \qquad \textit{Ans.}$$

*Velocity.* The *displacement* from $t = 0$ to $t = 3.5$ s is

$$\Delta s = s|_{t=3.5\,s} - s|_{t=0} = 6.12 - 0 = 6.12 \text{ m}$$

and so the average velocity is

$$v_{\text{avg}} = \frac{\Delta s}{\Delta t} = \frac{6.12}{3.5 - 0} = 1.75 \text{ m/s} \rightarrow \qquad \textit{Ans.}$$

The average speed is defined in terms of the *distance traveled* $s_T$. This positive scalar is

$$(v_{\text{sp}})_{\text{avg}} = \frac{s_T}{\Delta t} = \frac{14.125}{3.5 - 0} = 4.04 \text{ m/s} \qquad \textit{Ans.}$$

# PROBLEMS

**12-1.** A bicyclist starts from rest and after traveling along a straight path a distance of 20 m reaches a speed of 30 km/h. Determine his acceleration if it is *constant*. Also, how long does it take to reach the speed of 30 km/h?

**12-2.** A car starts from rest and reaches a speed of 20 m/s after traveling 125 m along a straight road. Determine its constant acceleration and the time of travel.

**12-3.** A baseball is thrown downward from a 12.5-m tower with an initial speed of 4.5 m/s. Determine the speed at which it hits the ground and the time of travel.

**\*12-4.** A particle travels along a straight line such that in 2 s it moves from an initial position $s_A = +0.5$ m to a position $s_B = -1.5$ m. Then in another 4 s it moves from $s_B$ to $s_C = +2.5$ m. Determine the particle's average velocity and average speed during the 6-s time interval.

**12-5.** Traveling with an initial speed of 70 km/h, a car accelerates at 6000 km/h² along a straight road. How long will it take to reach a speed of 120 km/h? Also, through what distance does the car travel during this time?

**12-6.** A freight train travels at $v = 20(1 - e^{-t})$ m/s, where $t$ is the elapsed time in seconds. Determine the distance traveled in three seconds, and the acceleration at this time.

Prob. 12–6

**12-7.** The position of a particle along a straight line is given by $s = (0.3t^3 - 2.7t^2 + 4.5t)$ m where $t$ is in seconds. Determine its maximum acceleration and maximum velocity during the time interval $0 \le t \le 10$ s.

**\*12-8.** From approximately what floor of a building must a car be dropped from an at-rest position so that it reaches a speed of 25 m/s (90 km/h) when it hits the ground? Each floor is 3.6 m higher than the one below it. (*Note:* You may want to remember this when traveling 90 km/h.)

**12-9.** A car is to be hoisted by elevator to the fourth floor of a parking garage, which is 16 m above the ground. If the elevator can accelerate at 0.2 m/s², decelerate at 0.1 m/s², and reach a maximum speed of 2.7 m/s, determine the shortest time to make the lift, starting from rest and ending at rest.

**12-10.** A particle travels in a straight line such that for a short time $2\,\text{s} \le t \le 6\,\text{s}$ its motion is described by $v = (2/a)$ m/s, where $a$ is in m/s². If $v = 3$ m/s when $t = 2$ s, determine the particle's acceleration when $t = 3$ s.

**12-11.** The acceleration of a particle as it moves along a straight line is given by $a = (2t - 1)$ m/s², where $t$ is in seconds. If $s = 1$ m and $v = 2$ m/s when $t = 0$, determine the particle's velocity and position when $t = 6$ s. Also, determine the total distance the particle travels during this time period.

**\*12-12.** When a train is traveling along a straight track at 2 m/s, it begins to accelerate at $a = (60\,v^{-4})$ m/s², where $v$ is in m/s. Determine its velocity $v$ and the position 3 s after the acceleration.

Prob. 12–12

**12-13.** The position of a particle along a straight line is given by $s = (0.3t^3 - 2.7t^2 + 4.5t)$ m, where $t$ is in seconds. Determine the position of the particle when $t = 6$ s and the total distance it travels during the 6-s time interval. *Hint*: Plot the path to determine the total distance traveled.

**12-14.** The position of a particle on a straight line is given by $s = (t^3 - 9t^2 + 15t)$ m, where $t$ is in seconds. Determine the position of the particle when $t = 6$ s and the total distance it travels during the 6-s time interval. *Hint:* Plot the path to determine the total distance traveled.

**12-15.** A particle travels to the right along a straight line with a velocity $v = [5/(4 + s)]$ m/s, where $s$ is in meters. Determine its position when $t = 6$ s if $s = 5$ m when $t = 0$.

**\*12-16.** A particle travels to the right along a straight line with a velocity $v = [5/(4 + s)]$ m/s, where $s$ is in meters. Determine its deceleration when $s = 2$ m.

**12-17.** Two particles $A$ and $B$ start from rest at the origin $s = 0$ and move along a straight line such that $a_A = (6t - 3)$ m/s$^2$, and $a_B = (12t^2 - 8)$ m/s$^2$, where $t$ is in seconds. Determine the distance between them when $t = 4$ s and the total distance each has traveled in $t = 4$ s.

**12-18.** A car starts from rest and moves along a straight line with an acceleration of $a = (3s^{-1/3})$ m/s$^2$, where $s$ is in meters. Determine the car's acceleration when $t = 4$ s.

**12-19.** A stone $A$ is dropped from rest down a well, and in 1 s another stone $B$ is dropped from rest. Determine the distance between the stones another second later.

**\*12-20.** A stone $A$ is dropped from rest down a well, and in 1 s another stone $B$ is dropped from rest. Determine the time interval between the instant $A$ strikes the water and the instant $B$ strikes the water. Also, at what speed do they strike the water?

80 m

Probs. 12–19/20

**12-21.** A particle travels in a straight line with accelerated motion such that $a = -ks$, where $s$ is the distance from the starting point and $k$ is a proportionality constant which is to be determined. For $s = 2$ m the velocity is 4 m/s, and for $s = 3.5$ m the velocity is 10 m/s. What is $s$ when $v = 0$?

**12-22.** The acceleration of a rocket traveling upward is given by $a = (6 + 0.02s)$ m/s$^2$, where $s$ is in meters. Determine the rocket's velocity when $s = 2$ km and the time needed to reach this altitude. Initially, $v = 0$ and $s = 0$ when $t = 0$.

$s$

Prob. 12–22

**12-23.** The acceleration of a rocket traveling upward is given by $a = (6 + 0.02s)$ m/s$^2$, where $s$ is in meters. Determine the time needed for the rocket to reach an altitude of $s = 100$ m. Initially, $v = 0$ and $s = 0$ when $t = 0$.

$s$

Prob. 12–23

**\*12-24.** At $t = 0$ bullet $A$ is fired vertically with an initial (muzzle) velocity of 450 m/s. When $t = 3$ s, bullet $B$ is fired upward with a muzzle velocity of 600 m/s. Determine the time $t$, after $A$ is fired, as to when bullet $B$ passes bullet $A$. At what altitude does this occur?

**■12-25.** A particle moves along a straight line with an acceleration of $a = 5/(3s^{1/3} + s^{5/2})$ m/s$^2$, where $s$ is in meters. Determine the particle's velocity when $s = 2$ m, if it starts from rest when $s = 1$ m. Use Simpson's rule to evaluate the integral.

**12-26.** Ball $A$ is released from rest at a height of 12 m at the same time that a second ball $B$ is thrown upward 1.5 m from the ground. If the balls pass one another at a height of 6 m, determine the speed at which ball $B$ was thrown upward.

12 m

1.5 m

Prob. 12–26

**■12-27.** A projectile, initially at the origin, moves vertically downward along a straight-line path through a fluid medium such that its velocity is defined as $v = 3(8e^{-t} + t)^{1/2}$ m/s, where $t$ is in seconds. Plot the position $s$ of the projectile during the first 2 s. Use the Runge-Kutta method to evaluate $s$ with incremental values of $h = 0.25$ s.

**\*12-28.** The acceleration of a particle along a straight line is defined by $a = (2t - 9)$ m/s$^2$, where $t$ is in seconds. At $t = 0$, $s = 1$ m and $v = 10$ m/s. When $t = 9$ s, determine (a) the particle's position, (b) the total distance traveled, and (c) the velocity.

**12-29.** A particle is moving along a straight line such that when it is at the origin it has a velocity of 4 m/s. If it begins to decelerate at the rate of $a = (-1.5v^{1/2})$ m/s$^2$, where $v$ is in m/s, determine the distance it travels before it stops.

**12-30.** A particle moves along a straight line with an acceleration of $a = 5/(3s^{1/3} + s^{5/2})$ m/s$^2$, where $s$ is in meters. Determine the particle's velocity when $s = 2$ m, if it starts from rest when $s = 1$ m. Use Simpson's rule to evaluate the integral.

**12-31.** Determine the time required for a car to travel 1 km along a road if the car starts from rest, reaches a maximum speed at some intermediate point, and then stops at the end of the road. The car can accelerate at 1.5 m/s$^2$ and decelerate at 2 m/s$^2$.

**\*12-32.** When two cars $A$ and $B$ are next to one another, they are traveling in the same direction with speeds $v_A$ and $v_B$, respectively. If $B$ maintains its constant speed, while $A$ begins to decelerate at $a_A$, determine the distance $d$ between the cars at the instant $A$ stops.

A

B

d

Prob. 12–32

**12-33.** If the effects of atmospheric resistance are accounted for, a freely falling body has an acceleration defined by the equation $a = 9.81[1 - v^2(10^{-4})]$ m/s$^2$, where $v$ is in m/s and the positive direction is downward. If the body is released from rest at a *very high altitude*, determine (a) the velocity when $t = 5$ s, and (b) the body's terminal or maximum attainable velocity (as $t \to \infty$).

**12-34.** As a body is projected to a high altitude above the earth's *surface*, the variation of the acceleration of gravity with respect to altitude $y$ must be taken into account. Neglecting air resistance, this acceleration is determined from the formula $a = -g_0[R^2/(R + y)^2]$, where $g_0$ is the constant gravitational acceleration at sea level, $R$ is the radius of the earth, and the positive direction is measured upward. If $g_0 = 9.81$ m/s$^2$ and $R = 6356$ km, determine the minimum initial velocity (escape velocity) at which a projectile should be shot vertically from the earth's surface so that it does not fall back to the earth. *Hint:* This requires that $v = 0$ as $y \to \infty$.

**12-35.** Accounting for the variation of gravitational acceleration $a$ with respect to altitude $y$ (see Prob. 12–34), derive an equation that relates the velocity of a freely falling particle to its altitude. Assume that the particle is released from rest at an altitude $y_0$ from the earth's surface. With what velocity does the particle strike the earth if it is released from rest at an altitude $y_0 = 500$ km? Use the numerical data in Prob. 12–34.

**\*12-36.** When a particle falls through the air, its initial acceleration $a = g$ diminishes until it is zero, and thereafter it falls at a constant or terminal velocity $v_f$. If this variation of the acceleration can be expressed as $a = (g/v^2_f)(v^2_f - v^2)$, determine the time needed for the velocity to become $v < v_f$. Initially the particle falls from rest.

## 12.3 Rectilinear Kinematics: Erratic Motion

When a particle's motion during a time period is erratic, it may be difficult to obtain a continuous mathematical function to describe its position, velocity, or acceleration. Instead, the motion may best be described graphically using a series of curves that can be generated experimentally from computer output. If the resulting graph describes the relationship between any two of the variables, *a, v, s, t*, a graph describing the relationship between the other variables can be established by using the kinematic equations $a = dv/dt$, $v = ds/dt$, $a\,ds = v\,dv$. Several situations occur frequently.

**Given the *s–t* Graph, Construct the *v–t* Graph.** If the position of a particle can be *determined experimentally* during a time period $t$, the $s$–$t$ graph for the particle can be plotted, Fig. 12–7a. To determine the particle's velocity as a function of time, i.e., the $v$–$t$ graph, we must use $v = ds/dt$ since this equation relates $v$, $s$, and $t$. Therefore, the velocity at any instant is determined by measuring the *slope* of the $s$–$t$ graph, i.e.,

$$\frac{ds}{dt} = v$$

slope of
$s$–$t$ graph = velocity

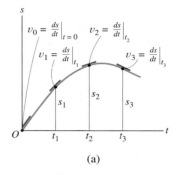

(a)

For example, measurement of the slopes $v_0$, $v_1$, $v_2$, $v_3$ at the intermediate points $(0, 0)$, $(t_1, s_1)$, $(t_2, s_2)$, $(t_3, s_3)$ on the $s$–$t$ graph, Fig. 12–7a, gives the corresponding points on the $v$–$t$ graph shown in Fig. 12–7b.

It may also be possible to establish the $v$–$t$ graph *mathematically*, provided the segments of the $s$–$t$ graph can be expressed in the form of equations $s = f(t)$. Corresponding equations describing the segments of the $v$–$t$ graph are then determined by time *differentiation*, since $v = ds/dt$.

**Given the *v–t* Graph, Construct the *a–t* Graph.** When the particle's $v$–$t$ graph is known, as in Fig. 12–8a, the acceleration as a function of time, i.e., the $a$–$t$ graph, can be determined using $a = dv/dt$. (Why?) Hence, the acceleration at any instant is determined by measuring the slope of the $v$–$t$ graph, i.e.,

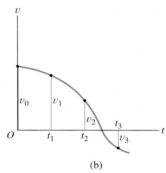

$$\frac{dv}{dt} = a$$

slope of
$v$–$t$ graph = acceleration

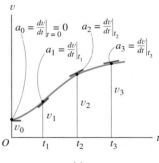

(b)

**Fig. 12–7**

For example, measurement of the slopes $a_0$, $a_1$, $a_2$, $a_3$ at the intermediate points $(0, v_0)$, $(t_1, v_1)$, $(t_2, v_2)$, $(t_3, v_3)$ on the $v$–$t$ graph, Fig. 12–8a, yields the corresponding points on the $a$–$t$ graph shown in Fig. 12–8b.

Any segments of the $a$–$t$ graph can also be determined *mathematically*, provided the equations of the corresponding segments of the $v$–$t$ graph are known, $v = g(t)$. This is done by simply taking the time *derivative* of $v = g(t)$, since $a = dv/dt$.

Since differentiation reduces a polynomial of degree $n$ to that of degree $n - 1$, then if the $s$–$t$ graph is parabolic (a second-degree curve), the $v$–$t$ graph will be a sloping line (a first-degree curve), and the $a$–$t$ graph will be a constant or a horizontal line (a zero-degree curve).

(a)

(b)

**Fig. 12–8**

E X A M P L E **12.6**

A bicycle moves along a straight road such that its position is described by the graph shown in Fig. 12–9a. Construct the v–t and a–t graphs for $0 \leq t \leq 30$ s.

s = 6t – 30

s = 0.3t²

Fig. 12–9

(a)

**Solution**

*v–t Graph.* Since $v = ds/dt$, the v–t graph can be determined by differentiating the equations defining the s–t graph, Fig. 12–9a. We have

$$0 \leq t < 10 \text{ s}; \qquad s = 0.3t^2 \qquad v = \frac{ds}{dt} = 0.6t$$

$$10 \text{ s} < t \leq 30 \text{ s}; \qquad s = 6t - 30 \qquad v = \frac{ds}{dt} = 6$$

The results are plotted in Fig. 12–9b. We can also obtain specific values of v by measuring the *slope* of the s–t graph at a given instant. For example, at $t = 20$ s, the slope of the s–t graph is determined from the straight line from 10 s to 30 s, i.e.,

$$t = 20 \text{ s}; \qquad v = \frac{\Delta s}{\Delta t} = \frac{150 - 30}{30 - 10} = 6 \text{ m/s}$$

*a–t Graph.* Since $a = dv/dt$, the a–t graph can be determined by differentiating the equations defining the lines of the v–t graph. This yields

$$0 \leq t < 10 \text{ s}; \qquad v = 0.6t \qquad a = \frac{dv}{dt} = 0.6$$

$$10 < t \leq 30 \text{ s}; \qquad v = 6 \qquad a = \frac{dv}{dt} = 0$$

The results are plotted in Fig. 12–9c. Show that $a = 0.6$ m/s² when $t = 5$ s by measuring the slope of the v–t graph.

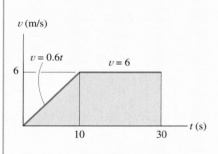

v = 0.6t

v = 6

(b)

a (m/s²)

(c)

Fig. 12–9

**Given the $a$–$t$ Graph, Construct the $v$–$t$ Graph.** If the $a$–$t$ graph is given, Fig. 12–10$a$, the $v$–$t$ graph may be constructed using $a = dv/dt$, written in integrated form as

$$\Delta v = \int a \, dt$$

$$\begin{array}{ccc} \text{change in} & = & \text{area under} \\ \text{velocity} & & a\text{–}t \text{ graph} \end{array}$$

Hence, to construct the $v$–$t$ graph, we begin by first knowing the particle's initial velocity $v_0$ and then add to this small increments of area ($\Delta v$) determined from the $a$–$t$ graph. In this manner, successive points, $v_1 = v_0 + \Delta v$, etc., for the $v$–$t$ graph are determined, Fig. 12–10$b$. Notices that an algebraic addition of the area increments is necessary, since areas lying above the $t$ axis correspond to an increase in $v$ ("positive" area), whereas those lying below the axis indicate a decrease in $v$ ("negative" area).

If segments of the $a$–$t$ graph can be described by a series of equations, then each of these equations may be *integrated* to yield equations describing the corresponding segments of the $v$–$t$ graph. Hence, if the $a$–$t$ graph is linear (a first-degree curve), integration will yield a $v$–$t$ graph that is parabolic (a second-degree curve), etc.

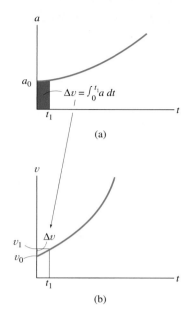

(a)

(b)

Fig. 12–10

**Given the $v$–$t$ Graph, Construct the $s$–$t$ Graph.** When the $v$–$t$ graph is given, Fig. 12–11$a$, it is possible to determine the $s$–$t$ graph using $v = ds/dt$, written in integrated form

$$\Delta s = \int v \, dt$$

$$\begin{array}{c} \text{displacement} = \text{area under} \\ v\text{–}t \text{ graph} \end{array}$$

In the same manner as stated above, we begin by knowing the particle's initial position $s_0$ and add (algebraically) to this small area increments $\Delta s$ determined from the $v$–$t$ graph, Fig. 12–11$b$.

If it is possible to describe segments of the $v$–$t$ graph by a series of equations, then each of these equations may be *integrated* to yield equations that describe corresponding segments of the $s$–$t$ graph.

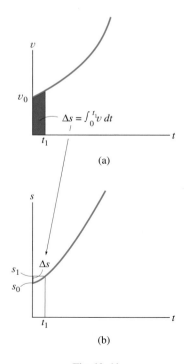

(a)

(b)

Fig. 12–11

**E X A M P L E  12.7**

(a)

(b)

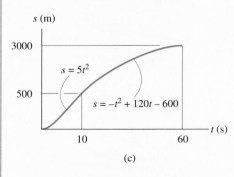

(c)

**Fig. 12–12**

The test car in Fig. 12–12a starts from rest and travels along a straight track such that it accelerates at a constant rate for 10 s and then decelerates at a constant rate. Draw the $v$–$t$ and $s$–$t$ graphs and determine the time $t'$ needed to stop the car. How far has the car traveled?

**Solution**

*v–t Graph.* Since $dv = a\,dt$, the $v$–$t$ graph is determined by integrating the straight-line segments of the $a$–$t$ graph. Using the *initial condition* $v = 0$ when $t = 0$, we have

$$0 \le t < 10 \text{ s}; \qquad a = 10; \qquad \int_0^v dv = \int_0^t 10\,dt, \qquad v = 10t$$

When $t = 10$ s, $v = 10(10) = 100$ m/s. Using this as the *initial condition* for the next time period, we have

$$10 \text{ s} < t \le t'; \qquad a = -2; \qquad \int_{100}^v dv = \int_{10}^t -2\,dt, \qquad v = -2t + 120$$

When $t = t'$ we require $v = 0$. This yields, Fig. 12–12b,

$$t' = 60 \text{ s} \qquad\qquad Ans.$$

A more direct solution for $t'$ is possible by realizing that the area under the $a$–$t$ graph is equal to the change in the car's velocity. We require $\Delta v = 0 = A_1 + A_2$, Fig. 12–12a. Thus

$$0 = 10 \text{ m/s}^2(10 \text{ s}) + (-2 \text{ m/s}^2)(t' - 10 \text{ s}) = 0$$
$$t' = 60 \text{ s} \qquad\qquad Ans.$$

*s–t Graph.* Since $ds = v\,dt$, integrating the equations of the $v$–$t$ graph yields the corresponding equations of the $s$–$t$ graph. Using the *initial conditions* $s = 0$ when $t = 0$, we have

$$0 \le t \le 10 \text{ s}; \qquad v = 10t; \qquad \int_0^s ds = \int_0^t 10t\,dt, \qquad s = 5t^2$$

When $t = 10$ s, $s = 5(10)^2 = 500$ m. Using this *initial condition*,

$$10 \text{ s} \le t \le 60 \text{ s}; \qquad v = -2t + 120; \qquad \int_{500}^s ds = \int_{10}^t (-2t + 120)\,dt$$
$$s - 500 = -t^2 + 120t - [-(10)^2 + 120(10)]$$
$$s = -t^2 + 120t - 600$$

When $t' = 60$ s, the position is

$$s = -(60)^2 + 120(60) - 600 = 3000 \text{ m} \qquad\qquad Ans.$$

The $s$–$t$ graph is shown in Fig. 12–12c. Note that a direct solution for $s$ is possible when $t' = 60$ s, since the *triangular area* under the $v$–$t$ graph would yield the displacement $\Delta s = s - 0$ from $t = 0$ to $t' = 60$ s. Hence,

$$\Delta s = \tfrac{1}{2}(60)(100) = 3000 \text{ m} \qquad\qquad Ans.$$

**Given the $a$–$s$ Graph, Construct the $v$–$s$ Graph.** In some cases an $a$–$s$ graph for the particle can be constructed, so that points on the $v$–$s$ graph can be determined by using $v\,dv = a\,ds$. Integrating this equation between the limits $v = v_0$ at $s = s_0$ and $v = v_1$ at $s = s_1$, we have,

$$\frac{1}{2}(v_1^2 - v_0^2) = \int_{s_0}^{s_1} a\,ds$$

area under
$a$–$s$ graph

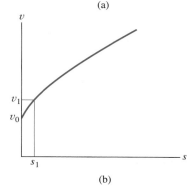

(a)

(b)

Fig. 12–13

Thus, the initial small segment of area under the $a$–$s$ graph, $\int_{s_0}^{s_1} a\,ds$, shown colored in Fig. 12–13a, equals one-half the difference in the squares of the speed, $\frac{1}{2}(v_1^2 - v_0^2)$. Therefore, if the area is determined and the initial value of $v_0$ at $s_0 = 0$ is known, then $v_1 = (2\int_{s_0}^{s_1} a\,ds + v_0^2)^{1/2}$, Fig. 12–13b. Successive points on the $v$–$s$ graph can be constructed in this manner starting from the initial velocity $v_0$.

Another way to construct the $v$–$s$ graph is to first determine the equations which define the segments of the $a$–$s$ graph. Then the corresponding equations defining the segments of the $v$–$s$ graph can be obtained directly from integration, using $v\,dv = a\,ds$.

**Given the $v$–$s$ Graph, Construct the $a$–$s$ Graph.** If the $v$–$s$ graph is known, the acceleration $a$ at any position $s$ can be determined using $a\,ds = v\,dv$, written as

$$a = v\left(\frac{dv}{ds}\right)$$

acceleration = velocity times
slope of
$v$–$s$ graph

(a)

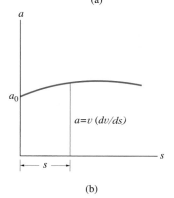

(b)

Fig. 12–14

Thus, at any point $(s, v)$ in Fig. 12–14a, the slope $dv/ds$ of the $v$–$s$ graph is measured. Then since $v$ and $dv/ds$ are known, the value of $a$ can be calculated, Fig. 12–14b.

We can also determine the segments describing the $a$–$s$ graph analytically, provided the equations of the corresponding segments of the $v$–$s$ graph are known. As above, this requires integration using $a\,ds = v\,dv$.

EXAMPLE 12.8

(b)

**Fig. 12–15**

The $v$–$s$ graph describing the motion of a motorcycle is shown in Fig. 12–15a. Construct the $a$–$s$ graph of the motion and determine the time needed for the motorcycle to reach the position $s = 120$ m.

**Solution**

*a–s Graph.* Since the equations for segments of the $v$–$s$ graph are given, the $a$–$s$ graph can be determined using $a\,ds = v\,dv$.

$$0 \le s < 60 \text{ m}; \qquad v = 0.2s + 3$$

$$a = v\frac{dv}{ds} = (0.2s + 3)\frac{d}{ds}(0.2s + 3) = 0.04s + 0.6$$

$$60 \text{ m} < s \le 120 \text{ m}; \qquad v = 15;$$

$$a = v\frac{dv}{ds} = (15)\frac{d}{ds}(15) = 0$$

The results are plotted in Fig. 12–15b.

*Time.* The time can be obtained using the $v$–$s$ graph and $v = ds/dt$, because this equation relates $v$, $s$, and $t$. For the first segment of motion, $s = 0$ at $t = 0$, so

$$0 \le s < 60 \text{ m}; \qquad v = 0.2s + 3; \qquad dt = \frac{ds}{v} = \frac{ds}{0.2s + 3}$$

$$\int_0^t dt = \int_0^s \frac{ds}{0.2s + 3}$$

$$t = 5\ln(0.2s + 3) - 5\ln 3$$

At $s = 60$ m, $t = 5\ln[0.2(60) + 3] - 5\ln 3 = 8.05$ s. Therefore, for the second segment of motion,

$$60 \text{ m} < s \le 120 \text{ m}; \qquad v = 15; \qquad dt = \frac{ds}{v} = \frac{ds}{15}$$

$$\int_{8.05}^t dt = \int_{60}^s \frac{ds}{15}$$

$$t - 8.05 = \frac{s}{15} - 4$$

$$t = \frac{s}{15} + 4.05$$

Therefore, at $s = 120$ m,

$$t = \frac{120}{15} + 4.05 = 12.0 \text{ s} \qquad \qquad Ans.$$

# PROBLEMS

**12-37.** An airplane starts from rest, travels 1500 m down a runway, and after uniform acceleration, takes off with a speed of 260 km/h. It then climbs in a straight line with a uniform acceleration of 0.9 m/s² until it reaches a constant speed of 353 km/h. Draw the *s–t, v–t,* and *a–t* graphs that describe the motion.

**12-38.** The elevator starts from rest at the first floor of the building. It can accelerate at 1.5 m/s² and then decelerate at 0.6 m/s². Determine the shortest time it takes to reach a floor 12 m above the ground. The elevator starts from rest and then stops. Draw the *a–t, v–t,* and *s–t* graphs for the motion.

12 m

Prob. 12–38

**12-39.** A freight train starts from rest and travels with a constant acceleration of 0.15 m/s². After a time *t′* it maintains a constant speed so that when *t* = 160 s it has traveled 600 m. Determine the time *t′* and draw the *v–t* graph for the motion.

***12-40.** If the position of a particle is defined by $s = [2 \sin(\pi/5)t + 4]$ m, where *t* is in seconds, construct the *s–t, v–t,* and *a–t* graphs for $0 \le t \le 10$ s.

**12-41.** The *v–t* graph for a particle moving through an electric field from one plate to another has the shape shown in the figure. The acceleration and deceleration that occur are constant and both have a magnitude of 4 m/s². If the plates are spaced 200 mm apart, determine the maximum velocity $v_{max}$ and the time *t′* for the particle to travel from one plate to the other. Also draw the *s–t* graph. When $t = t'/2$ the particle is at $s = 100$ mm.

**12-42.** The *v–t* graph for a particle moving through an electric field from one plate to another has the shape shown in the figure, where $t' = 0.2$ s and $v_{max} = 10$ m/s. Draw the *s–t* and *a–t* graphs for the particle. When $t = t'/2$ the particle is at $s = 0.5$ m.

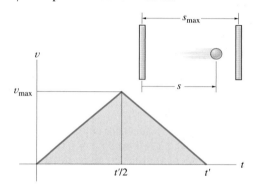

Probs. 12–41/42

**12-43.** The *a–s* graph for a jeep traveling along a straight road is given for the first 300 m of its motion. Construct the *v–s* graph. At $s = 0$, $v = 0$.

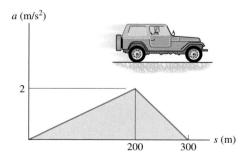

Prob. 12–43

***12-44.** A motorcycle starts from rest at $s = 0$ and travels along a straight road with the speed shown by the $v$–$t$ graph. Determine the motorcycle's acceleration and position when $t = 8$ s and $t = 12$ s.

**12-46.** A race cars starting from rest travels along a straight road and for 10 s has the acceleration shown. Construct the $v$–$t$ graph that describes the motion and find the distance traveled in 10 s.

**Prob. 12–44**

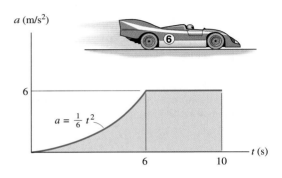

**Prob. 12–46**

**12-45.** An airplane lands on the straight runway, originally traveling at 33 m/s when $s = 0$. If it is subjected to the decelerations shown, determine the time $t'$ needed to stop the plane and construct the $s$–$t$ graph for the motion.

**12-47.** The $v$–$t$ graph for the motion of a train as it moves from station $A$ to station $B$ is shown. Draw the $a$–$t$ graph and determine the average speed and the distance between the stations.

**Prob. 12–45**

**Prob. 12–47**

*12-48. The velocity of a car is plotted as shown. Determine the total distance the car moves until it stops ($t = 80$ s). Construct the $a$–$t$ graph.

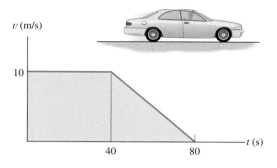

**Prob. 12–48**

12-49. The $v$–$t$ graph for the motion of a car as if moves along a straight road is shown. Draw the $a$–$t$ graph and determine the maximum acceleration during the 30-s time interval. The car starts from rest at $s = 0$.

12-50. The $v$–$t$ graph for the motion of a car as it moves along a straight road is shown. Draw the $s$–$t$ graph and determine the average speed and the distance traveled for the 30-s time interval. The car starts from rest at $s = 0$.

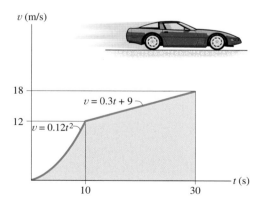

**Probs. 12–49/50**

12-51. A car travels along a straight road with the speed shown by the $v$–$t$ graph. Determine the total distance the car travels until it stops when $t = 48$ s. Also plot the $s$–$t$ and $a$–$t$ graphs.

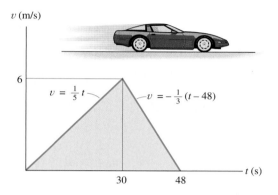

**Prob. 12–51**

*12-52. A man riding upward in a freight elevator accidentally drops a package off the elevator when it is 30 m from the ground. If the elevator maintains a constant upward speed of 1.2 m/s, determine how high the elevator is from the ground the instant the package hits the ground. Draw the $v$–$t$ curve for the package during the time it is in motion. Assume that the package was released with the same upward speed as the elevator.

12-53. Two cars start from rest side by side and travel along a straight road. Car $A$ accelerates at 4 m/s$^2$ for 10 s and then maintains a constant speed. Car $B$ accelerates at 5 m/s$^2$ until reaching a constant speed of 25 m/s and then maintains this speed. Construct the $a$–$t$, $v$–$t$, and $s$–$t$ graphs for each car until $t = 15$ s. What is the distance between the two cars when $t = 15$ s?

**12-54.** A two-stage rocket is fired vertically from rest at $s = 0$ with an acceleration as shown. After 30 s the first stage $A$ burns out and the second stage $B$ ignites. Plot the $v$–$t$ and $s$–$t$ graphs which describe the motion of the second stage for $0 \leq t \leq 60$ s.

**Prob. 12–54**

**12-55.** The $a$–$s$ graph for a boat moving along a straight path is given. If the boat starts at $s = 0$ when $v = 0$, determine its speed when it is at $s = 75$ m, and 125 m respectively. Use Simpson's rule with $n = 100$ to evaluate $v$ at $s = 125$ m.

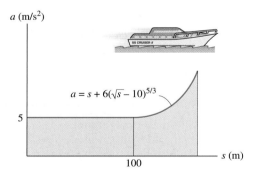

**Prob. 12–55**

**\*12-56.** The jet plane starts from rest at $s = 0$ and is subjected to the acceleration shown. Determine the speed of the plane when it has traveled 60 m. Also, how much time is required for it to travel 60 m?

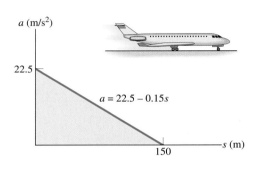

**Prob. 12–56**

**12-57.** The $v$–$t$ graph of a car while traveling along a road is shown. Draw the $s$–$t$ and $a$–$t$ graphs for the motion.

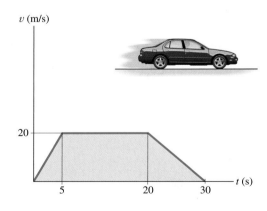

**Prob. 12–57**

**12-58.** A motorcyclist at $A$ is traveling at 18 m/s when he wishes to pass the truck $T$ which is traveling at a constant speed of 18 m/s. To do so the motorcyclist accelerates at 1.8 m/s² until reaching a maximum speed of 25.5 m/s. If he then maintains this speed, determine the time needed for him to reach a point located 30 m in front of the truck. Draw the $v$–$t$ and $s$–$t$ graphs for the motorcycle during this time.

Prob. 12–58

**12-59.** The $v$–$s$ graph for a go-cart traveling on a straight road is shown. Determine the acceleration of the go-cart at $s = 50$ m and $s = 150$ m. Draw the $a$–$s$ graph.

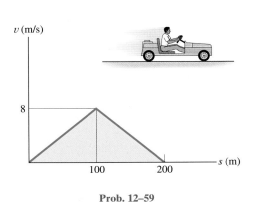

Prob. 12–59

**\*12-60.** The $v$–$s$ graph for the car is given for the first 150 m of its motion. Construct the $a$–$s$ graph for $0 \le s \le 150$ m. How long does it take to travel the 150-m distance? The car starts at $s = 0$ when $t = 0$.

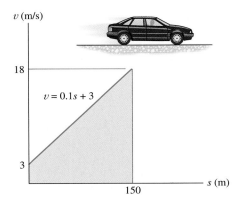

Prob. 12–60

**12-61.** The $a$–$s$ graph for a train traveling along a straight track is given for the first 400 m of its motion. Plot the $v$–$s$ graph. $v = 0$ at $s = 0$.

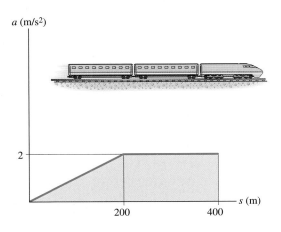

Prob. 12–61

**12-62.** The $v$–$s$ graph for an airplane traveling on a straight runway is shown. Determine the acceleration of the plane at $s = 100$ m and $s = 150$ m. Draw the $a$–$s$ graph.

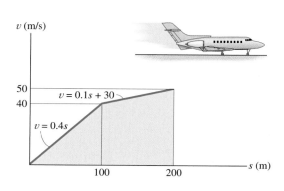

Prob. 12–62

**12-63.** Starting from rest at $s = 0$, a boat travels in a straight line with an acceleration as shown by the $a$–$s$ graph. Determine the boat's speed when $s = 40$, 90, and 200 m.

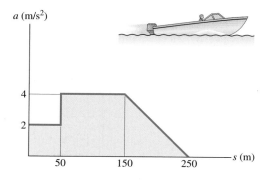

Prob. 12–63

**\*12-64.** The test car starts from rest and is subjected to a constant acceleration of $a_c = 5$ m/s² for $0 \le t < 10$ s. The brakes are then applied, which causes a deceleration at the rate shown until the car stops. Determine the car's maximum speed and the time $t$ when it stops.

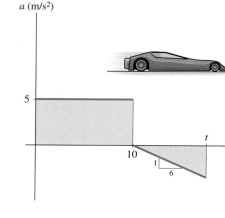

Prob. 12–64

**12-65.** The $a$–$s$ graph for a race car moving along a straight track has been experimentally determined. If the car starts from rest at $s = 0$, determine its speed when $s = 15$ m, 45 m, and 60 m, respectively.

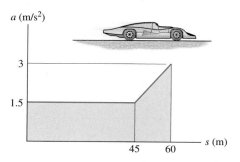

Prob. 12–65

## 12.4 General Curvilinear Motion

*Curvilinear motion* occurs when the particle moves along a curved path. Since this path is often described in three dimensions, vector analysis will be used to formulate the particle's position, velocity, and acceleration.* In this section the general aspects of curvilinear motion are discussed, and in subsequent sections three types of coordinate systems often used to analyze this motion will be introduced.

**Position.** Consider a particle located at point $P$ on a space curve defined by the path function $s$, Fig. 12–16a. The position of the particle, measured from a fixed point $O$, will be designated by the *position vector* $\mathbf{r} = \mathbf{r}(t)$. This vector is a function of time since, in general, both its magnitude and direction change as the particle moves along the curve.

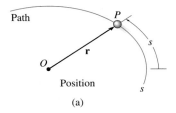

Position

(a)

**Displacement.** Suppose that during a small time interval $\Delta t$ the particle moves a distance $\Delta s$ along the curve to a new position $P'$, defined by $\mathbf{r}' = \mathbf{r} + \Delta\mathbf{r}$, Fig. 12–16b. The *displacement* $\Delta\mathbf{r}$ represents the change in the particle's position and is determined by vector subtraction; i.e., $\Delta\mathbf{r} = \mathbf{r}' - \mathbf{r}$.

**Velocity.** During the time $\Delta t$, the *average velocity* of the particle is defined as

$$\mathbf{v}_{avg} = \frac{\Delta\mathbf{r}}{\Delta t}$$

The *instantaneous velocity* is determined from this equation by letting $\Delta t \to 0$, and consequently the direction of $\Delta\mathbf{r}$ *approaches* the *tangent* to the curve at point $P$. Hence, $\mathbf{v} = \lim_{\Delta t \to 0} (\Delta\mathbf{r}/\Delta t)$ or

$$\mathbf{v} = \frac{d\mathbf{r}}{dt} \qquad (12\text{–}7)$$

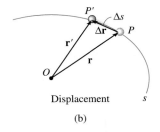

Displacement

(b)

Since $d\mathbf{r}$ will be tangent to the curve at $P$, the *direction* of $\mathbf{v}$ is also *tangent to the curve*, Fig. 12–16c. The *magnitude* of $\mathbf{v}$, which is called the *speed*, may be obtained by noting that the magnitude of the displacement $\Delta\mathbf{r}$ is the length of the straight line segment from $P$ to $P'$, Fig. 12–16b. Realizing that this length, $\Delta r$, approaches the arc length $\Delta s$ as $\Delta t \to 0$, we have $v = \lim_{\Delta t \to 0} (\Delta r/\Delta t) = \lim_{\Delta t \to 0} (\Delta s/\Delta t)$, or

$$v = \frac{ds}{dt} \qquad (12\text{–}8)$$

Thus, the *speed* can be obtained by differentiating the path function $s$ with respect to time.

*A summary of some of the important concepts of vector analysis is given in Appendix C.

Velocity

(c)

**Fig. 12–16**

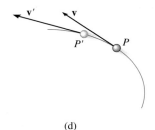

(d)

**Acceleration.** If the particle has a velocity **v** at time $t$ and a velocity $\mathbf{v}' = \mathbf{v} + \Delta\mathbf{v}$ at $t + \Delta t$, Fig. 12–16d, then the *average acceleration* of the particle during the time interval $\Delta t$ is

$$\mathbf{a}_{\text{avg}} = \frac{\Delta\mathbf{v}}{\Delta t}$$

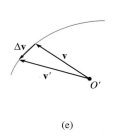

(e)

where $\Delta\mathbf{v} = \mathbf{v}' - \mathbf{v}$. To study this time rate of change, the two velocity vectors in Fig. 12–16d are plotted in Fig. 12–16e such that their tails are located at the fixed point $O'$ and their arrowheads touch points on the curve. This curve is called a *hodograph*, and when constructed, it describes the locus of points for the arrowhead of the velocity vector in the same manner as the *path s* describes the locus of points for the arrowhead of the position vector, Fig. 12–16a.

To obtain the *instantaneous acceleration*, let $\Delta t \rightarrow 0$ in the above equation. In the limit $\Delta\mathbf{v}$ will approach the *tangent to the hodograph*, and so $\mathbf{a} = \lim_{\Delta t \to 0} (\Delta\mathbf{v}/\Delta t)$, or

$$\boxed{\mathbf{a} = \frac{d\mathbf{v}}{dt}} \qquad (12\text{–}9)$$

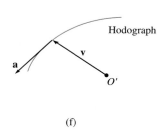

(f)

Substituting Eq. 12–7 into this result, we can also write

$$\mathbf{a} = \frac{d^2\mathbf{r}}{dt^2}$$

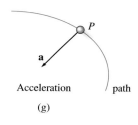

Acceleration    path

(g)

**Fig. 12–16**

By definition of the derivative, **a** acts *tangent to the hodograph*, Fig. 12–16f, and therefore, *in general,* **a** *is not tangent to the path of motion*, Fig. 12–16g. To clarify this point, realize that $\Delta\mathbf{v}$ and consequently **a** must account for the change made in *both* the magnitude *and* direction of the velocity **v** as the particle moves from $P$ to $P'$, Fig. 12–16d. Just a magnitude change increases (or decreases) the "length" of **v**, and this in itself would allow **a** to remain tangent to the path. However, in order for the particle to follow the path, the directional change always "swings" the velocity vector toward the "inside" or "concave side" of the path, and therefore **a** *cannot* remain tangent to the path. In summary, **v** is always tangent to the *path* and **a** is always tangent to the *hodograph*.

## 12.5 Curvilinear Motion: Rectangular Components

Occasionally the motion of a particle can best be described along a path that is represented using a fixed $x, y, z$ frame of reference.

**Position.**   If at a given instant the particle $P$ is at point $(x, y, z)$ on the curved path $s$, Fig. 12–17a, its location is then defined by the *position vector*

$$\boxed{\mathbf{r} = x\mathbf{i} + y\mathbf{j} + z\mathbf{k}} \qquad (12\text{–}10)$$

Because of the particle motion and the shape of the path, the $x, y, z$ components of $\mathbf{r}$ are generally all functions of time; i.e., $x = x(t)$, $y = y(t)$, $z = z(t)$, so that $\mathbf{r} = \mathbf{r}(t)$.

In accordance with the discussion in Appendix C, the *magnitude* of $\mathbf{r}$ is *always positive* and defined from Eq. C–3 as

$$r = \sqrt{x^2 + y^2 + z^2}$$

The *direction* of $\mathbf{r}$ is specified by the components of the unit vector $\mathbf{u}_r = \mathbf{r}/r$.

Position

(a)

**Velocity.**   The first time derivative of $\mathbf{r}$ yields the velocity $\mathbf{v}$ of the particle. Hence,

$$\mathbf{v} = \frac{d\mathbf{r}}{dt} = \frac{d}{dt}(x\mathbf{i}) + \frac{d}{dt}(y\mathbf{j}) + \frac{d}{dt}(z\mathbf{k})$$

When taking this derivative, it is necessary to account for changes in *both* the magnitude and direction of each of the vector's components. The derivative of the $\mathbf{i}$ component of $\mathbf{v}$ is therefore

$$\frac{d}{dt}(x\mathbf{i}) = \frac{dx}{dt}\mathbf{i} + x\frac{d\mathbf{i}}{dt}$$

The second term on the right side is zero, since the $x, y, z$ reference frame is *fixed*, and therefore the *direction* (and the *magnitude*) of $\mathbf{i}$ does not change with time. Differentiation of the $\mathbf{j}$ and $\mathbf{k}$ components may be carried out in a similar manner, which yields the final result,

$$\boxed{\mathbf{v} = \frac{d\mathbf{r}}{dt} = v_x\mathbf{i} + v_y\mathbf{j} + v_z\mathbf{k}} \qquad (12\text{–}11)$$

where

$$\boxed{v_x = \dot{x} \quad v_y = \dot{y} \quad v_z = \dot{z}} \qquad (12\text{–}12)$$

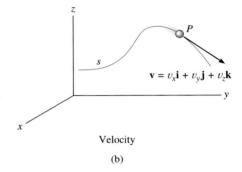

Velocity

(b)

**Fig. 12–17**

The "dot" notation $\dot{x}$, $\dot{y}$, $\dot{z}$ represents the first time derivatives of the parametric equations $x = x(t)$, $y = y(t)$, $z = z(t)$, respectively.

The velocity has a *magnitude* defined as the positive value of

$$v = \sqrt{v_x^2 + v_y^2 + v_z^2}$$

and a *direction* that is specified by the components of the unit vector $\mathbf{u}_v = \mathbf{v}/v$. This direction is *always tangent to the path*, as shown in Fig. 12–17b.

**Acceleration.**   The acceleration of the particle is obtained by taking the first time derivative of Eq. 12–11 (or the second time derivative of Eq. 12–10). Using dots to represent the derivatives of the components, we have

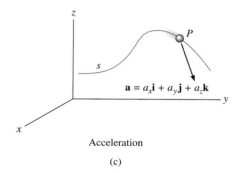

$$\boxed{\mathbf{a} = \frac{d\mathbf{v}}{dt} = a_x\mathbf{i} + a_y\mathbf{j} + a_z\mathbf{k}} \qquad (12\text{--}13)$$

where

$$\boxed{\begin{aligned} a_x &= \dot{v}_x = \ddot{x} \\ a_y &= \dot{v}_y = \ddot{y} \\ a_z &= \dot{v}_z = \ddot{z} \end{aligned}} \qquad (12\text{--}14)$$

$\mathbf{a} = a_x\mathbf{i} + a_y\mathbf{j} + a_z\mathbf{k}$

Acceleration

(c)

**Fig. 12–17**

Here $a_x$, $a_y$, $a_z$ represent, respectively, the first time derivatives of the functions $v_x = v_x(t)$,  $v_y = v_y(t)$,  $v_z = v_z(t)$,  or the second time derivatives of the functions $x = x(t)$, $y = y(t)$, $z = z(t)$.

The acceleration has a *magnitude* defined by the positive value of

$$a = \sqrt{a_x^2 + a_y^2 + a_z^2}$$

and a *direction* specified by the components of the unit vector $\mathbf{u}_a = \mathbf{a}/a$. Since $\mathbf{a}$ represents the time rate of *change* in velocity, in general $\mathbf{a}$ will *not* be tangent to the path, Fig. 12–17c.

## IMPORTANT POINTS

- Curvilinear motion can cause changes in *both* the magnitude and direction of the position, velocity, and acceleration vectors.
- The velocity vector is always directed *tangent* to the path.
- In general, the acceleration vector is *not* tangent to the path, but rather, it is tangent to the hodograph.
- If the motion is described using rectangular coordinates, then the components along each of the axes do not change direction, only their magnitude and sense (algebraic sign) will change.
- By considering the component motions, the direction of motion of the particle is automatically taken into account.

## PROCEDURE FOR ANALYSIS

### Coordinate System

- A rectangular coordinate system can be used to solve problems for which the motion can conveniently be expressed in terms of its $x, y, z$ components.

### Kinematic Quantities

- Since *rectilinear motion* occurs along *each* coordinate axis, the motion of each component is found using $v = ds/dt$ and $a = dv/dt$; or in cases where the motion is not expressed as a function of time, the equation $a \, ds = v \, dv$ can be used.
- Once the $x, y, z$ components of **v** and **a** have been determined, the magnitudes of these vectors are found from the Pythagorean theorem, Eq. C–3, and their directions from the components of their unit vectors, Eqs. C–4 and C–5.

As the airplane takes off, its path of motion can be established by knowing its horizontal position $x = x(t)$, and its vertical position or altitude $y = y(t)$, both of which can be found from navigation equipment. By plotting the results from these equations the path can be shown, and by taking the time derivatives, the velocity and acceleration of the plane at any instant can be determined.

**E X A M P L E  12.9**

(a)

(b)

(c)

Fig. 12–18

At any instant the horizontal position of the weather balloon in Fig. 12–18a is defined by $x = (9t)$ m, where $t$ is in seconds. If the equation of the path is $y = x^2/30$, determine (a) the distance of the balloon from the station at $A$ when $t = 2$ s, (b) the magnitude and direction of the velocity when $t = 2$ s, and (c) the magnitude and direction of the acceleration when $t = 2$ s.

**Solution**

*Position.*  When $t = 2$ s, $x = 9(2)$ m $= 18$ m and so

$$y = (18)^2/30 = 10.8 \text{ m}$$

The straight-line distance from $A$ to $B$ is therefore

$$r = \sqrt{(18)^2 + (10.8)^2} = 21 \text{ m} \qquad \textit{Ans.}$$

*Velocity.*  Using Eqs. 12–12 and application of the chain rule of calculus the components of velocity when $t = 2$ s are

$$v_x = \dot{x} = \frac{d}{dt}(9t) = 9 \text{ m/s} \rightarrow$$

$$v_y = \dot{y} = \frac{d}{dt}(x^2/30) = 2x\dot{x}/30 = 2(18)(9)/30 = 10.8 \text{ m/s} \uparrow$$

When $t = 2$ s, the magnitude of velocity is therefore

$$v = \sqrt{(9)^2 + (10.8)^2} = 14.1 \text{ m/s} \qquad \textit{Ans.}$$

The direction is tangent to the path, Fig. 12–18b, where

$$\theta_v = \tan^{-1}\frac{v_y}{v_x} = \tan^{-1}\frac{10.8}{9} = 50.2° \qquad \textit{Ans.}$$

*Acceleration.*  The components of acceleration are determined from Eqs. 12–14 and application of the chain rule, noting that $\ddot{x} = d^2(9t)/dt^2 = 0$. We have

$$a_x = \dot{v}_x = 0$$

$$a_y = \dot{v}_y = \frac{d}{dt}(2x\dot{x}/30) = 2(\dot{x})\dot{x}/30 + 2x(\ddot{x})/30$$

$$= 2(9)^2/30 + 2(18)(0)/30 = 5.4 \text{ m/s}^2 \uparrow$$

Thus

$$a = \sqrt{(0)^2 + (5.4)^2} = 5.4 \text{ m/s}^2 \qquad \textit{Ans.}$$

The direction of **a**, as shown in Fig. 12–18c, is

$$\theta_a = \tan^{-1}\frac{5.4}{0} = 90° \qquad \textit{Ans.}$$

*Note:* It is also possible to obtain $v_y$ and $a_y$ by first expressing $y = f(t) = (9t)^2/30 = 2.7t^2$ and then taking successive time derivatives.

# EXAMPLE 12.10

The motion of a box $B$ moving along the spiral conveyor shown in Fig. 12–19 is defined by the position vector $\mathbf{r} = \{0.5 \sin(2t)\mathbf{i} + 0.5 \cos(2t)\mathbf{j} - 0.2t\mathbf{k}\}$ m, where $t$ is in seconds and the arguments for sine and cosine are in radians ($\pi$ rad = 180°). Determine the location of the box when $t = 0.75$ s and the magnitudes of its velocity and acceleration at this instant.

### Solution

*Position.* Evaluating $\mathbf{r}$ when $t = 0.75$ s yields

$$\mathbf{r}|_{t=0.75\,s} = \{0.5 \sin(1.5\text{ rad})\mathbf{i} + 0.5 \cos(1.5\text{ rad})\mathbf{j} - 0.2(0.75)\mathbf{k}\} \text{ m}$$
$$= \{0.499\mathbf{i} + 0.0354\mathbf{j} - 0.150\mathbf{k}\} \text{ m} \qquad \textit{Ans.}$$

The distance of the box from the origin $O$ is

$$r = \sqrt{(0.499)^2 + (0.0354)^2 + (-0.150)^2} = 0.522 \text{ m} \qquad \textit{Ans.}$$

**Fig. 12–19**

The direction of $\mathbf{r}$ is obtained from the components of the unit vector,

$$\mathbf{u}_r = \frac{\mathbf{r}}{r} = \frac{0.499}{0.522}\mathbf{i} + \frac{0.0354}{0.522}\mathbf{j} - \frac{0.150}{0.522}\mathbf{k}$$
$$= 0.955\mathbf{i} + 0.0678\mathbf{j} - 0.287\mathbf{k}$$

Hence, the coordinate direction angles $\alpha$, $\beta$, $\gamma$, Fig. 12–19, are

$$\alpha = \cos^{-1}(0.955) = 17.2° \qquad \textit{Ans.}$$
$$\beta = \cos^{-1}(0.0678) = 86.1° \qquad \textit{Ans.}$$
$$\gamma = \cos^{-1}(-0.287) = 107° \qquad \textit{Ans.}$$

*Velocity.* The velocity is defined by

$$\mathbf{v} = \frac{d\mathbf{r}}{dt} = \frac{d}{dt}[0.5 \sin(2t)\mathbf{i} + 0.5 \cos(2t)\mathbf{j} - 0.2t\mathbf{k}]$$
$$= \{1 \cos(2t)\mathbf{i} - 1 \sin(2t)\mathbf{j} - 0.2\mathbf{k}\} \text{ m/s}$$

Hence, when $t = 0.75$ s the magnitude of velocity, or the speed, is

$$v = \sqrt{v_x^2 + v_y^2 + v_z^2}$$
$$= \sqrt{[1 \cos(1.5\text{ rad})]^2 + [-1 \sin(1.5\text{ rad})]^2 + (-0.2)^2}$$
$$= 1.02 \text{ m/s} \qquad \textit{Ans.}$$

The velocity is tangent to the path as shown in Fig. 12–19. Its coordinate direction angles can be determined from $\mathbf{u}_v = \mathbf{v}/v$.

*Acceleration.* The acceleration $\mathbf{a}$ of the box, which is shown in Fig. 12–19, is *not* tangent to the path. Show that

$$\mathbf{a} = \frac{d\mathbf{v}}{dt} = \{-2 \sin(2t)\mathbf{i} - 2 \cos(2t)\mathbf{j}\} \text{ m/s}^2$$

At $t = 0.75s$, $a = 2$ m/s$^2$ \qquad \textit{Ans.}

## 12.6 Motion of a Projectile

The free-flight motion of a projectile is often studied in terms of its rectangular components, since the projectile's acceleration *always* acts in the vertical direction. To illustrate the kinematic analysis, consider a projectile launched at point $(x_0, y_0)$, as shown in Fig. 12–20. The path is defined in the *x–y* plane such that the initial velocity is $\mathbf{v}_0$, having components $(\mathbf{v}_0)_x$ and $(\mathbf{v}_0)_y$. When air resistance is neglected, the only force acting on the projectile is its weight, which causes the projectile to have a *constant downward acceleration* of approximately $a_c = g = 9.81 \text{ m/s}^2$.*

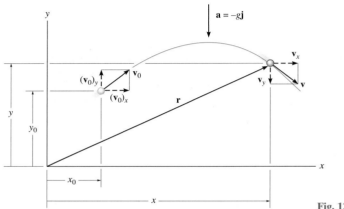

Fig. 12–20

**Horizontal Motion.** Since $a_x = 0$, application of the constant acceleration equations, 12–4 to 12–6, yields

$$( \xrightarrow{+} )v = v_0 + a_c t; \qquad\qquad v_x = (v_0)_x$$
$$( \xrightarrow{+} )x = x_0 + v_0 t + \tfrac{1}{2} a_c t^2; \qquad x = x_0 + (v_0)_x t$$
$$( \xrightarrow{+} )v^2 = v_0^2 + 2a_c(s - s_0); \qquad v_x = (v_0)_x$$

The first and last equations indicate that *the horizontal component of velocity always remains constant during the motion.*

**Vertical Motion.** Since the positive *y* axis is directed upward, then $a_y = -g$. Applying Eqs. 12–4 to 12–6, we get

$$(+\uparrow)v = v_0 + a_c t; \qquad\qquad v_y = (v_0)_y - gt$$
$$(+\uparrow)y = y_0 + v_0 t + \tfrac{1}{2} a_c t^2; \qquad y = y_0 + (v_0)_y t - \tfrac{1}{2} gt^2$$
$$(+\uparrow)v^2 = v_0^2 + 2a_c(y - y_0); \qquad v_y^2 = (v_0)_y^2 - 2g(y - y_0)$$

Recall that the last equation can be formulated on the basis of eliminating the time *t* between the first two equations, and therefore *only two of the above three equations are independent of one another.*

*This assumes that the earth's gravitational field does not vary with altitude.

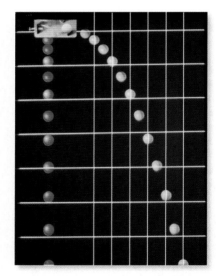

Each picture in this sequence is taken after the same time interval. The red ball falls from rest, whereas the yellow ball is given a horizontal velocity when released. Notice both balls are subjected to the same downward acceleration since they remain at the same elevation at any instant. This acceleration causes the difference in elevation to increase between successive photos. Also, note the horizontal distance between successive photos of the yellow ball is constant since the velocity in the horizontal direction remains constant.

To summarize, problems involving the motion of a projectile can have at most three unknowns since only three independent equations can be written; that is, *one* equation in the *horizontal direction* and *two* in the *vertical direction*. Once $\mathbf{v}_x$ and $\mathbf{v}_y$ are obtained, the resultant velocity $\mathbf{v}$, which is *always tangent* to the path, is defined by the *vector sum* as shown in Fig. 12–20.

## PROCEDURE FOR ANALYSIS

Free-flight projectile motion problems can be solved using the following procedure.

### *Coordinate System*

- Establish the fixed *x, y* coordinate axes and sketch the trajectory of the particle. Between any *two points* on the path specify the given problem data and the *three unknowns*. In all cases the acceleration of gravity acts downward. The particle's initial and final velocities should be represented in terms of their *x* and *y* components.

- Remember that positive and negative position, velocity, and acceleration components always act in accordance with their associated coordinate directions.

### *Kinematic Equations*

- Depending upon the known data and what is to be determined, a choice should be made as to which three of the following four equations should be applied between the two points on the path to obtain the most direct solution to the problem.

### *Horizontal Motion*

- The *velocity* in the horizontal or *x* direction is *constant*, i.e., $(v_x) = (v_0)_x$, and

$$x = x_0 + (v_0)_x t$$

### *Vertical Motion*

- In the vertical or *y* direction *only two* of the following three equations can be used for solution.

$$v_y = (v_0)_y + a_c t$$
$$y = y_0 + (v_0)_y t + \tfrac{1}{2} a_c t^2$$
$$v_y^2 = (v_0)_y^2 + 2a_c(y - y_0)$$

- For example, if the particle's final velocity $v_y$ is not needed, then the first and third of these equations (for *y*) will not be useful.

Gravel falling off the end of this conveyor belt follows a path that can be predicted using the equations of constant acceleration. In this way the location of the accumulated pile can be determined. Rectilinear coordinates are used for the analysis since the acceleration is only in the vertical direction.

E X A M P L E **12.11**

A sack slides off the ramp, shown in Fig. 12–21, with a horizontal velocity of 12 m/s. If the height of the ramp is 6 m from the floor, determine the time needed for the sack to strike the floor and the range $R$ where sacks begin to pile up.

**Fig. 12–21**

**Solution**

*Coordinate System.* The origin of coordinates is established at the beginning of the path, point $A$, Fig. 12–21. The initial velocity of a sack has components $(v_A)_x = 12$ m/s and $(v_A)_y = 0$. Also, between points $A$ and $B$ the acceleration is $a_y = -9.81$ m/s². Since $(v_B)_x = (v_A)_x = 12$ m/s, the three unknowns are $(v_B)_y$, $R$, and the time of flight $t_{AB}$. Here we do not need to determine $(v_B)_y$.

*Vertical Motion.* The vertical distance from $A$ to $B$ is known, and therefore we can obtain a direct solution for $t_{AB}$ by using the equation

$(+\uparrow)$ $\qquad\qquad y = y_0 + (v_0)_y t_{AB} + \frac{1}{2} a_c t_{AB}^2$

$$-6\text{ m} = 0 + 0 + \tfrac{1}{2}(-9.81\text{ m/s}^2)t_{AB}^2$$

$$t_{AB} = 1.11\text{ s} \qquad\qquad\qquad\qquad Ans.$$

This calculation also indicates that if a sack were released *from rest* at $A$, it would take the same amount of time to strike the floor at $C$, Fig. 12–21.

*Horizontal Motion.* Since $t$ has been calculated, $R$ is determined as follows:

$(\overset{+}{\rightarrow})$ $\qquad\qquad\qquad x = x_0 + (v_0)_x t_{AB}$

$$R = 0 + 12\text{ m/s }(1.11\text{ s})$$

$$R = 13.3\text{ m} \qquad\qquad\qquad\qquad Ans.$$

# EXAMPLE 12.12

The chipping machine is designed to eject wood chips at $v_O = 7.5$ m/s as shown in Fig. 12–22. If the tube is oriented at 30° from the horizontal, determine how high, $h$, the chips strike the pile if they land on the pile 6 m from the tube.

**Fig. 12–22**

## Solution

*Coordinate System.* When the motion is analyzed between points $O$ and $A$, the three unknowns are represented as the height $h$, time of flight $t_{OA}$, and vertical component of velocity $(v_A)_y$. (Note that $(v_A)_x = (v_O)_x$.) With the origin of coordinates at $O$, Fig. 12–22, the initial velocity of a chip has components of

$$(v_O)_x = (7.5 \cos 30°) \text{ m/s} = 6.5 \text{ m/s} \rightarrow$$
$$(v_O)_y = (7.5 \sin 30°) \text{ m/s} = 3.75 \text{ m/s} \uparrow$$

Also, $(v_A)_x = (v_O)_x = 6.5$ m/s and $a_y = -9.81$ m/s$^2$. Since we do not need to determine $(v_A)_y$, we have

*Horizontal Motion*
$(\xrightarrow{+})$
$$x_A = x_O + (v_O)_x t_{OA}$$
$$6 \text{ m} = 0 + (6.5 \text{ m/s}) t_{OA}$$
$$t_{OA} = 0.9231 \text{ s}$$

*Vertical Motion.* Relating $t_{OA}$ to the initial and final elevations of a chip, we have

$(+\uparrow)$  $$y_A = y_O + (v_O)_y t_{OA} + \tfrac{1}{2} a_c t_{OA}^2$$
$$(h - 2.1 \text{ m}) = 0 + (3.75 \text{ m/s})(0.9231 \text{ s}) + \tfrac{1}{2}(-9.81 \text{ m/s}^2)(0.9231 \text{ s})^2$$
$$h = 1.38 \text{ m} \hspace{2cm} Ans.$$

# E X A M P L E 12.13

The track for this racing event was designed so that riders jump off the slope at 30°, from a height of 1 m. During a race it was observed that the rider shown in Fig. 12–23a remained in mid air for 1.5 s. Determine the speed at which he was traveling off the slope, the horizontal distance he travels before striking the ground, and the maximum height he attains. Neglect the size of the bike and rider.

(a)

**Fig. 12–23**

(b)

### Solution

*Coordinate System.* As shown in Fig. 12–23b, the origin of the coordinates is established at $A$. Between the end points of the path $AB$ the three unknowns are the initial speed $v_A$, range $R$, and the vertical component of velocity $v_B$.

*Vertical Motion.* Since the time of flight and the vertical distance between the ends of the path are known, we can determine $v_A$.

$$(+\uparrow) \qquad (s_B)_y = (s_A)_y + (v_A)_y t_{AB} + \tfrac{1}{2} a_c t^2_{AB}$$
$$-1 = 0 + v_A \sin 30° \,(1.5) + \tfrac{1}{2}(-9.81)(1.5)^2$$
$$v_A = 13.38 \text{ m/s} = 13.4 \text{ m/s} \qquad\qquad Ans.$$

*Horizontal Motion.* The range $R$ can now be determined.

$$(\overset{+}{\to}) \qquad\qquad (s_B)_x = (s_A)_x + (v_A)_x t_{AB}$$
$$R = 0 + 13.38 \cos 30°(1.5)$$
$$= 17.4 \text{ m} \qquad\qquad Ans.$$

In order to find the maximum height $h$ we will consider the path $AC$, Fig. 12–23b. Here the three unknowns become the time of flight $t_{AC}$, the horizontal distance from $A$ to $C$, and the height $h$. At the maximum height $(v_C)_y = 0$, and since $v_A$ is known, we can determine $h$ *directly* without considering $t_{AC}$ using the following equation.

$$(v_C)^2_y = (v_A)^2_y + 2a_c[(s_C)_y - (s_A)_y]$$
$$(0)^2 = (13.38 \sin 30°)^2 + 2(-9.81)\,[(h-1) - 0]$$
$$h = 3.28 \text{ m} \qquad\qquad Ans.$$

Show that the bike will strike the ground at $B$ with a velocity having components of

$$(v_B)_x = 11.6 \text{ m/s} \to, \quad (v_B)_y = 8.02 \text{ m/s} \downarrow$$

# PROBLEMS

**12-66.** A particle, originally at rest and located at point (3 m, 2 m, 5 m), is subjected to an acceleration of $a = \{6t\mathbf{i} + 12t^2\mathbf{k}\}$ m/s². Determine the particle's position $(x, y, z)$ at $t = 1$ s.

**12-67.** The velocity of a particle is given by $v = \{16t^2\mathbf{i} + 4t^3\mathbf{j} + (5t + 2)\mathbf{k}\}$ m/s, where $t$ is in seconds. If the particle is at the origin when $t = 0$, determine the magnitude of the particle's acceleration when $t = 2$ s. Also, what is the $x, y, z$ coordinate position of the particle at this instant?

**■*12-68.** A particle is traveling with a velocity of $\mathbf{v} = \{3\sqrt{t}e^{-0.2t}\mathbf{i} + 4e^{-0.8t^2}\mathbf{j}\}$ m/s, where $t$ is in seconds. Determine the magnitude of the particle's displacement from $t = 0$ to $t = 3$ s. Use Simpson's rule with $n = 100$ to evaluate the integrals. What is the magnitude of the particle's acceleration when $t = 2$ s?

**12-69.** The position of a particle is defined by $r = \{5(\cos 2t)\mathbf{i} + 4(\sin 2t)\mathbf{j}\}$ m, where $t$ is in seconds and the arguments for the sine and cosine are given in radians. Determine the magnitudes of the velocity and acceleration of the particle when $t = 1$ s. Also, prove that the path of the particle is elliptical.

**12-70.** The car travels from $A$ to $B$, and then from $B$ to $C$, as shown in the figure. Determine the magnitude of the displacement of the car and the distance traveled.

Prob. 12–70

**12-71.** A particle travels along the curve from $A$ to $B$ in 2 s. It takes 4 s for it to go from $B$ to $C$ and then 3 s to go from $C$ to $D$. Determine its average speed when it goes from $A$ to $D$.

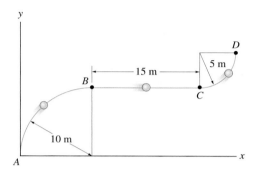

Prob. 12–71

**\*12-72.** A car travels east 2 km for 5 minutes, then north 3 km for 8 minutes, and then west 4 km for 10 minutes. Determine the total distance traveled and the magnitude of displacement of the car. Also, what is the magnitude of the average velocity and the average speed?

**12-73.** A car traveling along the straight portions of the road has the velocities indicated in the figure when it arrives at points $A$, $B$, and $C$. If it takes 3 s to go from $A$ to $B$, and then 5 s to go from $B$ to $C$, determine the average acceleration between points $A$ and $B$ and between points $A$ and $C$.

Prob. 12–73

**12-74.** A particle moves along the curve $y = e^{2x}$ such that its velocity has a constant magnitude of $v = 4$ m/s. Determine the $x$ and $y$ components of velocity when the particle is at $y = 5$ m.

**12-75.** The path of a particle is defined by $y^2 = 4kx$, and the component of velocity along the $y$ axis is $v_y = ct$, where both $k$ and $c$ are constants. Determine the $x$ and $y$ components of acceleration.

**\*12-76.** A particle is moving along the curve $y = x - (x^2/400)$, where $x$ and $y$ are in ft. If the velocity component in the $x$ direction is $v_x = 2$ m/s and remains *constant*, determine the magnitudes of the velocity and acceleration when $x = 20$ m.

**12-77.** The motorcycle travels with constant speed $v_0$ along the path that, for a short distance, takes the form of a sine curve. Determine the $x$ and $y$ components of its velocity at any instant on the curve.

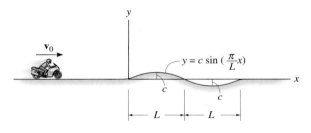

Prob. 12–77

**12-78.** The particle travels along the path defined by the parabola $y = 0.5x^2$. If the component of velocity along the $x$ axis is $v_x = (5t)$ m/s, where $t$ is in seconds, determine the particle's distance from the origin $O$ and the magnitude of its acceleration when $t = 1$ s. When $t = 0$, $x = 0$, $y = 0$.

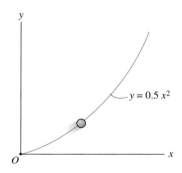

Prob. 12–78

**12-79.** When a rocket reaches an altitude of 40 m it begins to travel along the parabolic path $(y - 40)^2 = 160x$, where the coordinates are measured in meters. If the component of velocity in the vertical direction is constant at $v_y = 180$ m/s, determine the magnitudes of the rocket's velocity and acceleration when it reaches an altitude of 80 m.

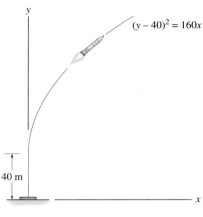

Prob. 12–79

**\*12-80.** The girl always throws the toys at an angle of 30° from point $A$ as shown. Determine the time between throws so that both toys strike the edges of the pool $B$ and $C$ at the same instant. With what speed must she throw each toy?

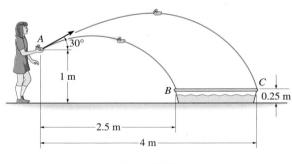

Prob. 12–80

**12-81.** The nozzle of a garden hose discharges water at the rate of 15 m/s. If the nozzle is held at ground level and directed $\theta = 30°$ from the ground, determine the maximum height reached by the water and the horizontal distance from the nozzle to where the water strikes the ground.

**12-82.** The balloon $A$ is ascending at the rate $v_A = 12$ km/h and is being carried horizontally by the wind at $v_w = 20$ km/h. If a ballast bag is dropped from the balloon at the instant $h = 50$ m, determine the time needed for it to strike the ground. Assume that the bag was released from the balloon with the same velocity as the balloon. Also, with what speed does the bag strike the ground?

$v_A = 12$ km/h

$v_w = 20$ km/h

$A$

$h$

Prob. 12–82

**12-83.** Determine the maximum height on the wall to which the firefighter can project water from the hose, if the speed of the water at the nozzle is $v_C = 16$ m/s.

■*12-84. Determine the smallest angle $\theta$, measured above the horizontal, that the hose should be directed so that the water stream strikes the bottom of the wall at $B$. The speed of the water at the nozzle is $v_C = 16$ m/s.

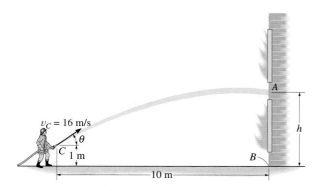

$v_C = 16$ m/s

$\theta$

$C$ 1 m

$A$

$h$

$B$

10 m

Probs. 12–83/84

**12-85.** From a videotape, it was observed that a pro football player kicked a football 42 m during a measured time of 3.6 seconds. Determine the initial speed of the ball and the angle $\theta$ at which it was kicked.

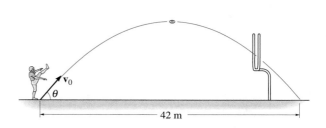

$\mathbf{v}_0$

$\theta$

42 m

Prob. 12–85

**12-86.** During a race the dirt bike was observed to leap up off the small hill at $A$ at an angle of 60° with the horizontal. If the point of landing is 6 m away, determine the approximate speed at which the bike was traveling just before it left the ground. Neglect the size of the bike for the calculation.

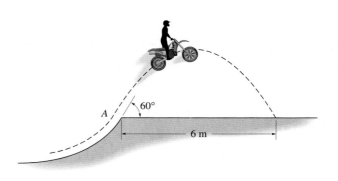

$A$

60°

6 m

Prob. 12–86

**12-87.** Measurements of a shot recorded on a videotape during a basketball game are shown. The ball passed through the hoop even though it barely cleared the hands of the player $B$ who attempted to block it. Neglecting the size of the ball, determine the magnitude $v_A$ of its initial velocity and the height $h$ of the ball when it passes over player $B$.

Prob. 12–87

**12-89.** The snowmobile is traveling at 10 m/s when it leaves the embankment at $A$. Determine the speed at which it strikes the ground at $B$ and its maximum acceleration along the trajectory $AB$.

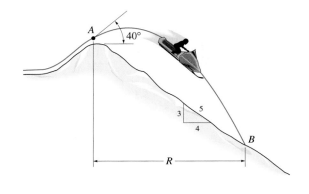

Prob. 12–89

**\*12-88.** The snowmobile is traveling at 10 m/s when it leaves the embankment at $A$. Determine the time of flight from $A$ to $B$ and the range $R$ of the trajectory.

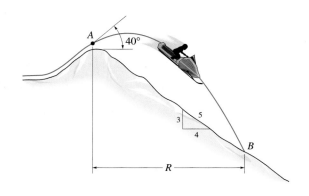

Prob. 12–88

**12-90.** A golf ball is struck with a velocity of 24 m/s as shown. Determine the distance $d$ to where it will land.

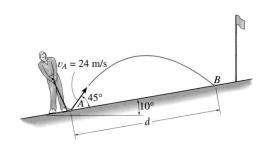

Prob. 12–90

**12-91.** It is observed that the skier leaves the ramp $A$ at an angle $\theta_A = 25°$ with the horizontal. If he strikes the ground at $B$, determine his initial speed $v_A$ and the time of flight $t_{AB}$.

**12-93.** The ball at $A$ is kicked with a speed $v_A = 24$ m/s and at an angle $\theta_A = 30°$. Determine the point $(x, -y)$ where it strikes the ground. Assume the ground has the shape of a parabola as shown.

**12-94.** The ball at $A$ is kicked such that $\theta_A = 30°$. If it strikes the ground at $B$ having coordinates $x = 4.5$ m, $y = -2.7$ m, determine the speed at which it is kicked and the speed at which it strikes the ground.

Prob. 12–91

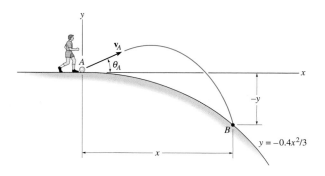

Probs. 12–93/94

*\*12-92.** The man stands 18 m from the wall and throws a ball at it with a speed $v_0 = 15$ m/s. Determine the angle $\theta$ at which he should release the ball so that it strikes the wall at the highest point possible. What is this height? The room has a ceiling height of 6 m.

**12-95.** Determine the horizontal velocity $v_A$ of a tennis ball at $A$ so that it just clears the net at $B$. Also, find the distance $s$ where the ball strikes the ground.

Prob. 12–92

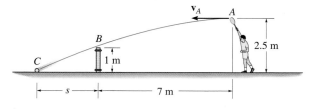

Prob. 12–95

**\*12-96.** A boy at $O$ throws a ball in the air with a speed $v_O$ at an angle $\theta_1$. If he then throws another ball at the same speed $v_O$ at an angle $\theta_2 < \theta_1$, determine the time between the throws so the balls collide in mid air at $B$.

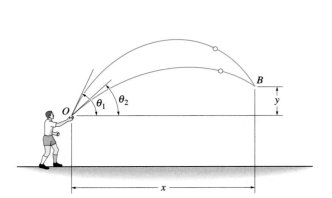

Prob. 12–96

**12-97.** The man at $A$ wishes to throw two darts at the target at $B$ so that they arrive at the *same time*. If each dart is thrown with a speed of 10 m/s, determine the angles $\theta_C$ and $\theta_D$ at which they should be thrown and the time between each throw. Note that the first dart must be thrown at $\theta_C (>\theta_D)$, then the second dart is thrown at $\theta_D$.

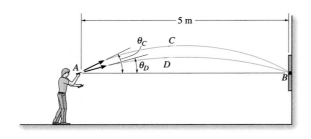

Prob. 12–97

**12-98.** The ball is thrown from the tower with a velocity of 6 m/s as shown. Determine the $x$ and $y$ coordinates to where the ball strikes the slope. Also, determine the speed at which the ball hits the ground.

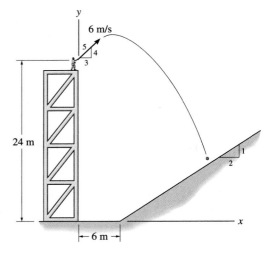

Prob. 12–98

**12-99.** The baseball player $A$ hits the baseball at $v_A = 12$ m/s and $\theta_A = 60°$ from the horizontal. When the ball is directly overhead of player $B$ he begins to run under it. Determine the constant speed at which $B$ must run and the distance $d$ in order to make the catch at the same elevation at which the ball was hit.

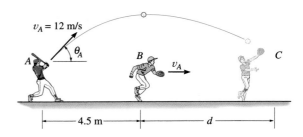

Prob. 12–99

## 12.7 Curvilinear Motion: Normal and Tangential Components

When the path along which a particle is moving is *known*, it is often convenient to describe the motion using *n* and *t* coordinates which act normal and tangent to the path, respectively, and at the instant considered have their *origin located at the particle.*

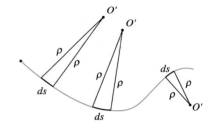

Position

(a)

**Planar Motion.** Consider the particle *P* shown in Fig. 12–24*a*, which is moving in a plane along a fixed curve, such that at a given instant it is at position *s*, measured from point *O*. We will now consider a coordinate system that has its origin at a *fixed point* on the curve, and at the instant considered this origin happens to *coincide* with the location of the particle. The *t* axis is *tangent* to the curve at *P* and is positive in the direction of *increasing s*. We will designate this positive direction with the unit vector $\mathbf{u}_t$. A unique choice for the *normal axis* can be made by noting that geometrically the curve is constructed from a series of differential arc segments *ds*, Fig. 12–24*b*. Each segment *ds* is formed from the arc of an associated circle having a *radius of curvature* ρ (rho) and *center of curvature O'*. The normal axis *n* is perpendicular to the *t* axis and is directed from *P* *toward* the center of curvature *O'*, Fig. 12–24*a*. This positive direction, which is *always* on the concave side of the curve, will be designated by the unit vector $\mathbf{u}_n$. The plane which contains the *n* and *t* axes is referred to as the *osculating plane*, and in this case it is fixed in the plane of motion.*

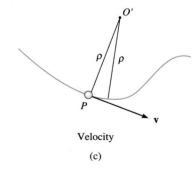

Radius of curvature

(b)

**Velocity.** Since the particle is moving, *s* is a function of time. As indicated in Sec. 12.4, the particle's velocity **v** has a *direction* that is *always tangent to the path*, Fig. 12–24*c*, and a *magnitude* that is determined by taking the time derivative of the path function $s = s(t)$, i.e., $v = ds/dt$ (Eq. 12–8). Hence

$$\mathbf{v} = v\mathbf{u}_t \tag{12–15}$$

where

$$v = \dot{s} \tag{12–16}$$

Velocity

(c)

Fig. 12–24

---

*The osculating plane may also be defined as that plane which has the greatest contact with the curve at a point. It is the limiting position of a plane contacting both the point and the arc segment *ds*. As noted above, the osculating plane is always coincident with a plane curve; however, each point on a three-dimensional curve has a unique osculating plane.

**Acceleration.** The acceleration of the particle is the time rate of change of the velocity. Thus,

$$\mathbf{a} = \dot{\mathbf{v}} = \dot{v}\mathbf{u}_t + v\dot{\mathbf{u}}_t \qquad (12\text{–}17)$$

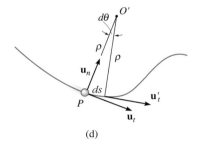

(d)

In order to determine the time derivative $\dot{\mathbf{u}}_t$, note that as the particle moves along the arc $ds$ in time $dt$, $\mathbf{u}_t$ preserves its magnitude of unity; however, its *direction* changes, and becomes $\mathbf{u}'_t$, Fig. 12–24d. As shown in Fig. 12–24e, we require $\mathbf{u}'_t = \mathbf{u}_t + d\mathbf{u}_t$. Here $d\mathbf{u}_t$ stretches between the arrowheads of $\mathbf{u}_t$ and $\mathbf{u}'_t$, which lie on an infinitesimal arc of radius $u_t = 1$. Hence, $d\mathbf{u}_t$ has a *magnitude* of $du_t = (1)\, d\theta$, and its *direction* is defined by $\mathbf{u}_n$. Consequently, $d\mathbf{u}_t = d\theta\mathbf{u}_n$, and therefore the time derivative becomes $\dot{\mathbf{u}}_t = \dot{\theta}\mathbf{u}_n$. Since $ds = \rho\, d\theta$, Fig. 12–24d, then $\dot{\theta} = \dot{s}/\rho$, and therefore

$$\dot{\mathbf{u}}_t = \dot{\theta}\mathbf{u}_n = \frac{\dot{s}}{\rho}\mathbf{u}_n = \frac{v}{\rho}\mathbf{u}_n$$

(e)

Substituting into Eq. 12–17, $\mathbf{a}$ can be written as the sum of its two components,

$$\boxed{\mathbf{a} = a_t\mathbf{u}_t + a_n\mathbf{u}_n} \qquad (12\text{–}18)$$

where

$$\boxed{a_t = \dot{v}} \quad \text{or} \quad \boxed{a_t\, ds = v\, dv} \qquad (12\text{–}19)$$

and

$$\boxed{a_n = \frac{v^2}{\rho}} \qquad (12\text{–}20)$$

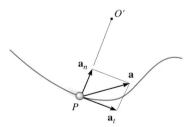

Acceleration

(f)

**Fig. 12–24**

These two mutually perpendicular components are shown in Fig. 12–24f, in which case the *magnitude* of acceleration is the positive value of

$$a = \sqrt{a_t^2 + a_n^2} \qquad (12\text{–}21)$$

To summarize these concepts, consider the following two special cases of motion.

1.  If the particle moves along a straight line, then $\rho \to \infty$ and from Eq. 12–20, $a_n = 0$. Thus $a = a_t = \dot{v}$, and we can conclude that the *tangential component of acceleration represents the time rate of change in the magnitude of the velocity*.

2.  If the particle moves along a curve with a constant speed, then $a_t = \dot{v} = 0$ and $a = a_n = v^2/\rho$. Therefore, the *normal component of acceleration represents the time rate of change in the direction of the velocity*. Since $\mathbf{a}_n$ *always* acts towards the center of curvature, this component is sometimes referred to as the *centripetal acceleration*.

As a result of these interpretations, a particle moving along the curved path in Fig. 12–25 will have accelerations directed as shown.

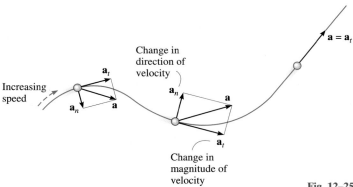

Fig. 12–25

**Three-Dimensional Motion.** If the particle is moving along a space curve, Fig. 12–26, then at a given instant the $t$ axis is uniquely specified; however, an infinite number of straight lines can be constructed normal to the tangent axis at $P$. As in the case of planar motion, we will choose the positive $n$ axis directed from $P$ toward the path's center of curvature $O'$. This axis is referred to as the *principal normal* to the curve at $P$. With the $n$ and $t$ axes so defined, Eqs. 12–15 to 12–21 can be used to determine $\mathbf{v}$ and $\mathbf{a}$. Since $\mathbf{u}_t$ and $\mathbf{u}_n$ are always perpendicular to one another and lie in the osculating plane, for spatial motion a third unit vector, $\mathbf{u}_b$, defines a *binormal axis* $b$ which is perpendicular to $\mathbf{u}_t$ and $\mathbf{u}_n$, Fig. 12–26.

Since the three unit vectors are related to one another by the vector cross product, e.g., $\mathbf{u}_b = \mathbf{u}_t \times \mathbf{u}_n$, Fig. 12–26, it may be possible to use this relation to establish the direction of one of the axes, if the directions of the other two are known. For example, no motion occurs in the $\mathbf{u}_b$ direction, and so if this direction and $\mathbf{u}_t$ are known, then $\mathbf{u}_n$ can be determined, where in this case $\mathbf{u}_n = \mathbf{u}_b \times \mathbf{u}_t$, Fig. 12–26. Remember, though, that $\mathbf{u}_n$ is always on the concave side of the curve.

Fig. 12–26

Motorists traveling along this clover-leaf interchange experience a normal acceleration due to the change in direction of their velocity. A tangential component of acceleration occurs when the cars' speed is increased or decreased.

## PROCEDURE FOR ANALYSIS

### Coordinate System

- Provided the *path* of the particle is *known*, we can establish a set of $n$ and $t$ coordinates having a *fixed origin* which is coincident with the particle at the instant considered.
- The positive tangent axis acts in the direction of motion and the positive normal axis is directed toward the path's center of curvature.
- The $n$ and $t$ axes are particularly advantageous for studying the velocity and acceleration of the particle, because the $t$ and $n$ components of **a** are expressed by Eqs. 12–19 and 12–20, respectively.

### Velocity

- The particle's *velocity* is always tangent to the path.
- The magnitude of velocity is found from the time derivative of the path function.

$$v = \dot{s}$$

### Tangential Acceleration

- The tangential component of acceleration is the result of the time rate of change in the magnitude of velocity. This component acts in the positive $s$ direction if the particle's speed is increasing or in the opposite direction if the speed is decreasing.
- The relations between $a_t$, $v$, $t$ and $s$ are the same as for rectilinear motion, namely,

$$a_t = \dot{v} \quad a_t\, ds = v\, dv$$

- If $a_t$ is constant, $a_t = (a_t)_c$, the above equations, when integrated, yield

$$s = s_0 + v_0 t + \tfrac{1}{2}(a_t)_c t^2$$
$$v = v_0 + (a_t)_c t$$
$$v^2 = v_0^2 + 2(a_t)_c(s - s_0)$$

### Normal Acceleration

- The normal component of acceleration is the result of the time rate of change in the direction of the particle's velocity. This component is *always* directed toward the center of curvature of the path, i.e., along the positive $n$ axis.
- The magnitude of this component is determined from

$$a_n = \frac{v^2}{\rho}$$

- If the path is expressed as $y = f(x)$, the radius of curvature $\rho$ at any point on the path is determined from the equation

$$\rho = \frac{[1 + (dy/dx)^2]^{3/2}}{|d^2y/dx^2|}$$

The derivation of this result is given in any standard calculus text.

## EXAMPLE 12.14

When the skier reaches point $A$ along the parabolic path in Fig. 12–27a, he has a speed of 6 m/s which is increasing at 2 m/s$^2$. Determine the direction of his velocity and the direction and magnitude of his acceleration at this instant. Neglect the size of the skier in the calculation.

### Solution

*Coordinate System.* Although the path has been expressed in terms of its $x$ and $y$ coordinates, we can still establish the origin of the $n, t$ axes at the fixed point $A$ on the path and determine the components of $\mathbf{v}$ and $\mathbf{a}$ along these axes, Fig. 12–27a.

*Velocity.* By definition, the velocity is always directed tangent to the path. Since $y = \frac{1}{20}x^2$, $dy/dx = \frac{1}{10}x$, then $dy/dx|_{x=10} = 1$. Hence, at $A$, $\mathbf{v}$ makes an angle of $\theta = \tan^{-1} 1 = 45°$ with the $x$ axis, Fig. 12–27. Therefore,

$$v_A = 6 \text{ m/s} \qquad 45° \nearrow v_A \qquad \qquad \textit{Ans.}$$

*Acceleration.* The acceleration is determined from $\mathbf{a} = \dot{v}\mathbf{u}_t + (v^2/\rho)\mathbf{u}_n$. However, it is first necessary to determine the radius of curvature of the path at $A$ (10 m, 5 m). Since $d^2y/dx^2 = \frac{1}{10}$, then

$$\rho = \frac{[1 + (dy/dx)^2]^{3/2}}{|d^2y/dx^2|} = \frac{[1 + (\frac{1}{10}x)^2]^{3/2}}{|\frac{1}{10}|} \bigg|_{x=10 \text{ m}} = 28.28 \text{ m}$$

The acceleration becomes

$$\mathbf{a}_A = \dot{v}\mathbf{u}_t + \frac{v^2}{\rho}\mathbf{u}_n$$

$$= 2\mathbf{u}_t + \frac{(6 \text{ m/s})^2}{28.28 \text{ m}}\mathbf{u}_n$$

$$= \{2\mathbf{u}_t + 1.273\mathbf{u}_n\} \text{ m/s}^2$$

As shown in Fig. 12–27b,

$$a = \sqrt{(2)^2 + (1.273)^2} = 2.37 \text{ m/s}^2$$

$$\phi = \tan^{-1}\frac{2}{1.273} = 57.5°$$

Thus, $57.5° - 45° = 12.5°$ so that,

$$a = 2.37 \text{ m/s}^2 \qquad 12.5° \nearrow \mathbf{a}_A \qquad \qquad \textit{Ans.}$$

*Note:* By using $n, t$ coordinates, we were able to readily solve this problem since the $n$ and $t$ components account for the *separate* changes in the magnitude and direction of $\mathbf{v}$.

(a)

(b)

Fig. 12–27

**E X A M P L E  12.15**

A race car $C$ travels around the horizontal circular track that has a radius of 90 m, Fig. 12–28. If the car increases its speed at a constant rate of 2.1 m/s$^2$, starting from rest, determine the time needed for it to reach an acceleration of 2.4 m/s$^2$. What is its speed at this instant?

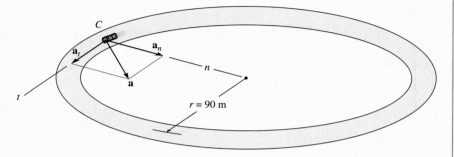

**Fig. 12–28**

**Solution**

*Coordinate System.* The origin of the $n$ and $t$ axes is coincident with the car at the instant considered. The $t$ axis is in the direction of motion, and the positive $n$ axis is directed toward the center of the circle. This coordinate system is selected since the path is known.

*Acceleration.* The magnitude of acceleration can be related to its components using $a = \sqrt{a_t^2 + a_n^2}$. Here $a_t = 2.1$ m/s$^2$. Since $a_n = v^2/\rho$, the velocity as a function of time is

$$v = v_0 + (a_t)_c t$$
$$v = 0 + 2.1t$$

Thus

$$a_n = \frac{v^2}{\rho} = \frac{(2.1t)^2}{90} = 0.049t^2 \text{ m/s}^2$$

The time needed for the acceleration to reach 2.4 m/s$^2$ is therefore

$$a = \sqrt{a_t^2 + a_n^2}$$
$$2.4 = \sqrt{(2.1)^2 + (0.049t^2)^2}$$

Solving for the positive value of $t$ yields

$$0.049t^2 = \sqrt{(2.4)^2 - (2.1)^2}$$
$$t = 4.87 \text{ s} \qquad Ans.$$

*Velocity.* The speed at time $t = 4.87$ s is

$$v = 2.1t = 2.1(4.87) = 10.2 \text{ m/s} \qquad Ans.$$

# E X A M P L E  12.16

The boxes in Fig. 12–29a travel along the industrial conveyor. If a box as in Fig. 12–29b starts from rest at $A$ and increases its speed such that $a_t = (0.2t)$ m/s$^2$, where $t$ is in seconds, determine the magnitude of its acceleration when it arrives at point $B$.

### Solution

*Coordinate System.*   The position of the box at any instant is defined from the fixed point $A$ using the position or path coordinate $s$, Fig. 12–29b. The acceleration is to be determined at $B$, so the origin of the $n$, $t$ axes is at this point.

*Acceleration.*   To determine the acceleration components $a_t = \dot{v}$ and $a_n = v^2/\rho$, it is first necessary to formulate $v$ and $\dot{v}$ so that they may be evaluated at $B$. Since $v_A = 0$ when $t = 0$, then

$$a_t = \dot{v} = 0.2t \qquad (1)$$

$$\int_0^v dv = \int_0^t 0.2t \, dt$$

$$v = 0.1t^2 \qquad (2)$$

The time needed for the box to reach point $B$ can be determined by realizing that the position of $B$ is $s_B = 3 + 2\pi(2)/4 = 6.142$ m, Fig. 12–29b, and since $s_A = 0$ when $t = 0$ we have

$$v = \frac{ds}{dt} = 0.1t^2$$

$$\int_0^{6.142} ds = \int_0^{t_B} 0.1t^2 \, dt$$

$$6.142 = 0.0333 t_B^3$$

$$t_B = 5.690 \text{ s}$$

Substituting into Eqs. 1 and 2 yields

$$(a_B)_t = \dot{v}_B = 0.2(5.690) = 1.138 \text{ m/s}^2$$

$$v_B = 0.1(5.69)^2 = 3.238 \text{ m/s}$$

At $B$, $\rho_B = 2$ m, so that

$$(a_B)_n = \frac{v_B^2}{\rho_B} = \frac{(3.238 \text{ m/s})^2}{2 \text{ m}} = 5.242 \text{ m/s}^2$$

The magnitude of $\mathbf{a}_B$, Fig. 12–29c, is therefore

$$a_B = \sqrt{(1.138)^2 + (5.242)^2} = 5.36 \text{ m/s}^2 \qquad Ans.$$

(a)

(b)

(c)

**Fig. 12–29**

## PROBLEMS

**\*12-100.** A car is traveling along a circular curve that has a radius of 50 m. If its speed is 16 m/s and is increasing uniformly at 8 m/s$^2$, determine the magnitude of its acceleration at this instant.

**12-101.** A car moves along a circular track of radius 75 m such that its speed for a short period of time $0 \le t \le 4$ s, is $v = 0.9(t + t^2)$ m/s, where $t$ is in seconds. Determine the magnitude of its acceleration when $t = 3$ s. How far has it traveled in $t = 3$ s?

**12-102.** At a given instant the jet plane has a speed of 120 m/s and an acceleration of 21 m/s$^2$ acting in the direction shown. Determine the rate of increase in the plane's speed and the radius of curvature $\rho$ of the path.

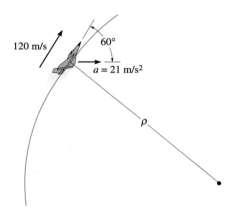

Prob. 12–102

**12-103.** A boat is traveling along a circular curve having a radius of 30 m. If its speed at $t = 0$ is 4.5 m/s and is increasing at $\dot{v} = (0.24t)$ m/s$^2$. determine the magnitude of its acceleration at the instant $t = 5$ s.

**\*12-104.** A boat is traveling along a circular path having a radius of 20 m. Determine the magnitude of the boat's acceleration when the speed is $v = 5$ m/s and the rate of increase in the speed is $\dot{v} = 2$ m/s$^2$.

**∎12-105.** Starting from rest, a bicyclist travels around a horizontal circular path, $\rho = 10$ m, at a speed of $v = (0.09t^2 + 0.1t)$ m/s, where $t$ is in seconds. Determine the magnitudes of his velocity and acceleration when he has traveled $s = 3$ m.

**12-106.** The jet plane travels along the vertical parabolic path. When it is at point $A$ it has a speed of 200 m/s, which is increasing at the rate of 0.8 m/s$^2$. Determine the magnitude of acceleration of the plane when it is at point $A$.

Prob. 12–106

**12-107.** Starting from rest, motorboat travels around the circular path, $\rho = 50$ m, at a speed $v = (0.8t)$ m/s, where $t$ is in seconds. Determine the magnitudes of the boats velocity and acceleration when it has traveled 20 m.

Prob. 12–107

*12-108. Starting from rest, the motorboat travels around the circular path, $\rho = 50$ m, at a speed $v = (0.2t^2)$ m/s, where $t$ is in seconds. Determine the magnitudes of the boats velocity and acceleration at the instant $t = 3$ s.

Prob. 12–108

12-109. A car moves along a circular track of radius 75 m, and its speed for a short period of time $0 \le t \le 2$ s is $v = 0.9(t + t^2)$ m/s, where $t$ is in seconds. Determine the magnitude of its acceleration when $t = 2$ s. How far has it traveled in $t = 2$ s?

■*12-110. The car travels along the curved path such that its speed is increased by $\dot{v} = (0.5e^t)$ m/s$^2$, where $t$ is in seconds. Determine the magnitudes of its velocity and acceleration after the car has traveled $s = 18$ m starting from rest. Neglect the size of the car.

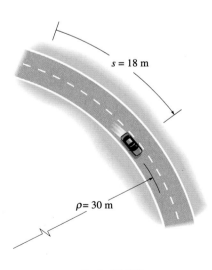

Prob. 12–110

12-111. At a given instant the train engine at $E$ has a speed of 20 m/s and an acceleration of 14 m/s$^2$ acting in the direction shown. Determine the rate of increase in the train's speed and the radius of curvature $\rho$ of the path.

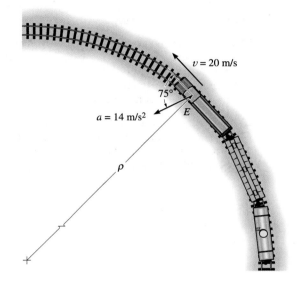

Prob. 12–111

*12-112. A toboggan is traveling down along a curve which can be approximated by the parabola $y = 0.01x^2$. Determine the magnitude of its acceleration when it reaches point $A$, where its speed is $v_A = 10$ m/s, and it is increasing at the rate of $\dot{v}_A = 3$ m/s$^2$.

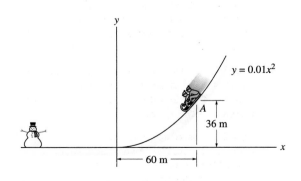

Prob. 12–112

**12-113.** The automobile is originally at rest at $s = 0$. If its speed is increased by $\dot{v} = (0.015t^2)$ m/s$^2$, where $t$ is in seconds, determine the magnitudes of its velocity and acceleration when $t = 18$ s.

**Prob. 12–113**

**12-114.** The automobile is originally at rest $s = 0$. If it then starts to increase its speed at $\dot{v} = (0.015t^2)$ m/s$^2$, where $t$ is in seconds, determine the magnitudes of its velocity and acceleration at $s = 165$ m.

**Prob. 12–114**

**12-115.** The truck travels in a circular path havng a radius of 50 m at a speed of $4 =$ m/s. For a short distance from $s = 0$, its speed is increased by $\dot{v} = (0.05s)$ m/s$^2$, where $s$ is in meters. Determine its speed and the magnitude of its acceleration when it has moved $s = 10$ m.

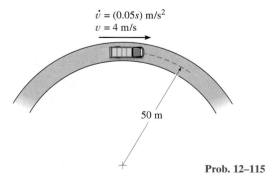

**Prob. 12–115**

*12-116.** The jet plane is traveling with a constant speed of 110 m/s along the curved path. Determine the magnitude of the acceleration of the plane at the instant it reaches point $A$ $(y = 0)$.

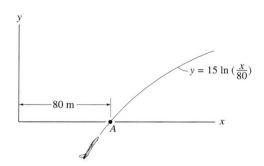

**Prob. 12–116**

**12-117.** A train is traveling with a constant speed of 14 m/s along the curved path. Determine the magnitude of the acceleration of the front of the train, $B$, at the instant it reaches point $A$ $(y = 0)$.

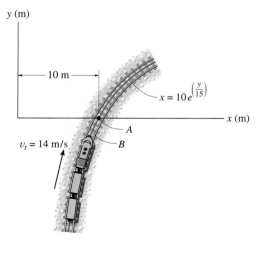

**Prob. 12–117**

**12-118.** When the motorcyclist is at $A$, he increases his speed along the vertical circular path at the rate of $\dot{v} = (0.1t)$ m/s², where $t$ is in seconds. If he starts from rest at $A$, determine the magnitudes of his velocity and acceleration when he reaches $B$.

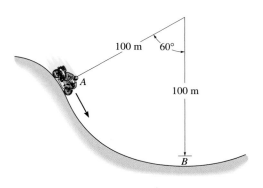

Prob. 12–118

**■12-119.** The car $B$ turns such that its speed is increased by $\dot{v}_B = (0.5e^t)$ m/s², where $t$ is in seconds. If the car starts from rest when $\theta = 0°$, determine the magnitudes of its velocity and acceleration when the arm $AB$ rotates $\theta = 30°$. Neglect the size of the car.

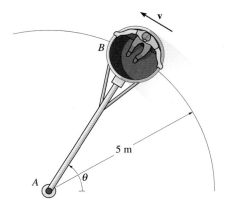

Prob. 12–119

**\*12-120.** The car $B$ turns such that its speed is increased by $\dot{v}_B = (0.5e^t)$ m/s², where $t$ is in seconds. If the car starts from rest when $\theta = 0°$, determine the magnitudes of its velocity and acceleration when $t = 2$ s. Neglect the size of the car. Also, through what angle $\theta$ has it traveled?

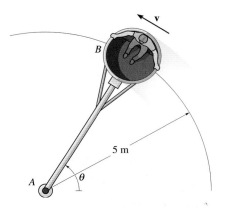

Prob. 12–120

**12-121.** The box of negligible size is sliding down along a curved path defined by the parabola $y = 0.4x^2$. When it is at $A$ ($x_A = 2$ m, $y_A = 1.6$ m), the speed is $v_B = 8$ m/s and the increase in speed is $dv_B/dt = 4$ m/s². Determine the magnitude of the acceleration of the box at this instant.

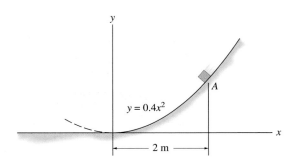

Prob. 12–121

**12-122.** The ball is ejected horizontally from the tube with a speed of 8 m/s. Find the equation of the path, $y = f(x)$, and then find the ball's velocity and the normal and tangential components of acceleration when $t = 0.25$ s.

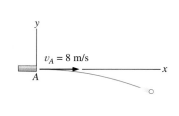

**Prob. 12–122**

**12-123.** The motion of a particle is defined by the equations $x = (2t + t^2)$ m and $y = (t^2)$ m, where $t$ is in seconds. Determine the normal and tangential components of the particle's velocity and acceleration when $t = 2$ s.

**\*12-124.** The motorcycle travels along the elliptical track at a constant speed $v$. Determine the greatest magnitude of the acceleration if $a > b$.

**Prob. 12–124**

**12-125.** The two particles $A$ and $B$ start at the origin $O$ and travel in opposite directions along the circular path at constant speeds $v_A = 0.7$ m/s and $v_B = 1.5$ m/s, respectively. Determine in $t = 2$ s, (a) the displacement along the path of each particle, (b) the position vector to each particle, and (c) the shortest distance between the particles.

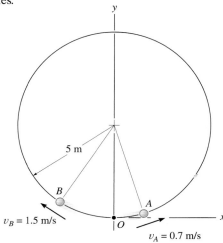

**Prob. 12–125**

**12-126.** The two particles $A$ and $B$ start at the origin $O$ and travel in opposite directions along the circular path at constant speeds $v_A = 0.7$ m/s and $v_B = 1.5$ m/s, respectively. Determine the time when they collide and the magnitude of the acceleration of $B$ just before this happens.

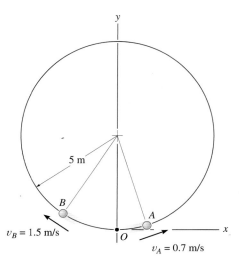

**Prob. 12–126**

**12-127.** The race car has an initial speed $v_A = 15$ m/s at $A$. If it increases its speed along the circular track at the rate $a_t = (0.4s)$ m/s$^2$, where $s$ is in meters, determine the time needed for the car to travel 20 m. Take $\rho = 150$ m.

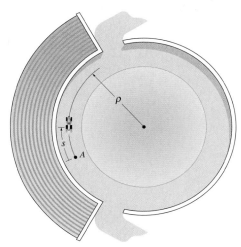

Prob. 12–127

***12-128.** A boy sits on a merry-go-round so that he is always located at $r = 2.4$ m from the center of rotation. The merry-go-round is originally at rest, and then due to rotation the boy's speed is increased at 0.6 m/s$^2$. Determine the time needed for his acceleration to become 1.2 m/s$^2$.

**12-129.** A particle travels along the path $y = a + bx + cx^2$, where $a, b, c$ are constants. If the speed of the particle is constant, $v = v_0$, determine the $x$ and $y$ components of velocity and the normal component of acceleration when $x = 0$.

**■12-130.** The ball is kicked with an initial speed $v_A = 8$ m/s at an angle $\theta_A = 40°$ with the horizontal. Find the equation of the path, $y = f(x)$, and then determine the ball's velocity and the normal and tangential components of its acceleration when $t = 0.25$ s.

Prob. 12–130

**■12-131.** Particles $A$ and $B$ are traveling counter-clockwise around a circular track at a constant speed of 8 m/s. If at the instant shown the speed of $A$ is increased by $\dot{v}_A = (4s_A)$ m/s$^2$, where $s_A$ is in meters, determine the distance measured counterclockwise along the track from $B$ to $A$ when $t = 1$ s. What is the magnitude of the acceleration of each particle at this instant?

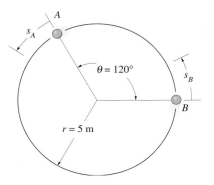

Prob. 12–131

***12-132.** Particles $A$ and $B$ are traveling around a circular track at a speed of 8 m/s at the instant shown. If the speed of $B$ is increased by $\dot{v}_B = 4$ m/s$^2$, and at the same instant $A$ has an increase in speed $\dot{v}_A = 0.8t$ m/s$^2$, determine how long it takes for a collision to occur. What is the magnitude of the acceleration of each particle just before the collision occurs?

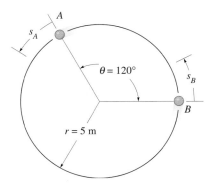

Prob. 12–132

**12-133.** The truck travels at a speed of 4 m/s along a circular road that has a radius of 50 m. For a short distance from $s = 0$, its speed is then increased by $\dot{v} = (0.05s)$ m/s², where $s$ is in meters. Determine its speed and the magnitude of its acceleration when it has moved $s = 10$ m.

50 m

Prob. 12–133

■**12-134.** A go-cart moves along a circular track of radius 30 m such that its speed for a short period of time, $0 \le t \le 4$ s, is $v = 18(1 - e^{-t^2})$ m/s. Determine the magnitude of its acceleration when $t = 2$ s. How far has it traveled in $t = 2$ s? Use Simpson's rule with $n = 50$ to evaluate the integral.

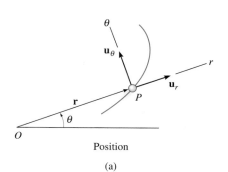

**12-135.** A particle $P$ travels along an elliptical spiral path such that its position vector $\mathbf{r}$ is defined by $\mathbf{r} = \{2 \cos(0.1t)\mathbf{i} + 1.5 \sin(0.1t)\mathbf{j} + (2t)\mathbf{k}\}$ m, where $t$ is in seconds and the arguments for the sine and cosine are given in radians. When $t = 8$ s, determine the coordinate direction angles $\alpha$, $\beta$, and $\gamma$, which the binormal axis to the osculating plane makes with the $x$, $y$, and $z$ axes. *Hint:* Solve for the velocity $\mathbf{v}_P$ and acceleration $\mathbf{a}_P$ of the particle in terms of their $\mathbf{i}, \mathbf{j}, \mathbf{k}$ components. The binormal is parallel to $\mathbf{v}_P \times \mathbf{a}_P$. Why?

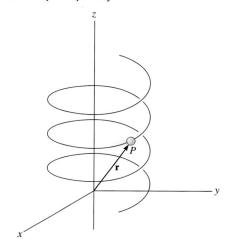

Prob. 12–135

## 12.8 Curvilinear Motion: Cylindrical Components

In some engineering problems it is often convenient to express the path of motion in terms of cylindrical coordinates, $r, \theta, z$. If motion is restricted to the plane, the polar coordinates $r$ and $\theta$ are used.

**Polar Coordinates.** We can specify the location of particle $P$ shown in Fig. 12–30a using both the *radial coordinate r*, which extends outward from the fixed origin $O$ to the particle, and a *transverse coordinate* $\theta$, which is the counterclockwise angle between a fixed reference line and the $r$ axis. The angle is generally measured in degrees or radians, where 1 rad = $180°/\pi$. The positive directions of the $r$ and $\theta$ coordinates are defined by the unit vectors $\mathbf{u}_r$ and $\mathbf{u}_\theta$, respectively. Here $\mathbf{u}_r$ or the radial direction $+r$ extends from $P$ along increasing $r$, when $\theta$ is held fixed, and $\mathbf{u}_\theta$ or $+\theta$ extends from $P$ in a direction that occurs when $r$ is held fixed and $\theta$ is increased. Note that these directions are perpendicular to one another.

Position

(a)

**Fig. 12–30**

**Position.** At any instant the position of the particle, Fig. 12–30a, is defined by the position vector

$$\mathbf{r} = r\mathbf{u}_r \tag{12-22}$$

**Velocity.** The instantaneous velocity $\mathbf{v}$ is obtained by taking the time derivative of $\mathbf{r}$. Using a dot to represent time differentiation, we have

$$\mathbf{v} = \dot{\mathbf{r}} = \dot{r}\mathbf{u}_r + r\dot{\mathbf{u}}_r$$

To evaluate $\dot{\mathbf{u}}_r$, notice that $\mathbf{u}_r$ changes only its direction with respect to time, since by definition the magnitude of this vector is always one unit. Hence, during the time $\Delta t$, a change $\Delta r$ will not cause a change in the direction of $\mathbf{u}_r$; however, a change $\Delta\theta$ will cause $\mathbf{u}_r$ to become $\mathbf{u}'_r$, where $\mathbf{u}'_r = \mathbf{u}_r + \Delta\mathbf{u}_r$, Fig. 12–30b. The time change in $\mathbf{u}_r$ is then $\Delta\mathbf{u}_r$. For small angles $\Delta\theta$ this vector has a magnitude $\Delta u_r \approx 1(\Delta\theta)$ and acts in the $\mathbf{u}_\theta$ direction. Therefore, $\Delta\mathbf{u}_r = \Delta\theta\mathbf{u}_\theta$, and so

$$\dot{\mathbf{u}}_r = \lim_{\Delta t \to 0} \frac{\Delta\mathbf{u}_r}{\Delta t} = \left(\lim_{\Delta t \to 0} \frac{\Delta\theta}{\Delta t}\right)\mathbf{u}_\theta$$

$$\dot{\mathbf{u}}_r = \dot{\theta}\mathbf{u}_\theta \tag{12-23}$$

Substituting into the above equation for $\mathbf{v}$, the velocity can be written in component form as

$$\boxed{\mathbf{v} = v_r\mathbf{u}_r + v_\theta\mathbf{u}_\theta} \tag{12-24}$$

where

$$\boxed{\begin{aligned} v_r &= \dot{r} \\ v_\theta &= r\dot{\theta} \end{aligned}} \tag{12-25}$$

These components are shown graphically in Fig. 12–30c. The *radial component* $\mathbf{v}_r$ is a measure of the rate of increase or decrease in the length of the radial coordinate, i.e., $\dot{r}$; whereas the *transverse component* $\mathbf{v}_\theta$ can be interpreted as the rate of motion along the circumference of a circle having a radius $r$. In particular, the term $\dot{\theta} = d\theta/dt$ is called the *angular velocity*, since it indicates the time rate of change of the angle $\theta$. Common units used for this measurement are rad/s.

Since $\mathbf{v}_r$ and $\mathbf{v}_\theta$ are mutually perpendicular, the *magnitude* of velocity or speed is simply the positive value of

$$v = \sqrt{(\dot{r})^2 + (r\dot{\theta})^2} \tag{12-26}$$

and the *direction* of $\mathbf{v}$ is, of course, tangent to the path at $P$, Fig. 12–30c.

Position

(a)

(b)

Velocity

(c)

**Fig. 12–30**

(d)

**Acceleration.** Taking the time derivatives of Eq. 12–24, using Eqs. 12–25, we obtain the particle's instantaneous acceleration,

$$\mathbf{a} = \dot{\mathbf{v}} = \ddot{r}\mathbf{u}_r + \dot{r}\dot{\mathbf{u}}_r + \dot{r}\dot{\theta}\mathbf{u}_\theta + r\ddot{\theta}\mathbf{u}_\theta + r\dot{\theta}\dot{\mathbf{u}}_\theta$$

To evaluate the term involving $\dot{\mathbf{u}}_\theta$, it is necessary only to find the change made in the direction of $\mathbf{u}_\theta$ since its magnitude is always unity. During the time $\Delta t$, a change $\Delta r$ will not change the direction of $\mathbf{u}_\theta$, although a change $\Delta\theta$ will cause $\mathbf{u}_\theta$ to become $\mathbf{u}'_\theta$, where $\mathbf{u}'_\theta = \mathbf{u}_\theta + \Delta\mathbf{u}_\theta$, Fig. 12–30d. The time change in $\mathbf{u}_\theta$ is thus $\Delta\mathbf{u}_\theta$. For small angles this vector has a magnitude $\Delta u_\theta \approx 1(\Delta\theta)$ and acts in the $-\mathbf{u}_r$, direction; i.e., $\Delta\mathbf{u}_\theta = -\Delta\theta\mathbf{u}_r$. Thus,

$$\dot{\mathbf{u}}_\theta = \lim_{\Delta t \to 0} \frac{\Delta\mathbf{u}_\theta}{\Delta t} = -\left(\lim_{\Delta t \to 0} \frac{\Delta\theta}{\Delta t}\right)\mathbf{u}_r$$

$$\dot{\mathbf{u}}_\theta = -\dot{\theta}\mathbf{u}_r \qquad (12\text{–}27)$$

Substituting this result and Eq. 12–23 into the above equation for $\mathbf{a}$, we can write the acceleration in component form as

$$\boxed{\mathbf{a} = a_r\mathbf{u}_r + a_\theta\mathbf{u}_\theta} \qquad (12\text{–}28)$$

where

$$\boxed{\begin{aligned} a_r &= \ddot{r} - r\dot{\theta}^2 \\ a_\theta &= r\ddot{\theta} + 2\dot{r}\dot{\theta} \end{aligned}} \qquad (12\text{–}29)$$

The term $\ddot{\theta} = d^2\theta/dt^2 = d/dt(d\theta/dt)$ is called the *angular acceleration* since it measures the change made in the angular velocity during an instant of time. Units for this measurement are rad/s$^2$.

Since $\mathbf{a}_r$, and $\mathbf{a}_\theta$ are always perpendicular, the *magnitude* of acceleration is simply the positive value of

$$a = \sqrt{(\ddot{r} - r\dot{\theta}^2)^2 + (r\ddot{\theta} + 2\dot{r}\dot{\theta})^2} \qquad (12\text{–}30)$$

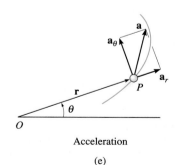

Acceleration

(e)

Fig. 12–30

The *direction* is determined from the vector addition of its two components. In general, $\mathbf{a}$ will *not* be tangent to the path, Fig. 12–30e.

**Cylindrical Coordinates.** If the particle $P$ moves along a space curve as shown in Fig. 12–31, then its location may be specified by the three *cylindrical coordinates, r $\theta$, z.* The $z$ coordinate is identical to that used for rectangular coordinates. Since the unit vector defining its direction, $\mathbf{u}_z$, is constant, the time derivatives of this vector are zero, and therefore the position, velocity, and acceleration of the particle can be written in terms of its cylindrical coordinates as follows:

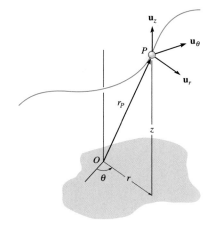

$$\mathbf{r}_p = r\mathbf{u}_r + z\mathbf{u}_z$$
$$\mathbf{v} = \dot{r}\mathbf{u}_r + r\dot{\theta}\mathbf{u}_\theta + \dot{z}\mathbf{u}_z$$
$$\mathbf{a} = (\ddot{r} - r\dot{\theta}^2)\mathbf{u}_r + (r\ddot{\theta} + 2\dot{r}\dot{\theta})\mathbf{u}_\theta + \ddot{z}\mathbf{u}_z$$

**Fig. 12–31**

**Time Derivatives.** The equations of kinematics require that we obtain the time derivatives $\dot{r}$, $\ddot{r}$, $\dot{\theta}$, and $\ddot{\theta}$ in order to evaluate the $r$ and $\theta$ components of $\mathbf{v}$ and $\mathbf{a}$. Two types of problems generally occur:

1. If the coordinates are specified as time parametric equations, $r = r(t)$ and $\theta = \theta(t)$, then the time derivatives can be found directly. For example, consider

$$r = 4t^2 \qquad \theta = (8t^3 + 6)$$
$$\dot{r} = 8t \qquad \dot{\theta} = 24t^2$$
$$\ddot{r} = 8 \qquad \ddot{\theta} = 48t$$

2. If the time-parametric equations are not given, then it will be necessary to specify the path $r = f(\theta)$ and find the *relationship* between the time derivatives using the chain rule of calculus. Consider the following examples.

$$r = 5\theta^2$$
$$\dot{r} = 10\theta\dot{\theta}$$
$$\ddot{r} = 10[(\dot{\theta})\dot{\theta} + \theta(\ddot{\theta})]$$
$$= 10\dot{\theta}^2 + 10\theta\ddot{\theta}$$

The spiral motion of this boy can be followed by using cylindrical components. Here the radial coordinate $r$ is constant, the transverse coordinate $\theta$ will increase with time as the boy rotates about the vertical, and his altitude $z$ will decrease with time.

or

$$r^2 = 6\theta^3$$

$$2r\dot{r} = 18\theta^2\dot{\theta}$$

$$2[(\dot{r})\dot{r} + r(\ddot{r})] = 18[(2\theta\dot{\theta})\dot{\theta} + \theta^2(\ddot{\theta})]$$

$$\dot{r}^2 + r\ddot{r} = 9(2\theta\dot{\theta}^2 + \theta^2\ddot{\theta})$$

If two of the *four* time derivatives $\dot{r}$, $\ddot{r}$, $\dot{\theta}$, and $\ddot{\theta}$ are *known*, then the other two can be obtained from the equations for first and second time derivatives of $r = f(\theta)$. See Example 12.19. In some problems, however, two of these time derivatives may *not* be known; instead the magnitude of the particle's velocity or acceleration may be specified. If this is the case, Eqs. 12–26 and 12–30 [$v^2 = \dot{r}^2 + (\dot{r}\dot{\theta})^2$ and $a^2 = (\ddot{r} - r\dot{\theta}^2)^2 + (r\ddot{\theta} + 2\dot{r}\dot{\theta})^2$] may be used to obtain the necessary relationships involving $\dot{r}$, $\ddot{r}$, $\dot{\theta}$, and $\ddot{\theta}$. See Example 12.20.

## PROCEDURE FOR ANALYSIS

### Coordinate System

- Polar coordinates are a suitable choice for solving problems for which data regarding the angular motion of the radial coordinate $r$ is given to describe the particle's motion. Also, some paths of motion can conveniently be described in terms of these coordinates.
- To use polar coordinates, the origin is established at a fixed point, and the radial line $r$ is directed to the particle.
- The transverse coordinate $\theta$ is measured from a fixed reference line to the radial line.

### Velocity and Acceleration

- Once $r$ and the four time derivatives $\dot{r}$, $\ddot{r}$, $\dot{\theta}$, and $\ddot{\theta}$ have been evaluated at the instant considered, their values can be substituted into Eqs. 12–25 and 12–29 to obtain the radial and transverse components of **v** and **a.**
- If it is necessary to take the time derivatives of $r = f(\theta)$, it is very important to use the chain rule of calculus.
- Motion in three dimensions requires a simple extension of the above procedure to include $\dot{z}$ and $\ddot{z}$.

Besides the examples which follow, further examples involving the calculation of $a_r$ and $a_\theta$ can be found in the "kinematics" sections of Examples 13.10 through 13.12.

# E X A M P L E  12.17

The amusement park ride shown in Fig. 12–32a consists of a chair that is rotating in a horizontal circular path of radius $r$ such that the arm $OB$ has an angular velocity $\dot{\theta}$ and angular acceleration $\ddot{\theta}$. Determine the radial and transverse components of velocity and acceleration of the passenger. Neglect his size in the calculation.

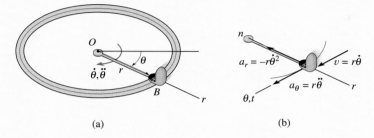

(a)                                      (b)

**Fig. 12–32**

## Solution

*Coordinate System.*   Since the angular motion of the arm is reported, polar coordinates are chosen for the solution, Fig. 12–32a. Here $\theta$ is not related to $r$, since the radius is constant for all $\theta$.

*Velocity and Acceleration.*   Equations 12–25 and 12–29 will be used for the solution, and so it is first necessary to specify the first and second time derivatives of $r$ and $\theta$. Since $r$ is *constant*, we have

$$r = r \qquad \dot{r} = 0 \qquad \ddot{r} = 0$$

Thus

$$v_r = \dot{r} = 0 \qquad\qquad Ans.$$
$$v_\theta = r\dot{\theta} \qquad\qquad Ans.$$
$$a_r = \ddot{r} - r\dot{\theta}^2 = -r\dot{\theta}^2 \qquad\qquad Ans.$$
$$a_\theta = r\ddot{\theta} + 2\dot{r}\dot{\theta} = r\ddot{\theta} \qquad\qquad Ans.$$

These results are shown in Fig. 12–32b. Also shown are the *n, t* axes, which in this special case of circular motion happen to be *colinear* with the $r$ and $\theta$ axes, respectively. In particular note that $v = v_\theta = v_t = r\dot{\theta}$. Also,

$$-a_r = a_n = \frac{v^2}{\rho} = \frac{(r\dot{\theta})^2}{r} = r\dot{\theta}^2$$

$$a_\theta = a_t = \frac{dv}{dt} = \frac{d}{dt}(r\dot{\theta}) = \frac{dr}{dt}\dot{\theta} + r\frac{d\dot{\theta}}{dt} = 0 + r\ddot{\theta}$$

E X A M P L E 12.18

(a)

(b)

(c)

**Fig. 12–33**

The rod $OA$ in Fig. 12–33$a$ is rotating in the horizontal plane such that $\theta = (t^3)$ rad. At the same time, the collar $B$ is sliding outward along $OA$ so that $r = (100t^2)$ mm. If in both cases $t$ is in seconds, determine the velocity and acceleration of the collar when $t = 1$ s.

## Solution

*Coordinate System.* Since time-parametric equations of the path are given, it is not necessary to relate $r$ to $\theta$.

*Velocity and Acceleration.* Determining the time derivatives and evaluating when $t = 1$ s, we have

$$r = 100t^2 \Big|_{t=1\,\text{s}} = 100 \text{ mm} \qquad \theta = t^3 \Big|_{t=1\,\text{s}} = 1 \text{ rad} = 57.3°$$

$$\dot{r} = 200t \Big|_{t=1\,\text{s}} = 200 \text{ mm/s} \qquad \dot{\theta} = 3t^2 \Big|_{t=1\,\text{s}} = 3 \text{ rad/s}$$

$$\ddot{r} = 200 \Big|_{t=1\,\text{s}} = 200 \text{ mm/s}^2 \qquad \ddot{\theta} = 6t \Big|_{t=1\,\text{s}} = 6 \text{ rad/s}^2.$$

As shown in Fig. 12–33$b$,

$$\mathbf{v} = \dot{r}\mathbf{u}_r + r\dot{\theta}\mathbf{u}_\theta$$
$$= 200\mathbf{u}_r + 100(3)\mathbf{u}_\theta$$
$$= \{200\mathbf{u}_r + 300\mathbf{u}_\theta\} \text{ mm/s}$$

The magnitude of $\mathbf{v}$ is

$$v = \sqrt{(200)^2 + (300)^2} = 361 \text{ mm/s} \qquad \textit{Ans.}$$

$$\delta = \tan^{-1}\left(\frac{300}{200}\right) = 56.3° \qquad \delta + 57.3° = 114° \qquad \textit{Ans.}$$

As shown in Fig. 12–33$c$,

$$\mathbf{a} = (\ddot{r} - r\dot{\theta}^2)\mathbf{u}_r + (r\ddot{\theta} + 2\dot{r}\dot{\theta})\mathbf{u}_\theta$$
$$= [200 - 100(3)^2]\mathbf{u}_r + [100(6) + 2(200)3]\mathbf{u}_\theta$$
$$= \{-700\mathbf{u}_r + 1800\mathbf{u}_\theta\} \text{ mm/s}^2$$

The magnitude of $\mathbf{a}$ is

$$a = \sqrt{(700)^2 + (1800)^2} = 1930 \text{ mm/s}^2 \qquad \textit{Ans.}$$

$$\phi = \tan^{-1}\left(\frac{1800}{700}\right) = 68.7° \qquad (180° - \phi) + 57.3° = 169° \qquad \textit{Ans.}$$

# EXAMPLE 12.19

The searchlight in Fig. 12–34a casts a spot of light along the face of a wall that is located 100 m from the searchlight. Determine the magnitudes of the velocity and acceleration at which the spot appears to travel across the wall at the instant $\theta = 45°$. The searchlight is rotating at a constant rate of $\dot\theta = 4$ rad/s.

(a)

## Solution

*Coordinate System.* Polar coordinates will be used to solve this problem since the angular rate of the searchlight is given. To find the necessary time derivatives it is first necessary to relate $r$ to $\theta$. From Fig. 12–34a, this relation is

$$r = 100/\cos\theta = 100\sec\theta$$

*Velocity and Acceleration.* Using the chain rule of calculus, noting that $d(\sec\theta) = \sec\theta\tan\theta\,d\theta$, and $d(\tan\theta) = \sec^2\theta\,d\theta$, we have

$$\dot r = 100(\sec\theta\tan\theta)\dot\theta$$
$$\ddot r = 100(\sec\theta\tan\theta)\dot\theta(\tan\theta)\dot\theta + 100\sec\theta(\sec^2\theta)\dot\theta(\dot\theta)$$
$$\quad + 100\sec\theta\tan\theta(\ddot\theta)$$
$$\quad = 100\sec\theta\tan^2\theta(\dot\theta)^2 + 100\sec^3\theta(\dot\theta)^2 + 100(\sec\theta\tan\theta)\ddot\theta$$

Since $\dot\theta = 4$ rad/s = constant, then $\ddot\theta = 0$, and the above equations, when $\theta = 45°$, become

$$r = 100\sec 45° = 141.4$$
$$\dot r = 400\sec 45°\tan 45° = 565.7$$
$$\ddot r = 1600(\sec 45°\tan^2 45° + \sec^3 45°) = 6788.2$$

As shown in Fig. 12–34b,

$$\mathbf{v} = \dot r\mathbf{u}_r + r\dot\theta\mathbf{u}_\theta$$
$$\quad = 565.7\mathbf{u}_r + 141.4(4)\mathbf{u}_\theta$$
$$\quad = \{565.7\mathbf{u}_r + 565.7\mathbf{u}_\theta\}\text{ m/s}$$
$$v = \sqrt{v_r^2 + v_\theta^2} = \sqrt{(565.7)^2 + (565.7)^2}$$
$$\quad = 800\text{ m/s} \qquad Ans.$$

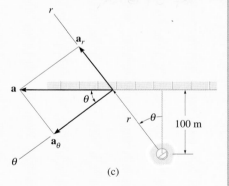

(b)

As shown in Fig. 12–34c,

$$\mathbf{a} = (\ddot r - r\dot\theta^2)\mathbf{u}_r + (r\ddot\theta + 2\dot r\dot\theta)\mathbf{u}_\theta$$
$$\quad = [6788.2 - 141.4(4)^2]\mathbf{u}_r + [141.4(0) + 2(565.7)4]\mathbf{u}_\theta$$
$$\quad = \{4525.5\mathbf{u}_r + 4525.5\mathbf{u}_\theta\}\text{ m/s}^2$$
$$a = \sqrt{a_r^2 + a_\theta^2} = \sqrt{(4525.5)^2 + (4525.5)^2}$$
$$\quad = 6400\text{ m/s}^2 \qquad Ans.$$

*Note:* It is also possible to find $a$ without having to calculate $\ddot r$ (or $a_r$). As shown in Fig. 12–34d, since $a_\theta = 4525.5$ m/s², then by vector resolution, $a = 4525.5/\cos 45° = 6400$ m/s².

(c)

(d)

**Fig. 12–34**

# E X A M P L E 12.20

$r = 0.15(1 - \cos\theta)$ m

(a)

Fig. 12–35

Due to the rotation of the forked rod, the ball $A$ in Fig. 12–35a travels around the slotted path, a portion of which is in the shape of a cardioid, $r = 0.15(1 - \cos\theta)$ m, where $\theta$ is in radians. If the ball's velocity is $v = 1.2$ m/s and its acceleration is $a = 9$ m/s² at the instant $\theta = 180°$, determine the angular velocity $\dot{\theta}$ and angular acceleration $\ddot{\theta}$ of the fork.

## Solution

*Coordinate System.* This path is most unusual, and mathematically it is best expressed using polar coordinates, as done here, rather than rectangular coordinates. Also, $\dot{\theta}$ and $\ddot{\theta}$ must be determined so $r, \theta$ coordinates are an obvious choice.

*Velocity and Acceleration.* Determining the time derivatives of $r$ using the chain rule of calculus yields

$$r = 0.15(1 - \cos\theta)$$
$$\dot{r} = 0.15(\sin\theta)\dot{\theta}$$
$$\ddot{r} = 0.15(\cos\theta)\dot{\theta}(\dot{\theta}) + 0.15(\sin\theta)\ddot{\theta}$$

Evaluating these results at $\theta = 180°$, we have

$$r = 0.3 \text{ m} \quad \dot{r} = 0 \quad \ddot{r} = -0.15\dot{\theta}^2$$

Since $v = 1.2$ m/s, using Eq. 12–26 to determine $\dot{\theta}$ yields

$$v = \sqrt{(\dot{r})^2 + (r\dot{\theta})^2}$$
$$1.2 = \sqrt{(0)^2 + (0.3\dot{\theta})^2}$$
$$\dot{\theta} = 4 \text{ rad/s} \qquad\qquad Ans.$$

In a similar manner, $\ddot{\theta}$ can be found using Eq. 12–30.

$$a = \sqrt{(\ddot{r} - r\dot{\theta}^2)^2 + (r\ddot{\theta} + 2\dot{r}\dot{\theta})^2}$$
$$9 = \sqrt{[-0.15(4)^2 - 0.3(4)^2]^2 + [0.3\ddot{\theta} + 2(0)(4)]^2}$$
$$(9)^2 = (-7.2)^2 + (0.3\ddot{\theta})^2$$
$$\ddot{\theta} = 18 \text{ rad/s}^2 \qquad\qquad Ans.$$

Vectors **a** and **v** are shown in Fig. 12–35b.

$r$

$v = 1.2$ m/s

$a = 9$ m/s²

$\theta$

(b)

# PROBLEMS

**\*12-136.** The time rate of change of acceleration is referred to as the *jerk*, which is often used as a means of measuring passenger discomfort. Calculate this vector, $\dot{\mathbf{a}}$, in terms of its cylindrical components, using Eq. 12–32.

**12-137.** If a particle's position is described by the polar coordinates $r = 4(1 + \sin t)$ m and $\theta = (2e^{-t})$ rad, where $t$ is in seconds and the argument for the sine is in radians, determine the radial and tangential components of the particle's velocity and acceleration when $t = 2$ s.

**12-138.** A particle is moving along a circular path having a radius of 4 m such that its position as a function of time is given by $\theta = \cos 2t$, where $\theta$ is in radians and $t$ is in seconds. Determine the magnitude of the acceleration of the particle when $\theta = 30°$.

**12-139.** A car is traveling along the circular curve of radius $r = 100$ m. At the instant shown, its angular rate of rotation is $\dot{\theta} = 0.4$ rad/s, which is increasing at the rate of $\ddot{\theta} = 0.2$ rad/s$^2$. Determine the magnitudes of the car's velocity and acceleration at this instant.

$\dot{\theta} = 0.4$ rad/s
$\ddot{\theta} = 0.2$ rad/s$^2$

$r = 100$ m

$\theta$

Prob. 12–139

**\*12-140.** If a particle moves along a path such that $r = (2 \cos t)$ m and $\theta = (t/2)$ rad, where $t$ is in seconds, plot the path $r = f(\theta)$ and determine the particle's radial and transverse components of velocity and acceleration.

**12-141.** If a particle's position is described by the polar coordinates $r = (2 \sin 2\theta)$ m and $\theta = (4t)$ rad, where $t$ is in seconds, determine the radial and tangential components of its velocity and acceleration when $t = 1$ s.

**12-142.** A particle is moving along a circular path having a 400-mm radius. Its position as a function of time is given by $\theta = (2t^2)$ rad, where $t$ is in seconds. Determine the magnitude of the particle's acceleration when $\theta = 30°$. The particle starts from rest when $\theta = 0°$.

**12-143.** A particle moves in the $x$–$y$ plane such that its position is defined by $r = \{2t\mathbf{i} + 4t^2\mathbf{j}\}$ m, where $t$ is in seconds. Determine the radial and tangential components of the particle's velocity and acceleration when $t = 2$ s.

**\*12-144.** A truck is traveling along the horizontal circular curve of radius $r = 60$ m with a constant speed $v = 20$ m/s. Determine the angular rate of rotation $\dot{\theta}$ of the radial line $r$ and the magnitude of the truck's acceleration.

**12-145.** A truck is traveling along the horizontal circular curve of radius $r = 60$ m with a speed of 20 m/s which is increasing at 3 m/s$^2$. Determine the truck's radial and transverse components of acceleration.

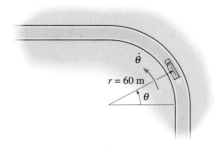

$\dot{\theta}$

$r = 60$ m

$\theta$

Probs. 12–144/145

**12-146.** A particle is moving along a circular path having a radius of 6 cm such that its position as a function of time is given by $\theta = \sin 3t$, where $\theta$ is in radians, the argument for the sine is in degrees, and $t$ is in seconds. Determine the acceleration of the particle at $\theta = 30°$. The particle starts from rest at $\theta = 0°$.

**12-147.** The slotted link is pinned at $O$, and as a result of the constant angular velocity $\dot{\theta} = 3$ rad/s it drives the peg $P$ for a short distance along the spiral guide $r = (0.4\,\theta)$ m, where $\theta$ is in radians. Determine the radial and transverse components of the velocity and acceleration of $P$ at the instant $\theta = \pi/3$ rad.

**\*12-148.** Solve Prob. 12–147 if the slotted link has an angular acceleration $\ddot{\theta} = 8$ rad/s² when $\dot{\theta} = 3$ rad/s at $\theta = \pi/3$ rad.

**12-149.** The slotted link is pinned at $O$, and as a result of the constant angular velocity $\dot{\theta} = 3$ rad/s it drives the peg $P$ for a short distance along the spiral guide $r = (0.4\,\theta)$ m, where $\theta$ is in radians. Determine the velocity and acceleration of the particle at the instant it leaves the slot in the link, i.e., when $r = 0.5$ m.

Probs. 12–147/148/149

**12-150.** A block moves outward along the slot in the platform with a speed of $\dot{r} = (4t)$ m/s, where $t$ is in seconds. The platform rotates at a constant rate of 6 rad/s. If the block starts from rest at the center, determine the magnitudes of its velocity and acceleration when $t = 1$ s.

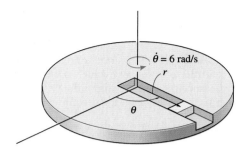

Prob. 12–150

**12-151.** The small washer is sliding down the cord $OA$. When it is at the midpoint, its speed is 200 mm/s and its acceleration is 10 mm/s². Express the velocity and acceleration of the washer at this point in terms of its cylindrical components.

Prob. 12–151

**\*12-152.** At the instant shown, the watersprinkler is rotating with an angular speed $\dot{\theta} = 2$ rad/s and an angular acceleration $\ddot{\theta} = 3$ rad/s². If the nozzle lies in the vertical plane and water is flowing through it at a constant rate of 3 m/s, determine the magnitudes of the velocity and acceleration of a water particle as it exits the open end, $r = 0.2$ m.

Prob. 12–152

**12-153.** The automobile is traveling from a parking deck down along a cylindrical spiral ramp at a constant speed of $v = 1.5$ m/s. If the ramp descends a distance of 12 m for every full revolution; $\theta = 2\pi$ rad, determine the magnitude of the car's acceleration as it moves along the ramp, $r = 10$ m. *Hint:* For part of the solution, note that the tangent to the ramp at any point is at an angle of $\phi = \tan^{-1}(12/[2\pi(10)]) = 10.81°$ from the horizontal. Use this to determine the velocity components $v_\theta$ and $v_z$, which in turn are used to determine $\dot{\theta}$ and $\dot{z}$.

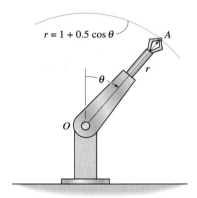

Prob. 12–153

**12-154.** Because of telescopic action, the end of the industrial robotic arm extends along the path of the limaçon $r = (1 + 0.5 \cos\theta)$ m. At the instant $\theta = \pi/4$, the arm has an angular rotation $\dot{\theta} = 0.6$ rad/s, which is increasing at $\ddot{\theta} = 0.25$ rad/s². Determine the radial and transverse components of the velocity and acceleration of the object $A$ held in its grip at this instant.

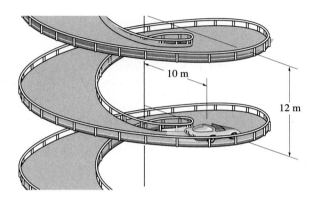

Prob. 12–154

**12-155.** For a short distance the train travels along a track having the shape of a spiral, $r = (1000/\theta)$ m, where $\theta$ is in radians. If it maintains a constant speed $v = 20$ m/s, determine the radial and transverse components of its velocity when $\theta = (9\pi/4)$ rad.

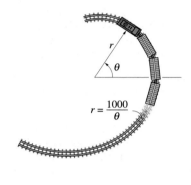

Prob. 12–155

*12-156.** For a short distance the train travels along a track having the shape of a spiral, $r = (1000/\theta)$ m, where $\theta$ is in radians. If the angular rate is constant, $\dot{\theta} = 0.2$ rad/s, determine the radial and transverse components of its velocity and acceleration when $\theta = (9\pi/4)$ rad.

Prob. 12–156

**12-157.** The arm of the robot has a fixed length so that $r = 1$ m and its grip $A$ moves along the path $z = (\sin 4\theta)$ m, where $\theta$ is in radians. If $\theta = (0.5t)$ rad, where $t$ is in seconds, determine the magnitudes of the grip's velocity and acceleration when $t = 3$ s.

**12-158.** For a short time the arm of the robot is extending at a constant rate such that $\dot{r} = 0.45$ m/s when $r = 0.9$ m, $z = (1.2t^2)$ m, and $\theta = 0.5t$ rad, where $t$ is in seconds. Determine the magnitudes of the velocity and acceleration of the grip $A$ when $t = 3$ s.

Probs. 12–157/158

**12-159.** The partial surface of the cam is that of a logarithmic spiral $r = (40e^{0.05\theta})$ mm, where $\theta$ is in radians. If the cam is rotating at a constant angular rate of $\dot{\theta} = 4$ rad/s, determine the magnitudes of the velocity and acceleration of the follower rod at the instant $\theta = 30°$.

**\*12-160.** Solve Prob. 12–159, if the cam has an angular acceleration of $\ddot{\theta} = 2$ rad/s$^2$ when its angular velocity is $\dot{\theta} = 4$ rad/s at $\theta = 30°$.

**12-161.** The searchlight on the boat anchored 600 m from shore is turned on the automobile, which is traveling along the straight road at a constant speed of 24 m/s. Determine the angular rate of rotation of the light when the automobile is $r = 900$ m from the boat.

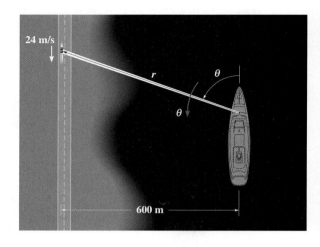

Prob. 12–161

**12-162.** If the boat in Prob. 12–161 is accelerating at 4.5 m/s$^2$ at the instant $r = 900$ m, determine the required angular acceleration $\ddot{\theta}$ of the light at this instant.

**12-163.** A particle $P$ moves along the spiral path $r = (3/\theta)$ m, where $\theta$ is in radians. If it maintains a constant speed of $v = 6$ m/s, determine the magnitudes $v_r$ and $v_\theta$ as functions of $\theta$ and evaluate each at $\theta = 1$ rad.

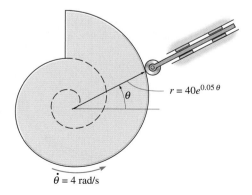

$r = 40e^{0.05\,\theta}$

$\dot{\theta} = 4$ rad/s

Probs. 12–159/160

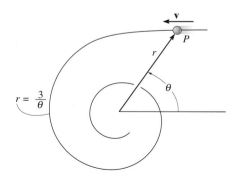

$r = \dfrac{3}{\theta}$

Prob. 12–163

*12-164. A particle travels along the portion of the "four-leaf rose" defined by the equation $r = (5 \cos 2\theta)$ m. If the angular velocity of the radial coordinate line is $\dot{\theta} = (3t^2)$ rad/s, where $t$ is in seconds, determine the radial and transverse components of the particle's velocity and acceleration at the instant $\theta = 30°$. When $t = 0$, $\theta = 0$.

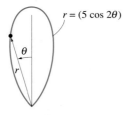

$r = (5 \cos 2\theta)$

**Prob. 12–164**

■12-165. The double collar $C$ is pin connected such that one collar slides over a fixed rod and the other slides over a rotating rod $AB$. If the angular velocity of $AB$ is given as $\dot{\theta} = (e^{0.5t^2})$ rad/s, where $t$ is in seconds, and the path defined by the fixed rod is $r = |0.4 \sin \theta + 0.2|$ m, determine the radial and transverse components of the collar's velocity and acceleration when $t = 1$ s. When $t = 0$, $\theta = 0°$. Use Simpson's rule to determine $\theta$ at $t = 1$ s.

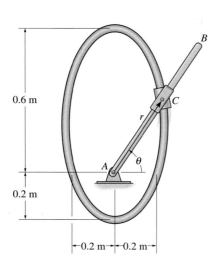

**Prob. 12–165**

12-166. The roller coaster is traveling down along the spiral ramp with a constant speed $v = 6$ m/s. If the track descends a distance of 10 m for every full revolution, $\theta = 2\pi$ rad, determine the magnitude of the roller coaster's acceleration as it moves along the track, $r = 5$ m. *Hint:* For part of the solution, note that the tangent to the ramp at any point is at an angle $\phi = \tan^{-1}[10/2\pi(5)] = 17.66°$ from the horizontal. Use this to determine the velocity components $v_\theta$ and $v_z$, which in turn are used to determine $\dot{\theta}$ and $\dot{z}$.

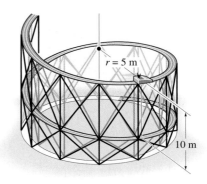

$r = 5$ m

10 m

**Prob. 12–166**

12-167. A cameraman standing at $A$ is following the movement of a race car, $B$, which is traveling around a curved track at a constant speed of 30 m/s. Determine the angular rate $\dot{\theta}$ at which the man must turn in order to keep the camera directed on the car at the instant $\theta = 30°$.

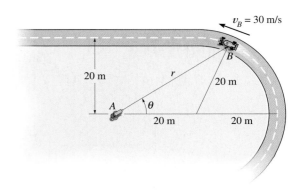

$v_B = 30$ m/s

20 m

$r$

20 m

$A$

$\theta$

20 m

20 m

**Prob. 12–167**

**\*12-168.** The pin follows the path described by the equation $r = (0.2 + 0.15 \cos \theta)$ m. At the instant $\theta = 30°$, $\dot{\theta} = 0.7$ rad/s and $\ddot{\theta} = 0.5$ rad/s². Determine the magnitudes of the pin's velocity and acceleration at this instant. Neglect the size of the pin.

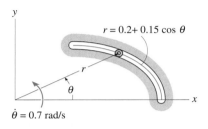

Prob. 12–168

**12-169.** For a short time the position of the roller-coaster car along its path is defined by the equations $r = 25$ m, $\theta = (0.3t)$ rad, and $z = (-8 \cos \theta)$ m, where $t$ is in seconds. Determine the magnitude of the car's velocity and acceleration when $t = 4$ s.

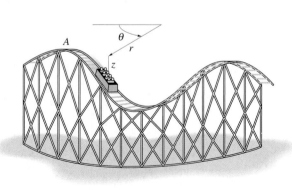

Prob. 12–169

**12-170.** The mechanism of a machine is constructed so that the roller at $A$ follows the surface of the cam described by the equation $r = (0.3 + 0.2 \cos \theta)$ m. If $\dot{\theta} = 0.5$ rad/s and $\ddot{\theta} = 0$, determine the magnitudes of the roller's velocity and acceleration when $\theta = 30°$. Neglect the size of the roller. Also compute the velocity components $(\mathbf{v}_A)_x$ and $(\mathbf{v}_A)_y$ of the roller at this instant. The rod to which the roller is attached remains vertical and can slide up or down along the guides while the guides translate horizontally to the left.

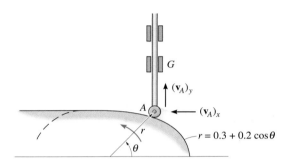

Prob. 12–170

**12-171.** The crate slides down the section of the spiral ramp such that $r = (0.5z)$ m and $z = (30 - 0.03t^2)$ m, where $t$ is in seconds. If the rate of rotation about the $z$ axis is $\dot{\theta} = 0.04\pi t$ rad/s, determine the magnitudes of the velocity and acceleration of the crate at the instant $z = 3$ m.

Prob. 12–171

## 12.9 Absolute Dependent Motion Analysis of Two Particles

In some types of problems the motion of one particle will *depend* on the corresponding motion of another particle. This dependency commonly occurs if the particles are interconnected by inextensible cords which are wrapped around pulleys. For example, the movement of block *A* downward along the inclined plane in Fig. 12–36 will cause a corresponding movement of block *B* up the other incline. We can show this mathematically by first specifying the location of the blocks using *position coordinates* $s_A$ and $s_B$. Note that each of the coordinate axes is (1) referenced from a *fixed* point (*O*) or *fixed* datum line, (2) measured along each inclined plane in the direction of motion of block *A* and block *B*, and (3) has a positive sense from *C* to *A* and *D* to *B*. If the total cord length is $l_T$, the position coordinates are related by the equation

$$s_A + l_{CD} + s_B = l_T$$

Here $l_{CD}$ is the length of the cord passing over arc *CD*. Taking the time derivative of this expression, realizing that $l_{CD}$ and $l_T$ *remain constant*, while $s_A$ and $s_B$ measure the lengths of the changing segments of the cord, we have

$$\frac{ds_A}{dt} + \frac{ds_B}{dt} = 0 \qquad \text{or} \qquad v_B = -v_A$$

The negative sign indicates that when block *A* has a velocity downward, i.e., in the direction of positive $s_A$, it causes a corresponding upward velocity of block *B*; i.e., *B* moves in the negative $s_B$ direction.

In a similar manner, time differentiation of the velocities yields the relation between the accelerations, i.e.,

$$a_B = -a_A$$

A more complicated example involving dependent motion of two blocks is shown in Fig. 12–37*a*. In this case, the position of block *A* is specified by $s_A$, and the position of the *end* of the cord from which block *B* is suspended is defined by $s_B$. Here we have chosen coordinate axes which are (1) referenced from fixed points or datums, (2) measured in the direction of motion of each block, and (3) positive to the right $(s_A)$ and positive downward $(s_B)$. During the motion, the red colored segments of the cord in Fig. 12–37*a remain constant*. If *l* represents the total length of cord minus these segments, then the position coordinates can be related by the equation

$$2s_B + h + s_A = l$$

Since *l* and *h* are constant during the motion, the two time derivatives yield

$$2v_B = -v_A \qquad 2a_B = -a_A$$

Hence, when *B* moves downward $(+s_B)$, *A* moves to the left $(-s_A)$ with two times the motion.

**Fig. 12–36**

(a)

**Fig. 12–37**

(b)

Fig. 12–37

The motion of the traveling block on this oil rig depends upon the motion of the cable connected to the winch which operates it. It is important to be able to relate these motions in order to determine the power requirements of the winch and the force in the cable caused by accelerated motion.

This example can also be worked by defining the position of block $B$ from the center of the bottom pulley (a fixed point), Fig. 12–37b. In this case

$$2(h - s_B) + h + s_A = l$$

Time differentiation yields

$$2v_B = v_A \quad 2a_B = a_A$$

Here the signs are the same. Why?

## PROCEDURE FOR ANALYSIS

The above method of relating the dependent motion of one particle to that of another can be performed using algebraic scalars or position coordinates provided each particle moves along a rectilinear path. When this is the case, only the magnitudes of the velocity and acceleration of the particles will change, not their line of direction. The following procedure is required.

### Position-Coordinate Equation

• Establish position coordinates which have their origin located at a *fixed* point or datum.

• The coordinates are directed along the path of motion and extend to a point having the same motion as each of the particles.

• It is *not necessary* that the *origin* be the *same* for each of the coordinates; however, it is *important* that each coordinate axis selected be directed along the *path of motion* of the particle.

• Using geometry or trigonometry, relate the coordinates to the total length of the cord, $l_T$, or to that portion of cord, $l$, which *excludes* the segments that do not change length as the particles move—such as arc segments wrapped over pulleys.

• If a problem involves a *system* of two or more cords wrapped around pulleys, then the position of a point on one cord must be related to the position of a point on another cord using the above procedure. Separate equations are written for a fixed length of each cord of the system and the positions of the two particles are then related by these equations (see Examples 12.22 and 12.23).

### Time Derivatives

• Two successive time derivatives of the position-coordinate equations yield the required velocity and acceleration equations which relate the motions of the particles.

• The signs of the terms in these equations will be consistent with those that specify the positive and negative sense of the position coordinates.

E X A M P L E **12.21**

Determine the speed of block $A$ in Fig. 12–38 if block $B$ has an upward speed of 2 m/s.

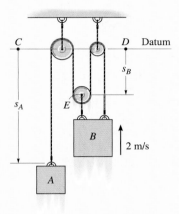

**Fig. 12–38**

## Solution

*Position-Coordinate Equation.*  There is *one cord* in this system having segments which are changing length. Position coordinates $s_A$ and $s_B$ will be used since each is measured from a fixed point ($C$ or $D$) and extends along each block's *path of motion*. In particular, $s_B$ is directed to point $E$ since motion of $B$ and $E$ is the *same*.

The red colored segments of the cord in Fig. 12–38 remain at a constant length and do not have to be considered as the blocks move. The remaining length of cord, $l$, is also constant and is related to the changing position coordinates $s_A$ and $s_B$ by the equation

$$s_A + 3s_B = l$$

*Time Derivative.*  Taking the time derivative yields

$$v_A + 3v_B = 0$$

so that when $v_B = -2$ m/s (upward),

$$v_A = 6 \text{ m/s} \downarrow \qquad\qquad Ans.$$

**E X A M P L E 12.22**

Determine the speed of block $A$ in Fig. 12–39 if block $B$ has an upward speed of 2 m/s.

**Fig. 12–39**

**Solution**

*Position-Coordinate Equation.* As shown, the positions of blocks $A$ and $B$ are defined using coordinates $s_A$ and $s_B$. Since the system has *two* cords which change length, it will be necessary to use a third coordinate, $s_C$, in order to relate $s_A$ to $s_B$. In other words, the length of one of the cords can be expressed in terms of $s_A$ and $s_C$, and the length of the other cord can be expressed in terms of $s_B$ and $s_C$.

The red colored segments of the cords in Fig. 12–39 do not have to be considered in the analysis. Why? For the remaining cord lengths, say $l_1$ and $l_2$, we have

$$s_A + 2s_C = l_1 \qquad s_B + (s_B - s_C) = l_2$$

Eliminating $s_C$ yields an equation defining the positions of both blocks, i.e.,

$$s_A + 4s_B = 2l_2 + l_1$$

*Time Derivative.* The time derivative gives

$$v_A + 4v_B = 0$$

so that when $v_B = -2$ m/s (upward),

$$v_B = +8 \text{ m/s} = 8 \text{ m/s} \downarrow \qquad\qquad\qquad Ans.$$

# EXAMPLE 12.23

Determine the speed with which block $B$ rises in Fig. 12–40 if the end of the cord at $A$ is pulled down with a speed of 2 m/s.

**Fig. 12–40**

## Solution

*Position-Coordinate Equation.*  The position of point $A$ is defined by $s_A$, and the position of block $B$ is specified by $s_B$ since point $E$ on the pulley will have the *same motion* as the block. Both coordinates are measured from a horizontal datum passing through the *fixed* pin at pulley $D$. Since the system consists of *two* cords, the coordinates $s_A$ and $s_B$ cannot be related directly. Instead, by establishing a third position coordinate, $s_C$, we can now express the length of one of the cords in terms of $s_B$ and $s_C$, and the length of the other cord in terms of $s_A$, $s_B$, and $s_C$.

Excluding the red colored segments of the cords in Fig. 12–40, the remaining constant cord lengths $l_1$ and $l_2$ (along with the hook and link dimensions) can be expressed as

$$s_C + s_B = l_1$$
$$(s_A - s_C) + (s_B - s_C) + s_B = l_2$$

Eliminating $s_C$ yields

$$s_A + 4s_B = l_2 + 2l_1$$

As required, this equation relates the position $s_B$ of block $B$ to the position $s_A$ of point $A$.

*Time Derivative.*  The time derivative gives

$$v_A + 4v_B = 0$$

so that when $v_A = 2$ m/s (downward),

$$v_B = -0.5 \text{ m/s} = 0.5 \text{ m/s} \uparrow \qquad \textit{Ans.}$$

EXAMPLE 12.24

**Fig. 12–41**

A man at $A$ is hoisting a safe $S$ as shown in Fig. 12–41 by walking to the right with a constant velocity $v_A = 0.5$ m/s. Determine the velocity and acceleration of the safe when it reaches the elevation at $E$. The rope is 30 m long and passes over a small pulley at $D$.

**Solution**

*Position-Coordinate Equation.* This problem is unlike the previous examples since rope segment $DA$ changes both direction and magnitude. However, the ends of the rope, which define the positions of $S$ and $A$, are specified by means of the $x$ and $y$ coordinates measured from a fixed point and *directed along the paths of motion* of the ends of the rope.

The $x$ and $y$ coordinates may be related since the rope has a fixed length $l = 30$ m, which at all times is equal to the length of segment $DA$ plus $CD$. Using the Pythagorean theorem to determine $l_{DA}$, we have $l_{DA} = \sqrt{(15)^2 + x^2}$; also, $l_{CD} = 15 - y$. Hence,

$$l = l_{DA} + l_{CD}$$

$$30 = \sqrt{(15)^2 + x^2} + (15 - y)$$

$$y = \sqrt{225 + x^2} - 15 \qquad (1)$$

*Time Derivatives.* Taking the time derivative, using the chain rule, where $v_S = dy/dt$ and $v_A = dx/dt$, yields

$$v_S = \frac{dy}{dt} = \left[ \frac{1}{2} \frac{2x}{\sqrt{225 + x^2}} \right] \frac{dx}{dt}$$

$$= \frac{x}{\sqrt{225 + x^2}} v_A. \qquad (2)$$

At $y = 10$ m, $x$ is determined from Eq. 1, i.e., $x = 20$ m. Hence, from Eq. 2 with $v_A = 0.5$ m/s,

$$v_S = \frac{20}{\sqrt{225 + (20)^2}}(0.5) = 0.4 \text{ m/s} = 400 \text{ mm/s}\uparrow \qquad Ans.$$

The acceleration is determined by taking the time derivative of Eq. 2. Since $v_A$ is constant, then $a_A = dv_A/dt = 0$, and we have

$$a_S = \frac{d^2y}{dt^2} = \left[ \frac{-x(dx/dt)}{(225 + x^2)^{3/2}} \right] x v_A + \left[ \frac{1}{\sqrt{225 + x^2}} \right] \left( \frac{dx}{dt} \right) v_A + \left[ \frac{1}{\sqrt{225 + x^2}} \right] x \frac{dv_A}{dt} = \frac{225 v_A^2}{(225 + x^2)^{3/2}}$$

At $x = 20$ m, with $v_A = 0.5$ m/s, the acceleration becomes

$$a_S = \frac{225(0.5 \text{ m/s})^2}{[225 + (20 \text{ m})^2]^{3/2}} = 0.00360 \text{ m/s}^2 = 3.60 \text{ mm/s}^2\uparrow \qquad Ans.$$

Note that the constant velocity at $A$ causes the other end $C$ of the rope to have an acceleration since $\mathbf{v}_A$ causes segment $DA$ to change its direction as well as its length.

# 12.10  Relative-Motion Analysis of Two Particles Using Translating Axes

Throughout this chapter the absolute motion of a particle has been determined using a single fixed reference frame for measurement. There are many cases, however, where the path of motion for a particle is complicated, so that it may be feasible to analyze the motion in parts by using two or more frames of reference. For example, the motion of a particle located at the tip of an airplane propeller, while the plane is in flight, is more easily described if one observes first the motion of the airplane from a fixed reference and then superimposes (vectorially) the circular motion of the particle measured from a reference attached to the airplane. Any type of coordinates—rectangular, cylindrical, etc.— may be chosen to describe these two different motions.

In this section only *translating frames of reference* will be considered for the analysis. Relative-motion analysis of particles using rotating frames of reference will be treated in Secs. 16.8 and 20.4, since such an analysis depends on prior knowledge of the kinematics of line segments.

**Position.**  Consider particles $A$ and $B$, which move along the arbitrary paths $aa$ and $bb$, respectively, as shown in Fig. 12–42a. The *absolute position* of each particle, $\mathbf{r}_A$ and $\mathbf{r}_B$, is measured from the common origin $O$ of the *fixed $x, y, z$* reference frame. The origin of a second frame of reference $x'$, $y'$, $z'$ is attached to and moves with particle $A$. The axes of this frame are *only permitted to translate* relative to the fixed frame. The *relative position* of "$B$ with respect to $A$" is designated by a *relative-position vector* $\mathbf{r}_{B/A}$. Using vector addition, the three vectors shown in Fig. 12–42a can be related by the equation*

$$\mathbf{r}_B = \mathbf{r}_A + \mathbf{r}_{B/A} \qquad (12\text{–}33)$$

**Velocity.**  An equation that relates the velocities of the particles can be determined by taking the time derivative of Eq. 12–33, i.e.,

$$\mathbf{v}_B = \mathbf{v}_A + \mathbf{v}_{B/A} \qquad (12\text{–}34)$$

Here $\mathbf{v}_B = d\mathbf{r}_B/dt$ and $\mathbf{v}_A = d\mathbf{r}_A/dt$ refer to *absolute velocities*, since they are observed from the fixed frame; whereas the *relative velocity* $\mathbf{v}_{B/A} = d\mathbf{r}_{B/A}/dt$ is observed from the translating frame. It is important

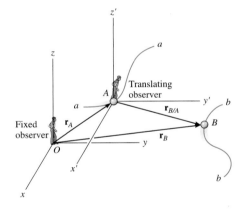

(a)

**Fig. 12–42**

---

*An easy way to remember the setup of this equation, and others like it, is to note the "cancellation" of the subscript $A$ between the two terms, i.e., $\mathbf{r}_B = \mathbf{r}_A + \mathbf{r}_{B/A}$.

(b)

(c)

**Fig. 12–42**

to note that since the $x'$, $y'$, $z'$ axes translate, the *components* of $\mathbf{r}_{B/A}$ will *not* change direction and therefore the time derivative of this vector's components will only have to account for the change in the vector's magnitude. Equation 12–34 therefore states that the velocity of $B$ is equal to the velocity of $A$ plus (vectorially) the relative velocity of "$B$ with respect to $A$," as measured by the *translating observer* fixed in the $x'$, $y'$, $z'$ reference, Fig. 12–42b.

**Acceleration.** The time derivative of Eq. 12–34 yields a similar vector relationship between the *absolute* and *relative accelerations* of particles $A$ and $B$.

$$\boxed{\mathbf{a}_B = \mathbf{a}_A + \mathbf{a}_{B/A}} \qquad (12\text{–}35)$$

Here $\mathbf{a}_{B/A}$ is the acceleration of $B$ as seen by the observer located at $A$ and translating with the $x'$, $y'$, $z'$ reference frame. The vector addition is shown in Fig. 12–42c.

## PROCEDURE FOR ANALYSIS

- When applying the relative-position equation, $\mathbf{r}_B = \mathbf{r}_A + \mathbf{r}_{B/A}$, it is first necessary to specify the locations of the fixed $x$, $y$, $z$, and translating $x'$, $y'$, $z'$ axes.
- Usually, the origin $A$ of the translating axes is located at a point having a *known position*, $\mathbf{r}_A$, Fig. 12–42a.
- A graphical representation of the vector addition $\mathbf{r}_B = \mathbf{r}_A + \mathbf{r}_{B/A}$ can be shown, and both the known and unknown quantities labeled on this sketch.
- Since vector addition forms a triangle, there can be at most *two unknowns*, represented by the magnitudes and/or directions of the vector quantities.
- These unknowns can be solved for either graphically, using trigonometry (law of sines, law of cosines), or by resolving each of the three vectors $\mathbf{r}_B$, $\mathbf{r}_A$, and $\mathbf{r}_{B/A}$ into rectangular or Cartesian components, thereby generating a set of scalar equations.
- The relative-motion equations $\mathbf{v}_B = \mathbf{v}_A + \mathbf{v}_{B/A}$ and $\mathbf{a}_B = \mathbf{a}_A + \mathbf{a}_{B/A}$ are applied in the same manner as explained above, except in this case the origin $O$ of the fixed $x$, $y$, $z$ axes does not have to be specified, Figs. 12–42b and 12–42c.

The pilots of these jet planes flying close to one another must be aware of their relative positions and velocities at all times in order to avoid a collision.

## E X A M P L E 12.25

A train, traveling at a constant speed of 90 km/h, crosses over a road as shown in Fig. 12–43a. If automobile $A$ is traveling at 67.5 km/h along the road, determine the magnitude and direction of the relative velocity of the train with respect to the automobile.

### Solution I

*Vector Analysis.* The relative velocity $\mathbf{v}_{T/A}$ is measured from the translating $x'$, $y'$ axes attached to the automobile, Fig. 12–43a. It is determined from $\mathbf{v}_T = \mathbf{v}_A + \mathbf{v}_{T/A}$. Since $\mathbf{v}_T$ and $\mathbf{v}_A$ are known in *both* magnitude and direction, the unknowns become the $x$ and $y$ components of $\mathbf{v}_{T/A}$. Using the $x$, $y$ axes in Fig. 12–43a and a Cartesian vector analysis, we have

$$\mathbf{v}_T = \mathbf{v}_A + \mathbf{v}_{T/A}$$
$$90\mathbf{i} = (67.5 \cos 45° \, \mathbf{i} + 67.5 \sin 45° \, \mathbf{j}) + \mathbf{v}_{T/A}$$
$$\mathbf{v}_{T/A} = \{42.3\mathbf{i} - 47.7\mathbf{j}\} \text{ km/h} \qquad \textit{Ans.}$$

(a)

The magnitude of $\mathbf{v}_{T/A}$ is thus

$$v_{T/A} = \sqrt{(42.3)^2 + (-47.7)^2]^2} = 63.8 \text{ km/h} \qquad \textit{Ans.}$$

From the direction of each component, Fig. 12–43b, the direction of $\mathbf{v}_{T/A}$ defined from the $x$ axis is

$$\tan \theta = \frac{(v_{T/A})_y}{(v_{T/A})_x} = \frac{47.7}{42.3}$$
$$\theta = 48.40° \, \searrow^\theta \qquad \textit{Ans.}$$

Note that the vector addition shown in Fig. 12–43b indicates the correct sense for $\mathbf{v}_{T/A}$. This figure anticipates the answer and can be used to check it.

(b)

### Solution II

*Scalar Analysis.* The unknown components of $\mathbf{v}_{T/A}$ can also be determined by applying a scalar analysis. We will assume these components act in the *positive* $x$ and $y$ directions. Thus,

$$\mathbf{v}_T = \mathbf{v}_A + \mathbf{v}_{T/A}$$

$$\begin{bmatrix} 90 \text{ km/h} \\ \rightarrow \end{bmatrix} = \begin{bmatrix} 67.5 \text{ km/h} \\ \nearrow 45° \end{bmatrix} + \begin{bmatrix} (v_{T/A})_x \\ \rightarrow \end{bmatrix} + \begin{bmatrix} (v_{T/A})_y \\ \uparrow \end{bmatrix}$$

Resolving each vector into its $x$ and $y$ components yields

$(\overset{+}{\rightarrow})$      $90 = 67.5 \cos 45° + (v_{T/A})_x + 0$
$(+\uparrow)$      $0 = 67.5 \sin 45° + 0 + (v_{T/A})_y$

Solving, we obtain the previous results,

$$(v_{T/A})_x = 42.3 \text{ km/h} = 42.3 \text{ km/h} \rightarrow$$
$$(v_{T/A})_y = -47.7 \text{ km/h} = 47.7 \text{ km/h} \downarrow \qquad \textit{Ans.}$$

(c)

Fig. 12–43

**EXAMPLE 12.26**

(a)

(b)

(c)

**Fig. 12–44**

Plane $A$ in Fig. 12–44$a$ is flying along a straight-line path, whereas plane $B$ is flying along a circular path having a radius of curvature of $\rho_B = 400$ km. Determine the velocity and acceleration of $B$ as measured by the pilot of $A$.

**Solution**

*Velocity.* The $x, y$ axes are located at an arbitrary fixed point. Since the motion relative to plane $A$ is to be determined, the *translating frame of reference* $x', y'$ is attached to it, Fig. 12–44$a$. Applying the relative-velocity equation in scalar form since the velocity vectors of both planes are parallel at the instant shown, we have

$$(+\uparrow) \qquad\qquad v_B = v_A + v_{B/A}$$
$$600 = 700 + v_{B/A}$$
$$v_{B/A} = -100 \text{ km/h} = 100 \text{ km/h} \downarrow \qquad\qquad Ans.$$

The vector addition is shown in Fig. 12–44$b$.

*Acceleration.* Plane $B$ has both tangential and normal components of acceleration, since it is flying along a *curved path*. From Eq. 12–20, the magnitude of the normal component is

$$(a_B)_n = \frac{v_B^2}{\rho} = \frac{(600 \text{ km/h})^2}{400 \text{ km}} = 900 \text{ km/h}^2$$

Applying the relative-acceleration equation, we have

$$\mathbf{a}_B = \mathbf{a}_A + \mathbf{a}_{B/A}$$
$$900\mathbf{i} - 100\mathbf{j} = 50\mathbf{j} + \mathbf{a}_{B/A}$$

Thus,

$$\mathbf{a}_{B/A} = \{900\mathbf{i} - 150\mathbf{j}\} \text{ km/h}^2$$

From Fig. 12–44$c$, the magnitude and direction of $\mathbf{a}_{B/A}$ are therefore

$$a_{B/A} = 912 \text{ km/h}^2 \quad \theta = \tan^{-1}\frac{150}{900} = 9.46° \ \searrow^\theta \qquad\qquad Ans.$$

Notice that the solution to this problem is possible using a translating frame of reference, since the pilot in plane $A$ is "translating." Observation of plane $A$ with respect to the pilot of plane $B$, however, must be obtained using a *rotating* set of axes attached to plane $B$. (This assumes, of course, that the pilot of $B$ is fixed in the rotating frame, so he does not turn his eyes to follow the motion of $A$.) The analysis for this case is given in Example 16.21.

## E X A M P L E 12.27

At the instant shown in Fig. 12–45 cars $A$ and $B$ are traveling with speeds of 18 m/s and 12 m/s, respectively. Also at this instant, $A$ has a decrease in speed of 2 m/s$^2$, and $B$ has an increase in speed of 3 m/s$^2$. Determine the velocity and acceleration of $B$ with respect to $A$.

(a)

### Solution

*Velocity.* The fixed $x, y$ axes are established at a point on the ground and the translating $x', y'$ axes are attached to car $A$, Fig. 12–45a. Why? The relative velocity is determined from $\mathbf{v}_B = \mathbf{v}_A + \mathbf{v}_{B/A}$. What are the two unknowns? Using a Cartesian vector analysis, we have

$$\mathbf{v}_B = \mathbf{v}_A + \mathbf{v}_{B/A}$$

$$-12\mathbf{j} = (-18\cos 60°\mathbf{i} - 18\sin 60°\mathbf{j}) + \mathbf{v}_{B/A}$$

$$\mathbf{v}_{B/A} = \{9\mathbf{i} + 3.588\mathbf{j}\} \text{ m/s}$$

Thus,

$$v_{B/A} = \sqrt{(9)^2 + (3.588)^2} = 9.69 \text{ m/s} \qquad Ans.$$

Noting that $\mathbf{v}_{B/A}$ has $+\mathbf{i}$ and $+\mathbf{j}$ components, Fig. 12–45b, its direction is

$$\tan\theta = \frac{(v_{B/A})_y}{(v_{B/A})_x} = \frac{3.588}{9}$$

$$\theta = 21.7° \nearrow \qquad Ans.$$

(b)

*Acceleration.* Car $B$ has both tangential and normal components of acceleration. Why? The magnitude of the normal component is

$$(a_B)_n = \frac{v_B^2}{\rho} = \frac{(12 \text{ m/s})^2}{100 \text{ m}} = 1.440 \text{ m/s}^2$$

Applying the equation for relative acceleration yields

$$\mathbf{a}_B = \mathbf{a}_A + \mathbf{a}_{B/A}$$

$$(-1.440\mathbf{i} - 3\mathbf{j}) = (2\cos 60°\mathbf{i} + 2\sin 60°\mathbf{j}) + \mathbf{a}_{B/A}$$

$$\mathbf{a}_{B/A} = \{-2.440\mathbf{i} - 4.732\mathbf{j}\} \text{ m/s}^2$$

Here $\mathbf{a}_{B/A}$ has $-\mathbf{i}$ and $-\mathbf{j}$ components. Thus, from Fig. 12–45c,

$$a_{B/A} = \sqrt{(2.440)^2 + (4.732)^2} = 5.32 \text{ m/s}^2 \qquad Ans.$$

$$\tan\phi = \frac{(a_{B/A})_y}{(a_{B/A})_x} = \frac{4.732}{2.440}$$

$$\phi = 62.7° \swarrow \qquad Ans.$$

(c)

**Fig. 12–45**

It is possible to obtain the relative acceleration of $\mathbf{a}_{A/B}$ using this method? Refer to the comment made at the end of Example 12.26.

# PROBLEMS

**\*12-172.** If the end of the cable at $A$ is pulled down with a speed of 2 m/s, determine the speed at which block $B$ rises.

Prob. 12–172

**12-173.** If the end of the cable at $A$ is pulled down with a speed of 2 m/s, determine the speed at which block $B$ rises.

Prob. 12–173

**12-174.** Determine the constant speed at which the cable at $A$ must be drawn in by the motor in order to hoist the load at $B$ 5 m in 5 s.

Prob. 12–174

**12-175.** Determine the time needed for the load at $B$ to attain a speed of 8 m/s, starting from rest, if the cable is drawn into the motor with an acceleration of $0.2$ m/s$^2$.

Prob. 12–175

**\*12-176.** Determine the displacement of the log if the truck at $C$ pulls the cable 1.2 m to the right.

Prob. 12–176

**12-177.** The crate is being lifted up the inclined plane using the motor $M$ and the rope and pulley arrangement shown. Determine the speed at which the cable must be taken up by the motor in order to move the crate up the plane with a constant speed of 1.2 m/s.

Prob. 12–177

**12-178.** Determine the displacement of the block at $B$ if $A$ is pulled down 1 m.

Prob. 12–178

**12-179.** The cable at $B$ is pulled downwards at 1.2 m/s, and is slowing at 0.6 m/s². Determine the velocity and acceleration of block $A$ at this instant.

Prob. 12–179

**\*12-180.** The pulley arrangement shown is designed for hoisting materials. If *BC remains fixed* while the plunger $P$ is pushed downward with a speed of 1.2 m/s, determine the speed of the load at $A$.

Prob. 12–180

**12-181.** If block $A$ is moving downward with a speed of 1.2 m/s while $C$ is moving up at 0.6 m/s, determine the speed of block $B$.

**12-182.** If block $A$ is moving downward at 2 m/s while block $C$ is moving down at 6 m/s, determine the relative velocity of block $B$ with respect to $C$.

Probs. 12–181/182

**12-183.** If the end of the cable at $A$ is pulled down with a speed of 2 m/s, determine the speed at which block $E$ rises.

Prob. 12–183

**\*12-184.** If block $A$ of the pulley system is moving downward with a speed of 1.2 m/s while block $C$ is moving up at 0.6 m/s, determine the speed of block $B$.

Prob. 12–184

**12-185.** The crane is used to hoist the load. If the motors at $A$ and $B$ are drawing in the cable at a speed of 0.6 m/s and 1.2 m/s, respectively, determine the speed of the load.

Prob. 12–185

**12-186.** The cylinder $C$ is being lifted using the cable and pulley system shown. If point $A$ on the cable is being drawn toward the drum with a speed of 2 m/s, determine the speed of the cylinder.

Prob. 12–186

**12-187.** The motion of the collar at $A$ is controlled by a motor at $B$ such that when the collar is at $s_A = 0.9$ m it is moving upwards at 0.6 m/s and slowing down at 0.3 m/s². Determine the velocity and acceleration of the cable as it is drawn into the motor $B$ at this instant.

Prob. 12–187

**\*12-188.** The roller at $A$ is moving upward with a velocity of $v_A = 0.9$ m/s and has an acceleration of $a_A = 1.2$ m/s² when $s_A = 1.2$ m. Determine the velocity and acceleration of block $B$ at this instant.

Prob. 12–188

**12-189.** The crate $C$ is being lifted by moving the roller at $A$ downward with a constant speed of $v_A = 2$ m/s along the guide. Determine the velocity and acceleration of the crate at the instant $s = 1$ m. When the roller is at $B$, the crate rests on the ground. Neglect the size of the pulley in the calculation. *Hint:* Relate the coordinates $x_C$ and $x_A$ using the problem geometry, then take the first and second time derivatives.

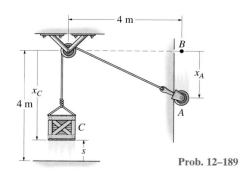

Prob. 12–189

**12-190.** The girl at $C$ stands near the edge of the pier and pulls in the rope *horizontally* at a constant speed of 1.8 m/s. Determine how fast the boat approaches the pier at the instant the rope length $AB$ is 15 m.

Prob. 12–190

**12-191.** The man pulls the boy up to the tree limb $C$ by walking backward. If he starts from rest when $x_A = 0$ and moves backward with a constant acceleration $a_A = 0.2 \text{ m/s}^2$, determine the speed of the boy at the instant $y_B = 4$ m. Neglect the size of the limb. When $x_A = 0$, $y_B = 8$ m, so that $A$ and $B$ are coincident, i.e., the rope is 16 m long.

Prob. 12–191

**\*12-192.** Collars $A$ and $B$ are connected to the cord that passes over the small pulley at $C$. When $A$ is located at $D$, $B$ is 7.2 m to the left of $D$. If $A$ moves at a constant speed of 0.6 m/s to the right, determine the speed of $B$ when $A$ is 1.2 m to the right of $D$.

Prob. 12–192

**12-193.** If block $B$ is moving down with a velocity $v_B$ and has an acceleration $a_B$, determine the velocity and acceleration of block $A$ in terms of the parameters shown.

Prob. 12–193

**12-194.** Vertical motion of the load is produced by movement of the piston at $A$ on the boom. Determine the distance the piston or pulley at $C$ must move to the left in order to lift the load 0.6 m. The cable is attached at $B$, passes over the pulley at $C$, then $D$, $E$, $F$, and again around $E$, and is attached at $G$.

Prob. 12–194

**12-195.** Sand falls from rest 0.5 m vertically onto a chute. If the sand then slides with a velocity of $v_C = 2$ m/s down the chute, determine the relative velocity of the sand just falling on the chute at $A$ with respect to the sand sliding down the chute. The chute is inclined at an angle of $40°$ with the horizontal.

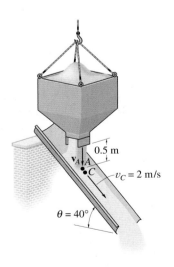

Prob. 12–195

**\*12-196.** Two planes, $A$ and $B$, are flying at the same altitude. If their velocities are $v_A = 600$ km/h and $v_B = 500$ km/h such that the angle between their straight-line courses is $\theta = 75°$, determine the velocity of plane $B$ with respect to plane $A$.

**Prob. 12–196**

**12-197.** At the instant shown, cars $A$ and $B$ are traveling at speeds of 48 km/h and 32 km/h, respectively. If $B$ is increasing its speed by 1920 km/h², while $A$ maintains a constant speed, determine the velocity and acceleration of $B$ with respect to $A$.

**12-198.** At the instant shown, cars $A$ and $B$ are traveling at speeds of 48 km/h and 32 km/h, respectively. If $A$ is increasing its speed at 640 km/h² whereas the speed of $B$ is decreasing at 1280 km/h², determine the velocity and acceleration of $B$ with respect to $A$.

**Probs. 12–197/198**

**12-199.** Two boats leave the shore at the same time and travel in the directions shown. If $v_A = 6$ m/s and $v_B = 4.5$ m/s, determine the speed of boat $A$ with respect to boat $B$. How long after leaving the shore will the boats be 240 m apart?

**Prob. 12–199**

**\*12-200.** Two planes $A$ and $B$ are flying side by side at a constant speed of 900 km/h. Maintaining this speed, plane $A$ begins to travel along the spiral path $r = (1500\theta)$ km, where $\theta$ is in radians, whereas plane $B$ continues to fly in a straight line. Determine the speed of plane $A$ with respect to plane $B$ when $r = 750$ km.

**Prob. 12–200**

**12-201.** At the instant shown, the bicyclist at $A$ is traveling at 7 m/s around the curve on the race track while increasing his speed at 0.5 m/s². The bicyclist at $B$ is traveling at 8.5 m/s along the straight-a-way and increasing his speed at 0.7 m/s². Determine the relative velocity and relative acceleration of $A$ with respect to $B$ at this instant.

**Prob. 12–201**

**12-202.** At the instant shown, cars $A$ and $B$ are traveling at speeds of 88 km/h and 64 km/h, respectively. If $B$ is increasing its speed by 1920 km/h², while $A$ maintains a constant speed, determine the velocity and acceleration of $B$ with respect to $A$. Car $B$ moves along a curve having a radius of curvature of 0.8 km.

**Prob. 12–202**

**12-203.** Cars $A$ and $B$ are traveling around the circular race track. At the instant shown, $A$ has a speed of 27 m/s and is increasing its speed at the rate of 4.5 m/s², whereas $B$ has a speed of 31.5 m/s and is decreasing its speed at 7.5 m/s². Determine the relative velocity and relative acceleration of car $A$ with respect to car $B$ at this instant.

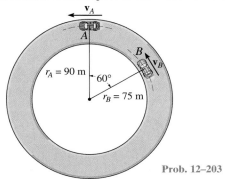

Prob. 12–203

**\*12-204.** The two cyclists $A$ and $B$ travel at the same constant speed $v$. Determine the speed of $A$ with respect to $B$ if $A$ travels along the circular track, while $B$ travels along the diameter of the circle.

Prob. 12–204

**12-205.** A man can row a boat at 5 m/s in still water. He wishes to cross a 50-m-wide river to point $B$, 50 m downstream. If the river flows with a velocity of 2 m/s, determine the speed of the boat and the time needed to make the crossing.

Prob. 12–205

**12-206.** A passenger in an automobile observes that raindrops make an angle of 30° with the horizontal as the auto travels forward with a speed of 60 km/h. Compute the terminal (constant) velocity $\mathbf{v}_r$ of the rain if it is assumed to fall vertically.

Prob. 12–206

**12-207.** At a given instant the football player at $A$ throws a football $C$ with a velocity of 20 m/s in the direction shown. Determine the constant speed at which the player at $B$ must run so that he can catch the football at the same elevation at which it was thrown. Also calculate the relative velocity and relative acceleration of the football with respect to $B$ at the instant the catch is made. Player $B$ is 15 m away from $A$ when $A$ starts to throw the football.

Prob. 12–207

**\*12-208.** A man can swim at 1.2 m/s in still water. He wishes to cross the 12-m-wide river to point $B$, 9 m downstream. If the river flows with a velocity of 0.6 m/s, determine the speed of the man and the time needed to make the crossing. *Note*: While in the water he must not direct himself towards point $B$ to reach this point. Why?

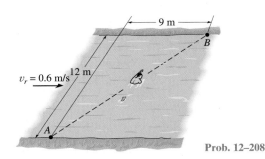

Prob. 12–208

# DESIGN PROJECT

**12–1D. DESIGN OF A MARBLE-SORTING DEVICE**

Marbles roll off the production chute at 0.15 m/s. Determine the range for the angle $0 \le \theta \le 30°$ for a selected position $s$ for the placement of the hopper relative to the end of the chute. Submit a drawing of the device that shows the path the marbles take.

**Fig. 12–1D**

# CHAPTER REVIEW

- **Rectilinear Kinematics.** Rectilinear kinematics refers to motion along a straight line. A position coordinate $s$ specifies the location of the particle on the line, and the displacement $\Delta s$ is the change in this position.

  The average velocity is a vector quantity, defined as the displacement divided by the time interval.

$$\mathbf{v}_{avg} = \frac{\Delta \mathbf{r}}{\Delta t}$$

  This is different than the average speed, which is a scalar and is the total distance traveled divided by the time of travel.

$$(v_{sp})_{avg} = \frac{s_T}{\Delta t}$$

  The time, position, instantaneous velocity, and instantaneous acceleration are related by the differential equations

$$v = ds/dt \qquad a = dv/dt \qquad a\,ds = v\,dv$$

  If the acceleration is known to be constant, then integration of these equations yields

$$v = v_0 + a_c t$$
$$s = s_0 + v_0 t + \tfrac{1}{2} a_c t^2$$
$$v^2 = v_0^2 + 2a_c(s - s_0)$$

- **Graphical Solutions.** If the motion is erratic, then it can be described by a graph. If one of these graphs is given, then the others can be established using the differential relations, $v = ds/dt$, $a = dv/dt$, or $a\,ds = v\,dv$. For example, if the $v$–$t$ graph is known, then values of the $s$–$t$ graph are determined from $\Delta s = \int v\,dt$ = area increments under the $v$–$t$ graph. Values of the $a$–$t$ graph are determined from $a = dv/dt$ = slope of $v$–$t$ graph.

- **Curvilinear Motion, x, y, z.** For this case, motion along the path is resolved into rectilinear motion along the $x$, $y$, $z$ axes. The equation of the path is used to relate the motion along each axis.

- *Projectile Motion.* Free flight motion of a projectile follows a parabolic path. It has a constant velocity in the horizontal direction and constant acceleration of $g = 9.81 \text{ m/s}^2$ in the vertical direction. Any two of the three equations for constant acceleration apply in the vertical direction, and in the horizontal direction only $x = x_0 + (v_0)_x t$ applies.

- *Curvilinear Motion n, t.* If normal and tangential axes are used for the analysis, then **v** is always in the positive $t$ direction. The acceleration has two components. The tangential component, $\mathbf{a}_t$, accounts for the change in the magnitude of the velocity; a slowing down is in the negative $t$ direction, and a speeding up is in the positive $t$ direction. The normal component $\mathbf{a}_n$ accounts for the change in the direction of the velocity. This component is always in the positive $n$ direction.

- *Curvilinear Motion, r, θ, z.* If the path of motion is expressed in polar coordinates, then the velocity and acceleration components can be written as

$$
\begin{aligned}
v_r &= \dot{r} & a_r &= \ddot{r} - r\dot{\theta}^2 \\
v_\theta &= r\dot{\theta} & a_\theta &= r\ddot{\theta} + 2\dot{r}\dot{\theta}
\end{aligned}
$$

To apply these equations, it is necessary to determine $r, \dot{r}, \ddot{r}, \dot{\theta}, \ddot{\theta}$ at the instant considered. If the path $r = f(\theta)$ is given, then the chain rule of calculus must be used to obtain the time derivatives. Once the data is substituted into the equations, then the algebraic sign of the results will indicate the direction of the components of $v$ or $a$ along each axis.

- *Absolute Dependent Motion of Two Particles.* The dependent motion of blocks that are suspended from pulleys and cables can be related by the geometry of the system. This is done by first establishing position coordinates, measured from a fixed origin to each block so that they are directed along the line of motion of the blocks. Using geometry and/or trigonometry, the coordinates are then related to the cable length in order to formulate a position coordinate equation. The first time derivative of this equation gives a relationship between the velocities of the blocks, and a second time derivative gives the relationship between their accelerations.

- *Relative Motion Analysis Using Translating Axes.* If two particles $A$ and $B$ undergo independent motions, then these motions can be related to their relative motion. Using a translating set of axes attached to one of the particles ($A$), the velocity and acceleration equations become

$$
\mathbf{v}_B = \mathbf{v}_A + \mathbf{v}_{B/A}
$$
$$
\mathbf{a}_B = \mathbf{a}_A + \mathbf{a}_{B/A}
$$

For planar motion, each of these equations produces two scalar equations, one in the $x$, and the other in the $y$ direction. For solution, the vectors can be expressed in Cartesian form or the $x$ and $y$ scalar components can be written directly.

The design of conveyors for a bottling plant requires knowledge of the forces that act on them and the ability to predict the motion of the bottles they transport.

# Kinetics of a Particle: Force and Acceleration

- To state Newton's Laws of Motion and Gravitational Attraction and to define mass and weight.
- To analyze the accelerated motion of a particle using the equation of motion with different coordinate systems.
- To investigate central-force motion and apply it to problems in space mechanics.

## 13.1 Newton's Laws of Motion

Many of the earlier notions about dynamics were dispelled after 1590 when Galileo performed experiments to study the motions of pendulums and falling bodies. The conclusions drawn from these experiments gave some insight as to the effects of forces acting on bodies in motion. The general laws of motion of a body subjected to forces were not known, however, until 1687, when Isaac Newton first presented three basic laws governing the motion of a particle. In a slightly reworded form, Newton's three laws of motion can be stated as follows:

*First Law: A particle originally at rest, or moving in a straight line with a constant velocity, will remain in this state provided the particle is not subjected to an unbalanced force.*

*Second Law: A particle acted upon by an unbalanced force* **F** *experiences an acceleration* **a** *that has the same direction as the force and a magnitude that is directly proportional to the force.** 

*Third Law: The mutual forces of action and reaction between two particles are equal, opposite, and collinear.*

*Stated another way, the unbalanced force acting on the particle is proportional to the time rate of change of the particle's linear momentum. See footnote † on next page.

The first and third laws were used extensively in developing the concepts of statics. Although these laws are also considered in dynamics, Newton's second law of motion forms the basis for most of this study, since this law relates the accelerated motion of a particle to the forces that act on it.

Measurements of force and acceleration can be recorded in a laboratory so that in accordance with the second law, if a known unbalanced force $\mathbf{F}$ is applied to a particle, the acceleration $\mathbf{a}$ of the particle may be measured. Since the force and acceleration are directly proportional, the constant of proportionality, $m$, may be determined from the ratio $m = F/a$.* The positive scalar $m$ is called the *mass* of the particle. Being constant during any acceleration, $m$ provides a quantitative measure of the resistance of the particle to a change in its velocity.

If the mass of the particle is $m$, Newton's second law of motion may be written in mathematical form as

$$\mathbf{F} = m\mathbf{a}$$

This equation, which is referred to as the *equation of motion*, is one of the most important formulations in mechanics.† As previously stated, its validity is based solely on *experimental evidence*. In 1905, however, Albert Einstein developed the theory of relativity and placed limitations on the use of Newton's second law for describing general particle motion. Through experiments it was proven that *time* is not an absolute quantity as assumed by Newton; as a result, the equation of motion fails to predict the exact behavior of a particle, especially when the particle's speed approaches the speed of light (0.3 Gm/s). Developments of the theory of quantum mechanics by Erwin Schrödinger and others indicate further that conclusions drawn from using this equation are also invalid when particles are the size of an atom and move close to one another. For the most part, however, these requirements regarding particle speed and size are not encountered in engineering problems, so their effects will not be considered in this book.

---

*Recall that the unit of force in the SI system is derived from this equation, where N = kg · m/s² (see Sec. 1.3 of *Statics*). If, however, the units of force, mass, length, and time were *all* selected arbitrarily, then it is necessary to write $F = kma$, where $k$ (a dimensionless constant) would have to be determined experimentally in order to preserve the equality.

†Since $m$ is constant, we can also write $\mathbf{F} = d(m\mathbf{v})/dt$, where $m\mathbf{v}$ is the particle's linear momentum.

**Newton's Law of Gravitational Attraction.** Shortly after formulating his three laws of motion, Newton postulated a law governing the mutual attraction between any two particles. In mathematical form this law can be expressed as

$$F = G\frac{m_1 m_2}{r^2} \tag{13–1}$$

where

$F$ = force of attraction between the two particles

$G$ = universal constant of gravitation; according to experimental evidence $G = 66.73(10^{-12})$ m$^3$/(kg $\cdot$ s$^2$)

$m_1, m_2$ = mass of each of the two particles

$r$ = distance between the centers of the two particles

Any two particles or bodies have a mutually attractive gravitational force acting between them. In the case of a particle located at or near the surface of the earth, however, the only gravitational force having any sizable magnitude is that between the earth and the particle. This force is termed the "weight" and, for our purpose, it will be the only gravitational force considered.

**Mass and Weight.** *Mass* is a property of matter by which we can compare the response of one body with that of another. As indicated above, this property manifests itself as a gravitational attraction between two bodies and provides a quantitative measure of the resistance of matter to a change in velocity. It is an *absolute* quantity since the measurement of mass can be made at any location. The weight of a body, however, is *not absolute* since it is measured in a gravitational field, and hence its magnitude depends on where the measurement is made. From Eq. 13–1, we can develop a general expression for finding the weight $W$ of a particle having a mass $m_1 = m$. Let $m_2$ be the mass of the earth and $r$ the distance between the earth's center and the particle. Then, if $g = Gm_2/r^2$, we have

$$W = mg$$

By comparison with $F = ma$, we term $g$ the acceleration due to gravity. For most engineering calculations $g$ is measured at a point on the surface of the earth at sea level, and at a latitude of 45°, considered the "standard location."

SI system

**Fig. 13–1**

**SI System of Units.**   In the SI system the mass of the body is specified in kilograms, and the weight must be calculated using the equation of motion, $F = ma$. Hence, if a body has a mass $m$ (kg) and is located at a point where the acceleration due to gravity is $g$ (m/s$^2$), then the weight is expressed in *newtons* as $W = mg$ (N), Fig. 13–1. In particular, if the body is located at the "standard location," the acceleration due to gravity is $g = 9.80665$ m/s$^2$. For calculations, the value $g = 9.81$ m/s$^2$ will be used, so that

$$W = mg \text{ (N)} \qquad (13\text{–}2)$$
$$(g = 9.81 \text{ m/s}^2) \qquad (13\text{–}3)$$

Therefore, a body of mass 1 kg has a weight of 9.81 N; a 2-kg body weighs 19.62 N; and so on.

## 13.2   The Equation of Motion

When more than one force acts on a particle, the resultant force is determined by a vector summation of all the forces; i.e., $\mathbf{F}_R = \Sigma\mathbf{F}$. For this more general case, the equation of motion may be written as

$$\boxed{\Sigma\mathbf{F} = m\mathbf{a}} \tag{13–4}$$

To illustrate application of this equation, consider the particle $P$ shown in Fig. 13–2a, which has a mass $m$ and is subjected to the action of two forces, $\mathbf{F}_1$ and $\mathbf{F}_2$. We can graphically account for the magnitude and direction of each force acting on the particle by drawing the particle's *free-body diagram*, Fig. 13–2b. Since the *resultant* of these forces *produces* the vector $m\mathbf{a}$, its magnitude and direction can be represented graphically on the *kinetic diagram*, shown in Fig. 13–2c.* The equal sign written between the diagrams symbolizes the *graphical* equivalency between the free-body diagram and the kinetic diagram; i.e., $\Sigma\mathbf{F} = m\mathbf{a}$.† In particular, note that if $\mathbf{F}_R = \Sigma\mathbf{F} = \mathbf{0}$, then the acceleration is also zero, so that the particle will either remain at *rest* or move along a straight-line path with *constant velocity*. Such are the conditions of *static equilibrium*, Newton's first law of motion.

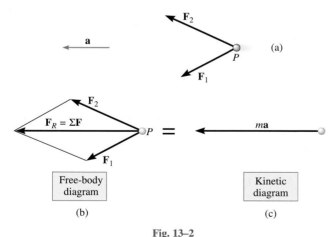

(a)

Free-body diagram

(b)

Kinetic diagram

(c)

**Fig. 13–2**

*Recall the free-body diagram considers the particle to be free of its surroundings and shows all the forces acting on the particle. The kinetic diagram pertains to the particle's motion as caused by the forces.

† The equation of motion can also be rewritten in the form $\Sigma\mathbf{F} - m\mathbf{a} = \mathbf{0}$. The vector $-m\mathbf{a}$ is referred to as the *inertia force vector*. If it is treated in the same way as a "force vector," then the state of "equilibrium" created is referred to as *dynamic equilibrium*. This method for application is often referred to as the *D'Alembert principle*, named after the French mathematician Jean le Rond d'Alembert.

**Inertial Frame of Reference.** Whenever the equation of motion is applied, it is required that measurements of the acceleration be made from a *Newtonian* or *inertial frame of reference. Such a coordinate system does not rotate and is either fixed or translates in a given direction with a constant velocity (zero acceleration).* This definition ensures that the particle's *acceleration* measured by observers in two different inertial frames of reference will always be the *same.* For example, consider the particle $P$ moving with an absolute acceleration $\mathbf{a}_P$ along a straight path as shown in Fig. 13–3. If the observer is *fixed* in the inertial $x, y$ frame of reference, this acceleration, $\mathbf{a}_P$, will be measured by the observer regardless of the direction and magnitude of the velocity $\mathbf{v}_O$ of the frame of reference. On the other hand, if the observer is *fixed* in the noninertial $x', y'$ frame of reference, Fig. 13–3, the observer will not measure the particle's acceleration as $\mathbf{a}_P$. Instead, if the frame is *accelerating* at $\mathbf{a}_{O'}$ the particle will appear to have an acceleration of $\mathbf{a}_{P/O'} = \mathbf{a}_P - \mathbf{a}_{O'}$. Also, if the frame is *rotating*, as indicated by the curl, then the particle will appear to move along a *curved path*, in which case it will appear to have other components of acceleration (see Sec. 16.8). In any case, the measured acceleration from this observer cannot be used in Newton's law of motion to determine the forces acting on the particle.

When studying the motions of rockets and satellites, it is justifiable to consider the inertial reference frame as fixed to the stars, whereas dynamics problems concerned with motions on or near the surface of the earth may be solved by using an inertial frame which is assumed fixed to the earth. Even though the earth both rotates about its own axis and revolves about the sun, the accelerations created by these rotations are relatively small and can be neglected in most computations.

**Fig. 13–3**

W

$N_2$

$N_1$

At rest or constant velocity

Fig. 1

We are all familiar with the sensation one feels when sitting in a car that is subjected to a forward acceleration. Often people think this is caused by a "force" which acts on them and tends to push them back in their seats; however, this is not the case. Instead, this sensation occurs due to their inertia or the resistance of their mass to a change in velocity.

Consider the passenger in Fig. 1 who is strapped to the seat of a rocket sled. Provided the sled is at rest or is moving with constant velocity, then no force is exerted on his back as shown on his free-body diagram.

W

$N_2$

$N_1$

F

Acceleration

Fig. 2

When the thrust of the rocket engine causes the sled to accelerate, then the seat upon which he is sitting exerts a force **F** on him which pushes him forward, Fig. 2. In the photo, notice that the inertia of his head resists this change in motion (acceleration), and so his head moves back against the seat and his face, which is nonrigid, tends to distort.

W

$N_2$

$N_1$

F'

Deceleration

Fig. 3

Upon deceleration, Fig. 3, the force of the seatbelt **F′** tends to pull him to a stop, and so his head leaves contact with the back of the seat and his face distorts forward, again due to his inertia or tendency to continue to move forward. No force is pulling him forward, although this is the sensation he receives.

## 13.3 Equation of Motion for a System of Particles

The equation of motion will now be extended to include a system of $n$ particles isolated within an enclosed region in space, as shown in Fig. 13–4a. In particular, there is no restriction in the way the particles are connected, and as a result the following analysis will apply equally well to the motion of a solid, liquid, or gas system. At the instant considered, the arbitrary $i$th particle, having a mass $m_i$, is subjected to a system of internal forces and a resultant external force. The *resultant internal force*, represented symbolically as $\mathbf{f}_i$, is determined from the forces which the other particles exert on the $i$th particle. Usually these forces are developed by direct contact, although the summation extends over all $n$ particles within the dashed boundary. The *resultant external force* $\mathbf{F}_i$ represents, for example, the effect of gravitational, electrical, magnetic, or contact forces between the $i$th particle and adjacent bodies or particles *not* included within the system.

The free-body and kinetic diagrams for the $i$th particle are shown in Fig. 13–4b. Applying the equation of motion yields

$$\Sigma \mathbf{F} = m\mathbf{a}; \qquad\qquad \mathbf{F}_i + \mathbf{f}_i = m_i \mathbf{a}_i$$

When the equation of motion is applied to each of the other particles of the system, similar equations will result. If all these equations are added together *vectorially*, we obtain

$$\Sigma \mathbf{F}_i + \Sigma \mathbf{f}_i = \Sigma m_i \mathbf{a}_i$$

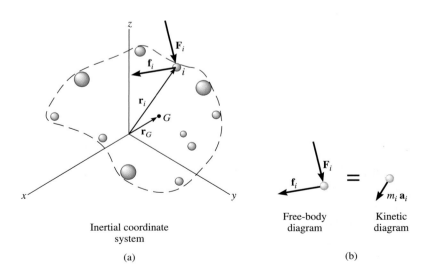

Inertial coordinate
system

(a)

Free-body
diagram

Kinetic
diagram

(b)

**Fig. 13–4**

The summation of the internal forces, if carried out, will equal zero, since internal forces between particles all occur in equal but opposite collinear pairs. Consequently, only the sum of the external forces will remain, and therefore the equation of motion, written for the system of particles, becomes

$$\Sigma \mathbf{F}_i = \Sigma m_i \mathbf{a}_i \tag{13-5}$$

If $\mathbf{r}_G$ is a position vector which locates the *center of mass G* of the particles, Fig. 13–4a, then by definition of the center of mass, $m\mathbf{r}_G = \Sigma m_i \mathbf{r}_i$, where $m = \Sigma m_i$ is the total mass of all the particles. Differentiating this equation twice with respect to time, assuming that no mass is entering or leaving the system, yields

$$m\mathbf{a}_G = \Sigma m_i \mathbf{a}_i$$

Substituting this result into Eq. 13–5, we obtain

$$\boxed{\Sigma \mathbf{F} = m\mathbf{a}_G} \tag{13-6}$$

Hence, the sum of the external forces acting on the system of particles is equal to the total mass of the particles times the acceleration of its center of mass $G$. Since in reality all particles must have a finite size to possess mass, Eq. 13–6 justifies application of the equation of motion to a *body* that is represented as a single particle.

## IMPORTANT POINTS

- The equation of motion is based on experimental evidence and is valid only when applied from an inertial frame of reference.
- The equation of motion states that the *unbalanced force* on a particle causes it to accelerate.
- An inertial frame of reference does not rotate, rather it has axes that either translate with constant velocity or are at rest.
- Mass is a property of matter that provides a quantitative measure of its resistance to a change in velocity. It is an absolute quantity.
- Weight is a force that is caused by the earth's gravitation. It is not absolute; rather it depends on the altitude of the mass from the earth's surface.

## 13.4 Equations of Motion: Rectangular Coordinates

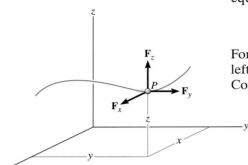

**Fig. 13–5**

When a particle is moving relative to an inertial $x, y, z$ frame of reference, the forces acting on the particle, as well as its acceleration, may be expressed in terms of their $\mathbf{i}, \mathbf{j}, \mathbf{k}$ components, Fig. 13–5. Applying the equation of motion, we have

$$\Sigma \mathbf{F} = m\mathbf{a}$$

$$\Sigma F_x \mathbf{i} + \Sigma F_y \mathbf{j} + \Sigma F_z \mathbf{k} = m(a_x \mathbf{i} + a_y \mathbf{j} + a_z \mathbf{k})$$

For this equation to be satisfied, the respective $\mathbf{i}, \mathbf{j}, \mathbf{k}$ components on the left side must equal the corresponding components on the right side. Consequently, we may write the following three scalar equations:

$$\begin{aligned}
\Sigma F_x &= ma_x \\
\Sigma F_y &= ma_y \\
\Sigma F_z &= ma_z
\end{aligned} \tag{13–7}$$

In particular, if the particle is constrained to move only in the $x$–$y$ plane, then the first two of these equations are used to specify the motion.

### PROCEDURE FOR ANALYSIS

The equations of motion are used to solve problems which require a relationship between the forces acting on a particle and the accelerated motion they cause.

*Free-Body Diagram*

- Select the inertial coordinate system. Most often, rectangular or $x, y, z$ coordinates are chosen to analyze problems for which the particle has *rectilinear motion*.

- Once the coordinates are established, draw the particle's free-body diagram. Drawing this diagram is *very important* since it provides a graphical representation that accounts for *all the forces* ($\Sigma \mathbf{F}$) which act on the particle, and thereby makes it possible to resolve these forces into their $x, y, z$ components.

- The direction and sense of the particle's acceleration $\mathbf{a}$ should also be established. If the senses of its components are unknown, for mathematical convenience assume that they are in the *same direction* as the *positive* inertial coordinate axes.

- The acceleration may be represented as the $m\mathbf{a}$ vector on the kinetic diagram.*

- Identify the unknowns in the problem.

*It is a convention in this text always to use the kinetic diagram as a graphical aid when developing the proofs and theory. The particle's acceleration or its components will be shown as blue colored vectors near the free-body diagram in the examples.

### Equations of Motion

- If the forces can be resolved directly from the free-body diagram, apply the equations of motion in their scalar component form.

- If the geometry of the problem appears complicated, which often occurs in three dimensions, Cartesian vector analysis can be used for the solution.

- *Friction.* If a moving particle contacts a rough surface, it may be necessary to use the *frictional equation*, which relates the coefficient of kinetic friction $\mu_k$ to the magnitudes of the frictional and normal forces $\mathbf{F}_f$ and $\mathbf{N}$ acting at the surfaces of contact, i.e., $F_f = \mu_k N$. Remember that $\mathbf{F}_f$ always acts on the free-body diagram such that it opposes the motion of the particle relative to the surface it contacts. If the particle is on the verge of relative motion then the coefficient of static friction should be used.

- *Spring.* If the particle is connected to an *elastic spring* having negligible mass, the spring force $F_s$ can be related to the deformation of the spring by the equation $F_s = ks$. Here $k$ is the spring's stiffness measured as a force per unit length, and $s$ is the stretch or compression defined as the difference between the deformed length $l$ and the undeformed length $l_0$, i.e., $s = l - l_0$.

### Kinematics

- If the velocity or position of the particle is to be found, it will be necessary to apply the proper kinematic equations once the particle's acceleration is determined from $\Sigma\mathbf{F} = m\mathbf{a}$.

- If *acceleration is a function of time*, use $a = dv/dt$ and $v = ds/dt$ which, when integrated, yield the particle's velocity and position.

- If *acceleration is a function of displacement*, integrate $a\,ds = v\,dv$ to obtain the velocity as a function of position.

- If *acceleration is constant*, use $v = v_0 + a_c t$, $s = s_0 + v_0 t + \frac{1}{2}a_c t^2$, $v^2 = v_0^2 + 2a_c(s - s_0)$ to determine the velocity or position of the particle.

- If the problem involves the dependent motion of several particles, use the method outlined in Sec. 12.9 to relate their accelerations.

- In all cases, make sure the positive inertial coordinate directions used for writing the kinematic equations are the same as those used for writing the equations of motion; otherwise, simultaneous solution of the equations will result in errors.

- If the solution for an unknown vector component yields a negative scalar, it indicates that the component acts in the direction opposite to that which was assumed.

# E X A M P L E 13.1

(a)

(b)

**Fig. 13–6**

The 50-kg crate shown in Fig. 13–6a rests on a horizontal plane for which the coefficient of kinetic friction is $\mu_k = 0.3$. If the crate is subjected to a 400-N towing force as shown, determine the velocity of the crate in 3 s starting from rest.

**Solution**

Using the equations of motion, we can relate the crate's acceleration to the force causing the motion. The crate's velocity can then be determined using kinematics.

*Free-Body Diagram.* The weight of the crate is $W = mg = 50 \text{ kg} (9.81 \text{ m/s}^2) = 490.5 \text{ N}$. As shown in Fig. 13–6b, the frictional force has a magnitude $F = \mu_k N_C$ and acts to the left, since it opposes the motion of the crate. The acceleration **a** is assumed to act horizontally, in the positive $x$ direction. There are two unknowns, namely $N_C$ and $a$. (We can also use the alternative procedure of drawing the crate's free-body *and* kinetic diagrams, Fig. 13–6c, prior to applying the equations of motion.)

*Equations of Motion.* Using the data shown on the free-body diagram, we have

$$\xrightarrow{+} \Sigma F_x = ma_x; \qquad 400 \cos 30° - 0.3 N_C = 50a \qquad (1)$$

$$+ \uparrow \Sigma F_y = ma_y; \qquad N_C - 490.5 + 400 \sin 30° = 0 \qquad (2)$$

Solving Eq. 2 for $N_C$, substituting the result into Eq. 1, and solving for $a$ yields

$$N_C = 290.5 \text{ N}$$
$$a = 5.19 \text{ m/s}^2$$

*Kinematics.* Note that the acceleration is *constant*, since the applied force **P** is constant. Since the initial velocity is zero, the velocity of the crate in 3 s is

$$(\xrightarrow{+}) \qquad v = v_0 + a_c t$$
$$= 0 + 5.19(3)$$
$$= 15.6 \text{ m/s} \rightarrow \qquad \qquad \textit{Ans.}$$

(c)

# E X A M P L E 13.2

A 10-kg projectile is fired vertically upward from the ground, with an initial velocity of 50 m/s, Fig. 13–7a. Determine the maximum height to which it will travel if (a) atmospheric resistance is neglected; and (b) atmospheric resistance is measured as $F_D = (0.01v^2)$ N, where $v$ is the speed at any instant, measured in m/s.

### Solution

In both cases the known force on the projectile can be related to its acceleration using the equation of motion. Kinematics can then be used to relate the projectile's acceleration to its position.

*Part (a) Free-Body Diagram.* As shown in Fig. 13–7b, the projectile's weight is $W = mg = 10(9.81) = 98.1$ N. We will assume the unknown acceleration **a** acts upward in the *positive z* direction.

*Equation of Motion*

$$+\uparrow \Sigma F_z = ma_z; \qquad -98.1 = 10a, \qquad a = -9.81 \text{ m/s}^2$$

The result indicates that the projectile, like every object having free-flight motion near the earth's surface, is subjected to a *constant* downward acceleration of 9.81 m/s².

*Kinematics.* Initially, $z_0 = 0$ and $v_0 = 50$ m/s, and at the maximum height $z = h$, $v = 0$. Since the acceleration is *constant*, then

$$(+\uparrow) \qquad v^2 = v_0^2 + 2a_c(z - z_0)$$
$$0 = (50)^2 + 2(-9.81)(h - 0)$$
$$h = 127 \text{ m} \qquad\qquad Ans.$$

*Part (b) Free-Body Diagram.* Since the force $F_D = (0.01v^2)$ N tends to retard the upward motion of the projectile, it acts downward as shown on the free-body diagram, Fig. 13–7c.

*Equation of Motion*

$$+\uparrow \Sigma F_z = ma_z; \quad -0.01v^2 - 98.1 = 10a, \quad a = -0.01v^2 - 9.81$$

*Kinematics.* Here the acceleration is *not constant* since $F_D$ depends on the velocity. Since $a = f(v)$, we can relate $a$ to position using

$$(+\uparrow) \ a \ dz = v \ dv; \quad (-0.001v^2 - 9.81) \ dz = v \ dv$$

Separating the variables and integrating, realizing that initially $z_0 = 0$, $v_0 = 50$ m/s (positive upward), and at $z = h$, $v = 0$, we have

$$\int_0^h dz = -\int_{50}^0 \frac{v \ dv}{0.001v^2 + 9.81} = -500 \ln(v^2 + 9810) \Big|_{50}^0$$
$$h = 114 \text{ m} \qquad\qquad Ans.$$

The answer indicates a lower elevation than that obtained in part (a) due to atmospheric resistance.

*Note that if the projectile were fired downward, with $z$ positive downward, the equation of motion would then be $-0.01v^2 + 98.1 = 10a$.

(a)

(b)

(c)

Fig. 13–7

EXAMPLE **13.3**

The baggage truck $A$ shown in the photo has a weight of 3600 N ($\approx$ 360 kg) and tows a 2200-N ($\approx$ 220-kg) cart $B$ and a 1300-N ($\approx$ 130-kg) cart $C$. For a short time the driving frictional force developed at the wheels of the truck is $F_A = (160t)$ N, where $t$ is in seconds. If the truck starts from rest, determine its speed in 2 seconds. Also, what is the horizontal force acting on the coupling between the truck and cart $B$ at this instant? Neglect the size of the truck and carts.

(a)

### Solution

*Free-Body Diagram.* As shown in Fig. 13–8a, it is the frictional driving force that gives both the truck and carts an acceleration. Here we have considered all three vehicles.

*Equation of Motion.* Only motion in the horizontal direction has to be considered.

$$\xrightarrow{+} \Sigma F_x = ma_x; \qquad 160t = \left(\frac{3600 + 2200 + 1300}{9.81}\right)a$$

$$a = 0.221t$$

*Kinematics.* Since the acceleration is a function of time, the velocity of the truck is obtained using $a = dv/dt$ with the initial condition that $v_0 = 0$ at $t = 0$. We have

$$\int_0^v dv = \int_0^2 (0.221t)\,dt; \qquad v = 0.1105t^2 \Big|_0^2 = 0.442 \text{ m/s} \qquad \textit{Ans.}$$

*Free-Body Diagram.* In order to determine the force between the truck and cart $B$, we can consider a free-body diagram of the truck so that we can "expose" the coupling force $\mathbf{T}$ as external to the free-body diagram, Fig. 13–8b.

*Equation of Motion.* When $t = 2$ s, then

$$\xrightarrow{+} \Sigma F_x = ma_x; \qquad 160(2) - T = \left(\frac{3600}{9.81}\right)[0.221(2)]$$

$$T = 157.8 \text{ N} \qquad \textit{Ans.}$$

Try and obtain this same result by considering a free-body diagram of carts $B$ and $C$.

(b)

**Fig. 13–8**

# EXAMPLE 13.4

A smooth 2-kg collar $C$, shown in Fig. 13–9a, is attached to a spring having a stiffness $k = 3$ N/m and an unstretched length of 0.75 m. If the collar is released from rest at $A$, determine its acceleration and the normal force of the rod on the collar at the instant $y = 1$ m.

(a)

## Solution

*Free-Body Diagram.* The free-body diagram of the collar when it is located at the arbitrary position $y$ is shown in Fig. 13–9b. Note that the weight is $W = 2(9.81) = 19.62$ N. Furthermore, the collar is *assumed* to be accelerating so that "**a**" acts downward in the *positive* $y$ direction. There are four unknowns, namely, $N_C$, $F_s$, $a$, and $\theta$.

*Equations of Motion*

$$\xrightarrow{+} \Sigma F_x = ma_x; \qquad -N_C + F_s \cos\theta = 0 \qquad (1)$$

$$+\downarrow \Sigma F_y = ma_y; \qquad 19.62 - F_s \sin\theta = 2a \qquad (2)$$

(b)

**Fig. 13–9**

From Eq. 2 it is seen that the acceleration depends on the magnitude and direction of the spring force. Solution for $N_C$ and $a$ is possible once $F_s$ and $\theta$ are known.

The magnitude of the spring force is a function of the stretch $s$ of the spring; i.e., $F_s = ks$. Here the unstretched length is $AB = 0.75$ m, Fig. 13–9a; therefore, $s = CB - AB = \sqrt{y^2 + (0.75)^2} - 0.75$. Since $k = 3$ N/m, then

$$F_s = ks = 3(\sqrt{y^2 + (0.75)^2} - 0.75) \qquad (3)$$

From Fig. 13–9a, the angle $\theta$ is related to $y$ by trigonometry.

$$\tan\theta = \frac{y}{0.75} \qquad (4)$$

Substituting $y = 1$ m into Eqs. 3 and 4 yields $F_s = 1.50$ N and $\theta = 53.1°$. Substituting these results into Eqs. 1 and 2, we obtain

$$N_C = 0.900 \text{ N} \qquad\qquad Ans.$$

$$a = 9.21 \text{ m/s}^2\downarrow \qquad\qquad Ans.$$

**EXAMPLE 13.5**

(a)

$T$  $T$

$2T$

(b)

$2T$

$\mathbf{a}_A$

$s_A$   981 N

(c)

$T$

$\mathbf{a}_B$

196.2 N

$s_B$

(d)

**Fig. 13–10**

The 100-kg block $A$ shown in Fig. 13–10a is released from rest. If the masses of the pulleys and the cord are neglected, determine the speed of the 20-kg block $B$ in 2 s.

**Solution**

*Free-Body Diagrams.* Since the mass of the pulleys is *neglected*, then for pulley $C$, $ma = 0$ and we can apply $\Sigma F_y = 0$ as shown in Fig. 13–10b. The free-body diagrams for blocks $A$ and $B$ are shown in Fig. 13–10c and d, respectively. One can see that for $A$ to remain static requires $T = 490.5$ N, whereas for $B$ to remain static requires $T = 196.2$ N. Hence $A$ will move down while $B$ moves up. Here we will *assume* both blocks accelerate downward, in the direction of $+s_A$ and $+s_B$. The three unknowns are $T$, $a_A$, and $a_B$.

*Equations of Motion.*

Block $A$ (Fig. 13–10c):

$$+\downarrow \Sigma F_y = ma_y; \qquad 981 - 2T = 100a_A \qquad (1)$$

Block $B$ (Fig. 13–10d):

$$+\downarrow \Sigma F_y = ma_y; \qquad 196.2 - T = 20a_B \qquad (2)$$

*Kinematics.* The necessary third equation is obtained by relating $a_A$ to $a_B$ using a dependent motion analysis. Using the technique developed in Sec. 12.9, the coordinates $s_A$ and $s_B$ measure the positions of $A$ and $B$ from the fixed datum, Fig. 13–10a. It is seen that

$$2s_A + s_B = l$$

where $l$ is constant and represents the total vertical length of cord. Differentiating this expression twice with respect to time yields

$$2a_A = -a_B \qquad (3)$$

Notice that in writing Eqs. 1 to 3, the *positive direction was always assumed downward*. It is very important to be *consistent* in this assumption since we are seeking a simultaneous solution of equations. The solution yields

$$T = 327.0 \text{ N}$$
$$a_A = 3.27 \text{ m/s}^2$$
$$a_B = -6.54 \text{ m/s}^2$$

Hence when block $A$ accelerates *downward*, block $B$ accelerates *upward*. Since $a_B$ is constant, the velocity of block $B$ in 2 s is thus

$$(+\downarrow) \qquad v = v_0 + a_B t$$
$$= 0 + (-6.54)(2)$$
$$= -13.1 \text{ m/s} \qquad \textit{Ans.}$$

The negative sign indicates that block $B$ is moving upward.

# PROBLEMS

**13-1.** The moon has a mass of $73.5(10^{21})$ kg, and the earth has a mass of $5.98(10^{24})$ kg. If their centers are $384(10^6)$ m apart, determine the gravitational attractive force between the two bodies.

**13-2.** The 100-N ($\approx$ 10-kg) block has an initial velocity of 2 m/s on the smooth plane. If a force $F = (25t)$ N, where $t$ is in seconds, acts on the block for 3 s, determine the final velocity of the block and the distance the block travels during this time.

**Prob. 13–2**

**13-3.** By using an inclined plane to retard the motion of a falling object, and thus make the observations more accurate, Galileo was able to determine experimentally that the distance through which an object moves in free fall is proportional to the square of the time for travel. Show that this is the case, i.e., $s \propto t^2$, by determining the time $t_B$, $t_C$, and $t_D$ needed for a block of mass $m$ to slide from rest at $A$ to points $B$, $C$, and $D$, respectively. Neglect the effects of friction.

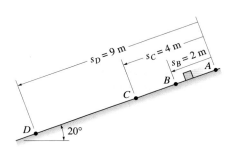

**Prob. 13–3**

**\*13-4.** The van is traveling at 20 km/h when the coupling of the trailer at $A$ fails. If the trailer has a mass of 250 kg and coasts 45 m before coming to rest, determine the constant horizontal force $F$ created by rolling friction which causes the trailer to stop.

**Prob. 13–4**

**13-5.** A block having a mass of 2 kg is placed on a spring scale located in an elevator that is moving downward. If the scale reading, which measures the force in the spring, is 20 N, determine the acceleration of the elevator. Neglect the mass of the scale.

**Prob. 13–5**

**13-6.** The baggage truck $A$ has a mass of 800 kg and is used to pull the two cars, each with mass 300 kg. If the tractive force $F$ on the truck is $F = 480$ N, determine the initial acceleration of the truck. What is the acceleration of the truck if the coupling at $C$ suddenly fails? The car wheels are free to roll. Neglect the mass of the wheels.

Prob. 13–6

**13-7.** The 500-kg fuel assembly for a nuclear reactor is being lifted out from the core of the nuclear reactor using the pulley system shown. It is hoisted upward with a constant acceleration such that $s = 0$ and $v = 0$ when $t = 0$, and $s = 2.5$ m when $t = 1.5$ s. Determine the tension in the cable at $A$ during the motion.

Prob. 13–7

***13-8.** The man weighs 900 N and supports the barbells which have a weight of 500 N. If he lifts them 0.6 m in the air in 1.5 s starting from rest, determine the reaction of *both* of his feet on the ground during the lift. Assume the motion is with uniform acceleration.

Prob. 13–8

**13-9.** The crate has a mass of 80 kg and is being towed by a chain which is always directed at 20° from the horizontal as shown. If the magnitude of $T$ is increased until the crate begins to slide, determine the crate's initial acceleration if the coefficient of static friction is $\mu_s = 0.5$ and the coefficient of kinetic friction is $\mu_k = 0.3$.

**13-10.** The crate has a mass of 80 kg and is being towed by a chain which is always directed at 20° from the horizontal as shown. Determine the crate's acceleration in $t = 2$ s if the coefficient of static friction is $\mu_s = 0.4$ and the coefficient of kinetic friction is $\mu_k = 0.3$ and the towing force is $T = (90t^2)$ N, where $t$ is in seconds.

Probs. 13–9/10

**13-11.** The water-park ride consists of an 8-kN ($\approx$ 800-kg) sled which slides from rest down the incline and then into the pool. If the frictional resistance on the incline is $F_r = 300$ N, and in the pool for a short distance $F_r = 800$ N, determine how fast the sled is traveling when $s = 1$ m.

20 m

20 m

$s$

Prob. 13–11

***13-12.** The 6-N ($\approx$ 0.6-kg) particle is subjected to the action of its weight and forces $\mathbf{F}_1 = \{2\mathbf{i} + 6\mathbf{j} - 2t\mathbf{k}\}$ N, $\mathbf{F}_2 = \{t^2\mathbf{i} + 4t\mathbf{j} - 1\mathbf{k}\}$ N, and $\mathbf{F}_3 = \{-2t\mathbf{i}\}$ N, where $t$ is in seconds. Determine the distance the ball is from the origin 2 s after being released from rest.

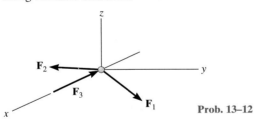

Prob. 13–12

**13-13.** The 2-N ($\approx$ 0.2-kg) particle $A$ is acted upon by its weight and the force system $\mathbf{F}_1 = \{2\mathbf{i} + 6\mathbf{j} - 2\mathbf{k}\}$ N, $\mathbf{F}_2 = \{3\mathbf{i} - 1\mathbf{k}\}$ N, and $\mathbf{F}_3 = \{1\mathbf{i} - t^2\mathbf{j} - 2\mathbf{k}\}$ N, where $t$ is in seconds. Determine the distance the particle is from the origin 3 s after it has been released from rest.

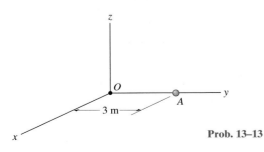

Prob. 13–13

**13-14.** Each of the two blocks has a mass $m$. The coefficient of kinetic friction at all surfaces of contact is $\mu$. If a horizontal force $\mathbf{P}$ moves the bottom block, determine the acceleration of the bottom block in each case.

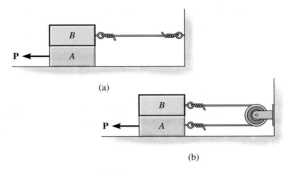

(a)

(b)

Prob. 13–14

**13-15.** The driver attempts to tow the crate using a rope that has a tensile strength of 1 kN. If the crate is originally at rest and has a weight of 2.5 kN ($\approx$ 250 kg), determine the greatest acceleration it can have if the coefficient of static friction between the crate and the road is $\mu_s = 0.4$, and the coefficient of kinetic friction is $\mu_k = 0.3$.

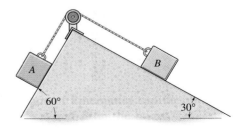

Prob. 13–15

***13-16.** The double inclined plane supports two blocks $A$ and $B$, each having a weight of 100 N ($\approx$ 10 kg). If the coefficient of kinetic friction between the blocks and the plane is $\mu_k = 0.1$, determine the acceleration of each block.

Prob. 13–16

**13-17.** The speed of the 17.5-kN ($\approx$ 1750-kg) sports car is plotted over the 30-s time period. Plot the variation of the traction force **F** needed to cause the motion.

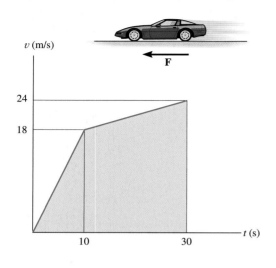

Prob. 13–17

**13-18.** The man pushes on the 600-N ($\approx$ 60-kg) crate with a force **F**. The force is always directed down at 30° from the horizontal as shown, and its magnitude is increased until the crate begins to slide. Determine the crate's initial acceleration if the static coefficient of friction is $\mu_s = 0.6$ and the kinetic coefficient of friction is $\mu_k = 0.3$.

Prob. 13–18

**13-19.** A 200-N ($\approx$ 20-kg) suitcase slides from rest 5 m down the smooth ramp. Determine the point where it strikes the ground at $C$. How long does it take to go from $A$ to $C$?

*13-20.** Solve Prob. 13–19 if the suitcase has an initial velocity down the ramp of $v_A = 2.5$ m/s and the coefficient of kinetic friction along $AB$ is $\mu_k = 0.2$.

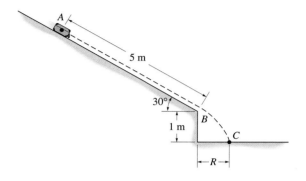

Probs. 13–19/20

**13-21.** The winding drum $D$ is drawing in the cable at an accelerated rate of 5 m/s². Determine the cable tension if the suspended crate has a mass of 800 kg.

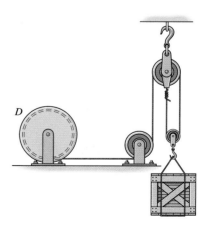

Prob. 13–21

**13-22.** The 100-N ($\approx$ 10-kg) block $A$ is traveling to the right at $v_A = 1$ m/s at the instant shown. If the coefficient of kinetic friction is $\mu_k = 0.2$ between the surface and $A$, determine the velocity of $A$ when it has moved 2 m. Block $B$ has a weight of 200 N ($\approx$ 20 kg).

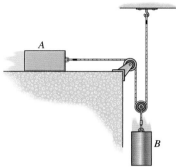

Prob. 13–22

**13-23.** A force $F = 150$ N is applied to the cord. Determine how high the 300-N ($\approx$ 30-kg) block $A$ rises in 2 s starting from rest. Neglect the weight of the pulleys and cord.

Prob. 13–23

**\*13-24.** At a given instant the 100-N ($\approx$ 10-kg) block $A$ is moving downward with a speed of 2 m/s. Determine its speed 2 s later. Block $B$ has a weight of 40 N ($\approx$ 4 kg), and the coefficient of kinetic friction between it and the horizontal plane is $\mu_k = 0.2$. Neglect the mass of the pulleys and cord.

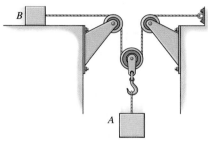

Prob. 13–24

**13-25.** Determine the required mass of block $A$ so that when it is released from rest it moves the 5-kg block $B$ 0.75 m up along the smooth inclined plane in $t = 2$ s. Neglect the mass of the pulleys and cords.

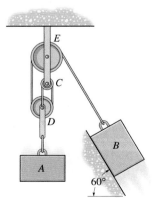

Prob. 13–25

**13-26.** A freight elevator, including its load, has a mass of 500 kg. It is prevented from rotating by using the track and wheels mounted along its sides. Starting from rest, in $t = 2$ s, the motor $M$ draws in the cable with a speed of 6 m/s, *measured relative to the elevator*. Determine the constant acceleration of the elevator and the tension in the cable. Neglect the mass of the pulleys and cables.

**Prob. 13–26**

**13-27.** The safe $S$ has a weight of 1 kN ($\approx$ 100 kg) and is supported by the rope and pulley arrangement shown. If the end of the rope is given to a boy $B$ of weight 450 N ($\approx$ 45 kg), determine his acceleration if in the confusion he doesn't let go of the rope. Neglect the mass of the pulleys and rope.

**Prob. 13–27**

**\*13-28.** The 400-kg mine car is hoisted up the incline using the cable and motor $M$. For a short time, the force in the cable is $F = (3200t^2)$ N, where $t$ is in seconds. If the car has an initial velocity $v_1 = 2$ m/s when $t = 0$, determine its velocity when $t = 2$ s.

**13-29.** The 400-kg mine car is hoisted up the incline using the cable and motor $M$. For a short time, the force in the cable is $F = (3200t^2)$ N, where $t$ is in seconds. If the car has an initial velocity $v_1 = 2$ m/s at $s = 0$ and $t = 0$, determine the distance it moves up the plane when $t = 2$ s.

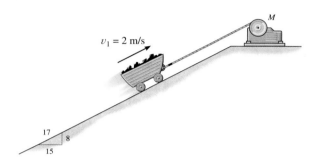

**Probs. 13–28/29**

**13-30.** Determine the tension developed in the cords attached to each block and the accelerations of the blocks. Neglect the mass of the pulleys and cords.

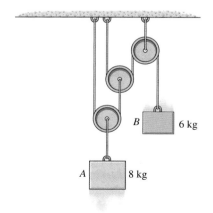

**Prob. 13–30**

**13-31.** The 2-kg shaft $CA$ passes through a smooth journal bearing at $B$. Initially, the springs, which are coiled loosely around the shaft, are unstretched when no force is applied to the shaft. In this position $s = s' = 250$ mm and the shaft is originally at rest. If a horizontal force of $F = 5$ kN is applied, determine the speed of the shaft at the instant $s = 50$ mm, $s' = 450$ mm. The ends of the springs are attached to the bearing at $B$ and the caps at $C$ and $A$.

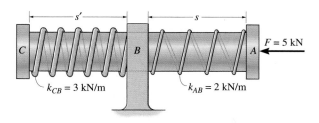

Prob. 13-31

**13-34.** The boy having a weight of 400 N ($\approx$ 40 kg) hangs uniformly from the bar. Determine the force in each of his arms in $t = 2$ s if the bar is moving upward with (a) a constant velocity of 1 m/s, and (b) a speed of $v = (1.2t^2)$ m/s where $t$ is in seconds.

Prob. 13-34

*13-32.** The 2-kg collar $C$ is free to slide along the smooth shaft $AB$. Determine the acceleration of collar $C$ if (a) the shaft is fixed from moving, (b) collar $A$, which is fixed to shaft $AB$, moves downward at constant velocity along the vertical rod, and (c) collar $A$ is subjected to a downward acceleration of 2 m/s². In all cases, the collar moves in the plane.

**13-33.** The 2-kg collar $C$ is free to slide along the smooth shaft $AB$. Determine the acceleration of collar $C$ if collar $A$ is subjected to an upward acceleration of 4 m/s².

Probs. 13-32/33

**13-35.** The 300-N ($\approx$ 30-kg) crate is being hoisted upward with a constant acceleration of 2 m/s². If the uniform beam $AB$ has a weight of 2 kN ($\approx$ 200 kg), determine the components of reaction at $A$. Neglect the size and mass of the pulley at $B$. *Hint:* First find the tension in the cable, then analyze the forces in the beam using statics.

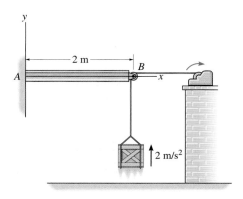

Prob. 13-35

**\*13-36.** If cylinders $B$ and $C$ have a mass of 15 kg and 10 kg, respectively, determine the required mass of $A$ so that it does not move when all the cylinders are released. Neglect the mass of the pulleys and the cords.

**13-38.** The 20-N ($\approx$ 2-kg) collar $C$ fits loosely on the smooth shaft. If the spring is unstretched when $s = 0$ and the collar is given a velocity of 5 m/s, determine the velocity of the collar when $s = 0.4$ m.

**Prob. 13–36**

**Prob. 13–38**

**13-37.** The conveyor belt is moving at 4 m/s. If the coefficient of static friction between the conveyor and the 10-kg package $B$ is $\mu_s = 0.2$, determine the shortest time the belt can stop so that the package does not slide on the belt.

**13-39.** The conveyor belt delivers each 12-kg crate to the ramp at $A$ such that the crate's speed is $v_A = 2.5$ m/s, directed down *along* the ramp. If the coefficient of kinetic friction between each crate and the ramp is $\mu_k = 0.3$, determine the speed at which each crate slides off the ramp at $B$. Assume that no tipping occurs. Take $\theta = 30°$.

**Prob. 13–37**

**Prob. 13–39**

**\*13-40.** A parachutist having a mass $m$ opens his parachute from an at-rest position at a very high altitude. If the atmospheric drag resistance is $F_D = kv^2$, where $k$ is a constant, determine his velocity when he has fallen for a time $t$. What is his velocity when he lands on the ground? This velocity is referred to as the *terminal velocity*, which is found by letting the time of fall $t \rightarrow \infty$ .

Prob. 13–40

**13-41.** If a horizontal force $P = 120$ N is applied to block $A$, determine the acceleration of block $B$. Neglect friction.

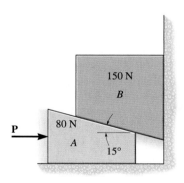

Prob. 13–41

**13-42.** Blocks $A$ and $B$ each have a mass $m$. Determine the largest horizontal force $P$ which can be applied to $B$ so that $A$ will not move relative to $B$. All surfaces are smooth.

**13-43.** Blocks $A$ and $B$ each have a mass $m$. Determine the largest horizontal force $P$ which can be applied to $B$ so that $A$ will not slip up $B$. The coefficient of static friction between $A$ and $B$ is $\mu_s$. Neglect any friction between $B$ and $C$.

Probs. 13–42/43

**\*13-44.** Each of the three plates has a mass of 10 kg. If the coefficients of static and kinetic friction at each surface of contact are $\mu_s = 0.3$ and $\mu_k = 0.2$, respectively, determine the acceleration of each plate when the three horizontal forces are applied.

Prob. 13–44

**13-45.** A projectile of mass $m$ is fired into a liquid at an angle $\theta_0$ with an initial velocity $\mathbf{v}_0$ as shown. If the liquid develops a frictional or drag resistance on the projectile which is proportional to its velocity, i.e., $F = kv$, where $k$ is a constant, determine the $x$ and $y$ components of its position at any instant. Also, what is the maximum distance $x_{max}$ that it travels?

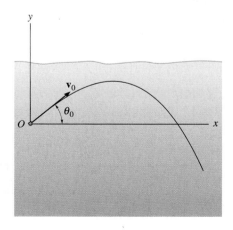

Prob. 13–45

■**13-46.** The tractor is used to lift the 150-kg load $B$ with the 24-m-long rope, boom, and pulley system. If the tractor is traveling to the right at a constant speed of 4 m/s, determine the tension in the rope when $s_A = 5$ m. When $s_A = 0$, $s_B = 0$.

**13-47.** The tractor is used to lift the 150-kg load $B$ with the 24-m-long rope, boom, and pulley system. If the tractor is traveling to the right with an acceleration of 3 m/s² and has a velocity of 4 m/s at the instant $s_A = 5$ m, determine the tension in the rope at this instant. When $s_A = 0$, $s_B = 0$.

12 m

$s_B$

$B$

$A$

$s_A$

**Probs. 13–46/47**

*13-48. The smooth block $B$ of negligible size has a mass $m$ and rests on the horizontal plane. If the board $AC$ pushes on the block at an angle $\theta$ with a constant acceleration $\mathbf{a}_0$, determine the velocity of the block along the board and the distance $s$ the block moves along the board as a function of time $t$. The block starts from rest when $s = 0$, $t = 0$.

$\mathbf{a}_0$

$\theta$

$C$

$A$

$B$

$s$

**Prob. 13–48**

**13-49.** Block $A$ has a mass $m_A$ and is attached to a spring having a stiffness $k$ and unstretched length $l_0$. If another block $B$, having a mass $m_B$, is pressed against $A$ so that the spring deforms a distance $d$, determine the distance both blocks slide on the smooth surface before they begin to separate. What is their velocity at this instant?

**13-50.** Block $A$ has a mass $m_A$ and is attached to a spring having a stiffness $k$ and unstretched length $l_0$. If another block $B$, having a mass $m_B$, is pressed against $A$ so that the spring deforms a distance $d$, show that for separation to occur it is necessary that $d > 2\mu_k g(m_A + m_B)/k$, where $\mu_k$ is the coefficient of kinetic friction between the blocks and the ground. Also, what is the distance the blocks slide on the surface before they separate?

$k$

$A$

$B$

**Probs. 13–49/50**

**13-51.** The block $A$ has a mass $m_A$ and rests on the pan $B$, which has a mass $m_B$. Both are supported by a spring having a stiffness $k$ that is attached to the bottom of the pan and to the ground. Determine the distance $d$ the pan should be pushed down from the equilibrium position and then released from rest so that separation of the block will take place from the surface of the pan at the instant the spring becomes unstretched.

$A$

$B$

$y$ $d$

$k$

**Prob. 13–51**

## 13.5   Equations of Motion: Normal and Tangential Coordinates

When a particle moves over a curved path which is known, the equation of motion for the particle may be written in the tangential, normal, and binormal directions. We have

$$\Sigma \mathbf{F} = m\mathbf{a}$$

$$\Sigma F_t \mathbf{u}_t + \Sigma F_n \mathbf{u}_n + \Sigma F_b \mathbf{u}_b = m\mathbf{a}_t + m\mathbf{a}_n$$

Here $\Sigma F_t$, $\Sigma F_n$, $\Sigma F_b$ represent the sums of all the force components acting on the particle in the tangential, normal, and binormal directions, respectively, Fig. 13–11. Note that there is no motion of the particle in the binormal direction, since the particle is constrained to move along the path. The above equation is satisfied provided

$$\boxed{\begin{aligned} \Sigma F_t &= ma_t \\ \Sigma F_n &= ma_n \\ \Sigma F_b &= 0 \end{aligned}} \qquad (13\text{–}8)$$

Recall that $a_t (= dv/dt)$ represents the time rate of change in the magnitude of velocity. Consequently, if $\Sigma \mathbf{F}_t$ acts in the direction of motion, the particle's speed will increase, whereas if it acts in the opposite direction, the particle will slow down. Likewise, $a_n (= v^2/\rho)$ represents the time rate of change in the velocity's direction. Since this vector *always* acts in the positive $n$ direction, i.e., toward the path's center of curvature, then $\Sigma \mathbf{F}_n$, which causes $\mathbf{a}_n$, also acts in this direction. For example, when the particle is constrained to travel in a circular path with a constant speed, there is a normal force exerted on the particle by the constraint in order to change the direction of the particle's velocity ($\mathbf{a}_n$). Since this force is always directed toward the center of the path, it is often referred to as the *centripetal force.*

The centrifuge is used to subject a passenger to very large normal accelerations caused by high rotations. Realize that these accelerations are caused by the unbalanced normal force exerted on the passenger by the seat of the centrifuge.

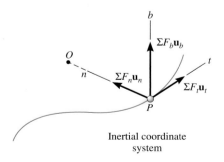

Inertial coordinate system

# PROCEDURE FOR ANALYSIS

When a problem involves the motion of a particle along a *known curved path*, normal and tangential coordinates should be considered for the analysis since the acceleration components can be readily formulated. The method for applying the equations of motion, which relate the forces to the acceleration, has been outlined in the procedure given in Sec. 13.4. Specifically, for *t, n, b* coordinates it may be stated as follows:

## Free-Body Diagram

- Establish the inertial *t, n, b* coordinate system at the particle and draw the particle's free-body diagram.

- The particle's normal acceleration $\mathbf{a}_n$ *always* acts in the positive *n* direction.

- If the tangential acceleration $\mathbf{a}_t$ is unknown, assume it acts in the positive *t* direction.

- Identify the unknowns in the problem.

## Equations of Motion

- Apply the equations of motion, Eqs. 13–8.

## Kinematics

- Formulate the tangential and normal components of acceleration; i.e., $a_t = dv/dt$ or $a_t = v\, dv/ds$ and $a_n = v^2/\rho$.

- If the path is defined as $y = f(x)$, the radius of curvature at the point where the particle is located can be obtained from $\rho = [1 + (dy/dx)^2]^{3/2}/|d^2y/dx^2|$.

# EXAMPLE 13.6

Determine the banking angle $\theta$ for the race track so that the wheels of the racing cars shown in Fig. 13–12a will not have to depend upon friction to prevent any car from sliding up or down the track. Assume the cars have negligible size a mass $m$, and travel around the curve of radius $\rho$ with a speed $v$.

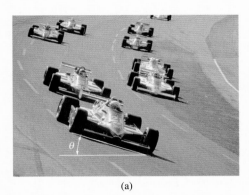

(a)

### Solution

Before looking at the following solution, give some thought as to why it should be solved using $t, n, b$ coordinates.

*Free-Body Diagram.* As shown in Fig. 13–12b, and as stated in the problem, no frictional force acts on the car. Here $\mathbf{N}_C$ represents the *resultant* of the ground on all four wheels. Since $a_n$ can be calculated, the unknowns are $N_C$ and $\theta$.

(b)

**Fig. 13–12**

*Equations of Motion.* Using the $n, b$ axes shown,

$$\xrightarrow{+} \Sigma F_n = ma_n; \qquad N_C \sin \theta = m \frac{v^2}{\rho} \qquad (1)$$

$$+\uparrow \Sigma F_b = 0; \qquad N_C \cos \theta - mg = 0 \qquad (2)$$

Eliminating $N_C$ and $m$ from these equations by dividing Eq. 1 by Eq. 2, we obtain

$$\tan \theta = \frac{v^2}{g\rho}$$

$$\theta = \tan^{-1}\left(\frac{v^2}{g\rho}\right) \qquad \textit{Ans.}$$

Notice that the result is independent of the mass of the car. Also, a force summation in the tangential direction is of no consequence to the solution. If it were considered, then $a_t = dv/dt = 0$, since the car moves with *constant speed*. A further analysis of this problem is discussed in Prob. 21–48.

## E X A M P L E 13.7

The 3-kg disk $D$ is attached to the end of a cord as shown in Fig. 13–13a. The other end of the cord is attached to a ball-and-socket joint located at the center of a platform. If the platform is rotating rapidly, and the disk is placed on it and released from rest as shown, determine the time it takes for the disk to reach a speed great enough to break the cord. The maximum tension the cord can sustain is 100 N, and the coefficient of kinetic friction between the disk and the platform is $\mu_k = 0.1$.

(a)

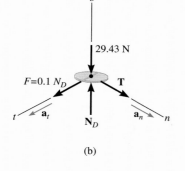

(b)

**Fig. 13–13**

### Solution

*Free-Body Diagram.* The frictional force has a magnitude $F = \mu_k N_D = 0.1 N_D$ and a sense of direction that opposes the *relative motion* of the disk with respect to the platform. It is this force that gives the disk a tangential component of acceleration causing $v$ to increase, thereby causing $T$ to increase until it reaches 100 N. The weight of the disk is $W = 3(9.81) = 29.43$ N. Since $a_n$ can be related to $v$, the unknowns are $N_D$, $a_t$, and $v$.

*Equations of Motion.*

$$\Sigma F_n = ma_n; \qquad\qquad T = 3\left(\frac{v^2}{1}\right) \tag{1}$$

$$\Sigma F_t = ma_t; \qquad\qquad 0.1 N_D = 3a_t \tag{2}$$

$$\Sigma F_b = 0; \qquad\qquad N_D - 29.43 = 0 \tag{3}$$

Setting $T = 100$ N, Eq. 1 can be solved for the critical speed $v_{cr}$ of the disk needed to break the cord. Solving all the equations, we obtain

$$N_D = 29.43 \text{ N}$$
$$a_t = 0.981 \text{ m/s}^2$$
$$v_{cr} = 5.77 \text{ m/s}$$

*Kinematics.* Since $a_t$ is *constant*, the time needed to break the cord is

$$v_{cr} = v_0 + a_t t$$
$$5.77 = 0 + (0.981)t$$
$$t = 5.89 \text{ s} \qquad\qquad Ans.$$

EXAMPLE 13.8

Design of the ski jump shown in the photo requires knowing the type of forces that will be exerted on the skier and his approximate trajectory. If in this case the jump can be approximated by the parabola shown in Fig. 13–14a, determine the normal force on the 600-N ($\approx$ 60-kg) skier the instant he arrives at the end of the jump, point $A$, where his velocity is 9 m/s. Also, what is his acceleration at this point?

### Solution
Why consider using $n, t$ coordinates to solve this problem?

*Free-Body Diagram.*   The free-body diagram for the skier when he is at $A$ is shown in Fig. 13–14b. Since the path is *curved*, there are two components of acceleration, $\mathbf{a}_n$ and $\mathbf{a}_t$. Since $a_n$ can be calculated, the unknowns are $a_t$ and $N_A$.

(a)

*Equations of Motion.*

$$+\uparrow \Sigma F_n = ma_n; \qquad N_A - 600 = \frac{600}{9.81}\left(\frac{(9)^2}{\rho}\right) \tag{1}$$

$$\xrightarrow{+} \Sigma F_t = ma_t; \qquad 0 = \frac{600}{9.81}a_t \tag{2}$$

The radius of curvature $\rho$ for the path must be determined at point $A(0, -15\text{ m})$. Here $y = \frac{1}{60}x^2 - 15$, $dy/dx = \frac{1}{30}x$, $d^2y/dx^2 = \frac{1}{30}$, so that at $x = 0$,

$$\rho = \frac{[1 + (dy/dx)^2]^{3/2}}{|d^2y/dx^2|}\bigg|_{x=0} = \frac{[1 + (0)^2]^{3/2}}{|\frac{1}{30}|} = 30\text{ m}$$

(b)

Fig. 13–14

Substituting into Eq. 1 and solving for $N_A$, we have

$$N_A = 765\text{ N} \qquad \qquad \textit{Ans.}$$

*Kinematics.*   From Eq. 2,

$$a_t = 0$$

Thus,

$$a_n = \frac{v^2}{\rho} = \frac{(9)^2}{30} = 2.7\text{ m/s}^2$$

$$a_A = a_n = 2.7\text{ m/s}^2 \uparrow \qquad \qquad \textit{Ans.}$$

Show that when the skier is in mid-air his acceleration is 9.81 m/s$^2$.

# EXAMPLE 13.9

(a)

(b)

**Fig. 13–15**

Packages, each having a mass of 2 kg, are delivered from a conveyor to a smooth circular ramp with a velocity of $v_0 = 1$ m/s as shown in Fig. 13–15a. If the effective radius of the ramp is 0.5 m, determine the angle $\theta = \theta_{max}$ at which each package begins to leave the surface.

## Solution

*Free-Body Diagram.* The free-body diagram for a package, when it is located at the *general position* $\theta$, is shown in Fig. 13–15b. The package must have a tangential acceleration $\mathbf{a}_t$, since its *speed* is always *increasing* as it slides downward. The weight is $W = 2(9.81) = 19.62$ N. Specify the three unknowns.

*Equations of Motion.*

$$+\swarrow \Sigma F_n = ma_n; \qquad -N_B + 19.62 \cos \theta = 2\frac{v^2}{0.5} \qquad (1)$$

$$+\searrow \Sigma F_t = ma_t; \qquad 19.62 \sin \theta = 2a_t \qquad (2)$$

At the instant $\theta = \theta_{max}$, the package leaves the surface of the ramp so that $N_B = 0$. Therefore, there are three unknowns, $v$, $a_t$, and $\theta$.

*Kinematics.* The third equation for the solution is obtained by noting that the magnitude of tangential acceleration $a_t$ may be related to the speed of the package $v$ and the angle $\theta$. Since $a_t \, ds = v \, dv$ and $ds = r \, d\theta = 0.5 \, d\theta$, Fig. 13–15a, we have

$$a_t = \frac{v \, dv}{0.5 \, d\theta} \qquad (3)$$

To solve, substitute Eq. 3 into Eq. 2 and separate the variables. This gives

$$v \, dv = 4.905 \sin \theta \, d\theta$$

Integrate both sides, realizing that when $\theta = 0°$, $v_0 = 1$ m/s.

$$\int_1^v v \, dv = 4.905 \int_{0°}^{\theta} \sin \theta \, d\theta$$

$$\left.\frac{v^2}{2}\right|_1^v = -4.905 \cos \theta \Big|_{0°}^{\theta}$$

$$v^2 = 9.81(1 - \cos \theta) + 1$$

Substituting into Eq. 1 with $N_B = 0$ and solving for $\cos \theta_{max}$ yields

$$19.62 \cos \theta_{max} = \frac{2}{0.5}[9.81(1 - \cos \theta_{max}) + 1]$$

$$\cos \theta_{max} = \frac{43.24}{58.86}$$

$$\theta_{max} = 42.7° \qquad \qquad Ans.$$

# PROBLEMS

**\*13-52.** Determine the mass of the sun, knowing that the distance from the earth to the sun is $149.6(10^6)$ km. *Hint:* Use Eq. 13–1 to represent the force of gravity acting on the earth.

**13-53.** The sports car, having a mass of 1700 kg, is traveling horizontally along a 20° banked track which is circular and has a radius of curvature of $\rho = 100$ m. If the coefficient of static friction between the tires and the road is $\mu_s = 0.2$, determine the *maximum constant speed* at which the car can travel without sliding up the slope. Neglect the size of the car.

**13-54.** Using the data in Prob. 13–53, determine the *minimum speed* at which the car can travel around the track without sliding down the slope.

$\theta = 20°$

Probs. 13–53/54

**13-55.** A girl, having a mass of 15 kg, sits motionless relative to the surface of a horizontal platform at a distance of $r = 5$ m from the platform's center. If the angular motion of the platform is *slowly* increased so that the girl's tangential component of acceleration can be neglected, determine the maximum speed which the girl will have before she begins to slip off the platform. The coefficient of static friction between the girl and the platform is $\mu = 0.2$.

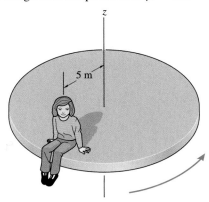

$z$

5 m

Prob. 13–55

**\*13-56.** Solve Prob. 13–55 assuming that the platform starts rotating from rest so that the girl's speed is increased uniformly at $\dot{v} = 0.5$ m/s$^2$.

**13-57.** The 600-kg wrecking ball is suspended from the crane by a cable having a negligible mass. If the ball has a speed $v = 8$ m/s at the instant it is at its lowest point, $\theta = 0°$, determine the tension in the cable at this instant. Also, determine the angle $\theta$ to which the ball swings before it stops.

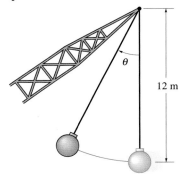

$\theta$

12 m

Prob. 13–57

**13-58.** Prove that if the block is released from rest at point $B$ of a smooth path of *arbitrary shape*, the speed it attains when it reaches point $A$ is equal to the speed it attains when it falls freely through a distance $h$; i.e., $v = \sqrt{2gh}$.

$B$

$h$

$A$

Prob. 13–58

**13-59.** At the instant $\theta = 60°$, the boy's center of mass $G$ has a downward speed $v_G = 3$ m/s. Determine the rate of increase in his speed and the tension in each of the two supporting cords of the swing at this instant. The boy has a weight of 300 N ($\approx 30$ kg). Neglect his size and the mass of the seat and cords.

**\*13-60.** At the instant $\theta = 60°$, the boy's center of mass $G$ is momentarily at rest. Determine his speed and the tension in each of the two supporting cords of the swing when $\theta = 90°$. The boy has a weight of 300 N ($\approx 30$ kg). Neglect his size and the mass of the seat and cords.

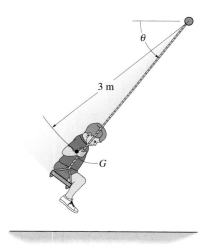

Probs. 13–59/60

**13-61.** An acrobat has a weight of 750 N ($\approx 75$ kg) and is sitting on a chair which is perched on top of a pole as shown. If by a mechanical drive the pole rotates downward at a constant rate from $\theta = 0°$, such that the acrobat's center of mass $G$ maintains a *constant speed* of $v_a = 3$ m/s, determine the angle $\theta$ at which he begins to "fly" out of the chair. Neglect friction and assume that the distance from the pivot $O$ to $G$ is $\rho = 3$ m.

**13-62.** Solve Prob. 13–61 if the speed of the acrobat's center of mass is increased from $(v_a)_0 = 3$ m/s at $\theta = 0°$ by a constant rate of $\dot{v}_a = 0.2$ m/s².

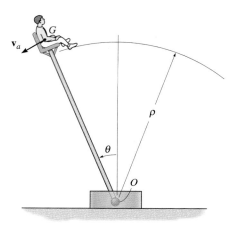

Probs. 13–61/62

**13-63.** If the crest of the hill has a radius of curvature $\rho = 100$ m, determine the maximum constant speed at which the car can travel over it without leaving the surface of the road. Neglect the size of the car in the calculation. The car has a weight of 17.5 kN ($\approx 1750$ kg).

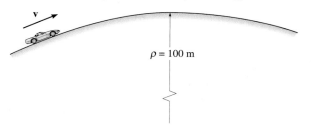

Prob. 13–63

**\*13-64.** The airplane, traveling at a constant speed of 50 m/s, is executing a horizontal turn. If the plane is banked at $\theta = 15°$, when the pilot experiences only a normal force on the seat of the plane, determine the radius of curvature $\rho$ of the turn. Also, what is the normal force of the seat on the pilot if he has a mass of 70 kg.

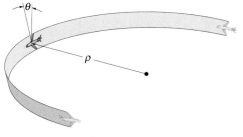

Prob. 13–64

**13-65.** The 750-N ($\approx$ 75-kg) man lies against the cushion for which the coefficient of static friction is $\mu_s = 0.5$. Determine the resultant normal and frictional forces the cushion exerts on him if, due to rotation about the $z$ axis, he has a constant speed $v = 6$ m/s. Neglect the size of the man. Take $\theta = 60°$.

**13-66.** The 750-N ($\approx$ 75-kg) man lies against the cushion for which the coefficient of static friction is $\mu_s = 0.5$. If he rotates about the $z$ axis with a constant speed $v = 10$ m/s, determine the smallest angle $\theta$ of the cushion at which he will begin to slip off.

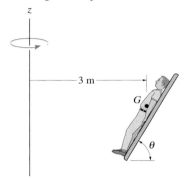

Probs. 13–65/66

**13-67.** Determine the constant speed of the passengers on the amusement-park ride if it is observed that the supporting cables are directed at $\theta = 30°$ from the vertical. Each chair including its passenger has a mass of 80 kg. Also, what are the components of force in the $n$, $t$, and $b$ directions which the chair exerts on a 50-kg passenger during the motion?

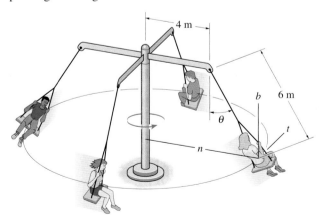

Prob. 13–67

**\*13-68.** If the ball has a mass of 30 kg and a speed $v = 4$ m/s at the instant it is at its lowest point, $\theta = 0°$, determine the tension in the cord at this instant. Also, determine the angle $\theta$ to which the ball swings at the instant it momentarily stops. Neglect the size of the ball.

**13-69.** The ball has a mass of 30 kg and a speed $v = 4$ m/s at the instant it is at its lowest point, $\theta = 0°$. Determine the tension in the cord and the rate at which the ball's speed is decreasing at the instant $\theta = 20°$. Neglect the size of the ball.

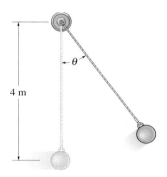

Probs. 13–68/69

**13-70.** The package has a weight of 50 N ($\approx$ 5 kg) and slides down the chute. When it reaches the curved portion $AB$, it is traveling at 2 m/s ($\theta = 0°$). If the chute is smooth, determine the speed of the package when it reaches the intermediate point $C$ ($\theta = 30°$) and when it reaches the horizontal plane ($\theta = 45°$). Also, find the normal force on the package at $C$.

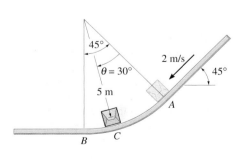

Prob. 13–70

**13-71.** Cartons having a mass of 5 kg are required to move along the assembly line at a constant speed of 8 m/s. Determine the smallest radius of curvature, $\rho$, for the conveyor so the cartons do not slip. The coefficients of static and kinetic friction between a carton and the conveyor are $\mu_s = 0.7$ and $\mu_k = 0.5$, respectively.

8 m/s

$\rho$

Prob. 13–71

**13-73.** The 0.8-Mg car is traveling over the hill having the shape of a parabola. If the driver maintains a constant speed of 9 m/s, determine both the resultant normal force and the resultant frictional force that all the wheels of the car exert on the road at the instant it reaches point $A$. Neglect the size of the car.

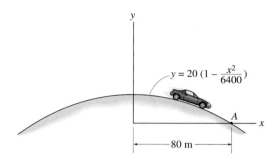

$y$

$y = 20 \left(1 - \dfrac{x^2}{6400}\right)$

$A$

$x$

80 m

Prob. 13–73

*13-72.** The smooth block $B$, having a mass of 0.2 kg, is attached to the vertex $A$ of the right circular cone using a light cord. The cone is rotating at a constant angular rate about the $z$ axis such that the block attains a speed of 0.5 m/s. At this speed, determine the tension in the cord and the reaction which the cone exerts on the block. Neglect the size of the block.

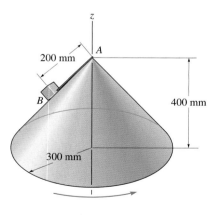

$z$

$A$

200 mm

$B$

400 mm

300 mm

Prob. 13–72

**13-74.** A girl having a mass of 25 kg sits at the edge of the merry-go-round so her center of mass $G$ is at a distance of 1.5 m from the axis of rotation. If the angular motion of the platform is *slowly* increased so that the girl's tangential component of acceleration can be neglected, determine the maximum speed which she can have before she begins to slip off the merry-go-round. The coefficient of static friction between the girl and the merry-go-round is $\mu_s = 0.3$.

$z$

1.5 m

$G$

Prob. 13–74

**13-75.** The 100-N ($\approx$ 10-kg) suitcase slides down the curved ramp for which the coefficient of kinetic friction is $\mu_k = 0.2$. If at the instant it reaches point $A$ it has a speed of 1 m/s, determine the normal force on the suitcase and the rate of increase of its speed.

$$y = \frac{5}{8}x^2$$

Prob. 13–75

**13-77.** The 2-kg spool $S$ fits loosely on the inclined rod for which the coefficient of static friction is $\mu_s = 0.2$. If the spool is located 0.25 m from $A$, determine the maximum constant speed the spool can have so that it does not slip up the rod.

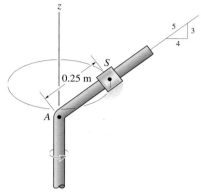

Prob. 13–77

***13-76.** The 2-kg spool $S$ fits loosely on the inclined rod for which the coefficient of static friction is $\mu_s = 0.2$. If the spool is located 0.25 m from $A$, determine the minimum constant speed the spool can have so that it does not slip down the rod.

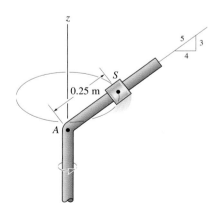

Prob. 13–76

**13-78.** The man has a mass of 80 kg and sits 3 m from the center of the rotating platform. Due to the rotation his speed is increased from rest by $\dot{v} = 0.4$ m/s². If the coefficient of static friction between his clothes and the platform is $\mu_s = 0.3$, determine the time required to cause him to slip.

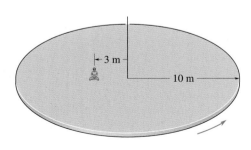

Prob. 13–78

**13-79.** The skier starts from rest at $A(10\text{ m}, 0)$ and descends the smooth slope, which may be approximated by a parabola. If she has a mass of 52 kg, determine the normal force she exerts on the ground at the instant she arrives at point $B$. Neglect the size of the skier. *Hint:* Use the result of Prob. 13–58.

**13-81.** If the bicycle and rider have a total weight of 900 N ($\approx$ 90 kg), determine the resultant normal force acting on the bicycle when it is at point $A$ while it is freely coasting at $v_A = 2$ m/s. Also, compute the increase in the bicyclist's speed at this point. Neglect the resistance due to the wind and the size of the bicycle and rider.

**Prob. 13–81**

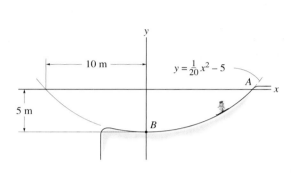

**Prob. 13–79**

*****13-80.** The block has a weight of 20 N ($\approx$ 2 kg) and it is free to move along the smooth slot in the rotating disk. The spring has a stiffness of 10 N/m and an unstretched length of 0.5 m. Determine the force of the spring on the block and the tangential component of force which the slot exerts on the side of the block, when the block is at rest with respect to the disk and is traveling with a constant speed of 4.8 m/s.

**13-82.** The collar has a mass of 5 kg and is confined to move along the smooth circular rod which lies in the horizontal plane. The attached spring has an unstretched length of 200 mm. If, at the instant $\theta = 30°$, the collar has a speed $v = 2$m/s, determine the magnitude of normal force of the rod on the collar and the collar's acceleration.

**Prob. 13–80**

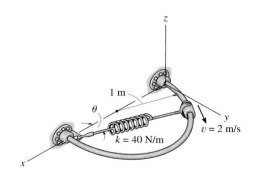

**Prob. 13–82**

# 13.6 Equations of Motion: Cylindrical Coordinates

When all the forces acting on a particle are resolved into cylindrical components, i.e., along the unit-vector directions $\mathbf{u}_r$, $\mathbf{u}_\theta$, $\mathbf{u}_z$, Fig. 13–16, the equation of motion may be expressed as

$$\Sigma \mathbf{F} = m\mathbf{a}$$

$$\Sigma F_r\mathbf{u}_r + \Sigma F_\theta\mathbf{u}_\theta + \Sigma F_z\mathbf{u}_z = ma_r\mathbf{u}_r + ma_\theta\mathbf{u}_\theta + ma_z\mathbf{u}_z$$

To satisfy this equation, the respective $\mathbf{u}_r$, $\mathbf{u}_\theta$, $\mathbf{u}_z$ components on the left side must equal the corresponding components on the right side. Consequently, we may write the following three scalar equations of motion:

$$\boxed{\begin{aligned} \Sigma F_r &= ma_r \\ \Sigma F_\theta &= ma_\theta \\ \Sigma F_z &= ma_z \end{aligned}}$$ (13–9)

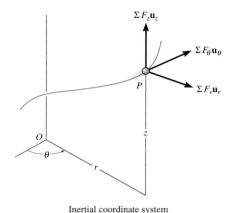

Inertial coordinate system

Fig. 13–16

If the particle is constrained to move only in the $r-\theta$ plane, then only the first two of Eqs. 13–9 are used to specify the motion.

**Tangential and Normal Forces.** The most straightforward type of problem involving cylindrical coordinates requires the determination of the resultant force components $\Sigma F_r$, $\Sigma F_\theta$, $\Sigma F_z$ causing a particle to move with a *known* acceleration. If, however, the particle's accelerated motion is not completely specified at the given instant, then some information regarding the directions or magnitudes of the forces acting on the particle must be known or computed in order to solve Eqs. 13–9. For example, the force $\mathbf{P}$ causes the particle in Fig. 13–17a to move along a path $r = f(\theta)$. The *normal force* $\mathbf{N}$ which the path exerts on the particle is always *perpendicular to the tangent of the path*, whereas the frictional force $\mathbf{F}$ always acts along the tangent in the opposite direction of motion. The *directions* of $\mathbf{N}$ and $\mathbf{F}$ can be specified relative to the radial coordinate by using the angle $\psi$ (psi), Fig. 13–17b, which is defined between the *extended* radial line and the tangent to the curve.

As the car of weight $W$ descends the spiral track, the resultant normal force which the track exerts on the car can be represented by its three cylindrical components. $-\mathbf{N}_r$ creates a radial acceleration, $-\mathbf{a}_r$, $\mathbf{N}_\theta$ creates a transverse acceleration $\mathbf{a}_\theta$, and the difference, $\mathbf{W} - \mathbf{N}_z$ creates an azimuthal acceleration $-\mathbf{a}_z$.

(a)

Fig. 13–17

(b)

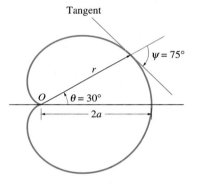

(c)

**Fig. 13–17**

Tangent

$\psi = 75°$

$r$

$O$  $\theta = 30°$

$2a$

**Fig. 13–18**

This angle can be obtained by noting that when the particle is displaced a distance $ds$ along the path, Fig. 13–17c, the component of displacement in the radial direction is $dr$ and the component of displacement in the transverse direction is $r\,d\theta$. Since these two components are mutually perpendicular, the angle $\psi$ can be determined from $\tan\psi = r\,d\theta/dr$, or

$$\tan\psi = \frac{r}{dr/d\theta} \tag{13–10}$$

If $\psi$ is calculated as a positive quantity, it is measured from the *extended radial line* to the tangent in a counterclockwise sense or in the positive direction of $\theta$. If it is negative, it is measured in the opposite direction to positive $\theta$. For example, consider the cardioid $r = a(1 + \cos\theta)$, shown in Fig. 13–18. Because $dr/d\theta = -a\sin\theta$, then when $\theta = 30°$, $\tan\psi = a(1 + \cos 30°)/(-a\sin 30°) = -3.732$, or $\psi = -75°$, measured clockwise, as shown in the figure.

## PROCEDURE FOR ANALYSIS

Cylindrical or polar coordinates are a suitable choice for the analysis of a problem for which data regarding the angular motion of the radial line $r$ are given, or in cases where the path can be conveniently expressed in terms of these coordinates. Once these coordinates have been established, the equations of motion can be applied in order to relate the forces acting on the particle to its acceleration components. The method for doing this has been outlined in the procedure for analysis given in Sec. 13.4. The following is a summary of this procedure.

*Free-Body Diagram*

- Establish the $r$, $\theta$, $z$ inertial coordinate system and draw the particle's free-body diagram.
- Assume that $\mathbf{a}_r$, $\mathbf{a}_\theta$, $\mathbf{a}_z$ act in the *positive directions* of $r$, $\theta$, $z$ if they are unknown.
- Identify all the unknowns in the problem.

*Equations of Motion*

- Apply the equations of motion, Eqs. 13–9.

*Kinematics*

- Use the methods of Sec. 12.8 to determine $r$ and the time derivatives $\dot{r}$, $\ddot{r}$, $\dot{\theta}$, $\ddot{\theta}$, $\ddot{z}$, and then evaluate the acceleration components $a_r = \ddot{r} - r\dot{\theta}^2$, $a_\theta = r\ddot{\theta} + 2\dot{r}\dot{\theta}$, $a_z = \ddot{z}$.
- If any of the acceleration components is computed as a negative quantity, it indicates that it acts in its negative coordinate direction.
- When taking the time derivatives of $r = f(\theta)$, it is very important to use the chain rule of calculus.

# EXAMPLE 13.10

The 2-kg block in Fig. 13–19a moves on a smooth horizontal track, such that its path is specified in polar coordinates by the parametric equations $r = (3t^2)$ m and $\theta = (0.5t)$ rad, where $t$ is in seconds. Determine the magnitude of the tangential force **F** causing the motion at the instant $t = 1$ s.

## Solution

*Free-Body Diagram.* As shown on the block's free-body diagram, Fig. 13–19b, the normal force of the track on the block, **N**, and the tangential force **F** are located at an angle $\psi$ from the $r$ and $\theta$ axes. This angle can be obtained from Eq. 13–10. To do so, we must first express the path as $r = f(\theta)$ by eliminating the parameter $t$ between $r$ and $\theta$. This yields $r = 12\theta^2$. Also, when $t = 1$ s, $\theta = 0.5(1 \text{ s}) = 0.5$ rad. Thus,

(a)

$$\tan \psi = \frac{r}{dr/d\theta} = \frac{12\theta^2}{12(2\theta)} \Big|_{\theta=0.5 \text{ rad}} = 0.25$$

$$\psi = 14.04°$$

Because $\psi$ is a positive quantity, it is measured counterclockwise from the $r$ axis to the tangent (the same direction as $\theta$) as shown in Fig. 13–19b. There are presently four unknowns: $F$, $N$, $a_r$ and $a_\theta$.

(b)

Fig. 13–19

## Equations of Motion.

$$+\downarrow \Sigma F_r = ma_r; \quad F \cos 14.04° - N \sin 14.04° = 2a_r \quad (1)$$

$$\uparrow+ \Sigma F_\theta = ma_\theta; \quad F \sin 14.04° + N \cos 14.04° = 2a_\theta \quad (2)$$

*Kinematics.* Since the motion is specified, the coordinates and the required time derivatives can be calculated and evaluated at $t = 1$ s.

$$r = 3t^2 \Big|_{t=1 \text{ s}} = 3 \text{ m} \qquad \theta = 0.5t \Big|_{t=1 \text{ s}} = 0.5 \text{ rad}$$

$$\dot{r} = 6t \Big|_{t=1 \text{ s}} = 6 \text{ m/s} \qquad \dot{\theta} = 0.5 \text{ rad/s}$$

$$\ddot{r} = 6 \text{ m/s}^2 \qquad\qquad \ddot{\theta} = 0$$

$$a_r = \ddot{r} - r\dot{\theta}^2 = 6 - 3(0.5)^2 = 5.25 \text{ m/s}^2$$

$$a_\theta = r\ddot{\theta} + 2\dot{r}\dot{\theta} = 3(0) + 2(6)(0.5) = 6 \text{ m/s}^2$$

Substituting into Eqs. 1 and 2 and solving, we get

$$F = 13.10 \text{ N} \qquad\qquad Ans.$$

$$N = 9.22 \text{ N}$$

# E X A M P L E 13.11

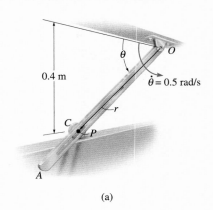

(a)

(b)

**Fig. 13–20**

The smooth 2-kg cylinder $C$ in Fig. 13–20a has a peg $P$ through its center which passes through the slot in arm $OA$. If the arm rotates in the *vertical plane* at a constant rate $\dot\theta = 0.5$ rad/s, determine the force that the arm exerts on the peg at the instant $\theta = 60°$.

**Solution**

Why is it a good idea to use polar coordinates to solve this problem?

*Free-Body Diagram.* The free-body diagram for the cylinder is shown in Fig. 13–20b. The force on the peg, $\mathbf{F}_P$, acts perpendicular to the slot in the arm. As usual, $\mathbf{a}_r$ and $\mathbf{a}_\theta$ are assumed to act in the directions of *positive r* and $\theta$, respectively. Identify the four unknowns.

*Equations of Motion.* Using the data in Fig. 13–20b, we have

$$+\searrow \Sigma F_r = ma_r; \qquad\qquad 19.62 \sin\theta - N_C \sin\theta = 2a_r \qquad (1)$$

$$+\swarrow \Sigma F_\theta = ma_\theta; \qquad 19.62 \cos\theta + F_P - N_C \cos\theta = 2a_\theta \qquad (2)$$

*Kinematics.* From Fig. 13–20a, $r$ can be related to $\theta$ by the equation

$$r = \frac{0.4}{\sin\theta} = 0.4 \csc\theta$$

Since $d(\csc\theta) = -(\csc\theta \cot\theta)\, d\theta$ and $d(\cot\theta) = -(\csc^2\theta)\, d\theta$, then $r$ and the necessary time derivatives become

$$\dot\theta = 0.5 \qquad r = 0.4 \csc\theta$$
$$\ddot\theta = 0 \qquad \dot r = -0.4(\csc\theta \cot\theta)\dot\theta$$
$$= -0.2 \csc\theta \cot\theta$$
$$\ddot r = -0.2(-\csc\theta \cot\theta)(\dot\theta)\cot\theta - 0.2\csc\theta(-\csc^2\theta)\dot\theta$$
$$= 0.1 \csc\theta(\cot^2\theta + \csc^2\theta)$$

Evaluating these formulas at $\theta = 60°$, we get

$$\dot\theta = 0.5 \qquad r = 0.462$$
$$\ddot\theta = 0 \qquad \dot r = -0.133$$
$$\ddot r = 0.192$$
$$a_r = \ddot r - r\dot\theta^2 = 0.192 - 0.462(0.5)^2 = 0.0770$$
$$a_\theta = r\ddot\theta + 2\dot r\dot\theta = 0 + 2(-0.133)(0.5) = -0.133$$

Substituting these results into Eqs. 1 and 2 with $\theta = 60°$ and solving yields

$$N_C = 19.4 \text{ N} \qquad F_P = -0.356 \text{ N} \qquad\qquad \textit{Ans.}$$

The negative sign indicates that $\mathbf{F}_P$ acts opposite to that shown in Fig. 13–20b.

# E X A M P L E 13.12

A can $C$, having a mass of 0.5 kg, moves along a grooved horizontal slot shown in Fig. 13–21a. The slot is in the form of a spiral, which is defined by the equation $r = (0.1\theta)$ m, where $\theta$ is in radians. If the arm $OA$ is rotating at a constant rate $\dot\theta = 4$ rad/s in the horizontal plane, determine the force it exerts on the can at the instant $\theta = \pi$ rad. Neglect friction and the size of the can.

(a)

### Solution

*Free-Body Diagram.* The driving force $\mathbf{F}_C$ acts perpendicular to the arm $OA$, whereas the normal force of the wall of the slot on the can, $\mathbf{N}_C$, acts perpendicular to the tangent to the curve at $\theta = \pi$ rad, Fig. 13–21b. As usual, $\mathbf{a}_r$ and $\mathbf{a}_\theta$ are assumed to act in the *positive directions* of $r$ and $\theta$, respectively. Since the path is specified, the angle $\psi$ which the extended radial line $r$ makes with the tangent, Fig. 13–21c, can be determined from Eq. 13–10. We have $r = 0.1\theta$, so that $dr/d\theta = 0.1$, and therefore

$$\tan\psi = \frac{r}{dr/d\theta} = \frac{0.1\theta}{0.1} = \theta$$

When $\theta = \pi$, $\psi = \tan^{-1}\pi = 72.3°$, so that $\phi = 90° - \psi = 17.7°$, as shown in Fig. 13–21c. Identify the four unknowns in Fig. 13–21b.

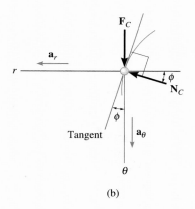

(b)

*Equations of Motion.* Using $\phi = 17.7°$ and the data shown in Fig. 13–21b, we have

$$\xleftarrow{+} \Sigma F_r = ma_r; \qquad N_C \cos 17.7° = 0.5a_r \qquad (1)$$

$$+\downarrow \Sigma F_\theta = ma_\theta; \qquad F_C - N_C \sin 17.7° = 0.5a_\theta \qquad (2)$$

*Kinematics.* The time derivatives of $r$ and $\theta$ are

$$\dot\theta = 4 \text{ rad/s} \qquad r = 0.1\theta$$
$$\ddot\theta = 0 \qquad \dot r = 0.1\dot\theta = 0.1(4) = 0.4 \text{ m/s}$$
$$\ddot r = 0.1\ddot\theta = 0$$

At the instant $\theta = \pi$ rad,

$$a_r = \ddot r - r\dot\theta^2 = 0 - 0.1(\pi)(4)^2 = -5.03 \text{ m/s}^2$$
$$a_\theta = r\ddot\theta + 2\dot r\dot\theta = 0 + 2(0.4)(4) = 3.20 \text{ m/s}^2$$

Substituting these results into Eqs. 1 and 2 and solving yields

$$N_C = -2.64 \text{ N}$$
$$F_C = 0.800 \text{ N} \qquad\qquad Ans.$$

What does the negative sign for $N_C$ indicate?

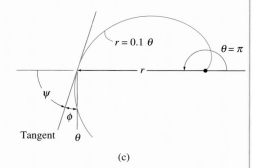

(c)

**Fig. 13–21**

# PROBLEMS

**13-83.** A particle, having a mass of 1.5 kg, moves along a path defined by the equations $r = (4 + 3t)$ m, $\theta = (t^2 + 2)$ rad, and $z = (6 - t^3)$ m, where $t$ is in seconds. Determine the $r$, $\theta$, and $z$ components of force which the path exerts on the particle when $t = 2$ s.

**\*13-84.** The path of motion of a 5-N ($\approx$ 0.5-kg) particle in the horizontal plane is described in terms of polar coordinates as $r = (2t + 1)$ m and $\theta = (0.5t^2 - t)$ rad, where $t$ is in seconds. Determine the magnitude of the unbalanced force acting on the particle when $t = 2$ s.

**13-85.** The spring-held follower $AB$ has a weight of 7.5 N ($\approx$ 0.75 kg) and moves back and forth as its end rolls on the contoured surface of the cam, where $r = 0.1$ m and $z = (0.05 \sin 2\theta)$ m. If the cam is rotating at a constant rate of 6 rad/s, determine the force at the end $A$ of the follower when $\theta = 90°$. In this position the spring is compressed 0.2 m. Neglect friction at the bearing $C$.

**13-86.** The spring-held follower $AB$ has a weight of 7.5 N ($\approx$ 0.75 kg) and moves back and forth as its end rolls on the contoured surface of the cam, where $r = 0.1$ m and $z = (0.05 \sin 2\theta)$ m. If the cam is rotating at a constant rate of 6 rad/s, determine the maximum and minimum force the follower exerts on the cam if the spring is compressed 0.2 m when $\theta = 45°$.

**Probs. 13–85/86**

**13-87.** The 2-kg rod $AB$ moves up and down as its end slides on the smooth contoured surface of the cam, where $r = 0.1$ m and $z = (0.02 \sin 2\theta)$ m. If the cam is rotating at a constant rate of 5 rad/s, determine the maximum and minimum force the cam exerts on the rod.

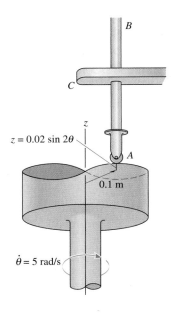

**Prob. 13–87**

**\*13-88.** The boy of mass 40 kg is sliding down the spiral slide at a constant speed such that his position, measured from the top of the chute, has components $r = 1.5$ m, $\theta = (0.7t)$ rad, and $z = (-0.5t)$ m, where $t$ is in seconds. Determine the components of force $\mathbf{F}_r$, $\mathbf{F}_\theta$, and $\mathbf{F}_z$ which the slide exerts on him at the instant $t = 2$ s. Neglect the size of the boy.

**Prob. 13–88**

**13-89.** Rod *OA* rotates counterclockwise with a constant angular velocity of $\dot{\theta} = 5$ rad/s. The double collar *B* is pin-connected together such that one collar slides over the rotating rod and the other slides over the *horizontal* curved rod, of which the shape is described by the equation $r = 0.5(2 - \cos\theta)$ m. If both collars weigh 7.5 N ($\approx 0.75$ kg), determine the normal force which the curved rod exerts on one collar at the instant $\theta = 120°$. Neglect friction.

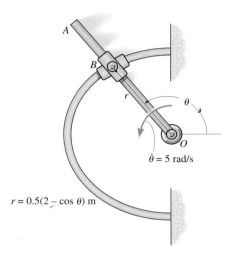

Prob. 13–89

**13-90.** The 5-N ($\approx 0.5$-kg) particle is guided along the circular path using the slotted arm guide. If the arm has an angular velocity $\dot{\theta} = 4$ rad/s and an angular acceleration $\ddot{\theta} = 8$ rad/s² at the instant $\theta = 30°$, determine the force of the guide on the particle. Motion occurs in the *horizontal plane*.

Prob. 13–90

**13-91.** The particle has a mass of 0.5 kg and is confined to move along the smooth horizontal slot due to the rotation of the arm *OA*. Determine the force of the rod on the particle and the normal force of the slot on the particle when $\theta = 30°$. The rod is rotating with a constant angular velocity $\dot{\theta} = 2$ rad/s. Assume the particle contacts only one side of the slot at any instant.

**\*13-92.** Solve Problem 13–91 if the arm has an angular acceleration of $\ddot{\theta} = 3$ rad/s² and $\dot{\theta} = 2$ rad/s at this instant. Assume the particle contacts only one side of the slot at any instant.

Probs. 13–91/92

**13-93.** The spool, which has a mass of 2 kg, slides along the smooth *horizontal* spiral rod, $r = (0.4\theta)$ m, where $\theta$ is in radians. If its angular rate of rotation is constant and equals $\dot{\theta} = 6$ rad/s, determine the horizontal tangential force *P* needed to cause the motion and the horizontal normal force component that the spool exerts on the rod at the instant $\theta = 45°$.

Prob. 13–93

**13-94.** The forked rod is used to move the smooth 20-N ($\approx$ 2-kg) particle around the horizontal path in the shape of a limaçon, $r = (2 + \cos\theta)$ m. If at all times $\dot\theta = 0.5$ rad/s, determine the force which the rod exerts on the particle at the instant $\theta = 90°$. The fork and path contact the particle on only one side.

**13-95.** Solve Prob. 13–94 at the instant $\theta = 60°$.

**\*13-96.** The forked rod is used to move the smooth 20-N ($\approx$ 2-kg) particle around the horizontal path in the shape of a limaçon, $r = (2 + \cos\theta)$ m. If $\theta = (0.5t^2)$ rad, where $t$ is in seconds, determine the force which the rod exerts on the particle at the instant $t = 1$ s. The fork and path contact the particle on only one side.

Probs. 13–94/95/96

**13-97.** The smooth particle has a mass of 80 g. It is attached to an elastic cord extending from $O$ to $P$ and due to the slotted arm guide moves along the *horizontal* circular path $r = (0.8\sin\theta)$ m. If the cord has a stiffness $k = 30$ N/m and an unstretched length of 0.25 m, determine the force of the guide on the particle when $\theta = 60°$. The guide has a constant angular velocity $\dot\theta = 5$ rad/s.

**13-98.** Solve Prob. 13–97 if $\ddot\theta = 2$ rad/s² when $\dot\theta = 5$ rad/s and $\theta = 60°$.

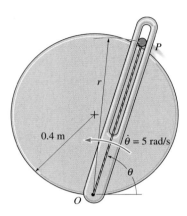

Probs. 13–97/98

**13-99.** For a short time, the 250-kg roller coaster car is traveling along the spiral track such that its position measured from the top of the track has components $r = 8$ m, $\theta = (0.1t + 0.5)$ rad, and $z = (-0.2t)$ m, where $t$ is in seconds. Determine the magnitudes of the components of force which the track exerts on the car in the $r$, $\theta$, and $z$ directions at the instant $t = 2$ s. Neglect the size of the car.

Prob. 13–99

**\*13-100.** Using a forked rod, a smooth cylinder $C$ having a mass of 0.5 kg is forced to move along the *vertical slotted* path $r = (0.5\theta)$ m, where $\theta$ is in radians. If the angular position of the arm is $\theta = (0.5t^2)$ rad, where $t$ is in seconds, determine the force of the rod on the cylinder and the normal force of the slot on the cylinder at the instant $t = 2$ s. The cylinder is in contact with only *one* edge of the rod and slot at any instant.

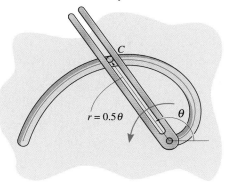

Prob. 13–100

**13-101.** The ball has a mass of 2 kg and a negligible size. It is originally traveling around the horizontal circular path of radius $r_0 = 0.5$ m such that the angular rate of rotation is $\dot{\theta}_0 = 1$ rad/s. If the attached cord $ABC$ is drawn down through the hole at a constant speed of 0.2 m/s, determine the tension the cord exerts on the ball at the instant $r = 0.25$ m. Also, compute the angular velocity of the ball at this instant. Neglect the effects of friction between the ball and horizontal plane. *Hint:* First show that the equation of motion in the $\theta$ direction yields $a_\theta = r\ddot{\theta} + 2\dot{r}\dot{\theta} = (1/r) (d(r^2\dot{\theta})/dt) = 0$. When integrated, $r^2\dot{\theta} = c$, where the constant $c$ is determined from the problem data.

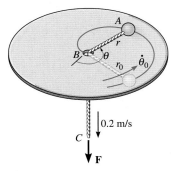

Prob. 13–101

**13-102.** The collar has a mass of 2 kg and travels along the smooth horizontal rod defined by the equiangular spiral $r = (e^\theta)$ m, where $\theta$ is in radians. Determine the tangential force $F$ and the normal force $N$ acting on the collar when $\theta = 45°$, if the force $F$ maintains a constant angular motion $\dot{\theta} = 2$ rad/s.

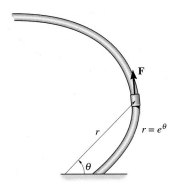

Prob. 13–102

**13-103.** The collar has a mass of 2 kg and travels along the smooth horizontal rod defined by the equiangular spiral $r = (e^\theta)$ m, where $\theta$ is in radians. Determine the tangential force $F$ and the normal force $N$ acting on the collar when $\theta = 90°$, if the force $F$ maintains a constant angular motion $\dot{\theta} = 2$ rad/s.

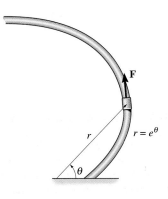

Prob. 13–103

*13-104. Using a forked rod, a smooth cylinder $P$, having a mass of 0.4 kg, is forced to move along the *vertical slotted* path $r = (0.6\theta)$ m, where $\theta$ is in radians. If the cylinder has a constant speed of $v_C = 2$ m/s, determine the force of the rod and the normal force of the slot on the cylinder at the instant $\theta = \pi$ rad. Assume the cylinder is in contact with only *one edge* of the rod and slot at any instant. *Hint:* To obtain the time derivatives necessary to compute the cylinder's acceleration components $a_r$ and $a_\theta$, take the first and second time derivatives of $r = 0.6\theta$. Then, for further information, use Eq. 12–26 to determine $\dot\theta$. Also, take the time derivative of Eq. 12–26, noting that $\dot v_C = 0$, to determine $\ddot\theta$.

Prob. 13–105

Prob. 13–104

13-106. Using air pressure, the 0.5-kg ball is forced to move through the tube lying in the *horizontal plane* and having the shape of a logarithmic spiral. If the tangential force exerted on the ball due to the air is 6 N, determine the rate of increase in the ball's speed at the instant $\theta = \pi/2$. What direction does it act in?

13-107. Solve Prob. 13–106 if the tube lies in a *vertical plane*.

13-105. A ride in an amusement park consists of a cart which is supported by small wheels. Initially the cart is traveling in a circular path of radius $r_0 = 6.4$ m such that the angular rate of rotation is $\dot\theta_0 = 0.2$ rad/s. If the attached cable $OC$ is drawn inward at a constant speed of $\dot r = -0.2$ m/s, determine the tension it exerts on the cart at the instant $r = 1.6$ m. The cart and its passengers have a total weight of 2 kN ($\approx 200$ kg). Neglect the effects of friction. *Hint:* First show that the equation of motion in the $\theta$ direction yields $a_\theta = r\ddot\theta + 2\dot r\dot\theta = (1/r)d(r^2\dot\theta)/dt = 0$. When integrated, $r^2\dot\theta = c$, where the constant $c$ is determined from the problem data.

Probs. 13–106/107

**\*13-108.** The arm is rotating at a rate of $\dot{\theta} = 5$ rad/s when $\ddot{\theta} = 2$ rad/s$^2$ and $\theta = 90°$. Determine the normal force it must exert on the 0.5-kg particle if the particle is confined to move along the slotted path defined by the *horizontal* hyperbolic spiral $r\theta = 0.2$ m.

**13-110.** The pilot of an airplane executes a vertical loop which in part follows the path of a cardioid, $r = 150(1 + \cos\theta)$ m, where $\theta$ is in radians. If his speed at $A$ $(\theta = 0°)$ is a constant $v_P = 20$ m/s, determine the vertical force the belt of his seat must exert on him to hold him to his seat when the plane is upside down at $A$. He weighs 750 N ($\approx$ 75 kg). See hint related to Prob. 13–104.

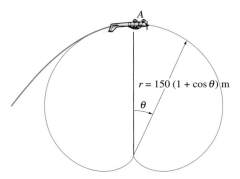

Prob. 13–108

Prob. 13–110

**13-109.** The collar, which has a weight of 30 N ($\approx$ 3 kg), slides along the smooth rod lying in the *horizontal plane* and having the shape of a parabola $r = 2/(1 - \cos\theta)$, where $\theta$ is in radians and $r$ is in metres. If the collar's angular rate is constant and equals $\dot{\theta} = 4$ rad/s, determine the tangential retarding force $P$ needed to cause the motion and the normal force that the collar exerts on the rod at the instant $\theta = 90°$.

**13-111.** A 0.2-kg spool slides down along a smooth rod. If the rod has a constant angular rate of rotation $\dot{\theta} = 2$ rad/s in the vertical plane, show that the equations of motion for the spool are $\ddot{r} - 4r - 9.81\sin\theta = 0$ and $0.8\dot{r} + N_s - 1.962\cos\theta = 0$, where $N_s$ is the magnitude of the normal force of the rod on the spool. Using the methods of differential equations, it can be shown that the solution of the first of these equations is $r = C_1 e^{-2t} + C_2 e^{2t} - (9.81/8)\sin 2t$. If $r, \dot{r}$, and $\theta$ are zero when $t = 0$, evaluate the constants $C_1$ and $C_2$ determine $r$ at the instant $\theta = \pi/4$ rad.

Prob. 13–109

Prob. 13–111

## *13.7 Central-Force Motion and Space Mechanics

(a)

(b)

**Fig. 13–22**

If a particle is moving only under the influence of a force having a line of action which is always directed toward a fixed point, the motion is called *central-force motion*. This type of motion is commonly caused by electrostatic and gravitational forces.

In order to determine the motion, we will consider the particle $P$ shown in Fig. 13–22a, which has a mass $m$ and is acted upon only by the central force **F**. The free-body diagram for the particle is shown in Fig. 13–22b. Using polar coordinates $(r, \theta)$, the equations of motion, Eqs. 13–9, become

$$-F = m\left[\frac{d^2 r}{dt^2} - r\left(\frac{d\theta}{dt}\right)^2\right]$$

$$0 = m\left(r\frac{d^2\theta}{dt^2} + 2\frac{dr}{dt}\frac{d\theta}{dt}\right) \qquad (13\text{–}11)$$

The second of these equations may be written in the form

$$\frac{1}{r}\left[\frac{d}{dt}\left(r^2\frac{d\theta}{dt}\right)\right] = 0$$

so that integrating yields

$$r^2\frac{d\theta}{dt} = h \qquad (13\text{–}12)$$

Here $h$ is a constant of integration. From Fig. 13–22a notice that the shaded area described by the radius $r$, as $r$ moves through an angle $d\theta$, is $dA = \frac{1}{2}r^2 d\theta$. If the *areal velocity* is defined as

$$\frac{dA}{dt} = \frac{1}{2}r^2\frac{d\theta}{dt} = \frac{h}{2} \qquad (13\text{–}13)$$

then, it is seen that the areal velocity for a particle subjected to central-force motion is *constant*. In other words, the particle will sweep out equal segments of area per unit of time as it travels along the path. To obtain the *path of motion*, $r = f(\theta)$, the independent variable $t$ must be eliminated from Eqs. 13–11. Using the chain rule of calculus and Eq. 13–12, the time derivatives of Eqs. 13–11 may be replaced by

$$\frac{dr}{dt} = \frac{dr}{d\theta}\frac{d\theta}{dt} = \frac{h}{r^2}\frac{dr}{d\theta}$$

$$\frac{d^2 r}{dt^2} = \frac{d}{dt}\left(\frac{h}{r^2}\frac{dr}{d\theta}\right) = \frac{d}{d\theta}\left(\frac{h}{r^2}\frac{dr}{d\theta}\right)\frac{d\theta}{dt} = \left[\frac{d}{d\theta}\left(\frac{h}{r^2}\frac{dr}{d\theta}\right)\right]\frac{h}{r^2}$$

Substituting a new dependent variable (xi) $\xi = 1/r$ into the second equation, we have

$$\frac{d^2r}{dt^2} = -h^2\xi^2\frac{d^2\xi}{d\theta^2}$$

Also, the square of Eq. 13–12 becomes

$$\left(\frac{d\theta}{dt}\right)^2 = h^2\xi^4$$

Substituting these last two equations into the first of Eqs. 13–11 yields

$$-h^2\xi^2\frac{d^2\xi}{d\theta^2} - h^2\xi^3 = -\frac{F}{m}$$

or

$$\frac{d^2\xi}{d\theta^2} + \xi = \frac{F}{mh^2\xi^2} \qquad (13\text{–}14)$$

This satellite is subjected to a central force and as such its orbital motion can be closely predicted using the equations developed in this section.

This differential equation defines the path over which the particle travels when it is subjected to the central force* **F**.

For application, the force of gravitational attraction will be considered. Some common examples of central-force systems which depend on gravitation include the motion of the moon and artificial satellites about the earth, and the motion of the planets about the sun. As a typical problem in space mechanics, consider the trajectory of a space satellite or space vehicle launched into free-flight orbit with an initial velocity $\mathbf{v}_0$, Fig. 13–23. It will be assumed that this velocity is initially *parallel* to the tangent at the surface of the earth, as shown in the figure.† Just after the satellite is released into free flight, the only force acting on it is the gravitational force of the earth. (Gravitational attractions involving other bodies such as the moon or sun will be neglected, since for orbits close to the earth their effect is small in comparison with the earth's gravitation.) According to Newton's law of gravitation, force **F** will always act between the mass centers of the earth and the satellite, Fig. 13–23. From Eq. 13–1, this force of attraction has a magnitude of

$$F = G\frac{M_e m}{r^2}$$

where $M_e$ and $m$ represent the mass of the earth and the satellite, respectively, $G$ is the gravitational constant, and $r$ is the distance between

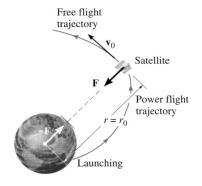

Fig. 13–23

---

*In the derivation, **F** is considered positive when it is directed toward point $O$. If **F** is oppositely directed, the right side of Eq. 13–14 should be negative.

†The case where $\mathbf{v}_0$ acts at some initial angle $\theta$ to the tangent is best described using the conservation of angular momentum (see Prob. 15–116).

the mass centers. Setting $\xi = 1/r$ in the foregoing equation and substituting the result into Eq. 13–14, we obtain

$$\frac{d^2\xi}{d\theta^2} + \xi = \frac{GM_e}{h^2} \qquad (13\text{–}15)$$

This second-order ordinary differential equation has constant coefficients and is nonhomogeneous. The solution is represented as the sum of the complementary and particular solutions. The complementary solution is obtained when the term on the right is equal to zero. It is

$$\xi_c = C \cos(\theta - \phi)$$

where $C$ and $\phi$ are constants of integration. The particular solution is

$$\xi_p = \frac{GM_e}{h^2}$$

Thus, the complete solution to Eq. 13–15 is

$$\xi = \xi_c + \xi_p$$
$$= \frac{1}{r} = C \cos(\theta - \phi) + \frac{GM_e}{h^2} \qquad (13\text{–}16)$$

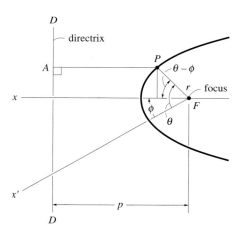

**Fig. 13–24**

The validity of this result may be checked by substitution into Eq. 13–15.

Equation 13–16 represents the *free-flight trajectory* of the satellite. It is the equation of a conic section expressed in terms of polar coordinates. As shown in Fig. 13–24, a *conic section* is defined as the locus of point $P$, which moves in a plane in such a way that the ratio of its distance from a fixed point $F$ to its distance from a fixed line is constant. The fixed point is called the *focus*, and the fixed line $DD$ is called the *directrix*. The constant ratio is called the *eccentricity* of the conic section and is denoted by $e$. Thus,

$$e = \frac{FP}{PA}$$

which may be written in the form

$$FP = r = e(PA) = e[p - r \cos(\theta - \phi)]$$

or

$$\frac{1}{r} = \frac{1}{p} \cos(\theta - \phi) + \frac{1}{ep}$$

Comparing this equation with Eq. 13–16, it is seen that the eccentricity of the conic section for the trajectory is

$$\boxed{e = \frac{Ch^2}{GM_e}} \qquad (13\text{–}17)$$

and the fixed distance from the focus to the directrix is

$$p = \frac{1}{C} \tag{13-18}$$

Provided the polar angle $\theta$ is measured from the $x$ axis (an axis of symmetry since it is perpendicular to the directrix), the angle $\phi$ is zero, Fig. 13–24, and therefore Eq. 13–16 reduces to

$$\frac{1}{r} = C \cos \theta + \frac{GM_e}{h^2} \tag{13-19}$$

The constants $h$ and $C$ are determined from the data obtained for the position and velocity of the satellite at the end of the *power-flight trajectory*. For example, if the initial height or distance to the space vehicle is $r_0$ (measured from the center of the earth) and its initial speed is $v_0$ at the beginning of its free flight, Fig. 13–25, then the constant $h$ may be obtained from Eq. 13–12. When $\theta = \phi = 0°$, the velocity $\mathbf{v}_0$ has no radial component; therefore, from Eq. 12–25, $v_0 = r_0(d\theta/dt)$, so that

$$h = r_0^2 \frac{d\theta}{dt}$$

or

$$\boxed{h = r_0 v_0} \tag{13-20}$$

To determine $C$, use Eq. 13–19 with $\theta = 0°$, $r = r_0$, and substitute Eq. 13–20 for $h$:

$$\boxed{C = \frac{1}{r_0}\left(1 - \frac{GM_e}{r_0 v_0^2}\right)} \tag{13-21}$$

The equation for the free-flight trajectory therefore becomes

$$\boxed{\frac{1}{r} = \frac{1}{r_0}\left(1 - \frac{GM_e}{r_0 v_0^2}\right)\cos \theta + \frac{GM_e}{r_0^2 v_0^2}} \tag{13-22}$$

The type of path taken by the satellite is determined from the value of the eccentricity of the conic section as given by Eq. 13–17. If

$$
\boxed{
\begin{array}{ll}
e = 0 & \text{free-flight trajectory is a circle} \\
e = 1 & \text{free-flight trajectory is a parabola} \\
e < 1 & \text{free-flight trajectory is an ellipse} \\
e > 1 & \text{free-flight trajectory is a hyperbola}
\end{array}
} \tag{13-23}
$$

Each of these trajectories is shown in Fig. 13–25. From the curves it is seen that when the satellite follows a parabolic path, it is "on the border" of never returning to its initial starting point. The initial launch velocity, $\mathbf{v}_0$, required for the satellite to follow a parabolic path is called the *escape velocity*. The speed, $v_e$, can be determined by using the second of Eqs. 13–23 with Eqs. 13–17, 13–20, and 13–21. It is left as an exercise to show that

$$v_e = \sqrt{\frac{2GM_e}{r_0}} \tag{13–24}$$

The speed $v_c$ required to launch a satellite into a *circular orbit* can be found using the first of Eqs. 13–23. Since $e$ is related to $h$ and $C$, Eq. 13–17, $C$ must be zero to satisfy this equation (from Eq. 13–20, $h$ cannot be zero); and therefore, using Eq. 13–21, we have

$$v_c = \sqrt{\frac{GM_e}{r_0}} \tag{13–25}$$

Provided $r_0$ represents a minimum height for launching, in which frictional resistance from the atmosphere is neglected, speeds at launch which are less than $v_c$ will cause the satellite to reenter the earth's atmosphere and either burn up or crash, Fig. 13–25.

**Fig. 13–25**

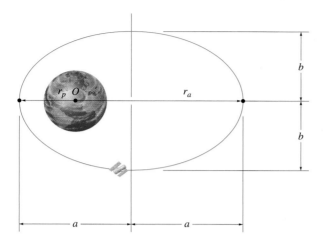

Fig. 13–26

All the trajectories attained by planets and most satellites are elliptical, Fig. 13–26. For a satellite's orbit about the earth, the *minimum distance* from the orbit to the center of the earth $O$ (which is located at one of the foci of the ellipse) is $r_p$ and can be found using Eq. 13–22 with $\theta = 0°$. Therefore;

$$r_p = r_0 \tag{13–26}$$

This minimum distance is called the *perigee* of the orbit. The *apogee* or maximum distance $r_a$ can be found using Eq. 13–22 with $\theta = 180°$.* Thus,

$$r_a = \frac{r_0}{(2GM_e/r_0 v_0^2) - 1} \tag{13–27}$$

With reference to Fig. 13–26, the semimajor axis $a$ of the ellipse is

$$a = \frac{r_p + r_a}{2} \tag{13–28}$$

Using analytical geometry, it can be shown that the minor axis $b$ is determined from the equation

$$b = \sqrt{r_p r_a} \tag{13–29}$$

*Actually, the terminology perigee and apogee pertains only to orbits about the *earth*. If any other heavenly body is located at the focus of an elliptical orbit, the minimum and maximum distances are referred to respectively as the *periapsis* and *apoapsis* of the orbit.

Furthermore, by direct integration, the area of an ellipse is

$$A = \pi ab = \frac{\pi}{2}(r_p + r_a)\sqrt{r_p r_a} \qquad (13\text{--}30)$$

The areal velocity has been defined by Eq. 13–13, $dA/dt = h/2$. Integrating yields $A = hT/2$, where $T$ is the *period* of time required to make one orbital revolution. From Eq. 13–30, the period is

$$T = \frac{\pi}{h}(r_p + r_a)\sqrt{r_p r_a} \qquad (13\text{--}31)$$

In addition to predicting the orbital trajectory of earth satellites, the theory developed in this section is valid, to a surprisingly close approximation, at predicting the actual motion of the planets traveling around the sun. In this case the mass of the sun, $M_s$, should be substituted for $M_e$ when the appropriate formulas are used.

The fact that the planets do indeed follow elliptic orbits about the sun was discovered by the German astronomer Johannes Kepler in the early seventeenth century. His discovery was made *before* Newton had developed the laws of motion and the law of gravitation, and so at the time it provided important proof as to the validity of these laws. Kepler's laws, developed after 20 years of planetary observation, are summarized as follows:

1. Every planet moves in its orbit such that the line joining it to the sun sweeps over equal areas in equal intervals of time, whatever the line's length.

2. The orbit of every planet is an ellipse with the sun placed at one of its foci.

3. The square of the period of any planet is directly proportional to the cube of the minor axis of its orbit.

A mathematical statement of the first and second laws is given by Eqs. 13–13 and 13–22, respectively. The third law can be shown from Eq. 13–31 using Eqs. 13–19, 13–28, and 13–29.

# EXAMPLE 13.13

A satellite is launched 600 km from the surface of the earth, with an initial velocity of 30 Mm/h acting parallel to the tangent at the surface of the earth, Fig. 13–27. Assuming that the radius of the earth is 6378 km and that its mass is $5.976(10^{24})$ kg, determine (a) the eccentricity of the orbital path, and (b) the velocity of the satellite at apogee.

**Solution**

*Part (a).* The eccentricity of the orbit is obtained using Eq. 13–17. The constants $h$ and $C$ are first determined from Eqs. 13–20 and 13–21. Since

$$r_p = r_0 = 6378 \text{ km} + 600 \text{ km} = 6.978(10^6) \text{ m}$$

$$v_0 = 30 \text{ Mm/h} = 8333.3 \text{ m/s}$$

then

$$h = r_p v_0 = 6.978(10^6)(8333.3) = 58.15(10^9) \text{ m}^2/\text{s}$$

$$C = \frac{1}{r_p}\left(1 - \frac{GM_e}{r_p v_0^2}\right)$$

$$= \frac{1}{6.978(10^6)}\left\{1 - \frac{66.73(10^{-12})[5.976(10^{24})]}{6.978(10^6)(8333.3)^2}\right\} = 25.4(10^{-9}) \text{ m}^{-1}$$

Hence,

$$e = \frac{Ch^2}{GM_e} = \frac{2.54(10^{-8})[58.15(10^9)]^2}{66.73(10^{-12})[5.976(10^{24})]} = 0.215 < 1 \qquad Ans.$$

From Eq. 13–23, observe that the orbit is an *ellipse*.

*Part (b).* If the satellite were launched at the apogee $A$ shown in Fig. 13–27, with a velocity $\mathbf{v}_A$, the same orbit would be maintained provided that

$$h = r_p v_0 = r_a v_A = 58.15(10^9) \text{ m}^2/\text{s}$$

Using Eq. 13–27, we have

$$r_a = \frac{r_p}{\dfrac{2GM_e}{r_p v_0^2} - 1} = \frac{6.978(10^6)}{\left\{\dfrac{2[66.73(10^{-12})][5.976(10^{24})]}{6.978(10^6)(8333.3)^2} - 1\right\}} = 10.804(10^6)$$

Thus,

$$v_A = \frac{58.15(10^9)}{10.804(10^6)} = 5382.2 \text{ m/s} = 19.4 \text{ Mm/h} \qquad Ans.$$

Fig. 13–27

# PROBLEMS

In the following problems, except where otherwise indicated, assume that the radius of the earth is 6378 km, the earth's mass is $5.976(10^{24})$ kg, the mass of the sun is $1.99(10^{30})$ kg, and the gravitational constant is $G = 66.73(10^{-12})$ m$^3$/(kg·s$^2$).

**\*13-112.** The rocket is in circular orbit about the earth at an altitude of $h = 4$ Mm. Determine the minimum increment in speed it must have in order to escape the earth's gravitational field.

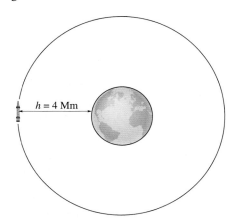

**Prob. 13–112**

**13-113.** Prove Kepler's third law of motion. *Hint:* Use Eqs. 13–19, 13–28, 13–29, and 13–31.

**13-114.** The satellite is moving in an elliptical orbit with an eccentricity $e = 0.25$. Determine its speed when it is at its maximum distance $A$ and minimum distance $B$ from the earth.

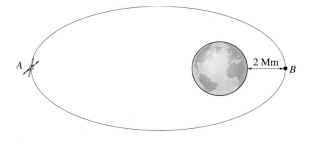

**Prob. 13–114**

**13-115.** The rocket is traveling in free flight along an elliptical trajectory $A'A$. The planet has a mass 0.60 times that of the earth's. If the rocket has an apoapsis and periapsis as shown in the figure, determine the speed of the rocket when it is at point $A$.

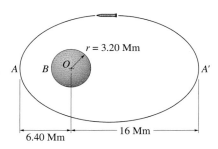

**Prob. 13–115**

**\*13-116.** An elliptical path of a satellite has an eccentricity $e = 0.130$. If it has a speed of 15 Mm/h when it is at perigee, $P$, determine its speed when it arrives at apogee, $A$. Also, how far is it from the earth's surface when it is at $A$?

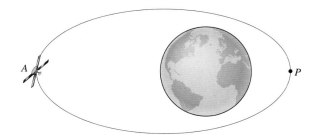

**Prob. 13–116**

**13-117.** A satellite is launched with an initial velocity $v_0 = 4000$ km/h parallel to the surface of the earth. Determine the required altitude (or range of altitudes) above the earth's surface for launching if the free-flight trajectory is to be (a) circular, (b) parabolic, (c) elliptical, and (d) hyperbolic. Take $G = 66.73(10^{-12})$ (N·m$^2$)/kg$^2$, $M_e = 5.976(10^{24})$ kg, the earth's radius $r_e = 6378$ km.

**13-118.** The rocket is docked next to a satellite located 18 Mm above the earth's surface. If the satellite is traveling in a circular orbit, determine the speed tangent to the earth's surface which must suddenly be given to the rocket, relative to the satellite, such that it travels in free flight away from the satellite along a parabolic trajectory as shown.

18 Mm

**Prob. 13–118**

**13-119.** The speed of a satellite launched into a circular orbit about the earth is given by Eq. 13–25. Determine the speed of a satellite launched parallel to the surface of the earth so that it travels in a circular orbit 800 km from the earth's surface.

**\*13-120.** The rocket is in a free-flight elliptical orbit about the earth such that the eccentricity of its orbit is $e$ and its perigee is $r_0$. Determine the minimum increment of speed it should have in order to escape the earth's gravitational field when it is at this point along its orbit.

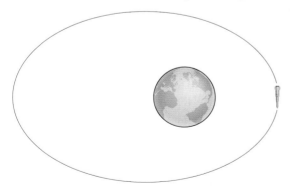

**Prob. 13–120**

**13-121.** The rocket is traveling in free flight along an elliptical trajectory $A'A$. The planet has no atmosphere, and its mass is 0.70 times that of the earth's. If the rocket has an apoapsis and periapsis as shown in the figure, determine the speed of the rocket when it is at point $A$.

**13-122.** If the rocket in Prob. 13–121 is to land on the surface of the planet, determine the required free-flight speed it must have at $A'$ so that it strikes the planet at $B$. How long does it take for the rocket to land, going from $A'$ to $B$ along an elliptical path?

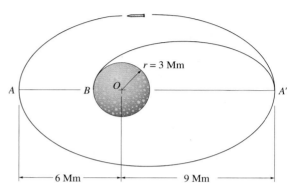

$r = 3$ Mm

$A$   $B$   $O$   $A'$

6 Mm   9 Mm

**Probs. 13–121/122**

**13-123.** A satellite $S$ travels in a circular orbit around the earth. A rocket is located at the apogee of its elliptical orbit for which $e = 0.58$. Determine the sudden change in speed that must occur at $A$ so that the rocket can enter the satellite's orbit while in free flight along the blue elliptical trajectory. When it arrives at $B$, determine the sudden adjustment in speed that must be given to the rocket in order to maintain the circular orbit.

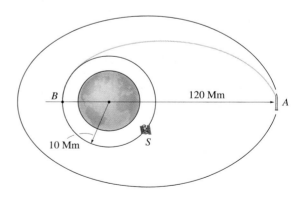

$B$   120 Mm   $A$

10 Mm   $S$

**Prob. 13–123**

**\*13-124.** An asteroid is in an elliptical orbit about the sun such that its perihelion distance is $9.30(10^9)$ km. If the eccentricity of the orbit is $e = 0.073$, determine the aphelion distance of the orbit.

**13-125.** The rocket is traveling in a free-flight elliptical orbit about the earth such that $e = 0.76$ as shown. Determine its speed when it is at point $A$. Also determine the sudden change in speed the rocket must experience at $B$ in order to travel in free flight along the orbit indicated by the dashed path.

**Prob. 13–125**

**13-126.** The rocket is traveling in a free-flight elliptical orbit about the earth such that $e = 0.76$ and its perigee is 9 Mm as shown. Determine its speed when it is at point $B$. Also determine the sudden decrease in speed the rocket must experience at $A$ in order to travel in a circular orbit about the earth.

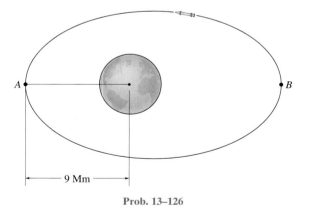

**Prob. 13–126**

**13-127.** The rocket shown is originally in a circular orbit 6 Mm above the surface of the earth. It is required that it travel in another circular orbit having an altitude of 14 Mm. To do this, the rocket is given a short pulse of power at $A$ so that it travels in free flight along the gray elliptical path from the first orbit to the second orbit.

Determine the necessary speed it must have at $A$ just after the power pulse, and at the time required to get to the outer orbit along the path $AA'$. What adjustment in speed must be made at $A'$ to maintain the second circular orbit?

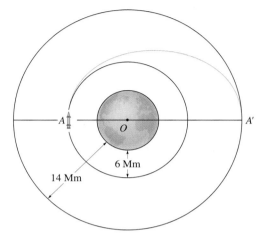

**Prob. 13–127**

---

# DESIGN PROJECTS

**13–1D. DESIGN OF A RAMP CATAPULT**

The block $B$ has a mass of 20 kg and is to be catapulted from the table. Design a catapulting mechanism that can be attached to the table and to the container of the block, using cables and pulleys. Neglect the mass of the container, assume the operator can exert a constant tension of 120 N on a single cable during operation, and that the maximum movement of his arm is 0.5 m. The coefficient of kinetic friction between the table and container is $\mu_k = 0.2$. Submit a drawing of your design, and calculate the maximum range $R$ to where the block will strike the ground. Compare your value with that of others in the class.

**Prob. 13–1D**

### 13–2D.  DESIGN OF A WATER-BALLOON LAUNCHER

Design a method for launching a 0.1-kg water balloon. Hold a contest with other students to see who can launch the balloon the farthest or hit a target. Materials should consist of a single rubber band of specified length and stiffness, and if necessary no more than three pieces of wood of specified size. Submit a report to show your calculations of where the balloon is predicted to strike the ground from the point at which it was launched.

Compare this with the actual value $R$ and discuss why the two distances may be different.

**Prob. 13–2D**

## CHAPTER REVIEW

- **Kinetics.**   Kinetics is the study of the relationship between forces and the acceleration they cause. This relationship is based on Newton's second law of motion, expressed mathematically as $\Sigma \mathbf{F} = m\mathbf{a}$. Here the mass $m$ is the proportionality constant between the resultant force $\Sigma \mathbf{F}$ acting on the particle and the acceleration $\mathbf{a}$ caused by this resultant. The mass represents the quantity of matter contained within the particle. It measures the resistance to a change in its motion.

  Before applying the equation of motion, it is important to draw the particle's free-body diagram first in order to account for all of the forces that act on the particle. Graphically, this diagram can be set equal to the kinetic diagram, which shows the result of the forces, that is, the $m\mathbf{a}$ vector.

- **Inertial Coordinate Systems.**   When applying the equation of motion, it is important to make measurements of the acceleration from an inertial coordinate system. This system has axes that do not rotate but are either fixed or translate with a constant velocity. Various types of inertial coordinate systems can be used to apply $\Sigma \mathbf{F} = m\mathbf{a}$ in component form. Rectangular $x, y, z$ axes are used to describe rectilinear motion along each of the axes. Normal and tangential $n, t$ axes are often used when the path is known. Recall that $\mathbf{a}_n$ is always directed in the $+n$ direction. It indicates the change in the velocity direction. And $\mathbf{a}_t$ is tangent to the path. It indicates the change in the velocity magnitude. Finally, cylindrical coordinates are useful when angular motion of the radial coordinate $r$ is specified or when the path can conveniently be described with these coordinates. For some problems, the direction of the forces on the free-body diagram will require finding the angle $\psi$ between the extended radial coordinate and the tangent to the curve. This angle can be determined using

$$\tan \psi = \frac{r}{dr/d\theta}$$

- **Central-Force Motion.**   When a single force acts upon a particle, such as the free-flight trajectory of a satellite in a gravitational field, then the motion is referred to as central-force motion. The orbit depends upon the eccentricity $e$, and as a result, the trajectory can either be circular, parabolic, elliptical, or hyperbolic.

In order to properly design the loop of this roller coaster it is necessary to ensure that the cars have enough energy to be able to make the loop without leaving the tracks.

# Kinetics of a Particle: Work and Energy

- To develop the principle of work and energy and apply it to solve problems that involve force, velocity, and displacement.
- To study problems that involve power and efficiency.
- To introduce the concept of a conservative force and apply the theorem of conservation of energy to solve kinetic problems.

## 14.1 The Work of a Force

In mechanics a force **F** does *work* on a particle only when the particle undergoes a *displacement in the direction of the force*. For example, consider the force **F** acting on the particle in Fig. 14–1. If the particle moves along the path $s$ from position **r** to a new position **r**′, the displacement is then $d\mathbf{r} = \mathbf{r}' - \mathbf{r}$. The magnitude of $d\mathbf{r}$ is represented by $ds$, the differential segment along the path. If the angle between the tails of $d\mathbf{r}$ and **F** is $\theta$, Fig. 14–1, then the work $dU$ which is done by **F** is a

Fig. 14–1

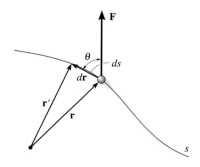

**Fig. 14–1**

*scalar quantity*, defined by

$$dU = F \, ds \cos \theta$$

By definition of the dot product (see Eq. C–14) this equation may also be written as

$$dU = \mathbf{F} \cdot d\mathbf{r}$$

This result may be interpreted in one of two ways: either as the product of $F$ and the component of displacement in the direction of the force, i.e., $ds \cos \theta$, or as the product of $ds$ and the component of force in the direction of displacement, i.e., $F \cos \theta$. Note that if $0° \le \theta < 90°$, then the force component and the displacement have the *same sense* so that the work is *positive*; whereas if $90° < \theta \le 180°$, these vectors have an *opposite sense*, and therefore the work is *negative*. Also, $dU = 0$ if the force is *perpendicular* to displacement, since $\cos 90° = 0$, or if the force is applied at a *fixed point*, in which case the displacement is zero.

The basic unit for work in the SI system is called a joule (J). This unit combines the units of force and displacement. Specifically, 1 *joule* of work is done when a force of 1 newton moves 1 meter along its line of action $(1 \text{ J} = 1 \text{ N} \cdot \text{m})$. The moment of a force has this same combination of units $(\text{N} \cdot \text{m})$; however, the concepts of moment and work are in no way related. A moment is a vector quantity, whereas work is a scalar.

**Work of a Variable Force.** If the particle undergoes a finite displacement along its path from $\mathbf{r}_1$ to $\mathbf{r}_2$ or $s_1$ to $s_2$, Fig. 14–2a, the work is determined by integration. If $\mathbf{F}$ is expressed as a function of position, $F = F(s)$, we have

$$U_{1-2} = \int_{\mathbf{r}_1}^{\mathbf{r}_2} \mathbf{F} \cdot d\mathbf{r} = \int_{s_1}^{s_2} F \cos \theta \, ds \qquad (14\text{–}1)$$

If the working component of the force, $F \cos \theta$, is plotted versus $s$, Fig. 14–2b, the integral in this equation can be interpreted as the *area under the curve* from position $s_1$ to position $s_2$.

(a)

(b)

**Fig. 14–2**

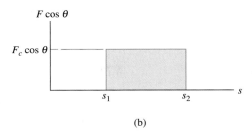

(a)                                                                                    (b)

Fig. 14–3

**Work of a Constant Force Moving Along a Straight Line.** If the force $\mathbf{F}_c$ has a constant magnitude and acts at a constant angle $\theta$ from its straight-line path, Fig. 14–3a, then the component of $\mathbf{F}_c$ in the direction of displacement is $F_c \cos \theta$. The work done by $\mathbf{F}_c$ when the particle is displaced from $s_1$ to $s_2$ is determined from Eq. 14–1, in which case

$$U_{1-2} = F_c \cos \theta \int_{s_1}^{s_2} ds$$

or

$$\boxed{U_{1-2} = F_c \cos \theta (s_2 - s_1)} \qquad (14\text{–}2)$$

Here the work of $\mathbf{F}_c$ represents the *area of the rectangle* in Fig. 14–3b.

**Work of a Weight.** Consider a particle which moves up along the path $s$ shown in Fig. 14–4 from position $s_1$ to position $s_2$. At an intermediate point, the displacement $d\mathbf{r} = dx\mathbf{i} + dy\mathbf{j} + dz\mathbf{k}$. Since $\mathbf{W} = -W\mathbf{j}$, applying Eq. 14–1 yields

$$U_{1-2} = \int \mathbf{F} \cdot d\mathbf{r} = \int_{\mathbf{r}_1}^{\mathbf{r}_2} (-W\mathbf{j}) \cdot (dx\mathbf{i} + dy\mathbf{j} + dz\mathbf{k})$$

$$= \int_{y_1}^{y_2} -W\,dy = -W(y_2 - y_1)$$

or

$$\boxed{U_{1-2} = -W\Delta y} \qquad (14\text{–}3)$$

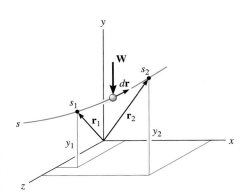

Thus, the work done is equal to the magnitude of the particle's weight times its vertical displacement. In the case shown in Fig. 14–4 the work is *negative*, since $W$ is downward and $\Delta y$ is upward. Note, however, that if the particle is displaced *downward* $(-\Delta y)$, the work of the weight is *positive*. Why?

Fig. 14–4

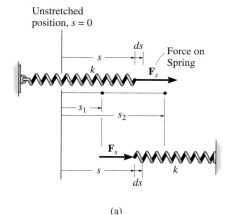

Unstretched position, $s = 0$

(a)

(b)

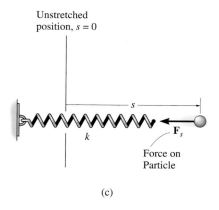

Unstretched position, $s = 0$

(c)

**Fig. 14–5**

**Work of a Spring Force.** The magnitude of force developed in a linear elastic spring when the spring is displaced a distance $s$ from its unstretched position is $F_s = ks$, where $k$ is the spring stiffness. If the spring is elongated or compressed from a position $s_1$ to a further position $s_2$, Fig. 14–5a, the work done *on the spring* by $\mathbf{F}_s$ is *positive*, since in each case the force and displacement are in the *same direction*. We require

$$U_{1-2} = \int_{s_1}^{s_2} F_s \, ds = \int_{s_1}^{s_2} ks \, ds$$
$$= \tfrac{1}{2}ks_2^2 - \tfrac{1}{2}ks_1^2$$

This equation represents the trapezoidal area under the line $F_s = ks$, Fig. 14–5b.

If a particle (or body) is attached to a spring, then the force $\mathbf{F}_s$ exerted on the particle is *opposite* to that exerted on the spring, Fig. 14–5c. Consequently, the force will do *negative work* on the particle when the particle is moving so as to further elongate (or compress) the spring. Hence, the above equation becomes

$$\boxed{U_{1-2} = -(\tfrac{1}{2}ks_2^2 - \tfrac{1}{2}ks_1^2)} \qquad (14\text{–}4)$$

When this equation is used, a mistake in sign can be eliminated if one simply notes the direction of the spring force acting on the particle and compares it with the direction of displacement of the particle—if both are in the *same direction, positive work* results; if they are *opposite* to one another, the *work is negative*.

The forces acting on the cart as it is pulled a distance $s$ up the incline, are shown on its free-body diagram. The constant towing force $\mathbf{T}$ does positive work of $U_T = (T \cos \phi)s$, the weight does negative work of $U_W = -(W \sin \theta)s$, and the normal force $\mathbf{N}$ does no work since there is no displacement of this force along its line of action.

# EXAMPLE 14.1

The 10-kg block shown in Fig. 14–6a rests on the smooth incline. If the spring is originally stretched 0.5 m, determine the total work done by all the forces acting on the block when a horizontal force $P = 400$ N pushes the block up the plane $s = 2$ m.

$s = 2$ m

Initial position of spring

$P = 400$ N

2 sin 30° m

$k = 30$ N/m

2 cos 30° m

30°

(a)

## Solution

First the free-body diagram of the block is drawn in order to account for all the forces that act on the block, Fig. 14–6b.

*Horizontal Force P.* Since this force is *constant*, the work is determined using Eq. 14–2. The result can be calculated as the force times the component of displacement in the direction of the force; i.e.,

$$U_P = 400 \text{ N } (2 \text{ m cos } 30°) = 692.8 \text{ J}$$

or the displacement times the component of force in the direction of displacement, i.e.,

$$U_P = 400 \text{ N cos } 30°(2 \text{ m}) = 692.8 \text{ J}$$

*Spring Force F$_s$.* In the initial position the spring is stretched $s_1 = 0.5$ m and in the final position it is stretched $s_2 = 0.5 + 2 = 2.5$ m. We require the work to be negative since the force and displacement are in opposite directions. The work of $\mathbf{F}_s$ is thus

$$U_s = -[\tfrac{1}{2}(30 \text{ N/M})(2.5 \text{ m})^2 - \tfrac{1}{2}(30 \text{ N/m})(0.5 \text{ m})^2] = -90 \text{ J}$$

*Weight W.* Since the weight acts in the opposite direction to its vertical displacement, the work is negative; i.e.,

$$U_W = -98.1 \text{ N } (2 \text{ m sin } 30°) = -98.1 \text{ J}$$

Note that it is also possible to consider the component of weight in the direction of displacement; i.e.,

$$U_W = -(98.1 \sin 30° \text{ N})2 \text{ m} = -98.1 \text{ J}$$

*Normal Force N$_B$.* This force does *no work* since it is *always* perpendicular to the displacement.

*Total Work.* The work of all the forces when the block is displaced 2 m is thus

$$U_T = 692.8 - 90 - 98.1 = 505 \text{ J} \qquad \textit{Ans.}$$

98.1 N  30°

$P = 400$ N

30°

$N_B$

$F_s$

(b)

**Fig. 14–6**

## 14.2 Principle of Work and Energy

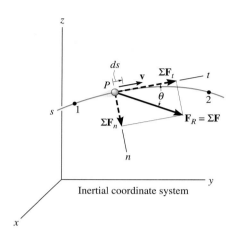

Inertial coordinate system

**Fig. 14–7**

Consider a particle $P$ in Fig. 14–7, which at the instant considered is located on the path as measured from an inertial coordinate system. If the particle has a mass $m$ and is subjected to a system of external forces represented by the resultant $\mathbf{F}_R = \Sigma\mathbf{F}$, then the equation of motion for the particle in the tangential direction is $\Sigma F_t = ma_t$. Applying the kinematic equation $a_t = v\,dv/ds$ and integrating both sides, assuming initially that the particle has a position $s = s_1$ and a speed $v = v_1$, and later at $s = s_2$, $v = v_2$, yields

$$\Sigma\int_{s_1}^{s_2} F_t\,ds = \int_{v_1}^{v_2} mv\,dv$$

$$\Sigma\int_{s_1}^{s_2} F_t\,ds = \tfrac{1}{2}mv_2^2 - \tfrac{1}{2}mv_1^2 \qquad (14\text{–}5)$$

From Fig. 14–7, $\Sigma F_t = \Sigma F\cos\theta$ and since work is defined from Eq. 14–1, the final result may be written as

$$\Sigma U_{1\text{-}2} = \tfrac{1}{2}mv_2^2 - \tfrac{1}{2}mv_1^2 \qquad (14\text{–}6)$$

This equation represents the *principle of work and energy* for the particle. The term on the left is the sum of the work done by *all* the forces acting on the particle as the particle moves from point 1 to point 2. The two terms on the right side, which are of the form $T = \tfrac{1}{2}mv^2$, define the particle's final and initial *kinetic energy*, respectively. These terms are always *positive* scalars. Furthermore, Eq. 14–6 must be dimensionally homogeneous so that the kinetic energy has the same units as work, e.g., joules (J).

When Eq. 14–6 is applied, it is often symbolized in the form

$$\boxed{T_1 + \Sigma U_{1\text{-}2} = T_2} \qquad (14\text{–}7)$$

which states that the particle's initial kinetic energy plus the work done by all the forces acting on the particle as it moves from its initial to its final position is equal to the particle's final kinetic energy.

As noted from the derivation, the principle of work and energy represents an integrated form of $\Sigma F_t = ma_t$, obtained by using the kinematic equation $a_t = v\,dv/ds$. As a result, this principle will provide a convenient *substitution* for $\Sigma F_t = ma_t$ when solving those types of kinetic problems which involve force, velocity, and displacement, since these variables are involved in the terms of Eq. 14–7. For example, if a particle's initial speed is known and the work of all the forces acting on the particle can be determined, then Eq. 14–7 provides a *direct means* of obtaining the final speed $v_2$ of the particle after it undergoes a specified

If an oncoming car strikes these crash barrels, the car's kinetic energy will be transformed into work, which causes the barrels, and to some extent the car, to be deformed. By knowing the amount of energy absorbed by each barrel it is possible to design a crash cushion such as this.

displacement. If instead $v_2$ is determined by means of the equation of motion, a two-step process is necessary; i.e., apply $\Sigma F_t = ma_t$ to obtain $a_t$, then integrate $a_t = v\,dv/ds$ to obtain $v_2$. Note that the principle of work and energy cannot be used, for example, to determine forces directed *normal* to the path of motion, since these forces do no work on the particle. Instead $\Sigma F_n = ma_n$ must be applied. For curved paths, however, the magnitude of the normal force is a function of speed. Hence, it may be easier to obtain this speed using the principle of work and energy, and then substitute this quantity into the equation of motion $\Sigma F_n = mv^2/\rho$ to obtain the normal force.

## PROCEDURE FOR ANALYSIS

The principle of work and energy is used to solve kinetic problems that involve *velocity, force*, and *displacement*, since these terms are involved in the equation. For application it is suggested that the following procedure be used.

### Work (Free-Body Diagram)

- Establish the inertial coordinate system and draw a free-body diagram of the particle in order to account for all the forces that do work on the particle as it moves along its path.

### Principle of Work and Energy

- Apply the principle of work and energy, $T_1 + \Sigma U_{1-2} = T_2$.
- The kinetic energy at the initial and final points is always positive, since it involves the speed squared ($T = \frac{1}{2}mv^2$).
- A force does work when it moves through a displacement in the direction of the force.
- Work is *positive* when the force component is in the *same direction* as its displacement, otherwise it is negative.
- Forces that are functions of displacement must be integrated to obtain the work. Graphically, the work is equal to the area under the force-displacement curve.
- The work of a weight is the product of the weight magnitude and the vertical displacement, $U_W = \pm Wy$. It is positive when the weight moves downwards.
- The work of a spring is of the form $U_s = \frac{1}{2}ks^2$, where $k$ is the spring stiffness and $s$ is the stretch or compression of the spring.

Numerical application of this procedure is illustrated in the examples following Sec. 14.3.

## 14.3 Principle of Work and Energy for a System of Particles

Inertial coordinate system

**Fig. 14–8**

The principle of work and energy can be extended to include a system of $n$ particles isolated within an enclosed region of space as shown in Fig. 14–8. Here the arbitrary $i$th particle, having a mass $m_i$, is subjected to a resultant external force $\mathbf{F}_i$ and a resultant internal force $\mathbf{f}_i$ which each of the other particles exerts on the $i$th particle. Using Eq. 14–5, which applies in the tangential direction, the principle of work and energy written for the $i$th particle is thus

$$\tfrac{1}{2}m_i v_{i1}^2 + \int_{s_{i1}}^{s_{i2}} (F_i)_t \, ds + \int_{s_{i1}}^{s_{i2}} (f_i)_t \, ds = \tfrac{1}{2}m_i v_{i2}^2.$$

Similar equations result if the principle of work and energy is applied to each of the other particles of the system. Since both work and kinetic energy are scalars, the results may be added together algebraically, so that

$$\Sigma \tfrac{1}{2}m_i v_{i1}^2 + \Sigma \int_{s_{i1}}^{s_{i2}} (F_i)_t \, ds + \Sigma \int_{s_{i1}}^{s_{i2}} (f_i)_t \, ds = \Sigma \tfrac{1}{2}m_i v_{i2}^2$$

We can write this equation symbolically as

$$\Sigma T_1 + \Sigma U_{1-2} = \Sigma T_2 \qquad (14\text{–}8)$$

This equation states that the system's initial kinetic energy ($\Sigma T_1$) plus the work done by all the external and internal forces acting on the particles of the system ($\Sigma U_{1-2}$) is equal to the system's final kinetic energy ($\Sigma T_2$). To maintain this balance of energy, strict accountability of the work done by all the forces must be made. In this regard, note that although the internal forces on adjacent particles occur in equal but opposite collinear pairs, the total work done by each of these forces will, in general, *not cancel* out since the paths over which corresponding particles travel will be *different*. There are, however, two important exceptions to this rule which often occur in practice. If the particles are contained within the boundary of a *translating rigid body*, the internal forces all undergo the same displacement, and therefore the internal work will be zero. Also, particles connected by inextensible cables make up a system that has internal forces which are displaced by an equal amount. In this case, adjacent particles exert equal but opposite internal forces that have components which undergo the same displacement, and therefore the work of these forces cancels. On the other hand, note that if the body is assumed to be *nonrigid*, the particles of the body are displaced along *different paths*, and some of the energy due to force interactions would be given off and lost as heat or stored in the body if permanent deformations occur. We will discuss these effects briefly at the end of this section and in Sec. 15.4. Throughout this text, however, the principle of work and energy will be applied to the solution of problems only when direct accountability of these energy losses does not have to be made.

The procedure for analysis outlined in Sec. 14.2 provides a method for applying Eq. 14–8; however, only one equation applies for the entire system. If the particles are connected by cords, other equations can generally be obtained by using the kinematic principles outlined in Sec. 12.9 in order to relate the particle's speeds. See Example 14.6.

**Work of Friction Caused by Sliding.** A special class of problems will now be investigated which requires a careful application of Eq. 14–8. These problems all involve cases where a body is sliding over the surface of another body in the presence of friction. Consider, for example, a block which is translating a distance $s$ over a rough surface as shown in Fig. 14–9a. If the applied force **P** just balances the *resultant* frictional force $\mu_k N$, Fig. 14–9b, then due to equilibrium a constant velocity **v** is maintained, and one would expect Eq. 14–8 to be applied as follows:

$$\tfrac{1}{2}mv^2 + Ps - \mu_k Ns = \tfrac{1}{2}mv^2$$

Indeed this equation is satisfied if $P = \mu_k N$; however, as one realizes from experience, the sliding motion will *generate heat*, a form of energy which seems not to be accounted for in the work-energy equation. In order to explain this paradox and thereby more closely represent the nature of friction, we should actually model the block so that the surfaces of contact are *deformable* (nonrigid.)* Recall that the rough portions at the bottom of the block act as "teeth," and when the block slides these teeth *deform slightly* and either break off or vibrate due to interlocking effects and pull away from "teeth" at the contacting surface, Fig. 14–9c. As a result, frictional forces that act on the block at these points are displaced slightly, due to the localized deformations, and then they are replaced by other frictional forces as other points of contact are made. At any instant, the *resultant* **F** of all these frictional forces remains essentially constant, i.e., $\mu_k N$; however, due to the many *localized deformations*, the actual displacement $s'$ of $\mu_k N$ is *not* the same displacement $s$ as the applied force **P**. Instead, $s'$ will be *less* than $s$ ($s' < s$), and therefore the *external work* done by the resultant frictional force will be $\mu_k Ns'$ and not $\mu_k Ns$. The remaining amount of work, $\mu_k N(s - s')$, manifests itself as an increase in *internal energy*, which in fact causes the block's temperature to rise. In summary then, Eq. 14–8 can be applied to problems involving sliding friction; however, it should be fully realized that the work of the resultant frictional force is not represented by $\mu_k Ns$; instead, this term represents *both* the external work of friction ($\mu_k Ns'$) and internal work $[\mu_k N(s - s')]$ which is converted into various forms of internal energy, such as heat.†

(a)

(b)

(c)

**Fig. 14–9**

---

*See Chapter 8 of *Engineering Mechanics: Statics.*

† See B. A. Sherwood and W. H. Bernard, "Work and Heat Transfer in the Presence of Sliding Friction," *Am. J. Phys.* 52, 1001 (1984).

E X A M P L E **14.2**

(a)

(b)

**Fig. 14–10**

The 17.5-kN ($\approx$ 1750-kg) automobile shown in Fig. 14–10a is traveling down the 10° inclined road at a speed of 6 m/s. If the driver jams on the brakes, causing his wheels to lock, determine how far $s$ his tires skid on the road. The coefficient of kinetic friction between the wheels and the road is $\mu_k = 0.5$.

**Solution I**

This problem can be solved using the principle of work and energy, since it involves force, velocity, and displacement.

*Work (Free-Body Diagram).* As shown in Fig. 14–10b, the normal force $\mathbf{N}_A$ does no work since it never undergoes displacement along its line of action. The weight, 17.5 kN, is displaced $s \sin 10°$ and does positive work. Why? The frictional force $\mathbf{F}_A$ does both external and internal work when it is *thought* to undergo a displacement $s$. This work is negative since it is in the opposite direction to displacement. Applying the equation of equilibrium normal to the road, we have

$$+\nwarrow \Sigma F_n = 0; \quad N_A - 17500 \cos 10° \text{ N} = 0 \quad N_A = 17234.1 \text{ N}$$

Thus,

$$F_A = 0.5 N_A = 8617.1 \text{ N}$$

*Principle of Work and Energy.*

$$T_1 + \Sigma U_{1-2} = T_2$$

$$\frac{1}{2}\left(\frac{17500 \text{ N}}{9.81 \text{ m/s}^2}\right)(6 \text{ m/s})^2 + \{17500 \text{ N}(s \sin 10°) - (8617.1 \text{ N})s\} = 0$$

Solving for $s$ yields

$$s = 5.75 \text{ m} \qquad\qquad Ans.$$

**Solution II**

If this problem is solved by using the equation of motion, *two steps* are involved. First, from the free-body diagram, Fig. 14–10b, the equation of motion is applied along the incline. This yields

$$+\swarrow \Sigma F_s = ma_s; \quad 17500 \sin 10° \text{ N} - 8617.1 \text{ N} = \frac{17500 \text{ N}}{9.81 \text{ m/s}^2} a$$

$$a = -3.13 \text{ m/s}^2$$

Then, using the integrated form of $a \, ds = v \, dv$ (kinematics), since $a$ is constant, we have

$$(+\swarrow) \quad v^2 = v_0^2 + 2a_c(s - s_0);$$

$$(0)^2 = (6 \text{ m/s})^2 + 2(-3.13 \text{ m/s}^2)(s - 0)$$

$$s = 5.75 \text{ m} \qquad\qquad Ans.$$

**E X A M P L E  14.3**

For a short time the crane in Fig. 14–11a lifts the 2.50-Mg beam with a force of $F = (28 + 3s^2)$ kN. Determine the speed of the beam when it has risen $s = 3$ m. Also, how much time does it take to attain this height starting from rest?

**Solution**

We can solve part of this problem using the principle of work and energy since it involves force, velocity, and displacement. Kinematics must be used to determine the time.

*Work (Free-Body Diagram).* As shown on the free-body diagram, Fig. 14–11b, the towing force **F** does positive work, which must be determined by integration since this force is a variable. Also, the weight is constant and will do negative work since the displacement is upwards.

*Principles of Work and Energy.*

$$T_1 + \Sigma U_{1-2} = T_2$$

$$0 + \int_0^s (28 + 3s^2)(10^3)ds - (2.50)(10^3)(9.81)s = \tfrac{1}{2}(2.50)(10^3)v^2$$

$$28(10^3)s + (10^3)s^3 - 24.525(10^3)s = 1.25(10^3)v^2$$

$$v = (2.78s + 0.8s^3)^{\frac{1}{2}}$$

When $s = 3$ m,

$$v = 5.47 \text{ m/s} \qquad \qquad Ans.$$

*Kinematics.* Since we were able to express the velocity as a function of displacement, the time can be determined using $v = ds/dt$. In this case,

$$(2.78s + 0.8s^3)^{\frac{1}{2}} = \frac{ds}{dt}$$

$$t = \int_0^3 \frac{ds}{(2.78s + 0.8s^3)^{\frac{1}{2}}}$$

The integration can be performed numerically using a pocket calculator. The result is

$$t = 1.79 \text{ s} \qquad \qquad Ans.$$

(a)

2.50 $(10^3)(9.81)$ N

(b)

**Fig. 14–11**

## E X A M P L E 14.4

The platform $P$, shown in Fig. 14–12a, has negligible mass and is tied down so that the 0.4-m-long cords keep a 1-m long spring compressed 0.6 m when *nothing* is on the platform. If a 2-kg block is placed on the platform and released from rest after the platform is pushed down 0.1 m, Fig. 14–12b, determine the maximum height $h$ the block rises in the air, measured from the ground.

(a)                                  (b)

**Fig. 14–12**

### Solution

*Work (Free-Body Diagram).*   Since the block is released from rest and later reaches its maximum height, the initial and final velocities are zero. The free-body diagram of the block when it is still in contact with the platform is shown in Fig. 14–12c. Note that the weight does negative work and the spring force does positive work. Why? In particular, the *initial compression* in the spring is $s_1 = 0.6$ m $+ 0.1$ m $= 0.7$ m. Due to the cords, the spring's *final compression* is $s_2 = 0.6$ m (after the block leaves the platform). The bottom of the block rises from a height of $(0.4$ m $- 0.1$ m$) = 0.3$ m to a final height $h$.

19.62 N

$F_s$

(c)

*Principle of Work and Energy.*

$$T_1 + \Sigma U_{1-2} = T_2$$

$$\tfrac{1}{2}mv_1^2 + \{-(\tfrac{1}{2}ks_2^2 - \tfrac{1}{2}ks_1^2) - W\Delta y\} = \tfrac{1}{2}mv_2^2$$

Note that here $s_1 = 0.7$ m $> s_2 = 0.6$ m and so the work of the spring as determined from Eq. 14–4 will indeed be positive once the calculation is made. Thus,

$$0 + \{-[\tfrac{1}{2}(200 \text{ N/m})(0.6 \text{ m})^2 - \tfrac{1}{2}(200 \text{ N/m})(0.7 \text{ m})^2]$$
$$- (19.62 \text{ N})[h - (0.3 \text{ m})]\} = 0$$

Solving yields

$$h = 0.963 \text{ m} \qquad\qquad Ans.$$

EXAMPLE 14.5

Packages having a mass of 2 kg are delivered from a conveyor to a smooth circular ramp with a velocity of $v_0 = 1$ m/s as shown in Fig. 14–13a. If the radius of the ramp is 0.5 m, determine the angle $\theta = \theta_{max}$ at which each package begins to leave the surface.

(a)

(b)

Fig. 14–13

## Solution

**Work (Free-Body Diagram).** The free-body diagram of the block is shown at the intermediate location $\theta$. The weight $W = 2(9.81) = 19.62$ N does positive work during the displacement. If a package is assumed to leave the surface when $\theta = \theta_{max}$ then the weight moves through a vertical displacement of $[0.5 - 0.5 \cos \theta_{max}]$ m, as shown in the figure.

**Principle of Work and Energy.**

$$T_1 + \Sigma U_{1-2} = T_2$$

$$\tfrac{1}{2}(2\text{ kg})(1\text{ m/s})^2 + \{19.62\text{ N}(0.5 - 0.5 \cos \theta_{max})\text{m}\} = \tfrac{1}{2}(2\text{ kg})v_2^2$$

$$v_2^2 = 9.81(1 - \cos \theta_{max}) + 1 \qquad (1)$$

**Equation of Motion.** There are two unknowns in Eq. 1, $\theta_{max}$ and $v_2$. A second equation relating these two variables may be obtained by applying the equation of motion in the *normal direction* to the forces on the free-body diagram. (The principle of work and energy has replaced application of $\Sigma F_t = ma_t$ as noted in the derivation.) Thus,

$$+\nearrow\Sigma F_n = ma_n; \qquad -N_B + 19.62\text{ N} \cos \theta = (2\text{ kg})\left(\frac{v^2}{0.5\text{ m}}\right)$$

When the package leaves the ramp at $\theta = \theta_{max}$, $N_B = 0$ and $v = v_2$; hence, this equation becomes

$$\cos \theta_{max} = \frac{v_2^2}{4.905} \qquad (2)$$

Eliminating the unknown $v_2^2$ between Eqs. 1 and 2 gives

$$4.905 \cos \theta_{max} = 9.81(1 - \cos \theta_{max}) + 1$$

Solving, we have

$$\cos \theta_{max} = 0.735$$

$$\theta_{max} = 42.7° \qquad \qquad Ans.$$

This problem has also been solved in Example 13.9. If the two methods of solution are compared, it will be apparent that a work-energy approach yields a more direct solution.

# EXAMPLE 14.6

(a)

(b)

**Fig. 14–14**

The blocks $A$ and $B$ shown in Fig. 14–14a have a mass of 10 kg and 100 kg, respectively. Determine the distance $B$ travels from the point where it is released from rest to the point where its speed becomes 2 m/s.

**Solution**

This problem may be solved by considering the blocks separately and applying the principle of work and energy to each block. However, the work of the (unknown) cable tension can be eliminated from the analysis by considering blocks $A$ and $B$ together as a *system*. The solution will require simultaneous solution of the equations of work and energy *and* kinematics. To be consistent with our sign convention, we will assume both blocks move in the positive *downward* direction.

*Work (Free-Body Diagram).* As shown on the free-body diagram of the system, Fig. 14–14b, the cable force $\mathbf{T}$ and reactions $\mathbf{R}_1$ and $\mathbf{R}_2$ do *no work*, since these forces represent the reactions at the supports and consequently do not move while the blocks are being displaced. The weights both do positive work since, as stated above, they are both assumed to move downward.

*Principle of Work and Energy.* Realizing the blocks are released from rest, we have

$$\Sigma T_1 + \Sigma U_{1-2} = \Sigma T_2$$

$$\{\tfrac{1}{2}m_A(v_A)_1^2 + \tfrac{1}{2}m_B(v_B)_1^2\} + \{W_A\,\Delta s_A + W_B\,\Delta s_B\} =$$
$$\{\tfrac{1}{2}m_A(v_A)_2^2 + \tfrac{1}{2}m_B(v_B)_2^2\}$$

$$\{0 + 0\} + \{98.1\,\text{N}(\Delta s_A) + 981\,\text{N}(\Delta s_B)\} =$$
$$\{\tfrac{1}{2}(10\,\text{kg})(v_A)_2^2 + \tfrac{1}{2}(100\,\text{kg})(2\,\text{m/s})^2\} \qquad (1)$$

*Kinematics.* Using the methods of kinematics discussed in Sec. 12.9, it may be seen from Fig. 14–14a that at any given instant the total length $l$ of all the vertical segments of cable may be expressed in terms of the position coordinates $s_A$ and $s_B$ as

$$s_A + 4s_B = l$$

Hence, a change in position yields the displacement equation

$$\Delta s_A + 4\,\Delta s_B = 0$$

$$\Delta s_A = -4\,\Delta s_B \qquad (2)$$

As required, both of these displacements are positive downward. Taking the time derivative yields

$$v_A = -4v_B = -4(2\,\text{m/s}) = -8\,\text{m/s}$$

*Retaining* the negative sign in Eq. 2 and substituting into Eq. 1 yields

$$\Delta s_B = 0.883\,\text{m}\!\downarrow \qquad\qquad\qquad Ans.$$

# PROBLEMS

**14-1.** A woman having a mass of 70 kg stands in an elevator which has a downward acceleration of $4 \text{ m/s}^2$ starting from rest. Determine the work done by her weight and the work of the normal force which the floor exerts on her when the elevator descends 6 m. Explain why the work of these forces is different.

**14-2.** The car having a mass of 2 Mg is originally traveling at 2 m/s. Determine the distance it must be towed by a force $F = 4 \text{ kN}$ in order to attain a speed of 5 m/s. Neglect friction and the mass of the wheels.

Prob. 14–2

**14-3.** The 20-kg crate is subjected to a force having a constant direction and a magnitude $F = 100 \text{ N}$, where $s$ is measured in meters. When $s = 15 \text{ m}$, the crate is moving to the right with a speed of 8 m/s. Determine its speed when $s = 25 \text{ m}$. The coefficient of kinetic friction between the crate and the ground is $\mu_k = 0.25$.

Prob. 14–3

**\*14-4.** The "air spring" $A$ is used to protect the support structure $B$ and prevent damage to the conveyor-belt tensioning weight $C$ in the event of a belt failure $D$. The force developed by the spring as a function of its deflection is shown by the graph. If the weight is 500 N ($\approx 50 \text{ kg}$) and is suspended a height $d = 0.3 \text{ m}$ above the top of the spring, determine the maximum deformation of the spring in the event the conveyor belt fails. Neglect the mass of the pulley and belt.

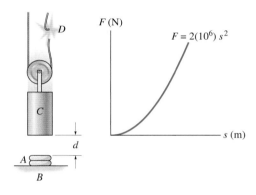

Prob. 14–4

**14-5.** The smooth plug has a weight of 200 N ($\approx 20 \text{ kg}$) and is pushed against a series of Belleville spring washers so that the compression in the spring is $s = 0.01 \text{ m}$. If the force of the spring on the plug is $F = (51s^{1/3}) \text{ N}$, where $s$ is given in metres, determine the speed of the plug after it moves away from the spring. Neglect friction.

Prob. 14–5

**14-6.** When a 7-kg projectile is fired from a cannon barrel that has a length of 2 m, the explosive force exerted on the projectile, while it is in the barrel, varies in the manner shown. Determine the approximate muzzle velocity of the projectile at the instant it leaves the barrel. Neglect the effects of friction inside the barrel and assume the barrel is horizontal.

Prob. 14–6

**14-7.** Design considerations for the bumper $B$ on the 5-Mg train car require use of a nonlinear spring having the load-deflection characteristics shown in the graph. Select the proper value of $k$ so that the maximum deflection of the spring is limited to 0.2 m when the car, traveling at 4 m/s, strikes the rigid stop. Neglect the mass of the car wheels.

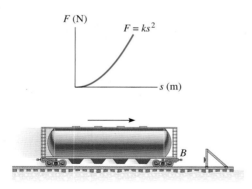

Prob. 14–7

**\*14-8.** The crate, which has a mass of 100 kg is subjected to the action of the two forces. If it is originally at rest, determine the distance it slides in order to attain a speed of 6 m/s. The coefficient of kinetic friction between the crate and the surface is $\mu_k = 0.2$.

Prob. 14–8

**14-9.** When the driver applies the brakes of a light truck traveling 40 km/h, it skids 3 m before stopping. How far will the truck skid if it is traveling 80 km/h when the brakes are applied?

Prob. 14–9

**14-10.** The 0.5-kg ball of negligible size is fired up the vertical circular track using the spring plunger. The plunger keeps the spring compressed 0.08 m when $s = 0$. Determine how far $s$ it must be pulled back and released so that the ball will begin to leave the track when $\theta = 135°$.

Prob. 14–10

■**14-11.** The force **F**, acting in a constant direction on the 20-kg block, has a magnitude which varies with the position *s* of the block. Determine how far the block slides before its velocity becomes 5 m/s. When *s* = 0 the block is moving to the right at 2 m/s. The coefficient of kinetic friction between the block and surface is $\mu_k = 0.3$.

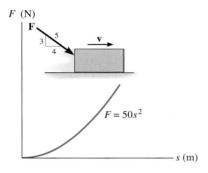

$F = 50s^2$

**Prob. 14–11**

**14-13.** As indicated by the derivation, the principle of work and energy is valid for observers in *any* inertial reference frame. Show that this is so, by considering the 10-kg block which rests on the smooth surface and is subjected to a horizontal force of 6 N. If observer *A* is in a *fixed* frame *x*, determine the final speed of the block if it has an initial speed of 5 m/s and travels 10 m, both directed to the right and measured from the fixed frame. Compare the result with that obtained by an observer *B*, attached to the *x′* axis and moving at a constant velocity of 2 m/s relative to *A*. *Hint:* The distance the block travels will first have to be computed for observer *B* before applying the principle of work and energy.

**Prob. 14–13**

*\*14-12.** The force **F**, acting in a constant direction on the 20-kg block, has a magnitude which varies with position *s* of the block. Determine the speed of the block after it slides 3 m. When *s* = 0 the block is moving to the right at 2 m/s. The coefficient of kinetic friction between the block and surface is $\mu_k = 0.3$.

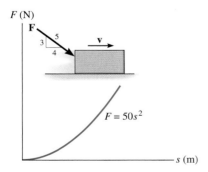

$F = 50s^2$

**Prob. 14–12**

**14-14.** Determine the velocity of the 20-kg block *A* after it is released from rest and moves 2 m down the plane. Block *B* has a mass of 10 kg and the coefficient of kinetic friction between the plane and block *A* is $\mu_k = 0.2$. Also, what is the tension in the cord?

**Prob. 14–14**

**14-15.** Block $A$ has a weight of 600 N ($\approx$ 60 kg) and block $B$ has a weight of 100 N ($\approx$ 10 kg). Determine the speed of block $A$ after it moves 1 m down the plane, starting from rest. Neglect friction and the mass of the cord and pulleys.

**Prob. 14–15**

**\*14-16.** The smooth plug has a weight of 200 N ($\approx$ 20 kg) and is pushed against a series of Belleville spring washers so that the compression in the spring is $s = 0.01$ m. If the force of the spring on the plug is $F = (1710s^{1/3})$ N, where $s$ is given in metres, determine the speed of the plug just after it moves away from the spring, i.e., at $s = 0$.

**Prob. 14–16**

**14-17.** The collar has a mass of 20 kg and rests on the smooth rod. Two springs are attached to it and the ends of the rod as shown. Each spring has an uncompressed length of 1 m. If the collar is displaced $s = 0.5$ m and released from rest, determine its velocity at the instant it returns to the point $s = 0$.

**Prob. 14–17**

**14-18.** Determine the height $h$ to the top of the incline $D$ to which the 200-kg roller coaster car will reach, if it is launched at $B$ with a speed just sufficient for it to round the top of the loop at $C$ without leaving the track. The radius of curvature at $C$ is $\rho_C = 25$ m.

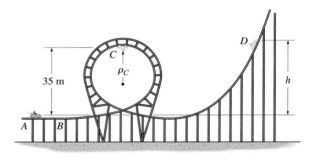

**Prob. 14–18**

**14-19.** The 2-kg block is subjected to a force having a constant direction and a magnitude $F = (300/(1 + s))$ N, where $s$ is in meters. When $s = 4$ m, the block is moving to the left with a speed of 8 m/s. Determine its speed when $s = 12$ m. The coefficient of kinetic friction between the block and the ground is $\mu_k = 0.25$.

**Prob. 14–19**

**\*14-20.** The motion of a truck is arrested using a bed of loose stones $AB$ and a set of crash barrels $BC$. If experiments show that the stones provide a rolling resistance of 800 N per wheel and the crash barrels provide a resistance as shown in the graph, determine the distance $x$ the 22.5-kN ($\approx$ 2250-kg) truck penetrates the barrels if the truck is coasting at 12 m/s when it approaches $A$. Take $s = 10$ m and neglect the size of the truck.

**Prob. 14–20**

**14-21.** The crash cushion for a highway barrier consists of a nest of barrels filled with an impact-absorbing material. The barrier stopping force is measured versus the vehicle penetration into the barrier. Determine the distance a car having a weight of 20 kN ($\approx$ 2000 kg) will penetrate the barrier if it is originally traveling at 11 m/s when it strikes the first barrel.

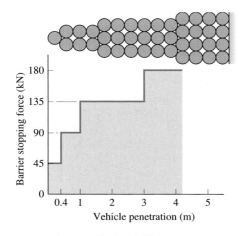

**Prob. 14–21**

**14-22.** The two blocks $A$ and $B$ have weights $W_A = 600$ N ($\approx$ 60 kg) and $W_B = 100$ N ($\approx$ 10 kg). If the kinetic coefficient of friction between the incline and block $A$ is $\mu_k = 0.2$, determine the speed of $A$ after it moves 1 m down the plane starting from rest. Neglect the mass of the cord and pulleys.

**Prob. 14–22**

**14-23.** Packages having a weight of 250 N ($\approx$ 25 kg) are delivered to the chute at $v_A = 0.9$ m/s using a conveyor belt. Determine their speeds when they reach points $B$, $C$, and $D$. Also calculate the normal force of the chute on the packages at $B$ and $C$. Neglect friction and the size of the packages.

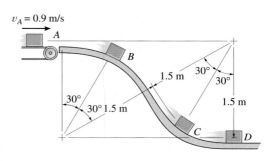

**Prob. 14–23**

**\*14-24.** The steel ingot has a mass of 1800 kg. It travels along the conveyor at a speed $v = 0.5$ m/s when it collides with the "nested" spring assembly. Determine the maximum deflection in each spring needed to stop the motion of the ingot. Take $k_A = 5$ kN/m, $k_B = 3$ kN/m.

**14-26.** Block $A$ has a weight of 600 N ($\approx$ 60 kg) and block $B$ has a weight of 100 N ($\approx$ 10 kg). Determine the distance $A$ must descend from rest before it obtains a speed of 2 m/s. Also, what is the tension in the cord supporting block $A$? Neglect the mass of the cord and pulleys.

**Prob. 14–26**

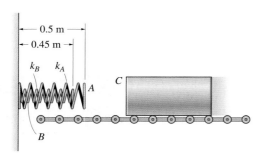

**Prob. 14–24**

**14-25.** The steel ingot has a mass of 1800 kg. It travels along the conveyor at a speed $v = 0.5$ m/s when it collides with the "nested" spring assembly. If the stiffness of the outer spring is $k_A = 5$ kN/m, determine the required stiffness $k_B$ of the inner spring so that the motion of the ingot is stopped at the moment the front, $C$, of the ingot is 0.3 m from the wall.

**14-27.** The 250-N ($\approx$ 25-kg) block has an initial speed of $v_0 = 5$ m/s when it is midway between springs $A$ and $B$. After striking spring $B$, it rebounds and slides across the horizontal plane toward spring $A$, etc. If the coefficient of kinetic friction between the plane and the block is $\mu_k = 0.4$, determine the total distance traveled by the block before it comes to rest.

**Prob. 14–25**

**Prob. 14–27**

*14-28. The 20-N ($\approx$ 2-kg) brick slides down a smooth roof, such that when it is at A it has a velocity of 2 m/s. Determine the speed of the block just before it leaves the surface at B, the distance d from the wall to where it strikes the ground, and the speed at which it hits the ground.

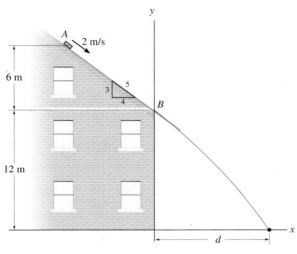

Prob. 14–28

14-29. Roller coasters are designed so that riders will not experience more than 3.5 times their weight as a normal force against the seat of the car. Determine the smallest radius of curvature $\rho$ of the track at its lowest point if the car has a speed of 1 m/s at the crest of the drop. Neglect friction.

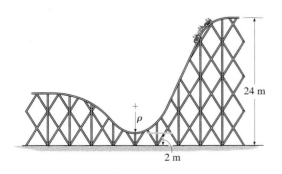

Prob. 14–29

14-30. The catapulting mechanism is used to propel the 10-kg slider A to the right along the smooth track. The propelling action is obtained by drawing the pulley attached to rod BC rapidly to the left by means of a piston P. If the piston applies a constant force $F = 20$ kN to rod BC such that it moves it 0.2 m, determine the speed attained by the slider if it was originally at rest. Neglect the mass of the pulleys, cable, piston, and rod BC.

Prob. 14–30

14-31. The collar has a mass of 20 kg and slides along the smooth rod. Two springs are attached to it and the ends of the rod as shown. If each spring has an uncompressed length of 1 m and the collar has a speed of 2 m/s when $s = 0$, determine the maximum compression of each spring due to the back-and-forth (oscillating) motion of the collar.

Prob. 14–31

***14-32.** The cyclist travels to point $A$, pedaling until he reaches a speed $v_A = 8$ m/s. He then coasts freely up the curved surface. Determine the normal force he exerts on the surface when he reaches point $B$. The total mass of the bike and man is 75 kg. Neglect friction, the mass of the wheels, and the size of the bicycle.

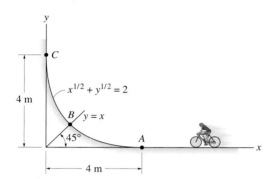

**Prob. 14–32**

**14-34.** The 300-N ($\approx$ 30-kg) box $A$ is released from rest and slides down along the smooth ramp and onto the surface of a cart. If the cart is *fixed from moving*, determine the distance $s$ from the end of the cart to where the box stops. The coefficient of kinetic friction between the cart and the box is $\mu_k = 0.6$.

**Prob. 14–34**

**14-33.** The cyclist travels to point $A$, pedaling until he reaches a speed $v_A = 4$ m/s. He then coasts freely up the curved surface. Determine how high he reaches up the surface before he comes to a stop. Also, what are the resultant normal force on the surface at this point and his acceleration? The total mass of the bike and man is 75 kg. Neglect friction, the mass of the wheels, and the size of the bicycle.

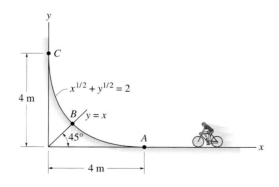

**Prob. 14–33**

**14-35.** The man at the window $A$ wishes to throw the 30-kg sack on the ground. To do this he allows it to swing from rest at $B$ to point $C$, when he releases the cord at $\theta = 30°$. Determine the speed at which it strikes the ground and the distance $R$.

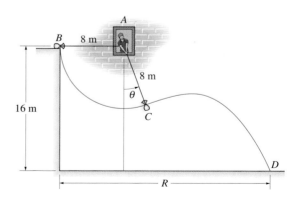

**Prob. 14–35**

*14-36. A 20-N ($\approx$ 2-kg) block rests on the smooth semicylindrical surface. An elastic cord having a stiffness $k = 60$ N/m is attached to the block at $B$ and to the base of the semicylinder at point $C$. If the block is released from rest at $A(\theta = 0°)$, determine the unstretched length of the cord so the block begins to leave the semicylinder at the instant $\theta = 45°$. Neglect the size of the block.

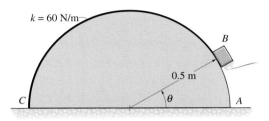

$k = 60$ N/m

$B$

0.5 m

$\theta$

$C$      $A$

**Prob. 14–36**

14-37. The spring bumper is used to arrest the motion of the 40-N ($\approx$ 4-kg) block, which is sliding toward it at $v = 3$ m/s. As shown, the spring is confined by the plate $P$ and wall using cables so that its length is 0.5 m. If the stiffness of the spring is $k = 1500$ N/m, determine the required unstretched length of the spring so that the plate is not displaced more than 0.1 m after the block collides into it. Neglect friction, the mass of the plate and spring, and the energy loss between the plate and block during the collision.

$k$   $P$             $v_A$

$A$

0.5 m    2 m

**Prob. 14–37**

14-38. Cylinder $A$ has a mass of 3 kg and cylinder $B$ has a mass of 8 kg. Determine the speed of $A$ after it moves upwards 2 m starting from rest. Neglect the mass of the cord and pulleys.

$A$

$B$

**Prob. 14-38**

14-39. The collar has a mass of 20 kg and is supported on the smooth rod. The attached springs are undeformed when $d = 0.5$ m. Determine the speed of the collar after the applied force $F = 100$ N causes it to be displaced so that $d = 0.3$ m. When $d = 0.5$ m the collar is at rest.

$k' = 15$ N/m

$F = 100$ N

$60°$

$d$

$k = 25$ N/m

*14-40. The skier starts from rest at $A$ and travels down the ramp. If friction and air resistance can be neglected, determine his speed $v_B$ when he reaches $B$. Also, find the distance $s$ to where he strikes the ground at $C$, if he makes the jump traveling horizontally at $B$. Neglect the skier's size. He has a mass of 70 kg.

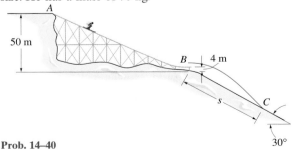

$A$

50 m

$B$ | 4 m

$s$

$C$

$30°$

**Prob. 14–40**

## 14.4 Power and Efficiency

**Power.** *Power* is defined as the amount of work performed per unit of time. Hence, the *power* generated by a machine or engine that performs an amount of work $dU$ within the time interval $dt$ is

$$P = \frac{dU}{dt} \qquad (14\text{--}9)$$

Provided the work $dU$ is expressed by $dU = \mathbf{F} \cdot d\mathbf{r}$, then it is also possible to write

$$P = \frac{dU}{dt} = \frac{\mathbf{F} \cdot d\mathbf{r}}{dt} = \mathbf{F} \cdot \frac{d\mathbf{r}}{dt}$$

or

$$P = \mathbf{F} \cdot \mathbf{v} \qquad (14\text{--}10)$$

Hence, power is a *scalar*, where in the formulation $\mathbf{v}$ represents the velocity of the point which is acted upon by the force $\mathbf{F}$.

The basic unit of power used in the SI system is the watt (W). This unit is defined as

$$1 \text{ W} = 1 \text{ J/s} = 1 \text{ N} \cdot \text{m/s}$$

The term "power" provides a useful basis for determining the type of motor or machine which is required to do a certain amount of work in a given time. For example, two pumps may each be able to empty a reservoir if given enough time; however, the pump having the larger power will complete the job sooner.

**Efficiency.** The *mechanical efficiency* of a machine is defined as the ratio of the output of useful power produced by the machine to the input of power supplied to the machine. Hence,

$$\epsilon = \frac{\text{power output}}{\text{power input}} \qquad (14\text{--}11)$$

The power output of this locomotive comes from the driving frictional force $\mathbf{F}$ developed at its wheels. It is this force that overcomes the frictional resistance of the cars in tow and is able to lift the weight of the train up the grade.

If energy applied to the machine occurs during the *same time interval* at which it is removed, then the efficiency may also be expressed in terms of the ratio of output energy to input energy; i.e.

$$\epsilon = \frac{\text{energy output}}{\text{energy input}} \qquad (14\text{--}12)$$

Since machines consist of a series of moving parts, frictional forces will always be developed within the machine, and as a result, extra energy or power is needed to overcome these forces. Consequently, *the efficiency of a machine is always less than 1.*

The power requirements of this elevator depend upon the vertical force **F** that acts on the elevator and causes it to move upwards. If the velocity of the elevator is **v**, then the power output is $P = \mathbf{F} \cdot \mathbf{v}$.

## PROCEDURE FOR ANALYSIS

The power supplied to a body can be computed using the following procedure.

- First determine the external force **F** acting on the body which causes the motion. This force is usually developed by a machine or engine placed either within or external to the body.
- If the body is accelerating, it may be necessary to draw its free-body diagram and apply the equation of motion ($\Sigma \mathbf{F} = m\mathbf{a}$) to determine **F**.
- Once **F** and the velocity **v** of the point where **F** is applied have been found, the power is determined by multiplying the force magnitude by the component of velocity acting in the direction of **F**, (i.e., $P = \mathbf{F} \cdot \mathbf{v} = Fv \cos \theta$).
- In some problems the power may be found by calculating the work done by **F** per unit of time ($P_{\text{avg}} = \Delta U / \Delta t$, or $P = dU/dt$).

## EXAMPLE 14.7

(a)

(b)

**Fig. 14–15**

The motor $M$ of the hoist shown in Fig. 14–15a operates with an efficiency of $\epsilon = 0.85$. Determine the power that must be supplied to the motor to lift the 375-N ($\approx$ 37.5-kg) crate $C$ at the instant point $P$ on the cable has an acceleration of 1.2 m/s², and a velocity of 0.6 m/s. Neglect the mass of the pulley and cable.

### Solution

In order to compute the power output of the motor, it is first necessary to determine the tension in the cable since this force is developed by the motor.

From the free-body diagram, Fig. 14–15b, we have

$$+\downarrow \quad \Sigma F_y = ma_y; \qquad -2T + 375\,\text{N} = \frac{375\,\text{N}}{9.81\,\text{m/s}^2}\,a_c \qquad (1)$$

The acceleration of the crate can be obtained by using kinematics to relate it to the known acceleration of point $P$, Fig. 14–15a. Using the methods of Sec. 12.9, the coordinates $s_C$ and $s_P$ in Fig. 14–15a can be related to a constant portion of cable length $l$ which is changing in the vertical and horizontal directions. We have $2s_C + s_P = l$. Taking the second time derivative of this equation yields

$$2a_C = -a_P \qquad (2)$$

Since $a_P = +1.2$ m/s², then $a_C = (-1.2$ m/s²$)/2 = -0.6$ m/s². What does the negative sign indicate? Substituting this result into Eq. 1 and *retaining* the negative sign since the acceleration in *both* Eqs. 1 and 2 is considered positive downward, we have

$$-2T + 375\,\text{N} = \frac{375\,\text{N}}{9.81\,\text{m/s}^2}\,(-0.6\,\text{m/s}^2)$$

$$T = 199.0\,\text{N}$$

The power output required to draw the cable in at a rate of 0.6 m/s is therefore

$$P = \mathbf{T} \cdot \mathbf{v} = (199\,\text{N})(0.6\,\text{m/s})$$

$$= 119.4\,\text{W}$$

This *power output* requires that the motor provide a *power input* of

$$\text{power input} = \frac{1}{\epsilon}(\text{power output})$$

$$= \frac{1}{0.85}(119.4\,\text{W}) = 140.5\,\text{W} \qquad \textit{Ans.}$$

Since the velocity of the crate is constantly changing, notice that this power requirement is *instantaneous*.

# EXAMPLE 14.8

The sports car shown in Fig. 14–16a has a mass of 2 Mg and is traveling at a speed of 25 m/s, when the brakes to all the wheels are applied. If the coefficient of kinetic friction is $\mu_k = 0.35$, determine the power developed by the friction force when the car skids. Then find the car's speed after it has slid 10 m.

(a)

(b)

**Fig. 14–16**

**Solution**
As shown on the free-body diagram, Fig. 14–16b, the normal force $\mathbf{N}_C$ and frictional force $\mathbf{F}_C$ represent the *resultant forces* of all four wheels.
Applying the equation of equilibrium in the $y$ direction to determine $N_C$, we have

$$+\uparrow \Sigma F_y = 0; \qquad N_C = 19.62 \text{ kN}$$

The kinetic frictional force is therefore

$$F_C = 0.35(19.62 \text{ kN}) = 6.867 \text{ kN}$$

The velocity of the car can be determined when $s = 10$ m by applying the principle of work and energy. Why?

$$T_1 + \Sigma U_{1-2} = T_2$$
$$\tfrac{1}{2}(2000 \text{ kg})(25 \text{ m/s})^2 - 6.867(10^3)\text{N}(10 \text{ m}) = \tfrac{1}{2}(2000 \text{ kg})v^2$$
$$v = 23.59 \text{ m/s}$$

The power of the frictional force at this instant is therefore

$$P = |\mathbf{F}_C \cdot \mathbf{v}| = 6.867(10^3)\text{N}(25 \text{ m/s}) = 172 \text{ kW} \qquad \textit{Ans.}$$

# PROBLEMS

**14-41.** The diesel engine of a 400-Mg train increases the train's speed uniformly from rest to 10 m/s in 100 s along a horizontal track. Determine the average power developed.

**14-42.** Determine the power input for a motor necessary to lift 3000 N ($\approx$ 300 kg) at a constant rate of 2 m/s. The efficiency of the motor is $\epsilon = 0.65$.

**14-43.** An electric streetcar has a weight of 75 kN ($\approx$ 7500 kg) and accelerates along a horizontal straight road from rest such that the power is always 75 kW. Determine how much time it takes to reach a speed of 10 m/s.

***14-44.** The jeep has a weight of 12.5 kN ($\approx$ 1250 kg) and an engine which transmits a power of 75 kW to *all* the wheels. Assuming the wheels do not slip on the ground, determine the angle $\theta$ of the largest incline the jeep can climb at a constant speed $v = 10$ m/s.

**Prob. 14–44**

**14-45.** An automobile having a mass of 2 Mg travels up a 7° slope at a constant speed of $v = 100$ km/h. If mechanical friction and wind resistance are neglected, determine the power developed by the engine if the automobile has an efficiency $\epsilon = 0.65$.

**Prob. 14–45**

**14-46.** A loaded truck weighs 80 kN ($\approx$ 8000 kg) and accelerates uniformly on a level road from 5 m/s to 10 m/s during 4 s. If the frictional resistance to motion is 1625 N, determine the maximum power that must be delivered to the wheels.

**14-47.** An electric streetcar has a weight of 75 kN ($\approx$ 7500 kg) and accelerates along a horizontal straight road from rest such that the power is always 75 kW. Determine how far it must travel to reach a speed of 10 m/s.

***14-48.** The escalator steps move with a constant speed of 0.6 m/s. If the steps are 125 mm high and 250 mm in length, determine the power of a motor needed to lift an average mass of 150 kg per step. There are 32 steps.

**14-49.** The 250-N ($\approx$ 25-kg) crate is given a speed of 3 m/s in $t = 4$ s starting from rest. If the acceleration is constant, determine the power that must be supplied to the motor when $t = 2$ s. The motor has an efficiency $\epsilon = 0.76$. Neglect the mass of the pulley and cable.

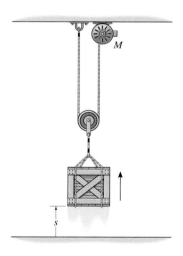

**Prob. 14–49**

**14-50.** A car has a mass $m$ and accelerates along a horizontal straight road from rest such that the power is always a constant amount $P$. Determine how far it must travel to reach a speed of $v$.

**14-51.** To dramatize the loss of energy in an automobile, consider a car having a weight of 25 kN ($\approx 2500$ kg) that is traveling at 56 km/h. If the car is brought to a stop, determine how long a 100-W light bulb must burn to expend the same amount of energy.

*__14-52.__ The motor $M$ is used to hoist the 500-kg elevator upward with a constant velocity $v_E = 8$ m/s. If the motor draws 60 kW of electrical power, determine the motor's efficiency. Neglect the mass of the pulleys and cable.

**14-53.** The 500-kg elevator starts from rest and travels upward with a constant acceleration $a_c = 2$ m/s$^2$. Determine the power output of the motor $M$ when $t = 3$ s. Neglect the mass of the pulleys and cable.

**Prob. 14–53**

**14-54.** The crate has a mass of 150 kg and rests on a surface for which the coefficients of static and kinetic friction are $\mu_s = 0.3$ and $\mu_k = 0.2$, respectively. If the motor $M$ supplies a cable force of $F = (8t^2 + 20)$ N, where $t$ is in seconds, determine the power output developed by the motor when $t = 5$ s.

**Prob. 14–52**

**Prob. 14–54**

**14-55.** The elevator $E$ and its freight have a total mass of 400 kg. Hoisting is provided by the motor $M$ and the 60-kg block $C$. If the motor has an efficiency of $\epsilon = 0.6$, determine the power that must be supplied to the motor when the elevator is hoisted upward at a constant speed of $v_E = 4$ m/s.

Prob. 14–55

*14-56.** The 50-kg crate is hoisted up the 30° incline by the pulley system and motor $M$. If the crate starts from rest and by constant acceleration attains a speed of 4 m/s after traveling 8 m along the plane, determine the power that must be supplied to the motor at this instant. Neglect friction along the plane. The motor has an efficiency of $\epsilon = 0.74$.

Prob. 14–56

**14-57.** The sports car has a mass of 2.3 Mg, and while it is traveling at 28 m/s the driver causes it to accelerate at 5 m/s². If the drag resistance on the car due to the wind is $F_D = (0.3v^2)$ N, where $v$ is the velocity in m/s, determine the power supplied to the engine at this instant. The engine has a running efficiency of $\epsilon = 0.68$.

**14-58.** The sports car has a mass of 2.3 Mg and accelerates at 6 m/s², starting from rest. If the drag resistance on the car due to the wind is $F_D = (10v)$ N, where $v$ is the velocity in m/s, determine the power supplied to the engine when $t = 5$ s. The engine has a running efficiency of $\epsilon = 0.68$.

Prob. 14–57/58

**14-59.** The 250-N ($\approx$ 25-kg) load is hoisted by the pulley system and motor $M$. If the motor exerts a constant force of 150 N on the cable, determine the power that must be supplied to the motor if the load has been hoisted $s = 3$ m starting from rest. The motor has an efficiency of $\epsilon = 0.76$.

Prob. 14–59

*14-60. The rocket sled has a mass of 4 Mg and travels from rest along the horizontal track for which the coefficient of kinetic friction is $\mu_k = 0.20$. If the engine provides a constant thrust $T = 150$ kN, determine the power output of the engine as a function of time. Neglect the loss of fuel mass and air resistance.

Prob. 14–60

14-61. The 50-N ($\approx$ 5-kg) collar starts from rest at $A$ and is lifted by applying a constant force of $F = 125$ N to the cord. If the rod is smooth, determine the power developed by the force at the instant $\theta = 60°$.

Prob. 14–61

14-62. An athlete pushes against an exercise machine with a force that varies with time as shown in the first graph. Also, the velocity of the athlete's arm acting in the same direction as the force varies with time as shown in the second graph. Determine the power applied as a function of time and the work done in $t = 0.3$ s.

14-63. An athlete pushes against an exercise machine with a force that varies with time as shown in the first graph. Also, the velocity of the athlete's arm acting in the same direction as the force varies with time as shown in the second graph. Determine the maximum power developed during the 0.3-second time period.

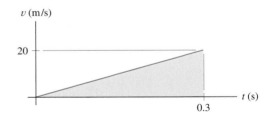

Probs. 14–62/63

## 14.5 Conservative Forces and Potential Energy

**Conservative Force.** When the work done by a force in moving a particle from one point to another is *independent of the path* followed by the particle, then this force is called a *conservative force*. The weight of a particle and the force of an elastic spring are two examples of conservative forces often encountered in mechanics. The work done by the weight of a particle is *independent of the path* since it depends only on the particle's *vertical displacement*. The work done by a spring force *acting on a particle* is *independent of the path* of the particle, since it depends only on the extension or compression *s* of the spring.

In contrast to a conservative force, consider the force of friction exerted *on a sliding object* by a fixed surface. The work done by the frictional force *depends on the path*—the longer the path, the greater the work. Consequently, *frictional forces are nonconservative*. The work is dissipated from the body in the form of heat.

**Potential Energy.** Energy may be defined as the capacity for doing work. When energy comes from the *motion* of the particle, it is referred to as *kinetic energy*. When it comes from the *position* of the particle, measured from a fixed datum or reference plane, it is called potential energy. Thus, *potential energy* is a measure of the amount of work a conservative force will do when it moves from a given position to the datum. In mechanics, the potential energy due to gravity (weight) or an elastic spring is important.

**Gravitational Potential Energy.** If a particle is located a distance *y above* an arbitrarily selected datum, as shown in Fig. 14–17, the particle's weight **W** has positive *gravitational potential energy*, $V_g$, since **W** has the capacity of doing positive work when the particle is moved back down to the datum. Likewise, if the particle is located a distance *y below* the datum, $V_g$ is negative since the weight does negative work when the particle is moved back up to the datum. At the datum $V_g = 0$.

In general, if *y* is *positive upward*, the gravitational potential energy of the particle of weight *W* is*

$$V_g = Wy \qquad (14\text{–}13)$$

---

*Here the weight is assumed to be *constant*. This assumption is suitable for small differences in elevation $\Delta y$. If the elevation change is significant, however, a variation of weight with elevation must be taken into account (see Prob. 14–97).

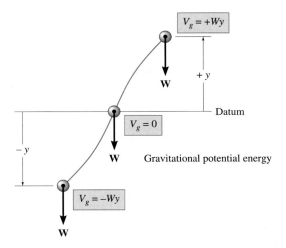

Fig. 14–17

**Elastic Potential Energy.** When an elastic spring is elongated or compressed a distance $s$ from its unstretched position, the elastic potential energy $V_e$ due to the spring's configuration can be expressed as

$$V_e = +\tfrac{1}{2}ks^2 \qquad (14\text{–}14)$$

Here $V_e$ is *always positive* since, in the deformed position, the force of the spring has the *capacity* for always doing positive work on the particle when the spring is returned to its unstretched position, Fig. 14–18.

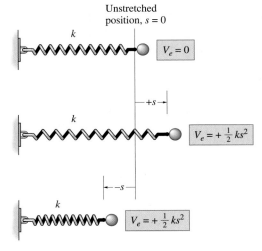

Elastic potential energy

**Fig. 14–18**

**Potential Function.** In the general case, if a particle is subjected to both gravitational and elastic forces, the particle's potential energy can be expressed as a *potential function*, which is the algebraic sum

$$V = V_g + V_e \tag{14-15}$$

Measurement of $V$ depends on the location of the particle with respect to a selected datum in accordance with Eqs. 14–13 and 14–14.

If the particle is located at an arbitrary point $(x, y, z)$ in space, this potential function is then $V = V(x, y, z)$. The work done by a conservative force in moving the particle from point $(x_1, y_1, z_1)$ to point $(x_2, y_2, z_2)$ is measured by the *difference* of this function, i.e.,

$$U_{1-2} = V_1 - V_2 \tag{14-16}$$

For example, the potential function for a particle of weight $W$ suspended from a spring can be expressed in terms of its position, $s$, measured from a datum located at the unstretched length of the spring, Fig. 14–19. We have

$$V = V_g + V_e$$
$$= -Ws + \tfrac{1}{2}ks^2$$

If the particle moves from $s_1$ to a lower position $s_2$, then applying Eq. 14–16 it can be seen that the work of $\mathbf{W}$ and $\mathbf{F}_s$ is

$$U_{1-2} = V_1 - V_2 = (-Ws_1 + \tfrac{1}{2}ks_1^2) - (-Ws_2 + \tfrac{1}{2}ks_2^2)$$
$$= W(s_2 - s_1) - (\tfrac{1}{2}ks_2^2 - \tfrac{1}{2}ks_1^2)$$

Fig. 14–19

When the displacement along the path is infinitesimal, i.e., from point $(x, y, z)$ to $(x + dx, y + dy, z + dz)$, Eq. 14–16 becomes

$$dU = V(x, y, z) - V(x + dx, y + dy, z + dz)$$
$$= -dV(x, y, z) \qquad (14\text{–}17)$$

Provided both the force and displacement are defined using rectangular coordinates, then the work can also be expressed as

$$dU = \mathbf{F} \cdot d\mathbf{r} = (F_x\mathbf{i} + F_y\mathbf{j} + F_z\mathbf{k}) \cdot (dx\mathbf{i} + dy\mathbf{j} + dz\mathbf{k})$$
$$= F_x dx + F_y dy + F_z dz$$

Substituting this result into Eq. 14–17 and expressing the differential $dV(x, y, z)$ in terms of its partial derivatives yields

$$F_x dx + F_y dy + F_z dz = -\left(\frac{\partial V}{\partial x}dx + \frac{\partial V}{\partial y}dy + \frac{\partial V}{\partial z}dz\right)$$

Since changes in $x$, $y$, and $z$ are all independent of one another, this equation is satisfied provided

$$F_x = -\frac{\partial V}{\partial x}, \qquad F_y = -\frac{\partial V}{\partial y}, \qquad F_z = -\frac{\partial V}{\partial z} \qquad (14\text{–}18)$$

Thus,

$$\mathbf{F} = -\frac{\partial V}{\partial x}\mathbf{i} - \frac{\partial V}{\partial y}\mathbf{j} - \frac{\partial V}{\partial z}\mathbf{k}$$
$$= -\left(\frac{\partial}{\partial x}\mathbf{i} + \frac{\partial}{\partial y}\mathbf{j} + \frac{\partial}{\partial z}\mathbf{k}\right)V$$

or

$$\mathbf{F} = -\nabla V \qquad (14\text{–}19)$$

where $\nabla$ (del) represents the vector operator $\nabla = (\partial/\partial x)\mathbf{i} + (\partial/\partial y)\mathbf{j} + (\partial/\partial z)\mathbf{k}$.

Equation 14–19 relates a force $\mathbf{F}$ to its potential function $V$ and thereby provides a mathematical criterion for proving that $\mathbf{F}$ is conservative. For example, the gravitational potential function for a weight located a distance $y$ above a datum is $V_g = Wy$. To prove that $\mathbf{W}$ is conservative, it is necessary to show that it satisfies Eq. 14–19 (or Eq. 14–18), in which case

$$F_y = -\frac{\partial V}{\partial y}; \qquad\qquad F = -\frac{\partial}{\partial y}(Wy) = -W$$

The negative sign indicates that $\mathbf{W}$ acts downward, opposite to positive $y$, which is upward.

## 14.6 Conservation of Energy

The weight of the sacks resting on this platform causes potential energy to be stored in the supporting springs. As each sack is removed, the platform will *rise* slightly since some of the potential energy within the springs will be transferred into an increase in gravitational potential energy of the remaining sacks. Such a device is useful for removing the sacks without having to bend over to pick them up as they are unloaded.

When a particle is acted upon by a system of *both* conservative and nonconservative forces, the portion of the work done by the *conservative forces* can be written in terms of the difference in their potential energies using Eq. 14–16, i.e., $(\Sigma U_{1-2})_{\text{cons.}} = V_1 - V_2$. As a result, the principle of work and energy can be written as

$$T_1 + V_1 + (\Sigma U_{1-2})_{\text{noncons.}} = T_2 + V_2 \qquad (14\text{–}20)$$

Here $(\Sigma U_{1-2})_{\text{noncons.}}$ represents the work of the nonconservative forces acting on the particle. If *only conservative forces* are applied to the body, this term is zero and then we have

$$\boxed{T_1 + V_1 = T_2 + V_2} \qquad (14\text{–}21)$$

This equation is referred to as the *conservation of mechanical energy* or simply the *conservation of energy*. It states that during the motion the sum of the particle's kinetic and potential energies remains *constant*. For this to occur, kinetic energy must be transformed into potential energy, and vice versa. For example, if a ball of weight **W** is dropped from a height $h$ above the ground (datum), Fig. 14–20, the potential energy of the ball is maximum before it is dropped, at which time its kinetic energy is zero. The total mechanical energy of the ball in its initial position is thus

$$E = T_1 + V_1 = 0 + Wh = Wh$$

When the ball has fallen a distance $h/2$, its speed can be determined by using $v^2 = v_0^2 + 2a_c(y - y_0)$, which yields $v = \sqrt{2g(h/2)} = \sqrt{gh}$. The energy of the ball at the mid-height position is therefore

$$E = T_2 + V_2 = \frac{1}{2}\frac{W}{g}(\sqrt{gh})^2 + W\frac{h}{2} = Wh$$

Just before the ball strikes the ground, its potential energy is zero and its speed is $v = \sqrt{2gh}$. Here, again, the total energy of the ball is

$$E = T_3 + V_3 = \frac{1}{2}\frac{W}{g}(\sqrt{2gh})^2 + 0 = Wh$$

Potential Energy (max)
Kinetic Energy (zero)

Potential Energy and
Kinetic Energy

Potential Energy (zero)
Kinetic Energy (max)

**Fig. 14–20**

Note that when the ball comes in contact with the ground, it deforms somewhat, and provided the ground is hard enough, the ball will rebound off the surface, reaching a new height $h'$, which will be less than the height $h$ from which it was first released. Neglecting air friction, the difference in height accounts for an energy loss, $E_l = W(h - h')$, which occurs during the collision. Portions of this loss produce noise, localized deformation of the ball and ground, and heat.

**System of Particles.**   If a system of particles is *subjected only to conservative forces*, then an equation similar to Eq. 14–21 can be written for the particles. Applying the ideas of the preceding discussion, Eq. 14–8 ($\Sigma T_1 + \Sigma U_{1-2} = \Sigma T_2$) becomes

$$\boxed{\Sigma T_1 + \Sigma V_1 = \Sigma T_2 + \Sigma V_2} \tag{14–22}$$

Here, the sum of the system's initial kinetic and potential energies is equal to the sum of the system's final kinetic and potential energies. In other words, $\Sigma T + \Sigma V =$ const.

It is important to remember that only problems involving conservative force systems (weights and springs) may be solved by using the conservation of energy theorem. As stated previously, friction or other drag-resistant forces, which depend upon velocity or acceleration, are nonconservative. A portion of the work done by such forces is transformed into thermal energy, and consequently this energy dissipates into the surroundings and may not be recovered.

## PROCEDURE FOR ANALYSIS

The conservation of energy equation is used to solve problems involving *velocity, displacement*, and *conservative force systems*. It is generally *easier to apply* than the principle of work and energy because the energy equation just requires specifying the particle's kinetic and potential energies at only *two points* along the path, rather than determining the work when the particle moves through a *displacement*. For application it is suggested that the following procedure be used.

*Potential Energy*

- Draw two diagrams showing the particle located at its initial and final points along the path.
- If the particle is subjected to a vertical displacement, establish the fixed horizontal datum from which to measure the particle's gravitational potential energy $V_g$.
- Data pertaining to the elevation $y$ of the particle from the datum and the extension or compression $s$ of any connecting springs can be determined from the geometry associated with the two diagrams.
- Recall $V_g = Wy$, where $y$ is positive upward from the datum and negative downward from the datum; also $V_e = \frac{1}{2}ks^2$, which is *always positive*.

*Conservation of Energy*

- Apply the equation $T_1 + V_1 = T_2 + V_2$.
- When determining the kinetic energy, $T = \frac{1}{2}mv^2$, the particle's speed $v$ must be measured from an inertial reference frame.

E X A M P L E **14.9**

The gantry structure in the photo is used to test the response of an airplane during a crash. As shown in Fig. 14–21a, the plane, having a mass of 8 Mg, is hoisted back until $\theta = 60°$, and then the pull-back cable *AC* is released when the plane is at rest. Determine the speed of the plane just before crashing into the ground, $\theta = 15°$. Also, what is the maximum tension developed in the supporting cable during the motion? Neglect the effect of lift caused by the wings during the motion and the size of the airplane.

(a)

(b)

**Fig. 14–21**

### Solution

Since the force of the cable does *no work* on the plane, it must be obtained using the equation of motion. First, however, we must determine the plane's speed at *B*.

*Potential Energy.*   For convenience, the datum has been established at the top of the gantry.

*Conservation of Energy.*

$$T_A + V_A = T_B + V_B$$

$$0 - 8000 \text{ kg } (9.81 \text{ m/s}^2)(20 \cos 60° \text{ m}) =$$

$$\tfrac{1}{2}(8000 \text{ kg})v_B^2 - 8000 \text{ kg } (9.81 \text{ m/s}^2)(20 \cos 15° \text{ m})$$

$$v_B = 13.5 \text{ m/s} \qquad \text{Ans.}$$

*Equation of Motion.*   Using the data tabulated on the free-body diagram when the plane is at *B*, Fig. 14–21b, we have

$$+\nwarrow \quad \Sigma F_n = ma_n;$$

$$T - 8000 \,(9.81)\text{N} \cos 15° = (8000 \text{ kg})\frac{(13.5 \text{ m/s})^2}{20 \text{ m}}$$

$$T = 149 \text{ kN} \qquad \text{Ans.}$$

# E X A M P L E 14.10

The ram $R$ shown in Fig. 14–22a has a mass of 100 kg and is released from rest 0.75 m from the top of a spring, $A$, that has a stiffness $k_A = 12$ kN/m. If a second spring $B$, having a stiffness $k_B = 15$ kN/m, is "nested" in $A$, determine the maximum displacement of $A$ needed to stop the downward motion of the ram. The unstretched length of each spring is indicated in the figure. Neglect the mass of the springs.

## Solution

*Potential Energy.* We will *assume* that the ram compresses *both* springs at the instant it comes to rest. The datum is located through the center of gravity of the ram at its initial position, Fig. 14–22b. When the kinetic energy is reduced to zero ($v_2 = 0$) $A$ is compressed a distance $s_A$ and $B$ compresses $s_B = s_A - 0.1$ m.

*Conservation of Energy.*

$$T_1 + V_1 = T_2 + V_2$$

$$0 + 0 = 0 + \{ \tfrac{1}{2}k_A s_A^2 + \tfrac{1}{2}k_B(s_A - 0.1)^2 - Wh \}$$

$$0 + 0 = 0 + \{ \tfrac{1}{2}(12\,000 \text{ N/m})s_A^2 + \tfrac{1}{2}(15\,000 \text{ N/m})(s_A - 0.1\text{m})^2$$
$$- 981 \text{ N}(0.75 \text{ m} + s_A) \}$$

Rearranging the terms,

$$13\,500s_A^2 - 2481s_A - 660.75 = 0$$

Using the quadratic formula and solving for the positive root,* we have

$$s_A = 0.331 \text{ m} \qquad \qquad Ans.$$

Since $s_B = 0.331$ m $- 0.1$ m $= 0.231$ m, which is positive, the assumption that *both* springs are compressed by the ram is correct.

---

*The second root, $s_A = -0.148$ m, does not represent the physical situation. Since positive $s$ is measured downward, the negative sign indicates that spring $A$ would have to be "extended" by an amount of 0.148 m to stop the ram.

$k_A = 12$ kN/m

$A$

$B$

$k_B = 15$ kN/m

0.75 m

0.4 m

0.3 m

(a)

981 N

Datum

0.75 m

981 N

1

2

$s_A$

$s_A$

$s_B = s_A - 0.1$ m

(b)

Fig. 14–22

E X A M P L E **14.11**

(a)

A smooth 2-kg collar $C$, shown in Fig. 14–23a, fits loosely on the vertical shaft. If the spring is unstretched when the collar is in the position $A$, determine the speed at which the collar is moving when $y = 1$ m, if (a) it is released from rest at $A$, and (b) it is released at $A$ with an *upward* velocity $v_A = 2$ m/s.

**Solution**

*Part (a)*

*Potential Energy.* For convenience, the datum is established through $AB$, Fig. 14–23b. When the collar is at $C$, the gravitational potential energy is $-(mg)y$, since the collar is *below* the datum, and the elastic potential energy is $\frac{1}{2}ks_{CB}^2$. Here $s_{CB} = 0.5$ m, which represents the *stretch* in the spring as shown in the figure.

*Conservation of Energy.*

$$T_A + V_A = T_C + V_C$$
$$0 + 0 = \tfrac{1}{2}mv_C^2 + \{\tfrac{1}{2}ks_{CB}^2 - mgy\}$$
$$0 + 0 = \{\tfrac{1}{2}(2\text{ kg})v_C^2\} + \{\tfrac{1}{2}(3\text{ N/m})(0.5\text{ m})^2 - 2(9.81)\text{ N}(1\text{ m})\}$$
$$v_C = 4.39\text{ m/s} \downarrow \qquad\qquad Ans.$$

This problem can also be solved by using the equation of motion or the principle of work and energy. Note that in *both* of these methods the variation of the magnitude and direction of the spring force must be taken into account (see Example 13.4). Here, however, the above method of solution is clearly advantageous since the calculations depend *only* on data calculated at the initial and final points of the path.

*Part (b)*

*Conservation of Energy.* If $v_A = 2$ m/s, using the data in Fig. 14–23b, we have

$$T_A + V_A = T_C + V_C$$
$$\tfrac{1}{2}mv_A^2 + 0 = \tfrac{1}{2}mv_C^2 + \{\tfrac{1}{2}ks_{CB}^2 - mgy\}$$
$$\tfrac{1}{2}(2\text{ kg})(2\text{ m/s})^2 + 0 = \tfrac{1}{2}(2\text{ kg})v_C^2 + \{\tfrac{1}{2}(3\text{ N/m})(0.5\text{ m})^2$$
$$- 2(9.81)\text{ N}(1\text{ m})\}$$
$$v_C = 4.82\text{ m/s}\downarrow \qquad\qquad Ans.$$

Note that the kinetic energy of the collar depends only on the *magnitude* of velocity, and therefore it is immaterial if the collar is moving up or down at 2 m/s when released at $A$.

(b)

**Fig. 14–23**

(Labels in figure (a): 0.75 m, A, B, $k = 3$ N/m, $y$, C)

(Labels in figure (b): W, 0.75 m, Datum, A, B, $y = 1$ m, W, $\sqrt{(1\text{ m})^2 + (0.75\text{ m})^2} = 1.25$ m, $v_C$, C, $s_{CB} = 1.25$ m $- 0.75$ m $= 0.5$ m)

# PROBLEMS

**\*14-64.** Solve Prob. 14–18 using the conservation of energy equation.

**14-65.** Solve Prob. 14–15 using the conservation of energy equation.

**14-66.** Solve Prob. 14–17 using the conservation of energy equation.

**14-67.** Solve Prob. 14–31 using the conservation of energy equation.

**\*14-68.** Solve Prob. 14–36 using the conservation of energy equation.

**14-69.** Solve Prob. 14–23 using the conservation of energy equation.

**14-70.** Two equal-length springs are "nested" together in order to form a shock absorber. If it is designed to arrest the motion of a 2-kg mass that is dropped $s = 0.5$ m above the top of the springs from an at-rest position, and the maximum compression of the springs is to be 0.2 m, determine the required stiffness of the inner spring, $k_B$, if the outer spring has a stiffness $k_A = 400$ N/m.

**14-71.** The block has a weight of 15 N ($\approx 1.5$ kg) and slides along the smooth chute $AB$. It is released from rest at $A$, which has coordinates of $A(2$ m, 0, 4 m). Determine the speed at which it slides off at $B$, which has coordinates of $B(0, 3.2$ m, 0).

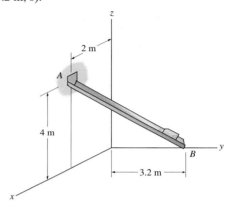

**Prob. 14–71**

**\*14-72.** The girl has a mass of 40 kg and center of mass at $G$. If she is swinging to a maximum height defined by $\theta = 60°$, determine the force developed along each of the four supporting posts such as $AB$ at the instant $\theta = 0°$. The swing is centrally located between the posts.

**Prob. 14–70**

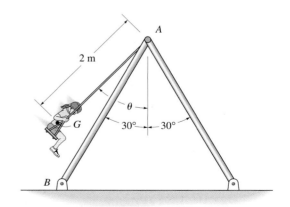

**Prob. 14–72**

**14-73.** The collar has a weight of 40 N ($\approx$ 4 kg). If it is pushed down so as to compress the spring 1 m and then released from rest ($h = 0$), determine its speed when it is displaced $h = 2$ m. The spring is not attached to the collar. Neglect friction.

**14-74.** The collar has a weight of 40 N ($\approx$ 4 kg). If it is released from rest at a height of $h = 1$ m from the top of the uncompressed spring, determine the speed of the collar after it falls and compresses the spring 0.1 m.

Probs. 14–73/74

**14-75.** The 2-kg collar is attached to a spring that has an unstretched length of 3 m. If the collar is drawn to point $B$ and released from rest, determine its speed when it arrives at point $A$.

Prob. 14–75

***14-76.** The 25-N ($\approx$ 2.5-kg) collar is released from rest at $A$ and travels along the smooth guide. Determine the speed of the collar just before it strikes the stop at $B$. The spring has an unstretched length of 30 cm.

**14-77.** The 25-N ($\approx$ 2.5-kg) collar is released from rest at $A$ and travels along the smooth guide. Determine its speed when its center reaches point $C$ and the normal force it exerts on the rod at this point. The spring has an unstretched length of 30 cm, and point $C$ is located just before the end of the curved portion of the rod.

Probs. 14–76/77

**14-78.** The 10-N ($\approx$ 1-kg) block is given an initial velocity of 10 m/s when it is at $A$. If the spring has an unstretched length of 1 m and a stiffness of $k = 1000$ N/m, determine the velocity of the block when $s = 0.5$ m.

Prob. 14–78

**14-79.** The roller-coaster car has a mass of 800 kg, including its passenger, and starts from the top of the hill $A$ with a speed $v_A = 3$ m/s. Determine the minimum height $h$ of the hill crest so that the car travels around both inside loops without leaving the track. Neglect friction, the mass of the wheels, and the size of the car. What is the normal reaction on the car when the car is at $B$ and when it is at $C$?

**\*14-80.** The roller-coaster car has a mass of 800 kg, including its passenger. If it is released from rest at the top of the hill $A$, determine the minimum height $h$ of the hill crest so that the car travels around both inside loops without leaving the track. Neglect friction, the mass of the wheels, and the size of the car. What is the normal reaction on the car when the car is at $B$ and when it is at $C$?

Probs. 14–79/80

**14-81.** Tarzan has a mass of 100 kg and from rest swings from the cliff by rigidly holding on to the tree vine, which is 10 m measured from the supporting limb $A$ to his center of mass. Determine his speed just after the vine strikes the lower limb at $B$. Also, with what force must he hold on to the vine just before and just after the vine contacts the limb at $B$?

Prob. 14–81

**14-82.** The spring has a stiffness $k = 30$ N/m and an unstretched length of 1 m. If it is attached to the 25-N ($\approx 2.5$-kg) smooth collar and the collar is released from rest at $A$, determine the speed of the collar just before it strikes the end of the rod at $B$. Neglect the size of the collar.

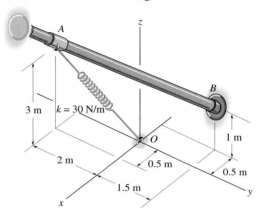

Prob. 14–82

**14-83.** Just for fun, two 750-N ($\approx 75$-kg) engineering students $A$ and $B$ intend to jump off the bridge from rest using an elastic cord (bungee cord) having a stiffness $k = 1200$ N/m. They wish to just reach the surface of the river, when $A$, attached to the cord, lets go of $B$ at the instant they touch the water. Determine the proper unstretched length of the cord to do the stunt, and calculate the maximum acceleration of student $A$ and the maximum height he reaches above the water after the rebound. From your results, comment on the feasibility of doing this stunt.

Prob. 14–83

**\*14-84.** Two equal-length springs having a stiffness $k_A = 300\,\text{N/m}$ and $k_B = 200\,\text{N/m}$ are "nested" together in order to form a shock absorber. If a 2-kg block is dropped from an at-rest position 0.6 m above the top of the springs, determine their deformation when the block momentarily stops.

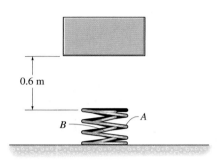

**Prob. 14–84**

**14-85.** The ride at an amusement park consists of a gondola which is lifted to a height of 60 m at $A$. If it is released from rest and falls along the parabolic track, determine the speed at the instant $y = 10$ m. Also determine the normal reaction of the tracks on the gondola at this instant. The gondola and passenger have a total weight of 2.5 kN ($\approx 250$ kg). Neglect the effects of friction and the mass of the wheels.

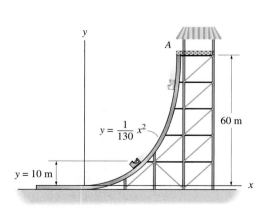

**Prob. 14–85**

**14-86.** When the 6-kg box reaches point $A$ it has a speed of $v_A = 2$ m/s. Determine the angle $\theta$ at which it leaves the smooth circular ramp and the distance $s$ to where it falls into the cart. Neglect friction.

**Prob. 14–86**

**14-87.** The 10-N ($\approx 1$-kg) box has a velocity of 2.5 m/s when it begins to slide down the smooth inclined surface at $A$. Determine the point $C\,(x, y)$ where it strikes the lower incline.

**\*14-88.** The 10-N ($\approx 1$-kg) box has a velocity of 2.5 m/s when it begins to slide down the smooth inclined surface at $A$. Determine its speed just before hitting the surface at $C$ and the time to travel from $A$ to $C$. The coordinates of point $C$ are $x = 8.83$ m, and $y = 4.416$ m.

**Probs. 14–87/88**

**14-89.** The 2-kg ball of negligible size is fired from point $A$ with an initial velocity of 10 m/s up the smooth inclined plane. Determine the distance from point $C$ to where it hits the horizontal surface at $D$. Also, what is its velocity when it strikes the surface?

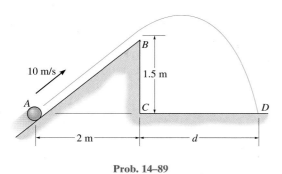

Prob. 14–89

**14-90.** The ball has a weight of 75 N ($\approx$ 7.5 kg) and is fixed to a rod having a negligible mass. If it is released from rest when $\theta = 0°$, determine the angle $\theta$ at which the compressive force in the rod becomes zero.

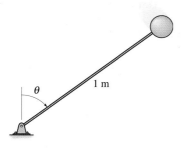

Prob. 14–90

**14-91.** The 5-N ($\approx$ 0.5-kg) ball is shot from the spring device shown. The spring has a stiffness $k = 40$ N/cm, and the four cords $C$ and plate $P$ keep the spring compressed 5 cm when no load is on the plate. The plate is pushed back 7.5 cm from its initial position. If it is then released from rest, determine the speed of the ball when it travels 75 cm up the smooth plane.

***14-92.** The 5-N ($\approx$ 0.5-kg) ball is shot from the spring device shown. Determine the smallest stiffness $k$ which is required to shoot the ball a maximum distance of 75 cm up the plane after the spring is pushed back 7.5 cm and the ball is released from rest. The four cords $C$ and plate $P$ keep the spring compressed 5 cm when no load is on the plate.

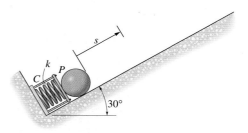

Probs. 14–91/92

**14-93.** Four inelastic cables $C$ are attached to a plate $P$ and hold the 0.4-m-long spring 0.1 m in compression when *no weight* is on the plate. There is also an undeformed spring nested within this compressed spring. If the block, having a weight of 50 N ($\approx$ 5 kg), is moving downward at $v = 1.6$ m/s, when it is 0.8 m above the plate, determine the maximum compression in each spring after it strikes the plate. Neglect the mass of the plate and spring and any energy lost in the collision.

Prob. 14–93

**14-94.** The double-spring bumper is used to stop the 7500-N ($\approx$ 750-kg) steel billet in the rolling mill. Determine the maximum deflection of the plate $A$ caused by the billet if it strikes the plate with a speed of 3 m/s. Neglect the mass of the springs, rollers and the plates $A$ and $B$. Take $k_1$ = 5000 N/m, $k_2$ = 7500 N/m.

$v = 3$ m/s

**Prob. 14–94**

**14-95.** If the mass of the earth is $M_e$, show that the gravitational potential energy of a body of mass $m$ located a distance $r$ from the center of the earth is $V_g = -GM_em/r$. Recall that the gravitational force acting between the earth and the body is $F = G(M_em/r^2)$, Eq. 13–1. For the calculation, locate the datum at $r \to \infty$. Also, prove that F is a conservative force.

**\*14-96.** A rocket of mass $m$ is fired vertically from the surface of the earth, i.e., at $r = r_1$. Assuming that no mass is lost as it travels upward, determine the work it must do against gravity to reach a distance $r_2$. The force of gravity is $F = GM_em/r^2$ (Eq. 13–1), where $M_e$ is the mass of the earth and $r$ the distance between the rocket and the center of the earth.

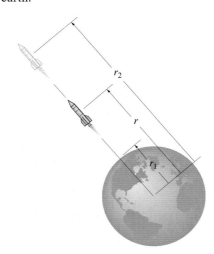

**Prob. 14–96**

# DESIGN PROJECTS

## 14–1D. DESIGN OF A CAR BUMPER

The body of an automobile is to be protected by a spring-loaded bumper, which is attached to the automobile's frame. Design the bumper so that it will stop a 17.5-kN ($\approx$ 1750-kg) car traveling freely at 8 km/h and not deform the springs more than 75 mm. Submit a sketch of your design showing the placement of the springs and their stiffness. Plot the load-deflection diagram for the bumper during a direct collision with a rigid wall, and also plot the deceleration of the car as a function of the springs' displacement.

8 km/h

**Prob. 14–1D**

## 14–2D. DESIGN OF AN ELEVATOR HOIST

It is required that an elevator and its contents, having a maximum weight of 2.5 kN ($\approx$ 250 kg), be lifted $y$ = 10 m, starting from rest and then stopping after 6 seconds. A single motor and cable-winding drum can be mounted anywhere and used for the operation. During any lift or descent the acceleration should not exceed 5 m/s$^2$. Design a cable-and-pulley system for the elevator, and estimate the material cost if the cable is $2.60/m and pulleys are $3.50 each. Submit a drawing of your design, and include plots of the power output required of the motor and the elevator's speed versus the height $y$ traveled.

**Prob. 14–2D**

## CHAPTER REVIEW

- **Work of a Force.** A force does work when it undergoes a displacement along its line of action. If the force varies with the displacement, then $U = \int F \, ds$. Graphically, this represents the area under the $F-s$ diagram. If the force is constant, then for a displacement $\Delta s$ in the direction of the force, $U = F\Delta s$.

  A typical example of this case is the work of weight, $U = W\Delta y$.

  Here, $\Delta y$ is the vertical displacement. A spring force, $F = ks$, depends upon the elongation or compression $s$ of the spring. The work is determined by integration to be $U = \frac{1}{2}ks^2$.

- **The Principle of Work and Energy.** If the equation of motion in the tangential direction, $\Sigma F_t = ma_t$, is combined with the kinematic equation, $a_t \, ds = v \, dv$, we obtain the principle of work and energy.

$$T_1 + \Sigma U_{1-2} = T_2$$

  Here, the initial kinetic energy of the particle $(T_1 = \frac{1}{2}mv_1^2)$, plus the work done by all the forces that act on the particle as it moves from its initial position to its final position $(\Sigma U_{1-2})$, is equal to the final kinetic energy of the particle $(T_1 = \frac{1}{2}mv_2^2)$.

  The principle of work and energy is useful for solving problems that involve force, velocity, and displacement. For application, the free-body diagram of the particle should be drawn in order to identify the forces that do work.

- **Power and Efficiency.** Power is the time-rate of doing work. It is defined by $P = dU/dt$, or $P = \mathbf{F} \cdot \mathbf{v}$. For application, the force $\mathbf{F}$ creating the power and its velocity $\mathbf{v}$ must be specified. Efficiency represents the ratio of power output to power input. Due to frictional losses, it is always less than one.

- **Conservation of Energy.** A conservative force is one that does work which is independent of its path. Two examples are the weight of a particle and the spring force. Friction is a nonconservative force since the work depends upon the length of the path. The longer the path is, the more work is done. The work done by a conservative force depends upon its position relative to a datum. When this work is referenced from a datum, it is called potential energy. For weight, it is $V_g = Wy$, and for a spring it is $V_e = \frac{1}{2}kx^2$.

  Mechanical energy consists of kinetic energy $T$ and gravitational and elastic potential energies $V$. According to the conservation of energy, this sum is constant and has the same value at any two positions on the path. That is,

$$T_1 + V_1 = T_2 + V_2$$

  If motion of the particle is caused only by gravitational and spring forces, then this equation can be used to solve problems involving displacement and velocity.

The velocities of the vehicles involved in this accident can be estimated using the principles of impulse and momentum.

# Kinetics of a Particle:
# Impulse and Momentum

- To develop the principle of linear impulse and momentum for a particle.
- To study the conservation of linear momentum for particles.
- To analyze the mechanics of impact.
- To introduce the concept of angular impulse and momentum.
- To solve problems involving steady fluid streams and propulsion with variable mass.

## 15.1  Principle of Linear Impulse and Momentum

In this section we will integrate the equation of motion with respect to time and thereby obtain the principle of impulse and momentum. It will then be shown that the resulting equation will be useful for solving problems involving force, velocity, and time.

The equation of motion for a particle of mass $m$ can be written as

$$\Sigma \mathbf{F} = m\mathbf{a} = m\frac{d\mathbf{v}}{dt} \qquad (15\text{--}1)$$

where $\mathbf{a}$ and $\mathbf{v}$ are both measured from an inertial frame of reference. Rearranging the terms and integrating between the limits $\mathbf{v} = \mathbf{v}_1$ at $t = t_1$ and $\mathbf{v} = \mathbf{v}_2$ at $t = t_2$, we have

$$\Sigma \int_{t_1}^{t_2} \mathbf{F}\, dt = m \int_{\mathbf{v}_1}^{\mathbf{v}_2} d\mathbf{v}$$

The impulse tool is used to remove the dent in the automobile fender. To do so its end is first screwed into a hole drilled in the fender, then the weight is gripped and jerked upwards, striking the stop ring. The impulse developed is transferred along the shaft of the tool and pulls suddenly on the dent.

or

$$\Sigma \int_{t_1}^{t_2} \mathbf{F} \, dt = m\mathbf{v}_2 - m\mathbf{v}_1 \qquad (15\text{--}2)$$

This equation is referred to as the *principle of linear impulse and momentum*. From the derivation it can be seen that it is simply a time integration of the equation of motion. It provides a *direct means* of obtaining the particle's final velocity $\mathbf{v}_2$ after a specified time period when the particle's initial velocity is known and the forces acting on the particle are either constant or can be expressed as functions of time. By comparison, if $\mathbf{v}_2$ was determined using the equation of motion, a two-step process would be necessary; i.e., apply $\Sigma \mathbf{F} = m\mathbf{a}$ to obtain $\mathbf{a}$, then integrate $\mathbf{a} = d\mathbf{v}/dt$ to obtain $\mathbf{v}_2$.

**Linear Momentum.** Each of the two vectors of the form $\mathbf{L} = m\mathbf{v}$ in Eq. 15–2 is referred to as the particle's *linear momentum*. Since $m$ is a positive scalar, the linear-momentum vector has the same direction as $\mathbf{v}$, and its magnitude $mv$ has unit of mass–velocity, e.g., kg $\cdot$ m/s.

**Linear Impulse.** The integral $\mathbf{I} = \int \mathbf{F} \, dt$ in Eq. 15–2 is referred to as the *linear impulse*. This term is a vector quantity which measures the effect of a force during the time the force acts. Since time is a positive scalar, the impulse acts in the same direction as the force, and its magnitude has unit of force–time, e.g., N $\cdot$ s.* If the force is expressed as a function of time, the impulse may be determined by direct evaluation of the integral. In particular, the magnitude of the impulse $\mathbf{I} = \int_{t_1}^{t_2} \mathbf{F} \, dt$ can be represented experimentally by the shaded area under the curve of force versus time, Fig. 15–1. When the force is constant in both magnitude and direction, the resulting impulse becomes $\mathbf{I} = \int_{t_1}^{t_2} \mathbf{F}_c \, dt = \mathbf{F}_c(t_2 - t_1)$, which represents the shaded rectangular area shown in Fig. 15–2.

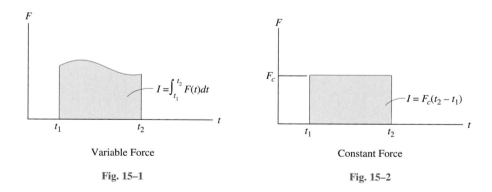

Variable Force

**Fig. 15–1**

Constant Force

**Fig. 15–2**

*Although the units for impulse and momentum are defined differently, one can show that Eq. 15–2 is dimensionally homogeneous.

**Principle of Linear Impulse and Momentum.** For problem solving, Eq. 15–2 will be rewritten in the form

$$mv_1 + \Sigma \int_{t_1}^{t_2} F \, dt = mv_2 \qquad (15\text{–}3)$$

Initial momentum diagram

which states that the initial momentum of the particle at $t_1$ plus the sum of all the impulses applied to the particle from $t_1$ to $t_2$ is equivalent to the final momentum of the particle at $t_2$. These three terms are illustrated graphically on the *impulse and momentum diagrams* shown in Fig. 15–3. The two *momentum diagrams* are simply outlined shapes of the particle which indicate the direction and magnitude of the particle's initial and final momenta, $mv_1$ and $mv_2$, respectively, Fig. 15–3. Similar to the free-body diagram, the *impulse diagram* is an outlined shape of the particle showing all the impulses that act on the particle when it is located at some intermediate point along its path. In general, whenever the magnitude or direction of a force *varies* with time, the impulse is represented on the impulse diagram as $\int_{t_1}^{t_2} F \, dt$. If the force is *constant*, the impulse applied to the particle is $F_c(t_2 - t_1)$, and it acts in the same direction as $F_c$.

+

$$\Sigma \int_{t_1}^{t_2} F \, dt$$

Impulse diagram

$$\|$$

**Scalar Equations.** If each of the vectors in Eq. 15–3 is resolved into its $x, y, z$ components, we can write symbolically the following three scalar equations:

$mv_2$

Final momentum diagram

Fig. 15–3

$$m(v_x)_1 + \Sigma \int_{t_1}^{t_2} F_x \, dt = m(v_x)_2$$

$$m(v_y)_1 + \Sigma \int_{t_1}^{t_2} F_y \, dt = m(v_y)_2 \qquad (15\text{–}4)$$

$$m(v_z)_1 + \Sigma \int_{t_1}^{t_2} F_z \, dt = m(v_z)_2$$

These equations represent the principle of linear impulse and momentum for the particle in the $x, y, z$ directions, respectively.

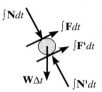

As the wheels of the pitching machine rotate, they apply frictional impulses to the ball, thereby giving it a linear momentum. These impulses are shown on the impulse diagram. Here both the frictional and normal impulses vary with time. By comparison, the weight impulse is constant and is very small since the time $\Delta t$ the ball is in contact with the wheels is very small.

# PROCEDURE FOR ANALYSIS

The principle of linear impulse and momentum is used to solve problems involving *force, time,* and *velocity*, since these terms are involved in the formulation. For application it is suggested that the following procedure be used.*

### *Free-Body Diagram*

- Establish the *x, y, z* inertial frame of reference and draw the particle's free-body diagram in order to account for all the forces that produce impulses on the particle.

- The direction and sense of the particle's initial and final velocities should be established.

- If a vector is unknown, assume that the sense of its components is in the direction of the positive inertial coordinate(s).

- As an alternative procedure, draw the impulse and momentum diagrams for the particle as discussed in reference to Fig. 15–3.

### *Principle of Impulse and Momentum*

- In accordance with the established coordinate system apply the principle of linear impulse and momentum, $m\mathbf{v}_1 + \Sigma \int_{t_1}^{t_2} \mathbf{F}\, dt = m\mathbf{v}_2$. If motion occurs in the *x–y* plane, the two scalar component equations can be formulated by either resolving the vector components of $\mathbf{F}$ from the free-body diagram, or by using the data on the impulse and momentum diagrams.

- Realize that every force acting on the particle's free-body diagram will create an impulse, even though some of these forces will do no work.

- Forces that are functions of time must be integrated to obtain the impulse. Graphically, the impulse is equal to the area under the force–time curve.

- If the problem involves the dependent motion of several particles, use the method outlined in Sec. 12.9 to relate their velocities. Make sure the positive coordinate directions used for writing these kinematic equations are the *same* as those used for writing the equations of impulse and momentum.

*This procedure will be followed when developing the proofs and theory in the text.

# E X A M P L E  **15.1**

The 100-kg stone shown in Fig. 15–4a is originally at rest on the smooth horizontal surface. If a towing force of 200 N, acting at an angle of 45°, is applied to the stone for 10 s, determine the final velocity and the normal force which the surface exerts on the stone during the time interval.

(a)

## Solution

This problem can be solved using the principle of impulse and momentum since it involves force, velocity, and time.

*Free-Body Diagram.*  See Fig. 15–4b. Since all the forces acting are *constant*, the impulses are simply the product of the force magnitude and 10 s [$\mathbf{I} = \mathbf{F}_c(t_2 - t_1)$]. Note the alternative procedure of drawing the stone's impulse and momentum diagrams, Fig. 15–4c.

*Principle of Impulse and Momentum.*  Resolving the vectors in Fig. 15–4b along the x, y axes and applying Eqs. 15–4 yields

(b)

$$(\xrightarrow{+}) \qquad m(v_x)_1 + \Sigma \int_{t_1}^{t_2} F_x \, dt = m(v_x)_2$$

$$0 + 200 \text{ N}(10 \text{ s}) \cos 45° = (100 \text{ kg})v_2$$

$$v_2 = 14.1 \text{ m/s} \qquad\qquad Ans.$$

$$(+\uparrow) \qquad m(v_y)_1 + \Sigma \int_{t_1}^{t_2} F_y \, dt = m(v_y)_2$$

$$0 + N_C(10 \text{ s}) - 981 \text{ N}(10 \text{ s}) + 200 \text{ N}(10 \text{ s}) \sin 45° = 0$$

$$N_C = 840 \text{ N} \qquad\qquad Ans.$$

Since no motion occurs in the y direction, direct application of the equilibrium equation $\Sigma F_y = 0$ gives the same result for $N_C$.

(c)

Fig. 15–4

$v_1 = 1$ m/s

P    30°

(a)

250 N

30°

$y$

v

$x$

$F = 0.3\,N_C$

$P = 100t$

$N_C$

(b)

**Fig. 15–5**

The 250-N ($\approx$ 25-kg) crate shown in Fig. 15–5$a$ is acted upon by a force having a variable magnitude $P = (100t)$ N, where $t$ is in seconds. Determine the crate's velocity 2 s after **P** has been applied. The initial velocity is $v_1 = 1$ m/s down the plane, and the coefficient of kinetic friction between the crate and the plane is $\mu_k = 0.3$.

**Solution**

*Free-Body Diagram.* See Fig. 15–5$b$. Since the magnitude of force $P = 100t$ varies with time, the impulse it creates must be determined by integrating over the 2-s time interval. The weight, normal force, and frictional force (which acts opposite to the direction of motion) are all *constant*, so that the impulse created by each of these forces is simply the magnitude of the force times 2 s.

*Principle of Impulse and Momentum.* Applying Eqs. 15–4 in the $x$ direction, we have

$$(+\swarrow) \qquad m(v_x)_1 + \Sigma \int_{t_1}^{t_2} F_x \, dt = m(v_x)_2$$

$$\frac{250 \text{ N}}{9.81 \text{ m/s}^2} (1 \text{ m/s}) + \int_0^2 (100t) \, dt - 0.3N_C(2 \text{ s}) + (250 \text{ N})(2 \text{ s}) \sin 30° = \frac{250 \text{ N}}{9.81 \text{ m/s}^2} v_2$$

$$25.5 + 200 - 0.6N_C + 250 = 25.5v_2$$

The equation of equilibrium can be applied in the $y$ direction. Why?

$$+\nwarrow \Sigma F_y = 0; \qquad N_C - 250 \cos 30° \text{ N} = 0$$

Solving,

$$N_C = 216.5 \text{ N}$$
$$v_2 = 13.6 \text{ m/s} \swarrow \qquad \qquad Ans.$$

*Note:* We can also solve this problem using the equation of motion. From Fig. 15–5$b$,

$$+\swarrow \Sigma F_x = ma_x; \qquad 100t - 0.3(216.5) + 250 \sin 30° = \frac{250}{9.81} a$$

$$a = 3.924t + 2.356$$

Using kinematics

$$+\swarrow dv = a \, dt; \qquad \int_3^v dv = \int_0^2 (3.924t + 2.356) \, dt$$

$$v = 12.56 \text{ m/s} \qquad \qquad Ans.$$

By comparison, application of the principle of impulse and momentum eliminates the need for using kinematics ($a = dv/dt$) and thereby yields an easier method for solution.

EXAMPLE **15.3**

Blocks $A$ and $B$ shown in Fig. 15–6a have a mass of 3 kg and 5 kg, respectively. If the system is released from rest, determine the velocity of block $B$ in 6 s. Neglect the mass of the pulleys and cord.

**Solution**

*Free-Body Diagram.* See Fig. 15–6b. Since the weight of each block is constant, the cord tensions will also be constant. Furthermore, since the mass of pulley $D$ is neglected, the cord tension $T_A = 2T_B$. Note that the blocks are both assumed to be traveling downward in the positive coordinate directions, $s_A$ and $s_B$.

*Principle of Impulse and Momentum.*

*Block A:*

$(+\downarrow)$ $\qquad m(v_A)_1 + \Sigma \int_{t_1}^{t_2} F_y \, dt = m(v_A)_2$

$\qquad 0 - 2T_B(6\text{ s}) + 3(9.81)\text{ N}(6\text{ s}) = (3\text{ kg})(v_A)_2 \qquad$ (1)

*Block B:*

$(+\downarrow)$ $\qquad m(v_B)_1 + \Sigma \int_{t_1}^{t_2} F_y \, dt = m(v_B)_2$

$\qquad 0 + 5(9.81)\text{ N}(6\text{ s}) - T_B(6\text{ s}) = (5\text{ kg})(v_B)_2 \qquad$ (2)

*Kinematics.* Since the blocks are subjected to dependent motion, the velocity of $A$ may be related to that of $B$ by using the kinematic analysis discussed in Sec. 12.9. A horizontal datum is established through the fixed point at $C$, Fig. 15–6a, and the position coordinates, $s_A$ and $s_B$, are related to the constant total length $l$ of the vertical segments of the cord by the equation

$$2s_A + s_B = l$$

Taking the time derivative yields

$$2v_A = -v_B \qquad (3)$$

As indicated by the negative sign, when $B$ moves downward $A$ moves upward. *Substituting this result into Eq. 1 and solving Eqs. 1 and 2 yields

$$(v_B)_2 = 35.8 \text{ m/s} \downarrow \qquad \text{Ans.}$$

$$T_B = 19.2 \text{ N}$$

*Realize that the *positive* (downward) direction for $\mathbf{v}_A$ and $\mathbf{v}_B$ is *consistent* in Figs. 15–6a and 15–6b and in Eqs. 1 to 3. Why is this important?

Datum

(a)

(b)

Fig. 15–6

## 15.2 Principle of Linear Impulse and Momentum for a System of Particles

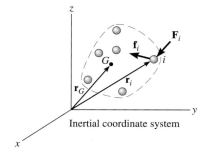

Inertial coordinate system

**Fig. 15–7**

The principle of linear impulse and momentum for a system of particles moving relative to an inertial reference, Fig. 15–7, is obtained from the equation of motion applied to all the particles in the system, i.e.,

$$\Sigma \mathbf{F}_i = \Sigma m_i \frac{d\mathbf{v}_i}{dt} \tag{15–5}$$

The term on the left side represents only the sum of the *external forces* acting on the system of particles. Recall that the internal forces $\mathbf{f}_i$ acting between particles do not appear with this summation, since by Newton's third law they occur in equal but opposite collinear pairs and therefore cancel out. Multiplying both sides of Eq. 15–5 by $dt$ and integrating between the limits $t = t_1$, $\mathbf{v}_i = (\mathbf{v}_i)_1$ and $t = t_2$, $\mathbf{v}_i = (\mathbf{v}_i)_2$ yields

$$\Sigma m_i(\mathbf{v}_i)_1 + \Sigma \int_{t_1}^{t_2} \mathbf{F}_i \, dt = \Sigma m_i(\mathbf{v}_i)_2 \tag{15–6}$$

This equation states that the initial linear momenta of the system plus the impulses of all the *external forces* acting on the system from $t_1$ to $t_2$ are equal to the system's final linear momenta.

Since the location of the mass center $G$ of the system is determined from $m\mathbf{r}_G = \Sigma m_i\mathbf{r}_i$, where $m = \Sigma m_i$ is the total mass of all the particles, Fig. 15–7, then taking the time derivatives, we have

$$m\mathbf{v}_G = \Sigma m_i\mathbf{v}_i$$

which states that the total linear momentum of the system of particles is equivalent to the linear momentum of a "fictitious" aggregate particle of mass $m = \Sigma m_i$ moving with the velocity of the mass center of the system. Substituting into Eq. 15–6 yields

$$m(\mathbf{v}_G)_1 + \Sigma \int_{t_1}^{t_2} \mathbf{F}_i \, dt = m(\mathbf{v}_G)_2 \tag{15–7}$$

Here the initial linear momentum of the aggregate particle plus the external impulses acting on the system of particles from $t_1$ to $t_2$ is equal to the aggregate particle's final linear momentum. Since in reality all particles must have nonzero size to possess mass, the above equation justifies application of the principle of linear impulse and momentum to a rigid body represented as a single particle.

# PROBLEMS

**15-1.** A 20-N ($\approx$ 2-kg) block slides down a 30° inclined plane with an initial velocity of 2 m/s. Determine the velocity of the block in 3 s if the coefficient of kinetic friction between the block and the plane is $\mu_k = 0.25$.

**15-2.** A 10-N ($\approx$ 1-kg) ball is thrown in the direction shown with an initial speed $v_A = 6$ m/s. Determine the time needed for it to reach its highest point $B$ and the speed at which it is traveling at $B$. Use the principle of impulse and momentum for the solution.

Prob. 15–2

**15-3.** A 50-N ($\approx$ 5-kg) block is given an initial velocity of 3 m/s up a 45° smooth slope. Determine the time it will take to travel up the slope before it stops.

**\*15-4.** The 900-N ($\approx$ 90-kg) iron worker is secured by a fall-arrest system consisting of a harness and lanyard $AB$, which is fixed to the beam. If the lanyard has a slack of 2 m, determine the average impulsive force developed in the lanyard if he happens to fall 2 meters. Neglect his size in the calculation and assume the impulse takes place in 0.6 seconds.

Prob. 15–4

**15-5.** The graph shows the vertical reaction force of the shoe-ground interaction as a function of time. The first peak acts on the heel, and the second peak acts on the forefoot. Determine the total impulse acting on the shoe during the interaction.

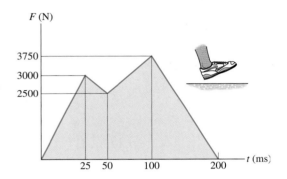

Prob. 15–5

**15-6.** A man hits the 50-g golf ball such that it leaves the tee at an angle of 40° with the horizontal and strikes the ground at the same elevation a distance of 20 m away. Determine the impulse of the club $C$ on the ball. Neglect the impulse caused by the ball's weight while the club is striking the ball.

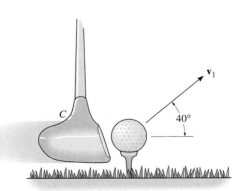

Prob. 15–6

**15-7.** A hammer head $H$ having a weight of 1 N ($\approx$ 0.1 kg) is moving vertically downward at 10 m/s when it strikes the head of a nail of negligible mass and drives it into a block of wood. Find the impulse on the nail if it is assumed that the grip at $A$ is loose, the handle has a negligible mass, and the hammer stays in contact with the nail while it comes to rest. Neglect the impulse caused by the weight of the hammer head during contact with the nail.

Prob. 15–7

**15-9.** When the 5-kg block is 6 m from the wall, it is sliding at $v_1 = 14$ m/s. If the coefficient of kinetic friction between the block and the horizontal plane is $\mu_k = 0.3$, determine the impulse of the wall on the block necessary to stop the block. Neglect the friction impulse acting on the block during the collision.

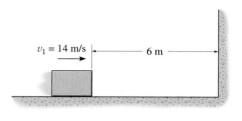

Prob. 15–9

***15-8.** During operation the breaker hammer develops on the concrete surface a force which is indicated in the graph. To achieve this the 10-N ($\approx$ 1-kg) spike $S$ is fired from rest into the surface at 60 m/s. Determine the speed of the spike just after rebounding.

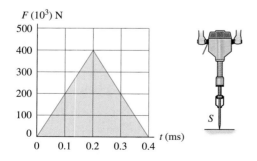

Prob. 15–8

**15-10.** A man kicks the 200-g ball such that it leaves the ground at an angle of 30° with the horizontal and strikes the ground at the same elevation a distance of 15 m away. Determine the impulse of his foot $F$ on the ball. Neglect the impulse caused by the ball's weight while its being kicked.

Prob. 15–10

**15-11.** The particle $P$ is acted upon by its weight of 30 N ($\approx$ 3 kg) and forces $\mathbf{F}_1$ and $\mathbf{F}_2$, where $t$ is in seconds. If the particle orginally has a velocity of $\mathbf{v}_1 = \{3\mathbf{i} + 1\mathbf{j} + 6\mathbf{k}\}$ m/s. determine its speed after 2 s.

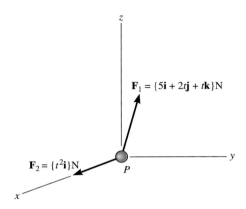

Prob. 15–11

**15-13.** Assuming that the force acting on a 2-g bullet, as it passes horizontally through the barrel of a rifle, varies with time in the manner shown, determine the maximum net force, $F_0$, applied to the bullet when it is fired. The muzzle velocity is 500 m/s when $t = 0.75$ ms. Neglect friction between the bullet and the rifle barrel.

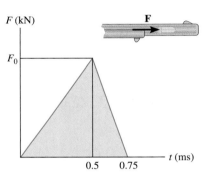

Prob. 15–13

**\*15-12.** The twitch in a muscle of the arm develops a force which can be measured as a function of time as shown in the graph. If the effective contraction of the muscle lasts for a time $t_0$, determine the impulse developed by the muscle.

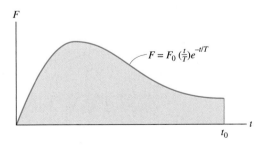

Prob. 15–12

**15-14.** As indicated by the derivation, the principle of impulse and momentum is valid for observers in *any* inertial reference frame. Show that this is so, by considering the 10-kg block which rests on the smooth surface and is subjected to a horizontal force of 6 N. If observer $A$ is in a *fixed* frame $x$, determine the final speed of the block in 4 s if it has an initial speed of 5 m/s measured from the fixed frame. Compare the result with that obtained by an observer $B$, attached to the $x'$ axis that moves at a constant velocity of 2 m/s relative to $A$.

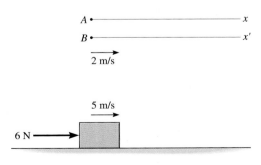

Prob. 15–14

**15-15.** The 20-N ($\approx$ 2-kg) cabinet is subjected to the force $F = 60/(t + 1)^2$ where $t$ is in seconds. If the cabinet is initially moving up the plane with a velocity of 3 m/s, determine how long it will take before the cabinet comes to a stop. **F** always acts parallel to the plane. Neglect the size of the rollers.

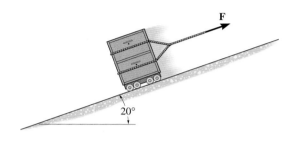

Prob. 15–15

**15-17.** The 5.5-Mg humpback whale is stuck on the shore due to changes in the tide. In an effort to rescue the whale, a 12-Mg tugboat is used to pull it free using an inextensible rope tied to its tail. To overcome the frictional force of the sand on the whale, the tug backs up so that the rope becomes slack and then the tug proceeds forward at 3 m/s. If the tug then turns the engines off, determine the average frictional force **F** on the whale if sliding occurs for 1.5 s before the tug stops after the rope becomes taut. Also, what is the average force on the rope during the tow?

Prob. 15–17

**\*15-16.** If it takes 35 s for the 50-Mg tugboat to increase its speed uniformly to 25 km/h, starting from rest, determine the force of the rope on the tugboat. The propeller provides the propulsion force **F** which gives the tugboat forward motion, whereas the barge moves freely. Also, determine $F$ acting on the tugboat. The barge has a mass of 75 Mg.

Prob. 15–16

**15-18.** The uniform beam has a weight of 25 kN ($\approx$ 2500 kg). Determine the average tension in each of the two cables $AB$ and $AC$ if the beam is given an upward speed of 4 m/s in 1.5 s starting from rest. Neglect the mass of the cables.

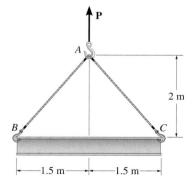

Prob. 15–18

**15-19.** The 5-kg block is moving downward at $v_1 = 2$ m/s when it is 8 m from the sandy surface. Determine the impulse of the sand on the block necessary to stop its motion. Neglect the distance the block dents into the sand and assume the block does not rebound. Neglect the weight of the block during the impact with the sand.

**\*15-20.** The 5-kg block is falling downward at $v_1 = 2$ m/s when it is 8 m from the sandy surface. Determine the average impulsive force acting on the block by the sand if the motion of the block is stopped in 0.9 s once the block strikes the sand. Neglect the distance the block dents into the sand and assume the block does not rebound. Neglect the weight of the block during the impact with the sand.

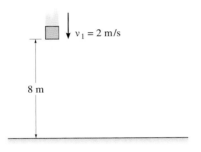

8 m

**Probs. 15–19/20**

**15-21.** A 300-N ($\approx$ 30-kg) block is initially moving along a smooth horizontal surface with a speed of $v_1 = 2$ m/s to the left. If it is acted upon by a force **F**, which varies in the manner shown, determine the velocity of the block in 15 s.

**15-22.** The rocket sled has a mass of 3 Mg and starts from rest when $t = 0$. If the engines provide a horizontal thrust $T$ which varies as shown in the graph, determine the sled's velocity in $t = 4$ s. Neglect air resistance, friction, and the loss of fuel during the motion.

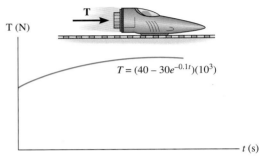

$$T = (40 - 30e^{-0.1t})(10^3)$$

**Prob. 15–22**

**15-23.** The tennis ball has a horizontal speed of 15 m/s when it is struck by the racket. If it then travels away at an angle of 25° from the horizontal and reaches a maximum altitude of 10 m, measured from the height of the racket, determine the magnitude of the net impulse of the racket on the ball. The ball has a mass of 180 g. Neglect the weight of the ball during the time the racket strikes the ball.

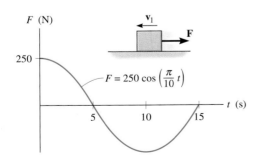

$$F = 250 \cos\left(\frac{\pi}{10} t\right)$$

**Prob. 15–21**

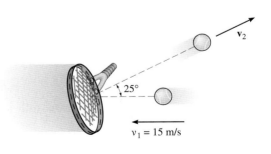

**Prob. 15–23**

**\*15-24.** The 40-kg slider block is moving to the right with a speed of 1.5 m/s when it is acted upon by the forces $F_1$ and $F_2$. If these loadings vary in the manner shown on the graph, determine the speed of the block at $t = 6$ s. Neglect friction and the mass of the pulleys and cords.

**Prob. 15–24**

**15-25.** Determine the velocities of blocks $A$ and $B$ 2 s after they are released from rest. Neglect the mass of the pulleys and cables.

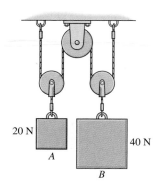

**Prob. 15–25**

**15-26.** The 5-kg package is released from rest at $A$. It slides down the smooth plane which is inclined at 30°, onto the rough surface having a coefficient of kinetic friction of $\mu_k = 0.2$. Determine the total time of travel before the package stops sliding. Neglect the size of the package.

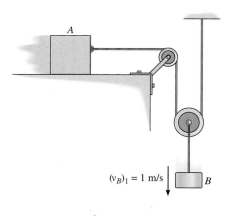

**Prob. 15–26**

**15-27.** Block $A$ weighs 100 N ($\approx$ 10 kg) and block $B$ weighs 30 N ($\approx$ 3 kg). If $B$ is moving downward with a velocity $(v_B)_1 = 1$ m/s at $t = 0$, determine the velocity of $A$ when $t = 1$ s. Assume that the horizontal plane is smooth. Neglect the mass of the pulleys and cords.

**Prob. 15–27**

**\*15-28.** Block $A$ weighs 100 N ($\approx$ 10 kg) and block $B$ weighs 30 N ($\approx$ 3 kg). If $B$ is moving downward with a velocity $(v_B)_1 = 1$ m/s at $t = 0$, determine the velocity of $A$ when $t = 1$ s. The coefficient of kinetic friction between the horizontal plane and block $A$ is $\mu_A = 0.15$.

Prob. 15–28

**15-29.** The winch delivers a horizontal towing force $F$ to its cable at $A$ which varies as shown in the graph. Determine the speed of the 70-kg bucket $B$ when $t = 18$ s. Originally the bucket is moving upward at $v_1 = 3$ m/s.

**15-30.** The winch delivers a horizontal towing force $F$ to its cable at $A$ which varies as shown in the graph. Determine the speed of the 80-kg bucket $B$ when $t = 24$ s. Originally the bucket is moving downward at 20 m/s.

Probs. 15–29/30

**15-31.** The log has a mass of 500 kg and rests on the ground for which the coefficients of static and kinetic friction are $\mu_s = 0.5$ and $\mu_k = 0.4$, respectively. The winch delivers a horizontal towing force $T$ to its cable at $A$ which varies as shown in the graph. Determine the speed of the log when $t = 5$ s. Originally the tension in the cable is zero. *Hint:* First determine the force needed to begin moving the log.

Prob. 15–31

## 15.3 Conservation of Linear Momentum for a System of Particles

When the sum of the *external impulses* acting on a system of particles is *zero*, Eq. 15–6 reduces to a simplified form, namely,

$$\Sigma m_i(\mathbf{v}_i)_1 = \Sigma m_i(\mathbf{v}_i)_2 \tag{15–8}$$

This equation is referred to as the *conservation of linear momentum*. It states that the total linear momentum for a system of particles remains constant during the time period $t_1$ to $t_2$. Substituting $m\mathbf{v}_G = \Sigma m_i\mathbf{v}_i$ into Eq. 15–8, we can also write

$$(\mathbf{v}_G)_1 = (\mathbf{v}_G)_2 \tag{15–9}$$

The hammer in the top photo applies an impulsive force to the stake. During this extremely short time of contact the weight of the stake can be considered nonimpulsive, and provided the stake is driven into soft ground, the impulse of the ground acting on the stake can also be considered nonimpulsive. By contrast, if the stake is used in a concrete chipper to break concrete, then two impulsive forces act on the stake: one at its top due to the chipper and the other on its bottom due to the rigidity of the concrete.

which indicates that the velocity $\mathbf{v}_G$ of the mass center for the system of particles does not change when no external impulses are applied to the system.

The conservation of linear momentum is often applied when particles collide or interact. For application, a careful study of the free-body diagram for the *entire* system of particles should be made in order to identify the forces which create either external or internal impulses and thereby determine in what direction(s) linear momentum is conserved. As stated earlier, the *internal impulses* for the system will always cancel out, since they occur in equal but opposite collinear pairs. If the time period over which the motion is studied is *very short*, some of the external impulses may also be neglected or considered approximately equal to zero. The forces causing these negligible impulses are called *nonimpulsive forces*. By comparison, forces which are very large and act for a very short period of time produce a significant change in momentum and are called *impulsive forces*. They, of course, cannot be neglected in the impulse-momentum analysis.

Impulsive forces normally occur due to an explosion or the striking of one body against another, whereas nonimpulsive forces may include the weight of a body, the force imparted by a slightly deformed spring having a relatively small stiffness, or for that matter, any force that is very small compared to other larger (impulsive) forces. When making this distinction between impulsive and nonimpulsive forces, it is important to realize that this only applies during the time $t_1$ to $t_2$. To illustrate, consider the effect of striking a tennis ball with a racket as shown in the photo. During the *very short* time of interaction, the force of the racket on the ball is impulsive since it changes the ball's momentum drastically. By comparison, the ball's weight will have a negligible effect on the change in momentum, and therefore it is nonimpulsive. Consequently, it can be neglected from an impulse-momentum analysis during this time. If an impulse-momentum analysis is considered during the much longer time of flight after the racket-ball interaction, then the impulse of the ball's weight is important since it, along with air resistance, causes the change in the momentum of the ball.

## PROCEDURE FOR ANALYSIS

Generally, the principle of linear impulse and momentum or the conservation of linear momentum is applied to a *system of particles* in order to determine the final velocities of the particles *just after* the time period considered. By applying these equations to the entire system, the internal impulses acting within the system, which may be unknown, are *eliminated* from the analysis. For application it is suggested that the following procedure be used.

*Free-Body Diagram.*

- Establish the *x, y, z* inertial frame of reference and draw the free-body diagram for each particle of the system in order to identify the internal and external forces.

- The conservation of linear momentum applies to the system in a given direction when no external forces or if nonimpulsive forces act on the system in that direction.

- Establish the direction and sense of the particles' initial and final velocities. If the sense is unknown, assume it is along a positive inertial coordinate axis.

- As an alternative procedure, draw the impulse and momentum diagrams for each particle of the system.

*Momentum Equations.*

- Apply the principle of linear impulse and momentum or the conservation of linear momentum in the appropriate directions.

- If it is necessary to determine the *internal impulse $\int F \, dt$* acting on only one particle of a system, then the particle must be *isolated* (free-body diagram), and the principle of linear impulse and momentum must be applied *to the particle*.

- After the impulse is calculated, and provided the time $\Delta t$ for which the impulse acts is known, then the *average impulsive force $F_{avg}$* can be determined from $F_{avg} = \int F \, dt / \Delta t$.

**E X A M P L E** **15.4**

The 15-Mg boxcar $A$ is coasting at 1.5 m/s on the horizontal track when it encounters a 12-Mg tank car $B$ coasting at 0.75 m/s toward it as shown in Fig. 15–8a. If the cars meet and couple together, determine (a) the speed of both cars just after the coupling, and (b) the average force between them if the coupling takes place in 0.8 s.

(a)

**Solution**

*Part (a)   Free-Body Diagram.*\*   Here we have considered *both* cars as a single system, Fig. 15–8b. By inspection, momentum is conserved in the $x$ direction since the coupling force **F** is *internal* to the system and will therefore cancel out. It is assumed both cars, when coupled, move at $\mathbf{v}_2$ in the positive $x$ direction.

*Conservation of Linear Momentum.*

$$( \xrightarrow{+} ) \qquad m_A(v_A)_1 + m_B(v_B)_1 = (m_A + m_B)v_2$$

$$(15\,000 \text{ kg})(1.5 \text{ m/s}) - 12\,000 \text{ kg}(0.75 \text{ m/s}) = (27\,000 \text{ kg})v_2$$

$$v_2 = 0.5 \text{ m/s} \rightarrow \qquad\qquad Ans.$$

*Part (b).*   The average (impulsive) coupling force, $\mathbf{F}_{avg}$, can be determined by applying the principle of linear momentum to *either one* of the cars.

*Free-Body Diagram.*   As shown in Fig. 15–8c, by isolating the boxcar the coupling force is *external* to the car.

*Principle of Impulse and Momentum.*   Since $\int F\,dt = F_{avg}\Delta t = F_{avg}(0.8)$, we have

$$( \xrightarrow{+} ) \qquad m_A(v_A)_1 + \Sigma \int F\,dt = m_A v_2$$

$$(15\,000 \text{ kg})(1.5 \text{ m/s}) - F_{avg}(0.8 \text{ s}) = (15\,000 \text{ kg})(0.5 \text{ m/s})$$

$$F_{avg} = 18.8 \text{ kN} \qquad\qquad Ans.$$

Solution was possible here since the boxcar's final velocity was obtained in Part (a). Try solving for $F_{avg}$ by applying the principle of impulse and momentum to the tank car.

\*Only horizontal forces are shown on the free-body diagram.

(b)

(c)

Fig. 15–8

# EXAMPLE 15.5

The 600-kg cannon shown in Fig. 15–9a fires an 4-kg projectile with a muzzle velocity of 450 m/s relative to the ground. If firing takes place in 0.03 s, determine (a) the recoil velocity of the cannon just after firing, and (b) the average impulsive force acting on the projectile. The cannon support is fixed to the ground, and the horizontal recoil of the cannon is absorbed by two springs.

Recoil spring

(a)

### Solution

*Part (a)  Free-Body Diagram.** As shown in Fig. 15–9b, we have considered the projectile and cannon as a single system, since the impulsive forces, **F**, between the cannon and projectile are *internal* to the system and will therefore cancel from the analysis. Furthermore, during the time $\Delta t = 0.03$ s, the two recoil springs which are attached to the support each exert a *nonimpulsive force* $\mathbf{F}_s$ on the cannon. This is because $\Delta t$ is very short, so that during this time the cannon only moves through a very small distances.† Consequently, $F_s = ks \approx 0$, where $k$ is the spring's stiffness. Hence it may be concluded that momentum for the system is conserved in the *horizontal direction*. Here we will assume that the cannon moves to the left, while the projectile moves to the right after firing.

$2\mathbf{F}_s$   $-\mathbf{F}$   $\mathbf{F}$

(b)

*Conservation of Linear Momentum.*

$(\overset{+}{\rightarrow})$     $m_c(v_c)_1 + m_p(v_p)_1 = -m_c(v_c)_2 + m_p(v_p)_2$

$$0 + 0 = -(600 \text{ kg})(v_c)_2 + (4 \text{ kg})(450 \text{ m/s})$$

$$(v_c)_2 = 3 \text{ m/s} \leftarrow \qquad \qquad Ans.$$

*Part (b).*   The average impulsive force exerted by the cannon on the projectile can be determined by applying the principle of linear impulse and momentum to the projectile (or to the cannon). Why?

*Principle of Impulse and Momentum.*   Using the data in Fig. 15–9c, noting that $\int F \, dt = F_{avg} \, \Delta t = F_{avg}(0.03)$, we have

(c)

Fig. 15–9

$(\overset{+}{\rightarrow})$     $m(v_p)_1 + \Sigma \int F \, dt = m(v_p)_2$

$$0 + F_{avg}(0.03 \text{ s}) = (4 \text{ kg})(450 \text{ m/s})$$

$$F_{avg} = 60(10^3) \text{ N} = 60.0 \text{ kN} \qquad \qquad Ans.$$

*Only horizontal forces are shown on the free-body diagram.

†If the cannon is firmly fixed to its support (no springs), the reactive force of the support on the cannon must be considered as an external impulse to the system, since the support would allow no movement of the cannon. This, of course, assumes the earth's movement is neglected.

**E X A M P L E** **15.6**

The 350-Mg tugboat $T$ shown in Fig. 15–10a is used to pull the 50-Mg barge $B$ with a rope $R$. If the barge is initially at rest and the tugboat is coasting freely with a velocity of $(v_T)_1 = 3$ m/s while the rope is *slack*, determine the velocity of the tugboat *directly after* the rope becomes taut. Assume the rope does not stretch. Neglect the frictional effects of the water.

(a)    (b)

**Solution**

*Free-Body Diagram.** As shown in Fig. 15–10b, we have considered the entire system (tugboat and barge). Hence, the impulsive force created between the tugboat and the barge is *internal* to the system, and therefore momentum of the system is conserved during the instant of towing.

The alternative procedure of drawing the system's impulse and momentum diagrams is shown in Fig. 15–10c.

*Conservation of Momentum.* Noting that $(v_B)_2 = (v_T)_2$, we have

$$(\overset{+}{\leftarrow}) \qquad m_T(v_T)_1 + m_B(v_B)_1 = m_T(v_T)_2 + m_B(v_B)_2$$
$$350(10^3) \text{ kg}(3 \text{ m/s}) + 0 = 350(10^3) \text{ kg}(v_T)_2 + 50(10^3) \text{ kg}(v_T)_2$$

Solving,

$$(v_T)_2 = 2.62 \text{ m/s} \leftarrow \qquad\qquad Ans.$$

This value represents the tugboat's velocity *just after* the towing impulse. Use this result and show that the towing *impulse* is 131 kN · s.

(c)

**Fig. 15–10**

*Only horizontal forces are shown on the free-body diagram.

# EXAMPLE 15.7

An 800-kg rigid pile $P$ shown in Fig. 15–11$a$ is driven into the ground using a 300-kg hammer $H$. The hammer falls from rest at a height $y_0 = 0.5$ m and strikes the top of the pile. Determine the impulse which the hammer imparts on the pile if the pile is surrounded entirely by loose sand so that after striking, the hammer does *not* rebound off the pile.

### Solution

*Conservation of Energy.* The velocity at which the hammer strikes the pile can be determined using the conservation of energy equation applied to the hammer. With the datum at the top of the pile, Fig. 15–11$a$, we have

$$T_0 + V_0 = T_1 + V_1$$

$$\tfrac{1}{2}m_H(v_H)_0^2 + W_H y_0 = \tfrac{1}{2}m_H(v_H)_1^2 + W_H y_1$$

$$0 + 300(9.81)\ \text{N}(0.5\ \text{m}) = \frac{1}{2}(300\ \text{kg})(v_H)_1^2 + 0$$

$$(v_H)_1 = 3.13\ \text{m/s}$$

*Free-Body Diagram.* From the physical aspects of the problem, the free-body diagram of the hammer and pile, Fig. 15–11$b$, indicates that during the *short time* occurring *just before* to *just after* the *collision*, the weights of the hammer and pile and the resistance force $\mathbf{F}_s$ of the sand are all *nonimpulsive*. The impulsive force $\mathbf{R}$ is internal to the system and therefore cancels. Consequently, momentum is conserved in the vertical direction during this short time.

*Conservation of Momentum.* Since the hammer does not rebound off the pile just after collision, then $(v_H)_2 = (v_P)_2 = v_2$.

$$(+\downarrow) \qquad m_H(v_H)_1 + m_P(v_P)_1 = m_H v_2 + m_P v_2$$

$$(300\ \text{kg})(3.13\ \text{m/s}) + 0 = (300\ \text{kg})v_2 + (800\ \text{kg})v_2$$

$$v_2 = 0.854\ \text{m/s}$$

*Principle of Impulse and Momentum.* The impulse which the pile imparts to the hammer can now be determined since $\mathbf{v}_2$ is known. From the free-body diagram for the hammer, Fig. 15–11$c$, we have

$$(+\downarrow) \qquad m_H(v_H)_1 + \Sigma \int_{t_1}^{t_2} F_y\, dt = m_H v_2$$

$$(300\ \text{kg})(3.13\ \text{m/s}) - \int R\, dt = (300\ \text{kg})(0.854\ \text{m/s})$$

$$\int R\, dt = 683\ \text{N}\cdot\text{s} \qquad\qquad Ans.$$

The equal but opposite impulse acts on the pile. Try finding this impulse by applying the principle of impulse and momentum to the pile.

(a)

(b)

(c)

**Fig. 15–11**

## EXAMPLE 15.8

(a)

(b)

(c)

Fig. 15–12

A boy having a mass of 40 kg stands on the back of a 15-kg toboggan which is originally at rest, Fig. 15–12a. If he walks to the front B and stops, determine the distance the toboggan moves. Neglect friction between the bottom of the toboggan and the ground (ice).

### Solution I

*Free-Body Diagram.* The unknown frictional force of the boy's shoes on the bottom of the toboggan can be *excluded* from the analysis if the toboggan and boy on it are considered as a single system. In this way the frictional force **F** becomes *internal* and the conservation of momentum applies, Fig. 15–12b.

*Conservation of Momentum.* Since both the initial and final momenta of the system are zero (because the initial and final velocities are zero), the system's momentum must also be zero when the boy is at some intermediate point between A and B. Thus

$$(\xrightarrow{+}) \qquad\qquad -m_b v_b + m_t v_t = 0 \qquad\qquad (1)$$

Here the two unknowns $v_b$ and $v_t$ represent the velocities of the boy moving to the left and the toboggan moving to the right. Both are measured from a *fixed inertial reference* on the ground.

At any instant the *position* of point A on the toboggan and the *position* of the boy must be determined by integration. Since $v = ds/dt$, then $-m_b ds_b + m_t ds_t = 0$. Assuming the initial position of point A to be at the origin, Fig. 15–12c, then at the final position we have $-m_b s_b + m_t s_t = 0$. Since $s_b + s_t = 2$ m, or $s_b = (2 - s_t)$ then

$$-m_b(2 - s_t) + m_t s_t = 0 \qquad\qquad (2)$$

$$s_t = \frac{2m_b}{m_b + m_t} = \frac{2(40)}{40 + 15} = 1.45 \text{ m} \qquad\qquad Ans.$$

### Solution II

The problem may also be solved by considering the relative motion of the boy with respect to the toboggan, $\mathbf{v}_{b/t}$. This velocity is related to the velocities of the boy and toboggan by the equation $\mathbf{v}_b = \mathbf{v}_t + \mathbf{v}_{b/t}$, Eq. 12–34. Since positive motion is assumed to be to the right in Eq. 1, $\mathbf{v}_b$ and $\mathbf{v}_{b/t}$ are negative, because the boy's motion is to the left. Hence, in scalar form, $-v_b = v_t - v_{b/t}$, and Eq. 1 then becomes $m_b(v_t - v_{b/t}) + m_t v_t = 0$. Integrating gives

$$m_b(s_t - s_{b/t}) + m_t s_t = 0$$

Realizing $s_{b/t} = 2$ m, we obtain Eq. 2.

# PROBLEMS

**\*15-32.** A railroad car having a mass of 15 Mg is coasting at 1.5 m/s on a horizontal track. At the same time another car having a mass of 12 Mg is coasting at 0.75 m/s in the opposite direction. If the cars meet and couple together, determine the speed of both cars just after the coupling. Find the difference between the total kinetic energy before and after coupling has occurred, and explain qualitatively what happened to this energy.

**15-33.** The car $A$ has a weight of 22.5 kN ($\approx$ 2250 kg) and is traveling to the right at 1 m/s. Meanwhile a 15-kN ($\approx$ 1500-kg) car $B$ is traveling at 2 m/s to the left. If the cars crash head-on and become entangled, determine their common velocity just after the collision. Assume that the brakes are not applied during collision.

**Prob. 15–33**

**15-34.** The bus $B$ has a weight of 75 kN ($\approx$ 7500 kg) and is traveling to the right at 2.5 m/s. Meanwhile a 15-kN ($\approx$ 1500-kg) car $A$ is traveling at 2 m/s to the left. If the vehicles crash head-on and become entangled, determine their common velocity just after the collision. Assume that the vehicles are free to roll during collision.

**Prob. 15–34**

**15-35.** The two blocks $A$ and $B$ each have a mass of 5 kg and are suspended from parallel cords. A spring, having a stiffness of $k = 60$ N/m, is attached to $B$ and is compressed 0.3 m against $A$ and $B$ as shown. Determine the maximum angles $\theta$ and $\phi$ of the cords when the blocks are released from rest and the spring becomes unstretched.

**Prob. 15–35**

**\*15-36.** Two men $A$ and $B$, each having a weight of 800 N ($\approx$ 80 kg), stand on the 1-kN ($\approx$ 100-kg) cart. Each runs with a speed of 1 m/s measured relative to the cart. Determine the final speed of the cart if (a) $A$ runs and jumps off, then $B$ runs and jumps off the same end, and (b) both run at the same time and jump off at the same time. Neglect the mass of the wheels and assume the jumps are made horizontally.

**Prob. 15–36**

**15-37.** A man wearing ice skates throws an 8-kg block with an initial velocity of 2 m/s, measured relative to himself, in the direction shown. If he is originally at rest and completes the throw in 1.5 s while keeping his legs rigid, determine the horizontal velocity of the man just after releasing the block. What is the vertical reaction of both his skates on the ice during the throw? The man has a mass of 70 kg. Neglect friction and the motion of his arms.

**Prob. 15–37**

**15-38.** The barge weighs 225 kN ($\approx$ 22 500 kg) and supports two automobiles $A$ and $B$, which weigh 20 kN ($\approx$ 2000 kg) and 15 kN ($\approx$ 1500 kg), respectively. If the automobiles start from rest and drive towards each other, accelerating at $a_A = 2$ m/s$^2$ and $a_B = 4$ m/s$^2$ until they reach a constant speed of 3 m/s relative to the barge, determine the speed of the barge just before the automobiles collide. How much time does this take? Originally the barge is at rest. Neglect water resistance.

Prob. 15–38

**15-39.** The barge $B$ weighs 150 kN ($\approx$ 15 000 kg) and supports an automobile weighing 15 kN ($\approx$ 1500 kg). If the barge is not tied to the pier $P$ and someone drives the automobile to the other side of the barge for unloading, determine how far the barge moves away from the pier. Neglect the resistance of the water.

Prob. 15–39

*15-40.** The block $A$ has a mass of 2 kg and slides smoothly into an open ended box $B$ with a velocity of 2 m/s. If the box has a mass of 3 kg and rests on top of a plate $P$ that has a mass of 3 kg, determine the distance the plate moves after it stops sliding on the floor. Also, how long is it after impact before all motion ceases? The coefficient of kinetic friction between the box and the plate is $\mu_k = 0.2$, and between the plate and the floor $\mu'_k = 0.4$. Also, the coefficient of static friction between the plate and the floor is $\mu'_s = 0.5$.

**15-41.** The block $A$ has a mass of 2 kg and slides smoothly into an open ended box $B$ with a velocity of 2 m/s. If the box has a mass of 3 kg and rests on top of a plate $P$ that has a mass of 3 kg, determine the distance the plate moves after it stops sliding on the floor. Also, how long is it after impact before all motion ceases? The coefficient of kinetic friction between the box and the plate is $\mu_k = 0.2$, and between the plate and the floor $\mu'_k = 0.1$. Also, the coefficient of static friction between the plate and the floor is $\mu'_s = 0.12$. Neglect friction within the box.

Probs. 15–40/41

**15-42.** The man $M$ weighs 750 kN ($\approx$ 75 kg) and jumps onto the boat $B$ which has a weight of 1 kN ($\approx$ 100 kg). If he has a horizontal component of velocity *relative to the boat* of 1.5 m/s, just before he enters the boat, and the boat is traveling $v_B = 1$ m/s away from the pier when he makes the jump, determine the resulting velocity of the man and boat.

**15-43.** The man $M$ weighs 750 N ($\approx$ 75 kg) and jumps onto the boat $B$ which is originally at rest. If he has a horizontal component of velocity of 1.5 m/s just before he enters the boat, determine the weight of the boat if it has a velocity of 1 m/s once the man enters it.

Probs. 15–42/43

**\*15-44.** A boy A having a weight of 400 N (≈ 40 kg) and a girl B having a weight of 325 N (≈ 32.5 kg) stand motionless at the ends of the toboggan, which has a weight of 100 N (≈ 10 kg). If A walks to B and stops, and both walk back together to the original position of A, determine the final position of the toboggan just after the motion stops. Neglect friction.

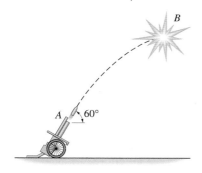

**Prob. 15–44**

**15-45.** The 5-kg projectile is fired from ground level with an initial velocity of $v_A = 20$ m/s in the direction shown. When it reaches its highest point B it explodes into two 2.5-kg fragments. If one fragment travels vertically upward at 3 m/s, determine the distance between the fragments after they strike the ground. Neglect the size of the gun.

**Prob. 15–45**

**15-46.** Two boxes A and B, each having a weight of 800 N (≈ 80 kg) sit on the 2500-N (≈ 250-kg) conveyor which is free to roll on the ground. If the belt starts from rest and begins to run with a speed of 1 m/s, determine the final speed of the conveyor if (a) the boxes are not stacked and A falls off then B falls off, and (b) A is stacked on top of B and both fall off together.

**Prob. 15–46**

**15-47.** The 10-kg block is held at rest on the smooth inclined plane by the stop block at A. If the 10-g bullet is traveling at 300 m/s when it becomes embedded in the 10-kg block, determine the distance the block will slide up along the plane before momentarily stopping.

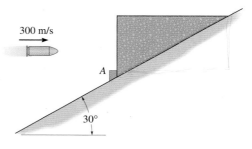

**Prob. 15–47**

**\*15-48.** A tugboat T having a mass of 19 Mg is tied to a barge B having a mass of 75 Mg. If the rope is "elastic" such that it has a stiffness $k = 600$ kN/m, determine the maximum stretch in the rope during the initial towing. Originally both the tugboat and barge are moving in the same direction with speeds $(v_T)_1 = 15$ km/h and $(v_B)_1 = 10$ km/h, respectively. Neglect the resistance of the water.

**Prob. 15–48**

**15-49.** The 10-kg cart $B$ is supported on rollers of negligible size. If a 5-kg suitcase $A$ is thrown horizontally on it at 3 m/s, determine the length of time that $A$ slides relative to $B$, and the final velocity of $A$ and $B$. The coefficient of kinetic friction between $A$ and $B$ is $\mu_k = 0.4$.

**15-50.** The 10-kg cart $B$ is supported on rollers of negligible size. If a 5-kg suitcase $A$ is thrown horizontally on it at 3 m/s, determine the time $t$ and the distance $B$ moves before $A$ stops relative to $B$. The coefficient of kinetic friction between $A$ and $B$ is $\mu_k = 0.4$.

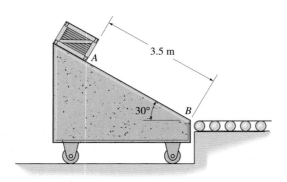

**Probs. 15–49/50**

**15-51.** The free-rolling ramp has a mass of 40 kg. A 10-kg crate is released from rest at $A$ and slides down 3.5 m to point $B$. If the surface of the ramp is smooth, determine the ramp's speed when the crate reaches $B$. Also, what is the velocity of the crate?

*15-52.** The block has a mass of 50 kg and rests on the surface of the cart having a mass of 75 kg. If the spring which is attached to the cart and not the block is compressed 0.2 m and the system is released from rest, determine the speed of the block after the spring becomes undeformed. Neglect the mass of the cart's wheels and the spring in the calculation. Also neglect friction. Take $k = 300$ N/m.

**15-53.** The block has a mass of 50 kg and rests on the surface of the cart having a mass of 75 kg. If the spring which is attached to the cart and not the block is compressed 0.2 m and the system is released from rest, determine the speed of the block with respect to the cart after the spring becomes undeformed. Neglect the mass of the wheels and the spring in the calculation. Also neglect friction. Take $k = 300$ N/m.

**Probs. 15–52/53**

**15-54.** Blocks $A$ and $B$ have masses of 40 kg and 60 kg, respectively. They are placed on a smooth surface and the spring connected between them is stretched 2 m. If they are released from rest, determine the speeds of both blocks the instant the spring becomes unstretched.

**Prob. 15–54**

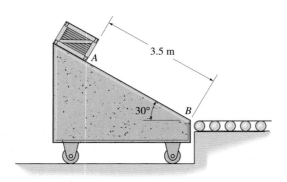

**Prob. 15–51**

# 15.4 Impact

*Impact* occurs when two bodies collide with each other during a very *short* period of time, causing relatively large (impulsive) forces to be exerted between the bodies. The striking of a hammer on a nail, or a golf club on a ball, are common examples of impact loadings.

In general, there are two types of impact. *Central impact* occurs when the direction of motion of the mass centers of the two colliding particles is along a line passing through the mass centers of the particles. This line is called the *line of impact*, Fig. 15–13a. When the motion of one or both of the particles is at an angle with the line of impact, Fig. 15–13b, the impact is said to be *oblique impact*.

**Central Impact.**   To illustrate the method for analyzing the mechanics of impact, consider the case involving the central impact of two *smooth* particles A and B shown in Fig. 15–14.

- The particles have the initial momenta shown in Fig. 15–14a. Provided $(v_A)_1 > (v_B)_1$, collision will eventually occur.

- During the collision the particles must be thought of as *deformable* or nonrigid. The particles will undergo a *period of deformation* such that they exert an equal but opposite deformation impulse $\int \mathbf{P} \, dt$ on each other, Fig. 15–14b.

- Only at the instant of *maximum deformation* will both particles move with a common velocity $\mathbf{v}$, since their relative motion is zero, Fig. 15–14c.

- Afterward a *period of restitution* occurs, in which case the particles will either return to their original shape or remain permanently deformed. The equal but opposite *restitution impulse* $\int \mathbf{R} \, dt$ pushes the particles apart from one another, Fig. 15–14d. In reality, the physical properties of any two bodies are such that the deformation impulse is *always greater* than that of restitution, i.e., $\int P \, dt > \int R \, dt$.

- Just after separation the particles will have the final momenta shown in Fig. 15–14e, where $(v_B)_2 > (v_A)_2$.

Central impact
(a)

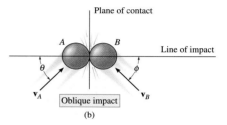

Oblique impact
(b)

**Fig. 15–13**

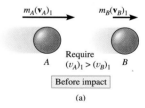

Require
$(v_A)_1 > (v_B)_1$

Before impact
(a)

**Fig. 15–14**

| $\int \mathbf{P} \, dt$     $-\int \mathbf{P} \, dt$ | $\mathbf{v}$ | $\int \mathbf{R} \, dt$     $-\int \mathbf{R} \, dt$ | $m_A(\mathbf{v}_A)_2$     $m_B(\mathbf{v}_B)_2$ |

Effect of A on B     Effect of B on A       A  B        Effect of A on B     Effect of B on A        A    $(v_B)_2 > (v_A)_2$    B

Deformation impulse        Maximum deformation        Restitution impulse        After impact

(b)        (c)        (d)        (e)

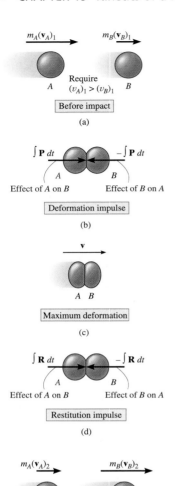

**Fig. 15–14**

In most problems the initial velocities of the particles will be *known*, and it will be necessary to determine their final velocities $(v_A)_2$ and $(v_B)_2$. In this regard, *momentum* for the *system of particles* is *conserved* since during collision the internal impulses of deformation and restitution cancel. Hence, referring to Fig. 15–14*a* and Fig. 15–14*e* we require

$$(\xrightarrow{+}) \qquad m_A(v_A)_1 + m_B(v_B)_1 = m_A(v_A)_2 + m_B(v_B)_2 \qquad (15\text{–}10)$$

In order to obtain a second equation necessary to solve for $(v_A)_2$ and $(v_B)_2$, we must apply the principle of impulse and momentum to *each particle*. For example, during the deformation phase for particle *A*, Figs. 15–14*a*, 15–14*b*, and 15–14*c*, we have

$$(\xrightarrow{+}) \qquad m_A(v_A)_1 - \int P \, dt = m_A v$$

For the restitution phase, Figs. 15–14*c*, 15–14*d*, and 15–14*e*,

$$(\xrightarrow{+}) \qquad m_A v - \int R \, dt = m_A(v_A)_2$$

The ratio of the restitution impulse to the deformation impulse is called the *coefficient of restitution*, *e*. From the above equations, this value for particle *A* is

$$e = \frac{\int R \, dt}{\int P \, dt} = \frac{v - (v_A)_2}{(v_A)_1 - v}$$

In a similar manner, we can establish *e* by considering particle *B*, Fig. 15–14. This yields

$$e = \frac{\int R \, dt}{\int P \, dt} = \frac{(v_B)_2 - v}{v - (v_B)_1}$$

If the unknown $v$ is eliminated from the above two equations, the coefficient of restitution can be expressed in terms of the particles' initial and final velocities as

$$(\xrightarrow{+}) \qquad \boxed{e = \frac{(v_B)_2 - (v_A)_2}{(v_A)_1 - (v_B)_1}} \qquad (15\text{–}11)$$

Provided a value for $e$ is specified, Eqs. 15–10 and 15–11 may be solved simultaneously to obtain $(v_A)_2$ and $(v_B)_2$. In doing so, however, it is important to carefully establish a sign convention for defining the positive direction for both $\mathbf{v}_A$ and $\mathbf{v}_B$ and then use it *consistently* when writing *both* equations. As noted from the application shown, and indicated symbolically by the arrow in parentheses, we have defined the positive direction to the right when referring to the motions of both $A$ and $B$. Consequently, if a negative value results from the solution of either $(v_A)_2$ or $(v_B)_2$, it indicates motion is to the left.

**Coefficient of Restitution.** With reference to Figs. 15–14a and 15–14e, it is seen that Eq. 15–11 states that $e$ is equal to the ratio of the relative velocity of the particles' separation *just after impact*, $(v_B)_2 - (v_A)_2$, to the relative velocity of the particles' approach *just before impact*, $(v_A)_1 - (v_B)_1$. By measuring these relative velocities experimentally, it has been found that $e$ varies appreciably with impact velocity as well as with the size and shape of the colliding bodies. For these reasons the coefficient of restitution is reliable only when used with data which closely approximate the conditions which were known to exist when measurements of it were made. In general $e$ has a value between zero and one, and one should be aware of the physical meaning of these two limits.

The quality of a manufactured tennis ball is measured by the height of its bounce, which can be related to its coefficient of restitution. Using the mechanics of oblique impact, engineers can design a separation device to maintain quality control of tennis balls after production.

**Elastic Impact** $(e = 1)$: If the collision between the two particles is *perfectly elastic*, the deformation impulse $(\int \mathbf{P}\, dt)$ is equal and opposite to the restitution impulse $(\int \mathbf{R}\, dt)$. Although in reality this can never be achieved, $e = 1$ for an elastic collision.

**Plastic Impact** $(e = 0)$: The impact is said to be *inelastic or plastic* when $e = 0$. In this case there is no restitution impulse given to the particles $(\int \mathbf{R}\, dt = \mathbf{0})$, so that after collision both particles couple or stick *together* and move with a common velocity.

From the above derivation it should be evident that the principle of work and energy cannot be used for the analysis of impact problems since it is not possible to know how the *internal forces* of deformation and restitution vary or displace during the collision. By knowing the particle's velocities before and after collision, however, the energy loss during collision can be calculated on the basis of the difference in the particle's kinetic energy. This energy loss, $\Sigma U_{1-2} = \Sigma T_2 - \Sigma T_1$, occurs because some of the initial kinetic energy of the particle is transformed into thermal energy as well as creating sound and localized deformation of the material when the collision occurs. In particular, if the impact is *perfectly elastic*, no energy is lost in the collision; whereas if the collision is *plastic*, the energy lost during collision is a maximum.

## PROCEDURE FOR ANALYSIS (CENTRAL IMPACT)

In most cases the *final velocities* of two smooth particles are to be determined *just after* they are subjected to direct central impact. Provided the coefficient of restitution, the mass of each particle, and each particle's initial velocity *just before* impact are known, the solution to the problem can be obtained using the following two equations:

- The conservation of momentum applies to the system of particles, $\Sigma m v_1 = \Sigma m v_2$.

- The coefficient of restitution, $e = [(v_B)_2 - (v_A)_2]/[(v_A)_1 - (v_B)_1]$, relates the relative velocities of the particles along the line of impact, just before and just after collision.

When applying these two equations, the sense of an unknown velocity can be assumed. If the solution yields a negative magnitude, the velocity acts in the opposite sense.

**Oblique Impact.**   When oblique impact occurs between two smooth particles, the particles move away from each other with velocities having unknown directions as well as unknown magnitudes. Provided the initial velocities are known, four unknowns are present in the problem. As shown in Fig. 15–15a, these unknowns may be represented either as $(v_A)_2$, $(v_B)_2$, $\theta_2$, and $\phi_2$, or as the x and y components of the final velocities.

## PROCEDURE FOR ANALYSIS (OBLIQUE IMPACT)

If the y axis is established within the plane of contact and the x axis along the line of impact, the impulsive forces of deformation and restitution act *only in the x direction*, Fig. 15–15b. Resolving the velocity or momentum vectors into components along the x and y axes, Fig. 15–15b, it is possible to write four independent scalar equations in order to determine $(v_{Ax})_2$, $(v_{Ay})_2$, $(v_{Bx})_2$, and $(v_{By})_2$.

- Momentum of the system is conserved *along the line of impact*, x axis, so that $\Sigma m(v_x)_1 = \Sigma m(v_x)_2$.

- The coefficient of restitution, $e = [(v_{Bx})_2 - (v_{Ax})_2]/[(v_{Ax})_1 - (v_{Bx})_1]$, relates the relative-velocity *components* of the particles *along the line of impact* (x axis).

- Momentum of particle A is conserved along the y axis, perpendicular to the line of impact, since no impulse acts on particle A in this direction.

- Momentum of particle B is conserved along the y axis, perpendicular to the line of impact, since no impulse acts on particle B in this direction.

Application of these four equations is illustrated numerically in Example 15.11.

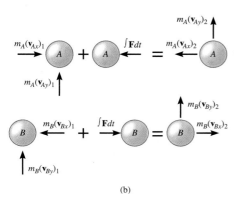

(a)

(b)

**Fig. 15–15**

## E X A M P L E 15.9

The bag $A$, having a mass of 6 kg, is released from rest at the position $\theta = 0°$, as shown in Fig. 15–16$a$. After falling to $\theta = 90°$, it strikes an 18-kg box $B$. If the coefficient of restitution between the bag and box is $e = 0.5$, determine the velocities of the bag and box just after impact and the loss of energy during collision.

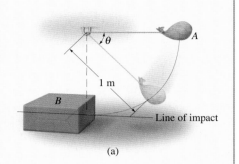

(a)

### Solution

This problem involves central impact. Why? Before analyzing the mechanics of the impact, however, it is first necessary to obtain the velocity of the bag *just before* it strikes the box.

*Conservation of Energy.* With the datum at $\theta = 0°$, Fig. 15–16$b$, we have

$$T_0 + V_0 = T_1 + V_1$$

$$0 + 0 = \frac{1}{2}(6\text{ kg})(v_A)_1^2 - 6\text{ kg }(9.81\text{ m/s}^2)(1\text{ m}); \quad (v_A)_1 = 4.43\text{ m/s}$$

(b)

*Conservation of Momentum.* After impact we will assume $A$ and $B$ travel to the left. Applying the conservation of momentum to the system, we have

$$(\xleftarrow{+}) \quad m_B(v_B)_1 + m_A(v_A)_1 = m_B(v_B)_2 + m_A(v_A)_2$$

$$0 + (6\text{ kg})(4.43\text{ m/s}) = (18\text{ kg})(v_B)_2 + 6\text{ kg }(v_A)_2$$

$$(v_A)_2 = 4.43 - 3(v_B)_2 \tag{1}$$

*Coefficient of Restitution.* Realizing that for separation to occur after collision $(v_B)_2 > (v_A)_2$, Fig. 15–16$c$, we have

$$(\xleftarrow{+}) \quad e = \frac{(v_B)_2 - (v_A)_2}{(v_A)_1 - (v_B)_1}; \quad 0.5 = \frac{(v_B)_2 - (v_A)_2}{4.43\text{ m/s} - 0}$$

$$(v_A)_2 = (v_B)_2 - 2.215 \tag{2}$$

$(v_B)_1 = 0$    $B$    $A$

$(v_A)_1$

Just before impact

Solving Eqs. 1 and 2 simultaneously yields

$$(v_A)_2 = -0.554\text{ m/s} = 0.554\text{ m/s} \rightarrow \quad \text{and} \quad (v_A)_2 = 1.66\text{ m/s} \leftarrow \quad \textit{Ans.}$$

*Loss of Energy.* Applying the principle of work and energy to the bag and box just before and just after collision, we have

$$\Sigma U_{1-2} = T_2 - T_1;$$

$$\Sigma U_{1-2} = \left[ \frac{1}{2}(18\text{ kg})(1.66\text{ m/s})^2 + \frac{1}{2}(6\text{ kg})(0.554\text{ m/s})^2 \right] -$$

$$\left[ \frac{1}{2}(6\text{ kg})(4.43\text{ m/s})^2 \right]$$

$$\Sigma U_{1-2} = -33.15\text{ J} \qquad \textit{Ans.}$$

Why is there an energy loss?

$B$    $A$

$(v_B)_2$    $(v_A)_2$

Just after impact

(c)

**Fig. 15–16**

**E X A M P L E   15.10**

Datum

$k = 800$ N/m    $y = (1 + 0.25)$ m

B

(a)

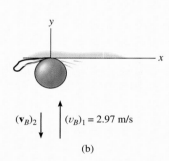

$y$

$x$

$(\mathbf{v}_B)_2$    $(v_B)_1 = 2.97$ m/s

(b)

$k = 800$ N/m    $y = (1 + s_3)$ m

(c)

**Fig. 15–17**

The ball $B$ shown in Fig. 15–17a has a mass of 1.5 kg and is suspended from the ceiling by a 1-m-long elastic cord. If the cord is *stretched* downward 0.25 m and the ball is released from rest, determine how far the cord stretches after the ball rebounds from the ceiling. The stiffness of the cord is $k = 800$ N/m, and the coefficient of restitution between the ball and ceiling is $e = 0.8$. The ball makes a central impact with the ceiling.

**Solution**

First we must obtain the velocity of the ball *just before* it strikes the ceiling using energy methods, then consider the impulse and momentum between the ball and ceiling, and finally again use energy methods to determine the stretch in the cord.

*Conservation of Energy.* With the datum located as shown in Fig. 15–17a, realizing that initially $y = y_0 = (1 + 0.25)$ m $= 1.25$ m, we have

$$T_0 + V_0 = T_1 + V_1$$
$$\tfrac{1}{2}m(v_B)_0^2 - W_B y_0 + \tfrac{1}{2}ks^2 = \tfrac{1}{2}m(v_B)_1^2 + 0$$
$$0 - 1.5(9.81)\text{ N}(1.25\text{ m}) + \tfrac{1}{2}(800\text{ N/m})(0.25\text{ m})^2 = \tfrac{1}{2}(1.5\text{ kg})(v_B)_1^2$$
$$(v_B)_1 = 2.97\text{ m/s} \uparrow$$

The interaction of the ball with the ceiling will now be considered using the principles of impact.* Since an unknown portion of the mass of the ceiling is involved in the impact, the conservation of momentum for the ball-ceiling system will not be written. The "velocity" of this portion of ceiling is zero since it (or the earth) are assumed to remain at rest *both* before and after impact.

*Coefficient of Restitution.* Fig. 15–17b.

$$(+\uparrow) \quad e = \frac{(v_B)_2 - (v_A)_2}{(v_A)_1 - (v_B)_1}; \qquad 0.8 = \frac{(v_B)_2 - 0}{0 - 2.97\text{ m/s}}$$
$$(v_B)_2 = -2.37\text{ m/s} = 2.37\text{ m/s} \downarrow$$

*Conservation of Energy.* The maximum stretch $s_3$ in the cord may be determined by again applying the conservation of energy equation to the ball just after collision. Assuming that $y = y_3 = (1 + s_3)$ m, Fig. 15–17c, then

$$T_2 + V_2 = T_3 + V_3$$
$$\tfrac{1}{2}m(v_B)_2^2 + 0 = \tfrac{1}{2}m(v_B)_3^2 - W_B y_3 + \tfrac{1}{2}ks_3^2$$
$$\tfrac{1}{2}(1.5\text{ kg})(2.37\text{ m/s})^2 = 0 - 9.81(1.5)\text{ N}(1\text{ m} + s_3) + \tfrac{1}{2}(800\text{ N/m})s_3^2$$
$$400s_3^2 - 14.72s_3 - 18.94 = 0$$

Solving this quadratic equation for the positive root yields
$$s_3 = 0.237\text{ m} = 237\text{ mm} \qquad\qquad Ans.$$

*The weight of the ball is considered a nonimpulsive force.

# EXAMPLE 15.11

Two smooth disks $A$ and $B$, having a mass of 1 kg and 2 kg, respectively, collide with the velocities shown in Fig. 15–18a. If the coefficient of restitution for the disks is $e = 0.75$, determine the $x$ and $y$ components of the final velocity of each disk just after collision.

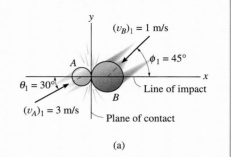

(a)

## Solution

The problem involves *oblique impact*. Why? In order to seek a solution, we have established the $x$ and $y$ axes along the line of impact and the plane of contact, respectively, Fig. 15–18a.

Resolving each of the initial velocities into $x$ and $y$ components, we have

$$(v_{Ax})_1 = 3\cos 30° = 2.60 \text{ m/s} \qquad (v_{Ay})_1 = 3\sin 30° = 1.50 \text{ m/s}$$
$$(v_{Bx})_1 = -1\cos 45° = -0.707 \text{ m/s} \quad (v_{By})_1 = -1\sin 45° = -0.707 \text{ m/s}$$

The four unknown velocity components after collision are assumed to act in the positive directions, Fig. 15–18b. Since the impact occurs only in the $x$ direction (line of impact), the conservation of momentum for *both* disks can be applied in this direction. Why?

(b)

*Conservation of "x" Momentum.* In reference to the momentum diagrams, we have

$$(\overset{+}{\rightarrow}) \qquad m_A(v_{Ax})_1 + m_B(v_{Bx})_1 = m_A(v_{Ax})_2 + m_B(v_{Bx})_2$$
$$1 \text{ kg}(2.60 \text{ m/s}) + 2 \text{ kg}(-0.707 \text{ m/s}) = 1 \text{ kg}(v_{Ax})_2 + 2 \text{ kg}(v_{Bx})_2$$
$$(v_{Ax})_2 + 2(v_{Bx})_2 = 1.18 \qquad (1)$$

*Coefficient of Restitution (x).* Both disks are *assumed* to have components of velocity in the $+x$ direction after collision, Fig. 15–18b.

$$(\overset{+}{\rightarrow}) \qquad e = \frac{(v_{Bx})_2 - (v_{Ax})_2}{(v_{Ax})_1 - (v_{Bx})_1}; \qquad 0.75 = \frac{(v_{Bx})_2 - (v_{Ax})_2}{2.60 \text{ m/s} - (-0.707 \text{ m/s})}$$
$$(v_{Bx})_2 - (v_{Ax})_2 = 2.48 \qquad (2)$$

Solving Eqs. 1 and 2 for $(v_{Ax})_2$ and $(v_{Bx})_2$ yields

$$(v_{Ax})_2 = -1.26 \text{ m/s} = 1.26 \text{ m/s} \leftarrow \qquad (v_{Bx})_2 = 1.22 \text{ m/s} \rightarrow \qquad Ans.$$

*Conservation of "y" Momentum.* The momentum of *each disk* is *conserved* in the $y$ direction (plane of contact), since the disks are smooth and therefore *no* external impulse acts in this direction. From Fig. 15–18b,

$$(+\uparrow) \; m_A(v_{Ay})_1 = m_A(v_{Ay})_2; \qquad (v_{Ay})_2 = 1.50 \text{ m/s}\uparrow \qquad Ans.$$
$$(+\uparrow) \; m_B(v_{By})_1 = m_B(v_{By})_2; \quad (v_{By})_2 = -0.707 \text{ m/s} = 0.707 \text{ m/s}\downarrow \; Ans.$$

Show that when the velocity components are summed, one obtains the results shown in Fig. 15–18c.

(c)

Fig. 15–18

# PROBLEMS

**15-55.** An ivory ball having a mass of 200 g is released from rest at a height of 400 mm above a very large fixed metal surface. If the ball rebounds to a height of 325 mm above the surface, determine the coefficient of restitution between the ball and the surface.

**\*15-56.** Block $A$ has a mass of 3 kg and is sliding on a rough horizontal surface with a velocity $(v_A)_1 = 2$ m/s when it makes a direct collision with block $B$, which has a mass of 2 kg and is originally at rest. If the collision is perfectly elastic $(e = 1)$, determine the velocity of each block just after collision and the distance between the blocks when they stop sliding. The coefficient of kinetic friction between the blocks and the plane is $\mu_k = 0.3$.

Prob. 15–56

**15-57.** Disk $A$ has a mass of 2 kg and is sliding forward on the *smooth* surface with a velocity $(v_A)_1 = 5$ m/s when it strikes the 4-kg disk $B$, which is sliding towards $A$ at $(v_B)_1 = 2$ m/s, with direct central impact. If the coefficient of restitution between the disks is $e = 0.4$, compute the velocities of $A$ and $B$ just after collision.

Prob. 15–57

**15-58.** The three balls each weigh 5 N ($\approx$ 0.5 kg) and have a coefficient of restitution of $e = 0.85$. If ball $A$ is released from rest and strikes ball $B$ and then ball $B$ strikes ball $C$, determine the velocity of each ball after the second collision has occurred. The balls slide without friction.

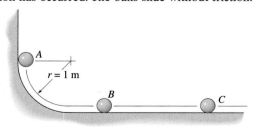

Prob. 15–58

**15-59.** If two disks $A$ and $B$ have the same mass and are subjected to direct central impact such that the collision is perfectly elastic $(e = 1)$, prove that the kinetic energy before collision equals the kinetic energy after collision. The surface upon which they slide is smooth.

**\*15-60.** Each ball has a mass $m$ and the coefficient of restitution between the balls is $e$. If they are moving towards one another with a velocity $v$, determine their speeds after collision. Also, determine their common velocity when they reach the state of maximum deformation. Neglect the size of each ball.

Prob. 15–60

**15-61.** The man $A$ has a weight of 700 N ($\approx$ 70 kg) and jumps from rest $h = 2$ m onto a platform $P$ that has a weight of 240 N ($\approx$ 24 kg). The platform is mounted on a spring, which has a stiffness $k = 3200$ N/m. Determine (a) the velocities of $A$ and $P$ just after impact and (b) the maximum compression imparted to the spring by the impact. Assume the coefficient of restitution between the man and the platform is $e = 0.6$, and the man holds himself rigid during the motion.

**15-62.** The man $A$ has a weight of 400 N ($\approx$ 40 kg) and jumps from rest onto the platform $P$ that has a weight of 240 N ($\approx$ 24 kg). The platform is mounted on a spring, which has a stiffness $k = 3200$ N/m. If the coefficient of restitution between the man and the platform is $e = 0.6$, and the man holds himself rigid during the motion, determine the required height $h$ of the jump if the maximum compression of the spring becomes 0.5 m.

Probs. 15–61/62

**15-63.** The three balls each have the same mass $m$. If $A$ has a speed $v$ just before a direct collision with $B$, determine the speed of $C$ after collision. The coefficient of restitution between each ball is $e$. Neglect the size of each ball.

Prob. 15–63

*15-64.** If the girl throws the ball with a horizontal velocity of 3 m/s, determine the distance $d$ so that the ball bounces once on the smooth surface and then lands in the cup at $C$. Take $e = 0.8$.

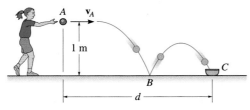

Prob. 15–64

**15-65.** The 1-kg ball is dropped from rest and falls a distance of 2 m before striking the smooth plane at $A$. If $e = 0.8$, determine the distance $d$ to where it again strikes the plane at $B$.

**15-66.** The 1-kg ball is dropped from rest and falls a distance of 2 m before striking the smooth plane at $A$. If it rebounds and in $t = 0.5$ s again strikes the plane at $B$, determine the coefficient of restitution $e$ between the ball and the plane. Also, what is the distance $d$?

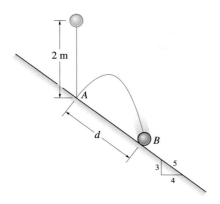

Probs. 15–65/66

**15-67.** The 2-kg ball is thrown at the suspended 20-kg block with a velocity of 4 m/s. If the coefficient of restitution between the ball and the block is $e = 0.8$, determine the maximum height $h$ to which the block will swing before it momentarily stops.

*15-68.** The 2-kg ball is thrown at the suspended 20-kg block with a velocity of 4 m/s. If the time of impact between the ball and the block is 0.005 s, determine the average normal force exerted on the block during this time. Take $e = 0.8$.

Probs. 15–67/68

**15-69.** A ball is thrown onto a rough floor at an angle $\theta$. If it rebounds at an angle $\phi$ and the coefficient of kinetic friction is $\mu$, determine the coefficient of restitution $e$. Neglect the size of the ball. *Hint:* Show that during impact, the average impulses in the $x$ and $y$ directions are related by $I_x = \mu I_y$. Since the time of impact is the same, $F_x \Delta t = \mu F_y \Delta t$ or $F_x = \mu F_y$.

**15-70.** A ball is thrown onto a rough floor at an angle of $\theta = 45°$. If it rebounds at the same angle $\phi = 45°$, determine the coefficient of kinetic friction between the floor and the ball. The coefficient of restitution is $e = 0.6$. *Hint:* Show that during impact, the average impulses in the $x$ and $y$ directions are related by $I_x = \mu I_y$. Since the time of impact is the same, $F_x \Delta t = \mu F_y \Delta t$ or $F_x = \mu F_y$.

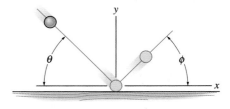

Probs. 15–69/70

**15-71.** Plates $A$ and $B$ each have a mass of 4 kg and are restricted to move along the smooth guides. If the coefficient of restitution between the plates is $e = 0.7$, determine (a) the speed of both plates just after collision and (b) the maximum compression of the spring. Plate $A$ has a velocity of 4 m/s just before striking $B$. Plate $B$ is originally at rest and the spring is unstretched.

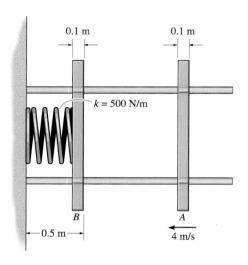

Prob. 15–71

*15-72.** The 4-kg ball is released from rest 3 m from the surface of a flat plate $P$ which has a mass of 3 kg. Determine the maximum compression in the spring if the impact is perfectly elastic.

Prob. 15–72

**15-73.** It was observed that a tennis ball when served horizontally 2.25 m above the ground strikes the smooth ground at $B$ 6 m away. Determine the initial velocity $\mathbf{v}_A$ of the ball and the velocity $\mathbf{v}_B$ (and $\theta$) of the ball just after it strikes the court at $B$. Take $e = 0.7$.

**15-74.** The tennis ball is struck with a horizontal velocity $\mathbf{v}_A$, strikes the smooth ground at $B$, and bounces upward at $\theta = 30°$. Determine the initial velocity $\mathbf{v}_A$, the final velocity $\mathbf{v}_B$, and the coefficient of restitution between the ball and the ground.

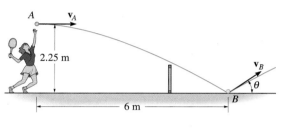

Probs. 15–73/74

**15-75.** The ping-pong ball has a mass of 2 g. If it is struck with the velocity shown, determine how high $h$ it rises above the end of the smooth table after the rebound. Take $e = 0.8$.

Prob. 15–75

**\*15-76.** The ball is ejected from the tube with a horizontal velocity of $v_1 = 3$ m/s as shown. If the coefficient of restitution between the ball and the ground is $e = 0.8$, determine (a) the velocity of the ball just after it rebounds from the ground and (b) the maximum height to which the ball rises after the first bounce.

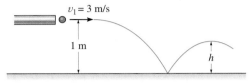

**Prob. 15–76**

**15-77.** The cue ball $A$ is given an initial velocity $(v_A)_1 = 5$ m/s. If it makes a direct collision with ball $B(e = 0.8)$, determine the velocity of $B$ and the angle $\theta$ just after it rebounds from the cushion at $C(e' = 0.6)$. Each ball has a mass of 0.4 kg. Assume the ball slides without rolling.

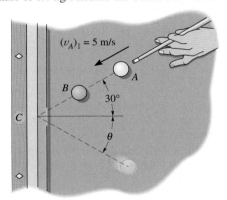

**Prob. 15–77**

**15-78.** The 20-kg box slides on the surface for which $\mu_k = 0.3$. The box has a velocity $v = 7.5$ m/s when it is 1 m from the plate. If it strikes the smooth plate, which has a mass of 10 kg and is held in position by an unstretched spring of stiffness $k = 4000$ N/m, determine the maximum compression imparted to the spring. Take $e = 0.8$ between the box and the plate. Assume that the plate slides smoothly.

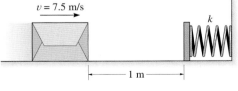

**Prob. 15–78**

**15-79.** The sphere of mass $m$ falls and strikes the triangular block with a vertical velocity $v$. If the block rests on a smooth surface and has a mass $3m$, determine its velocity just after the collision. The coefficient of restitution is $e$.

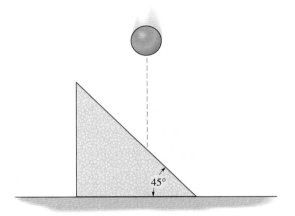

**Prob. 15–79**

**\*15-80.** Block $A$, having a mass $m$, is released from rest, falls a distance $h$ and strikes the plate $B$ having a mass $2m$. If the coefficient of restitution between $A$ and $B$ is $e$, determine the velocity of the plate just after collision. The spring has a stiffness $k$.

**Prob. 15–80**

**15-81.** Before a cranberry can make it to your dinner plate, it must pass a bouncing test which rates its quality. If cranberries having an $e \geq 0.8$ are to be accepted, determine the dimensions $d$ and $h$ for the barrier so that when a cranberry falls from rest at $A$ it strikes the plate at $B$ and bounces over the barrier at $C$.

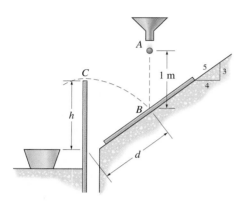

**Prob. 15–81**

**15-82.** If disk $A$ is sliding along the tangent to disk $B$ and strikes $B$ with a velocity $\mathbf{v}$, determine the velocity of $B$ after the collision and compute the loss of kinetic energy during the collision. Neglect friction. Disk $B$ is originally at rest. The coefficient of restitution is $e$, and each disk has the same size and mass $m$.

**15-83.** Two smooth coins $A$ and $B$, each having the same mass, slide on a smooth surface with the motion shown. Determine the speed of each coin after collision if they move off along the dashed paths. *Hint:* Since the line of impact has not been defined, apply the conservation of momentum along the $x$ and $y$ axes, respectively.

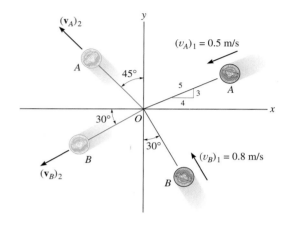

**Prob. 15–83**

**\*15-84.** Two coins $A$ and $B$ have the initial velocities shown just before they collide at point $O$. If they have masses of $M_A = 6.6$ g and $M_B = 3.3$ g and the surface upon which they slide is smooth, determine their speeds just after impact. The coefficient of restitution is $e = 0.65$.

**Prob. 15–82**

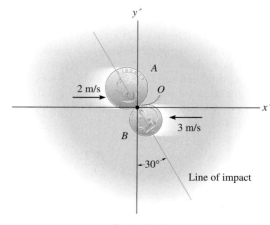

**Prob. 15–84**

**15-85.** Two smooth disks $A$ and $B$ each have a mass of 0.5 kg. If both disks are moving with the velocities shown when they collide, determine their final velocities just after collision. The coefficient of restitution is $e = 0.75$.

**15-86.** Two smooth disks $A$ and $B$ each have a mass of 0.5 kg. If both disks are moving with the velocities shown when they collide, determine the coefficient of restitution between the disks if after collision $B$ travels along a line, 30° counterclockwise from the $y$ axis.

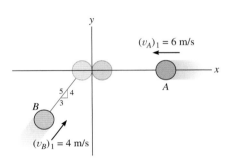

Probs. 15–85/86

**15-87.** Two smooth disks $A$ and $B$ have the initial velocities shown just before they collide at $O$. If they have masses $m_A = 8$ kg and $m_B = 6$ kg, determine their speeds just after impact. The coefficient of restitution is $e = 0.5$.

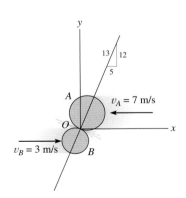

Prob. 15–87

*15-88. The "stone" $A$ used in the sport of curling slides over the ice track and strikes another "stone" $B$ as shown. If each "stone" is smooth and has a mass of 20 kg, and the coefficient of restitution between the "stones" is $e = 0.8$, determine their speeds just after collision. Initially $A$ has a velocity of 3 m/s and $B$ is at rest. Neglect friction.

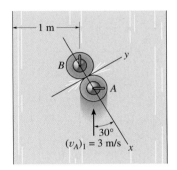

Prob. 15–88

**15-89.** Ball $A$ strikes ball $B$ with an initial velocity of $(\mathbf{v}_A)_1$ as shown. If both balls have the same mass and the collision is perfectly elastic, determine the angle $\theta$ after collision. Ball $B$ is originally at rest. Neglect the size of each ball.

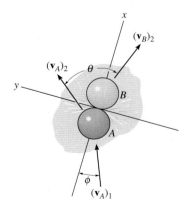

Prob. 15–89

## 15.5 Angular Momentum

The *angular momentum* of a particle about point $O$ is defined as the "moment" of the particle's linear momentum about $O$. Since this concept is analogous to finding the moment of a force about a point, the angular momentum, $\mathbf{H}_O$, is sometimes referred to as the *moment of momentum*.

**Scalar Formulation.** If a particle is moving along a curve lying in the $x$-$y$ plane, Fig. 15–19, the angular momentum at any instant can be determined about point $O$ (actually the $z$ axis) by using a scalar formulation. The *magnitude* of $\mathbf{H}_O$ is

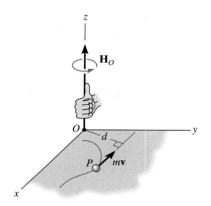

**Fig. 15–19**

$$(H_O)_z = (d)(mv) \tag{15–12}$$

Here $d$ is the moment arm or perpendicular distance from $O$ to the line of action of $m\mathbf{v}$. Common unit for $(H_O)_z$ is $kg \cdot m^2/s$. The *direction* of $\mathbf{H}_O$ is defined by the right-hand rule. As shown, the curl of the fingers of the right hand indicates the sense of rotation of $m\mathbf{v}$ about $O$, so that in this case the thumb (or $\mathbf{H}_O$) is directed perpendicular to the $x$-$y$ plane along the $+z$ axis.

**Vector Formulation.** If the particle is moving along a space curve, Fig. 15–20, the vector cross product can be used to determine the *angular momentum* about $O$. In this case

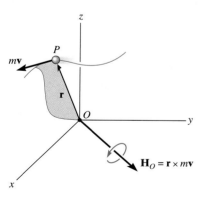

**Fig. 15–20**

$$\mathbf{H}_O = \mathbf{r} \times m\mathbf{v} \tag{15–13}$$

Here $\mathbf{r}$ denotes a position vector drawn from point $O$ to the particle $P$. As shown in the figure, $\mathbf{H}_O$ is *perpendicular* to the shaded plane containing $\mathbf{r}$ and $m\mathbf{v}$.

In order to evaluate the cross product, $\mathbf{r}$ and $m\mathbf{v}$ should be expressed in terms of their Cartesian components, so that the angular momentum is determined by evaluating the determinant:

$$\mathbf{H}_O = \begin{vmatrix} \mathbf{i} & \mathbf{j} & \mathbf{k} \\ r_x & r_y & r_z \\ mv_x & mv_y & mv_z \end{vmatrix} \tag{15–14}$$

## 15.6  Relation Between Moment of a Force and Angular Momentum

The moments about point $O$ of all the forces acting on the particle in Fig. 15–21$a$ may be related to the particle's angular momentum by using the equation of motion. If the mass of the particle is constant, we may write

$$\Sigma\mathbf{F} = m\dot{\mathbf{v}}$$

The moments of the forces about point $O$ can be obtained by performing a cross-product multiplication of each side of this equation by the position vector $\mathbf{r}$, which is measured in the $x$, $y$, $z$ inertial frame of reference. We have

$$\Sigma\mathbf{M}_O = \mathbf{r} \times \Sigma\mathbf{F} = \mathbf{r} \times m\dot{\mathbf{v}}$$

From Appendix C, the derivative of $\mathbf{r} \times m\mathbf{v}$ can be written as

$$\dot{\mathbf{H}}_O = \frac{d}{dt}(\mathbf{r} \times m\mathbf{v}) = \dot{\mathbf{r}} \times m\mathbf{v} + \mathbf{r} \times m\dot{\mathbf{v}}$$

The first term on the right side, $\dot{\mathbf{r}} \times m\mathbf{v} = m(\dot{\mathbf{r}} \times \dot{\mathbf{r}}) = \mathbf{0}$, since the cross product of a vector with itself is zero. Hence, the above equation becomes

$$\boxed{\Sigma\mathbf{M}_O = \dot{\mathbf{H}}_O} \qquad (15\text{–}15)$$

This equation states that *the resultant moment about point $O$ of all the forces acting on the particle is equal to the time rate of change of the particle's angular momentum about point $O$.* This result is similar to Eq. 15–1, i.e.,

$$\boxed{\Sigma\mathbf{F} = \dot{\mathbf{L}}} \qquad (15\text{–}16)$$

Here $\mathbf{L} = m\mathbf{v}$, so *the resultant force acting on the particle is equal to the time rate of change of the particle's linear momentum.*

From the derivations, it is seen that Eqs. 15–15 and 15–16 are actually another way of stating Newton's second law of motion. In other sections of this book it will be shown that these equations have many practical applications when extended and applied to the solution of problems involving either a system of particles or a rigid body.

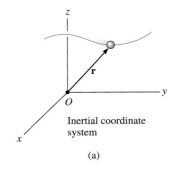

Inertial coordinate system

(a)

Fig. 15–21

**System of Particles.** An equation having the same form as Eq. 15–15 may be derived for the system of particles shown in Fig. 15–21$b$. The forces acting on the arbitrary $i$th particle of the system consist of a resultant *external force* $\mathbf{F}_i$ and a resultant *internal force* $\mathbf{f}_i$. Expressing the moments of these forces about point $O$, using the form of Eq. 15–15, we have

$$(\mathbf{r}_i \times \mathbf{F}_i) + (\mathbf{r}_i \times \mathbf{f}_i) = (\dot{\mathbf{H}}_i)_O$$

Here $\mathbf{r}_i$ is the position vector drawn from the origin $O$ of an inertial frame of reference to the $i$th particle, and $(\dot{\mathbf{H}}_i)_O$ is the time rate of change in the angular momentum of the $i$th particle about $O$. Similar equations can be written for each of the other particles of the system. When the results are summed vectorially, the result is

$$\Sigma(\mathbf{r}_i \times \mathbf{F}_i) + \Sigma(\mathbf{r}_i \times \mathbf{f}_i) = \Sigma(\dot{\mathbf{H}}_i)_O$$

The second term is zero since the internal forces occur in equal but opposite collinear pairs, and hence the moment of each pair about point $O$ is zero. Dropping the index notation, the above equation can be written in a simplified form as

$$\Sigma\mathbf{M}_O = \dot{\mathbf{H}}_O \tag{15–17}$$

which states that *the sum of the moments about point O of all the external forces acting on a system of particles is equal to the time rate of change of the total angular momentum of the system about point O.* Although $O$ has been chosen here as the origin of coordinates, it actually can represent any *fixed point* in the inertial frame of reference.

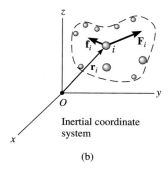

Inertial coordinate
system

(b)

Fig. 15–21

E X A M P L E  **15.12**

The box shown in Fig. 15–22a has a mass $m$ and is traveling down the smooth circular ramp such that when it is at the angle $\theta$ it has a speed $v$. Determine its angular momentum about point $O$ at this instant and the rate of increase in its speed, i.e., $a_t$.

Fig. 15–22

**Solution**

Since $\mathbf{v}$ is tangent to the path, applying Eq. 15–12 the angular momentum is

$$H_O = rmv \downarrow \qquad \qquad Ans.$$

The rate of increase in its speed ($dv/dt$) can be found by applying Eq. 15–15. From the free-body diagram of the block, Fig. 15–22b, it is seen that only the weight $W = mg$ contributes a moment about point $O$. We have

$$\uparrow + \Sigma M_O = \dot{H}_O; \qquad mg(r \sin \theta) = \frac{d}{dt}(rmv)$$

Since $r$ and $m$ are constant,

$$mgr \sin \theta = rm\frac{dv}{dt}$$

$$\frac{dv}{dt} = g \sin \theta \qquad \qquad Ans.$$

This same result can, of course, be obtained from the equation of motion applied in the tangential direction, Fig. 15–22b, i.e.,

$$+\swarrow \Sigma F_t = ma_t; \qquad mg \sin \theta = m\left(\frac{dv}{dt}\right)$$

$$\frac{dv}{dt} = g \sin \theta \qquad \qquad Ans.$$

## 15.7 Angular Impulse and Momentum Principles

**Principle of Angular Impulse and Momentum.** If Eq. 15–15 is rewritten in the form $\Sigma \mathbf{M}_O \, dt = d\mathbf{H}_O$ and integrated, we have, assuming that at time $t = t_1$, $\mathbf{H}_O = (\mathbf{H}_O)_1$ and at time $t = t_2$, $\mathbf{H}_O = (\mathbf{H}_O)_2$,

$$\Sigma \int_{t_1}^{t_2} \mathbf{M}_O \, dt = (\mathbf{H}_O)_2 - (\mathbf{H}_O)_1$$

or

$$(\mathbf{H}_O)_1 + \Sigma \int_{t_1}^{t_2} \mathbf{M}_O \, dt = (\mathbf{H}_O)_2 \qquad (15\text{–}18)$$

This equation is referred to as the *principle of angular impulse and momentum*. The initial and final angular momenta $(\mathbf{H}_O)_1$ and $(\mathbf{H}_O)_2$ are defined as the moment of the linear momentum of the particle $(\mathbf{H}_O = \mathbf{r} \times m\mathbf{v})$ at the instants $t_1$ and $t_2$, respectively. The second term on the left side, $\Sigma \int \mathbf{M}_O \, dt$, is called the *angular impulse*. It is determined by integrating, with respect to time, the moments of all the forces acting on the particle over the time period $t_1$ to $t_2$. Since the moment of a force about point $O$ is $\mathbf{M}_O = \mathbf{r} \times \mathbf{F}$, the angular impulse may be expressed in vector form as

$$\text{angular impulse} = \int_{t_1}^{t_2} \mathbf{M}_O \, dt = \int_{t_1}^{t_2} (\mathbf{r} \times \mathbf{F}) \, dt \qquad (15\text{–}19)$$

Here $\mathbf{r}$ is a position vector which extends from point $O$ to any point on the line of action of $\mathbf{F}$.

In a similar manner, using Eq. 15–18, the principle of angular impulse and momentum for a system of particles may be written as

$$\Sigma(\mathbf{H}_O)_1 + \Sigma \int_{t_1}^{t_2} \mathbf{M}_O \, dt = \Sigma(\mathbf{H}_O)_2 \qquad (15\text{–}20)$$

Here the first and third terms represent the angular momenta of the system of particles $[\Sigma \mathbf{H}_O = \Sigma(\mathbf{r}_i \times m\mathbf{v}_i)]$ at the instants $t_1$ and $t_2$. The second term is the sum of the angular impulses given to all the particles from $t_1$ to $t_2$. Recall that these impulses are created only by the moments of the external forces acting on the system where, for the $i$th particle, $\mathbf{M}_O = \mathbf{r}_i \times \mathbf{F}_i$.

**Vector Formulation.** Using impulse and momentum principles, it is therefore possible to write two equations which define the particle's motion, namely, Eqs. 15–3 and 15–18, restated as

$$m\mathbf{v}_1 + \Sigma \int_{t_1}^{t_2} \mathbf{F}\, dt = m\mathbf{v}_2$$

$$(\mathbf{H}_O)_1 + \Sigma \int_{t_1}^{t_2} \mathbf{M}_O\, dt = (\mathbf{H}_O)_2$$

(15–21)

**Scalar Formulation.** In general, the above equations may be expressed in $x, y, z$ component form, yielding a total of six independent scalar equations. If the particle is confined to move in the $x$–$y$ plane, three independent scalar equations may be written to express the motion, namely,

$$m(v_x)_1 + \Sigma \int_{t_1}^{t_2} F_x\, dt = m(v_x)_2$$

$$m(v_y)_1 + \Sigma \int_{t_1}^{t_2} F_y\, dt = m(v_y)_2$$

$$(H_O)_1 + \Sigma \int_{t_1}^{t_2} M_O\, dt = (H_O)_2$$

(15–22)

The first two of these equations represent the principle of linear impulse and momentum in the $x$ and $y$ directions, which has been discussed in Sec. 15.1, and the third equation represents the principle of angular impulse and momentum about the $z$ axis.

**Fig. 15–23**

Provided air resistance is neglected, the passengers on this amusement-park ride are subjected to a conservation of angular momentum about the axis of rotation. As shown on the free-body diagram, the line of action of the normal force **N** of the seat on the passenger passes through the axis, and the passenger's weight **W** is parallel to it. No angular impulse acts around the z axis.

**Conservation of Angular Momentum.** When the angular impulses acting on a particle are all zero during the time $t_1$ to $t_2$, Eq. 15–18 reduces to the following simplified form:

$$(\mathbf{H}_O)_1 = (\mathbf{H}_O)_2 \qquad (15\text{–}23)$$

This equation is known as the *conservation of angular momentum*. It states that from $t_1$ to $t_2$ the particle's angular momentum remains constant. Obviously, if no external impulse is applied to the particle, both linear and angular momentum will be conserved. In some cases, however, the particle's angular momentum will be conserved and linear momentum may not. An example of this occurs when the particle is subjected *only* to a *central force* (see Sec. 13.7). As shown in Fig. 15–23, the impulsive central force **F** is always directed toward point $O$ as the particle moves along the path. Hence, the angular impulse (moment) created by **F** about the z axis passing through point $O$ is always zero, and therefore angular momentum of the particle is conserved about this axis.

From Eq. 15–20, we can also write the conservation of angular momentum for a system of particles, namely,

$$\Sigma(\mathbf{H}_O)_1 = \Sigma(\mathbf{H}_O)_2 \qquad (15\text{–}24)$$

In this case the summation must include the angular momenta of all particles in the system.

## PROCEDURE FOR ANALYSIS

When applying the principles of angular impulse and momentum, or the conservation of angular momentum, it is suggested that the following procedure be used.

### Free-Body Diagram.

- Draw the particle's free-body diagram in order to determine any axis about which angular momentum may be conserved. For this to occur, the moments of the forces (or impulses) must be parallel or pass through the axis so as to create zero moment throughout the time period $t_1$ to $t_2$.

- The direction and sense of the particle's initial and final velocities should also be established.

- An alternative procedure would be to draw the impulse and momentum diagrams for the particle.

### Momentum Equations.

- Apply the principle of angular impulse and momentum, $(\mathbf{H}_o)_1$ $\Sigma \int_{t_1}^{t_2} \mathbf{M}_O \, dt = (\mathbf{H}_O)_2$, or if appropriate, the conservation of angular momentum, $(\mathbf{H}_O)_1 = (\mathbf{H}_O)_2$.

E X A M P L E  15.13

The 5-kg block of negligible size rests on the smooth horizontal plane, Fig. 15–24a. It is attached at $A$ to a slender rod of negligible mass. The rod is attached to a ball-and-socket joint at $B$. If a moment $M = (3t)$ N·m, where $t$ is in seconds, is applied to the rod and a horizontal force $P = 10$ N is applied to the block, determine the speed of the block in 4 s starting from rest.

Fig. 15–24

Solution

*Free-Body Diagram.* If we consider the system of both the rod and block, Fig. 15–24b, then the resultant force reaction $\mathbf{F}_B$ at the ball-and-socket can be eliminated from the analysis by applying the principle of angular impulse and momentum about the $z$ axis. If this is done, the angular impulses created by the weight and normal reaction $\mathbf{N}_A$ are also eliminated, since they act parallel to the $z$ axis and therefore create zero moment about this axis.

*Principle of Angular Impulse and Momentum.*

$$(H_z)_1 + \Sigma \int_{t_1}^{t_2} M_z \, dt = (H_z)_2$$

$$(H_z)_1 + \int_{t_1}^{t_2} M \, dt + r_{BA}P(\Delta t) = (H_z)_2$$

$$0 + \int_0^4 3t \, dt + (0.4 \text{ m})(10 \text{ N})(4 \text{ s}) = 5 \text{ kg}(v_A)_2 \,(0.4 \text{ m})$$

$$24 + 16 = 2(v_A)_2$$

$$(v_A)_2 = 20 \text{ m/s} \qquad\qquad Ans.$$

**E X A M P L E  15.14**

(a)

(b)

**Fig. 15–25**

The 0.4-kg ball $B$, shown in Fig. 15–25$a$, is attached to a cord which passes through a hole at $A$ in a smooth table. When the ball is $r_1 = 0.5$ m from the hole, it is rotating around in a circle such that its speed is $v_1 = 1.2$ m/s. By applying a force $\mathbf{F}$ the cord is pulled downward through the hole with a constant speed $v_c = 2$ m/s. Determine (a) the speed of the ball at the instant it is $r_2 = 0.2$ m from the hole, and (b) the amount of work done by $\mathbf{F}$ in shortening the radial distance from $r_1$ to $r_2$. Neglect the size of the ball.

**Solution**

*Part (a)  Free-Body Diagram.*  As the ball moves from $r_1$ to $r_2$, Fig. 15–25$b$, the cord force $\mathbf{F}$ on the ball always passes through the $z$ axis, and the weight and $\mathbf{N}_B$ are parallel to it. Hence the moments, or angular impulses created by these forces, are all *zero* about this axis. Therefore, the conservation of angular momentum applies about the $z$ axis.

*Conservation of Angular Momentum.*  The ball's velocity $\mathbf{v}_2$ is resolved into two components. The radial component, 2 m/s, is known; however, it produces zero angular momentum about the $z$ axis. Thus,

$$\mathbf{H}_1 = \mathbf{H}_2$$

$$r_1 m_B v_1 = r_2 m_B v_2'$$

$$(0.5 \text{ m})(0.4 \text{ kg})(1.2 \text{ m/s}) = (0.2 \text{ m})(0.4 \text{ kg})v_2'$$

$$v_2' = 3 \text{ m/s}$$

The speed of the ball is thus

$$v_2 = \sqrt{(3.0)^2 + (2)^2}$$
$$= 3.606 \text{ m/s}$$

*Part (b).*  The only force that does work on the ball is $\mathbf{F}$. (The normal force and weight do not move vertically.) The initial and final kinetic energies of the ball can be determined so that from the principle of work and energy we have

$$T_1 + \Sigma U_{1-2} = T_2$$

$$\frac{1}{2}(0.4 \text{ kg})(1.2 \text{ m/s})^2 + U_F = \frac{1}{2}(0.4 \text{ kg})(3.606 \text{ m/s})^2$$

$$U_F = 2.312 \text{ J} \qquad\qquad Ans.$$

# E X A M P L E 15.15

The 2-kg disk shown in Fig. 15–26a rests on a smooth horizontal surface and is attached to an elastic cord that has a stiffness $k_c = 20$ N/m and is initially unstretched. If the disk is given a velocity $(v_D)_1 = 1.5$ m/s, perpendicular to the cord, determine the rate at which the cord is being stretched and the speed of the disk at the instant the cord is stretched 0.2 m.

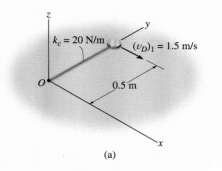

(a)

### Solution

*Free-Body Diagram.* After the disk has been launched, it slides along the path shown in Fig. 15–26b. By inspection, angular momentum about point $O$ (or the $z$ axis) is *conserved*, since none of the forces produce an angular impulse about this axis. Also, when the distance is 0.7 m, only the component $(\mathbf{v}'_D)_2$ produces angular momentum of the disk about $O$.

*Conservation of Angular Momentum.* The component $(\mathbf{v}'_D)_2$ can be obtained by applying the conservation of angular momentum about $O$ (the $z$ axis), i.e.,

$$(\mathbf{H}_O)_1 = (\mathbf{H}_O)_2$$
$$r_1 m_D (v_D)_1 = r_2 m_D (v'_D)_2$$
$$(\uparrow +) \qquad 0.5 \text{ m}(2 \text{ kg})(1.5 \text{ m/s}) = 0.7 \text{ m}(2 \text{ kg})(v'_D)_2$$
$$(v'_D)_2 = 1.07 \text{ m/s}$$

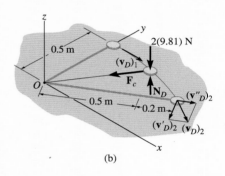

(b)

Fig. 15–26

*Conservation of Energy.* The speed of the disk may be obtained by applying the conservation of energy equation at the point where the disk was launched and at the point where the cord is stretched 0.2 m.

$$T_1 + V_1 = T_2 + V_2$$
$$\tfrac{1}{2}(2 \text{ kg})(1.5 \text{ m/s})^2 + 0 = \tfrac{1}{2}(2 \text{ kg})(v_D)_2^2 + \tfrac{1}{2}(20 \text{ N/m})(0.2 \text{ m})^2$$

Thus,

$$(v_D)_2 = 1.36 \text{ m/s} \qquad \textit{Ans.}$$

Having determined $(v_D)_2$ and its component $(v'_D)_2$, the rate of stretch of the cord $(v''_D)_2$ is determined from the Pythagorean theorem,

$$(v''_D)_2 = \sqrt{(v_D)_2^2 - (v'_D)_2^2}$$
$$= \sqrt{(1.36)^2 - (1.07)^2}$$
$$= 0.838 \text{ m/s} \qquad \textit{Ans.}$$

# PROBLEMS

**15-90.** Determine the angular momentum of the 2-kg particle $A$ about point $O$. Use a Cartesian vector solution.

**\*15-92.** Determine the angular momentum $\mathbf{H}_O$ of each of the particles about point $O$.

**15-93.** Determine the angular momentum $\mathbf{H}_P$ of each of the particles about point $P$.

Prob. 15-90

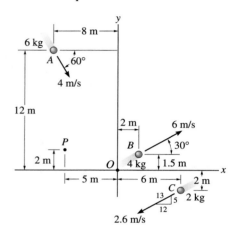

Probs. 15-92/93

**15-91.** Determine the angular momentum $\mathbf{H}_O$ of the particle about point $O$.

**15-94.** Determine the angular momentum $\mathbf{H}_O$ of the particle about point $O$.

**15-95.** Determine the angular momentum $\mathbf{H}_P$ of the particle about point $P$.

Prob. 15-91

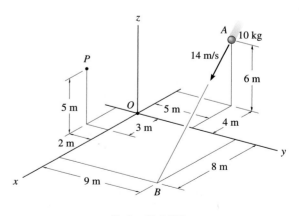

Probs. 15-94/95

**\*15-96.** Determine the total angular momentum $\mathbf{H}_O$ for the system of three particles about point $O$. All the particles are moving in the $x$–$y$ plane.

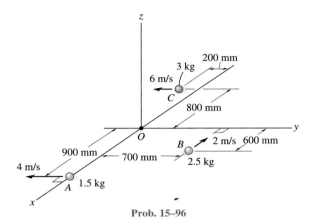

Prob. 15–96

**15-97.** Determine the angular momentum $\mathbf{H}_O$ of each of the two particles about point $O$. Use a scalar solution.

**15-98.** Determine the angular momentum $\mathbf{H}_P$ of each of the two particles about point $P$. Use a scalar solution.

Probs. 15–97/98

**15-99.** The ball $B$ has a mass of 10 kg and is attached to the end of a rod whose mass may be neglected. If the rod is subjected to a torque $M = (3t^2 + 5t + 2)\,\mathrm{N}\cdot\mathrm{m}$, where $t$ is in seconds, determine the speed of the ball when $t = 2$ s. The ball has a speed $v = 2$ m/s when $t = 0$.

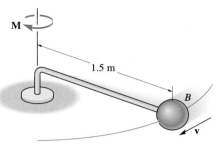

Prob. 15–99

**\*15-100.** The 3-kg ball located at $A$ is released from rest and slides smoothly down the curved path. If the ball exerts a normal force of 50 N on the path when it reaches point $B$, determine the angular momentum of the ball about the center of curvature, point $O$. *Hint:* The radius of curvature at point $B$ must be determined.

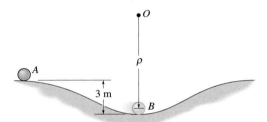

Prob. 15–100

**15-101.** The small cylinder $C$ has a mass of 10 kg and is attached to the end of a rod whose mass may be neglected. If the frame is subjected to a couple $M = (8t^2 + 5)\,\mathrm{N}\cdot\mathrm{m}$, where $t$ is in seconds, and the cylinder is subjected to a force of 60 N, which is always directed as shown, determine the speed of the cylinder when $t = 2$ s. The cylinder has a speed $v_0 = 2$ m/s when $t = 0$.

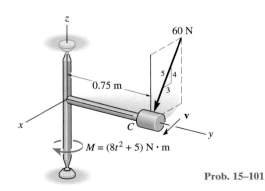

Prob. 15–101

**15-102.** The four 5-kg spheres are rigidly attached to the crossbar frame having a negligible weight. If a couple moment $M = (0.5t + 0.8)$ N · m, where $t$ is in seconds, is applied as shown, determine the speed of each of the spheres in 4 seconds starting from rest. Neglect the size of the spheres.

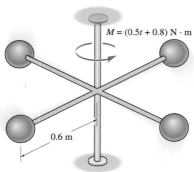

**Prob. 15–102**

**15-103.** An earth satellite of mass 700 kg is launched into a free-flight trajectory about the earth with an initial speed of $v_A = 10$ km/s when the distance from the center of the earth is $r_A = 15$ Mm. If the launch angle at this position is $\phi_A = 70°$, determine the speed $v_B$ of the satellite and its closest distance $r_B$ from the center of the earth. The earth has a mass $M_e = 5.976(10^{24})$ kg. *Hint:* Under these conditions, the satellite is subjected only to the earth's gravitational force, $F = GM_em_s/r^2$, Eq. 13–1. For part of the solution, use the conservation of energy (see Prob. 14–97).

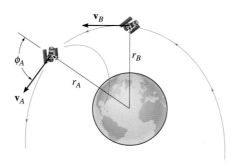

**Prob. 15–103**

*****15-104.** The ball $B$ has a mass of 5 kg and is originally rotating in a circle. As shown, the cord $AB$ has a length of 1.5 m and passes through the hole $A$, which is 1 m above the plane of motion. If 0.75 m of cord is pulled through the hole, determine the speed of the ball when it moves in a circular path at $C$.

**Prob. 15–104**

**15-105.** A 4-kg ball $B$ is traveling around in a circle of radius $r_1 = 1.5$ m with a speed $(v_B)_1 = 3$ m/s. If the attached cord is pulled down through the hole with a constant speed $v_r = 1$ m/s, determine the ball's speed at the instant $r_2 = 1$ m. How much work has to be done to pull down the cord? Neglect friction and the size of the ball.

**15-106.** A 4-kg ball $B$ is traveling around in a circle of radius $r_1 = 1.5$ m with a speed $(v_B)_1 = 3$ m/s. If the attached cord is pulled down through the hole with a constant speed $v_r = 1$ m/s, determine how much time is required for the ball to reach a speed of 6 m/s. How far $r_2$ is the ball from the hole when this occurs? Neglect friction and the size of the ball.

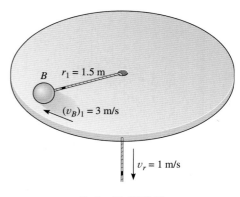

**Probs. 15–105/106**

**15-107.** An amusement park ride consists of a car which is attached to the cable $OA$. The car rotates in a horizontal circular path and is brought to a speed $v_1 = 2$ m/s, when $r = 6$ m. The cable is then pulled in at the constant rate of 0.25 m/s. Determine the speed of the car in 3 s.

**Prob. 15–107**

**15-109.** The 400-kg roller-coaster car starts from rest on the track having the shape of a cylindrical helix. If the helix descends 4 m for every one revolution, determine the speed of the car in $t = 4$ s. Also, how far has the car descended in this time? Neglect friction and the size of the car.

**Prob. 15–109**

**\*15-108.** A child having a mass of 50 kg holds her legs up as shown as she swings downward from rest at $\theta_1 = 30°$. Her center of mass is located at point $G_1$. When she is at the bottom position $\theta = 0°$, she *suddenly* lets her legs come down, shifting her center of mass to position $G_2$. Determine her speed in the upswing due to this sudden movement and the angle $\theta_2$ to which she swings before momentarily coming to rest. Treat the child's body as a particle.

**Prob. 15–108**

**15-110.** A small block having a mass of 0.1 kg is given a horizontal velocity of $v_1 = 0.4$ m/s when $r_1 = 500$ mm. It slides along the smooth conical surface. Determine the distance $h$ it must descend for it to reach a speed of $v_2 = 2$ m/s. Also, what is the angle of descent $\theta$, that is, the angle measured from the horizontal to the tangent of the path?

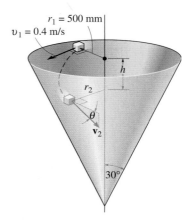

**Prob. 15–110**

## *15.8 Steady Fluid Streams

Knowledge of the forces developed by steadily moving fluid streams is of importance in the design and analysis of turbines, pumps, blades, and fans. To illustrate how the principle of impulse and momentum may be used to determine these forces, consider the diversion of a steady stream of fluid (liquid or gas) by a fixed pipe, Fig. 15–27a. The fluid enters the pipe with a velocity $\mathbf{v}_A$ and exits with a velocity $\mathbf{v}_B$. The impulse and momentum diagrams for the fluid stream are shown in Fig. 15–27b. The force $\Sigma\mathbf{F}$, shown on the impulse diagram, represents the resultant of all the external forces acting on the fluid stream. It is this loading which gives the fluid stream an impulse whereby the original momentum of the fluid is changed in both its magnitude and direction. Since the flow is steady, $\Sigma\mathbf{F}$ will be *constant* during the time interval $dt$. During this time the fluid stream is in motion, and as a result a small amount of fluid, having a mass $dm$, is about to enter the pipe with a velocity $\mathbf{v}_A$ at time $t$. If this element of mass and the mass of fluid in the pipe are considered as a "closed system," then at time $t + dt$ a corresponding element of mass $dm$ must leave the pipe with a velocity $\mathbf{v}_B$. Also, the fluid stream *within* the pipe section has a mass $m$ and an *average velocity* $\mathbf{v}$ which is constant during the time interval $dt$. Applying the principle of linear impulse and momentum to the fluid stream, we have

$$dm\,\mathbf{v}_A + m\mathbf{v} + \Sigma\mathbf{F}\,dt = dm\,\mathbf{v}_B + m\mathbf{v}$$

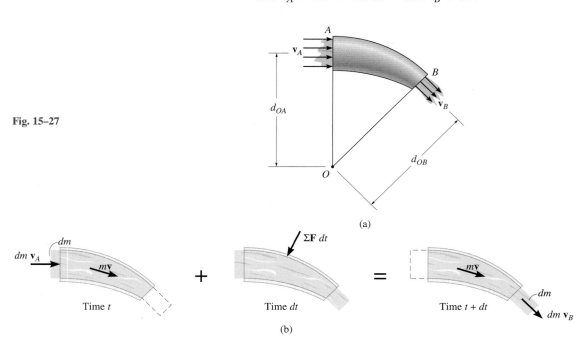

**Fig. 15–27**

(a)

(b)

**Force Resultant.**   Solving for the resultant force yields

$$\Sigma \mathbf{F} = \frac{dm}{dt}(\mathbf{v}_B - \mathbf{v}_A) \qquad (15\text{–}25)$$

Provided the motion of the fluid can be represented in the $x$–$y$ plane, it is usually convenient to express this vector equation in the form of two scalar component equations, i.e.,

$$\Sigma F_x = \frac{dm}{dt}(v_{Bx} - v_{Ax})$$
$$\Sigma F_y = \frac{dm}{dt}(v_{By} - v_{Ay}) \qquad (15\text{–}26)$$

The term $dm/dt$ is called the *mass flow* and indicates the constant amount of fluid which flows either into or out of the pipe per unit of time. If the cross-sectional areas and densities of the fluid at the entrance $A$ and exit $B$ are $A_A$, $\rho_A$ and $A_B$, $\rho_B$, respectively, Fig. 15–27c, then *continuity of mass* requires that $dm = \rho \, dV = \rho_A(ds_A A_A) = \rho_B(ds_B A_B)$. Hence, during the time $dt$, since $v_A = ds_A/dt$ and $v_B = ds_B/dt$, we have

$$\frac{dm}{dt} = \rho_A v_A A_A = \rho_B v_B A_B = \rho_A Q_A = \rho_B Q_B \qquad (15\text{–}27)$$

Here $Q = vA$ is the volumetric *flow rate*, which measures the volume of fluid flowing per unit of time.

(c)

The conveyor belt must supply frictional forces to the gravel that falls upon it in order to change the momentum of the gravel stream, so that it begins to travel along the belt.

The air on one side of this fan is essentially at rest, and as it passes through the blades its momentum is increased. To change the momentum of the air flow in this manner, the blades must exert a horizontal thrust on the air stream. As the blades turn faster, the equal but opposite thrust of the air on the blades could overcome the rolling resistance of the wheels on the ground and begin to move the frame of the fan.

**Moment Resultant.** In some cases it is necessary to obtain the support reactions on the fluid-carrying device. If Eq. 15–25 does not provide enough information to do this, the principle of angular impulse and momentum must be used. The formulation of this principle applied to fluid streams can be obtained from Eq. 15–17, $\Sigma \mathbf{M}_O = \dot{\mathbf{H}}_O$, which states that the moment of all the external forces acting on the system about point $O$ is equal to the time rate of change of angular momentum about $O$. In the case of the pipe shown in Fig. 15–27a, the flow is steady in the $x$–$y$ plane; hence we have

$(\curvearrowleft +)$

$$\Sigma M_O = \frac{dm}{dt}(d_{OB}v_B - d_{OA}v_A) \qquad (15\text{–}28)$$

where the moment arms $d_{OB}$ and $d_{OA}$ are directed from $O$ to the *geometric center* or *centroid* of the openings at $A$ and $B$.

## PROCEDURE FOR ANALYSIS

Problems involving steady flow can be solved using the following procedure.

### Kinematic Diagram.

- If the device is *moving*, a *kinematic diagram* may be helpful for determining the entrance and exit velocities of the fluid flowing onto the device, since a *relative-motion analysis* of velocity will be involved.
- The measurement of velocities $v_A$ and $v_B$ must be made by an observer fixed in an inertial frame of reference.
- Once the velocity of the fluid flowing onto the device is determined, the mass flow is calculated using Eq. 15–27.

### Free-Body Diagram.

- Draw a free-body diagram of the device which is directing the fluid in order to establish the forces $\Sigma \mathbf{F}$ that act on it. These external forces will include the support reactions, the weight of the device and the fluid contained within it, and the static pressure forces of the fluid at the entrance and exit sections of the device.*

### Equations of Steady Flow.

- Apply the equations of steady flow, Eqs. 15–26 and 15–28, using the appropriate components of velocity and force shown on the kinematic and free-body diagrams.

*In the SI system pressure is measured using the *pascal* (Pa), where $1 \text{ Pa} = 1 \text{ N/m}^2$.

# E X A M P L E  15.16

Determine the components of reaction which the fixed pipe joint at $A$ exerts on the elbow in Fig. 15–28a, if water flowing through the pipe is subjected to a static gauge pressure of 100 kPa at $A$. The discharge at $B$ is $Q_B = 0.2$ m$^3$/s. Water has a density $\rho_w = 1000$ kg/m$^3$, and the water-filled elbow has a mass of 20 kg and center of mass at $G$.

(a)

## Solution

Using a fixed inertial coordinate system, the velocity of flow at $A$ and $B$ and the mass flow rate can be obtained from Eq. 15–27. Since the density of water is constant, $Q_B = Q_A = Q$. Hence,

$$\frac{dm}{dt} = \rho_w Q = (1000 \text{ kg/m}^3)(0.2 \text{ m}^3/\text{s}) = 200 \text{ kg/s}$$

$$v_B = \frac{Q}{A_B} = \frac{0.2 \text{ m}^3/\text{s}}{\pi(0.05 \text{ m})^2} = 25.46 \text{ m/s} \downarrow$$

$$v_A = \frac{Q}{A_A} = \frac{0.2 \text{ m}^3/\text{s}}{\pi(0.1 \text{ m})^2} = 6.37 \text{ m/s} \rightarrow$$

*Free-Body Diagram.*   As shown on the free-body diagram, Fig. 15–28b, the *fixed* connection at $A$ exerts a resultant couple moment $\mathbf{M}_O$ and force components $\mathbf{F}_x$ and $\mathbf{F}_y$ on the elbow. Due to the static pressure of water in the pipe, the pressure force acting on the fluid at $A$ is $F_A = p_A A_A$. Since 1 kPa = 1000 N/m$^2$,

$$F_A = p_A A_A = [100(10^3) \text{ N/m}^2][\pi(0.1 \text{ m})^2] = 3141.6 \text{ N}$$

There is no static pressure acting at $B$, since the water is discharged at atmospheric pressure; i.e., the pressure measured by a gauge at $B$ is equal to zero, $p_B = 0$.

(b)

**Fig. 15–28**

*Equations of Steady Flow.*

$$\xrightarrow{+} \Sigma F_x = \frac{dm}{dt}(v_{Bx} - v_{Ax}); \quad -F_x + 3141.6 \text{ N} = 200 \text{ kg/s}(0 - 6.37 \text{ m/s})$$

$$F_x = 4.41 \text{ kN} \qquad\qquad\qquad Ans.$$

$$+\uparrow \Sigma F_y = \frac{dm}{dt}(v_{By} - v_{Ay}); \quad -F_y - 20(9.81) \text{ N} = 200 \text{ kg/s}(-25.46 \text{ m/s} - 0)$$

$$F_y = 4.90 \text{ kN} \qquad\qquad\qquad Ans.$$

If moments are summed about point $O$, Fig. 15–28b, then $\mathbf{F}_x$, $\mathbf{F}_y$, and the static pressure $\mathbf{F}_A$ are eliminated, as well as the moment of momentum of the water entering at $A$, Fig. 15–28a. Hence,

$$\curvearrowleft + \Sigma M_O = \frac{dm}{dt}(d_{OB}v_B - d_{OA}v_A)$$

$$M_O + 20(9.81) \text{ N}(0.125 \text{ m}) = 200 \text{ kg/s}[(0.3 \text{ m})(25.46 \text{ m/s}) - 0]$$

$$M_O = 1.50 \text{ kN} \cdot \text{m} \qquad\qquad Ans.$$

**EXAMPLE 15.17**

(a)

A 50-mm-diameter water jet having a velocity of 7.5 m/s impinges upon a single moving blade, Fig. 15–29a. If the blade is moving at 1.5 m/s away from the jet, determine the horizontal and vertical components of force which the blade is exerting on the water. What power does the water generate on the blade? Water has a specific weight of $\gamma_w = 10 \text{ kN/m}^3$.

**Solution**

*Kinematic Diagram.* From a fixed inertial coordinate system, Fig. 15–29b, the rate at which water enters the blade is

$$\mathbf{v}_A = \{7.5\mathbf{i}\} \text{ m/s}$$

The *relative-flow velocity* of the water onto the blade is $\mathbf{v}_{w/bl} = \mathbf{v}_w - \mathbf{v}_{bl} = 7.5\mathbf{i} - 1.5\mathbf{i} = \{6\mathbf{i}\}$ m/s. Since the blade is moving with a velocity of $\mathbf{v}_{bl} = \{1.5\mathbf{i}\}$ m/s, the velocity of flow at $B$ measured from $x, y$ is the vector sum, shown in Fig. 15–29b. Here,

$$\mathbf{v}_B = \mathbf{v}_{bl} + \mathbf{v}_{w/bl}$$
$$= \{1.5\mathbf{i} + 6\mathbf{j}\} \text{ m/s}$$

Thus, the mass flow of water *onto* the blade that undergoes a momentum change is

$$\frac{dm}{dt} = \rho_w(v_{w/bl})A_A = \frac{10(10^3)}{9.81}\,(6)\left[\pi\left(\frac{25}{1000}\right)^2\right] = 12.0 \text{ kg/s}$$

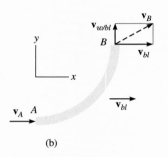

(b)

*Free-Body Diagram.* The free-body diagram of a section of water acting on the blade is shown in Fig. 15–29c. The weight of the water will be neglected in the calculation, since this force will be small compared to the reactive components $\mathbf{F}_x$ and $\mathbf{F}_y$.

*Equations of Steady Flow.*

$$\Sigma \mathbf{F} = \frac{dm}{dt}(\mathbf{v}_B - \mathbf{v}_A)$$

$$-F_x\mathbf{i} + F_y\mathbf{j} = 12.0(1.5\mathbf{i} + 6\mathbf{j} - 7.5\mathbf{i})$$

Equating the respective **i** and **j** components gives

(c)

**Fig. 15–29**

$$F_x = 12.0(6) = 72.0 \text{ N} \leftarrow \qquad Ans.$$
$$F_y = 12.0(6) = 72.0 \text{ N} \uparrow \qquad Ans.$$

The water exerts equal but opposite forces on the blade.

Since the water force which causes the blade to move forward horizontally with a velocity of 1.5 m/s is $F_x = 72.0$ N, then from Eq. 14–10 the power is

$$P = \mathbf{F} \cdot \mathbf{v}; \qquad P = (72.0 \text{ N})(1.5 \text{ m/s}) = 108 \text{ W} \qquad Ans.$$

## *15.9 Propulsion with Variable Mass

In the previous section we considered the case in which a *constant* amount of mass $dm$ enters and leaves a "*closed system.*" There are, however, two other important cases involving mass flow, which are represented by a system that is either gaining or losing mass. In this section we will discuss each of these cases separately.

**A System That Loses Mass.** Consider a device such as a rocket which at an instant of time has a mass $m$ and is moving forward with a velocity $\mathbf{v}$, Fig. 15–30a. At this same instant the device is expelling an amount of mass $m_e$ with a mass flow velocity $\mathbf{v}_e$. For the analysis, the "*closed system*" includes *both the mass m of the device and the expelled mass* $m_e$. The impulse and momentum diagrams for the system are shown in Fig. 15–30b. During the time $dt$, the velocity of the device is increased from $\mathbf{v}$ to $\mathbf{v} + d\mathbf{v}$ since an amount of mass $dm_e$ has been ejected and thereby gained in the exhaust. This increase in forward velocity, however, does not change the velocity $\mathbf{v}_e$ of the expelled mass, since this mass moves at a constant speed once it has been ejected. The impulses are created by $\Sigma\mathbf{F}_s$, which represents the resultant of all the external forces that *act on the system* in the direction of motion. This force resultant *does not include* the force which causes the device to move forward, since this force (called a *thrust*) is *internal to the system*; that is, the thrust acts with equal magnitude but opposite direction on the mass $m$ of the device and the expelled exhaust mass $m_e$.* Applying the principle of impulse and momentum to the system, Fig. 15–30b, we have

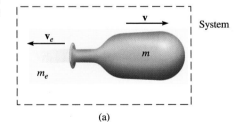

$$(\overset{+}{\rightarrow}) \quad mv - m_e v_e + \Sigma F_s \, dt = (m - dm_e)(v + dv) - (m_e + dm_e)v_e$$

or

$$\Sigma F_s \, dt = -v \, dm_e + m \, dv - dm_e \, dv - v_e \, dm_e$$

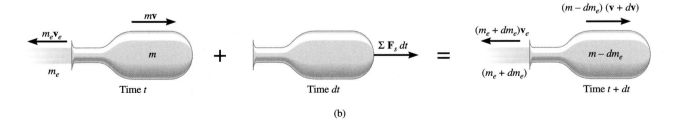

(b)

**Fig. 15–30**

*$\Sigma\mathbf{F}_s$ represents the external resultant force *acting on the system*, which is different from $\Sigma\mathbf{F}$, the resultant force acting only on the device.

Fig. 15–31

Without loss of accuracy, the third term on the right side may be neglected since it is a "second-order" differential. Dividing by $dt$ gives

$$\Sigma F_s = m\frac{dv}{dt} - (v + v_e)\frac{dm_e}{dt}$$

The relative velocity of the device as seen by an observer moving with the particles of the ejected mass is $v_{D/e} = (v + v_e)$, and so the final result can be written as

$$\boxed{\Sigma F_s = m\frac{dv}{dt} - v_{D/e}\frac{dm_e}{dt}} \qquad (15\text{–}29)$$

Here the term $dm_e/dt$ represents the rate at which mass is being ejected.

To illustrate an application of Eq. 15–29, consider the rocket shown in Fig. 15–31, which has a weight $\mathbf{W}$ and is moving upward against an atmospheric drag force $\mathbf{F}_D$. The system to be considered consists of the mass of the rocket and the mass of ejected gas $m_e$. Applying Eq. 15–29 to this system gives

$$(+\uparrow) \qquad -F_D - W = \frac{W}{g}\frac{dv}{dt} - v_{D/e}\frac{dm_e}{dt}$$

The last term of this equation represents the *thrust* $\mathbf{T}$ which the engine exhaust exerts on the rocket, Fig. 15–31. Recognizing that $dv/dt = a$, we may therefore write

$$(+\uparrow) \qquad T - F_D - W = \frac{W}{g}a$$

If a free-body diagram of the rocket is drawn, it becomes obvious that this equation represents an application of $\Sigma\mathbf{F} = m\mathbf{a}$ for the rocket.

**A System That Gains Mass.** A device such as a scoop or a shovel may gain mass as it moves forward. For example, the device shown in Fig. 15–32a has a mass $m$ and is moving forward with a velocity $\mathbf{v}$. At this instant, the device is collecting a particle stream of mass $m_i$. The flow velocity $\mathbf{v}_i$ of this injected mass is constant and independent of the velocity $\mathbf{v}$ such that $v > v_i$. The system to be considered includes both the mass of the device and the mass of the injected particles. The impulse and momentum diagrams for this system are shown in Fig. 15–32b. Along with an increase in mass $dm_i$ gained by the device, there is an assumed increase in velocity $d\mathbf{v}$ during the time interval $dt$. This increase is caused by the impulse created by $\Sigma\mathbf{F}_s$, the resultant of all the external forces *acting on the system* in the direction of motion. The force summation does not

(a)

Fig. 15–32

Time $t$

(b)

Time $t + dt$

include the retarding force of the injected mass acting on the device. Why? Applying the principle of impulse and momentum to the system, we have

$(\xrightarrow{+})$   $mv + m_i v_i + \Sigma F_s \, dt = (m + dm_i)(v + dv) + (m_i - dm_i)v_i$

Using the same procedure as in the previous case, we may write this equation as

$$\Sigma F_s = m\frac{dv}{dt} + (v - v_i)\frac{dm_i}{dt}$$

Since the relative velocity of the device as seen by an observer moving with the particles of the injected mass is $v_{D/i} = (v - v_i)$, the final result can be written as

$$\Sigma F_s = m\frac{dv}{dt} + v_{D/i}\frac{dm_i}{dt} \qquad (15\text{–}30)$$

where $dm_i/dt$ is the rate of mass injected into the device. The last term in this equation represents the magnitude of force **R**, which the injected mass *exerts on the device*. Since $dv/dt = a$, Eq. 15–30 becomes

$$\Sigma F_s - R = ma$$

This is the application of $\Sigma F = ma$, Fig. 15–32c.

As in the case of steady flow, problems which are solved using Eqs. 15–29 and 15–30 should be accompanied by the necessary free-body diagram. With this diagram one can then determine $\Sigma F_s$ *for the system* and isolate the force exerted on the device by the particle stream.

(c)

The scraper box behind this tractor represents a device that gains mass. If the tractor maintains a constant velocity $v$, then $dv/dt = 0$ and, because the soil is originally at rest, $v_{D/i} = v$. By Eq. 15–30, the horizontal towing force on the scraper box is then $T = 0 + v(dm/dt)$, where $dm/dt$ is the rate of soil accumulation in the box.

# E X A M P L E  15.18

System

W

T

**Fig. 15–33**

The initial combined mass of a rocket and its fuel is $m_0$. A total mass $m_f$ of fuel is consumed at a constant rate of $dm_e/dt = c$ and expelled at a constant speed of $u$ relative to the rocket. Determine the maximum velocity of the rocket, i.e., at the instant the fuel runs out. Neglect the change in the rocket's weight with altitude and the drag resistance of the air. The rocket is fired vertically from rest.

**Solution**

Since the rocket is losing mass as it moves upward, Eq. 15–29 can be used for the solution. The only *external force* acting on the *system* consisting of the rocket and a portion of the expelled mass is the weight **W**, Fig. 15–33. Hence,

$$+\uparrow \Sigma F_s = m\frac{dv}{dt} - v_{D/e}\frac{dm_e}{dt}; \qquad -W = m\frac{dv}{dt} - uc \qquad (1)$$

The rocket's velocity is obtained by integrating this equation.

At any given instant $t$ during the flight, the mass of the rocket can be expressed as $m = m_0 - (dm_e/dt)t = m_0 - ct$. Since $W = mg$, Eq. 1 becomes

$$-(m_0 - ct)g = (m_0 - ct)\frac{dv}{dt} - uc$$

Separating the variables and integrating, realizing that $v = 0$ at $t = 0$, we have

$$\int_0^v dv = \int_0^t \left(\frac{uc}{m_0 - ct} - g\right) dt$$

$$v = -u \ln(m_0 - ct) - gt \Big|_0^t = u \ln\left(\frac{m_0}{m_0 - ct}\right) - gt \qquad (2)$$

Note that lift off requires the first term on the right to be greater than the second during the initial phase of motion. The time $t'$ needed to consume all the fuel is given by

$$m_f = \left(\frac{dm_e}{dt}\right)t' = ct'$$

Hence,

$$t' = m_f/c$$

Substituting into Eq. 2 yields

$$v_{\max} = u \ln\left(\frac{m_0}{m_0 - m_f}\right) - \frac{gm_f}{c} \qquad Ans.$$

# EXAMPLE 15.19

A chain of length $l$, Fig. 15–34a, has a mass $m$. Determine the magnitude of force **F** required to (a) raise the chain with a constant speed $v_c$, starting from rest when $y = 0$; and (b) lower the chain with a constant speed $v_c$, starting from rest when $y = l$.

## Solution

*Part (a).* As the chain is raised, all the suspended links are given a sudden impulse downward by each added link which is lifted off the ground. Thus, the *suspended portion* of the chain may be considered as a device which is *gaining mass*. The system to be considered is the length of chain $y$ which is suspended by **F** at any instant, including the next link which is about to be added but is still at rest, Fig. 15–34b. The forces acting on this system *exclude* the internal forces **P** and $-$**P**, which act between the added link and the suspended portion of the chain. Hence, $\Sigma F_s = F - mg(y/l)$.

To apply Eq. 15–30, it is also necessary to find the rate at which mass is being added to the system. The velocity $\mathbf{v}_c$ of the chain is equivalent to $\mathbf{v}_{D/i}$. Why? Since $v_c$ is constant, $dv_c/dt = 0$ and $dy/dt = v_c$. Integrating, using the initial condition that $y = 0$ at $t = 0$, gives $y = v_ct$. Thus, the mass of the system at any instant is $m_s = m(y/l) = m(v_ct/l)$, and therefore the *rate* at which mass is *added* to the suspended chain is

$$\frac{dm_i}{dt} = m\left(\frac{v_c}{l}\right)$$

Applying Eq. 15–30 to the system, using this data, we have

$$+\uparrow \Sigma F_s = m\frac{dv_c}{dt} + v_{D/i}\frac{dm_i}{dt}$$

$$F - mg\left(\frac{y}{l}\right) = 0 + v_cm\left(\frac{v_c}{l}\right)$$

Hence,

$$F = (m/l)(gy + v_c^2) \qquad \text{Ans.}$$

*Part (b).* When the chain is being lowered, the links which are expelled (given zero velocity) *do not* impart an impulse to the *remaining* suspended links. Why? Thus, the system in Part (a) cannot be considered. Instead, the equation of motion will be used to obtain the solution. At time $t$ the portion of chain still off the floor is $y$. The free-body diagram for a suspended portion of the chain is shown in Fig. 15–34c. Thus,

$$+\uparrow \Sigma F = ma; \qquad F - mg\left(\frac{y}{l}\right) = 0$$

$$F = mg\left(\frac{y}{l}\right) \qquad \text{Ans.}$$

(a)

(b)

(c)

Fig. 15–34

# PROBLEMS

**15-111.** The 75-kg fireman is holding a hose which has a nozzle diameter of 2.5 cm and hose diameter of 5 cm. If the velocity of the water at discharge is 20 m/s, determine the resultant normal and frictional force acting on the man's feet at the ground. Neglect the weight of the hose and the water within it. $\gamma_w = 10$ kN/m$^3$.

**Prob. 15–111**

**\*15-112.** A jet of water having a cross-sectional area of 25 cm$^2$ strikes the fixed blade with a speed of 8 m/s. Determine the horizontal and vertical components of force which the blade exerts on the water. $\gamma_w = 10$ kN/m$^3$.

**Prob. 15–112**

**15-113.** Water is flowing from the 150-mm-diameter fire hydrant with a velocity $v_B = 15$ m/s. Determine the horizontal and vertical components of force and the moment developed at the base joint $A$, if the static (gauge) pressure at $A$ is 50 kPa. The diameter of the fire hydrant at $A$ is 200 mm. $\rho_w = 1$ Mg/m$^3$.

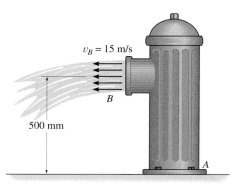

**Prob. 15–113**

**15-114.** The blade divides the jet of water having a diameter of 7.5 cm. If one-fourth of the water flows downward while the other three-fourths flows upwards, and the total flow is $Q = 0.015$ m$^3$/s, determine the horizontal and vertical components of force exerted on the blade by the jet, $\gamma_w = 10$ kN/m$^3$.

**Prob. 15–114**

**15-115.** The fan draws air through a vent with a speed of 4 m/s. If the cross-sectional area of the vent is 0.2 m², determine the horizontal thrust on the blade. The specific weight of the air is $\gamma_a = 12$ N/m³.

**Prob. 15–115**

**\*15-116.** The buckets on the *Pelton wheel* are subjected to a 5-cm-diameter jet of water, which has a velocity of 60 m/s. If each bucket is traveling at 38 m/s when the water strikes it, determine the power developed by the wheel. $\gamma_w = 10$ kN/m³.

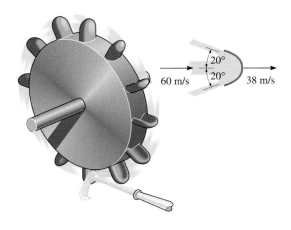

**Prob. 15–116**

**15-117.** The static pressure of water at $C$ is 32 N/cm². If water flows out of the pipe at $A$ and $B$ with velocities $v_A = 3.6$ m/s and $v_B = 7.5$ m/s, determine the horizontal and vertical components of force exerted on the elbow at $C$ necessary to hold the pipe assembly in equilibrium. Neglect the weight of water within the pipe and the weight of the pipe. The pipe has a diameter of 2 cm at $C$, and at $A$ and $B$ the diameter is 1.25 cm. $\gamma_w = 10$ kN/m³.

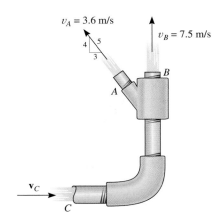

**Prob. 15–117**

**15-118.** The 200-kg boat is powered by the fan which develops a slipstream having a diameter of 0.75 m. If the fan ejects air with a speed of 14 m/s, measured relative to the boat, determine the initial acceleration of the boat if it is initially at rest. Assume that air has a constant density of $\rho_a = 1.22$ kg/m³ and that the entering air is essentially at rest. Neglect the drag resistance of the water.

**Prob. 15–118**

**15-119.** A power lawn mower hovers very close over the ground. This is done by drawing air in at a speed of 6 m/s through an intake unit A, which has a cross-sectional area of $A_A = 0.25$ m², and then discharging it at the ground, B, where the cross-sectional area is $A_B = 0.35$ m². If air at A is subjected only to atmospheric pressure, determine the air pressure which the lawn mower exerts on the ground when the weight of the mower is freely supported and no load is placed on the handle. The mower has a mass of 15 kg with center of mass at G. Assume that air has a constant density of $\rho_a = 1.22$ kg/m³.

Prob. 15–119

*15-120.** The elbow for a 12-cm-diameter buried pipe is subjected to a static pressure of 8 N/cm². The speed of the water passing through it is $v = 4$ m/s. Assuming the pipe connection at A and B do not offer any vertical force resistance on the elbow, determine the resultant vertical force **F** that the soil must then exert on the elbow in order to hold it in equilibrium. Neglect the weight of the elbow and the water within it. $\gamma_w = 10$ kN/m³.

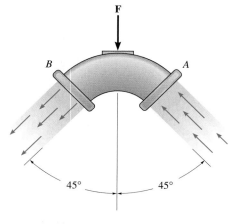

Prob. 15–120

**15-121.** The car is used to scoop up water that is lying in a trough at the tracks. Determine the force needed to pull the car forward at constant velocity **v** for each of the three cases. The scoop has a cross-sectional area A and the density of water is $\rho_w$.

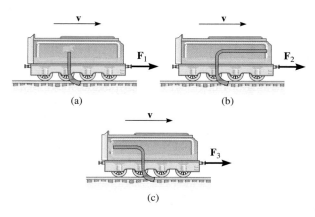

Prob. 15–121

**15-122.** A plow located on the front of a locomotive scoops up snow at the rate of 0.4 m³/s and stores it in the train. If the locomotive is traveling at a constant speed of 4 m/s, determine the resistance to motion caused by the shoveling. The specific weight of snow is $\gamma_s = 1$ kN/m³.

**15-123.** The boat has a mass of 180 kg and is traveling forward on a river with a constant velocity of 70 km/h, measured *relative* to the river. The river is flowing in the opposite direction at 5 km/h. If a tube is placed in the water, as shown, and it collects 40 kg of water in the boat in 80 s, determine the horizontal thrust T on the tube that is required to overcome the resistance to the water collection. $\rho_w = 1$ Mg/m³.

Prob. 15–123

*15-124. The second stage of the two-stage rocket has a mass of 1000 kg (empty) and is launched from the first stage with a velocity of 4800 km/h. The fuel in the second stage has a mass of 500 kg. If it is consumed at the rate of 25 kg/s and ejected with a relative velocity of 2400 m/s, determine the acceleration of the second stage just after the engine is fired. What is the rocket's acceleration just before all the fuel is consumed? Neglect the effect of gravitation.

15-125. The missile has a mass of 20 000 kg. The constant thrust provided by the turbojet engine is $T = 75$ kN. Additional thrust is provided by *two* rocket boosters $B$. The propellant in each booster is burned at a constant rate of 75 kg/s, with a relative exhaust velocity of 1000 m/s. If the mass of the propellant lost by the turbojet engine can be neglected, determine the velocity of the missile after the 4-s burn time of the boosters. The initial velocity of the missile is 480 km/h.

Prob. 15–125

15-126. The earthmover initially carries 10 m³ of sand having a density of 1520 kg/m³. The sand is unloaded horizontally through a 2.5-m² dumping port $P$ at a rate of 900 kg/s measured relative to the port. Determine the resultant tractive force **F** at its front wheels if the acceleration of the earthmover is 0.1 m/s² when half the sand is dumped. When empty, the earthmover has a mass of 30 Mg. Neglect any resistance to forward motion and the mass of the wheels. The rear wheels are free to roll.

Prob. 15–126

15-127. The 10-Mg helicopter carries a bucket containing 500 kg of water, which is used to fight fires. If it hovers over the land in a fixed position and then releases 50 kg/s of water at 10 m/s, measured relative to the helicopter, determine the initial upward acceleration the helicopter experiences as the water is being released.

Prob. 15–127

*15-128. The rocket has a mass of 32 500 kg including the fuel. Determine the constant rate at which the fuel must be burned so that its thrust gives the rocket a speed of 60 m/s in 10 s starting from rest. The fuel is expelled from the rocket at a relative speed of 900 m/s. Neglect the effects of air resistance and assume that $g$ is constant.

Prob. 15–128

**15-129.** The rocket has an initial mass $m_0$, including the fuel. For practical reasons desired for the crew, it is required that it maintain a constant upward acceleration $a_0$. If the fuel is expelled from the rocket at a relative speed $v_{e/r}$ determine the rate at which the fuel should be consumed to maintain the motion. Neglect air resistance, and assume that the gravitational acceleration is constant.

**Prob. 15–129**

**15-130.** The 12-Mg jet airplane has a constant speed of 950 km/h when it is flying along a horizontal straight line. Air enters the intake scoops $S$ at the rate of 50 m³/s. If the engine burns fuel at the rate of 0.4 kg/s and the gas (air and fuel) is exhausted relative to the plane with a speed of 450 m/s, determine the resultant drag force exerted on the plane by air resistance. Assume that air has a constant density of 1.22 kg/m³. *Hint*: Since mass both enters and exits the plane, Eqs. 15–29 and 15–30 must be combined to yield

$$\Sigma F_s = m\frac{dv}{dt} - v_{D/e}\frac{dm_e}{dt} + v_{D/i}\frac{dm_i}{dt}$$

$v = 950$ km/h

**Prob. 15–130**

**15-131.** The jet is traveling at a speed of 800 km/h, 30° with the horizontal. If the fuel is being spent at 1.5 kg/s, and the engine takes in air at 200 kg/s, whereas the exhaust gas (air and fuel) has a relative speed of 9800 m/s, determine the acceleration of the plane at this instant. The drag resistance of the air is $F_D = (40v^2)$ N, where the speed is measured in m/s. The jet has a mass of 7500 kg. *Hint*: See Prob. 15–130.

800 km/h

30°

**Prob. 15–131**

***15-132.** The truck has a mass of 50 Mg when empty. When it is unloading 5 m³ of sand at a constant rate of 0.8 m³/s, the sand flows out the back at a speed of 7 m/s, measured relative to the truck, in the direction shown. If the truck is free to roll, determine its initial acceleration just as the load begins to empty. Neglect the mass of the wheels and any frictional resistance to motion. The density of sand is $\rho_s = 1520$ kg/m³.

a

45°

7 m/s

**Prob. 15–132**

**15-133.** The car has a mass $m_0$ and is used to tow the smooth chain having a total length $l$ and a mass per unit of length $m'$. If the chain is originally piled up, determine the tractive force $F$ that must be supplied by the rear wheels of the car, necessary to maintain a constant speed $v$ while the chain is being drawn out.

**15-134.** Determine the magnitude of force **F** as a function of time, which must be applied to the end of the cord at $A$ to raise the hook $H$ with a constant speed $v = 0.4$ m/s. Initially the chain is at rest on the ground. Neglect the mass of the cord and the hook. The chain has a mass of 2 kg/m.

Prob. 15–133

Prob. 15–134

# DESIGN PROJECT

### 15–1D.  DESIGN OF A CRANBERRY SELECTOR

The quality of a cranberry depends upon its firmness, which in turn is related to its bounce. Through experiment, it is found that berries that bounce to a height of $0.75$ m $\leq h' \leq 0.975$ m when released from rest at a height of $h = 1.2$ m, are appropriate for processing. Using this information, determine the berry's range of the allowable coefficient of restitution, and then design a manner in which good and bad berries can be separated. Submit a drawing of your design, and show calculations as to how the selection and collection of berries is made from your established geometry.

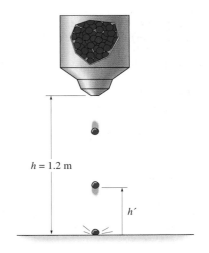

Prob. 15–1D

## CHAPTER REVIEW

- *Impulse.* An impulse that acts on the particle is defined by

$$\mathbf{I} = \int \mathbf{F} \, dt$$

  Graphically this represents the area under the $F$–$t$ diagram. If the force is constant, then the impulse becomes

$$\mathbf{I} = \mathbf{F}_c(t_2 - t_1)$$

- *Principle of Impulse and Momentum.* When the equation of motion, $\Sigma \mathbf{F} = m\mathbf{a}$, and the kinematic equation, $a = dv/dt$, are combined, we obtain the principle of impulse and momentum.

$$m\mathbf{v}_1 + \Sigma \int_{t_1}^{t_2} \mathbf{F} \, dt = m\mathbf{v}_2$$

  Here, the initial momentum of the particle, $m\mathbf{v}_1$, plus all of the impulses that are applied to the particle during the time $t_1$ to $t_2$, $\Sigma \int \mathbf{F} \, dt$, equals the final momentum $m\mathbf{v}_2$ of the particle. This is a vector equation that can be resolved into components and is used to solve problems that involve force, velocity, and time. For application, the free-body diagram should be drawn in order to account for all the impulses that act on the particle.

- *Conservation of Linear Momentum.* If the principle of impulse and momentum is applied to a system of particles, then the collisions between the particles produce internal impulses that are equal, opposite, and collinear, and therefore cancel from the equation. Furthermore, if an external impulse is small, that is, the force is small and the time is short, then the impulse can be classified as nonimpulsive and can be neglected. Consequently, momentum for the system of particles is conserved, and so

$$\Sigma(m\mathbf{v}_i)_1 = \Sigma(m\mathbf{v}_i)_2$$

  This equation is useful for finding the final velocity of a particle when internal impulses are exerted between two particles. If the internal impulse is to be determined, then one of the particles is isolated and the principle of impulse and momentum is applied to this particle.

- *Impact.* When two particles collide ($A$ and $B$), the internal impulse between them is equal, opposite, and collinear. Consequently, the conservation of momentum for this system applies along the line of impact. If the final velocities are unknown, a second equation is needed for solution. Here, we use the coefficient of restitution, $e$. This experimentally determined coefficient depends upon the physical properties of the colliding particles. It can be expressed as the ratio of the relative velocity after collision to the relative velocity before collision

$$e = \frac{(v_B)_2 - (v_A)_2}{(v_A)_1 - (v_B)_1}$$

  If the collision is elastic, no energy is lost and $e = 1$. For a plastic collision $e = 0$.

  If the impact is oblique, then conservation of momentum for the system and the coefficient of restitution equation apply along the line of impact. Also, conservation of momentum for each particle applies perpendicular to this line, because no impulse acts on the particles in this direction.

- *Principle of Angular Impulse and Momentum.* The moment of the linear momentum about an axis $(z)$ is called the angular momentum. Its magnitude is

$$(H_O)_z = (d)(mv)$$

In three dimensions, the cross product is used.

$$\mathbf{H}_O = \mathbf{r} \times m\mathbf{v}$$

The principle of angular impulse and momentum is derived from taking moments of the equation of motion about an inertial axis, using $\mathbf{a} = d\mathbf{v}/dt$. The result is

$$(\mathbf{H}_O)_1 + \Sigma \int_{t_1}^{t_2} \mathbf{M}_O \, dt = (\mathbf{H}_O)_2$$

This equation is often used to eliminate unknown impulses by summing the moments about an axis through which the lines of action of these impulses produce no moment. For this reason, a free-body diagram should accompany the solution.

- *Steady Fluid Streams.* Impulse and momentum methods are often used to determine the forces that a device exerts on the mass flow of a fluid—liquid or gas. To do so, a free-body diagram of the fluid mass in contact with the device is drawn in order to identify these forces. Also, the velocity of the fluid as it flows into and out of of the device is calculated. The equations of steady flow involve summing the forces and the moments to determine these reactions. These equations are

$$\Sigma F_x = \frac{dm}{dt}(v_{Bx} - v_{Ax})$$

$$\Sigma F_y = \frac{dm}{dt}(v_{By} - v_{Ay})$$

$$\Sigma M_O = \frac{dm}{dt}(d_{OB}v_B - d_{OA}v_A)$$

- *Propulsion with Variable Mass.* Some devices, such as a rocket, lose mass as they are propelled forward. Others gain mass, such as a shovel. We can account for this mass loss or gain by applying the principle of impulse and momentum to the device. From this equation, the force exerted on the device by the mass flow can then be determined. For a mass loss, the equation is

$$\Sigma F_s = m\frac{dv}{dt} - v_{D/e}\frac{dm_e}{dt}$$

And for a mass gain, it is

$$\Sigma F_s = m\frac{dv}{dt} + v_{D/i}\frac{dm_i}{dt}$$

# Kinematics and Kinetics of a Particle

The topics and problems pressented in Chapters 12 through 15 have all been *categorized* in order to provide a *clear focus* for learning the various problem-solving principles involved. In engineering practice, however, it is most important to be able to *identify* an appropriate method for the solution of a particular problem. In this regard, one must fully understand the limitations and use of the equations of dynamics, and be able to recognize which equations and principles to use for the problem's soluton. For these reasons, we will now summarize the equations and principles of particle dynamics and provide the opportunity for applying them to a variety of problems.

**Kinematics.** Problems in kinematics require a study only of the geometry of motion, and do not account for the forces causing the motion. When the equations of kinematics are applied, one should clearly establish a fixed origin and select an appropriate coordinate system used to define the position of the particle. Once the positive direction of each coordinate axis is established, then the directions of the components of position, velocity, and acceleration can be determined from the algebraic sign of their numerical quantities.

**Rectilinear Motion.**

*Variable Acceleration.* If a mathematical (or graphical) relationship is established between *any two* of the *four* variables $s$, $v$, $a$, and $t$, then a third variable can be determined by solving one of the following equations which relates all three variables.

$$v = \frac{ds}{dt} \qquad a = \frac{dv}{dt} \qquad a\,ds = v\,dv$$

*Constant Acceleration.* Be *absolutely certain* that the acceleration is constant when using the following equations:

$$s = s_0 + v_0 t + \tfrac{1}{2}a_c t^2 \qquad v = v_0 + a_c t \qquad v^2 = v_0^2 + 2a_c(s - s_0)$$

**Curvilinear Motion.**

*x, y, z Coordinates.* These coordinates are often used when the motion can be resolved into horizontal and vertical components. They are also useful for studying projectile motion since the acceleration of the projectile is *always* downward.

$$v_x = \dot{x} \qquad a_x = \dot{v}_x$$
$$v_y = \dot{y} \qquad a_y = \dot{v}_y$$
$$v_z = \dot{z} \qquad a_z = \dot{v}_z$$

*n, t, b Coordinates.* These coordinates are particularly advantageous for studying the particle's *acceleration* along a known path. This is because the $t$ and $n$ components of **a** represent the separate changes in the magnitude and direction of the velocity, respectively, and these components can be readily formulated.

$$v = \dot{s}$$
$$a_t = \dot{v} = v\frac{dv}{ds}$$
$$a_n = \frac{v^2}{\rho}$$

where

$$\rho = \left| \frac{[1 + (dy/dx)^2]^{3/2}}{d^2y/dx^2} \right|$$

when the path $y = f(x)$ is given.

*r, θ, z Coordinates.* These coordinates are used when data regarding the angular motion of the radial coordinate $r$ is given to describe the particle's motion. Also, some paths of motion can conveniently be described using these coordinates.

$$v_r = \dot{r} \qquad a_r = \ddot{r} - r\dot{\theta}^2$$
$$v_\theta = r\dot{\theta} \qquad a_\theta = r\ddot{\theta} + 2\dot{r}\dot{\theta}$$
$$v_z = \dot{z} \qquad a_z = \ddot{z}$$

**Relative Motion.** If the origin of a *translating* coordinate system is established at particle $A$, then for particle $B$,

$$\mathbf{r}_B = \mathbf{r}_A + \mathbf{r}_{B/A}$$
$$\mathbf{v}_B = \mathbf{v}_A + \mathbf{v}_{B/A}$$
$$\mathbf{a}_B = \mathbf{a}_A + \mathbf{a}_{B/A}$$

Here the relative motion is measured by an observer fixed in the translating coordinate system.

**Kinetics.** Problems in kinetics involve the analysis of forces which cause the motion. When applying the equations of kinetics, it is absolutely necessary that measurements of the motion be made from an *inertial coordinate system*, i.e., one that does not rotate and is either fixed or translates with constant velocity. If a problem requires *simultaneous solution* of the equations of kinetics and kinematics, then it is important that the coordinate systems selected for writing each of the equations define the *positive directions* of the axes in the *same* manner.

**Equations of Motion.** These equations are used to solve for the particle's acceleration or the forces causing the motion. If they are used to determine a particle's position, velocity, or time of motion, then kinematics will also have to be considered in the solution. Before applying the equations of motion, *always draw a free-body diagram* to identify all the forces acting on the particle. Also, establish the direction of the particle's acceleration or its components. (A kinetic diagram may accompany the solution in order to graphically account for the $m\mathbf{a}$ vector.)

$$\Sigma F_x = ma_x \quad \Sigma F_n = ma_n \quad \Sigma F_r = ma_r$$
$$\Sigma F_y = ma_y \quad \Sigma F_t = ma_t \quad \Sigma F_\theta = ma_\theta$$
$$\Sigma F_z = ma_z \quad \Sigma F_b = 0 \quad \Sigma F_z = ma_z$$

**Work and Energy.** The equation of work and energy represents an integrated form of the tangential equation of motion, $\Sigma F_t = ma_t$, combined with kinematics ($a_t \, ds = v \, dv$). It is used to solve problems involving force, velocity, and displacement. Before applying this equation, *always draw a free-body diagram* in order to identify the forces which do work on the particle.

$$T_1 + \Sigma U_{1-2} = T_2$$

where

$$T = \tfrac{1}{2}mv^2 \quad \text{(kinetic energy)}$$

$$U_F = \int_{s_1}^{s_2} F \cos \theta \, ds \quad \text{(work of a variable force)}$$

$$U_{F_c} = F_c \cos \theta \, (s_2 - s_1) \quad \text{(work of a constant force)}$$

$$U_W = -W \, \Delta y \quad \text{(work of a weight)}$$

$$U_s = -(\tfrac{1}{2}ks_2^2 - \tfrac{1}{2}ks_1^2) \quad \text{(work of an elastic spring)}$$

If the forces acting on the particle are *conservative forces*, i.e., those that *do not* cause a dissipation of energy, such as friction, then apply the conservation of energy equation. This equation is easier to use than the equation of work and energy since it applies only at *two points* on the path and *does not* require calculation of the work done by a force as the particle moves along the path.

$$T_1 + V_1 = T_2 + V_2$$

where

$$V_g = Wy \qquad \text{(gravitational potential energy)}$$

$$V_e = \tfrac{1}{2}ks^2 \qquad \text{(elastic potential energy)}$$

If the *power* developed by a force is to be determined, use

$$P = \frac{dU}{dt} = \mathbf{F} \cdot \mathbf{v}$$

where $\mathbf{v}$ is the velocity of a particle acted upon by the force $\mathbf{F}$.

**Impulse and Momentum.** The equation of *linear impulse and momentum* is an integrated form of the equation of motion, $\Sigma\mathbf{F} = m\mathbf{a}$, combined with kinematics ($\mathbf{a} = d\mathbf{v}/dt$). *It is used to solve problems involving force, velocity, and time.* Before applying this equation, one should *always draw the free-body diagram*, in order to identify all the forces that cause impulses on the particle. From the diagram the impulsive and nonimpulsive forces should be identified. Recall that the nonimpulsive forces can be neglected in the analysis during the time of impact. Also, establish the direction of the particle's velocity just before and just after the impulses are applied. As an alternative procedure, impulse and momentum diagrams may accompany the solution in order to graphically account for the terms in the equation.

$$m\mathbf{v}_1 + \Sigma \int_{t_1}^{t_2} \mathbf{F}\, dt = m\mathbf{v}_2$$

If several particles are involved in the problem, consider applying the *conservation of momentum* to the system in order to eliminate the internal impulses from the analysis. This can be done in a specified direction, provided no external impulses act on the particles in that direction.

$$\Sigma m\mathbf{v}_1 = \Sigma m\mathbf{v}_2$$

If the problem involves impact and the coefficient of restitution $e$ is given, then apply the following equation.

$$e = \frac{(v_B)_2 - (v_A)_2}{(v_A)_1 - (v_B)_1} \qquad \text{(along line of impact)}$$

Remember that during impact the principle of work and energy cannot be used, since the particles deform and therefore the work due to the internal forces will be unknown. The principle of work and energy can be used, however, to determine the energy loss during the collision once the particle's initial and final velocities are determined.

The *principle of angular impulse and momentum* and the *conservation of angular momentum* may be applied about an axis in order to *eliminate* some of the unknown impulses acting on the particle during the time period when its motion is studied. Investigation of the particle's free-body diagram (or the impulse diagram) will aid in choosing the axis for application.

$$(\mathbf{H}_O)_1 + \Sigma \int_{t_1}^{t_2} \mathbf{M}_O \, dt = (\mathbf{H}_O)_2$$

$$(\mathbf{H}_O)_1 = (\mathbf{H}_O)_2$$

The following problems provide an opportunity for applying the above concepts. They are presented in *random order* so that practice may be gained in identifying the various types of problems and developing the skills necessary for their solution.

# REVIEW PROBLEMS

**R1-1.** A sports car can accelerate at 6 m/s² and decelerate at 8 m/s². If the maximum speed it can attain is 60 m/s, determine the shortest time it takes to travel 900 m starting from rest and then stopping when s = 900 m.

**R1-2.** A 2-kg particle rests on a smooth horizontal plane and is acted upon by forces $F_x = 0$ and $F_y = 3$ N. If $x = 0$, $y = 0$, $v_x = 6$ m/s, and $v_y = 2$ m/s when $t = 0$, determine the equation $y = f(x)$ which describes the path.

**R1-3.** Determine the velocity of each block 2 s after the blocks are released from rest. Neglect the mass of the pulleys and cord.

A | 10 kg   B | 50 kg

Prob. R1–3

**\*R1-4.** To test the manufactured properties of 2-kg steel balls, each ball is released from rest as shown and strikes a 45° inclined surface. If the coefficient of restitution is to be e = 0.8, determine the distance s to where the ball must strike the horizontal plane at A. At what speed does the ball strike A?

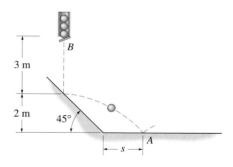

Prob. R1–4

**R1-5.** The 450-N force is required to drag the 1-kN ($\approx$ 100-kg) block 24 m up the *rough* inclined plane at constant velocity. If the force is removed when the block reaches point $B$, and the block is then released from rest, determine the block's velocity when it slides back down the plane and reaches point $A$.

Prob. R1–5

**R1-6.** The motor at $C$ pulls in the cable with an acceleration $a_c = (3t^2)$ m/s$^2$, where $t$ is in seconds. The motor at $D$ draws in its cable at $a_D = 5$ m/s$^2$. If both motors start at the same instant from rest when $d = 3$ m, determine (a) the time needed for $d = 0$, and (b) the relative velocity of block $A$ with respect to block $B$ when this occurs.

Prob. R1–6

**R1-7.** A spring having a stiffness of 5 kN/m is compressed 400 mm. The stored energy in the spring is used to drive a machine which requires 80 W of power. Determine how long the spring can supply energy at the required rate.

*R1-8.** The baggage truck $A$ has a mass of 800 kg annd is used to pull each of the 300-kg cars. Determine the tension in the couplings at $B$ and $C$ if the tractive force $\mathbf{F}$ on the truck is $F = 480$ N. What is the speed of the truck when $t = 2$ s, starting from the rest? The car wheels are free to roll. Neglect the mass of the wheels.

Prob. R1–8

**R1-9.** The baggage truck $A$ has a mass of 800 kg and is used to pull each of the 300-kg cars. If the tractive force $\mathbf{F}$ on the truck is $F = 480$ N, determine the initial acceleration of the truck. What is the acceleration of the truck if the coupling at $C$ suddenly fails? The car wheels are free to roll. Neglect the mass of the wheels.

Prob. R1–9

**R1-10.** A 2-kg particle rests on a smooth horizontal plane and is acted upon by forces $F_x = (8x)$ N, where $x$ is in meters, and $F_y = 0$. If $x = 0$, $y = 0$, $v_x = 4$ m/s, and $v_y = 6$ m/s when $t = 0$, determine the equation $y = f(x)$ which describes the path.

**R1-11.** Determine the speed of block $B$ if the end of the cable at $C$ is pulled downward with a speed of 3 m/s. What is the relative velocity of the block with respect to $C$.

**Prob. R1–11**

*■**R1-12.** Packages having a mass of 2.5 kg ride on the surface of the conveyor belt. If the belt starts from rest and with constant acceleration increases to a speed of 0.75 m/s in 2 s, determine the maximum angle of tilt, $\theta$, so that none of the packages slip on the inclined surface $AB$ of the belt. The coefficient of static friction between the belt and each package is $\mu_s = 0.3$. At what angle $\phi$ do the packages first begin to slip off the surface of the belt if the belt is moving at a constant speed of 0.75 m/s?

**Prob. R1–12**

**R1-13.** A projectile, initially at the origin, moves along a straight-line path through a fluid medium such that its velocity is $v = 1800(1 - e^{-0.3t})$ mm/s, where $t$ is in seconds. Determine the displacement of the projectile during the first 3 s.

**R1-14.** The speed of a train during the first minute of its motion has been recorded as follows:

| $t$ (s) | 0 | 20 | 40 | 60 |
|---|---|---|---|---|
| $v$ (m/s) | 0 | 16 | 21 | 24 |

Plot the $v$–$t$ graph, approximating the curve as straight line segments between the given points. Determine the total distance traveled.

**R1-15.** A train car, having a mass of 25 Mg, travels up a 10° incline with a constant speed of 80 km/h. Determine the power required to overcome the force of gravity.

*∗**R1-16.** The slotted arm $AB$ drives the pin $C$ through the spiral groove described by the equation $r = (1.5\theta)$ m, where $\theta$ is in radians. If the arm starts from rest when $\theta = 60°$ and is driven at an angular rate of $\dot{\theta} = (4t)$ rad/s, where $t$ is in seconds, determine the radial and transverse components of velocity and acceleration of the pin when $t = 1$ s.

**Prob. R1–16**

**R1-17.** The chain has a mass of 3 kg/m. If the coefficient of kinetic friction between the chain and the plane is $\mu_k = 0.2$, determine the velocity at which the end $A$ will pass point $B$ when the chain is released from rest.

Prob. R1–17

**R1-18.** The 30-N ($\approx$ 3-kg) ball is fired from a tube by a spring having a stiffness $k = 40$ N/cm. Determine how far the spring must be compressed to fire the ball from the compressed position to a height of 4 m, at which point it has a velocity of 3 m/s.

Prob. R1–18

**R1-19.** The collar of negligible size has a mass of 0.25 kg and is attached to a spring having an unstretched length of 100 mm. If the collar is released from rest at $A$ and travels along the smooth guide, determine its speed just before it strikes $B$.

Prob. R1–19

**\*R1-20.** A crate has a weight of 7.5 kN ($\approx$ 750 kg). If it is pulled along the ground at a constant speed for a distance of 10 m, and the towing cable makes an angle of 15° with the horizontal, determine the tension in the cable and the work done by the towing force. The coefficient of kinetic friction between the crate and the ground is $\mu_k = 0.55$.

**R1-21.** Disk $A$ has a mass of 2 kg and is sliding on a smooth horizontal plane with a velocity of 3 m/s. Disk $B$ has a mass of 11 kg and is initially at rest. If after the impact $A$ has a velocity of 1 m/s directed along the positive $x$ axis, determine the velocity of $B$ after impact. How much kinetic energy is lost in the collision?

Prob. R1–21

**R1-22.** A particle is moving along a circular path of 2-m radius such that its position as a function of time is given by $\theta = (5t^2)$ rad, where $t$ is in seconds. Determine the magnitude of the particle's acceleration when $\theta = 30°$. The particle starts from rest when $\theta = 0°$.

**R1-23.** If the end of the cable at $A$ is pulled down with a speed of 2 m/s, determine the speed at which block $B$ rises.

**R1-26.** The 20-kg block $B$ rests on the surface of a table for which the coefficient of kinetic friction is $\mu_k = 0.1$. Determine the speed of the 10-kg block $A$ after it has moved downward 1 m from rest. Neglect the mass of the pulleys and cords.

Prob. R1–26

Prob. R1–23

**\*R1-24.** A rifle has a mass of 2.5 kg. If it is loosely gripped and a 1.5-g bullet is fired from it with a horizontal muzzle velocity of 1400 m/s, determine the recoil velocity of the rifle just after firing.

**R1-25.** The drinking fountain is designed such that the nozzle is located from the edge of the basin as shown. Determine the maximum and minimum speed at which water can be ejected from the nozzle so that it does not splash over the sides of the basin at $B$ and $C$.

**R1-27.** The 2-kg ball, attached to the cord, is struck by the boy. Determine the smallest speed he must impart to the ball so that it will swing around in a vertical circle, without causing the cord to become slack.

Prob. R1–25

Prob. R1–27

**\*R1-28.** Two winding drum $D$ is drawing in the cable at an accelerated rate of $5\,\text{m/s}^2$. Determine the cable tension if the suspended crate has a mass of 800 kg.

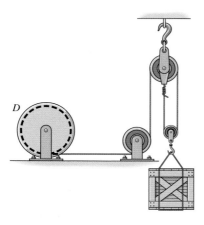

**Prob. R1–28**

**R1-29.** The particle $P$ travels with a constant speed of 300 mm/s along the curve. Determine its acceleration when it is located at point (200 mm, 100 mm).

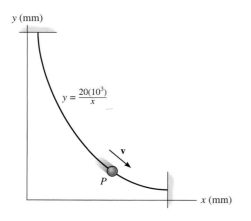

**Prob. R1–29**

**R1-30.** The block has a mass of 0.5 kg and moves within the smooth vertical slot. If the block starts from rest when the *attached* spring is in the unstretched position at $A$, determine the *constant* vertical force $F$ which must be applied to the cord so that the block attains a speed $v_B = 2.5$ m/s when it reaches $B$; $s_B = 0.15$ m. Neglect the mass of the cord and pulley.

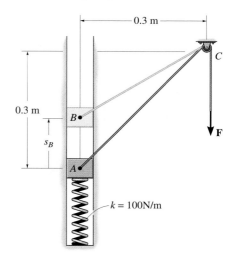

**Prob. R1–30**

**R1-31.** The rocket sled has a mass of 4 Mg and travels from rest along the smooth horizontal track such that it maintains a constant power output of 450 kW. Neglect the loss of fuel mass and air resistance, and determine how far it must travel to reach a speed of $v = 60$ m/s.

**Prob. R1–31**

**\*R1-32.** The spool, which has a mass of 4 kg, slides along the rotating rod. At the instant shown, the angular rate of rotation of the rod is $\dot{\theta} = 6$ rad/s and this rotation is increasing at $\ddot{\theta} = 2$ rad/s². At this same instant, the spool has a velocity of 3 m/s and an acceleration of 1 m/s², both measured relative to the rod and directed away from the center $O$ when $r = 0.5$ m. Determine the radial frictional force and the normal force, both exerted by the rod on the spool at this instant.

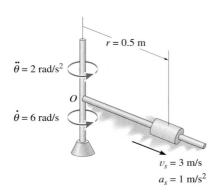

**Prob. R1–32**

**R1-33.** A skier starts from rest at $A$ (10 m, 0) and descends the smooth slope, which may be approximated by a parabola. If she has a weight of 600 N ($\approx 60$ kg), determine the normal force she exerts on the ground at the instant she arrives at point $B$.

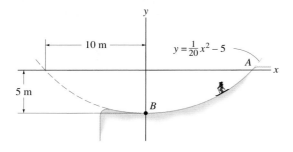

**Prob. R1–33**

**R1-34.** The small 2-kg collar starting from rest at $A$ slides down along the smooth rod. During the motion, the collar is acted upon by a force $F = \{10\mathbf{i} + 6y\mathbf{j} + 2z\mathbf{k}\}$ N, where $x$, $y$, $z$ are in meters. Determine the collar's speed when it strikes the wall at $B$.

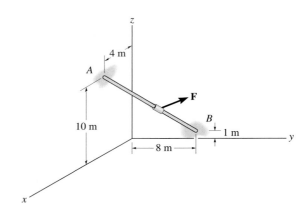

**Prob. R1–34**

**R1-35.** A ball having a mass of 200 g is released from rest at a height of 400 mm above a very large fixed metal surface. If the ball rebounds to a height of 325 mm above the surface, determine the coefficient of restitution between the ball and the surface.

**\*R1-36.** Packages having a mass of 6 kg slide down a smooth chute and land horizontally with a speed of 3 m/s on the surface of a conveyor belt. If the coefficient of kinetic friction between the belt and a package is $\mu_k = 0.2$, determine the time needed to bring the package to rest on the belt if the belt is moving in the same direction as the package with a speed $v = 1$ m/s.

**Prob. R1–36**

**R1-37.** The blocks $A$ and $B$ has masses of 10 kg and 30 kg, respectively. They are connected together by a light cord and ride in the frictionless grooves. Determine the speed of each block after block $A$ moves 3 m up along the plane. The blocks are released from rest.

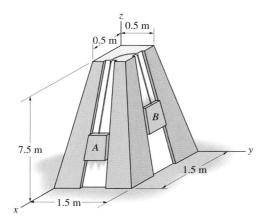

**Prob. R1–37**

**R1-38.** The motor $M$ pulls in its attached rope with an acceleration $a_p = 6$ m/s$^2$. Determine the towing force exerted by $M$ on the rope in order to move the 50-kg crate up the inclined plane. The coefficient of kinetic friction between the crate and the plane is $\mu_k = 0.3$. Neglect the mass of the pulleys and rope.

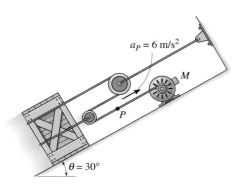

**Prob. R1–38**

**R1-39.** If a particle has an initial velocity $v_0 = 12$ m/s to the right, and a constant acceleration of 2 m/s$^2$ to the left, determine the particle's displacement in 10 s. Originally $s_0 = 0$.

*****R1-40.** A 3-kg block, initially at rest at point $A$, slides along the smooth parabolic surface. Determine the normal force acting on the block when it reaches $B$. Neglect the size of the block.

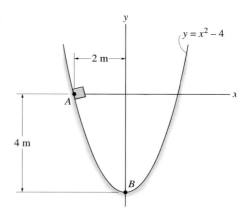

**Prob. R1–40**

**R1-41.** At a given instant the 10-kg block $A$ is moving downward with a speed of 2 m/s. Determine its speed 2 s later. Block $B$ has a mass of 4 kg, and the coefficient of kinetic friction between it and the horizontal plane is $\mu_k = 0.2$. Neglect the mass of the pulleys and cord.

**Prob. R1–41**

**R1-42.** A freight train starts from rest and travels with a constant acceleration of 0.5 m/s². After a time $t'$ it maintains a constant speed so that when $t = 160$ s it has traveled 2000 m. Determine the time $t'$ and draw the $v$–$t$ graph for the motion.

**R1-43.** The crate, having a weight of 500 N ($\approx$ 50 kg), is hoisted by the pulley system and motor $M$. If the crate starts from rest and, by constant acceleration, attains a speed of 6 m/s after rising 5 m, determine the power that must be supplied to the motor at the instant s = 5 m. The motor has an efficiency $\epsilon = 0.74$.

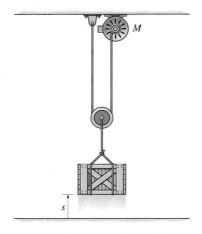

**Prob. R1–43**

**\*R1-44.** An automobile is traveling with a *constant speed* along a horizontal circular curve that has a radius $\rho = 225$ m. If the magnitude of acceleration is $a = 2.4$ m/s², determine the speed at which the automobile is traveling.

**R1-45.** Block $B$ rests on a smooth surface. If the coefficients of friction between $A$ and $B$ are $\mu_s = 0.4$ and $\mu_k = 0.3$, determine the acceleration of each block if (a) $F = 60$ N, and (b)$F = 500$ N.

**Prob. R1–45**

**R1-46.** The 100-kg crate is subjected to the action of two forces, $F_1 = 800$ N and $F_2 = 1.5$ kN, as shown. If it is originally at rest, determine the distance it slides in order to attain a speed of 6 m/s. The coefficient of kinetic friction between the crate and the surface is $\mu_k = 0.2$.

**Prob. R1–46**

**R1-47.** A 20-kg block is originally at rest on a horizontal surface for which the coefficient of static friction is $\mu_s = 0.6$ and the coefficient of kinetic friction is $\mu_k = 0.5$. If a horizontal force $F$ is applied such that it varies with time as shown, determine the speed of the block in 10 s. *Hint:* First determine the time needed to overcome friction and start the block moving.

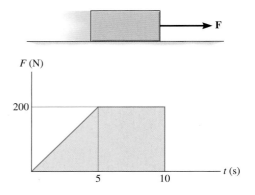

**Prob. R1–47**

**\*R1-48.** Two smooth billiard balls $A$ and $B$ have an equal mass of $m = 200$ g. If $A$ strikes $B$ with a velocity of $(v_A)_1 = 2$ m/s as shown, determine their final velocities just after collision. Ball $B$ is originally at rest and the coefficient of restitution is $e = 0.75$.

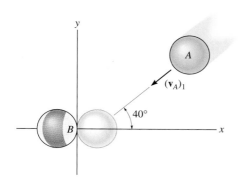

Prob. R1–48

**R1-49.** If a 75-kg crate is released from rest at $A$, determine its speed after it slides 10 m down the plane. The coefficient of kinetic friction between the crate and plane is $\mu_k = 0.3$.

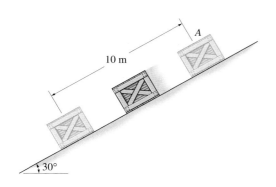

Prob. R1–49

**R1-50.** Determine the tension developed in the two cords and the acceleration of each block. Neglect the mass of the pulleys and cords. *Hint:* Since the system consists of *two* cords, relate the motion of block $A$ to $C$, and of block $B$ to $C$. Then, by elimination, relate the motion of $A$ to $B$.

Prob. R1–50

**R1-51.** The bottle rests at a distance of 1.5 m from the center of the horizontal platform. If the coefficient of static friction between the bottle and the platform is $\mu_s = 0.3$, determine the maximum speed that the bottle can attain before slipping. Assume the angular motion of the platform is slowly increasing.

**\*R1-52.** Work Prob. R1–51 assuming that the platform starts rotating from rest so that the speed of the bottle is increased at 1 m/s².

Probs. R1–51/R1–52

The wind turbine rotates about a fixed axis with variable angular motion.

# Planar Kinematics of a Rigid Body

- To classify the various types of rigid-body planar motion.
- To investigate rigid-body translation and show how to analyze motion about a fixed axis.
- To study planar motion using an absolute motion analysis.
- To provide a relative motion analysis of velocity and acceleration using a translating frame of reference.
- To show how to find the instantaneous center of zero velocity and determine the velocity of a point on a body using this method.
- To provide a relative motion analysis of velocity and acceleration using a rotating frame of reference.

## 16.1   Rigid-Body Motion

In this chapter, the planar kinematics of a rigid body will be discussed. This study is important for the design of gears, cams, and mechanisms used for many mechanical operations. Furthermore, once the kinematics of a rigid body is thoroughly understood, then it will be possible to apply the equations of motion, which relate the forces on the body to the body's motion.

When all the particles of a rigid body move along paths which are equidistant from a fixed plane, the body is said to undergo *planar motion*. There are three types of rigid body planar motion: in order of increasing complexity, they are

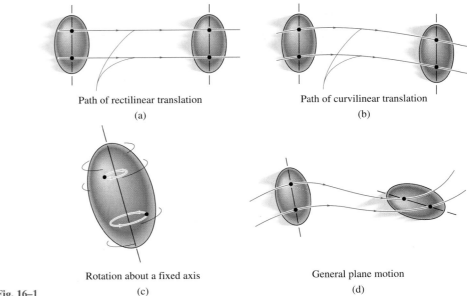

Path of rectilinear translation

(a)

Path of curvilinear translation

(b)

Rotation about a fixed axis

(c)

General plane motion

(d)

**Fig. 16–1**

1. *Translation.* This type of motion occurs if every line segment on the body remains parallel to its original direction during the motion. When the paths of motion for any two particles of the body are along equidistant straight lines the motion is called *rectilinear translation*, Fig. 16–1a. However, if the paths of motion are along curved lines which are equidistant the motion is called *curvilinear translation*, Fig. 16–1b.

2. *Rotation about a fixed axis.* When a rigid body rotates about a fixed axis, all the particles of the body, except those which lie on the axis of rotation, move along circular paths, Fig. 16–1c.

3. *General plane motion.* When a body is subjected to general plane motion, it undergoes a combination of translation *and* rotation, Fig. 16–1d. The translation occurs within a reference plane, and the rotation occurs about an axis perpendicular to the reference plane.

In the following sections we will consider each of these motions in detail. Examples of bodies undergoing these motions are shown in Fig. 16–2.

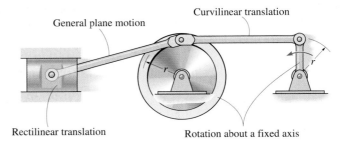

General plane motion

Curvilinear translation

Rectilinear translation

Rotation about a fixed axis

**Fig. 16–2**

## 16.2 Translation

Consider a rigid body which is subjected to either rectilinear or curvilinear translation in the $x$–$y$ plane, Fig. 16–3.

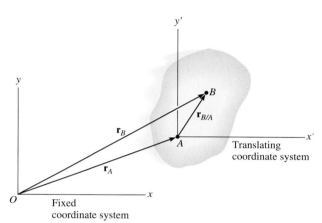

Fig. 16–3

**Position.** The locations of points $A$ and $B$ in the body are defined from the fixed $x$, $y$ reference frame by using *position vectors* $\mathbf{r}_A$ and $\mathbf{r}_B$. The translating $x'$, $y'$ coordinate system is *fixed in the body* and has its origin located at $A$, hereafter referred to as the *base point*. The position of $B$ with respect to $A$ is denoted by the *relative-position vector* $\mathbf{r}_{B/A}$ ("$\mathbf{r}$ of $B$ with respect to $A$"). By vector addition,

$$\mathbf{r}_B = \mathbf{r}_A + \mathbf{r}_{B/A}$$

**Velocity.** A relationship between the instantaneous velocities of $A$ and $B$ is obtained by taking the time derivative of the position equation, which yields $\mathbf{v}_B = \mathbf{v}_A + d\mathbf{r}_{B/A}/dt$. Here $\mathbf{v}_A$ and $\mathbf{v}_B$ denote *absolute velocities* since these vectors are measured from the $x$, $y$ axes. The term $d\mathbf{r}_{B/A}/dt = \mathbf{0}$, since the *magnitude* of $\mathbf{r}_{B/A}$ is *constant* by definition of a rigid body, and because the body is translating the *direction* of $\mathbf{r}_{B/A}$ is *constant*. Therefore,

$$\mathbf{v}_B = \mathbf{v}_A$$

**Acceleration.** Taking the time derivative of the velocity equation yields a similar relationship between the instantaneous accelerations of $A$ and $B$:

$$\mathbf{a}_B = \mathbf{a}_A$$

The above two equations indicate that *all points in a rigid body subjected to either rectilinear or curvilinear translation move with the same velocity and acceleration*. As a result, the kinematics of particle motion, discussed in Chapter 12, may also be used to specify the kinematics of points located in a translating rigid body.

Passengers on this amusement ride are subjected to curvilinear translation since the vehicle moves in a circular path yet it always remains in an upright position.

## 16.3 Rotation About a Fixed Axis

When a body is rotating about a fixed axis, any point $P$ located in the body travels along a *circular path*. To study this motion it is first necessary to discuss the angular motion of the body about the axis.

**Angular Motion.** A point is without dimension, and so it has no angular motion. *Only lines or bodies undergo angular motion.* For example, consider the body shown in Fig. 16–4a and the angular motion of a radial line $r$ located within the shaded plane and directed from point $O$ on the axis of rotation to point $P$.

**Angular Position.** At the instant shown, the *angular position* of $r$ is defined by the angle $\theta$, measured between a *fixed* reference line and $r$.

**Angular Displacement.** The change in the angular position, which can be measured as a differential $d\theta$, is called the *angular displacement*.* This vector has a *magnitude* of $d\theta$, measured in degrees, radians, or revolutions, where 1 rev $= 2\pi$ rad. Since motion is about a *fixed axis*, the direction of $d\theta$ is *always* along the axis. Specifically, the *direction* is determined by the right-hand rule; that is, the fingers of the right hand are curled with the sense of rotation, so that in this case the thumb, or $d\theta$, points upward, Fig. 16–4a. In two dimensions, as shown by the top view of the shaded plane, Fig. 16–4b, both $\theta$ and $d\theta$ are directed counterclockwise, and so the thumb points outward from the page.

**Angular Velocity.** The time rate of change in the angular position is called the *angular velocity* $\boldsymbol{\omega}$ (omega). Since $d\theta$ occurs during an instant of time $dt$, then,

$(\curvearrowright+)$
$$\omega = \frac{d\theta}{dt} \qquad (16\text{--}1)$$

This vector has a *magnitude* which is often measured in rad/s. It is expressed here in scalar form since its *direction* is always along the axis of rotation, i.e., in the same direction as $d\theta$, Fig. 16–4a. When indicating the angular motion in the shaded plane, Fig. 16–4b, we can refer to the sense of rotation as clockwise or counterclockwise. Here we have *arbitrarily* chosen counterclockwise rotations as *positive* and indicated this by the curl shown in parentheses next to Eq. 16–1. Realize, however, that the directional sense of $\boldsymbol{\omega}$ is actually outward from the page.

(a)

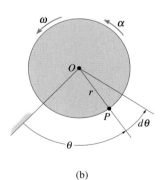

(b)

**Fig. 16–4**

---

*It is shown in Sec. 20.1 that finite rotations or finite angular displacements are *not* vector quantities, although differential rotations $d\theta$ are vectors.

**Angular Acceleration.**  The *angular acceleration* $\boldsymbol{\alpha}$ (alpha) measures the time rate of change of the angular velocity. The *magnitude* of this vector may be written as

$(\zeta+)$

$$\alpha = \frac{d\omega}{dt}$$

(16–2)

Using Eq. 16–1, it is possible to express $\alpha$ as

$(\zeta+)$

$$\alpha = \frac{d^2\theta}{dt^2}$$

(16–3)

The line of action of $\boldsymbol{\alpha}$ is the same as that for $\boldsymbol{\omega}$, Fig. 16–4a; however, its sense of *direction* depends on whether $\boldsymbol{\omega}$ is increasing or decreasing. In particular, if $\boldsymbol{\omega}$ is decreasing, then $\boldsymbol{\alpha}$ is called an *angular deceleration* and it therefore has a sense of direction which is opposite to $\boldsymbol{\omega}$.

By eliminating $dt$ from Eqs. 16–1 and 16–2, we obtain a differential relation between the angular acceleration, angular velocity, and angular displacement, namely,

$(\zeta+)$

$$\alpha \, d\theta = \omega \, d\omega$$

(16–4)

The similarity between the differential relations for angular motion and those developed for rectilinear motion of a particle ($v = ds/dt$, $a = dv/dt$, and $a \, ds = v \, dv$) should be apparent.

**Constant Angular Acceleration.**  If the angular acceleration of the body is constant, $\boldsymbol{\alpha} = \alpha_c$, then Eqs. 16–1, 16–2, and 16–4, when integrated, yield a set of formulas which relate the body's angular velocity, angular position, and time. These equations are similar to Eqs. 12–4 to 12–6 used for rectilinear motion. The results are

$(\zeta+)$
$(\zeta+)$
$(\zeta+)$

$$\omega = \omega_0 + \alpha_c t$$

(16–5)

$$\theta = \theta_0 + \omega_0 t + \tfrac{1}{2}\alpha_c t^2$$

(16–6)

$$\omega^2 = \omega_0^2 + 2\alpha_c(\theta - \theta_0)$$

(16–7)

Constant Angular Acceleration

Here $\theta_0$ and $\omega_0$ are the initial values of the body's angular position and angular velocity, respectively.

(c)

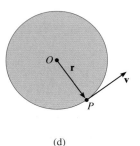

(d)

**Fig. 16–4**

**Motion of Point P.**  As the rigid body in Fig. 16–4c rotates, point $P$ travels along a *circular path* of radius $r$ and center at point $O$. This path is contained within the shaded plane shown in top view, Fig. 16–4d.

**Position.**  The position of $P$ is defined by the position vector $\mathbf{r}$, which extends from $O$ to $P$.

**Velocity.**  The velocity of $P$ has a magnitude which can be found from its polar coordinate components $v_r = \dot{r}$ and $v_\theta = r\dot{\theta}$, Eqs. 12–25. Since $r$ is constant, the radial component $v_r = \dot{r} = 0$, and so $v = v_\theta = r\dot{\theta}$. Because $\omega = \dot{\theta}$, Eq. 16–1, the velocity is

$$v = \omega r \tag{16–8}$$

As shown in Figs. 16–4c and 16–4d, the *direction* of $\mathbf{v}$ is *tangent* to the circular path.

Both the magnitude and direction of $\mathbf{v}$ can also be accounted for by using the cross product of $\boldsymbol{\omega}$ and $\mathbf{r}_P$ (see Appendix C). Here, $\mathbf{r}_P$ is directed from *any point* on the axis of rotation to point $P$, Fig. 16–4c. We have

$$\mathbf{v} = \boldsymbol{\omega} \times \mathbf{r}_P \tag{16–9}$$

The order of the vectors in this formulation is important, since the cross product is not commutative, i.e., $\boldsymbol{\omega} \times \mathbf{r}_P \neq \mathbf{r}_P \times \boldsymbol{\omega}$. In this regard, notice in Fig. 16–4c how the correct direction of $\mathbf{v}$ is established by the right-hand rule. The fingers of the right hand are curled from $\boldsymbol{\omega}$ toward $\mathbf{r}_P$ ($\boldsymbol{\omega}$ "cross" $\mathbf{r}_P$). The thumb indicates the correct direction of $\mathbf{v}$, which is tangent to the path in the direction of motion. From Eq. C–8, the magnitude of $\mathbf{v}$ in Eq. 16–9 is $v = \omega r_P \sin \phi$, and since $r = r_P \sin \phi$, Fig. 16–4c, then $v = \omega r$, which agrees with Eq. 16–8. As a special case, the position vector $\mathbf{r}$ can be chosen for $\mathbf{r}_P$. Here $\mathbf{r}$ lies in the plane of motion and again the velocity of point $P$ is

$$\mathbf{v} = \boldsymbol{\omega} \times \mathbf{r} \tag{16–10}$$

**Acceleration.** The acceleration of $P$ can be expressed in terms of its normal and tangential components.* Since $a_t = dv/dt$ and $a_n = v^2/\rho$, where $\rho = r$, $v = \omega r$, and $\alpha = d\omega/dt$, we have

$$a_t = \alpha r \tag{16–11}$$

$$a_n = \omega^2 r \tag{16–12}$$

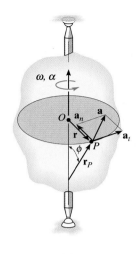

The *tangential component of acceleration*, Figs. 16–4e and 16–4f, represents the time rate of change in the velocity's magnitude. If the speed of $P$ is increasing, then $\mathbf{a}_t$ acts in the same direction as $\mathbf{v}$; if the speed is decreasing, $\mathbf{a}_t$ acts in the opposite direction of $\mathbf{v}$; and finally, if the speed is constant, $\mathbf{a}_t$ is zero.

The *normal component of acceleration* represents the time rate of change in the velocity's direction. The *direction* of $\mathbf{a}_n$ is always toward $O$, the center of the circular path, Figs. 16–4e and 16–4f.

Like the velocity, the acceleration of point $P$ may be expressed in terms of the vector cross product. Taking the time derivative of Eq. 16–9 we have

$$\mathbf{a} = \frac{d\mathbf{v}}{dt} = \frac{d\boldsymbol{\omega}}{dt} \times \mathbf{r}_P + \boldsymbol{\omega} \times \frac{d\mathbf{r}_P}{dt}$$

Recalling that $\boldsymbol{\alpha} = d\boldsymbol{\omega}/dt$, and using Eq. 16–9 ($d\mathbf{r}_P/dt = \mathbf{v} = \boldsymbol{\omega} \times \mathbf{r}_P$), yields

$$\mathbf{a} = \boldsymbol{\alpha} \times \mathbf{r}_P + \boldsymbol{\omega} \times (\boldsymbol{\omega} \times \mathbf{r}_P) \tag{16–13}$$

(e)

From the definition of the cross product, the first term on the right has a magnitude $a_t = \alpha r_P \sin \phi = \alpha r$, and by the right-hand rule, $\boldsymbol{\alpha} \times \mathbf{r}_P$ is in the direction of $\mathbf{a}_t$, Fig. 16–4e. Likewise, the second term has a magnitude $a_n = \omega^2 r_P \sin \phi = \omega^2 r$, and applying the right-hand rule twice, first to determine the result $\mathbf{v}_P = \boldsymbol{\omega} \times \mathbf{r}_P$ then $\boldsymbol{\omega} \times \mathbf{v}_P$, it can be seen that this result is in the same direction as $\mathbf{a}_n$, shown in Fig. 16–4e. Noting that this is also the *same* direction as $-\mathbf{r}$, which lies in the plane of motion, we can express $\mathbf{a}_n$ in a much simpler form as $\mathbf{a}_n = -\omega^2 \mathbf{r}$. Hence, Eq. 16–12 can be identified by its two components as

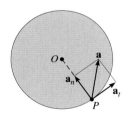

(f)

**Fig. 16–4**

$$\mathbf{a} = \mathbf{a}_t + \mathbf{a}_n$$
$$= \boldsymbol{\alpha} \times \mathbf{r} - \omega^2 \mathbf{r} \tag{16–14}$$

Since $\mathbf{a}_t$ and $\mathbf{a}_n$ are perpendicular to one another, if needed the magnitude of acceleration can be determined from the Pythagorean theorem; namely, $a = \sqrt{a_n^2 + a_t^2}$, Fig. 16–4f.

---

*Polar coordinates can also be used. Since $a_r = \ddot{r} - r\dot{\theta}^2$ and $a_\theta = r\ddot{\theta} + 2\dot{r}\dot{\theta}$, substituting $\dot{r} = \ddot{r} = 0$, $\dot{\theta} = \omega$, $\ddot{\theta} = \alpha$, we obtain Eqs. 16–11 and 16–12.

The many gears used in the operation of a crane all rotate about fixed axes. Engineers must be able to relate their angular motions in order to properly design this gear system.

## IMPORTANT POINTS

- A body can undergo two types of translation. During rectilinear translation all points follow parallel straight-line paths, and during curvilinear translation the points follow curved paths that are the same shape and are equidistant from one another.

- All the points on a translating body move with the same velocity and acceleration.

- Points located on a body that rotates about a fixed axis follow circular paths.

- The relationship $\alpha \, d\theta = \omega \, d\omega$ is derived from $\alpha = d\omega/dt$ and $\omega = d\theta/dt$ by eliminating $dt$.

- Once the angular motions $\omega$ and $\alpha$ are known, the velocity and acceleration of any point on the body can be determined.

- The velocity always acts tangent to the path of motion.

- The acceleration has two components. The tangential acceleration measures the rate of change in the magnitude of the velocity and can be determined using $a_t = \alpha r$. The normal acceleration measures the rate of change in the direction of the velocity and can be determined from $a_n = \omega^2 r$.

# PROCEDURE FOR ANALYSIS

The velocity and acceleration of a point located on a rigid body that is rotating about a fixed axis can be determined using the following procedure.

## *Angular Motion.*

- Establish the positive sense of direction along the axis of rotation and show it alongside each kinematic equation as it is applied.

- If a relationship is known between any *two* of the four variables $\alpha$, $\omega$, $\theta$, and $t$, then a third variable can be obtained by using one of the following kinematic equations which relates all three variables.

$$\omega = \frac{d\theta}{dt} \quad \alpha = \frac{d\omega}{dt} \quad \alpha\, d\theta = \omega\, d\omega$$

- If the body's angular acceleration is *constant*, then the following equations can be used:

$$\omega = \omega_0 + \alpha_c t$$
$$\theta = \theta_0 + \omega_0 t + \tfrac{1}{2}\alpha_c t^2$$
$$\omega^2 = \omega_0^2 + 2\alpha_c(\theta - \theta_0)$$

- Once the solution is obtained, the sense of $\theta$, $\omega$, and $\alpha$ is determined from the algebraic signs of their numerical quantities.

## *Motion of P.*

- In most cases the velocity of $P$ and its two components of acceleration can be determined from the scalar equations

$$v = \omega r$$
$$a_t = \alpha r$$
$$a_n = \omega^2 r$$

- If the geometry of the problem is difficult to visualize, the following vector equations should be used:

$$\mathbf{v} = \boldsymbol{\omega} \times \mathbf{r}_P = \boldsymbol{\omega} \times \mathbf{r}$$
$$\mathbf{a}_t = \boldsymbol{\alpha} \times \mathbf{r}_P = \boldsymbol{\alpha} \times \mathbf{r}$$
$$\mathbf{a}_n = \boldsymbol{\omega} \times (\boldsymbol{\omega} \times \mathbf{r}_P) = -\omega^2 \mathbf{r}$$

Here $\mathbf{r}_P$ is directed from any point on the axis of rotation to point $P$, whereas $\mathbf{r}$ lies in the plane of motion of $P$. Either of these vectors, along with $\boldsymbol{\omega}$ and $\boldsymbol{\alpha}$, should be expressed in terms of its $\mathbf{i}$, $\mathbf{j}$, $\mathbf{k}$ components, and, if necessary, the cross products determined by using a determinant expansion (see Eq. C–12).

E X A M P L E 16.1

Fig. 16–5

A cord is wrapped around a wheel which is initially at rest as shown in Fig. 16–5. If a force is applied to the cord and gives it an acceleration $a = (4t)$ m/s$^2$, where $t$ is in seconds, determine as a function of time (a) the angular velocity of the wheel, and (b) the angular position of line $OP$ in radians.

**Solution**

*Part (a).* The wheel is subjected to rotation about a fixed axis passing through point $O$. Thus, point $P$ on the wheel has motion about a circular path, and the acceleration of this point has *both* tangential and normal components. The tangential component is $(a_P)_t = (4t)$ m/s$^2$, since the cord is wrapped around the wheel and moves *tangent* to it. Hence the angular acceleration of the wheel is

$(\curvearrowright+)$
$$(a_P)_t = \alpha r$$
$$(4t) \text{ m/s}^2 = \alpha(0.2 \text{ m})$$
$$\alpha = 20t \text{ rad/s}^2 \downarrow$$

Using this result, the wheel's angular velocity $\omega$ can now be determined from $\alpha = d\omega/dt$, since this equation relates $\alpha$, $t$, and $\omega$. Integrating, with the initial condition that $\omega = 0$ at $t = 0$, yields

$(\curvearrowright+)$
$$\alpha = \frac{d\omega}{dt} = (20t) \text{ rad/s}^2$$
$$\int_0^\omega d\omega = \int_0^t 20t \, dt$$
$$\omega = 10t^2 \text{ rad/s} \downarrow \qquad \qquad Ans.$$

Why not use Eq. 16–5 ($\omega = \omega_0 + \alpha_c t$) to obtain this result?

*Part (b).* Using this result, the angular position $\theta$ of $OP$ can be found from $\omega = d\theta/dt$, since this equation relates $\theta$, $\omega$, and $t$. Integrating, with the initial condition $\theta = 0$ at $t = 0$, we have

$(\curvearrowright+)$
$$\frac{d\theta}{dt} = \omega = (10t^2) \text{ rad/s}$$
$$\int_0^\theta d\theta = \int_0^t 10t^2 \, dt$$
$$\theta = 3.33t^3 \text{ rad} \qquad \qquad Ans.$$

# EXAMPLE 16.2

The motor shown in the photo is used to turn a wheel and attached blower contained within the housing. The details of the design are shown in Fig. 16–6a. If the pulley $A$ connected to the motor begins rotating from rest with an angular acceleration of $\alpha_A = 2 \text{ rad/s}^2$, determine the magnitudes of the velocity and acceleration of point $P$ on the wheel, after the wheel $B$ has turned one revolution. Assume the transmission belt does not slip on the pulley and wheel.

**Solution**

*Angular Motion.*   First we will convert the one revolution to radians. Since there are $2\pi$ rad in one revolution, then

$$\theta_B = 1 \text{ rev} \left( \frac{2\pi \text{ rad}}{1 \text{ rev}} \right) = 6.283 \text{ rad}$$

We can find the angular velocity of pulley $A$ provided we first find its angular displacement. Since the belt does not slip, an equivalent length of belt $s$ must be unraveled from both the pulley and wheel at all times. Thus,

$$s = \theta_A r_A = \theta_B r_B; \qquad \theta_A(0.15 \text{ m}) = 6.283(0.4 \text{ m})$$
$$\theta_A = 16.76 \text{ rad}$$

Since $\alpha_A$ is constant, the angular velocity of pulley $A$ is therefore

$$(\curvearrowright +) \qquad \omega^2 = \omega_0^2 + 2\alpha_c(\theta - \theta_0)$$
$$\omega_A^2 = 0 + 2(2 \text{ rad/s}^2)(16.76 \text{ rad} - 0)$$
$$\omega_A = 8.188 \text{ rad/s}$$

The belt has the same speed and tangential component of acceleration as it passes over the pulley and wheel. Thus,

$$v = \omega_A r_A = \omega_B r_B; \qquad 8.188 \text{ rad/s}(0.15 \text{ m}) = \omega_B(0.4 \text{ m})$$
$$\omega_B = 3.070 \text{ rad/s}$$

$$a_t = \alpha_A r_A = \alpha_B r_B; \qquad 2 \text{ rad/s}^2(0.15 \text{ m}) = \alpha_B(0.4 \text{ m})$$
$$\alpha_B = 0.750 \text{ rad/s}^2$$

*Motion of P.*   As shown on the kinematic diagram in Fig. 16–6b, we have

$$v_P = \omega_B r_B = 3.070 \text{ rad/s}(0.4 \text{ m}) = 1.23 \text{ m/s} \qquad Ans.$$
$$(a_P)_t = \alpha_B r_B = 0.750 \text{ rad/s}^2(0.4 \text{ m}) = 0.3 \text{ m/s}^2$$
$$(a_P)_n = \omega_B^2 r_B = (3.070 \text{ rad/s})^2(0.4 \text{ m}) = 3.77 \text{ m/s}^2$$

Thus

$$a_P = \sqrt{(0.3)^2 + (3.77)^2} = 3.78 \text{ m/s}^2 \qquad Ans.$$

0.15 m
$A$     $\alpha_A = 2 \text{ rad/s}^2$

0.4 m

$B$

$P$

(a)

$\mathbf{a}_P$

$(\mathbf{a}_P)_n$

$(\mathbf{a}_P)_t$     $P$

$\mathbf{v}_P$

(b)

**Fig. 16–6**

# PROBLEMS

**16-1.** A wheel has an initial clockwise angular velocity of 10 rad/s and a constant angular acceleration of 3 rad/s². Determine the number of revolutions it must undergo to acquire a clockwise angular velocity of 15 rad/s. What time is required?

**16-2.** A flywheel has its angular speed increased uniformly from 15 rad/s to 60 rad/s in 80 s. If the diameter of the wheel is 0.6 m, determine the magnitudes of the normal and tangential components of acceleration of a point on the rim of the wheel when $t = 80$ s, and the total distance the point travels during the time period.

**16-3.** The angular velocity of the disk is defined by $\omega = (5t^2 + 2)$ rad/s, where $t$ is in seconds. Determine the magnitudes of the velocity and acceleration of point $A$ on the disk when $t = 0.5$ s.

**Prob. 16-3**

**\*16-4.** Just after the fan is turned on, the motor gives the blade an angular acceleration $\alpha = (20e^{-0.6t})$ rad/s², where $t$ is in seconds. Determine the speed of the tip $P$ of one of the blades when $t = 3$ s. How many revolutions has the blade turned in 3 s? When $t = 0$ the blade is at rest.

**Prob. 16-4**

**16-5.** Due to an increase in power, the motor $M$ rotates the shaft $A$ with an angular acceleration of $\alpha = (0.06\theta^2)$ rad/s², where $\theta$ is in radians. If the shaft is initially turning at $\omega_0 = 50$ rad/s, determine the angular velocity of gear $B$ after the shaft undergoes an angular displacement $\Delta\theta = 10$ rev.

**Prob. 16-5**

**16-6.** The hook moves from rest with an acceleration of 10 m/s². If it is attached to a cord which is wound around the drum, determine the angular acceleration of the drum and its angular velocity after the drum has completed 10 rev. How many more revolutions will the drum turn after it has first completed 10 rev and the hook continues to move downward for 4 s?

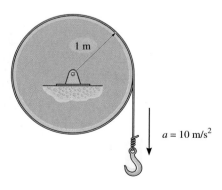

**Prob. 16-6**

**16-7.** The disk is driven by a motor such that the angular position of the disk is defined by $\theta = (20t + 4t^2)$ rad, where $t$ is in seconds. Determine the number of revolutions, the angular velocity, and angular acceleration of the disk when $t = 90$ s.

0.5 m

$\theta$

Prob. 16–7

**16-9.** The motor $M$ begins rotating at an angular rate of $\omega = 4(1 - e^{-t})$ rad/s, where $t$ is in seconds. If the pulleys and fan have the radii shown, determine the magnitudes of the velocity and acceleration of point $P$ on the fan blade when $t = 0.5$ s. Also, what is the maximum speed of this point?

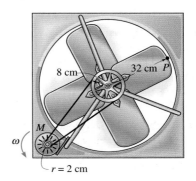

8 cm

32 cm  $P$

$M$

$\omega$

$r = 2$ cm

Prob. 16–9

***16-8.** The pinion gear $A$ on the motor shaft is given a constant angular acceleration $\alpha = 3$ rad/s$^2$. If the gears $A$ and $B$ have the dimensions shown, determine the angular velocity and angular displacement of the output shaft $C$, when $t = 2$ s starting from rest. The shaft is fixed to $B$ and turns with it.

$B$

$C$

125 mm

35 mm

$A$

Prob. 16–8

**16-10.** The disk is originally rotating at $\omega_0 = 8$ rad/s. If it is subjected to a constant angular acceleration of $\alpha = 6$ rad/s$^2$, determine the magnitudes of the velocity and the $n$ and $t$ components of acceleration of point $A$ at the instant $t = 0.5$ s.

**16-11.** The disk is originally rotating at $\omega_0 = 8$ rad/s. If it is subjected to a constant angular acceleration of $\alpha = 6$ rad/s$^2$, determine the magnitudes of the velocity and the $n$ and $t$ components of acceleration of point $B$ just after the wheel undergoes 2 revolutions.

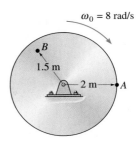

$\omega_0 = 8$ rad/s

$B$

1.5 m

2 m  $A$

Probs. 16–10/11

**\*16-12.** When only two gears are in mesh, the driving gear $A$ and the driven gear $B$ will always turn in opposite directions. In order to get them to turn in the *same direction* an idler gear $C$ is used. In the case shown, determine the angular velocity of gear $B$ when $t = 5$ s, if gear $A$ starts from rest and has an angular acceleration of $\alpha_A = (3t + 2)$ rad/s$^2$, where $t$ is in seconds.

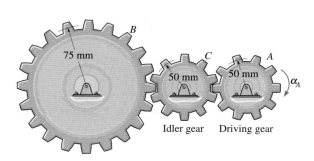

Prob. 16–12

**16-14.** The disk is originally rotating at $\omega_0 = 8$ rad/s. If it is subjected to a constant angular acceleration $\alpha_c = 6$ rad/s$^2$, determine the magnitudes of the velocity and the $n$ and $t$ components of acceleration of point $A$ at the instant $t = 3$ s.

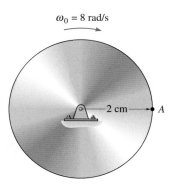

Prob. 16–14

**16-13.** A motor gives disk $A$ an angular acceleration of $\alpha_A = (0.6t^2 + 0.75)$ rad/s$^2$, where $t$ is in seconds. If the initial angular velocity of the disk is $\omega_0 = 6$ rad/s, determine the magnitudes of the velocity and acceleration of block $B$ when $t = 2$ s.

Prob. 16–13

**16-15.** Gear $A$ is in mesh with gear $B$ as shown. If $A$ starts from rest and has a constant angular acceleration of $\alpha_A = 2$ rad/s$^2$, determine the time needed for $B$ to attain an angular velocity of $\omega_B = 50$ rad/s.

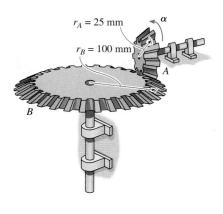

Prob. 16–15

*16-16. The gear $A$ on the drive shaft of the outboard motor has a radius $r_A = 2$ cm and the meshed pinion gear $B$ on the propeller shaft has a radius $r_B = 4$ cm. Determine the angular velocity of the propeller in $t = 1.3$ s if the drive shaft rotates with an angular acceleration $\alpha = (300\sqrt{t})$ rad/s$^2$, where $t$ is in seconds. The propeller is originally at rest and the motor frame does not move.

16-17. For the outboard motor in Prob. 16–16, determine the magnitudes of the velocity and acceleration of a point $P$ located on the tip of the propeller at the instant $t = 0.75$ s.

Probs. 16–16/17

16-18. Starting from rest when $s = 0$, pulley $A$ is given an angular acceleration $\alpha = (6\theta)$ rad/s$^2$, where $\theta$ is in radians. Determine the speed of block $B$ when it has risen $s = 6$ m. The pulley has an inner hub $D$ which is fixed to $C$ and turns with it.

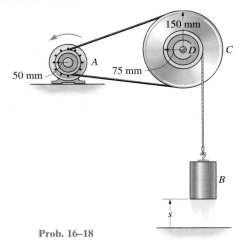

Prob. 16–18

16-19. Starting from rest when $s = 0$, pulley $A$ is given a constant angular acceleration $\alpha_c = 6$ rad/s$^2$. Determine the speed of block $B$ when it has risen $s = 6$ m. The pulley has an inner hub $D$ which is fixed to $C$ and turns with it.

Prob. 16–19

*16-20. Initially the motor on the circular saw turns its drive shaft at $\omega = (20t^{2/3})$ rad/s, where $t$ is in seconds. If the radii of gears $A$ and $B$ are 1 cm and 4 cm, respectively, determine the magnitudes of the velocity and acceleration of a tooth $C$ on the saw blade after the drive shaft rotates $\theta = 5$ rad starting from rest.

Prob. 16–20

**16-21.** Due to the screw at $E$, the actuator provides linear motion to the arm at $F$ when the motor turns the gear at $A$. If the gears have the radii listed in the figure, and the screw at $E$ has a pitch $p = 2$ mm, determine the speed at $F$ when the motor turns $A$ at $\omega_A = 20$ rad/s. *Hint:* The screw pitch indicates the amount of advance of the screw for each full revolution.

$r_A = 10$ mm
$r_B = 50$ mm
$r_C = 15$ mm
$r_D = 60$ mm

**Prob. 16–21**

**16-22.** A motor gives gear $A$ an angular acceleration of $\alpha_A = (0.25\theta^3 + 0.5)$ rad/s$^2$, where $\theta$ is in radians. If this gear is initially turning at $(\omega_A)_0 = 20$ rad/s, determine the angular velocity of gear $B$ after $A$ undergoes an angular displacement of 10 rev.

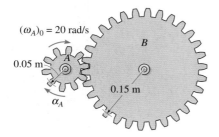

**Prob. 16–22**

**16-23.** A motor gives gear $A$ an angular acceleration of $\alpha_A = (4t^3)$ rad/s$^2$, where $t$ is in seconds. If this gear is initially turning at $(\omega_A)_0 = 20$ rad/s, determine the angular velocity of gear $B$ when $t = 2$ s.

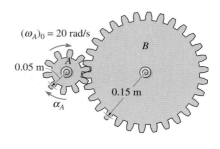

$(\omega_A)_0 = 20$ rad/s

0.05 m

$B$

0.15 m

$\alpha_A$

**Prob. 16–23**

*\*16-24.** The disk starts from rest and is given an angular acceleration $\alpha = (10\theta^{1/3})$ rad/s$^2$, where $\theta$ is in radians. Determine the angular velocity of the disk and its angular displacement when $t = 4$ s.

$P$

0.4 m

**Prob. 16–24**

**16-25.** The disk starts from rest and is given an angular acceleration $\alpha = (10\theta^{1/3})$ rad/s², where $\theta$ is in radians. Determine the magnitudes of the normal and tangential components of acceleration of a point $P$ on the rim of the disk when $t = 4$ s.

**16-27.** The operation of "reverse" for a three-speed automotive transmission is illustrated schematically in the figure. If the crank shaft $G$ is turning with an angular speed of 60 rad/s, determine the angular speed of the drive shaft $H$. Each of the gears rotates about a fixed axis. Note that gears $A$ and $B$, $C$ and $D$, $E$ and $F$ are in mesh. The radii of each of these gears are reported in the figure.

$$r_A = 90 \text{ mm}$$
$$r_B = r_C = 30 \text{ mm}$$
$$r_D = 50 \text{ mm}$$
$$r_E = 70 \text{ mm}$$
$$r_F = 60 \text{ mm}$$

**Prob. 16–27**

**Prob. 16–25**

**16-26.** If the angular velocity of the drum is increased uniformly from 6 rad/s when $t = 0$ to 12 rad/s when $t = 5$ s, determine the magnitudes of the velocity and acceleration of points $A$ and $B$ on the belt when $t = 1$ s. At this instant the points are located as shown.

**\*16-28.** Rotation of the robotic arm occurs due to linear movement of the hydraulic cylinders $A$ and $B$. If cylinder $A$ is extending at the constant rate 0.25 m/s while $B$ is held fixed, determine the magnitude of velocity and acceleration of the part $C$ held in the grips of the arm. The gear at $D$ has a radius of 0.05 m.

**Prob. 16–26**

**Prob. 16–28**

**16-29.** At the instant shown, gear $A$ is rotating with a constant angular velocity of $\omega_A = 6$ rad/s. Determine the largest angular velocity of gear $B$ and the maximum speed of point $C$.

**16-31.** The rope of diameter $d$ is wrapped around the tapered drum which has the dimensions shown. If the drum is rotating at a constant rate of $\omega$, determine the upward acceleration of the block. Neglect the small horizontal displacement of the block.

Prob. 16–29

Prob. 16–31

**16-30.** A mill in a textile plant uses the belt-and-pulley arrangement shown to transmit power. When $t = 0$ an electric motor is turning pulley $A$ with an angular velocity of $\omega_A = 5$ rad/s. If this pulley is subjected to a constant angular acceleration 2 rad/s$^2$, determine the angular velocity of pulley $B$ after $B$ turns 6 revolutions. The hub at $D$ is rigidly *connected* to pulley $C$ and turns with it.

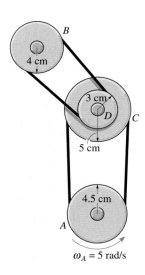

Prob. 16–30

*16-32. The rod assembly is supported by ball-and-socket joints at $A$ and $B$. At the instant shown it is rotating about the $y$ axis with an angular velocity $\omega = 5$ rad/s and has an angular acceleration $\alpha = 8$ rad/s$^2$. Determine the magnitudes of the velocity and acceleration of point $C$ at this instant. Solve the problem using Cartesian vectors and Eqs. 16–9 and 16–13.

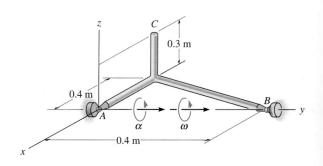

Prob. 16–32

# *16.4 Absolute Motion Analysis

A body subjected to *general plane motion* undergoes a *simultaneous* translation and rotation. If the body is represented by a thin slab, the slab translates in the plane and rotates about an axis perpendicular to the plane. The motion can be completely specified by knowing *both* the angular rotation of a line fixed in the body and the motion of a point on the body. One way to define these motions is to use a rectilinear position coordinate $s$ to locate the point along its path and an angular position coordinate $\theta$ to specify the orientation of the line. The two coordinates are then related using the geometry of the problem. By *direct application* of the time-differential equations $v = ds/dt$, $a = dv/dt$, $\omega = d\theta/dt$, and $\alpha = d\omega/dt$, the *motion* of the point and the *angular motion* of the line can then be related. In some cases, this procedure may also be used to relate the motions of one body to those of a connected body, or to study the motion of a body subjected to rotation about a fixed axis.

## PROCEDURE FOR ANALYSIS

The velocity and acceleration of a point $P$ undergoing rectilinear motion can be related to the angular velocity and angular acceleration of a line contained within a body using the following procedure.

### Position Coordinate Equation.

- Locate point $P$ using a position coordinate $s$, which is measured from a *fixed origin* and is *directed along the straight-line path of motion* of point $P$.
- Measure from a fixed reference line the angular position $\theta$ of a line lying in the body.
- From the dimensions of the body, relate $s$ to $\theta$, $s = f(\theta)$, using geometry and/or trigonometry.

### Time Derivatives.

- Take the first derivative of $s = f(\theta)$ with respect to time to get a relationship between $v$ and $\omega$.
- Take the second time derivative to get a relationship between $a$ and $\alpha$.
- In each case the chain rule of calculus must be used when taking the derivatives of the position coordinate equation.

The dumping bin on the truck rotates about a fixed axis passing through the pin at $A$. It is operated by the extension of the hydraulic cylinder $BC$. The angular position of the bin can be specified using the angular position coordinate $\theta$, and the position of point $C$ on the bin is specified using the rectilinear coordinate $s$. Since $a$ and $b$ are fixed lengths, then the coordinates can be related by the cosine law, $s = \sqrt{a^2 + b^2 - 2ab \cos \theta}$. Using the chain rule, the time derivative of this equation relates the speed at which the hydraulic cylinder extends, to the angular velocity of the bin, i.e.,

$$v = \frac{1}{2}(a^2 + b^2 - 2ab \cos \theta)^{-\frac{1}{2}}(2ab \sin \theta)\,\omega.$$

**EXAMPLE** **16.3**

The end of rod $R$ shown in Fig. 16–7 maintains contact with the cam by means of a spring. If the cam rotates about an axis through point $O$ with an angular acceleration $\boldsymbol{\alpha}$ and angular velocity $\boldsymbol{\omega}$, determine the velocity and acceleration of the rod when the cam is in the arbitrary position $\theta$.

**Fig. 16–7**

**Solution**

*Position Coordinate Equation.* Coordinates $\theta$ and $x$ are chosen in order to relate the *rotational motion* of the line segment $OA$ on the cam to the *rectilinear motion* of the rod. These coordinates are measured from the *fixed point $O$* and may be related to each other using trigonometry. Since $OC = CB = r \cos \theta$, Fig. 16–7, then

$$x = 2r \cos \theta$$

*Time Derivatives.* Using the chain rule of calculus, we have

$$\frac{dx}{dt} = -2r(\sin \theta)\frac{d\theta}{dt}$$

$$v = -2r\omega \sin \theta \qquad\qquad Ans.$$

$$\frac{dv}{dt} = -2r\left(\frac{d\omega}{dt}\right) \sin \theta - 2r\omega(\cos \theta)\frac{d\theta}{dt}$$

$$a = -2r(\alpha \sin \theta + \omega^2 \cos \theta) \qquad\qquad Ans.$$

The negative signs indicate that $v$ and $a$ are opposite to the direction of positive $x$.

# E X A M P L E  16.4

At a given instant, the cylinder of radius $r$, shown in Fig. 16–8, has an angular velocity $\omega$ and angular acceleration $\alpha$. Determine the velocity and acceleration of its center $G$ if the cylinder rolls without slipping.

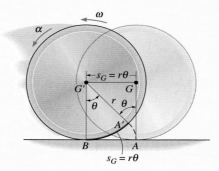

Fig. 16–8

## Solution

*Position Coordinate Equation.*  By inspection, point $G$ moves *horizontally* to the left from $G$ to $G'$ as the cylinder rolls, Fig. 16–8. Consequently its new location $G'$ will be specified by the *horizontal* position coordinate $s_G$, which is measured from the original position $(G)$ of the cylinder's center. Notice also, that as the cylinder rolls (without slipping), points on its surface contact the ground such that the arc length $A'B$ of contact must be equal to the distance $s_G$. Consequently, the motion requires the radial line $GA$ to rotate $\theta$ to the position $G'A'$. Since the arc $A'B = r\theta$, then $G$ travels a distance

$$s_G = r\theta$$

*Time Derivatives.*  Taking successive time derivatives of this equation, realizing that $r$ is constant, $\omega = d\theta/dt$, and $\alpha = d\omega/dt$, gives the necessary relationships:

$$s_G = r\theta$$
$$v_G = r\omega \qquad\qquad Ans.$$
$$a_G = r\alpha \qquad\qquad Ans.$$

Remember that these relationships are valid only if the cylinder (disk, wheel, ball, etc.) rolls *without* slipping.

E X A M P L E  **16.5**

**Fig. 16–9**

The large window in Fig. 16–9 is opened using a hydraulic cylinder *AB*. If the cylinder extends at a constant rate of 0.5 m/s, determine the angular velocity and angular acceleration of the window at the instant $\theta = 30°$.

**Solution**

*Position Coordinate Equation.*   The angular motion of the window can be obtained using the coordinate $\theta$, whereas the extension or motion *along the hydraulic cylinder* is defined using a coordinate $s$, which measures the length from the fixed point $A$ to the moving point $B$. These coordinates can be related using the law of cosines, namely,

$$s^2 = (2 \text{ m})^2 + (1 \text{ m})^2 - 2(2 \text{ m})(1 \text{ m}) \cos \theta$$

$$s^2 = 5 - 4 \cos \theta \tag{1}$$

When $\theta = 30°$,

$$s = 1.239 \text{ m}$$

*Time Derivatives.*   Taking the time derivatives of Eq. 1, we have

$$2s \frac{ds}{dt} = 0 - 4(-\sin \theta) \frac{d\theta}{dt}$$

$$s(v_s) = 2(\sin \theta)\omega \tag{2}$$

Since $v_s = 0.5$ m/s, then at $\theta = 30°$,

$$(1.239 \text{ m})(0.5 \text{ m/s}) = 2 \sin 30°\omega$$

$$\omega = 0.620 \text{ rad/s} \qquad \textit{Ans.}$$

Taking the time derivative of Eq. 2 yields

$$\frac{ds}{dt} v_s + s \frac{dv_s}{dt} = 2(\cos \theta) \frac{d\theta}{dt} \omega + 2(\sin \theta) \frac{d\omega}{dt}$$

$$v_s^2 + s a_s = 2(\cos \theta)\omega^2 + 2(\sin \theta)\alpha$$

Since $a_s = dv_s/dt = 0$, then

$$(0.5 \text{ m/s})^2 + 0 = 2 \cos 30°(0.620 \text{ rad/s})^2 + 2 \sin 30°\alpha$$

$$\alpha = -0.415 \text{ rad/s}^2 \qquad \textit{Ans.}$$

Because the result is negative, it indicates the window has an angular deceleration.

# PROBLEMS

**16-33.** The bar $DC$ rotates uniformly about the shaft at $D$ with a constant angular velocity $\omega$. Determine the velocity and acceleration of the bar $AB$, which is confined by the guides to move vertically.

**16-35.** The mechanism is used to convert the constant circular motion $\omega$ of rod $AB$ into translating motion of rod $CD$. Determine the velocity and acceleration of $CD$ for any angle $\theta$ of $AB$.

Prob. 16–33

Prob. 16–35

**16-34.** The scaffold $S$ is raised hydraulically by moving the roller at $A$ toward the pin at $B$. If $A$ is approaching $B$ with a speed of 0.6 m/s, determine the speed at which the platform is rising as a function of $\theta$. The 1.6-m links are pin-connected at their midpoint.

**\*16-36.** The block moves to the left with a constant velocity $\mathbf{v}_0$. Determine the angular velocity and angular acceleration of the bar as a function of $\theta$.

Prob. 16–34

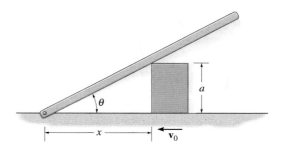

Prob. 16–36

**16-37.** Determine the velocity of rod $R$ for any angle $\theta$ of the cam $C$ if the cam rotates with a constant angular velocity $\omega$. The pin connection at $O$ does not cause an interference with the motion of $A$ on $C$.

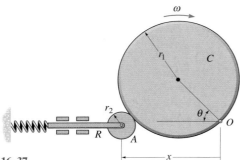

**Prob. 16–37**

**16-38.** The crankshaft $AB$ is rotating at a constant angular velocity of $\omega = 150$ rad/s. Determine the velocity of the piston $P$ at the instant $\theta = 30°$.

**Prob. 16–38**

**16-39.** At the instant $\theta = 50°$, the slotted guide is moving upward with an acceleration of $3$ m/s$^2$ and a velocity of $2$ m/s. Determine the angular acceleration and angular velocity of link $AB$ at this instant. *Note:* The upward motion of the guide is in the negative $y$ direction.

**Prob. 16–39**

**\*16-40.** Disk $A$ rolls without slipping over the surface of the *fixed* cylinder $B$. Determine the angular velocity of $A$ if its center $C$ has a speed $v_C = 5$ m/s. How many revolutions will $A$ have made about its center just after link $DC$ completes one revolution?

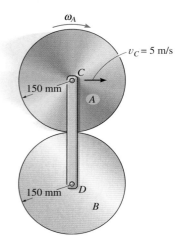

**Prob. 16–40**

**16-41.** Arm $AB$ has an angular velocity of $\omega$ and an angular acceleration of $\alpha$. If no slipping occurs between the disk and the fixed curved surface, determine the angular velocity and angular acceleration of the disk.

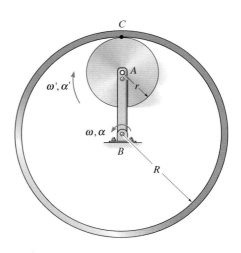

**Prob. 16–41**

**16-42.** The inclined plate moves to the left with a constant velocity **v**. Determine the angular velocity and angular acceleration of the slender rod of length *l*. The rod pivots about the step at *C* as it slides on the plate.

Prob. 16–42

***16-44.** The pins at *A* and *B* are confined to move in the vertical and horizontal tracks. If the slotted arm is causing *A* to move downward at $\mathbf{v}_A$, determine the velocity of *B* at the instant shown.

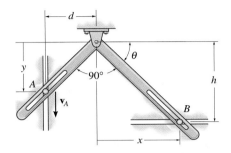

Prob. 16–44

**16-43.** The end *A* of the bar is moving to the left with a constant velocity $\mathbf{v}_A$. Determine the angular velocity $\boldsymbol{\omega}$ and angular acceleration $\boldsymbol{\alpha}$ of the bar as a function of its position *x*.

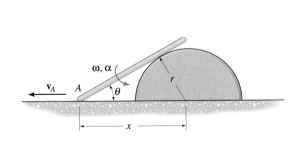

Prob. 16–43

**16-45.** Bar *AB* rotates uniformly about the fixed pin *A* with a constant angular velocity $\boldsymbol{\omega}$. Determine the velocity and acceleration of block *C*, at the instant $\theta = 60°$.

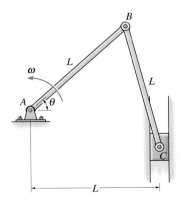

Prob. 16–45

**16-46.** The bar is confined to move along the vertical and inclined planes. If the velocity of the roller at $A$ is $v_A = 6$ m/s when $\theta = 45°$, determine the bar's angular velocity and the velocity of roller $B$ at this instant.

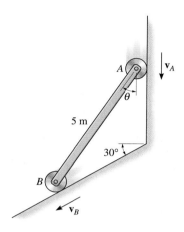

Prob. 16–46

**16-47.** The disk is rotating with an angular velocity of $\omega$ and has an angular acceleration of $\alpha$. Determine the velocity and acceleration of cylinder $B$. Neglect the size of the pulley at $C$.

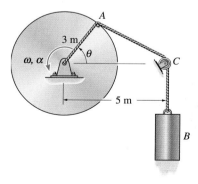

Prob. 16–47

**\*16-48.** The slotted yoke is pinned at $A$ while end $B$ is used to move the ram $R$ horizontally. If the disk rotates with a constant angular velocity $\omega$, determine the velocity and acceleration of the ram. The crank pin $C$ is fixed to the disk and turns with it.

Prob. 16–48

**16-49.** The Geneva wheel $A$ provides intermittent rotary motion $\omega_A$ for continuous motion $\omega_D = 2$ rad/s of disk $D$. By choosing $d = 100\sqrt{2}$ mm, the wheel has zero angular velocity at the instant pin $B$ enters or leaves one of the four slots. Determine the magnitude of the angular velocity $\omega_A$ of the Geneva wheel at any angle $\theta$ for which pin $B$ is in contact with the slot.

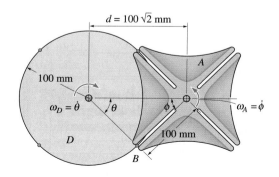

Prob. 16–49

## 16.5 Relative-Motion Analysis: Velocity

The general plane motion of a rigid body can be described as a *combination* of translation and rotation. To view these "component" motions *separately* we will use a *relative-motion analysis* involving two sets of coordinate axes. The $x, y$ coordinate system is fixed and measures the *absolute* position of two points $A$ and $B$ on the body, Fig. 16–10$a$. The origin of the $x', y'$ coordinate system will be attached to the selected "base point" $A$, which generally has a *known* motion. The axes of this coordinate system do not rotate with the body; rather they will only be allowed to *translate* with respect to the fixed frame.

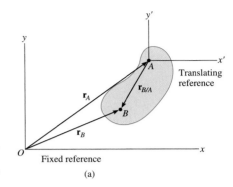

Fig. 16–10

**Position.** The position vector $\mathbf{r}_A$ in Fig. 16–10$a$ specifies the location of the "base point" $A$, and the relative-position vector $\mathbf{r}_{B/A}$ locates point $B$ with respect to point $A$. By vector addition, the *position* of $B$ is then

$$\mathbf{r}_B = \mathbf{r}_A + \mathbf{r}_{B/A}$$

**Displacement.** During an instant of time $dt$, points $A$ and $B$ undergo displacements $d\mathbf{r}_A$ and $d\mathbf{r}_B$ as shown in Fig. 16–10$b$. If we consider the general plane motion by its component parts then the *entire body* first *translates* by an amount $d\mathbf{r}_A$ so that $A$, the base point, moves to its *final position* and point $B$ moves to $B'$, Fig. 16–10$c$. The body is then *rotated* about $A$ by an amount $d\theta$ so that $B'$ undergoes a *relative displacement* $d\mathbf{r}_{B/A}$ and thus moves to its final position $B$. Due to the rotation about $A$, $dr_{B/A} = r_{B/A}\, d\theta$, and the displacement of $B$ is

$$d\mathbf{r}_B = d\mathbf{r}_A + d\mathbf{r}_{B/A}$$

| due to rotation about $A$
| due to translation of $A$
due to translation and rotation

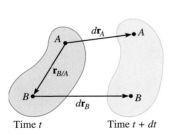

Time $t$                  Time $t + dt$

General plane
motion

(b)

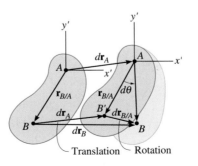

Translation    Rotation

(c)

As the slider block $A$ moves horizontally to the left with a velocity $\mathbf{v}_A$, it causes the link $CB$ to rotate counterclockwise, such that $\mathbf{v}_B$ is directed tangent to its circular path, i.e., upward to the left. The connecting rod $AB$ is subjected to general plane motion, and at the instant shown it has an angular velocity $\boldsymbol{\omega}$.

**Velocity.**  To determine the relationship between the velocities of points $A$ and $B$, it is necessary to take the time derivative of the position equation, or simply divide the displacement equation by $dt$. This yields

$$\frac{d\mathbf{r}_B}{dt} = \frac{d\mathbf{r}_A}{dt} + \frac{d\mathbf{r}_{B/A}}{dt}$$

The terms $d\mathbf{r}_B/dt = \mathbf{v}_B$ and $d\mathbf{r}_A/dt = \mathbf{v}_A$ are measured from the fixed $x$, $y$ axes and represent the *absolute velocities* of points $A$ and $B$, respectively. The magnitude of the third term is $r_{B/A}d\theta/dt = r_{B/A}\dot{\theta} = r_{B/A}\omega$, where $\omega$ is the angular velocity of the body at the instant considered. We will denote this term as the *relative velocity* $\mathbf{v}_{B/A}$, since it represents the velocity of $B$ with respect to $A$ as measured by an observer fixed to the translating $x'$, $y'$ axes. Since the body is rigid, realize that this observer only sees point $B$ move along a *circular arc* that has a radius of curvature $r_{B/A}$. In other words, *the body appears to move as if it were rotating with an angular velocity* $\boldsymbol{\omega}$ *about the $z'$ axis passing through $A$*. Consequently, $\mathbf{v}_{B/A}$ has a magnitude of $v_{B/A} = \omega r_{B/A}$ and a *direction* which is perpendicular to $\mathbf{r}_{B/A}$. We therefore have

$$\boxed{\mathbf{v}_B = \mathbf{v}_A + \mathbf{v}_{B/A}} \qquad (16\text{--}15)$$

where

$\mathbf{v}_B$ = velocity of point $B$

$\mathbf{v}_A$ = velocity of the base point $A$

$\mathbf{v}_{B/A}$ = relative velocity of "$B$ with respect to $A$"

This relative motion is *circular*, the *magnitude* is $v_{B/A} = \omega r_{B/A}$ and the *direction* is perpendicular to $\mathbf{r}_{B/A}$.

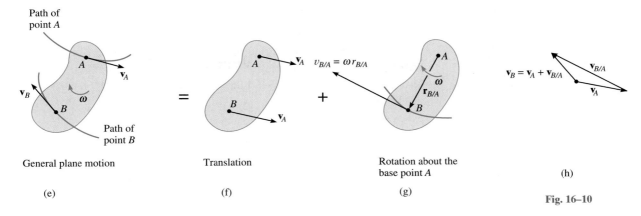

General plane motion

(e)

Translation

(f)

Rotation about the base point $A$

(g)

(h)

Fig. 16–10

Each of the three terms in Eq. 16–15 is represented graphically on the *kinematic diagrams* in Figs. 16–10e, 16–10f, and 16–10g. Here it is seen that the velocity of $B$, Fig. 16–10e, is determined by considering the entire body to translate with a velocity of $\mathbf{v}_A$, Fig. 16–10f, and rotate about $A$ with an angular velocity $\boldsymbol{\omega}$, Fig. 16–10g. Vector addition of these two effects, applied to $B$, yields $\mathbf{v}_B$, as shown in Fig. 16–10h.

Since the relative velocity $\mathbf{v}_{B/A}$ represents the effect of *circular motion*, about $A$, this term can be expressed by the cross product $\mathbf{v}_{B/A} = \boldsymbol{\omega} \times \mathbf{r}_{B/A}$, Eq. 16–9. Hence, for application, we can also write Eq. 16–15 as

(a)

$$\mathbf{v}_B = \mathbf{v}_A + \boldsymbol{\omega} \times \mathbf{r}_{B/A} \qquad (16\text{–}16)$$

where

$\mathbf{v}_B$ = velocity of $B$

$\mathbf{v}_A$ = velocity of the base point $A$

$\boldsymbol{\omega}$ = angular velocity of the body

$\mathbf{r}_{B/A}$ = relative-position vector drawn from $A$ to $B$

(b)

Fig. 16–11

The velocity equation 16–15 or 16–16 may be used in a practical manner to study the general plane motion of a rigid body which is either pin-connected to or in contact with other moving bodies. When applying this equation, points $A$ and $B$ should generally be selected as points on the body which are pin-connected to other bodies, or as points in contact with adjacent bodies which have a *known motion*. For example, both points $A$ and $B$ on link $AB$, Fig. 16–11a, have circular paths of motion since the wheel and link $CB$ move in circular paths. The *directions* of $\mathbf{v}_A$ and $\mathbf{v}_B$ can therefore be established since they are always *tangent* to their paths of motion, Fig. 16–11b. In the case of the wheel in Fig. 16–12, which rolls without slipping, point $A$ can be selected at the ground. Here $A$ (momentarily) has zero velocity since the ground does not move. Furthermore, the center of the wheel, $B$, moves along a horizontal path so that $\mathbf{v}_B$ is horizontal.

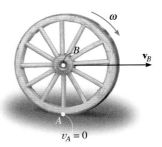

Fig. 16–12

# PROCEDURE FOR ANALYSIS

The relative velocity equation can be applied either by using Cartesian vector analysis, or by writing the $x$ and $y$ scalar component equations directly. For application, it is suggested that the following procedure be used.

**VECTOR ANALYSIS**

### Kinematic Diagram.

- Establish the directions of the fixed $x$, $y$ coordinates and draw a kinematic diagram of the body. Indicate on it the velocities $\mathbf{v}_A$, $\mathbf{v}_B$ of points $A$ and $B$, the angular velocity $\boldsymbol{\omega}$, and the relative-position vector $\mathbf{r}_{B/A}$.
- If the magnitudes of $\mathbf{v}_A$, $\mathbf{v}_B$, or $\boldsymbol{\omega}$ are unknown, the sense of direction of these vectors may be assumed.

### Velocity Equation.

- To apply $\mathbf{v}_B = \mathbf{v}_A + \boldsymbol{\omega} \times \mathbf{r}_{B/A}$, express the vectors in Cartesian vector form and substitute them into the equation. Evaluate the cross product and then equate the respective $\mathbf{i}$ and $\mathbf{j}$ components to obtain two scalar equations.
- If the solution yields a *negative* answer for an *unknown* magnitude, it indicates the sense of direction of the vector is opposite to that shown on the kinematic diagram.

**SCALAR ANALYSIS**

### Kinematic Diagram.

- If the velocity equation is to be applied in scalar form, then the magnitude and direction of the relative velocity $\mathbf{v}_{B/A}$ must be established. Draw a kinematic diagram such as shown in Fig. 16–10g, which shows the relative motion. Since the body is considered to be "pinned" momentarily at the base point $A$, the magnitude is $v_{B/A} = \omega r_{B/A}$. The sense of direction of $\mathbf{v}_{B/A}$ is established from the diagram, such that $\mathbf{v}_{B/A}$ acts perpendicular to $\mathbf{r}_{B/A}$ in accordance with the rotational motion $\boldsymbol{\omega}$ of the body.*

### Velocity Equation.

- Write Eq. 16–15 in symbolic form, $\mathbf{v}_B = \mathbf{v}_A + \mathbf{v}_{B/A}$, and underneath each of the terms represent the vectors graphically by showing their magnitudes and directions. The scalar equations are determined from the $x$ and $y$ components of these vectors.

*The notation $\mathbf{v}_B = \mathbf{v}_A + \mathbf{v}_{B/A\text{(pin)}}$ may be helpful in recalling that $A$ is "pinned."

# EXAMPLE 16.6

The link shown in Fig. 16–13a is guided by two blocks at A and B, which move in the fixed slots. If the velocity of A is 2 m/s downward, determine the velocity of B at the instant $\theta = 45°$.

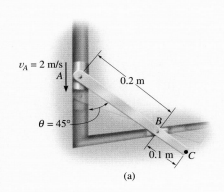

(a)

### Solution (Vector Analysis)

*Kinematic Diagram.* Since points A and B are restricted to move along the fixed slots and $\mathbf{v}_A$ is directed downward, the velocity $\mathbf{v}_B$ must be directed horizontally to the right, Fig. 16–13b. This motion causes the link to rotate counterclockwise; that is, by the right-hand rule the angular velocity $\boldsymbol{\omega}$ is directed outward, perpendicular to the plane of motion. Knowing the magnitude and direction of $\mathbf{v}_A$ and the lines of action of $\mathbf{v}_B$ and $\boldsymbol{\omega}$, it is possible to apply the velocity equation $\mathbf{v}_B = \mathbf{v}_A + \boldsymbol{\omega} \times \mathbf{r}_{B/A}$ to points A and B in order to solve for the two unknown magnitudes $v_B$ and $\omega$. Since $\mathbf{r}_{B/A}$ is needed, it is also shown in Fig. 16–13b.

*Velocity Equation.* Expressing each of the vectors in Fig. 16–13b in terms of their **i, j, k** components and applying Eq. 16–16 to A, the base point, and B, we have

(b)

$$\mathbf{v}_B = \mathbf{v}_A + \boldsymbol{\omega} \times \mathbf{r}_{B/A}$$
$$v_B\mathbf{i} = -2\mathbf{j} + [\omega\mathbf{k} \times (0.2 \sin 45°\mathbf{i} - 0.2 \cos 45°\mathbf{j})]$$
$$v_B\mathbf{i} = -2\mathbf{j} + 0.2\omega \sin 45°\mathbf{j} + 0.2\omega \cos 45°\mathbf{i}$$

Equating the **i** and **j** components gives

$$v_B = 0.2\omega \cos 45° \qquad 0 = -2 + 0.2\omega \sin 45°$$

Thus,

$$\omega = 14.1 \text{ rad/s} \circlearrowleft$$
$$v_B = 2 \text{ m/s} \rightarrow \qquad\qquad Ans.$$

**Fig. 16–13**

Since both results are *positive*, the *directions* of $\mathbf{v}_B$ and $\boldsymbol{\omega}$ are indeed *correct* as shown in Fig. 16–13b. It should be emphasized that these results are *valid only* at the instant $\theta = 45°$. A recalculation for $\theta = 44°$ yields $v_B = 2.07$ m/s and $\omega = 14.4$ rad/s; whereas when $\theta = 46°$, $v_B = 1.93$ m/s and $\omega = 13.9$ rad/s, etc.

Now that once the velocity of a point (A) on the link and the angular velocity are *known*, the velocity of any other point on the link can be determined. As an exercise, see if you can apply Eq. 16–16 to points A and C or to points B and C and show that when when $\theta = 45°$, $v_C = 3.16$ m/s, directed at $\theta = 18.4°$ up from the horizontal.

**E X A M P L E  16.7**

(a)

(b)

Relative motion
(c)

**Fig. 16–14**

The cylinder shown in Fig. 16–14a rolls without slipping on the surface of a conveyor belt which is moving at 2 m/s. Determine the velocity of point A. The cylinder has a clockwise angular velocity $\omega = 15$ rad/s at the instant shown.

### Solution I (Vector Analysis)

*Kinematic Diagram.* Since no slipping occurs, point $B$ on the cylinder has the same velocity as the conveyor, Fig. 16–14b. Also, the angular velocity of the cylinder is known, so we can apply the velocity equation to $B$, the base point, and $A$ to determine $\mathbf{v}_A$.

*Velocity Equation.*

$$\mathbf{v}_A = \mathbf{v}_B + \boldsymbol{\omega} \times \mathbf{r}_{A/B}$$
$$(v_A)_x\mathbf{i} + (v_A)_y\mathbf{j} = 2\mathbf{i} + (-15\mathbf{k}) \times (-0.5\mathbf{i} + 0.5\mathbf{j})$$
$$(v_A)_x\mathbf{i} + (v_A)_y\mathbf{j} = 2\mathbf{i} + 7.50\mathbf{j} + 7.50\mathbf{i}$$

so that

$$(v_A)_x = 2 + 7.50 = 9.50 \text{ m/s} \qquad (1)$$
$$(v_A)_y = 7.50 \text{ m/s} \qquad (2)$$

Thus,

$$v_A = \sqrt{(9.50)^2 + (7.50)^2} = 12.1 \text{ m/s} \qquad \textit{Ans.}$$

$$\theta = \tan^{-1}\frac{7.50}{9.50} = 38.3° \qquad \textit{Ans.}$$

### Solution II (Scalar Analysis)

As an alternative procedure, the scalar components of $\mathbf{v}_A = \mathbf{v}_B + \mathbf{v}_{A/B}$ can be obtained directly. From the kinematic diagram showing the relative "circular" motion $\mathbf{v}_{A/B}$, Fig. 16–14c, we have

$$v_{A/B} = \omega r_{A/B} = (15 \text{ rad/s})\left(\frac{0.5 \text{ m}}{\cos 45°}\right) = 10.6 \text{ m/s} \, \angle^{45°}$$

Thus

$$\mathbf{v}_A = \mathbf{v}_B + \mathbf{v}_{A/B}$$

$$\begin{bmatrix} (v_A)_x \\ \rightarrow \end{bmatrix} + \begin{bmatrix} (v_A)_y \\ \uparrow \end{bmatrix} = \begin{bmatrix} 2 \text{ m/s} \\ \rightarrow \end{bmatrix} + \begin{bmatrix} 10.6 \text{ m/s} \\ \angle^{45°} \end{bmatrix}$$

Equating the x and y components gives the same results as before, namely,

$$(\xrightarrow{+}) \qquad (v_A)_x = 2 + 10.6 \cos 45° = 9.50 \text{ m/s}$$
$$(+\uparrow) \qquad (v_A)_y = 0 + 10.6 \sin 45° = 7.50 \text{ m/s}$$

# EXAMPLE 16.8

The collar $C$ in Fig. 16–15$a$ is moving downward with a velocity of 2 m/s. Determine the angular velocities of $CB$ and $AB$ at this instant.

### Solution I (Vector Analysis)

*Kinematic Diagram.*   The downward motion of $C$ causes $B$ to move to the right. Also, $CB$ and $AB$ rotate counterclockwise. To solve, we will write the appropriate kinematic equation for each link.

*Velocity Equation.*

Link $CB$   (general plane motion): See Fig. 16–15$b$.

$$\mathbf{v}_B = \mathbf{v}_C + \boldsymbol{\omega}_{CB} \times \mathbf{r}_{B/C}$$
$$v_B\mathbf{i} = -2\mathbf{j} + \omega_{CB}\mathbf{k} \times (0.2\mathbf{i} - 0.2\mathbf{j})$$
$$v_B\mathbf{i} = -2\mathbf{j} + 0.2\omega_{CB}\mathbf{j} + 0.2\omega_{CB}\mathbf{i}$$

$$v_B = 0.2\omega_{CB} \tag{1}$$
$$0 = -2 + 0.2\omega_{CB} \tag{2}$$
$$\omega_{CB} = 10 \text{ rad/s}\circlearrowleft \qquad Ans.$$
$$v_B = 2 \text{ m/s} \rightarrow$$

Link $AB$   (rotation about a fixed axis): See Fig. 16–15$c$.

$$\mathbf{v}_B = \boldsymbol{\omega}_{AB} \times \mathbf{r}_B$$
$$2\mathbf{i} = \omega_{AB}\mathbf{k} \times (-0.2\mathbf{j})$$
$$2 = 0.2\omega_{AB}$$
$$\omega_{AB} = 10 \text{ rad/s}\circlearrowleft \qquad Ans.$$

### Solution II (Scalar Analysis)

The scalar component equations of $\mathbf{v}_B = \mathbf{v}_C + \mathbf{v}_{B/C}$ can be obtained directly. The kinematic diagram in Fig. 16–15$d$ shows the relative "circular" motion $\mathbf{v}_{B/C}$. We have

$$\mathbf{v}_B = \mathbf{v}_C + \mathbf{v}_{B/C}$$

$$\begin{bmatrix} v_B \\ \rightarrow \end{bmatrix} = \begin{bmatrix} 2 \text{ m/s} \\ \downarrow \end{bmatrix} + \begin{bmatrix} \omega_{CB}(0.2\sqrt{2} \text{ m}) \\ \measuredangle\, 45° \end{bmatrix}$$

Resolving these vectors in the $x$ and $y$ directions yields

$$(\xrightarrow{+}) \qquad v_B = 0 + \omega_{CB}(0.2\sqrt{2}\cos 45°)$$
$$(+\uparrow) \qquad 0 = -2 + \omega_{CB}(0.2\sqrt{2}\sin 45°)$$

which is the same as Eqs. 1 and 2.

(a)

(b)

(c)

Relative motion

(d)

**Fig. 16–15**

## EXAMPLE 16.9

(a)

Fig. 16–16

(b)

The bar $AB$ of the linkage shown in Fig. 16–16a has a clockwise angular velocity of 30 rad/s when $\theta = 60°$. Determine the angular velocities of member $BC$ and the wheel at this instant.

### Solution (Vector Analysis)

*Kinematic Diagram.* By inspection, the velocities of points $B$ and $C$ are defined by the rotation of link $AB$ and the wheel about their fixed axes. The position vectors and the angular velocity of each member are shown on the kinematic diagram in Fig. 16–16b. To solve, we will write the appropriate kinematic equation for each member.

*Velocity Equation.*

Link $AB$ (rotation about a fixed axis):

$$\mathbf{v}_B = \boldsymbol{\omega}_{AB} \times \mathbf{r}_B$$
$$= (-30\mathbf{k}) \times (0.2 \cos 60°\mathbf{i} + 0.2 \sin 60°\mathbf{j})$$
$$= \{5.20\mathbf{i} - 3.0\mathbf{j}\} \text{ m/s}$$

Link $BC$ (general plane motion):

$$\mathbf{v}_C = \mathbf{v}_B + \boldsymbol{\omega}_{BC} \times \mathbf{r}_{C/B}$$
$$v_C\mathbf{i} = 5.20\mathbf{i} - 3.0\mathbf{j} + (\omega_{BC}\mathbf{k}) \times (0.2\mathbf{i})$$
$$v_C\mathbf{i} = 5.20\mathbf{i} + (0.2\omega_{BC} - 3.0)\mathbf{j}$$
$$v_C = 5.20 \text{ m/s}$$
$$0 = 0.2\omega_{BC} - 3.0$$
$$\omega_{BC} = 15 \text{ rad/s} \curvearrowright \qquad\qquad Ans.$$

Wheel (rotation about a fixed axis):

$$\mathbf{v}_C = \boldsymbol{\omega}_D \times \mathbf{r}_C$$
$$5.20\mathbf{i} = (\omega_D\mathbf{k}) \times (-0.1\mathbf{j})$$
$$5.20 = 0.1\omega_D$$
$$\omega_D = 52 \text{ rad/s} \curvearrowright \qquad\qquad Ans.$$

Note that, by inspection, Fig. 16–16a, $v_B = (0.2)(30) = 6$ m/s, $\measuredangle^{30°}$ and $\mathbf{v}_C$ is directed to the right. As an exercise, use this information and try to obtain $\omega_{BC}$ by applying $\mathbf{v}_C = \mathbf{v}_B + \mathbf{v}_{C/B}$ using scalar components.

# PROBLEMS

**16-50.** At the instant shown the boomerang has an angular velocity $\omega = 4$ rad/s, and its mass center $G$ has a velocity $v_G = 12$ cm/s. Determine the velocity of point $B$ at this instant.

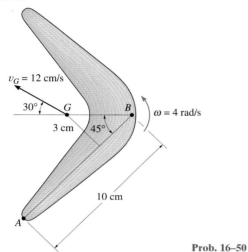

**Prob. 16–50**

**16-51.** The crankshaft $AB$ is rotating at 500 rad/s about a fixed axis passing through $A$. Determine the speed of the piston $P$ at the instant it is in the position shown.

**Prob. 16–51**

**\*16-52.** The pinion gear $A$ rolls on the fixed gear rack $B$ with an angular velocity $\omega = 4$ rad/s. Determine the velocity of the gear rack $C$.

**16-53.** The pinion gear rolls on the gear racks. If $B$ is moving to the right at 4 m/s and $C$ is moving to the left at 2 m/s, determine the angular velocity of the pinion gear and the velocity of its center $A$.

**Probs. 16–52/53**

**16-54.** The shaper mechanism is designed to give a slow cutting stroke and a quick return to a blade attached to the slider at $C$. Determine the velocity of the slider block $C$ at the instant $\theta = 60°$, if link $AB$ is rotating at 4 rad/s.

**16-55.** Determine the velocity of the slider block at $C$ at the instant $\theta = 45°$, if link $AB$ is rotating at 4 rad/s.

**Probs. 16–54/55**

**\*16-56.** The velocity of the slider block $C$ is 4 m/s up the inclined groove. Determine the angular velocity of links $AB$ and $BC$ and the velocity of point $B$ at the instant shown.

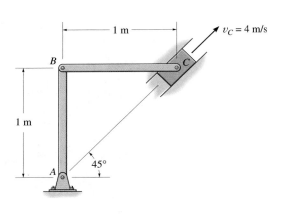

Prob. 16–56

**16-58.** If link $AB$ is rotating at $\omega_{AB} = 3$ rad/s, determine the angular velocity of link $CD$ at the instant shown.

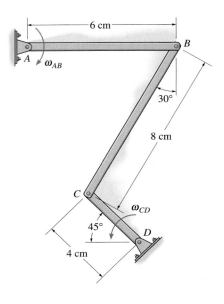

Prob. 16–58

**16-57.** If the block at $C$ is moving downward at 4 m/s, determine the angular velocity of bar $AB$ at the instant shown.

Prob. 16–57

**16-59.** The planetary gear $A$ is pinned at $B$. Link $BC$ rotates clockwise with an angular velocity of 8 rad/s, while the outer gear rack rotates counterclockwise with an angular velocity of 2 rad/s. Determine the angular velocity of gear $A$.

Prob. 16–59

***16-60.** The rotation of link $AB$ creates an oscillating movement of gear $F$. If $AB$ has an angular velocity of $\omega_{AB} = 6$ rad/s, determine the angular velocity of gear $F$ at the instant shown. Gear $E$ is rigidly attached to arm $CD$ and pinned at $D$ to a fixed point.

Prob. 16–60

**16-61.** At the instant shown, the truck is traveling to the right at 3 m/s, while the pipe is rolling counterclockwise at $\omega = 8$ rad/s without slipping at $B$. Determine the velocity of the pipe's center $G$.

**16-62.** At the instant shown, the truck is traveling to the right at 8 m/s. If the spool does not slip at $B$, determine its angular velocity so that its mass center $G$ appears to an observer on the ground to remain stationary.

Probs. 16–61/62

**16-63.** The planetary gear system is used in an automatic transmission for an automobile. By locking or releasing certain gears, it has the advantage of operating the car at different speeds. Consider the case where the ring gear $R$ is held fixed, $\omega_R = 0$, and the sun gear $S$ is rotating at $\omega_S = 5$ rad/s. Determine the angular velocity of each of the planet gears $P$ and shaft $A$.

Prob. 16–63

***16-64.** If the link $AB$ is rotating about the pin at $A$ with an angular velocity $\omega_{AB} = 5$ rad/s, determine the velocities of blocks $C$ and $E$ at the instant shown.

Prob. 16–64

**16-65.** If disk $D$ has a constant angular velocity $\omega_D = 2$ rad/s, determine the angular velocity of disk $A$ at the instant $\theta = 60°$.

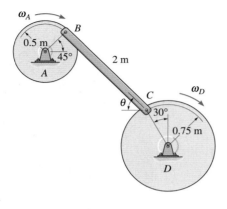

**Prob. 16–65**

**16-67.** If the angular velocity of link $AB$ is $\omega_{AB} = 3$ rad/s, determine the velocity of the block at $C$ and the angular velocity of the connecting link $CB$ at the instant $\theta = 45°$ and $\phi = 30°$.

**Prob. 16–67**

**16-66.** The bicycle has a velocity $v = 1$ m/s, and at the same instant the rear wheel has a clockwise angular velocity $\omega = 3$ rad/s, which causes it to slip at its contact point $A$. Determine the velocity of point $A$.

**Prob. 16–66**

**\*16-68.** If the end of the cord is pulled downward with a speed $v_C = 120$ mm/s, determine the angular velocities of pulleys $A$ and $B$ and the speed of block $D$. Assume that the cord does not slip on the pulleys.

**Prob. 16–68**

**16-69.** At the instant shown, the truck is traveling to the right at 8t m/s, while the pipe is rolling counterclockwise at $\omega = 2t$ rad/s without slipping at B, where t is in seconds. Determine the velocity of the pipe's center G as a function of time.

**16-70.** At the instant shown, the truck is traveling to the right at 12 m/s. If the pipe does not slip at B, determine its angular velocity if its mass center G appears to an observer on the ground to be moving to the right at 3 m/s.

**\*16-72.** Part of an automatic transmission consists of a *fixed* ring gear R, three equal planet gears P, the sun gear S, and the planet carrier C, which is shaded. If the sun gear is rotating at $\omega_S = 6$ rad/s, determine the angular velocity $\omega_C$ of the *planet carrier*. Note that C is pin-connected to the center of each of the planet gears.

Prob. 16–72

Probs. 16–69/70

**16-71.** The top view of an automatic service window at a fast-food restaurant is shown in the figure. During operation, a motor drives the pin-connected link CB with an angular velocity $\omega_{CB} = 0.5$ rad/s. Determine the velocity at the instant shown of the end A, which moves along the slotted guide.

**16-73.** The mechanism shown is used in a riveting machine. It consists of a driving piston A, three links, and a riveter which is attached to the slider block D. Determine the velocity of D at the instant shown, when the piston at A is traveling at $v_A = 20$ m/s.

Prob. 16–71

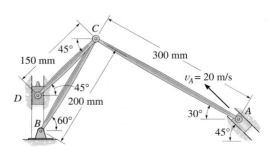

Prob. 16–73

**16-74.** In an automobile transmission the planet pinions *A* and *B* rotate on shafts that are mounted on the planet-pinion carrier *CD*. As shown, *CD* is attached to a shaft at *E* which is aligned with the center of the *fixed* sun-gear *S*. This shaft is not attached to the sun gear. If *CD* is rotating at $\omega_{CD} = 8$ rad/s, determine the angular velocity of the ring gear *R*.

Prob. 16–74

*16-76.** If the slider block *A* is moving downward at $v_A = 4$ m/s, determine the velocities of blocks *B* and *C* at the instant shown.

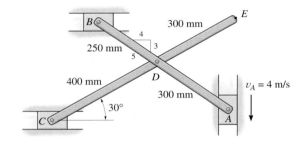

Prob. 16–76

**16-75.** The two-cylinder engine is designed so that the pistons are connected to the crankshaft *BE* using a master rod *ABC* and articulated rod *AD*. If the crankshaft is rotating at $\omega = 30$ rad/s, determine the velocities of the pistons *C* and *D* at the instant shown.

Prob. 16–75

**16-77.** Mechanical toy animals often use a walking mechanism as shown idealized in the figure. If the driving crank *AB* is propelled by a spring motor such that $\omega_{AB} = 5$ rad/s, determine the velocity of the rear foot *E* at the instant shown. Although not part of this problem, the upper end of the foreleg has a slotted guide which is constrained by the fixed pin at *G*.

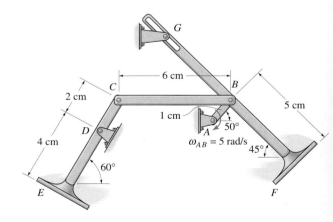

Prob. 16–77

# 16.6   Instantaneous Center of Zero Velocity

The velocity of any point $B$ located on a rigid body can be obtained in a very direct way if one chooses the base point $A$ to be a point that has *zero velocity* at the instant considered. In this case, $\mathbf{v}_A = \mathbf{0}$, and therefore the velocity equation, $\mathbf{v}_B = \mathbf{v}_A + \boldsymbol{\omega} \times \mathbf{r}_{B/A}$, becomes $\mathbf{v}_B = \boldsymbol{\omega} \times \mathbf{r}_{B/A}$. For a body having general plane motion, point $A$ so chosen is called the *instantaneous center of zero velocity (IC)*, and it lies on the *instantaneous axis of zero velocity*. This axis is always perpendicular to the plane of motion, and the intersection of the axis with this plane defines the location of the *IC*. Since point $A$ is coincident with the *IC*, then $\mathbf{v}_B = \boldsymbol{\omega} \times \mathbf{r}_{B/IC}$ and so point $B$ moves momentarily about the *IC* in a *circular path;* in other words, the body appears to rotate about the instantaneous axis. The *magnitude* of $\mathbf{v}_B$ is simply $v_B = \omega r_{B/IC}$, where $\omega$ is the angular velocity of the body. Due to the circular motion, the *direction* of $\mathbf{v}_B$ must always be *perpendicular* to $\mathbf{r}_{B/IC}$.

For example, consider the wheel in Fig. 16–17a. If it rolls *without slipping*, then the point of *contact* with the ground has *zero velocity*. Hence this point represents the *IC* for the wheel, Fig. 16–17b. If it is imagined that the wheel is momentarily pinned at this point, the velocities of points $B$, $C$, $O$, and so on, can be found using $v = \omega r$. Here the radial distances $r_{B/IC}$, $r_{C/IC}$, and $r_{O/IC}$, shown in Fig. 16–17b, must be determined from the geometry of the wheel.

(a)

(b)

Fig. 16–17

The *IC* for this bicycle wheel is at the ground. There the spokes are somewhat visible, whereas at the top of the wheel they become blurred. Note also how points on the side portions of the wheel move as shown by their velocities.

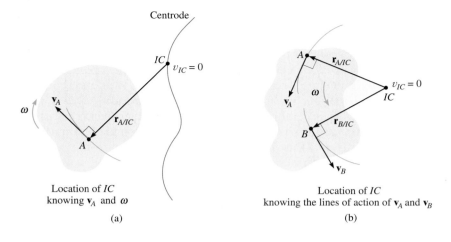

Location of *IC*
knowing $\mathbf{v}_A$ and $\boldsymbol{\omega}$

(a)

Location of *IC*
knowing the lines of action of $\mathbf{v}_A$ and $\mathbf{v}_B$

(b)

**Fig. 16–18**

**Location of the IC.** To locate the *IC* we can use the fact that the *velocity* of a point on the body is *always perpendicular* to the *relative-position vector* extending from the *IC* to the point. Several possibilities exist:

- *Given the velocity $\mathbf{v}_A$ of a point A on the body, and the angular velocity $\boldsymbol{\omega}$ of the body,* Fig. 16–18a. In this case, the *IC* is located along the line drawn perpendicular to $\mathbf{v}_A$ at *A*, such that the distance from *A* to the *IC* is $r_{A/IC} = v_A/\omega$. Note that the *IC* lies up and to the right of *A* since $\mathbf{v}_A$ must cause a clockwise angular velocity $\boldsymbol{\omega}$ about the *IC*.

- *Given the lines of action of two nonparallel velocities $\mathbf{v}_A$ and $\mathbf{v}_B$,* Fig. 16–18b. Construct at points *A* and *B* line segments that are perpendicular to $\mathbf{v}_A$ and $\mathbf{v}_B$. Extending these perpendiculars to their *point of intersection* as shown locates the *IC* at the instant considered.

- *Given the magnitude and direction of two parallel velocities $\mathbf{v}_A$ and $\mathbf{v}_B$.* Here the location of the *IC* is determined by proportional triangles. Examples are shown in Fig. 16–18c and d. In both cases $r_{A/IC} = v_A/\omega$ and $r_{B/IC} = v_B/\omega$. If *d* is a known distance between points *A* and *B*, then in Fig. 16–18c, $r_{A/IC} + r_{B/IC} = d$ and in Fig. 16–18d, $r_{B/IC} - r_{A/IC} = d$. As a special case, note that if the body is *translating*, $\mathbf{v}_A = \mathbf{v}_B$, then the *IC* would be located at infinity, in which case $r_{A/IC} = r_{B/IC} \rightarrow \infty$. This being the case, $\omega = (v_A/r_{A/IC}) = (v_B/r_{B/IC}) \rightarrow 0$, as expected.

(c)

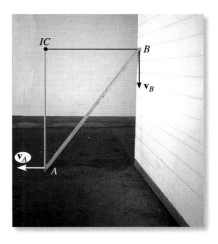

Location of *IC*
knowing $\mathbf{v}_A$ and $\mathbf{v}_B$

(d)

**Fig. 16–18**

Realize that the point chosen as the instantaneous center of zero velocity for the body *can only be used for an instant of time* since the body changes its position from one instant to the next. The locus of points which define the location of the *IC* during the body's motion is called a *centrode*, Fig. 16–18a, and so each point on the centrode acts as the *IC* for the body only for an instant.

Although the *IC* may be conveniently used to determine the velocity of any point in a body, it generally *does not have zero acceleration* and therefore it *should not* be used for finding the accelerations of points in a body.

As the board slides downward to the left it is subjected to general plane motion. Since the directions of the velocities of its ends *A* and *B* are known, the *IC* is located as shown. At this instant the board will momentarily rotate about this point. Draw the board in several other positions, establish the *IC* for each case and sketch the centrode.

## PROCEDURE FOR ANALYSIS

The velocity of a point on a body which is subjected to general plane motion can be determined with reference to its instantaneous center of zero velocity provided the location of the *IC* is first established using one of the three methods described above.

- As shown on the kinematic diagram in Fig. 16–19, the body is imagined as "extended and pinned" at the *IC* such that, at the instant considered, it rotates about this pin with its angular velocity $\boldsymbol{\omega}$.

- The *magnitude* of velocity for each of the arbitrary points *A*, *B*, and *C* on the body can be determined by using the equation $v = \omega r$, where $r$ is the radial distance from the *IC* to each point.

- The line of action of each velocity vector $\mathbf{v}$ is *perpendicular* to its associated radial line $\mathbf{r}$, and the velocity has a *sense of direction* which tends to move the point in a manner consistent with the angular rotation $\boldsymbol{\omega}$ of the radial line, Fig. 16–19.

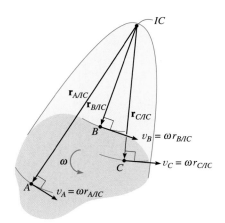

**Fig. 16–19**

## EXAMPLE 16.10

Show how to determine the location of the instantaneous center of zero velocity for (a) member $BC$ shown in Fig. 16–20a; and (b) the link $CB$ shown in Fig. 16–20b.

(a)

(b)

**Fig. 16–20**

(c)

(d)

### Solution

*Part (a).* As shown in Fig. 16–20a, point $B$ has a velocity $\mathbf{v}_B$, which is caused by the clockwise rotation of link $AB$. Point $B$ moves in a circular path such that $\mathbf{v}_B$ is perpendicular to $AB$, and so it acts at an angle $\theta$ from the horizontal as shown in Fig. 16–20c. The motion of point $B$ causes the piston to move forward *horizontally* with a velocity $\mathbf{v}_C$. When lines are drawn perpendicular to $\mathbf{v}_B$ and $\mathbf{v}_C$, Fig. 16–20c, they intersect at the *IC*.

*Part (b).* Points $B$ and $C$ follow circular paths of motion since rods $AB$ and $DC$ are each subjected to rotation about a fixed axis, Fig. 16–20b. Since the velocity is always tangent to the path, at the instant considered, $\mathbf{v}_C$ on rod $DC$ and $\mathbf{v}_B$ on rod $AB$ are both directed vertically downward, along the axis of link $CB$, Fig. 16–20d. Radial lines drawn perpendicular to these two velocities form parallel lines which intersect at "infinity;" i.e., $r_{C/IC} \to \infty$ and $r_{B/IC} \to \infty$. Thus, $\omega_{CB} = (v_C/r_{C/IC}) = \to 0$. As a result, rod $CB$ momentarily *translates*. An instant later, however, $CB$ will move to a tilted position, causing the instantaneous center to move to some finite location.

E X A M P L E  **16.11**

Block $D$ shown in Fig. 16–21$a$ moves with a speed of 3 m/s. Determine the angular velocities of links $BD$ and $AB$, at the instant shown.

(a)

Fig. 16–21

**Solution**

As $D$ moves to the right, it causes arm $AB$ to rotate clockwise about point $A$. Hence, $\mathbf{v}_B$ is directed perpendicular to $AB$. The instantaneous center of zero velocity for $BD$ is located at the intersection of the line segments drawn perpendicular to $\mathbf{v}_B$ and $\mathbf{v}_D$, Fig. 16–21$b$. From the geometry,

$$r_{B/IC} = 0.4 \tan 45°\,\text{m} = 0.4\,\text{m}$$

$$r_{D/IC} = \frac{0.4\,\text{m}}{\cos 45°} = 0.566\,\text{m}$$

(b)

Since the magnitude of $\mathbf{v}_D$ is known, the angular velocity of link $BD$ is

$$\omega_{BD} = \frac{v_D}{r_{D/IC}} = \frac{3\,\text{m/s}}{0.566\,\text{m}} = 5.30\,\text{rad/s}\,\text{↰}\qquad Ans.$$

The velocity of $B$ is therefore

$$v_B = \omega_{BD}(r_{B/IC}) = 5.30\,\text{rad/s}(0.4\,\text{m}) = 2.12\,\text{m/s}\,\text{↘}^{45°}$$

From Fig. 16–21$c$, the angular velocity of $AB$ is

(c)

$$\omega_{AB} = \frac{v_B}{r_{B/A}} = \frac{2.12\,\text{m/s}}{0.4\,\text{m}} = 5.30\,\text{rad/s}\,\text{↓}\qquad Ans.$$

**EXAMPLE 16.12**

The cylinder shown in Fig. 16–22a rolls without slipping between the two moving plates $E$ and $D$. Determine the angular velocity of the cylinder and the velocity of its center $C$ at the instant shown.

(a)

**Fig. 16–22**

**Solution**

Since no slipping occurs, the contact points $A$ and $B$ on the cylinder have the same velocities as the plates $E$ and $D$, respectively. Furthermore, the velocities $\mathbf{v}_A$ and $\mathbf{v}_B$ are *parallel*, so that by the proportionality of right triangles the $IC$ is located at a point on line $AB$, Fig. 16–22b. Assuming this point to be a distance $x$ from $B$, we have

(b)

$$v_B = \omega x; \qquad\qquad 0.4 \text{ m/s} = \omega x$$

$$v_A = \omega(0.25 \text{ m} - x); \qquad 0.25 \text{ m/s} = \omega(0.25 \text{ m} - x)$$

Dividing one equation into the other eliminates $\omega$ and yields

$$0.4(0.25 - x) = 0.25x$$

$$x = \frac{0.1}{0.65} = 0.154 \text{ m}$$

Hence, the angular velocity of the cylinder is

$$\omega = \frac{v_B}{x} = \frac{0.4 \text{ m/s}}{0.154 \text{ m}} = 2.60 \text{ rad/s}\downarrow \qquad\qquad Ans.$$

The velocity of point $C$ is therefore

$$v_C = \omega r_{C/IC} = 2.60 \text{ rad/s}(0.154 \text{ m} - 0.125 \text{ m})$$
$$= 0.0750 \text{ m/s} \leftarrow \qquad\qquad Ans.$$

# PROBLEMS

**16-78.** Solve Prob. 16–51 using the method of instantaneous center of zero velocity.

**16-79.** Solve Prob. 16–54 using the method of instantaneous center of zero velocity.

**\*16-80.** Solve Prob. 16–60 using the method of instantaneous center of zero velocity.

**16-81.** Solve Prob. 16–61 using the method of instantaneous center of zero velocity.

**16-82.** Solve Prob. 16–62 using the method of instantaneous center of zero velocity.

**16-83.** Solve Prob. 16–63 using the method of instantaneous center of zero velocity.

**\*16-84.** Solve Prob. 16–65 using the method of instantaneous center of zero velocity.

**16-85.** Solve Prob. 16–66 using the method of instantaneous center of zero velocity.

**16-86.** In each case show graphically how to locate the instantaneous center of zero velocity of link $AB$. Assume the geometry is known.

**16-87.** The shaper mechanism is designed to give a slow cutting stroke and a quick return to a blade attached to the slider at $C$. Determine the angular velocity of the link $CB$ at the instant shown, if the link $AB$ is rotating at 4 rad/s.

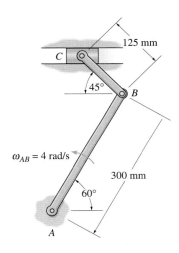

Prob. 16–87

**\*16-88.** At the instant shown, the disk is rotating at $\omega = 4$ rad/s. Determine the velocities of points $A$, $B$, and $C$.

Prob. 16–86

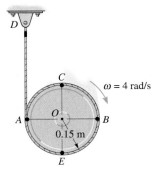

Prob. 16–88

**16-89.** The wheel rolls on its hub without slipping on the horizontal surface. If the velocity of the center of the wheel is $v_C = 0.6$ m/s to the right, determine the velocities of points $A$ and $B$ at the instant shown.

Prob. 16–89

**16-90.** If link $CD$ has an angular velocity of $\omega_{CD} = 6$ rad/s, determine the velocity of point $E$ on link $BC$ and the angular velocity of link $AB$ at the instant shown.

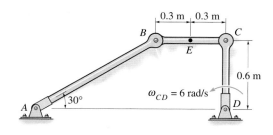

Prob. 16–90

**16-91.** If link $AB$ is rotating at $\omega_{AB} = 6$ rad/s, determine the angular velocities of links $BC$ and $CD$ at the instant $\theta = 60°$.

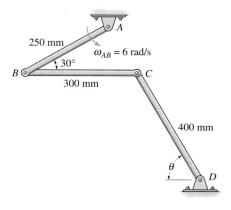

Prob. 16–91

**\*16-92.** Determine the angular velocity of link $AB$ at the instant shown if block $C$ is moving upward at 12 cm/s.

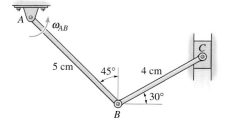

Prob. 16–92

**16-93.** As the car travels forward at 24 m/s on a wet road, due to slipping, the rear wheels have an angular velocity $\omega = 100$ rad/s. Determine the speeds of points $A$, $B$, and $C$ caused by the motion.

**\*16-96.** Due to slipping, points $A$ and $B$ on the rim of the disk have the velocities shown. Determine the velocities of the center point $C$ and point $D$ at this instant.

**16-97.** Due to slipping, points $A$ and $B$ on the rim of the disk have the velocities shown. Determine the velocities of the center point $C$ and point $E$ at this instant.

Prob. 16–93

Probs. 16–96/97

**16-94.** Knowing that the angular velocity of link $AB$ is $\omega_{AB} = 4$ rad/s, determine the velocity of the collar at $C$ and the angular velocity of link $CB$ at the instant shown. Link $CB$ is horizontal at this instant.

**16-95.** If the collar at $C$ is moving downward to the left at $v_C = 8$ m/s, determine the angular velocity of link $AB$ at the instant shown.

**16-98.** The mechanism used in a marine engine consists of a single crank $AB$ and two connecting rods $BC$ and $BD$. Determine the velocity of the piston at $C$ the instant the crank is in the position shown and has an angular velocity of 5 rad/s.

**16-99.** The mechanism used in a marine engine consists of a single crank $AB$ and two connecting rods $BC$ and $BD$. Determine the velocity of the piston at $D$ the instant the crank is in the position shown and has an angular velocity of 5 rad/s.

Probs. 16–94/95

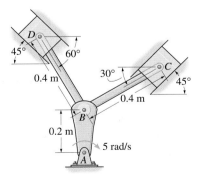

Probs. 16–98/99

**\*16-100.** The square plate is confined within the slots at $A$ and $B$. When $\theta = 30°$, point $A$ is moving at $v_A = 8$ m/s. Determine the velocity of point $C$ at this instant.

**16-101.** The square plate is confined within the slots at $A$ and $B$. When $\theta = 30°$, point $A$ is moving at $v_A = 8$ m/s. Determine the velocity of point $D$ at this instant.

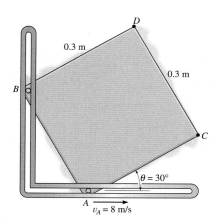

**Probs. 16–100/101**

**16-102.** The epicyclic gear train is driven by the rotating link $DE$, which has an angular velocity $\omega_{DE} = 5$ rad/s. If the ring gear $F$ is fixed, determine the angular velocities of gears $A$, $B$, and $C$.

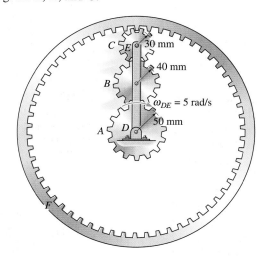

**Prob. 16–102**

**16-103.** The mechanism produces intermittent motion of link $AB$. If the sprocket $S$ is turning with an angular velocity of $\omega_s = 6$ rad/s, determine the angular velocity of link $AB$ at this instant. The sprocket $S$ is mounted on a shaft which is separate from a collinear shaft attached to $AB$ at $A$. The pin at $C$ is attached to one of the chain links.

**Prob. 16–103**

**\*16-104.** The similar links $AB$ and $CD$ rotate about the fixed pins at $A$ and $C$. If $AB$ has an angular velocity $\omega_{AB} = 8$ rad/s, determine the angular velocity of $BDP$ and the velocity of point $P$.

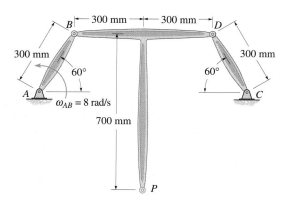

**Prob. 16–104**

# 16.7 Relative-Motion Analysis: Acceleration

An equation that relates the accelerations of two points on a rigid body subjected to general plane motion may be determined by differentiating the velocity equation $\mathbf{v}_B = \mathbf{v}_A + \mathbf{v}_{B/A}$ with respect to time. This yields

$$\frac{d\mathbf{v}_B}{dt} = \frac{d\mathbf{v}_A}{dt} + \frac{d\mathbf{v}_{B/A}}{dt}$$

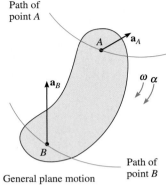

Path of point A

Path of point B

General plane motion

(a)

The terms $d\mathbf{v}_B/dt = \mathbf{a}_B$ and $d\mathbf{v}_A/dt = \mathbf{a}_A$ are measured from a set of *fixed x, y axes* and represent the *absolute accelerations* of points $B$ and $A$. The last term represents the acceleration of $B$ with respect to $A$ as measured by an observer fixed to translating $x'$, $y'$ axes which have their origin at the base point $A$. In Sec. 16.5 it was shown that to this observer point $B$ appears to move along a *circular arc* that has a radius of curvature $r_{B/A}$. Consequently, $\mathbf{a}_{B/A}$ can be expressed in terms of its tangential and normal components of motion; i.e., $\mathbf{a}_{B/A} = (\mathbf{a}_{B/A})_t + (\mathbf{a}_{B/A})_n$, where $(a_{B/A})_t = \alpha r_{B/A}$ and $(a_{B/A})_n = \omega^2 r_{B/A}$. Hence, the relative-acceleration equation can be written in the form

$$\boxed{\mathbf{a}_B = \mathbf{a}_A + (\mathbf{a}_{B/A})_t + (\mathbf{a}_{B/A})_n} \qquad (16\text{--}17)$$

where

$\mathbf{a}_B$ = acceleration of point $B$

$\mathbf{a}_A$ = acceleration of point $A$

$(\mathbf{a}_{B/A})_t$ = relative tangential acceleration component of "$B$ with respect to $A$." The *magnitude* is $(a_{B/A})_t = \alpha r_{B/A}$, and the *direction* is perpendicular to $\mathbf{r}_{B/A}$.

$(\mathbf{a}_{B/A})_n$ = relative normal acceleration component of "$B$ with respect to $A$." The *magnitude* is $(a_{B/A})_n = \omega^2 r_{B/A}$ and the *direction* is always from $B$ towards $A$.

Translation

(b)

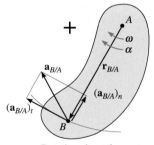

Rotation about the base point $A$

(c)

Each of the four terms in Eq. 16–17 is represented graphically on the *kinematic diagrams* shown in Fig. 16–23. Here it is seen that at a given instant the acceleration of $B$, Fig. 16–23a, is determined by considering the body to translate with an acceleration $\mathbf{a}_A$, Fig. 16–23b, and simultaneously rotate about the base point $A$ with an instantaneous angular velocity $\boldsymbol{\omega}$ and angular acceleration $\boldsymbol{\alpha}$, Fig. 16–23c. Vector addition of these two effects, applied to $B$, yields $\mathbf{a}_B$, as shown in Fig. 16–23d. It should be noted from Fig. 16–23a that since points $A$ and $B$ move along *curved paths*, the accelerations of these points will have *both tangential and normal components*. (Recall that the acceleration of a point is *tangent to the path only* when the path is *rectilinear* or when it is an inflection point on a curve.)

$$\mathbf{a}_B = \mathbf{a}_A + (\mathbf{a}_{B/A})_t + (\mathbf{a}_{B/A})_n$$

(d)

Fig. 16–23

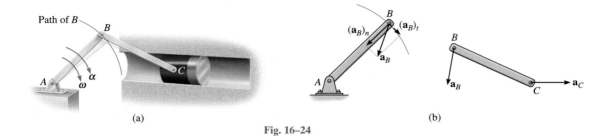

**Fig. 16–24**

Since the relative-acceleration components represent the effect of *circular motion* observed from translating axes having their origin at the base point $A$, these terms can be expressed as $(\mathbf{a}_{B/A})_t = \boldsymbol{\alpha} \times \mathbf{r}_{B/A}$ and $(\mathbf{a}_{B/A})_n = -\omega^2\mathbf{r}_{B/A}$, Eq. 16–14. Hence, Eq. 16–17 becomes

$$\mathbf{a}_B = \mathbf{a}_A + \boldsymbol{\alpha} \times \mathbf{r}_{B/A} - \omega^2\mathbf{r}_{B/A} \qquad (16\text{–}18)$$

where

$\mathbf{a}_B$ = acceleration of point $B$

$\mathbf{a}_A$ = acceleration of the base point $A$

$\boldsymbol{\alpha}$ = angular acceleration of the body

$\boldsymbol{\omega}$ = angular velocity of the body

$\mathbf{r}_{B/A}$ = relative-position vector drawn from $A$ to $B$

If Eq. 16–17 or 16–18 is applied in a practical manner to study the accelerated motion of a rigid body which is pin connected to two other bodies, it should be realized that points which are *coincident at the pin* move with the *same acceleration*, since the path of motion over which they travel is the *same*. For example, point $B$ lying on either rod $AB$ or $BC$ of the crank mechanism shown in Fig. 16–24a has the same acceleration, since the rods are pin connected at $B$. Here the motion of $B$ is along a *curved path*, so that $\mathbf{a}_B$ can be expressed in terms of its tangential and normal components. At the other end of rod $BC$ point $C$ moves along a *straight-lined path*, which is defined by the piston. Hence, $\mathbf{a}_C$ is horizontal, Fig. 16–24b.

If two bodies contact one another *without slipping*, and the *points in contact* move along *different paths*, the *tangential components* of acceleration of the points will be the *same*; however, the *normal components* will *not* be the same. For example, consider the two meshed gears in Fig. 16–25a. Point $A$ is located on gear $B$ and a coincident point $A'$ is located on gear $C$. Due to the rotational motion, $(\mathbf{a}_A)_t = (\mathbf{a}_{A'})_t$; however, since both points follow different curved paths, $(\mathbf{a}_A)_n \neq (\mathbf{a}_{A'})_n$ and therefore $\mathbf{a}_A \neq \mathbf{a}_{A'}$, Fig. 16–25b.

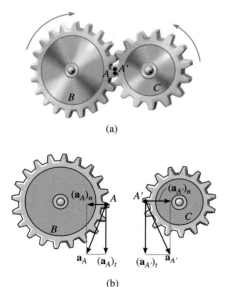

**Fig. 16–25**

## PROCEDURE FOR ANALYSIS

The relative acceleration equation can be applied between any two points $A$ and $B$ on a body either by using a Cartesian vector analysis, or by writing the $x$ and $y$ scalar component equations directly.

*Velocity Analysis.*

- Determine the angular velocity $\boldsymbol{\omega}$ of the body by using a velocity analysis as discussed in Sec. 16.5 or 16.6. Also, determine the velocities $\mathbf{v}_A$ and $\mathbf{v}_B$ of points $A$ and $B$ *if these points move along curved paths.*

**VECTOR ANALYSIS**

*Kinematic Diagram.*

- Establish the directions of the fixed $x$, $y$ coordinates and draw the kinematic diagram of the body. Indicate on it $\mathbf{a}_A$, $\mathbf{a}_B$, $\boldsymbol{\omega}$, $\boldsymbol{\alpha}$, and $\mathbf{r}_{B/A}$.

- If points $A$ and $B$ move along *curved paths*, then their accelerations should be indicated in terms of their tangential and normal components, i.e., $\mathbf{a}_A = (\mathbf{a}_A)_t + (\mathbf{a}_A)_n$ and $\mathbf{a}_B = (\mathbf{a}_B)_t + (\mathbf{a}_B)_n$.

*Acceleration Equation.*

- To apply $\mathbf{a}_B = \mathbf{a}_A + \boldsymbol{\alpha} \times \mathbf{r}_{B/A} - \omega^2 \mathbf{r}_{B/A}$ express the vectors in Cartesian vector form and substitute them into the equation. Evaluate the cross product and then equate the respective $\mathbf{i}$ and $\mathbf{j}$ components to obtain two scalar equations.

- If the solution yields a *negative* answer for an *unknown* magnitude, it indicates that the sense of direction of the vector is opposite to that shown on the kinematic diagram.

**SCALAR ANALYSIS**

*Kinematic Diagram.*

- If the equation $\mathbf{a}_B = \mathbf{a}_A + (\mathbf{a}_{B/A})_t + (\mathbf{a}_{B/A})_n$ is applied, then the magnitudes and directions of the relative-acceleration components $(\mathbf{a}_{B/A})_t$ and $(\mathbf{a}_{B/A})_n$ must be established. To do this draw a kinematic diagram such as shown in Fig. 16–23c. Since the body is considered to be momentarily "pinned" at the base point $A$, the *magnitudes* are $(a_{B/A})_t = \alpha r_{B/A}$ and $(a_{B/A})_n = \omega^2 r_{B/A}$. Their *sense of direction* is established from the diagram such that $(\mathbf{a}_{B/A})_t$ acts perpendicular to $\mathbf{r}_{B/A}$, in accordance with the rotational motion $\boldsymbol{\alpha}$ of the body, and $(\mathbf{a}_{B/A})_n$ is directed from $B$ towards $A$.*

*Acceleration Equation.*

- Represent the vectors in $\mathbf{a}_B = \mathbf{a}_A + (\mathbf{a}_{B/A})_t + (\mathbf{a}_{B/A})_n$ graphically by showing their magnitudes and directions underneath each term. The scalar equations are determined from the $x$ and $y$ components of these vectors.

*The notation $\mathbf{a}_B = \mathbf{a}_A + (\mathbf{a}_{B/A(\text{pin})})_t + (\mathbf{a}_{B/A(\text{pin})})_n$ may be helpful in recalling that $A$ is assumed to be pinned.

The mechanism for a window is shown. Here $CA$ rotates about a fixed axis through $C$, and $AB$ undergoes general plane motion. Since point $A$ moves along a curved path it has two components of acceleration, whereas point $B$ moves along a straight track and the direction of its acceleration is specified.

**EXAMPLE 16.13**

(a)

(b)

The rod $AB$ shown in Fig. 16–26a is confined to move along the inclined planes at $A$ and $B$. If point $A$ has an acceleration of 3 m/s$^2$ and a velocity of 2 m/s, both directed down the plane at the instant the rod becomes horizontal, determine the angular acceleration of the rod at this instant.

**Solution I (Vector Analysis)**

We will apply the acceleration equation to points $A$ and $B$ on the rod. To do so it is first necessary to determine the angular velocity of the rod. Show that it is $\omega = 0.283$ rad/s ↑ using either the velocity equation or the method of instantaneous centers.

*Kinematic Diagram.* Since points $A$ and $B$ both move along straight-line paths, they have *no* components of acceleration normal to the paths. There are two unknowns in Fig. 16–26b, namely, $a_B$ and $\alpha$.

*Acceleration Equation.* Applying Eq. 16–18 to points $A$ and $B$ on the rod, and expressing each of the vectors in Cartesian vector form, we have

$$\mathbf{a}_B = \mathbf{a}_A + \boldsymbol{\alpha} \times \mathbf{r}_{B/A} - \omega^2 \mathbf{r}_{B/A}$$

$$a_B \cos 45°\mathbf{i} + a_B \sin 45°\mathbf{j} = 3 \cos 45°\mathbf{i} - 3 \sin 45°\mathbf{j} + (\alpha\mathbf{k}) \times (10\mathbf{i}) - (0.283)^2(10\mathbf{i})$$

Carrying out the cross product and equating the **i** and **j** components yields

$$a_B \cos 45° = 3 \cos 45° - (0.283)^2(10) \tag{1}$$

$$a_B \sin 45° = -3 \sin 45° + \alpha(10) \tag{2}$$

Solving, we have

$$a_B = 1.87 \text{ m/s}^2 \angle{}^{45°}$$

$$\alpha = 0.344 \text{ rad/s}^2\!\uparrow \qquad\qquad Ans.$$

**Solution II (Scalar Analysis)**

As an alternative procedure, the scalar component equations 1 and 2 can be obtained directly. From the kinematic diagram, showing the relative-acceleration components $(\mathbf{a}_{B/A})_t$ and $(\mathbf{a}_{B/A})_n$, Fig. 16–26c, we have

$$\mathbf{a}_B = \mathbf{a}_A + (\mathbf{a}_{B/A})_t + (\mathbf{a}_{B/A})_n$$

$$\begin{bmatrix} a_B \\ \nearrow^{45°} \end{bmatrix} = \begin{bmatrix} 3 \text{ m/s}^2 \\ \searrow^{45°} \end{bmatrix} + \begin{bmatrix} \alpha(10 \text{ m}) \\ \uparrow \end{bmatrix} + \begin{bmatrix} (0.283 \text{ rad/s})^2(10 \text{ m}) \\ \leftarrow \end{bmatrix}$$

(c)

Fig. 16–26

Equating the $x$ and $y$ components yields Eqs. 1 and 2, and the solution proceeds as before.

**E X A M P L E  16.14**

At a given instant, the cylinder of radius $r$, shown in Fig. 16–27$a$, has an angular velocity $\omega$ and angular acceleration $\alpha$. Determine the velocity and acceleration of its center $G$ if it rolls without slipping.

(a)

**Solution (Vector Analysis)**

As the cylinder rolls, point $G$ moves along a straight line, and point $A$, located on the rim of the cylinder, moves along a curved path called a *cycloid*, Fig. 16–27$b$. We will apply the velocity and acceleration equations to these two points.

*Velocity Analysis.*  Since no slipping occurs, at the instant $A$ contacts the ground, $\mathbf{v}_A = \mathbf{0}$. Thus, from the kinematic diagram in Fig. 16–27$c$ we have

$$\mathbf{v}_G = \mathbf{v}_A + \omega \times \mathbf{r}_{G/A}$$
$$v_G\mathbf{i} = \mathbf{0} + (-\omega\mathbf{k}) \times (r\mathbf{j})$$
$$v_G = \omega r \qquad (1) \quad Ans.$$

(b)

This same result can also be obtained directly by noting that point $A$ represents the instantaneous center of zero velocity.

*Kinematic Diagram.*  The acceleration of point $G$ is horizontal since it moves along a *straight-line path. Just before* point $A$ touches the ground, its velocity is directed downward along the $y$ axis, Fig. 16–27$b$, and just after contact, its velocity is directed *upward*. For this reason, point $A$ begins to accelerate upward when it leaves the ground at $A$, Fig. 16–27$d$. The magnitudes of $\mathbf{a}_A$ and $\mathbf{a}_G$ are unknown.

(c)

*Acceleration Equation.*

$$\mathbf{a}_G = \mathbf{a}_A + \alpha \times \mathbf{r}_{G/A} - \omega^2\mathbf{r}_{G/A}$$
$$a_G\mathbf{i} = a_A\mathbf{j} + (-\alpha\mathbf{k}) \times (r\mathbf{j}) - \omega^2(r\mathbf{j})$$

Evaluating the cross product and equating the $\mathbf{i}$ and $\mathbf{j}$ components yields

$$a_G = \alpha r \qquad (2) \quad Ans.$$
$$a_A = \omega^2 r \qquad (3)$$

(d)

Fig. 16–27

These important results, that $v_G = \omega r$ and $a_G = \alpha r$, were also obtained in Example 16.4. They apply to any circular object, such as a ball, pulley, disk, etc., that rolls *without* slipping. Also, the fact that $a_A = \omega^2 r$ indicates that the instantaneous center of zero velocity, point $A$, *is not* a point of zero acceleration.

EXAMPLE **16.15**

The ball rolls without slipping and has the angular motion shown in Fig. 16–28a. Determine the accelerations of point $B$ and point $A$ at this instant.

(a)

(b)                                  (c)

**Fig. 16–28**

**Solution (Vector Analysis)**

*Kinematic Diagram.* Using the results of the previous example, the center of the ball has an acceleration of $a_O = \alpha r = (4 \text{ rad/s}^2)(0.15 \text{ m}) = 0.6 \text{ m/s}^2$. We will apply the acceleration equation to points $O$ and $B$ and points $O$ and $A$.

*Acceleration Equation.*

For point $B$, Fig. 16–28b,

$$\mathbf{a}_B = \mathbf{a}_O + \boldsymbol{\alpha} \times \mathbf{r}_{B/O} - \omega^2 \mathbf{r}_{B/O}$$
$$\mathbf{a}_B = -0.6\mathbf{i} + (4\mathbf{k}) \times (0.15\mathbf{i}) - (6)^2(0.15\mathbf{i})$$
$$\mathbf{a}_B = \{-6\mathbf{i} + 0.6\mathbf{j}\} \text{ m/s}^2 \qquad \qquad \qquad Ans.$$

For point $A$, Fig. 16–28c,

$$\mathbf{a}_A = \mathbf{a}_O + \boldsymbol{\alpha} \times \mathbf{r}_{A/O} - \omega^2 \mathbf{r}_{A/O}$$
$$\mathbf{a}_A = -0.6\mathbf{i} + (4\mathbf{k}) \times (0.15\mathbf{j}) - (6)^2(0.15\mathbf{j})$$
$$\mathbf{a}_A = \{-1.2\mathbf{i} - 5.4\mathbf{j}\} \text{ m/s}^2 \qquad \qquad \qquad Ans.$$

## EXAMPLE 16.16

The spool shown in Fig. 16–29a unravels from the cord, such that at the instant shown it has an angular velocity of 3 rad/s and an angular acceleration of 4 rad/s². Determine the acceleration of point B.

### Solution I (Vector Analysis)

The spool "appears" to be rolling downward without slipping at point A. Therefore, we can use the results of Example 16.14 to determine the acceleration of point G, i.e.,

$$a_G = \alpha r = 4 \text{ rad/s}^2 (150 \text{ mm}) = 600 \text{ mm/s}^2 = 0.6 \text{ m/s}^2$$

We will apply the acceleration equation at points G and B.

*Kinematic Diagram.* Point B moves along a *curved path* having an *unknown* radius of curvature.* Its acceleration will be represented by its unknown x and y components as shown in Fig. 16–29b.

*Acceleration Equation.*

$$\mathbf{a}_B = \mathbf{a}_G + \boldsymbol{\alpha} \times \mathbf{r}_{B/G} - \omega^2 \mathbf{r}_{B/G}$$
$$(a_B)_x \mathbf{i} + (a_B)_y \mathbf{j} = -600 \mathbf{j} + (-4\mathbf{k}) \times (225\mathbf{j}) - (3)^2 (225\mathbf{j})$$

Equating the **i** and **j** terms, the component equations are

$$(a_B)_x = 4(225) = 900 \text{ mm/s}^2 = 0.9 \text{ m/s}^2 \rightarrow \qquad (1)$$

$$(a_B)_y = -600 - 2025 = -2625 \text{ mm/s}^2 = 2.625 \text{ m/s}^2 \downarrow \qquad (2)$$

The magnitude and direction of $\mathbf{a}_B$ are therefore

$$a_B = \sqrt{(0.9)^2 + (2.625)^2} = 2.775 \text{ m/s}^2 \qquad Ans.$$

$$\theta = \tan^{-1} \frac{2.625}{0.9} = 71.1° \qquad Ans.$$

### Solution II (Scalar Analysis)

This problem may be solved by writing the scalar component equations directly. The kinematic diagram in Fig. 16–29c shows the relative-acceleration components $(\mathbf{a}_{B/G})_t$ and $(\mathbf{a}_{B/G})_n$. Thus,

$$\mathbf{a}_B = \mathbf{a}_G + (\mathbf{a}_{B/G})_t + (\mathbf{a}_{B/G})_n$$

$$\begin{bmatrix} (a_B)_x \\ \rightarrow \end{bmatrix} + \begin{bmatrix} (a_B)_y \\ \uparrow \end{bmatrix}$$

$$= \begin{bmatrix} 0.6 \text{ m/s}^2 \\ \downarrow \end{bmatrix} + \begin{bmatrix} 4 \text{ rad/s}^2 (0.225 \text{ m}) \\ \rightarrow \end{bmatrix} + \begin{bmatrix} (3 \text{ rad/s})^2 (0.225 \text{ m}) \\ \downarrow \end{bmatrix}$$

The x and y components yield Eqs. 1 and 2 above.

*Realize that the path's radius of curvature ρ is *not* equal to the radius of the spool since the spool is *not* rotating about point G. Furthermore, ρ is *not* defined as the distance from A (IC) to B, since the location of the IC depends only on the velocity of a point and *not* the geometry of its path.

(a)

(b)

(c)

Fig. 16–29

**EXAMPLE 16.17**

The collar $C$ in Fig. 16–30$a$ is moving downward with an acceleration of 1 m/s$^2$. At the instant shown, it has a speed of 2 m/s which gives links $CB$ and $AB$ an angular velocity $\omega_{AB} = \omega_{CB} = 10$ rad/s. (See Example 16.8.) Determine the angular accelerations of $CB$ and $AB$ at this instant.

(a)

**Solution (Vector Analysis)**

*Kinematic Diagram.* The kinematic diagrams of *both* links $AB$ and $CB$ are shown in Fig. 16–30$b$. To solve, we will apply the appropriate kinematic equation to each link.

*Acceleration Equation.*
Link $AB$ (rotation about a fixed axis):

$$\mathbf{a}_B = \boldsymbol{\alpha}_{AB} \times \mathbf{r}_B - \omega_{AB}^2 \mathbf{r}_B$$
$$\mathbf{a}_B = (\alpha_{AB}\mathbf{k}) \times (-0.2\mathbf{j}) - (10)^2(-0.2\mathbf{j})$$
$$\mathbf{a}_B = 0.2\alpha_{AB}\mathbf{i} + 20\mathbf{j}$$

Note that $\mathbf{a}_B$ has two components since it moves along a *curved path*.

Link $BC$ (general plane motion): Using the result for $\mathbf{a}_B$ and applying Eq. 16–18, we have

$$\mathbf{a}_B = \mathbf{a}_C + \boldsymbol{\alpha}_{CB} \times \mathbf{r}_{B/C} - \omega_{CB}^2 \mathbf{r}_{B/C}$$
$$0.2\alpha_{AB}\mathbf{i} + 20\mathbf{j} = -1\mathbf{j} + (\alpha_{CB}\mathbf{k}) \times (0.2\mathbf{i} - 0.2\mathbf{j}) - (10)^2(0.2\mathbf{i} - 0.2\mathbf{j})$$
$$0.2\alpha_{AB}\mathbf{i} + 20\mathbf{j} = -1\mathbf{j} + 0.2\alpha_{CB}\mathbf{j} + 0.2\alpha_{CB}\mathbf{i} - 20\mathbf{i} + 20\mathbf{j}$$

Thus,

$$0.2\alpha_{AB} = 0.2\alpha_{CB} - 20$$
$$20 = -1 + 0.2\alpha_{CB} + 20$$

Solving,

$$\alpha_{CB} = 5 \text{ rad/s}^2 \curvearrowright \qquad\qquad Ans.$$
$$\alpha_{AB} = -95 \text{ rad/s}^2 = 95 \text{ rad/s}^2 \curvearrowleft \qquad\qquad Ans.$$

(b)

Fig. 16–30

# EXAMPLE 16.18

The crankshaft $AB$ of an engine turns with a clockwise angular acceleration of 20 rad/s$^2$, Fig. 16–31a. Determine the acceleration of the piston at the instant $AB$ is in the position shown. At this instant $\omega_{AB} = 10$ rad/s and $\omega_{BC} = 2.43$ rad/s.

**Solution (Vector Analysis)**

*Kinematic Diagram.* The kinematic diagrams for both $AB$ and $BC$ are shown in Fig. 16–31b. Here $\mathbf{a}_C$ is vertical since $C$ moves along a straight-line path.

*Acceleration Equation.* Expressing each of the position vectors in Cartesian vector form

$$\mathbf{r}_B = \{-0.25 \sin 45°\mathbf{i} + 0.25 \cos 45°\mathbf{j}\} \text{ m} = \{-0.177\mathbf{i} + 0.177\mathbf{j}\} \text{ m}$$
$$\mathbf{r}_{C/B} = \{0.75 \sin 13.6°\mathbf{i} + 0.75 \cos 13.6°\mathbf{j}\} \text{ m} = \{0.176\mathbf{i} + 0.729\mathbf{j}\} \text{ m}$$

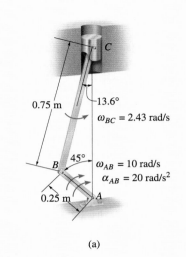

(a)

Crankshaft $AB$ (rotation about a fixed axis):

$$\mathbf{a}_B = \boldsymbol{\alpha}_{AB} \times \mathbf{r}_B - \omega_{AB}^2\mathbf{r}_B$$
$$= (-20\mathbf{k}) \times (-0.177\mathbf{i} + 0.177\mathbf{j}) - (10)^2(-0.177\mathbf{i} + 0.177\mathbf{j})$$
$$= \{21.21\mathbf{i} - 14.14\mathbf{j}\} \text{ m/s}^2$$

Connecting Rod $BC$ (general plane motion): Using the result for $\mathbf{a}_B$ and noting that $\mathbf{a}_C$ is in the vertical direction, we have

$$\mathbf{a}_C = \mathbf{a}_B + \boldsymbol{\alpha}_{BC} \times \mathbf{r}_{C/B} - \omega_{BC}^2\mathbf{r}_{C/B}$$
$$a_C\mathbf{j} = 21.21\mathbf{i} - 14.14\mathbf{j} + (\alpha_{BC}\mathbf{k}) \times (0.176\mathbf{i} + 0.729\mathbf{j}) - (2.43)^2(0.176\mathbf{i} + 0.729\mathbf{j})$$
$$a_C\mathbf{j} = 21.21\mathbf{i} - 14.14\mathbf{j} + 0.176\alpha_{BC}\mathbf{j} - 0.729\alpha_{BC}\mathbf{i} - 1.04\mathbf{i} - 4.30\mathbf{j}$$
$$0 = 20.17 - 0.729\alpha_{BC}$$
$$a_C = 0.176\alpha_{BC} - 18.45$$

(b)

Fig. 16–31

Solving yields

$$\alpha_{BC} = 27.7 \text{ rad/s}^2 \downturn$$
$$a_C = -13.6 \text{ m/s}^2 \qquad\qquad Ans.$$

Since the piston is moving upward, the negative sign for $a_C$ indicates that the piston is decelerating, i.e., $\mathbf{a}_C = \{-13.6\mathbf{j}\} \text{ m/s}^2$. This causes the speed of the piston to decrease until $AB$ becomes vertical, at which time the piston is momentarily at rest.

# PROBLEMS

**16-105.** At a given instant the bottom $A$ of the ladder has an acceleration $a_A = 2$ m/s$^2$ and velocity $v_A = 3$ m/s, both acting to the left. Determine the acceleration of the top of the ladder, $B$, and the ladder's angular acceleration at this same instant.

**16-106.** At a given instant the top $B$ of the ladder has an acceleration $a_B = 1$ m/s$^2$ and a velocity of $v_B = 2$ m/s, both acting downward. Determine the acceleration of the bottom $A$ of the ladder, and the ladder's angular acceleration at this instant.

**Probs. 16–105/106**

**16-107.** At a given instant the top end $A$ of the bar has the velocity and acceleration shown. Determine the acceleration of the bottom $B$ and the bar's angular acceleration at this instant.

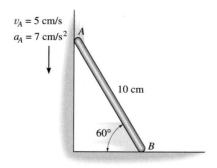

**Prob. 16–107**

**\*16-108.** At a given instant, the slider block $A$ has the velocity and deceleration shown. Determine the acceleration of block $B$ and the angular acceleration of the link at this instant.

**Prob. 16–108**

**16-109.** The wheel is moving to the right such that it has an angular velocity $\omega = 2$ rad/s and angular acceleration $\alpha = 4$ rad/s$^2$ at the instant shown. If it does not slip at $A$, determine the acceleration of point $B$.

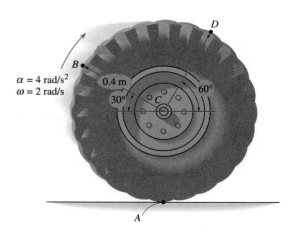

**Prob. 16–109**

**16-110.** At a given instant the wheel is rotating with the angular motions shown. Determine the acceleration of the collar at $A$ at this instant.

*16-112.** At a given instant the wheel is rotating with the angular velocity and angular acceleration shown. Determine the acceleration of block $B$ at this instant.

**Prob. 16–110**

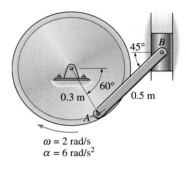

**Prob. 16–112**

**16-113.** The disk is moving to the left such that it has an angular acceleration $\alpha = 8 \text{ rad/s}^2$ and angular velocity $\omega = 3 \text{ rad/s}$ at the instant shown. If it does not slip at $A$, determine the acceleration of point $B$.

**16-111.** The flywheel rotates with an angular velocity $\omega = 2 \text{ rad/s}$ and an angular acceleration $\alpha = 6 \text{ rad/s}^2$. Determine the angular acceleration of links $AB$ and $BC$ at this instant. The slope of the line from $A$ to $B$ is $-3/4$.

**16-114.** The disk is moving to the left such that it has an angular acceleration $\alpha = 8 \text{ rad/s}^2$ and angular velocity $\omega = 3 \text{ rad/s}$ at the instant shown. If it does not slip at $A$, determine the acceleration of point $D$.

**Prob. 16–111**

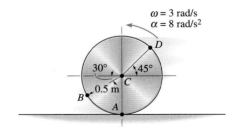

**Probs. 16–113/114**

**16-115.** The hoop is cast on the rough surface such that it has an angular velocity $\omega = 4$ rad/s and an angular acceleration $\alpha = 5$ rad/s$^2$. Also, its center has a velocity $v_O = 5$ m/s and a deceleration $a_O = 2$ m/s$^2$. Determine the acceleration of point $A$ at this instant.

**\*16-116.** The hoop is cast on the rough surface such that it has an angular velocity $\omega = 4$ rad/s and an angular acceleration $\alpha = 5$ rad/s$^2$. Also, its center has a velocity of $v_O = 5$ m/s and a deceleration $a_O = 2$ m/s$^2$. Determine the acceleration of point $B$ at this instant.

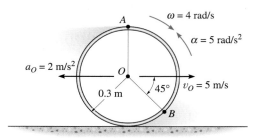

**Probs. 16–115/116**

**16-117.** The disk rotates with an angular velocity $\omega = 5$ rad/s and an angular acceleration $\alpha = 6$ rad/s$^2$. Determine the angular acceleration of link $CB$ at this instant.

**Prob. 16–117**

**16-118.** At a given instant, the slider block $B$ is traveling to the right with the velocity and acceleration shown. Determine the angular acceleration of the wheel at this instant.

**Prob. 16–118**

**16-119.** The ends of the bar $AB$ are confined to move along the paths shown. At a given instant, $A$ has a velocity of 8 m/s and an acceleration of 3 m/s$^2$. Determine the angular velocity and angular acceleration of $AB$ at this instant.

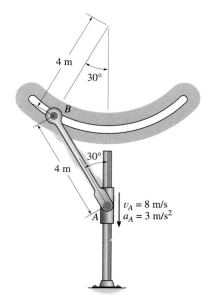

**Prob. 16–119**

**\*16-120.** Rod *AB* has the angular motion shown. Determine the acceleration of the collar *C* at this instant.

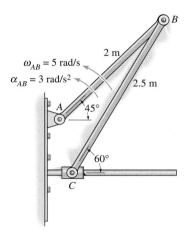

Prob. 16–120

**16-121.** At the given instant member *AB* has the angular motions shown. Determine the velocity and acceleration of the slider block *C* at this instant.

Prob. 16–121

**16-122.** At a given instant gears *A* and *B* have the angular motions shown. Determine the angular acceleration of gear *C* and the acceleration of its center point *D* at this instant. Note that the inner hub of gear *C* is in mesh with gear *A* and its outer rim is in mesh with gear *B*.

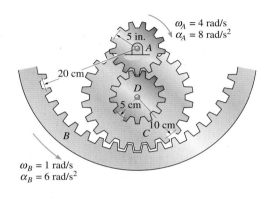

Prob. 16–122

**16-123.** The tied crank and gear mechanism gives rocking motion to crank *AC*, necessary for the operation of a printing press. If link *DE* has the angular motion shown, determine the respective angular velocities of gear *F* and crank *AC* at this instant, and the angular acceleration of crank *AC*.

Prob. 16–123

**\*16-124.** As the cord unravels from the cylinder, the cylinder has an angular acceleration of $\alpha = 4$ rad/s$^2$ and an angular velocity of $\omega = 2$ rad/s at the instant shown. Determine the accelerations of points $A$ and $B$ at this instant.

**16-126.** At a given instant, the gear has the angular motion shown. Determine the accelerations of points $A$ and $B$ on the link and the link's angular acceleration at this instant.

**Prob. 16–124**

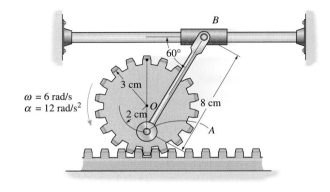

**Prob. 16–126**

**16-125.** The wheel rolls without slipping such that at the instant shown it has an angular velocity $\omega$ and angular acceleration $\alpha$. Determine the velocity and acceleration of point $B$ on the rod at this instant.

**16-127.** Determine the angular acceleration of link $AB$ if link $CD$ has the angular velocity and angular deceleration shown.

**Prob. 16–125**

**Prob. 16–127**

**\*16-128.** The slider block $B$ is moving to the right with an acceleration of 2 m/s². At the instant shown, its velocity is 6 m/s. Determine the angular acceleration of link $AB$ and the acceleration of point $A$ at this instant.

**16-130.** At a given instant, the cables supporting the pipe have the motions shown. Determine the angular velocity and angular acceleration of the pipe and the velocity and acceleration of point $B$ located on the pipe.

Prob. 16–130

Prob. 16–128

**16-129.** The ends of the bar $AB$ are confined to move along the paths shown. At a given instant, $A$ has a velocity of $v_A = 4$ m/s and an acceleration of $a_A = 7$ m/s². Determine the angular velocity and angular acceleration of $AB$ at this instant.

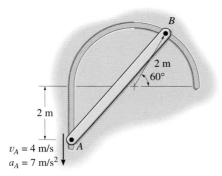

Prob. 16–129

## 16.8 Relative-Motion Analysis Using Rotating Axes

In the previous sections the relative-motion analysis for velocity and acceleration was described using a translating coordinate system. This type of analysis is useful for determining the motion of points on the *same* rigid body, or the motion of points located on several pin-connected rigid bodies. In some problems, however, rigid bodies (mechanisms) are constructed such that *sliding* will occur at their connections. The kinematic analysis for such cases is best performed if the motion is analyzed using a coordinate system which both *translates* and *rotates*. Furthermore, this frame of reference is useful for analyzing the motions of two points on a mechanism which are *not* located in the *same* rigid body and for specifying the kinematics of particle motion when the particle is moving along a rotating path.

In the following analysis two equations are developed which relate the velocity and acceleration of two points, one of which is the origin of a moving frame of reference subjected to both a translation and a rotation in the plane.* Due to the generality in the derivation which follows, these two points may represent either two particles moving independently of one another or two points located on the same (or different) rigid bodies.

**Position.**   Consider the two points $A$ and $B$ shown in Fig. 16–32a. Their location is specified by the position vectors $\mathbf{r}_A$ and $\mathbf{r}_B$, which are measured from the fixed $X, Y, Z$ coordinate system. As shown in the figure, the "base point" $A$ represents the origin of the $x, y, z$ coordinate system, which is assumed to be both translating and rotating with respect to the $X, Y, Z$ system. The position of $B$ with respect to $A$ is specified by the relative-position vector $\mathbf{r}_{B/A}$. The components of this vector may be expressed either in terms of unit vectors along the $X, Y$ axes, i.e., $\mathbf{I}$ and $\mathbf{J}$, or by unit vectors along the $x, y$ axes, i.e., $\mathbf{i}$ and $\mathbf{j}$. For the development which follows, $\mathbf{r}_{B/A}$ will be measured relative to the moving $x, y$ frame of reference. Thus, if $B$ has coordinates $(x_B, y_B)$, Fig. 16–32a, then

$$\mathbf{r}_{B/A} = x_B\mathbf{i} + y_B\mathbf{j}$$

Using vector addition, the three position vectors in Fig. 16–32a are related by the equation

$$\boxed{\mathbf{r}_B = \mathbf{r}_A + \mathbf{r}_{B/A}} \tag{16–19}$$

At the instant considered, point $A$ has a velocity $\mathbf{v}_A$ and an acceleration $\mathbf{a}_A$, while the angular velocity and angular acceleration of the $x, y$ axes are $\mathbf{\Omega}$ (omega) and $\dot{\mathbf{\Omega}} = d\mathbf{\Omega}/dt$, respectively. All these vectors are measured from the $X, Y, Z$ frame of reference, although they may be

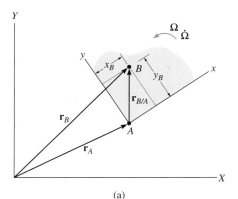

(a)

Fig. 16–32

*The more general, three-dimensional motion of the points is developed in Sec. 20.4.

expressed in terms of either **I, J, K** or **i, j, k** components. Since planar motion is specified, by the right-hand rule $\Omega$ and $\dot{\Omega}$ are always directed *perpendicular* to the reference plane of motion, whereas $\mathbf{v}_A$ and $\mathbf{a}_A$ lie in this plane.

**Velocity.** The velocity of point $B$ is determined by taking the time derivative of Eq. 16–19, which yields

$$\mathbf{v}_B = \mathbf{v}_A + \frac{d\mathbf{r}_{B/A}}{dt} \tag{16–20}$$

The last term in this equation is evaluated as follows:

$$\frac{d\mathbf{r}_{B/A}}{dt} = \frac{d}{dt}(x_B\mathbf{i} + y_B\mathbf{j})$$

$$= \frac{dx_B}{dt}\mathbf{i} + x_B\frac{d\mathbf{i}}{dt} + \frac{dy_B}{dt}\mathbf{j} + y_B\frac{d\mathbf{j}}{dt}$$

$$= \left(\frac{dx_B}{dt}\mathbf{i} + \frac{dy_B}{dt}\mathbf{j}\right) + \left(x_B\frac{d\mathbf{i}}{dt} + y_B\frac{d\mathbf{j}}{dt}\right) \tag{16–21}$$

The two terms in the first set of parentheses represent the components of velocity of point $B$ as measured by an observer attached to the moving $x, y, z$ coordinate system. These terms will be denoted by vector $(\mathbf{v}_{B/A})_{xyz}$. In the second set of parentheses the instantaneous time rate of change of the unit vectors $\mathbf{i}$ and $\mathbf{j}$ is measured by an observer located in the fixed $X, Y, Z$ coordinate system. These changes, $d\mathbf{i}$ and $d\mathbf{j}$, are due *only* to the instantaneous *rotation* $d\theta$ of the $x, y, z$ axes, causing $\mathbf{i}$ to become $\mathbf{i}' = \mathbf{i} + d\mathbf{i}$ and $\mathbf{j}$ to become $\mathbf{j}' = \mathbf{j} + d\mathbf{j}$, Fig. 16–32b. As shown, the *magnitudes* of both $d\mathbf{i}$ and $d\mathbf{j}$ equal $1 (d\theta)$, since $i = i' = j = j' = 1$. The *direction* of $d\mathbf{i}$ is defined by $+\mathbf{j}$, since $d\mathbf{i}$ is tangent to the path described by the arrowhead of $\mathbf{i}$ in the limit as $\Delta t \to dt$. Likewise, $d\mathbf{j}$ acts in the $-\mathbf{i}$ direction, Fig. 16–32b. Hence,

$$\frac{d\mathbf{i}}{dt} = \frac{d\theta}{dt}(\mathbf{j}) = \Omega\mathbf{j} \qquad \frac{d\mathbf{j}}{dt} = \frac{d\theta}{dt}(-\mathbf{i}) = -\Omega\mathbf{i}$$

Viewing the axes in three dimensions, Fig. 16–32c, and nothing that $\Omega = \Omega\mathbf{k}$, we can express the above derivatives in terms of the cross product as

$$\frac{d\mathbf{i}}{dt} = \Omega \times \mathbf{i} \qquad \frac{d\mathbf{j}}{dt} = \Omega \times \mathbf{j} \tag{16–22}$$

Substituting these results into Eq. 16–21 and using the distributive property of the vector cross product, we obtain

$$\frac{d\mathbf{r}_{B/A}}{dt} = (\mathbf{v}_{B/A})_{xyz} + \Omega \times (x_B\mathbf{i} + y_B\mathbf{j}) = (\mathbf{v}_{B/A})_{xyz} + \Omega \times \mathbf{r}_{B/A} \tag{16–23}$$

(b)

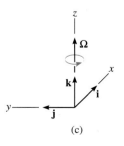

(c)

**Fig. 16–32**

Hence, Eq. 16–20 becomes

$$\mathbf{v}_B = \mathbf{v}_A + \mathbf{\Omega} \times \mathbf{r}_{B/A} + (\mathbf{v}_{B/A})_{xyz} \tag{16–24}$$

where

$\mathbf{v}_B$ = velocity of $B$, measured from the $X, Y, Z$ reference

$\mathbf{v}_A$ = velocity of the origin $A$ of the $x, y, z$ reference, measured from the $X, Y, Z$ reference

$(\mathbf{v}_{B/A})_{xyz}$ = relative velocity of "$B$ with respect to $A$," as measured by an observer attached to the *rotating* $x, y, z$ reference

$\mathbf{\Omega}$ = angular velocity of the $x, y, z$ reference, measured from the $X, Y, Z$ reference

$\mathbf{r}_{B/A}$ = relative position of "$B$ with respect to $A$"

Comparing Eq. 16–24 with Eq. 16–16 ($\mathbf{v}_B = \mathbf{v}_A + \mathbf{\Omega} \times \mathbf{r}_{B/A}$), which is valid for a translating frame of reference, it can be seen that the only difference between the equations is represented by the term $(\mathbf{v}_{B/A})_{xyz}$.

When applying Eq. 16–24 it is often useful to understand what each of the terms represents. In order of appearance, they are as follows:

$\mathbf{v}_B$ $\left\{ \text{absolute velocity of } B \right.$ $\left. \right\} \begin{array}{l} \text{motion of } B \text{ observed} \\ \text{from the } X, Y, Z \text{ frame} \end{array}$

(equals)

$\mathbf{v}_A$ $\left\{ \begin{array}{l} \text{absolute velocity of origin} \\ \text{of } x, y, z \text{ frame} \end{array} \right.$

(plus)

$\begin{array}{l} \text{motion of } x, y, z \text{ frame} \\ \text{observed from the } X, Y, Z \\ \text{frame} \end{array}$

$\mathbf{\Omega} \times \mathbf{r}_{B/A}$ $\left\{ \begin{array}{l} \text{angular velocity effect caused} \\ \text{by rotation of } x, y, z \text{ frame} \end{array} \right.$

(plus)

$(\mathbf{v}_{B/A})_{xyz}$ $\left\{ \begin{array}{l} \text{relative velocity of } B \\ \text{with respect to } A \end{array} \right.$ $\left. \right\} \begin{array}{l} \text{motion of } B \text{ observed} \\ \text{from the } x, y, z \text{ frame} \end{array}$

**Acceleration.** The acceleration of $B$, observed from the $X, Y, Z$ coordinate system, may be expressed in terms of its motion measured with respect to the rotating or moving system of coordinates by taking the time derivative of Eq. 16–24, i.e.,

$$\frac{d\mathbf{v}_B}{dt} = \frac{d\mathbf{v}_A}{dt} + \frac{d\mathbf{\Omega}}{dt} \times \mathbf{r}_{B/A} + \mathbf{\Omega} \times \frac{d\mathbf{r}_{B/A}}{dt} + \frac{d(\mathbf{v}_{B/A})_{xyz}}{dt}$$

$$\mathbf{a}_B = \mathbf{a}_A + \dot{\mathbf{\Omega}} \times \mathbf{r}_{B/A} + \mathbf{\Omega} \times \frac{d\mathbf{r}_{B/A}}{dt} + \frac{d(\mathbf{v}_{B/A})_{xyz}}{dt} \quad (16\text{–}25)$$

Here $\dot{\mathbf{\Omega}} = d\mathbf{\Omega}/dt$ is the angular acceleration of the $x, y, z$ coordinate system. For planar motion $\mathbf{\Omega}$ is always perpendicular to the plane of motion, and therefore $\dot{\mathbf{\Omega}}$ measures *only the change in magnitude* of $\mathbf{\Omega}$. The derivative $d\mathbf{r}_{B/A}/dt$ in Eq. 16–25 is defined by Eq. 16–23, so that

$$\mathbf{\Omega} \times \frac{d\mathbf{r}_{B/A}}{dt} = \mathbf{\Omega} \times (\mathbf{v}_{B/A})_{xyz} + \mathbf{\Omega} \times (\mathbf{\Omega} \times \mathbf{r}_{B/A}) \quad (16\text{–}26)$$

Finding the time derivative of $(\mathbf{v}_{B/A})_{xyz} = (v_{B/A})_x \mathbf{i} + (v_{B/A})_y \mathbf{j}$,

$$\frac{d(\mathbf{v}_{B/A})_{xyz}}{dt} = \left[ \frac{d(v_{B/A})_x}{dt} \mathbf{i} + \frac{d(v_{B/A})_y}{dt} \mathbf{j} \right] + \left[ (v_{B/A})_x \frac{d\mathbf{i}}{dt} + (v_{B/A})_y \frac{d\mathbf{j}}{dt} \right]$$

The two terms in the first set of brackets represent the components of acceleration of point $B$ as measured by an observer attached to the moving coordinate system. These terms will be denoted by $(\mathbf{a}_{B/A})_{xyz}$. The terms in the second set of brackets can be simplified using Eqs. 16–22.

$$\frac{d(\mathbf{v}_{B/A})_{xyz}}{dt} = (\mathbf{a}_{B/A})_{xyz} + \mathbf{\Omega} \times (\mathbf{v}_{B/A})_{xyz}$$

Substituting this and Eq. 16–26 into Eq. 16–25 and rearranging terms,

$$\boxed{\mathbf{a}_B = \mathbf{a}_A + \dot{\mathbf{\Omega}} \times \mathbf{r}_{B/A} + \mathbf{\Omega} \times (\mathbf{\Omega} \times \mathbf{r}_{B/A}) + 2\mathbf{\Omega} \times (\mathbf{v}_{B/A})_{xyz} + (\mathbf{a}_{B/A})_{xyz}}$$

$$(16\text{–}27)$$

where

$$\mathbf{a}_B = \text{acceleration of } B \text{, measured from the } X, Y, Z \text{ reference}$$

$$\mathbf{a}_A = \text{acceleration of the origin } A \text{ of the } x, y, z \text{ reference, measured from the } X, Y, Z \text{ reference}$$

$$(\mathbf{a}_{B/A})_{xyz}, (\mathbf{v}_{B/A})_{xyz} = \text{relative acceleration and relative velocity of "} B \text{ with respect to } A \text{," as measured by an observer attached to the } rotating \ x, y, z \text{ reference}$$

$$\dot{\mathbf{\Omega}}, \mathbf{\Omega} = \text{angular acceleration and angular velocity of the } x, y, z \text{ reference, measured from the } X, Y, Z \text{ reference}$$

$$\mathbf{r}_{B/A} = \text{relative position of "} B \text{ with respect to } A \text{"}$$

If Eq. 16–27 is compared with Eq. 16–18, written in the form $\mathbf{a}_B = \mathbf{a}_A + \dot{\boldsymbol{\Omega}} \times \mathbf{r}_{B/A} + \boldsymbol{\Omega} \times (\boldsymbol{\Omega} \times \mathbf{r}_{B/A})$, which is valid for a translating frame of reference, it can be seen that the difference between the equations is represented by the terms $2\boldsymbol{\Omega} \times (\mathbf{v}_{B/A})_{xyz}$ and $(\mathbf{a}_{B/A})_{xyz}$. In particular, $2\boldsymbol{\Omega} \times (\mathbf{v}_{B/A})_{xyz}$ is called the *Coriolis acceleration*, named after the French engineer G. C. Coriolis, who was the first to determine it. This term represents the difference in the acceleration of *B* as measured from nonrotating and rotating *x, y, z* axes. As indicated by the vector cross product, the Coriolis acceleration will *always* be perpendicular to both $\boldsymbol{\Omega}$ and $(\mathbf{v}_{B/A})_{xyz}$. It is an important component of the acceleration which must be considered whenever rotating reference frames are used. This often occurs, for example, when studying the accelerations and forces which act on rockets, long-range projectiles, or other bodies having motions whose measurements are significantly affected by the rotation of the earth.

The following interpretation of the terms in Eq. 16–27 may be useful when applying this equation to the solution of problems.

| | | |
|---|---|---|
| $\mathbf{a}_B$ | {absolute acceleration of *B* | } motion of *B* observed from the *X, Y, Z* frame |
| | (equals) | |
| $\mathbf{a}_A$ | {absolute acceleration of origin of *x, y, z* frame | |
| | (plus) | |
| $\dot{\boldsymbol{\Omega}} \times \mathbf{r}_{B/A}$ | {angular acceleration effect caused by rotation of *x, y, z* frame | motion of *x, y, z* frame observed from the *X, Y, Z* frame |
| | (plus) | |
| $\boldsymbol{\Omega} \times (\boldsymbol{\Omega} \times \mathbf{r}_{B/A})$ | {angular velocity effect caused by rotation of *x, y, z* frame | |
| | (plus) | |
| $2\boldsymbol{\Omega} \times (\mathbf{v}_{B/A})_{xyz}$ | {combined effect of *B* moving relative to *x, y, z* coordinates and rotation of *x, y, z* frame | } interacting motion |
| | (plus) | |
| $(\mathbf{a}_{B/A})_{xyz}$ | {relative acceleration of *B* with respect to *A* | } motion of *B* observed from the *x, y, z* frame |

## PROCEDURE FOR ANALYSIS

Equations 16–24 and 16–27 can be applied to the solution of problems involving the planar motion of particles or rigid bodies using the following procedure.

### Coordinate Axes.

- Choose an appropriate location for the origin and proper orientation of the axes for both the $X, Y, Z$ and moving $x, y, z$ reference frames.
- Most often solutions are easily obtained if at the instant considered:
  (1) the origins are coincident
  (2) the corresponding axes are collinear
  (3) the corresponding axes are parallel
- The moving frame should be selected fixed to the body or device along which the relative motion occurs.

### Kinematic Equations.

- After defining the origin $A$ of the moving reference and specifying the moving point $B$, Eqs. 16–24 and 16–27 should be written in symbolic form

$$\mathbf{v}_B = \mathbf{v}_A + \mathbf{\Omega} \times \mathbf{r}_{B/A} + (\mathbf{v}_{B/A})_{xyz}$$

$$\mathbf{a}_B = \mathbf{a}_A + \dot{\mathbf{\Omega}} \times \mathbf{r}_{B/A} + \mathbf{\Omega} \times (\mathbf{\Omega} \times \mathbf{r}_{B/A}) + 2\mathbf{\Omega} \times (\mathbf{v}_{B/A})_{xyz} + (\mathbf{a}_{B/A})_{xyz}$$

- The Cartesian components of all these vectors may be expressed along either the $X, Y, Z$ axes or the $x, y, z$ axes. The choice is arbitrary provided a consistent set of unit vectors is used.
- Motion of the moving reference, is expressed by $\mathbf{v}_A$, $\mathbf{a}_A$, $\mathbf{\Omega}$, and $\dot{\mathbf{\Omega}}$; and motion of $B$ with respect to the moving reference, is expressed by $\mathbf{r}_{B/A}$, $(\mathbf{v}_{B/A})_{xyz}$, and $(\mathbf{a}_{B/A})_{xyz}$.

The rotation of the dumping bin of the truck about point $C$ is operated by the extension of the hydraulic cylinder $AB$. To determine the rotation of the bin due to this extension, we can use the equations of relative motion and fix the $x, y$ axes to the cylinder so that the relative motion of the cylinder's extension occurs along the $y$ axis.

EXAMPLE 16.19

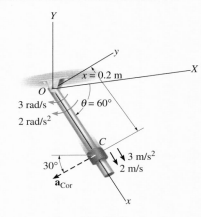

Fig. 16–33

At the instant $\theta = 60°$, the rod in Fig. 16–33 has an angular velocity of 3 rad/s and an angular acceleration of 2 rad/s². At this same instant, the collar $C$ is traveling outward along the rod such that when $x = 0.2$ m the velocity is 2 m/s and the acceleration is 3 m/s², both measured relative to the rod. Determine the Coriolis acceleration and the velocity and acceleration of the collar at this instant.

Solution

*Coordinate Axes.* The origin of both coordinate systems is located at point $O$, Fig. 16–33. Since motion of the collar is reported relative to the rod, the moving $x, y, z$ frame of reference is *attached* to the rod.

*Kinematic Equations.*

$$\mathbf{v}_C = \mathbf{v}_O + \mathbf{\Omega} \times \mathbf{r}_{C/O} + (\mathbf{v}_{C/O})_{xyz} \tag{1}$$

$$\mathbf{a}_C = \mathbf{a}_O + \dot{\mathbf{\Omega}} \times \mathbf{r}_{C/O} + \mathbf{\Omega} \times (\mathbf{\Omega} \times \mathbf{r}_{C/O}) + 2\mathbf{\Omega} \times (\mathbf{v}_{C/O})_{xyz} + (\mathbf{a}_{C/O})_{xyz} \tag{2}$$

It will be simpler to express the data in terms of $\mathbf{i}, \mathbf{j}, \mathbf{k}$ component vectors rather than $\mathbf{I}, \mathbf{J}, \mathbf{K}$ components. Hence,

| *Motion of moving reference* | *Motion of C with respect to moving reference* |
|---|---|
| $\mathbf{v}_O = \mathbf{0}$ | $\mathbf{r}_{C/O} = \{0.2\mathbf{i}\}$ m |
| $\mathbf{a}_O = \mathbf{0}$ | $(\mathbf{v}_{C/O})_{xyz} = \{2\mathbf{i}\}$ m/s |
| $\mathbf{\Omega} = \{-3\mathbf{k}\}$ rad/s | $(\mathbf{a}_{C/O})_{xyz} = \{3\mathbf{i}\}$ m/s² |
| $\dot{\mathbf{\Omega}} = \{-2\mathbf{k}\}$ rad/s² | |

From Eq. 2, the Coriolis acceleration is defined as

$$\mathbf{a}_{Cor} = 2\mathbf{\Omega} \times (\mathbf{v}_{C/O})_{xyz} = 2(-3\mathbf{k}) \times (2\mathbf{i}) = \{-12\mathbf{j}\} \text{ m/s}^2 \quad Ans.$$

This vector is shown dashed in Fig. 16–33. If desired, it may be resolved into $\mathbf{I}, \mathbf{J}$ components acting along the $X$ and $Y$ axes, respectively.

The velocity and acceleration of the collar are determined by substituting the data into Eqs. 1 and 2 and evaluating the cross products, which yields

$$\mathbf{v}_C = \mathbf{v}_O + \mathbf{\Omega} \times \mathbf{r}_{C/O} + (\mathbf{v}_{C/O})_{xyz}$$
$$= \mathbf{0} + (-3\mathbf{k}) \times (0.2\mathbf{i}) + 2\mathbf{i}$$
$$= \{2\mathbf{i} - 0.6\mathbf{j}\} \text{ m/s} \quad Ans.$$

$$\mathbf{a}_C = \mathbf{a}_O + \dot{\mathbf{\Omega}} \times \mathbf{r}_{C/O} + \mathbf{\Omega} \times (\mathbf{\Omega} \times \mathbf{r}_{C/O}) + 2\mathbf{\Omega} \times (\mathbf{v}_{C/O})_{xyz} + (\mathbf{a}_{C/O})_{xyz}$$
$$= \mathbf{0} + (-2\mathbf{k}) \times (0.2\mathbf{i}) + (-3\mathbf{k}) \times [(-3\mathbf{k}) \times (0.2\mathbf{i})] + 2(-3\mathbf{k}) \times (2\mathbf{i}) + 3\mathbf{i}$$
$$= \mathbf{0} - 0.4\mathbf{j} - 1.80\mathbf{i} - 12\mathbf{j} + 3\mathbf{i}$$
$$= \{1.20\mathbf{i} - 12.4\mathbf{j}\} \text{ m/s}^2 \quad Ans.$$

## E X A M P L E   16.20

The rod $AB$, shown in Fig. 16–34, rotates clockwise such that it has an angular velocity $\omega_{AB} = 3$ rad/s and angular acceleration $\alpha_{AB} = 4$ rad/s$^2$ when $\theta = 45°$. Determine the angular motion of rod $DE$ at this instant. The collar at $C$ is pin connected to $AB$ and slides over rod $DE$.

### Solution

*Coordinate Axes.*   The origin of both the fixed and moving frames of reference is located at $D$, Fig. 16–34. Furthermore, the $x, y, z$ reference is attached to and rotates with rod $DE$ so that the relative motion of the collar is easy to follow.

*Kinematic Equations.*

$$\mathbf{v}_C = \mathbf{v}_D + \boldsymbol{\Omega} \times \mathbf{r}_{C/D} + (\mathbf{v}_{C/D})_{xyz} \qquad (1)$$

$$\mathbf{a}_C = \mathbf{a}_D + \dot{\boldsymbol{\Omega}} \times \mathbf{r}_{C/D} + \boldsymbol{\Omega} \times (\boldsymbol{\Omega} \times \mathbf{r}_{C/D}) + 2\boldsymbol{\Omega} \times (\mathbf{v}_{C/D})_{xyz} + (\mathbf{a}_{C/D})_{xyz} \qquad (2)$$

All vectors will be expressed in terms of $\mathbf{i}, \mathbf{j}, \mathbf{k}$ components.

| Motion of moving reference | Motion of C with respect to moving reference |
|---|---|
| $\mathbf{v}_D = \mathbf{0}$ | $\mathbf{r}_{C/D} = \{0.4\mathbf{i}\}$ m |
| $\mathbf{a}_D = \mathbf{0}$ | $(\mathbf{v}_{C/D})_{xyz} = (v_{C/D})_{xyz}\mathbf{i}$ |
| $\boldsymbol{\Omega} = -\omega_{DE}\mathbf{k}$ | $(\mathbf{a}_{C/D})_{xyz} = (a_{C/D})_{xyz}\mathbf{i}$ |
| $\dot{\boldsymbol{\Omega}} = -\alpha_{DE}\mathbf{k}$ | |

**Fig. 16–34**

*Motion of C:* Since the collar moves along a *circular path*, its velocity and acceleration can be determined using Eqs. 16–9 and 16–14.

$$\mathbf{v}_C = \boldsymbol{\omega}_{AB} \times \mathbf{r}_{C/A} = (-3\mathbf{k}) \times (0.4\mathbf{i} + 0.4\mathbf{j}) = \{1.2\mathbf{i} - 1.2\mathbf{j}\} \text{ m/s}$$

$$\mathbf{a}_C = \boldsymbol{\alpha}_{AB} \times \mathbf{r}_{C/A} - \omega_{AB}^2 \mathbf{r}_{C/A}$$
$$= (-4\mathbf{k}) \times (0.4\mathbf{i} + 0.4\mathbf{j}) - (3)^2(0.4\mathbf{i} + 0.4\mathbf{j}) = \{-2\mathbf{i} - 5.2\mathbf{j}\} \text{ m/s}^2$$

Substituting the data into Eqs. 1 and 2, we have

$$\mathbf{v}_C = \mathbf{v}_D + \boldsymbol{\Omega} \times \mathbf{r}_{C/D} + (\mathbf{v}_{C/D})_{xyz}$$

$$1.2\mathbf{i} - 1.2\mathbf{j} = \mathbf{0} + (-\omega_{DE}\mathbf{k}) \times (0.4\mathbf{i}) + (v_{C/D})_{xyz}\mathbf{i}$$

$$1.2\mathbf{i} - 1.2\mathbf{j} = \mathbf{0} - 0.4\omega_{DE}\mathbf{j} + (v_{C/D})_{xyz}\mathbf{i}$$

$$(v_{C/D})_{xyz} = 1.2 \text{ m/s}$$

$$\omega_{DE} = 3 \text{ rad/s}\downarrow \qquad\qquad\qquad Ans.$$

$$\mathbf{a}_C = \mathbf{a}_D + \dot{\boldsymbol{\Omega}} \times \mathbf{r}_{C/D} + \boldsymbol{\Omega} \times (\boldsymbol{\Omega} \times \mathbf{r}_{C/D}) + 2\boldsymbol{\Omega} \times (\mathbf{v}_{C/D})_{xyz} + (\mathbf{a}_{C/D})_{xyz}$$

$$-2\mathbf{i} - 5.2\mathbf{j} = \mathbf{0} + (-\alpha_{DE}\mathbf{k}) \times (0.4\mathbf{i}) + (-3\mathbf{k}) \times [(-3\mathbf{k}) \times (0.4\mathbf{i})]$$
$$+ 2(-3\mathbf{k}) \times (1.2\mathbf{i}) + (a_{C/D})_{xyz}\mathbf{i}$$

$$-2\mathbf{i} - 5.2\mathbf{j} = -0.4\alpha_{DE}\mathbf{j} - 3.6\mathbf{i} - 7.2\mathbf{j} + (a_{C/D})_{xyz}\mathbf{i}$$

$$(a_{C/D})_{xyz} = 1.6 \text{ m/s}^2$$

$$\alpha_{DE} = -5 \text{ rad/s}^2 = 5 \text{ rad/s}^2\uparrow \qquad\qquad Ans.$$

EXAMPLE **16.21**

Two planes $A$ and $B$ are flying at the same elevation and have the motions shown in Fig. 16–35. Determine the velocity and acceleration of $A$ as measured by the pilot of $B$.

**Solution**

***Coordinate Axes.*** Since the relative motion of $A$ with respect to the pilot in $B$ is being sought, the $x, y, z$ axes are attached to plane $B$, Fig. 16–35. At the *instant* considered, the origin $B$ coincides with the origin of the fixed $X, Y, Z$ frame.

***Kinematic Equations.***

$$\mathbf{v}_A = \mathbf{v}_B + \boldsymbol{\Omega} \times \mathbf{r}_{A/B} + (\mathbf{v}_{A/B})_{xyz} \tag{1}$$

$$\mathbf{a}_A = \mathbf{a}_B + \dot{\boldsymbol{\Omega}} \times \mathbf{r}_{A/B} + \boldsymbol{\Omega} \times (\boldsymbol{\Omega} \times \mathbf{r}_{A/B}) + 2\boldsymbol{\Omega} \times (\mathbf{v}_{A/B})_{xyz} + (\mathbf{a}_{A/B})_{xyz} \tag{2}$$

*Motion of moving reference:*

$$\mathbf{v}_B = \{600\mathbf{j}\} \text{ km/h}$$

$$(a_B)_n = \frac{v_B^2}{\rho} = \frac{(600)^2}{400} = 900 \text{ km/h}^2$$

$$\mathbf{a}_B = (\mathbf{a}_B)_n + (\mathbf{a}_B)_t = \{900\mathbf{i} - 100\mathbf{j}\} \text{ km/h}^2$$

$$\Omega = \frac{v_B}{\rho} = \frac{600 \text{ km/h}}{400 \text{ km}} = 1.5 \text{ rad/h} \downarrow \qquad \boldsymbol{\Omega} = \{-1.5\mathbf{k}\} \text{ rad/h}$$

$$\dot{\Omega} = \frac{(a_B)_t}{\rho} = \frac{100 \text{ km/h}^2}{400 \text{ km}} = 0.25 \text{ rad/h}^2 \uparrow \qquad \dot{\boldsymbol{\Omega}} = \{0.25\mathbf{k}\} \text{ rad/h}^2$$

*Motion of A with respect to moving reference:*

$$\mathbf{r}_{A/B} = \{-4\mathbf{i}\} \text{ km} \qquad (\mathbf{v}_{A/B})_{xyz} = ? \qquad (\mathbf{a}_{A/B})_{xyz} = ?$$

Substituting the data into Eqs. 1 and 2, realizing that $\mathbf{v}_A = \{700\mathbf{j}\}$ km/h and $\mathbf{a}_A = \{50\mathbf{j}\}$ km/h$^2$, we have

$$\mathbf{v}_A = \mathbf{v}_B + \boldsymbol{\Omega} \times \mathbf{r}_{A/B} + (\mathbf{v}_{A/B})_{xyz}$$

$$700\mathbf{j} = 600\mathbf{j} + (-1.5\mathbf{k}) \times (-4\mathbf{i}) + (\mathbf{v}_{A/B})_{xyz}$$

$$(\mathbf{v}_{A/B})_{xyz} = \{94\mathbf{j}\} \text{ km/h} \qquad \qquad Ans.$$

$$\mathbf{a}_A = \mathbf{a}_B + \dot{\boldsymbol{\Omega}} \times \mathbf{r}_{A/B} + \boldsymbol{\Omega} \times (\boldsymbol{\Omega} \times \mathbf{r}_{A/B}) + 2\boldsymbol{\Omega} \times (\mathbf{v}_{A/B})_{xyz} + (\mathbf{a}_{A/B})_{xyz}$$

$$50\mathbf{j} = (900\mathbf{i} - 100\mathbf{j}) + (0.25\mathbf{k}) \times (-4\mathbf{i})$$

$$+ (-1.5\mathbf{k}) \times [(-1.5\mathbf{k}) \times (-4\mathbf{i})] + 2(-1.5\mathbf{k}) \times (94\mathbf{j}) + (\mathbf{a}_{A/B})_{xyz}$$

$$(\mathbf{a}_{A/B})_{xyz} = \{-1191\mathbf{i} + 151\mathbf{j}\} \text{ km/h}^2 \qquad \qquad Ans.$$

The solution of this problem should be compared with that of Example 12.26.

**Fig. 16–35**

# PROBLEMS

**16-131.** Block $A$, which is attached to a cord, moves along the slot of a horizontal forked rod. At the instant shown, the cord is pulled down through the hole at $O$ with an acceleration of $4 \, \text{m/s}^2$ and its velocity is $2 \, \text{m/s}$. Determine the acceleration of the block at this instant. The rod rotates about $O$ with a constant angular velocity $\omega = 4 \, \text{rad/s}$.

**Prob. 16–131**

*\*16-132.** The ball $B$ of negligible size rolls through the tube such that at the instant shown it has a velocity of $5 \, \text{m/s}$ and an acceleration of $3 \, \text{m/s}^2$, measured relative to the tube. If the tube has an angular velocity of $\omega = 3 \, \text{rad/s}$ and an angular acceleration of $\alpha = 5 \, \text{rad/s}^2$ at this same instant, determine the velocity and acceleration of the ball.

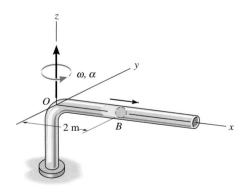

**Prob. 16–132**

**16-133.** The man stands on the platform at $O$ and runs out toward the edge such that when he is at $A$, $y = 5 \, \text{m}$, his mass center has a velocity of $2 \, \text{m/s}$ and an acceleration of $3 \, \text{m/s}^2$, both measured with respect to the platform and directed along the $y$ axis. If the platform has the angular motions shown, determine the velocity and acceleration of his mass center at this instant.

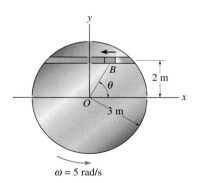

**Prob. 16–133**

**16-134.** Block $B$ moves along the slot in the platform with a constant speed of $2 \, \text{m/s}$, measured relative to the platform in the direction shown. If the platform is rotating at a constant rate of $\omega = 5 \, \text{rad/s}$, determine the velocity and acceleration of the block at the instant $\theta = 60°$.

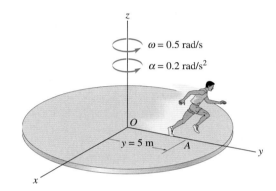

**Prob. 16–134**

**16-135.** While the swing bridge is closing with a constant rotation of 0.5 rad/s, a man runs along the roadway at a constant speed of 2 m/s relative to the roadway. Determine his velocity and acceleration at the instant $d = 6$ m.

**16-137.** A girl stands at $A$ on a platform which is rotating with a constant angular velocity $\omega = 0.5$ rad/s. If she walks at a constant speed of $v = 0.75$ m/s measured relative to the platform, determine her acceleration (a) when she reaches point $D$ in going along the path $ADC$, $d = 1$ m; and (b) when she reaches point $B$ if she follows the path $ABC$, $r = 3$ m.

Prob. 16–137

Prob. 16–135

***16-136.** While the swing bridge is closing with a constant rotation of 0.5 rad/s, a man runs along the roadway such that when $d = 4$ m he is running outward from the center at 2 m/s with an acceleration of 0.8 m/s², both measured relative to the roadway. Determine his velocity and acceleration at this instant.

**16-138.** A girl stands at $A$ on a platform which is rotating with an angular acceleration $\alpha = 0.2$ rad/s² and at the instant shown has an angular velocity $\omega = 0.5$ rad/s. If she walks at a constant speed $v = 0.75$ m/s measured relative to the platform, determine her acceleration (a) when she reaches point $D$ in going along the path $ADC$, $d = 1$ m; and (b) when she reaches point $B$ if she follows the path $ABC$, $r = 3$ m.

Prob. 16–138

Prob. 16–136

**16-139.** Rod $AB$ rotates counterclockwise with a constant angular velocity $\omega = 3$ rad/s. Determine the velocity and acceleration of point $C$ located on the double collar when $\theta = 45°$. The collar consists of two pin-connected slider blocks which are constrained to move along the circular path and the rod $AB$.

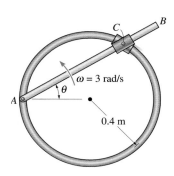

**Prob. 16–139**

**16-141.** Block $B$ of the mechanism is confined to move within the slot member $CD$. If $AB$ is rotating at a constant rate of $\omega_{AB} = 3$ rad/s, determine the angular velocity and angular acceleration of member $CD$ at the instant shown.

**Prob. 16–141**

*\**16-140.** A ride in an amusement park consists of a rotating platform $P$, having a constant angular velocity $\omega_P = 1.5$ rad/s, and four cars, $C$, mounted on the platform, which have constant angular velocities $\omega_{C/P} = 2$ rad/s measured relative to the platform. Determine the velocity and acceleration of the passenger at $B$ at the instant shown.

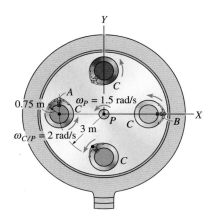

**Prob. 16–140**

**16-142.** At the instant shown, the robotic arm $AB$ is rotating counterclockwise at $\omega = 5$ rad/s and has an angular acceleration $\alpha = 2$ rad/s$^2$. Simultaneously, the grip $BC$ is rotating counterclockwise at $\omega' = 6$ rad/s and $\alpha' = 2$ rad/s$^2$, both measured relative to a *fixed* reference. Determine the velocity and acceleration of the object held at the grip $C$.

**Prob. 16–142**

**16-143.** The two-link mechanism serves to amplify angular motion. Link $AB$ has a pin at $B$ which is confined to move within the slot of link $CD$. If at the instant shown, $AB$ (input) has an angular velocity of $\omega_{AB} = 2.5$ rad/s and an angular acceleration of $\alpha_{AB} = 3$ rad/s², determine the angular velocity and angular acceleration of $CD$ (output) at this instant.

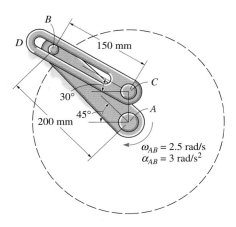

**Prob. 16–143**

***16-144.** At the instant shown, rod $AB$ has an angular velocity $\omega_{AB} = 3$ rad/s and an angular acceleration $\alpha_{AB} = 5$ rad/s². Determine the angular velocity and angular acceleration of rod $CD$ at this instant. The collar at $C$ is pin-connected to $CD$ and slides over $AB$.

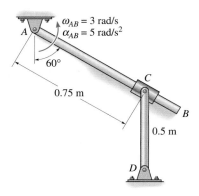

**Prob. 16–144**

**16-145.** The gear has the angular motion shown. Determine the angular velocity and angular acceleration of the slotted link $BC$ at this instant. The peg at $A$ is fixed to the gear.

**Prob. 16–145**

**16-146.** The quick-return mechanism consists of a crank $AB$, slider block $B$, and slotted link $CD$. If the crank has the angular motion shown, determine the angular motion of the slotted link at this instant.

**Prob. 16–146**

**16-147.** A ride in an amusement park consists of a rotating arm $AB$ having a constant angular velocity $\omega_{AB} = 2$ rad/s about point $A$ and a car mounted at the end of the arm which has a constant angular velocity $\boldsymbol{\omega}' = \{-0.5\mathbf{k}\}$ rad/s, measured relative to the arm. At the instant shown, determine the velocity and acceleration of the passenger at $C$.

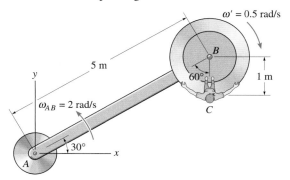

**Prob. 16–147**

*16-148.** A ride in an amusement park consists of a rotating arm $AB$ that has an angular acceleration of $\alpha_{AB} = 1$ rad/s$^2$ when $\omega_{AB} = 2$ rad/s at the instant shown. Also at this instant the car mounted at the end of the arm has a relative angular acceleration of $\boldsymbol{\alpha}' = \{-0.6\mathbf{k}\}$ rad/s$^2$ when $\boldsymbol{\omega}' = \{-0.5\mathbf{k}\}$ rad/s. Determine the velocity and acceleration of the passenger $C$ at this instant.

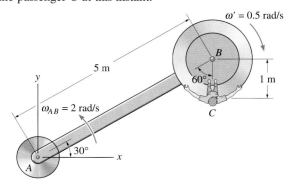

**Prob. 16–148**

**16-149.** The cars on the amusement-park ride rotate around the axle at $A$ with a constant angular velocity $\omega_{A/f} = 2$ rad/s, measured relative to the frame $AB$. At the same time the frame rotates around the main axle support at $B$ with a constant angular velocity $\omega_f = 1$ rad/s. Determine the velocity and acceleration of the passenger at $C$ at the instant shown.

**Prob. 16–149**

**16-150.** The cars on the amusement-park ride rotate around the axle at $A$ with a constant angular velocity $\omega_{A/f} = 2$ rad/s, measured relative to the frame $AB$. At the same time the frame rotates around the main axle support at $B$ with a constant angular velocity $\omega_f = 1$ rad/s. Determine the velocity and acceleration of the passenger at $D$ at the instant shown.

**Prob. 16–150**

# DESIGN PROJECTS

### 16–1D. DESIGN OF A BELT TRANSMISSION SYSTEM

The wheel $A$ is used in a textile mill and must be rotated counterclockwise at 4 rad/s. This can be done using a motor which is mounted on the platform at the location shown. If the shaft $B$ on the motor can rotate clockwise 50 rad/s, design a method for transmitting the rotation from $B$ to $A$. Use a series of belts and pulleys as a basis for your design. A belt drives the rotation of wheel $A$ by wrapping around its outer surface, and a pulley can be attached to the shaft of the motor as well as anywhere else. Do not let the length of any belt be longer than 6 ft. Submit a drawing of your design and the calculations of the kinematics. Also, determine the total cost of materials if any belt costs $2.50, and any pulley costs $0.1$r$, where $r$ is the radius of the pulley in metres.

**Prob. 16–1D**

### 16–2D. DESIGN OF AN OSCILLATING LINK MECHANISM

The operation of a sewing machine requires the 200-mm-long bar to oscillate back-and-forth through an angle of 60° every 0.2 seconds. A motor having a drive shaft which turns at 40 rad/s is available to provide the necessary power. Specify the location of the motor and design a mechanism required to perform the motion. Submit a drawing of your design, showing the placement of the motor, and compute the velocity and acceleration of the end $A$ of the link as a function of its angle of rotation $0° \le \theta \le 60°$.

**Prob. 16–2D**

## 16–3D. DESIGN OF A RETRACTABLE AIRCRAFT LANDING-GEAR MECHANISM

The nose wheel of a small plane is attached to member $AB$, which is pinned to the aircraft frame at $B$. Design a mechanism that will allow the wheel to be fully retracted forward; i.e., rotated clockwise 90°, in $t \leq 4$ seconds. Use a hydraulic cylinder which has a closed length of 0.5 m and, if needed, a fully extended length of 0.8 m. Make sure that your design holds the wheel in a stable position when the wheel is on the ground. Show plots of the angular velocity and angular acceleration of $AB$ versus its angular position $0° \leq \theta \leq 90°$.

**Prob. 16–3D**

## 16–4D. DESIGN OF A SAW LINK MECHANISM

The saw blade in a lumber mill is required to remain in the horizontal position and undergo a complete back-and-forth motion in 2 seconds. An electric motor, having a shaft rotation of 50 rad/s, is available to power the saw and can be located anywhere. Design a mechanism that will transfer the rotation of the motor's shaft to the saw blade. Submit drawings of your design and calculations of the kinematics of the saw blade. Include a plot of the velocity and acceleration of the saw blade as a function of it horizontal position. Note that to cut through the log the blade must be allowed to move freely downward as well as back and forth.

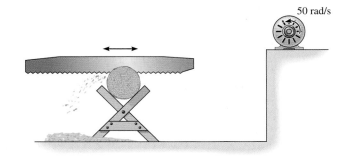

**Prob. 16–4D**

## CHAPTER REVIEW

- *Rigid-Body Planar Motion.* A rigid body undergoes three types of planar motion: translation, rotation about a fixed axis, and general plane motion.

- *Translation.* When a body has rectilinear translation, all the particles of the body travel along straight-line paths. If the paths have the same radius of curvature, then curvilinear translation occurs. Provided we know the motion of one of the particles, then the motion of all of the others is also known.

- *Rotation about a Fixed Axis.* For this type of motion, all of the particles move along circular paths. Here, all line segments in the body undergo the same angular displacement, angular velocity, and angular acceleration. The differential relationships between these kinematic quantities are

$$\omega = d\theta/dt \qquad \alpha = d\omega/dt \qquad \alpha \, d\theta = \omega \, d\omega$$

If the angular acceleration is constant, $\alpha = \alpha_c$, then these equations can be integrated and become

$$\omega = \omega_0 + \alpha_c t$$
$$\theta = \theta_0 + \omega_0 t + \tfrac{1}{2}\alpha_c t^2$$
$$\omega^2 = \omega_0^2 + 2\alpha_c(\theta - \theta_0)$$

Once the angular motion of the body is known, then the velocity of any particle a distance $r$ from the axis of rotation is

$$v = \omega r \qquad \text{or} \qquad \mathbf{v} = \boldsymbol{\omega} \times \mathbf{r}$$

The acceleration of the particle has two components. The tangential component accounts for the change in the magnitude of the velocity

$$a_t = \alpha r \qquad \text{or} \qquad \mathbf{a}_t = \boldsymbol{\alpha} \times \mathbf{r}$$

The normal component accounts for the change in the velocity direction

$$a_n = \omega^2 r \qquad \text{or} \qquad \mathbf{a}_n = -\omega^2 \mathbf{r}$$

- *General Plane Motion.* When a body undergoes general plane motion, it simultaneously translates and rotates. A typical example is a wheel that rolls without slipping. There are several methods for analyzing this motion.

*Absolute Motion Analysis.* If the motion of a point on a body or the angular motion of a line is known, then it may be possible to relate this motion to that of another point or line using an absolute motion analysis. To do so, linear position coordinates $s$ or angular position coordinates $\theta$ are established (measured from a fixed point or line). These position coordinates are then related using the geometry of the body. The time derivative of this equation gives the relationship between the velocities and/or the angular velocities. A second time derivative relates the accelerations and/or the angular accelerations.

*Relative Velocity Analysis.* General plane motion can also be analyzed using a relative-motion analysis between two points $A$ and $B$. This method considers the motion in parts: first a translation of the selected base point $A$, then a relative "rotation" of the body about point $A$, measured from a translating axis. The velocities of the two points $A$ and $B$ are then related using

$$\mathbf{v}_B = \mathbf{v}_A + \mathbf{v}_{B/A}$$

This equation can be applied in Cartesian vector form, written as

$$\mathbf{v}_B = \mathbf{v}_A + \boldsymbol{\omega} \times \mathbf{r}_{B/A}$$

In a similar manner, for acceleration,

$$\mathbf{a}_B = \mathbf{a}_A + (\mathbf{a}_{B/A})_t + (\mathbf{a}_{B/A})_n$$

or

$$\mathbf{a}_B = \mathbf{a}_A + \boldsymbol{\alpha} \times \mathbf{r}_{B/A} - \omega^2 \mathbf{r}_{B/A}$$

Since the relative motion is viewed as circular motion about the base point, point $B$ will have a velocity $\mathbf{v}_{B/A}$, that is tangent to the circle. It also has two components of acceleration, $(\mathbf{a}_{B/A})_t$, and $(\mathbf{a}_{B/A})_n$. It is important to also realize that $\mathbf{a}_A$ and $\mathbf{a}_B$ may have two components if these points move along curved paths.

*Instantaneous Center of Zero Velocity.* If the base point $A$ is selected as having zero velocity, then the relative velocity equation becomes

$$\mathbf{v}_B = \boldsymbol{\omega} \times \mathbf{r}_{B/A}$$

In this case, motion appears as if the body is rotating about an instantaneous axis.

The instantaneous center of rotation (*IC*) can be established provided the directions of the velocities of any two points on the body are known. Since the radial line $r$ will always be perpendicular to each velocity, then the *IC* is at the point of intersection of these two radial lines. Its measured location is determined from the geometry of the body. Once it is established, then the velocity of any point $P$ on the body can be determined from $v = \omega r$, where $r$ extends from the *IC* to point $P$.

• *Relative Motion Using Rotating Axes.* Problems that involve connected members that slide relative to one another, or points not located on the same body, can be analyzed using a relative-motion analysis referenced from a rotating frame. The equations of relative motion are

$$\mathbf{v}_B = \mathbf{v}_A + \boldsymbol{\Omega} \times \mathbf{r}_{B/A} + (\mathbf{v}_{B/A})_{xyz}$$

$$\mathbf{a}_B = \mathbf{a}_A + \dot{\boldsymbol{\Omega}} \times \mathbf{r}_{B/A} + \boldsymbol{\Omega} \times (\boldsymbol{\Omega} \times \mathbf{r}_{B/A}) + 2\boldsymbol{\Omega} \times (\mathbf{v}_{B/A})_{xyz} + (\mathbf{a}_{B/A})_{xyz}$$

In particular, the term $2\boldsymbol{\Omega} \times (\mathbf{v}_{B/A})_{xyz}$ is called the Coriolis acceleration.

The forces acting on this dragster as it begins to accelerate are quite severe
and must be accounted for in the design of its structure.

# Planar Kinetics of a Rigid Body: Force and Acceleration

- To introduce the methods used to determine the mass moment of inertia of a body.
- To develop the planar kinetic equations of motion for a symmetric rigid body.
- To discuss applications of these equations to bodies undergoing translation, rotation about a fixed axis, and general plane motion.

## 17.1 Moment of Inertia

Since a body has a definite size and shape, an applied non-concurrent force system may cause the body to both translate and rotate. The translational aspects of the motion were studied in Chapter 13 and are governed by the equation $\mathbf{F} = m\mathbf{a}$. It will be shown in Sec. 17.2 that the rotational aspects, caused by a moment $\mathbf{M}$, are governed by an equation of the form $\mathbf{M} = I\boldsymbol{\alpha}$. The symbol $I$ in this equation is termed the moment of inertia. By comparison, the *moment of inertia* is a measure of the resistance of a body to *angular acceleration* ($\mathbf{M} = I\boldsymbol{\alpha}$) in the same way that *mass* is a measure of the body's resistance to *acceleration* ($\mathbf{F} = m\mathbf{a}$).

The flywheel on the engine of this tractor has a large moment of inertia about its axis of rotation. Once it is set into motion, it will be difficult to stop, and this in turn will prevent the engine from stalling and instead it will allow it to maintain a constant power.

We define the *moment of inertia* as the integral of the "second moment" about an axis of all the elements of mass *dm* which compose the body.* For example, the body's moment of inertia about the *z* axis in Fig. 17–1 is

$$I = \int_m r^2 \, dm. \tag{17–1}$$

**Fig. 17–1**

Here the "moment arm" *r* is the perpendicular distance from the *z* axis to the arbitrary element *dm*. Since the formulation involves *r*, the value of *I* is different for each axis about which it is computed. In the study of planar kinetics, the axis which is generally chosen for analysis passes through the body's mass center *G* and is always perpendicular to the plane of motion. The moment of inertia computed about this axis will be denoted as $I_G$. Realize that because *r* is squared in Eq. 17–1, the mass moment of inertia is always a *positive* quantity. The common unit used for its measurement is $kg \cdot m^2$.

If the body consists of material having a variable density, $\rho = \rho\,(x, y, z)$, the elemental mass *dm* of the body may be expressed in terms of its density and volume as $dm = \rho \, dV$. Substituting *dm* into Eq. 17–1, the body's moment of inertia is then computed using *volume elements* for integration; i.e.,

$$I = \int_V r^2 \rho \, dV \tag{17–2}$$

*Another property of the body, which measures the symmetry of the body's mass with respect to a coordinate system, is the product of inertia. This property applies to the three-dimensional motion of a body and will be discussed in Chapter 21.

In the special case of $\rho$ being a *constant*, this term may be factored out of the integral, and the integration is then purely a function of geometry,

$$I = \rho \int_V r^2 \, dV \qquad (17\text{--}3)$$

When the elemental volume chosen for integration has infinitesimal dimensions in all three directions, e.g., $dV = dx \, dy \, dz$, Fig. 17–2a, the moment of inertia of the body must be determined using "triple integration." The integration process can, however, be simplified to a *single integration* provided the chosen elemental volume has a differential size or thickness in only *one direction*. Shell or disk elements are often used for this purpose.

(a)

(b)

## PROCEDURE FOR ANALYSIS

For integration, we will consider only symmetric bodies having surfaces which are generated by revolving a curve about an axis. An example of such a body which is generated about the $z$ axis is shown in Fig. 17–2a. Two types of differential elements can be chosen.

*Shell Element.*

- If a *shell element* having a height $z$, radius $r = y$, and thickness $dy$ is chosen for integration, Fig. 17–2b, then the volume is $dV = (2\pi y)(z) \, dy$.
- This element may be used in Eq. 17–2 or 17–3 for determining the moment of inertia $I_z$ of the body about the $z$ axis, since the *entire element*, due to its "thinness," lies at the *same* perpendicular distance $r = y$ from the $z$ axis (see Example 17.1).

*Disk Element.*

- If a disk element having a radius $y$ and a thickness $dz$ is chosen for integration, Fig. 17–2c, then the volume is $dV = (\pi y^2) \, dz$.
- This element is *finite* in the radial direction, and consequently its parts *do not* all lie at the *same radial distance r* from the $z$ axis. As a result, Eq. 17–2 or 17–3 *cannot* be used to determine $I_z$ directly. Instead, to perform the integration it is first necessary to determine the moment of inertia *of the element* about the $z$ axis and then integrate this result (see Example 17.2).

(c)

**Fig. 17–2**

**EXAMPLE** 17.1

Determine the moment of inertia of the cylinder shown in Fig. 17–3a about the z axis. The density of the material, $\rho$, is constant.

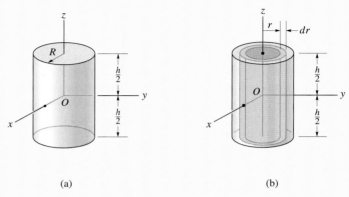

Fig. 17–3

**Solution**

*Shell Element.* This problem may be solved using the *shell element* in Fig. 17–3b and single integration. The volume of the element is $dV = (2\pi r)(h)\,dr$, so that its mass is $dm = \rho\,dV = \rho(2\pi hr\,dr)$. Since the *entire element* lies at the same distance $r$ from the $z$ axis, the moment of inertia *of the element* is

$$dI_z = r^2\,dm = \rho 2\pi hr^3\,dr$$

Integrating over the entire region of the cylinder yields

$$I_z = \int_m r^2\,dm = \rho 2\pi h \int_0^R r^3\,dr = \frac{\rho\pi}{2}R^4 h$$

The mass of the cylinder is

$$m = \int_m dm = \rho 2\pi h \int_0^R r\,dr = \rho\pi hR^2$$

so that

$$I_z = \frac{1}{2}mR^2 \qquad \qquad Ans.$$

# EXAMPLE 17.2

A solid is formed by revolving the shaded area shown in Fig. 17–4a about the $y$ axis. If the density of the material is 5 Mg/m³, determine the moment of inertia about the $y$ axis.

Fig. 17–4

**Solution**

*Disk Element.* The moment of inertia will be computed using a *disk element*, as shown in Fig. 17–4b. Here the element intersects the curve at the arbitrary point $(x, y)$ and has a mass

$$dm = \rho \, dV = \rho(\pi x^2) \, dy$$

Although all portions of the element are *not* located at the same distance from the $y$ axis, it is still possible to determine the moment of inertia $dI_y$ *of the element* about the $y$ axis. In the preceding example it was shown that the moment of inertia of a cylinder about its longitudinal axis is $I = \frac{1}{2}mR^2$, where $m$ and $R$ are the mass and radius of the cylinder. Since the height of the cylinder is not involved in this formula, the cylinder itself can be thought of as a disk. Thus, for the disk element in Fig. 17–4b, we have

$$dI_y = \tfrac{1}{2}(dm)x^2 = \tfrac{1}{2}[\rho(\pi x^2) \, dy]x^2$$

Substituting $x = y^2$, $\rho = 5$ Mg/m³, and integrating with respect to $y$, from $y = 0$ to $y = 1$ m, yields the moment of inertia for the entire solid.

$$I_y = \frac{\pi(5)}{2} \int_0^1 x^4 \, dy = \frac{\pi(5)}{2} \int_0^1 y^8 \, dy = 0.873 \text{ Mg} \cdot \text{m}^2 \qquad Ans.$$

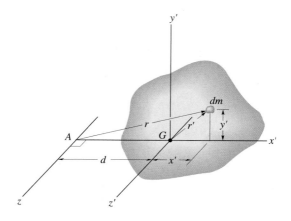

**Fig. 17–5**

**Parallel-Axis Theorem.** If the moment of inertia of the body about an axis passing through the body's mass center is known, then the moment of inertia about any other *parallel axis* may be determined by using the *parallel-axis theorem*. This theorem can be derived by considering the body shown in Fig. 17–5. The $z'$ axis passes through the mass center $G$, whereas the corresponding *parallel z axis* lies at a constant distance $d$ away. Selecting the differential element of mass $dm$, which is located at point $(x', y')$, and using the Pythagorean theorem, $r^2 = (d + x')^2 + y'^2$, we can express the moment of inertia of the body about the $z$ axis as

$$I = \int_m r^2\, dm = \int_m [(d + x')^2 + y'^2]\, dm$$

$$= \int_m (x'^2 + y'^2)\, dm + 2d \int_m x'\, dm + d^2 \int_m dm$$

Since $r'^2 = x'^2 + y'^2$, the first integral represents $I_G$. The second integral equals *zero*, since the $z'$ axis passes through the body's mass center, i.e., $\int x'\, dm = \bar{x}' \int dm = 0$ since $\bar{x}' = 0$. Finally, the third integral represents the total mass $m$ of the body. Hence, the moment of inertia about the *z* axis can be written as

$$I = I_G + md^2 \qquad (17\text{--}4)$$

where

$I_G$ = moment of inertia about the $z'$ axis passing through the mass center $G$

$m$ = mass of the body

$d$ = perpendicular distance between the parallel axes

**Radius of Gyration.**   Occasionally, the moment of inertia of a body about a specified axis is reported in handbooks using the *radius of gyration, k*. This value has units of length, and when it and the body's mass $m$ are known, the body's moment of inertia is determined from the equation

$$I = mk^2 \quad \text{or} \quad k = \sqrt{\frac{I}{m}} \qquad (17\text{--}5)$$

Note the *similarity* between the definition of $k$ in this formula and $r$ in the equation $dI = r^2\, dm$, which defines the moment of inertia of an elemental mass $dm$ of the body about an axis.

**Composite Bodies.**   If a body is constructed of a number of simple shapes such as disks, spheres, and rods, the moment of inertia of the body about any axis $z$ can be determined by adding algebraically the moments of inertia of all the composite shapes computed about the $z$ axis. Algebraic addition is necessary since a composite part must be considered as a negative quantity if it has already been counted as a piece of another part—for example, a "hole" subtracted from a solid plate. The parallel-axis theorem is needed for the calculations if the center of mass of each composite part does not lie on the $z$ axis. For the calculation, then, $I = \Sigma(I_G + md^2)$. Here $I_G$ for each of the composite parts is computed by integration or can be determined from a table, such as the one given on the inside back cover of this book.

E X A M P L E  **17.3**

If the plate shown in Fig. 17–6a has a density of 8000 kg/m³ and a thickness of 10 mm, determine its moment of inertia about an axis directed perpendicular to the page and passing through point $O$.

(a)                                                     (b)

**Fig. 17–6**

### Solution

The plate consists of two composite parts, the 250-mm-radius disk *minus* a 125-mm-radius disk, Fig. 17–6b. The moment of inertia about $O$ can be determined by computing the moment of inertia of each of these parts about $O$ and then adding the results *algebraically*. The calculations are performed by using the parallel-axis theorem in conjunction with the data listed in the table on the inside back cover.

*Disk.* The moment of inertia of a disk about the centroidal axis perpendicular to the plane of the disk is $I_G = \frac{1}{2}mr^2$. The mass center of the disk is located at a distance of 0.25 m from point $O$. Thus,

$$m_d = \rho_d V_d = 8000 \text{ kg/m}^3[\pi(0.25 \text{ m})^2(0.01 \text{ m})] = 15.71 \text{ kg}$$
$$(I_d)_O = \tfrac{1}{2}m_d r_d^2 + m_d d^2$$
$$= \frac{1}{2}(15.71 \text{ kg})(0.25 \text{ m})^2 + (15.71 \text{ kg})(0.25 \text{ m})^2$$
$$= 1.473 \text{ kg} \cdot \text{m}^2$$

*Hole.* For the 125-mm-radius disk (hole), we have

$$m_h = \rho_h V_h = 8000 \text{ kg/m}^3[\pi(0.125 \text{ m})^2(0.01 \text{ m})] = 3.93 \text{ kg}$$
$$(I_h)_O = \tfrac{1}{2}m_h r_h^2 + m_h d^2$$
$$= \frac{1}{2}(3.93 \text{ kg})(0.125 \text{ m})^2 + (3.93 \text{ kg})(0.25 \text{ m})^2$$
$$= 0.276 \text{ kg} \cdot \text{m}^2$$

The moment of inertia of the plate about point $O$ is therefore

$$I_O = (I_d)_O - (I_h)_O$$
$$= 1.473 \text{ kg} \cdot \text{m}^2 - 0.276 \text{ kg} \cdot \text{m}^2$$
$$= 1.20 \text{ kg} \cdot \text{m}^2 \qquad \qquad Ans.$$

# E X A M P L E  17.4

The pendulum in Fig. 17–7 is suspended from point $O$ and consists of two thin rods, each having a weight of 50 N ($\approx$ 5 kg). Determine the pendulum's moment of inertia about an axis passing through (a) the pin at $O$, and (b) the mass center $G$ of the pendulum.

**Solution**

*Part (a).*   Using the table on the inside back cover, the moment of inertia of rod $OA$ about an axis perpendicular to the page and passing through the end point $O$ of the rod is $I_O = \frac{1}{3}ml^2$. Hence,

$$(I_{OA})_O = \frac{1}{3}ml^2 = \frac{1}{3}\left(\frac{50\text{ N}}{9.81\text{ m/s}^2}\right)(1\text{ m})^2 = 1.699\text{ kg·m}^2$$

**Fig. 17–7**

This same value is obtained using $I_G = \frac{1}{12}ml^2$ and the parallel-axis theorem.

$$(I_{OA})_O = \frac{1}{12}ml^2 + md^2 = \frac{1}{12}\left(\frac{50\text{ N}}{9.81\text{ m/s}^2}\right)(1\text{ m})^2 + \left(\frac{50\text{ N}}{9.81\text{ m/s}^2}\right)(0.5\text{ m})^2$$

$$= 1.699\text{ kg · m}^2$$

For rod $BC$ we have

$$(I_{BC})_O = \frac{1}{12}ml^2 + md^2 = \frac{1}{12}\left(\frac{50\text{ N}}{9.81\text{ m/s}^2}\right)(1\text{ m})^2 + \left(\frac{50\text{ N}}{9.81\text{ m/s}^2}\right)(1\text{ m})^2$$

$$= 5.522\text{ kg · m}^2$$

The moment of inertia of the pendulum about $O$ is therefore

$$I_O = 1.699 + 5.522 = 7.22\text{ kg · m}^2 \qquad\qquad Ans.$$

*Part (b).*   The mass center $G$ will be located relative to the pin at $O$. Assuming this distance to be $\bar{y}$, Fig. 17–7, and using the formula for determining the mass center, we have

$$\bar{y} = \frac{\Sigma\tilde{y}m}{\Sigma m} = \frac{0.5(50/9.81) + 1(50/9.81)}{(50/9.81) + (50/9.81)} = 0.75\text{ m}$$

The moment of inertia $I_G$ may be computed in the same manner as $I_O$, which requires successive applications of the parallel-axis theorem to transfer the moments of inertia of rods $OA$ and $BC$ to $G$. A more direct solution, however, involves using the result for $I_O$, i.e.,

$$I_O = I_G + md^2; \qquad 7.22\text{ kg ·m}^2 = I_G + \left(\frac{100\text{ N}}{9.81\text{ m/s}^2}\right)(0.75\text{ m})^2$$

$$I_G = 1.486\text{ kg · m}^2 \qquad\qquad Ans.$$

# PROBLEMS

**17-1.** Determine the moment of inertia $I_y$ for the slender rod. The rod's density $\rho$ and cross-sectional area $A$ are constant. Express the result in terms of the rod's total mass $m$.

**17-3.** The right circular cone is formed by revolving the shaded area around the $x$ axis. Determine the moment of inertia $I_x$ and express the result in terms of the total mass $m$ of the cone. The cone has a constant density $\rho$.

Prob. 17–1

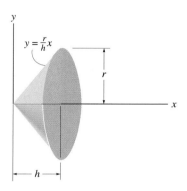

Prob. 17–3

*17-4.** A semiellipsoid is formed by rotating the shaded area about the $x$ axis. Determine the moment of inertia of this solid with respect to the $x$ axis and express the result in terms of the mass $m$ of the solid. The material has a constant density $\rho$.

**17-2.** Determine the moment of inertia of the thin ring about the $z$ axis. The ring has a mass $m$.

Prob. 17–2

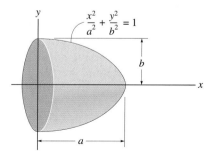

Prob. 17–4

**17-5.** The solid is formed by revolving the shaded area around the $y$ axis. Determine the radius of gyration $k_y$. The material has a constant density $\rho$.

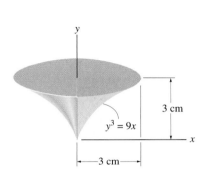

3 cm

$y^3 = 9x$

3 cm

Prob. 17–5

**17-7.** Determine the moment of inertia $I_z$ of the torus. The mass of the torus is $m$ and the density $\rho$ is constant. *Suggestion:* Use a shell element.

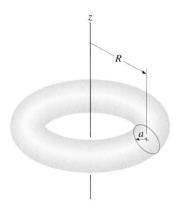

$R$

$a$

Prob. 17–7

**17-6.** The sphere is formed by revolving the shaded area around the $x$ axis. Determine the moment of inertia $I_x$ and express the result in terms of the total mass $m$ of the sphere. The material has a constant density $\rho$.

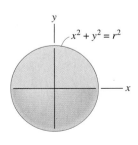

$x^2 + y^2 = r^2$

Prob. 17–6

**\*17-8.** The solid cylinder has an outer radius $R$, height $h$, and is made from a material having a density that varies from its center as $\rho = k + ar^2$, where $k$ and $a$ are constants. Determine the mass of the cylinder and its moment of inertia about the $z$ axis.

$R$

$h$

Prob. 17–8

**17-9.** The concrete shape is formed by rotating the shaded area about the $y$ axis. Determine the moment of inertia $I_y$. The specific weight of concrete is $\gamma = 24$ kN/m$^3$.

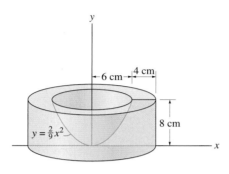

**Prob. 17–9**

**17-10.** The frustum is formed by rotating the shaded area around the $x$ axis. Determine the moment of inertia $I_x$ and express the result in terms of the total mass $m$ of the frustum. The frustum has a constant density.

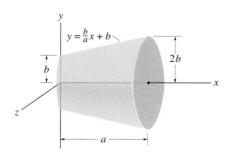

**Prob. 17–10**

**17-11.** Determine the moment of inertia of the homogeneous triangular prism with respect to the $y$ axis. Express the result in terms of the mass $m$ of the prism. *Hint:* For integration, use thin plate elements parallel to the $x$–$y$ plane and having a thickness $dz$.

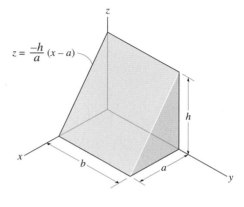

**Prob. 17–11**

**\*17-12.** Determine the moment of inertia of the assembly about an axis which is perpendicular to the page and passes through point $O$. The material has a specific weight of $\gamma = 15$ kN/m$^3$.

**Prob. 17–12**

**17-13.** The assembly consists of a disk having a mass of 6 kg and slender rods $AB$ and $DC$ which have a mass of 2 kg/m. Determine the length $L$ of $DC$ so that the center of mass is at the bearing $O$. What is the moment of inertia of the assembly about an axis perpendicular to the page and passing through $O$?

**17-14.** The assembly consists of a disk having a mass of 6 kg and slender rods $AB$ and $DC$ which have a mass of 2 kg/m. If $L = 0.75$ m, determine the moment of inertia of the assembly about an axis perpendicular to the page and passing through $O$.

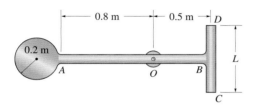

Probs. 17–13/14

*17-16.** The pendulum consists of the 3-kg slender rod and the 5-kg thin plate. Determine the location $\bar{y}$ of the center of mass $G$ of the pendulum; then calculate the moment of inertia of the pendulum about an axis perpendicular to the page and passing through $G$.

Prob. 17–16

**17-15.** The wheel consists of a thin ring having a mass of 10 kg and four spokes made from slender rods and each having a mass of 2 kg. Determine the wheel's moment of inertia about an axis perpendicular to the page and passing through point $A$.

**17-17.** Each of the three rods has a mass $m$. Determine the moment of inertia of the assembly about an axis which is perpendicular to the page and passes through the center point $O$.

Prob. 17–15

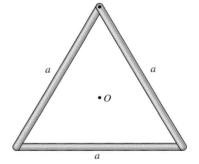

Prob. 17–17

**17-18.** The slender rods have a weight of 45 N/m. Determine the moment of inertia of the assembly about an axis perpendicular to the page and passing through the pin at $A$.

**Prob. 17–18**

**17-19.** The pendulum consists of a plate having a weight of 120 N ($\approx 12$ kg) and a slender rod having a weight of 40 N ($\approx 4$ kg). Determine the radius of gyration of the pendulum about an axis perpendicular to the page and passing through point $O$.

**Prob. 17–19**

**\*17-20.** The pendulum consists of two slender rods $AB$ and $OC$ which have a mass of 3 kg/m. The thin plate has a mass of 12 kg/m². Determine the location $\overline{y}$ of the center of mass $G$ of the pendulum, then calculate the moment of inertia of the pendulum about an axis perpendicular to the page and passing through $G$.

**17-21.** The pendulum consists of two slender rods $AB$ and $OC$ which have a mass of 3 kg/m. The thin plate has a mass of 12 kg/m². Determine the moment of inertia of the pendulum about an axis perpendicular to the page and passing through the pin at $O$.

**Probs. 17–20/21**

**17-22.** Determine the moment of inertia of the solid steel assembly about the $x$ axis. Steel has a specific weight of $\gamma_{st} = 78$ kN/m³.

**Prob. 17–22**

**17-23.** Determine the moment of inertia about an axis perpendicular to the page and passing through the pin at $O$. The thin plate has a hole in its center. Its thickness is 50 mm, and the material has a density $\rho = 50$ kg/m³.

**Prob. 17–23**

## 17.2 Planar Kinetic Equations of Motion

In the following analysis we will limit our study of planar kinetics to rigid bodies which, along with their loadings, are considered to be *symmetrical with respect to a fixed reference plane.*\* In this case the path of motion of each particle of the body is a plane curve parallel to a fixed reference plane. Since the motion of the body may be viewed within the reference plane, all the forces (and couple moments) acting on the body can then be projected onto the plane. An example of an arbitrary body of this type is shown in Fig. 17–8a. Here the *inertial frame of reference x, y, z* has its origin *coincident* with the arbitrary point *P* in the body. By definition, *these axes do not rotate and are either fixed or translate with constant velocity.*

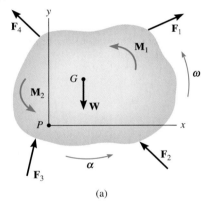

(a)

Fig. 17–8

**Equation of Translational Motion.**    The external forces shown on the body in Fig. 17–8a represent the effect of gravitational, electrical, magnetic, or contact forces between adjacent bodies. Since this force system has been considered previously in Sec. 13.3 for the analysis of a system of particles, the resulting Eq. 13–6 may be used here, in which case

$$\Sigma \mathbf{F} = m \mathbf{a}_G$$

This equation is referred to as the *translational equation of motion* for the mass center of a rigid body. It states that *the sum of all the external forces acting on the body is equal to the body's mass times the acceleration of its mass center G.*

For motion of the body in the *x–y* plane, the translational equation of motion may be written in the form of two independent scalar equations, namely,

$$\Sigma F_x = m(a_G)_x$$
$$\Sigma F_y = m(a_G)_y$$

\*By doing this, the rotational equation of motion reduces to a rather simplified form. The more general case of body shape and loading is considered in Chapter 21.

Particle free-body diagram

(b)

Particle kinetic diagram

(c)

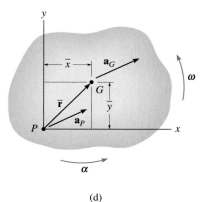

(d)

**Fig. 17–8**

**Equation of Rotational Motion.** We will now determine the effects caused by the moments of the external force system computed about an axis perpendicular to the plane of motion (the $z$ axis) and passing through point $P$. As shown on the free-body diagram of the $i$th particle, Fig. 17–8$b$, $\mathbf{F}_i$, represents the *resultant external force* acting on the particle, and $\mathbf{f}_i$ is the *resultant of the internal forces* caused by interactions with adjacent particles. If the particle has a mass $m_i$ and at the instant considered its acceleration is $\mathbf{a}_i$, then the kinetic diagram is constructed as shown in Fig. 17–8$c$. If moments of the forces acting on the particle are summed about point $P$, we require

$$\mathbf{r} \times \mathbf{F}_i + \mathbf{r} \times \mathbf{f}_i = \mathbf{r} \times m_i\mathbf{a}_i$$

or

$$(\mathbf{M}_P)_i = \mathbf{r} \times m_i\mathbf{a}_i$$

The moments about $P$ can be expressed in terms of the acceleration of point $P$, Fig. 17–8$d$. If the body has an angular acceleration $\boldsymbol{\alpha}$ and angular velocity $\boldsymbol{\omega}$, then using Eq. 16–18 we have

$$(\mathbf{M}_P)_i = m_i\mathbf{r} \times (\mathbf{a}_P + \boldsymbol{\alpha} \times \mathbf{r} - \omega^2\mathbf{r})$$
$$= m_i[\mathbf{r} \times \mathbf{a}_P + \mathbf{r} \times (\boldsymbol{\alpha} \times \mathbf{r}) - \omega^2(\mathbf{r} \times \mathbf{r})]$$

The last term is zero, since $\mathbf{r} \times \mathbf{r} = \mathbf{0}$. Expressing the vectors with Cartesian components and carrying out the cross-product operations yields

$$(M_P)_i\mathbf{k} = m_i\{(x\mathbf{i} + y\mathbf{j}) \times [(a_P)_x\mathbf{i} + (a_P)_y\mathbf{j}]$$
$$+ (x\mathbf{i} + y\mathbf{j}) \times [\alpha\mathbf{k} \times (x\mathbf{i} + y\mathbf{j})]\}$$
$$(M_P)_i\mathbf{k} = m_i[-y(a_P)_x + x(a_P)_y + \alpha x^2 + \alpha y^2]\mathbf{k}$$
$$\rotatebox{0}{$\downarrow$}(M_P)_i = m_i[-y(a_P)_x + x(a_P)_y + \alpha r^2]$$

Letting $m_i \to dm$ and integrating with respect to the entire mass $m$ of the body, we obtain the resultant moment equation

$$\rotatebox{0}{$\downarrow$}\Sigma M_P = -\left(\int_m y\, dm\right)(a_P)_x + \left(\int_m x\, dm\right)(a_P)_y + \left(\int_m r^2\, dm\right)\alpha$$

Here $\Sigma M_P$ represents only the moment of the *external forces* acting on the body about point $P$. The resultant moment of the internal forces is zero, since for the entire body these forces occur in equal and opposite collinear pairs and thus the moment of each pair of forces about $P$ cancels. The integrals in the first and second terms on the right are used to locate the body's center of mass $G$ with respect to $P$, since $\bar{y}m = \int y\, dm$ and $\bar{x}m = \int x\, dm$, Fig. 17–8$d$. Also, the last integral represents the body's moment of inertia computed about the $z$ axis, i.e., $I_P = \int r^2 dm$. Thus,

$$\rotatebox{0}{$\downarrow$}\Sigma M_P = -\bar{y}m(a_P)_x + \bar{x}m(a_P)_y + I_P\alpha \qquad (17\text{–}6)$$

It is possible to reduce this equation to a simpler form if point $P$ coincides with the mass center $G$ for the body. If this is the case, then $\bar{x} = \bar{y} = 0$, and therefore*

$$\boxed{\Sigma M_G = I_G \alpha} \qquad (17\text{–}7)$$

*This rotational equation of motion states that the sum of the moments of all the external forces computed about the body's mass center $G$ is equal to the product of the moment of inertia of the body about an axis passing through $G$ and the body's angular acceleration.*

Equation 17–6 can also be rewritten in terms of the $x$ and $y$ components of $\mathbf{a}_G$ and the body's moment of inertia $I_G$. If point $G$ is located at point $(\bar{x}, \bar{y})$, Fig. 17–8d, then by the parallel-axis theorem, $I_p = I_G + m(\bar{x}^2 + \bar{y}^2)$. Substituting into Eq. 17–6 and rearranging terms, we get

$$\curvearrowleft \Sigma M_P = \bar{y}m[-(a_P)_x + \bar{y}\alpha] + \bar{x}m[(a_P)_y + \bar{x}\alpha] + I_G\alpha \qquad (17\text{–}8)$$

From the kinematic diagram of Fig. 17–8d, $\mathbf{a}_P$ can be expressed in terms of $\mathbf{a}_G$ as

$$\mathbf{a}_G = \mathbf{a}_P + \boldsymbol{\alpha} \times \bar{\mathbf{r}} - \omega^2 \bar{\mathbf{r}}$$
$$(a_G)_x\mathbf{i} + (a_G)_y\mathbf{j} = (a_P)_x\mathbf{i} + (a_P)_y\mathbf{j} + \alpha\mathbf{k} \times (\bar{x}\mathbf{i} + \bar{y}\mathbf{j}) - \omega^2(\bar{x}\mathbf{i} + \bar{y}\mathbf{j})$$

Carrying out the cross product and equating the respective $\mathbf{i}$ and $\mathbf{j}$ components yields the two scalar equations

$$(a_G)_x = (a_P)_x - \bar{y}\alpha - \bar{x}\omega^2$$
$$(a_G)_y = (a_P)_y + \bar{x}\alpha - \bar{y}\omega^2$$

From these equations, $[-(a_P)_x + \bar{y}\alpha] = [-(a_G)_x - \bar{x}\omega^2]$ and $[(a_P)_y + \bar{x}\alpha] = [(a_G)_y + \bar{y}\omega^2]$. Substituting these results into Eq. 17–8 and simplifying gives

$$\curvearrowleft \Sigma M_P = -\bar{y}m(a_G)_x + \bar{x}m(a_G)_y + I_G\alpha \qquad (17\text{–}9)$$

*This important result indicates that when moments of the external forces shown on the free-body diagram are summed about point $P$, Fig. 17–8e, they are equivalent to the sum of the "kinetic moments" of the components of $m\mathbf{a}_G$ about $P$ plus the "kinetic moment" of $I_G\alpha$, Fig. 17–8f. In other words, when the "kinetic moments," $\Sigma(\mathcal{M}_k)_P$, are computed, Fig. 17–8f, the vectors $m(\mathbf{a}_G)_x$ and $m(\mathbf{a}_G)_y$ are treated as sliding vectors; that is, they can act at any point along their line of action. In a similar manner, $I_G\alpha$ can be treated as a free vector and can therefore act at any point. It is important to keep in mind that $m\mathbf{a}_G$ and $I_G\alpha$ are not the same as a force or a couple moment. Instead, they are caused by the external effects of forces and couple moments acting on the body.* With this in mind we can therefore write Eq. 17–9 in a more general form as

$$\boxed{\Sigma M_P = \Sigma(\mathcal{M}_k)_P} \qquad (17\text{–}10)$$

*It also reduces to this same simple form $\Sigma M_P = I_p\alpha$ if point $P$ is a *fixed* point (see Eq. 17–16) or the acceleration of point $P$ is directed along the line $PG$.

Free-body diagram

(e)

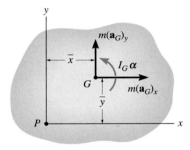

Kinetic diagram

(f)

**Fig. 17–8**

**General Application of the Equations of Motion.** To summarize this analysis, *three* independent scalar equations may be written to describe the general plane motion of a symmetrical rigid body.

$$\Sigma F_x = m(a_G)_x$$
$$\Sigma F_y = m(a_G)_y$$
$$\Sigma M_G = I_G\alpha \quad \text{or} \quad \Sigma M_P = \Sigma(\mathcal{M}_k)_P \qquad (17\text{–}11)$$

When applying these equations, one should *always* draw a free-body diagram, Fig. 17–8e, in order to account for the terms involved in $\Sigma F_x$, $\Sigma F_y$, $\Sigma M_G$, or $\Sigma M_P$. In some problems it may also be helpful to draw the *kinetic diagram* for the body. This diagram graphically accounts for the terms $m(\mathbf{a}_G)_x$, $m(\mathbf{a}_G)_y$, and $I_G\boldsymbol{\alpha}$, and it is especially convenient when used to determine the components of $m\mathbf{a}_G$ and the moment terms in $\Sigma(\mathcal{M}_k)_P$.*

## 17.3 Equations of Motion: Translation

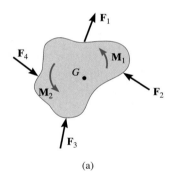

(a)

**Fig. 17–9**

When a rigid body undergoes a *translation*, Fig. 17–9a, all the particles of the body have the *same acceleration*, so that $\mathbf{a}_G = \mathbf{a}$. Furthermore, $\boldsymbol{\alpha} = \mathbf{0}$, in which case the rotational equation of motion applied at point $G$ reduces to a simplified form, namely, $\Sigma M_G = 0$. Application of this and the translational equations of motion will now be discussed for each of the two types of translation.

**Rectilinear Translation.** When a body is subjected to *rectilinear translation*, all the particles of the body (slab) travel along parallel straight-line paths. The free-body and kinetic diagrams are shown in Fig. 17–9b. Since $I_G\boldsymbol{\alpha} = \mathbf{0}$, only $m\mathbf{a}_G$ is shown on the kinetic diagram. Hence, the equations of motion which apply in this case become

$$\boxed{\begin{aligned} \Sigma F_x &= m(a_G)_x \\ \Sigma F_y &= m(a_G)_y \\ \Sigma M_G &= 0 \end{aligned}} \qquad (17\text{–}12)$$

The last equation requires that the sum of the moments of all the external forces (and couple moments) computed about the body's center of mass be equal to zero. It is possible, of course, to sum moments about other points on or off the body, in which case the moment of $m\mathbf{a}_G$ must be

---

*For this reason, the kinetic diagram will be used in the solution of an example problem whenever $\Sigma M_P = \Sigma(\mathcal{M}_k)_P$ is applied.

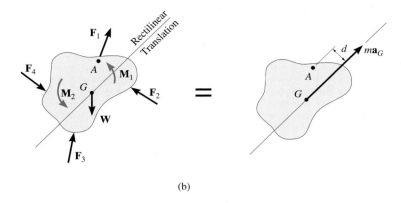

(b)

**Fig. 17–9**

taken into account. For example, if point $A$ is chosen, which lies at a perpendicular distance $d$ from the line of action of $m\mathbf{a}_G$, the following moment equation applies:

$$\zeta + \Sigma M_A = \Sigma(\mathcal{M}_k)_A; \qquad \Sigma M_A = (ma_G)d$$

Here the sum of moments of the external forces and couple moments about $A$ ($\Sigma M_A$, free-body diagram) equals the moment of $m\mathbf{a}_G$ about $A$ ($\Sigma(\mathcal{M}_k)_A$, kinetic diagram).

**Curvilinear Translation.** When a rigid body is subjected to *curvilinear translation*, all the particles of the body travel along *parallel curved paths*. For analysis, it is often convenient to use an inertial coordinate system having an origin which is coincident with the body's mass center at the instant considered, and axes which are oriented in the normal and tangential directions to the path of motion, Fig. 17–9c. The three scalar equations of motion are then

$$\boxed{\begin{aligned} \Sigma F_n &= m(a_G)_n \\ \Sigma F_t &= m(a_G)_t \\ \Sigma M_G &= 0 \end{aligned}} \qquad (17\text{–}13)$$

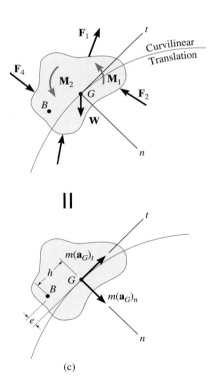

Here $(a_G)_t$ and $(a_G)_n$ represent, respectively, the magnitudes of the tangential and normal components of acceleration of point $G$.

If the moment equation $\Sigma M_G = 0$ is replaced by a moment summation about the arbitrary point $B$, Fig. 17–9c, it is necessary to account for the moments, $\Sigma(\mathcal{M}_k)_B$, of the two components $m(\mathbf{a}_G)_n$ and $m(\mathbf{a}_G)_t$ about this point. From the kinetic diagram, $h$ and $e$ represent the perpendicular distances (or "moment arms") from $B$ to the lines of action of the components. The required moment equation therefore becomes

$$\zeta + \Sigma M_B = \Sigma(\mathcal{M}_k)_B; \qquad \Sigma M_B = e[m(a_G)_t] - h[m(a_G)_n]$$

The free-body and kinetic diagrams for this boat and trailer are first drawn in order to apply the equations of motion. Here the forces on the free-body diagram cause the effect shown on the kinetic diagram. If moments are summed about the mass center, $G$, then $\Sigma M_G = 0$. However, if moments are summed about point $B$ then $\curvearrowright + \Sigma M_B = m a_G(d)$.

## PROCEDURE FOR ANALYSIS

Kinetic problems involving rigid-body *translation* can be solved using the following procedure.

### Free-Body Diagram.

- Establish the *x, y* or *n, t* inertial coordinate system and draw the free-body diagram in order to account for all the external forces and couple moments that act on the body.
- The direction and sense of the acceleration of the body's mass center $\mathbf{a}_G$ should be established.
- Identify the unknowns in the problem.
- If it is decided that the rotational equation of motion $\Sigma M_P = \Sigma(\mathcal{M}_k)_P$ is to be used in the solution, then consider drawing the kinetic diagram, since it graphically accounts for the components $m(\mathbf{a}_G)_x, m(\mathbf{a}_G)_y$ or $m(\mathbf{a}_G)_t, m(\mathbf{a}_G)_n$ and is therefore convenient for "visualizing" the terms needed in the moment sum $\Sigma(\mathcal{M}_k)_P$.

### Equations of Motion.

- Apply the three equations of motion in accordance with the established sign convention.
- To simplify the analysis, the moment equation $\Sigma M_G = 0$ can be replaced by the more general equation $\Sigma M_P = \Sigma(\mathcal{M}_k)_P$, where point $P$ is usually located at the intersection of the lines of action of as many unknown forces as possible.
- If the body is in contact with a *rough surface* and slipping occurs, use the frictional equation $F = \mu_k N$. Remember, $\mathbf{F}$ always acts on the body so as to oppose the motion of the body relative to the surface it contacts.

### Kinematics.

- Use kinematics if the velocity and position of the body are to be determined.
- For *rectilinear translation* with *variable acceleration*, use
$$a_G = dv_G/dt \quad a_G ds_G = v_G dv_G \quad v_G = ds_G/dt$$
- For *rectilinear translation* with *constant acceleration*, use
$$v_G = (v_G)_0 + a_G t \qquad v_G^2 = (v_G)_0^2 + 2a_G[s_G - (s_G)_0]$$
$$s_G = (s_G)_0 + (v_G)_0 t + \tfrac{1}{2}a_G t^2$$
- For *curvilinear translation*, use $(a_G)_n = v_G^2/\rho = \omega^2\rho, (a_G)_t = dv_G/dt, (a_G)_t ds_G = v_G dv_G, (a_G)_t = \alpha\rho$

# EXAMPLE 17.5

The car shown in Fig. 17–10a has a mass of 2 Mg and a center of mass at $G$. Determine the car's acceleration if the "driving" wheels in the back are always slipping, whereas the front wheels freely rotate. Neglect the mass of the wheels. The coefficient of kinetic friction between the wheels and the road is $\mu_k = 0.25$.

## Solution I

*Free-Body Diagram.* As shown in Fig. 17–10b, the rear-wheel frictional force $\mathbf{F}_B$ pushes the car forward, and since *slipping occurs*, $F_B = 0.25N_B$. The frictional forces acting on the *front wheels* are *zero*, since these wheels have negligible mass.* There are three unknowns in the problem, $N_A$, $N_B$, and $a_G$. Here we will sum moments about the mass center. The car (point $G$) is assumed to accelerate to the left, i.e., in the negative $x$ direction, Fig. 17–10b.

*Equations of Motion.*

$$\xrightarrow{+} \Sigma F_x = m(a_G)_x; \qquad -0.25N_B = -(2000 \text{ kg})a_G \qquad (1)$$

$$+\uparrow \Sigma F_y = m(a_G)_y; \qquad N_A + N_B - 2000(9.81) \text{ N} = 0 \qquad (2)$$

$$\zeta + \Sigma M_G = 0; \quad -N_A(1.25 \text{ m}) - 0.25N_B(0.3 \text{ m}) + N_B(0.75 \text{ m}) = 0 \quad (3)$$

Solving,

$$a_G = 1.59 \text{ m/s}^2 \leftarrow \qquad\qquad Ans.$$
$$N_A = 6.88 \text{ kN}$$
$$N_B = 12.7 \text{ kN}$$

## Solution II

*Free-Body and Kinetic Diagrams.* If the "moment" equation is applied about point $A$, then the unknown $N_A$ will be eliminated from the equation. To "visualize" the moment of $m\mathbf{a}_G$ about $A$, we will include the kinetic diagram as part of the analysis, Fig. 17–10c.

*Equation of Motion.* We require

$$\zeta + \Sigma M_A = \Sigma(\mathcal{M}_k)_A; \qquad N_B(2 \text{ m}) - 2000(9.81) \text{ N}(1.25 \text{ m}) =$$
$$(2000 \text{ kg})a_G(0.3 \text{ m})$$

Solving this and Eq. 1 for $a_G$ leads to a simpler solution than that obtained from Eqs. 1 to 3.

*With negligible wheel mass, $I\alpha = 0$ and the frictional force at $A$ required to turn the wheel is zero. If the wheels' mass were included, then the problem solution for this case would be more involved, since a general-plane-motion analysis of the wheels would have to be considered (see Sec. 17.5).

(a)

(b)

(c)

Fig. 17–10

E X A M P L E **17.6**

The motorcycle shown in Fig. 17–11a has a mass of 125 kg and a center of mass at $G_1$, while the rider has a mass of 75 kg and a center of mass at $G_2$. Determine the minimum coefficient of static friction between the wheels and the pavement in order for the rider to do a "wheely," i.e., lift the front wheel off the ground as shown in the photo. What acceleration is necessary to do this? Neglect the mass of the wheels and assume that the front wheel is free to roll.

(a)

**Solution**

*Free-Body and Kinetic Diagrams.* In this problem we will consider both the motorcycle and the rider as the "system" to be analyzed. It is possible first to determine the location of the center of mass for this "system" by using the equations $\bar{x} = \Sigma \tilde{x}m/\Sigma m$ and $\bar{y} = \Sigma \tilde{y}m/\Sigma m$. Here, however, we will consider the separate weight and mass of each of its *component parts* as shown on the free-body and kinetic diagrams, Fig. 17–11b. Both parts move with the *same* acceleration and we have assumed that the front wheel is *about* to leave the ground, so that the normal reaction $N_A \approx 0$. The three unknowns in the problem are $N_B$, $F_B$, and $a_G$.

*Equations of Motion.*

$$\xrightarrow{+} \Sigma F_x = m(a_G)_x; \qquad F_B = (75 \text{ kg} + 125 \text{ kg})a_G \qquad (1)$$

$$+\uparrow \Sigma F_y = m(a_G)_y; \qquad N_B - 735.75 \text{ N} - 1226.25 \text{ N} = 0 \qquad (2)$$

$$\zeta+ \Sigma M_B = \Sigma(\mathcal{M}_k)_B; \quad -(735.75 \text{ N})(0.4 \text{ m}) - (1226.25 \text{ N})(0.8 \text{ m}) = \\ -(75 \text{ kg } a_G)(0.9 \text{ m}) - (125 \text{ kg } a_G)(0.6 \text{ m})$$

Solving,

$$a_G = 8.95 \text{ m/s}^2 \rightarrow \qquad Ans.$$
$$N_B = 1962 \text{ N}$$
$$F_B = 1790 \text{ N}$$

Thus the minimum coefficient of static friction is

$$(\mu_s)_{min} = \frac{F_B}{N_B} = \frac{1790 \text{ N}}{1962 \text{ N}} = 0.912 \qquad Ans.$$

(b)

**Fig. 17–11**

## EXAMPLE 17.7

A uniform 50-kg crate rests on a horizontal surface for which the coefficient of kinetic friction is $\mu_k = 0.2$. Determine the crate's acceleration if a force of $P = 600$ N is applied to the crate as shown in Fig. 17–12a.

(a)

### Solution

*Free-Body Diagram.* The force **P** can cause the crate either to slide or to tip over. As shown in Fig. 17–12b, it is assumed that the crate slides, so that $F = \mu_k N_C = 0.2N_C$. Also, the resultant normal force $\mathbf{N}_C$ acts at $O$, a distance $x$ (where $0 < x \le 0.5$ m) from the crate's center line.* The three unknowns are $N_C$, $x$, and $a_G$.

*Equations of Motion*

$$\overset{+}{\rightarrow} \Sigma F_x = m(a_G)_x; \qquad 600\text{ N} - 0.2N_C = (50\text{ kg})a_G \qquad (1)$$
$$+\uparrow \Sigma F_y = m(a_G)_y; \qquad N_C - 490.5\text{ N} = 0 \qquad (2)$$
$$\zeta + \Sigma M_G = 0; \qquad -600\text{ N}(0.3\text{ m}) + N_C(x) - 0.2N_C(0.5\text{ m}) = 0 \qquad (3)$$

Solving, we obtain

$$N_C = 490\text{ N}$$
$$x = 0.467\text{ m}$$
$$a_G = 10.0\text{ m/s}^2 \rightarrow \qquad\qquad\qquad Ans.$$

Since $x = 0.467$ m $< 0.5$ m, indeed the crate slides as originally assumed. If the solution had given a value of $x > 0.5$ m, the problem would have to be reworked with the assumption that tipping occurred. If this were the case, $\mathbf{N}_C$ would act at the *corner point A* and $F \le 0.2N_C$.

**Fig. 17–12**

---

*The line of action of $\mathbf{N}_C$ does not necessarily pass through the mass center $G$ ($x = 0$), since $\mathbf{N}_C$ must counteract the tendency for tipping caused by **P**. See Sec. 8.1 of *Engineering Mechanics: Statics.*

## EXAMPLE 17.8

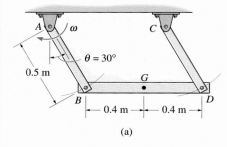

(a)

The 100-kg beam $BD$ shown in Fig. 17–13a is supported by two rods having negligible mass. Determine the force created in each rod if at the instant $\theta = 30°$ and $\omega = 6$ rad/s.

### Solution

*Free-Body Diagram.*   The beam moves with *curvilinear translation* since points $B$ and $D$ and the center of mass $G$ all move along circular paths, each path having the same radius of 0.5 m. Using normal and tangential coordinates, the free-body diagram for the beam is shown in Fig. 17–13b. Because of the *translation*, $G$ has the *same* motion as the pin at $B$, which is connected to both the rod and the beam. By studying the angular motion of rod $AB$, Fig. 17–13c, note that the tangential component of acceleration acts downward to the left due to the clockwise direction of $\alpha$. Furthermore, the normal component of acceleration is *always* directed toward the center of curvature (toward point $A$ for rod $AB$). Since the angular velocity of $AB$ is 6 rad/s, then

$$(a_G)_n = \omega^2 r = (6 \text{ rad/s})^2 (0.5 \text{ m}) = 18 \text{ m/s}^2$$

The three unknowns are $T_B$, $T_D$, and $(a_G)_t$. The directions of $(\mathbf{a}_G)_n$ and $(\mathbf{a}_G)_t$ have been established, and are indicated on the coordinate axes.

(b)

981 N

(c)

**Fig. 17–13**

### Equations of Motion.

$$+\nwarrow \Sigma F_n = m(a_G)_n; \quad T_B + T_D - 981 \cos 30° \text{ N} = 100 \text{ kg}(18 \text{ m/s}^2) \quad (1)$$

$$+\swarrow \Sigma F_t = m(a_G)_t; \quad\quad\quad\quad 981 \sin 30° = 100 \text{ kg}(a_G)_t \quad\quad (2)$$

$$\zeta + \Sigma M_G = 0; \quad -(T_B \cos 30°)(0.4 \text{ m}) + (T_D \cos 30°)(0.4 \text{ m}) = 0 \quad (3)$$

Simultaneous solution of these three equations gives

$$T_B = T_D = 1.32 \text{ kN} \searrow^{30°} \quad\quad\quad\quad Ans.$$

$$(a_G)_t = 4.90 \text{ m/s}^2$$

# PROBLEMS

**\*17-24.** The 4-Mg canister contains nuclear waste material encased in concrete. If the mass of the spreader beam *BD* is 50 kg, determine the force in each of the links *AB, CD, EF,* and *GH* when the system is lifted with an acceleration of *a* = 2 m/s² for a short period of time.

**17-25.** The 4-Mg canister contains nuclear waste material encased in concrete. If the mass of the spreader beam *BD* is 50 kg, determine the largest vertical acceleration **a** of the system so that each of the links *AB* and *CD* are not subjected to a force greater than 30 kN and links *EF* and *GH* are not subjected to a force greater than 34 kN.

Probs. 17–24/25

**17-26.** The 20-N (≈ 2-kg) bottle rests on the check-out conveyor at a grocery store. If the coefficient of static friction is $\mu_s$ = 0.2, determine the largest acceleration the conveyor can have without causing the bottle to slip or tip. The center of gravity is at *G*.

Prob. 17–26

**17-27.** The assembly has a mass of 8 Mg and is hoisted using the boom and pulley system. If the winch at *B* draws in the cable with an acceleration of 2 m/s², determine the compressive force in the hydraulic cylinder needed to support the boom. The boom has a mass of 2 Mg and mass center at *G*.

Prob. 17–27

**\*17-28.** The jet aircraft has a total mass of 22 Mg and a center of mass at *G*. Initially at take-off the engines provide a thrust 2*T* = 4 kN and *T'* = 1.5 kN. Determine the acceleration of the plane and the normal reactions on the nose wheel and each of the *two* wing wheels located at *B*. Neglect the mass of the wheels and, due to low velocity, neglect any lift caused by the wings.

Prob. 17–28

**17-29.** The lift truck has a mass of 70 kg and mass center at $G$. If it lifts the 120-kg spool with an acceleration of 3 m/s², determine the reactions of each of the four wheels on the ground. The loading is symmetric. Neglect the mass of the movable arm $CD$.

**17-30.** The lift truck has a mass of 70 kg and mass center at $G$. Determine the largest upward acceleration of the 120-kg spool so that no reaction of the wheels on the ground exceeds 600 N.

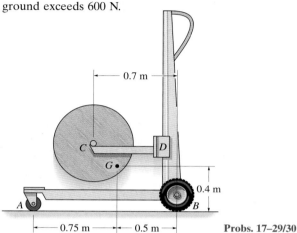

Probs. 17–29/30

**17-31.** The door has a weight of 1 kN ($\approx$ 100 kg) and a center of gravity at $G$. Determine how far the door moves in 2 s, starting from rest, if a man pushes on it at $C$ with a horizontal force $F = 150$ N. Also, find the vertical reactions at the rollers $A$ and $B$.

**\*17-32.** The door has a weight of 1 kN ($\approx$ 100 kg) and a center of gravity at $G$. Determine the constant force $F$ that must be applied to the door to push it open 3.6 m to the right in 5 s, starting from rest. Also, find the vertical reactions at the rollers $A$ and $B$.

Probs. 17–31/32

**17-33.** The uniform pipe has a weight of 7.5 kN/m ($\approx$ 750 kg/m) and diameter of 2 m. If it is hoisted as shown with an acceleration of 0.5 m/s², determine the internal moment at the center $A$ of the pipe due to the lift.

Prob. 17–33

**17-34.** The pipe has a mass of 800 kg and is being towed behind the truck. If the acceleration of the truck is $a_t = 0.5$ m/s², determine the angle $\theta$ and the tension in the cable. The coefficient of kinetic friction between the pipe and the ground is $\mu_k = 0.1$.

**17-35.** The pipe has a mass of 800 kg and is being towed behind a truck. If the angle $\theta = 30°$, determine the acceleration of the truck and the tension in the cable. The coefficient of kinetic friction between the pipe and the ground is $\mu_k = 0.1$.

Probs. 17–34/35

**\*17-36.** The pipe has a length of 3 m and a mass of 500 kg. It is attached to the back of the truck using a 0.6-m-long chain *AB*. If the coefficient of kinetic friction at *C* is $\mu_k = 0.4$, determine the acceleration of the truck if the angle $\theta = 10°$ with the road as shown.

**17-38.** The sports car has a mass of 1.5 Mg and a center of mass at *G*. Determine the shortest time it takes for it to reach a speed of 80 km/h, starting from rest, if the engine only drives the rear wheels, whereas the front wheels are free rolling. The coefficient of static friction between the wheels and the road is $\mu_s = 0.2$. Neglect the mass of the wheels for the calculation. If driving power could be supplied to all four wheels, what would be the shortest time for the car to reach a speed of 80 km/h?

Prob. 17–36

Prob. 17–38

**17-37.** The drop gate at the end of the trailer has a mass of 1.25 Mg and mass center at *G*. If it is supported by the cable *AB* and hinge at *C*, determine the tension in the cable when the truck begins to accelerate at 5 m/s². Also, what are the horizontal and vertical components of reaction at the hinge *C*?

**17-39.** The sports car has a weight of 22.5 kN ($\approx$ 2250 kg) and center of gravity at *G*. If it starts from rest it causes the rear wheels to slip as it accelerates. Determine how long it takes for it to reach a speed of 3 m/s. Also, what are the normal reactions at *each* of the four wheels on the road? The coefficients of static and kinetic friction at the road are $\mu_s = 0.5$ and $\mu_k = 0.3$, respectively. Neglect the mass of the wheels.

Prob. 17–37

Prob. 17–39

**\*17-40.** The car accelerates uniformly from rest to 26.4 m/s in 15 seconds. If it has a weight of 19 kN ($\approx$ 1900 kg) and a center of gravity at $G$, determine the normal reaction of *each wheel* on the pavement during the motion. Power is developed at the front wheels, whereas the rear wheels are free to roll. Neglect the mass of the wheels and take the coefficients of static and kinetic friction to be $\mu_s = 0.4$ and $\mu_k = 0.2$, respectively.

Prob. 17–40

**17-41.** The drum truck supports the 3-kN ($\approx$ 300-kg) drum that has a center of gravity at $G$. If the operator pushes it forward with a horizontal force of 100 N, determine the acceleration of the truck and the normal reactions at each of the four wheels. Neglect the mass of the wheels.

Prob. 17–41

**17-42.** The uniform crate has a mass $m$ and rests on a rough pallet for which the coefficient of static friction between the crate and pallet is $\mu_s$. If the pallet is given an acceleration of $a_p$, show that the crate will tip and slip at the same time provided $\mu_s = b/h$.

Prob. 17–42

**17-43.** The forklift and operator have a combined weight of 50 000 N ($\approx$ 5000 kg) and center of mass at $G$. If the forklift is used to lift the 10 000-N ($\approx$ 1000-kg) concrete pipe, determine the maximum vertical acceleration it can give to the pipe so that it does not tip forward on its front wheels.

**\*17-44.** The forklift and operator have a combined weight of 50 000 N ($\approx$ 5000 kg) and center of mass at $G$. If the forklift is used to lift the 10 000-N ($\approx$ 1000-kg) concrete pipe, determine the normal reactions on each of its four wheels if the pipe is given an upward acceleration of 1.2 m/s$^2$.

Probs. 17–43/44

**17-45.** The van has a weight of 22 500 N ($\approx$ 2250 kg) and center of gravity at $G_v$. It carries a fixed 4000-N ($\approx$ 400-kg) load which has a center of gravity at $G_l$. If the van is traveling at 12 m/s, determine the distance it skids before stopping. The brakes cause *all* the wheels to lock or skid. The coefficient of kinetic friction between the wheels and the pavement is $\mu_k = 0.3$. Compare this distance with that of the van being empty. Neglect the mass of the wheels.

**17-47.** The handcart has a mass of 200 kg and center of mass at $G$. Determine the normal reactions at each of the two wheels at $A$ and the two wheels at $B$ if a force of $P = 50$ N is applied to the handle. Neglect the mass of the wheels.

***17-48.** The handcart has a mass of 200 kg and center of mass at $G$. Determine the magnitude of the largest force **P** that can be applied to the handle so that the wheels at $A$ or $B$ continue to maintain contact with the ground. Neglect the mass of the wheels.

Probs. 17–47/48

Prob. 17–45

**17-46.** The crate has a mass of 50 kg and rests on the cart having an inclined surface. Determine if the crate will tip over or slide relative to the cart when the cart is subjected to the smallest acceleration necessary to cause one of these relative motions. What is the magnitude of this acceleration? The coefficient of static friction between the crate and the cart is $\mu_s = 0.5$.

**17-49.** The arched pipe has a mass of 80 kg and rests on the surface of the platform. As it is hoisted from one level to the next, $\alpha = 0.25$ rad/s$^2$ and $\omega = 0.5$ rad/s at the instant $\theta = 30°$. If it does not slip, determine the normal reactions of the arch on the platform at this instant.

**17-50.** The arched pipe has a mass of 80 kg and rests on the surface of the platform for which the coefficient of static friction is $\mu_s = 0.3$. Determine the greatest angular acceleration $\alpha$ of the platform, starting from rest when $\theta = 45°$, without causing the pipe to slip on the platform.

Prob. 17–46

Probs. 17–49/50

**17-51.** The crate $C$ has a weight of 1500 N ($\approx$ 150 kg) and rests on the truck elevator for which the coefficient of static friction is $\mu_s = 0.4$. Determine the largest initial angular acceleration $\alpha$, starting from rest, which the parallel links $AB$ and $DE$ can have without causing the crate to slip. No tipping occurs.

***17-52.** The arm $BDE$ of the industrial robot manufactured by Cincinnati Milacron is activated by applying the torque of $M = 50$ N·m to link $CD$. Determine the reactions at the pins $B$ and $D$ when the links are in the position shown and have an angular velocity of 2 rad/s. The uniform arm $BDE$ has a mass of 10 kg and a center of mass at $G_1$. The container held in its grip at $E$ has a mass of 12 kg and center of mass at $G_2$. Neglect the mass of links $AB$ and $CD$.

Prob. 17–52

Prob. 17–51

## 17.4 Equations of Motion: Rotation About a Fixed Axis

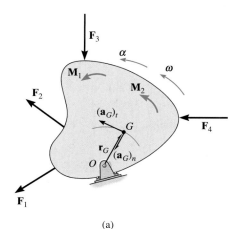

(a)

Fig. 17–14

Consider the rigid body (or slab) shown in Fig. 17–14a, which is constrained to rotate in the vertical plane about a fixed axis perpendicular to the page and passing through the pin at $O$. The angular velocity and angular acceleration are caused by the external force and couple moment system acting on the body. Because the body's center of mass $G$ moves in a *circular path*, the acceleration of this point is represented by its tangential and normal components. The *tangential component of acceleration* has a *magnitude* of $(a_G)_t = \alpha r_G$ and must act in a *direction* which is *consistent* with the body's angular acceleration $\alpha$. The *magnitude* of the *normal component of acceleration* is $(a_G)_n = \omega^2 r_G$. This component is *always directed* from point $G$ to $O$, regardless of the direction of $\omega$.

The free-body and kinetic diagrams for the body are shown in Fig. 17–14b. The weight of the body, $W = mg$, and the pin reaction $\mathbf{F}_O$ are included on the free-body diagram since they represent external forces acting on the body. The two components $m(\mathbf{a}_G)_t$ and $m(\mathbf{a}_G)_n$, shown on the kinetic diagram, are associated with the tangential and normal acceleration components of the body's mass center. These vectors act in the same *direction* as the acceleration components and have *magnitudes* of $m(a_G)_t$ and $m(a_G)_n$. The $I_G\boldsymbol{\alpha}$ vector acts in the same *direction* as $\boldsymbol{\alpha}$ and has a *magnitude* of $I_G\alpha$, where $I_G$ is the body's moment of inertia calculated about an axis which is perpendicular to the page and passing through $G$. From the derivation given in Sec. 17.2, the equations of motion which apply to the body may be written in the form

$$\Sigma F_n = m(a_G)_n = m\omega^2 r_G$$
$$\Sigma F_t = m(a_G)_t = m\alpha r_G \qquad (17\text{--}14)$$
$$\Sigma M_G = I_G\alpha$$

The moment equation may be replaced by a moment summation about any arbitrary point $P$ on or off the body provided one accounts for the moments $\Sigma(\mathcal{M}_k)_P$ produced by $I_G\boldsymbol{\alpha}$, $m(\mathbf{a}_G)_t$, and $m(\mathbf{a}_G)_n$ about the point. In many problems it is convenient to sum moments about the pin at $O$ in order to eliminate the *unknown* force $\mathbf{F}_O$. From the kinetic diagram, Fig. 17–14b, this requires

$$\zeta+\Sigma M_O = \Sigma(\mathcal{M}_k)_O; \quad \Sigma M_O = r_G m(a_G)_t + I_G\alpha \qquad (17\text{--}15)$$

Note that the moment of $m(\mathbf{a}_G)_n$ is not included in the summation since the line of action of this vector passes through $O$. Substituting $(a_G)_t = r_G\alpha$, we may rewrite the above equation as $\zeta+\Sigma M_O = (I_G + mr_G^2)\alpha$. From the parallel-axis theorem, $I_O = I_G + md^2$, and therefore the term in parentheses represents the *moment of inertia of the body about the fixed axis of rotation passing through $O$.* Consequently, we can write the three equations of motion for the body as

$$\Sigma F_n = m(a_G)_n = m\omega^2 r_G$$
$$\Sigma F_t = m(a_G)_t = m\alpha r_G \qquad (17\text{--}16)$$
$$\Sigma M_O = I_O\alpha$$

For applications, one should remember that "$I_O\alpha$" accounts for the "moment" of *both $m(\mathbf{a}_G)_t$ and $I_G\boldsymbol{\alpha}$* about point $O$, Fig. 17–14b. In other words, $\Sigma M_O = \Sigma(\mathcal{M}_k)_O = I_O\alpha$, as indicated by Eqs. 17–15 and 17–16.

*The result $\Sigma M_O = I_O\alpha$ can also be obtained *directly* from Eq. 17–6 by selecting point $P$ to coincide with $O$, realizing that $(a_P)_x = (a_P)_y = 0$.

(a)

(b)

**Fig. 17–14**

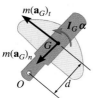

The crank on the oil-pumping rig undergoes rotation about a fixed axis which is caused by a driving torque **M** of the motor. The loadings shown on the free-body diagram cause the effects shown on the kinetic diagram. If moments are summed about the mass center, $G$, then $\Sigma M_G = I_G \alpha$. However, if moments are summed about point $O$, noting that $(a_G)_t = \alpha d$, then $\zeta + \Sigma M_O = I_G \alpha + m(a_G)_t d + m(a_G)_n (0) = (I_G + md^2)\alpha = I_O \alpha$.

## PROCEDURE FOR ANALYSIS

Kinetic problems which involve the rotation of a body about a fixed axis can be solved using the following procedure.

### Free-Body Diagram.

- Establish the inertial $x$, $y$ or $n$, $t$ coordinate system and specify the direction and sense of the accelerations $(\mathbf{a}_G)_n$ and $(\mathbf{a}_G)_t$ and the angular acceleration $\boldsymbol{\alpha}$ of the body. Recall that $(\mathbf{a}_G)_t$ must act in a direction which is in accordance with $\boldsymbol{\alpha}$, whereas $(\mathbf{a}_G)_n$ always acts toward the axis of rotation, point $O$.

- Draw the free-body diagram to account for all the external forces and couple moments that act on the body.

- Compute the moment of inertia $I_G$ or $I_O$.

- Identify the unknowns in the problem.

- If it is decided that the rotational equation of motion $\Sigma M_P = \Sigma (\mathcal{M}_k)_P$ is to be used, i.e., $P$ is a point other than $G$ or $O$, then consider drawing the kinetic diagram in order to help "visualize" the "moments" developed by the components $m(\mathbf{a}_G)_n$, $m(\mathbf{a}_G)_t$, and $I_G \boldsymbol{\alpha}$ when writing the terms for the moment sum $\Sigma (\mathcal{M}_k)_P$.

### Equations of Motion.

- Apply the three equations of motion in accordance with the established sign convention.

- If moments are summed about the body's mass center, $G$, then $\Sigma M_G = I_G \alpha$, since $(m\mathbf{a}_G)_t$ and $(m\mathbf{a}_G)_n$ create no moment about $G$.

- If moments are summed about the pin support $O$ on the axis of rotation, then $(m\mathbf{a}_G)_n$ creates no moment about $G$, and it can be shown that $\Sigma M_O = I_O \alpha$.

### Kinematics.

- Use kinematics if a complete solution cannot be obtained strictly from the equations of motion.

- If the *angular acceleration is variable*, use

$$\alpha = \frac{d\omega}{dt} \qquad \alpha \, d\theta = \omega \, d\omega \qquad \omega = \frac{d\theta}{dt}$$

- If the *angular acceleration is constant*, use

$$\omega = \omega_0 + \alpha_c t$$
$$\theta = \theta_0 + \omega_0 t + \tfrac{1}{2}\alpha_c t^2$$
$$\omega^2 = \omega_0^2 + 2\alpha_c(\theta - \theta_0)$$

# E X A M P L E  **17.9**

The 30-kg uniform disk shown in Fig. 17–15a is pin supported at its center. If it starts from rest, determine the number of revolutions it must make to attain an angular velocity of 20 rad/s. Also, what are the reactions at the pin? The disk is acted upon by a constant force $F = 10$ N, which is applied to a cord wrapped around its periphery, and a constant couple moment $M = 5$ N·m. Neglect the mass of the cord in the calculation.

(a)

**Solution**

*Free-Body Diagram.*  Fig. 17–15b. Note that the mass center is not subjected to an acceleration; however, the disk has a clockwise angular acceleration.

The moment of inertia of the disk about the pin is

$$I_O = \tfrac{1}{2}mr^2 = \frac{1}{2}(30 \text{ kg})(0.2 \text{ m})^2 = 0.6 \text{ kg} \cdot \text{m}^2$$

The three unknowns are $O_x$, $O_y$, and $\alpha$.

(b)

**Fig. 17–15**

*Equations of Motion.*

$$\xrightarrow{+} \Sigma F_x = m(a_G)_x; \qquad O_x = 0 \qquad\qquad Ans.$$
$$+\uparrow\Sigma F_y = m(a_G)_y; \quad O_y - 294.3 \text{ N} - 10 \text{ N} = 0$$
$$O_y = 304 \text{ N} \qquad\qquad Ans.$$
$$\zeta+\Sigma M_O = I_O\alpha; \quad -10 \text{ N}(0.2 \text{ m}) - 5 \text{ N}\cdot\text{m} = -(0.6 \text{ kg}\cdot\text{m}^2)\alpha$$
$$\alpha = 11.7 \text{ rad/s}^2\downarrow$$

*Kinematics.*  Since $\alpha$ is constant and is clockwise, the number of radians the disk must turn to obtain a clockwise angular velocity of 20 rad/s is

$$\zeta+$$
$$\omega^2 = \omega_0^2 + 2\alpha_c(\theta - \theta_0)$$
$$(-20 \text{ rad/s})^2 = 0 + 2(-11.7 \text{ rad/s}^2)(\theta - 0)$$
$$\theta = -17.1 \text{ rad} = 17.1 \text{ rad}\downarrow$$

Hence,

$$\theta = 17.1 \text{ rad}\left(\frac{1 \text{ rev}}{2\pi \text{ rad}}\right) = 2.73 \text{ rev}\downarrow \qquad\qquad Ans.$$

# E X A M P L E 17.10

The 20-kg slender rod shown in Fig. 17–16a is rotating in the vertical plane, and at the instant shown it has an angular velocity of $\omega = 5$ rad/s. Determine the rod's angular acceleration and the horizontal and vertical components of reaction at the pin at this instant.

(a)

||

(b)

**Fig. 17–16**

## Solution

*Free-Body and Kinetic Diagrams.*   Fig. 17–16b. As shown on the kinetic diagram, point *G* moves in a circular path and so has two components of acceleration. It is important that the tangential component $a_t = \alpha r_G$ act downward since it must be in accordance with the angular acceleration $\alpha$ of the rod. The three unknowns are $O_n$, $O_t$, and $\alpha$.

*Equations of Motion.*

$$\xleftarrow{\pm} \Sigma F_n = m\omega^2 r_G; \qquad O_n = (20 \text{ kg})(5 \text{ rad/s})^2(1.5 \text{ m})$$

$$+\downarrow\Sigma F_t = m\alpha r_G; \qquad -O_t + 20(9.81) \text{ N} = (20 \text{ kg})(\alpha)(1.5 \text{ m})$$

$$\zeta+\Sigma M_G = I_G\alpha; \quad O_t(1.5 \text{ m}) + 60 \text{ N}\cdot\text{m} = [\tfrac{1}{12}(20 \text{ kg})(3 \text{ m})^2]\alpha$$

Solving

$$O_n = 750 \text{ N} \qquad O_t = 19.0 \text{ N} \qquad \alpha = 5.90 \text{ rad/s}^2 \qquad Ans.$$

A more direct solution to this problem would be to sum moments about point *O* to eliminate $\mathbf{O}_n$ and $\mathbf{O}_t$ and obtain a *direct solution* for $\alpha$. Here,

$$\zeta+\Sigma M_O = \Sigma(\mathcal{M}_k)_O; \quad 60 \text{ N}\cdot\text{m} + 20(9.81) \text{ N}(1.5 \text{ m}) =$$
$$[\tfrac{1}{12}(20 \text{ kg})(3 \text{ m})^2]\alpha + [20 \text{ kg}(\alpha)(1.5 \text{ m})](1.5 \text{ m})$$
$$\alpha = 5.90 \text{ rad/s}^2 \qquad Ans.$$

Also, since $I_O = \tfrac{1}{3}ml^2$ for a slender rod, we can apply

$$\zeta+\Sigma M_O = I_O\alpha; \quad 60 \text{ N}\cdot\text{m} + 20(9.81) \text{ N}(1.5 \text{ m}) = [\tfrac{1}{3}(20 \text{ kg})(3 \text{ m})^2]\alpha$$
$$\alpha = 5.90 \text{ rad/s}^2 \qquad Ans.$$

By comparison, the last equation provides the simplest solution for $\alpha$ and *does not* require use of the kinetic diagram.

# EXAMPLE 17.11

The drum shown in Fig. 17–17a has a mass of 60 kg and a radius of gyration $k_O = 0.25$ m. A cord of negligible mass is wrapped around the periphery of the drum and attached to a block having a mass of 20 kg. If the block is released, determine the drum's angular acceleration.

(a)

### Solution I

*Free-Body Diagram.*   Here we will consider the drum and block separately, Fig. 17–17b. Assuming the block accelerates *downward* at **a**, it creates a *counterclockwise* angular acceleration $\boldsymbol{\alpha}$ of the drum.
   The moment of inertia of the drum is

$$I_O = mk_O^2 = (60 \text{ kg})(0.25 \text{ m})^2 = 3.75 \text{ kg} \cdot \text{m}^2$$

There are five unknowns, namely $O_x$, $O_y$, $T$, $a$, and $\alpha$.

*Equations of Motion.*   Applying the translational equations of motion $\Sigma F_x = m(a_G)_x$ and $\Sigma F_y = m(a_G)_y$ to the drum is of no consequence to the solution, since these equations involve the unknowns $O_x$ and $O_y$. Thus, for the drum and block, respectively,

$$\zeta + \Sigma M_O = I_O \alpha; \qquad T(0.4 \text{ m}) = (3.75 \text{ kg} \cdot \text{m}^2)\alpha \qquad (1)$$
$$+\uparrow \Sigma F_y = m(a_G)_y; \qquad -20(9.81) \text{ N} + T = -20a \qquad (2)$$

*Kinematics.*   Since the point of contact $A$ between the cord and drum has a tangential component of acceleration **a**, Fig. 17–17a, then

$$\zeta + a = \alpha r; \qquad\qquad a = \alpha(0.4) \qquad (3)$$

Solving the above equations,

$$T = 106 \text{ N}$$
$$a = 4.52 \text{ m/s}^2$$
$$\alpha = 11.3 \text{ rad/s}^2 \zeta \qquad\qquad Ans.$$

(b)

### Solution II

*Free-Body and Kinetic Diagrams.*   The cable tension $T$ can be eliminated from the analysis by considering the drum and block as a *single system*, Fig. 17–17c. The kinetic diagram is shown since moments will be summed about point $O$.

*Equations of Motion.*   Using Eq. 3 and applying the moment equation about $O$ to eliminate the unknowns $O_x$ and $O_y$, we have

$$\zeta + \Sigma M_O = \Sigma(\mathcal{M}_k)_O; \qquad 20(9.81) \text{ N}(0.4 \text{ m}) =$$
$$(3.75 \text{ kg} \cdot \text{m}^2)\alpha + [20 \text{ kg}(0.4 \text{ m } \alpha)](0.4 \text{ m})$$
$$\alpha = 11.3 \text{ rad/s}^2 \zeta \qquad\qquad Ans.$$

(c)

**Fig. 17–17**

*Note:* If the block were *removed* and a force of 20(9.81) N were applied to the cord, show that $\alpha = 20.9$ rad/s$^2$ and explain the reason for the difference in the results.

EXAMPLE 17.12

$\omega = 8$ rad/s

120 N·m  0.15 m

(a)

$n$

$t$

120 N·m  0.15 m

$O_n$

$O_t$  25 (9.81) N

$\parallel$

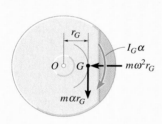

$r_G$

$I_G\alpha$

$m\omega^2 r_G$

$m\alpha r_G$

(b)

Fig. 17–18

The unbalanced 25-kg flywheel shown in Fig. 17–18a has a radius of gyration of $k_G = 0.18$ m about an axis passing through its mass center $G$. If it has a clockwise angular velocity of 8 rad/s at the instant shown, determine the horizontal and vertical components of reaction at the pin $O$.

### Solution

*Free-Body and Kinetic Diagrams.* Since $G$ moves in a circular path, it will have both normal and tangential components of acceleration. Also, since $\alpha$, which is caused by the flywheel's weight, acts clockwise, the tangential component of acceleration will act downward. Why? The vectors $m(a_G)_t = m\alpha r_G$, $m(a_G)_n = m\omega^2 r_G$, and $I_G\alpha$ are shown on the kinematic diagram in Fig. 17–18b. Here, the moment of inertia of the flywheel about its mass center is determined from the radius of gyration and the flywheel's mass; i.e., $I_G = mk_G^2 = (25 \text{ kg})(0.18 \text{ m})^2 = 0.18 \text{ kg} \cdot \text{m}^2$.

The three unknowns are $O_n$, $O_t$, and $\alpha$.

*Equations of Motion.*

$$\xleftrightarrow{} \Sigma F_n = m\omega^2 r_G; \qquad O_n = (25 \text{ kg})(8 \text{ rad/s})^2(0.15 \text{ m}) \qquad (1)$$

$$+\downarrow \Sigma F_t = m\alpha r_G; \quad -O_n + 25(9.81) \text{ N} = (25 \text{ kg})(\alpha)(0.15 \text{ m}) \qquad (2)$$

$$\overset{\curvearrowright}{+}\Sigma M_G = I_G\alpha; \quad 120 \text{ N} \cdot \text{m} + O_t(0.15 \text{ m}) = (0.81 \text{ kg} \cdot \text{m}^2)\alpha \qquad (3)$$

Solving, $\alpha = 114.2 \text{ rad/s}^2$ $\quad O_n = 240 \text{ N} \quad O_t = -183.1 \text{ N}$ *Ans.*

Moments can also be summed about point $O$ in order to eliminate $\mathbf{O}_n$ and $\mathbf{O}_t$ and thereby obtain a *direct solution* for $\alpha$, Fig. 17–18b. This can be done in one of *two* ways, i.e., by using either $\Sigma M_O = \Sigma(\mathcal{M}_k)_O$ or $\Sigma M_O = I_O\alpha$. If the first of these equations is applied, we have

$$\overset{\curvearrowright}{+}\Sigma M_O = \Sigma(\mathcal{M}_k)_O; \quad 120 \text{ N} \cdot \text{m} + 25(9.81 \text{ N})(0.15 \text{ m}) =$$

$$(0.81 \text{ kg} \cdot \text{m}^2)\alpha + [(25 \text{ kg})\alpha(0.15 \text{ m})](0.15 \text{ m})$$

$$156.7875 = 1.3725\alpha \qquad (4)$$

If $\Sigma M_O = I_O\alpha$ is applied, then by the parallel-axis theorem the moment of inertia of the flywheel about $O$ is

$$I_O = I_G + mr_G^2 = 0.81 + (25)(0.15)^2 = 1.3725 \text{ kg} \cdot \text{m}^2$$

Hence, from the free-body diagram, Fig. 17–18b, we require

$$\overset{\curvearrowright}{+}\Sigma M_O = I_O\alpha; \quad 120 \text{ N} \cdot \text{m} + (25(9.81) \text{ N})(0.15 \text{ m}) = (1.3725 \text{ kg} \cdot \text{m}^2)\alpha$$

which is the same as Eq. 4. Solving for $\alpha$ and substituting into Eq. 2 yields the answer for $O_t$ obtained previously.

**EXAMPLE 17.13**

The slender rod shown in Fig. 17–19a has a mass $m$ and length $l$ and is released from rest when $\theta = 0°$. Determine the horizontal and vertical components of force which the pin at $A$ exerts on the rod at the instant $\theta = 90°$.

(a)

### Solution

*Free-Body Diagram.* The free-body diagram for the rod is shown when the rod is in the general position $\theta$, Fig. 17–19b. For convenience, the force components at $A$ are shown acting in the $n$ and $t$ directions. Note that $\boldsymbol{\alpha}$ acts clockwise.

The moment of inertia of the rod about point $A$ is $I_A = \frac{1}{3}ml^2$.

*Equations of Motion.* Moments will be summed about $A$ in order to eliminate the reactive forces there.*

$$+\nwarrow\Sigma F_n = m\omega^2 r_G; \qquad A_n - mg\sin\theta = m\omega^2(l/2) \qquad (1)$$

$$+\swarrow\Sigma F_t = m\alpha r_G; \qquad A_t + mg\cos\theta = m\alpha(l/2) \qquad (2)$$

$$\curvearrowright+\Sigma M_A = I_A\alpha; \qquad mg\cos\theta(l/2) = (\tfrac{1}{3}ml^2)\alpha \qquad (3)$$

(b)

Fig. 17–19

*Kinematics.* For a given angle $\theta$ there are four unknowns in the above three equations: $A_n$, $A_t$, $\omega$, and $\alpha$. As shown by Eq. 3, $\alpha$ is *not constant;* rather, it depends on the position $\theta$ of the rod. The necessary fourth equation is obtained using kinematics, where $\alpha$ and $\omega$ can be related to $\theta$ by the equation

$$(\curvearrowright+) \qquad\qquad \omega\,d\omega = \alpha\,d\theta \qquad\qquad (4)$$

Note that the positive clockwise direction for this equation *agrees* with that of Eq. 3. This is important since we are seeking a simultaneous solution.

In order to solve for $\omega$ at $\theta = 90°$, eliminate $\alpha$ from Eqs. 3 and 4, which yields

$$\omega\,d\omega = (1.5\,g/l)\cos\theta\,d\theta$$

Since $\omega = 0$ at $\theta = 0°$, we have

$$\int_0^\omega \omega\,d\omega = (1.5\,g/l)\int_{0°}^{90°}\cos\theta\,d\theta$$

$$\omega^2 = 3\,g/l$$

Substituting this value into Eq. 1 with $\theta = 90°$ and solving Eqs. 1 to 3 yields

$$\alpha = 0 \qquad A_t = 0 \qquad A_n = 2.5\,mg \qquad\qquad Ans.$$

*If $\Sigma M_A = \Sigma(\mathcal{M}_k)_A$ is used, one must account for the moments of $I_G\alpha$ and $m(\mathbf{a}_G)_t$ about $A$. Here, however, we have used $\Sigma M_A = I_A\alpha$.

# PROBLEMS

**17-53.** The 80-kg disk is supported by a pin at $A$. If it is released from rest from the position shown, determine the initial horizontal and vertical components of reaction at the pin.

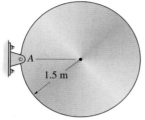

1.5 m

**Prob. 17–53**

**17-54.** The 10-kg wheel has a radius of gyration $k_A = 200$ mm. If the wheel is subjected to a moment $M = (5t)$ N·m, where $t$ is in seconds, determine its angular velocity when $t = 3$ s starting from rest. Also, compute the reactions which the fixed pin $A$ exerts on the wheel during the motion.

M

A

**Prob. 17–54**

**17-55.** The fan blade has a mass of 2 kg and a moment of inertia $I_O = 0.18$ kg·m² about an axis passing through its center $O$. If it is subjected to a moment of $M = 3(1 - e^{-0.2t})$ N·m, where $t$ is in seconds, determine its angular velocity when $t = 4$ s starting from rest.

O   M

**Prob. 17–55**

**\*17-56.** The drum has a weight of 400 N ($\approx$ 40 kg) and a radius of gyration $k_O = 0.4$ m. If the cable, which is wrapped around the drum, is subjected to a vertical force $P = 75$ N, determine the time needed to increase the drum's angular velocity from $\omega_1 = 5$ rad/s to $\omega_2 = 25$ rad/s. Neglect the mass of the cable.

$\omega$

0.5 m

O

P

**Prob. 17–56**

**17-57.** The spool is supported on small rollers at $A$ and $B$. Determine the constant force $P$ that must be applied to the cable in order to unwind 8 m of cable in 4 s starting from rest. Also calculate the normal forces at $A$ and $B$ during this time. The spool has a mass of 60 kg and a radius of gyration $k_O = 0.65$ m. For the calculation neglect the mass of the cable and the mass of the rollers at $A$ and $B$.

0.8 m

O

1 m

15°   15°

A   B

P

**Prob. 17–57**

**17-58.** A cord is wrapped around the inner core of a spool. If the cord is pulled with a constant tension of 300 N and the spool is originally at rest, determine the spool's angular velocity when $s = 0.8$ m of cord has unwound. Neglect the weight of the 0.8-m portion of cord. The spool and the entire cord have a total weight of 4000 N ($\approx 400$ kg), and the radius of gyration about the axle $A$ is $k_A = 0.13$ m.

**Prob. 17–58**

**17-59.** The 100-N ($\approx 10$-kg) bar is pinned at its center $O$ and connected to a torsional spring. The spring has a stiffness $k = 50$ N · m/rad, so that the torque developed is $M = (50\theta)$ N · m, where $\theta$ is in radians. If the bar is released from rest when it is vertical at $\theta = 90°$, determine its angular velocity at the instant $\theta = 0°$.

**\*17-60.** The 100-N ($\approx 10$-kg) bar is pinned at its center $O$ and connected to a torsional spring. The spring has a stiffness $k = 50$ N · m/rad, so that the torque developed is $M = (50\theta)$ N · m, where $\theta$ is in radians. If the bar is released from rest when it is vertical at $\theta = 90°$, determine its angular velocity at the instant $\theta = 45°$.

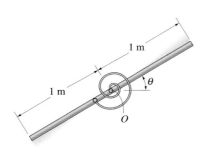

**Probs. 17–59/60**

**17-61.** The 20-kg roll of paper has a radius of gyration $k_A = 90$ mm about an axis passing through point $A$. It is pin-supported at both ends by two brackets $AB$. If the roll rests against a wall for which the coefficient of kinetic friction is $\mu_k = 0.2$ and a vertical force $F = 30$ N is applied to the end of the paper, determine the angular acceleration of the roll as the paper unrolls.

**Prob. 17–61**

**17-62.** Cable is unwound from a spool supported on small rollers at $A$ and $B$ by exerting a force of $T = 300$ N on the cable in the direction shown. Compute the time needed to unravel 5 m of cable from the spool if the spool and cable have a total mass of 600 kg and a centroidal radius of gyration of $k_O = 1.2$ m. For the calculation, neglect the mass of the cable being unwound and the mass of rollers at $A$ and $B$. The rollers turn with no friction.

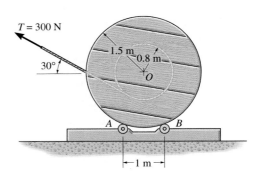

**Prob. 17–62**

**17-63.** The door will close automatically using torsional springs mounted on the hinges. Each spring has a stiffness $k = 50$ N·m/rad so that the torque on each hinge is $M = (50\theta)$ N·m, where $\theta$ is measured in radians. If the door is released from rest when it is open at $\theta = 90°$, determine its angular velocity at the instant $\theta = 0°$. For the calculation, treat the door as a thin plate having a mass of 70 kg.

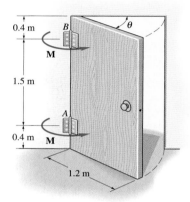

**Prob. 17–63**

*17-64.** The door will close automatically using torsional springs mounted on the hinges. If the torque on each hinge is $M = k\theta$, where $\theta$ is measured in radians, determine the required torsional stiffness $k$ so that the door will close $(\theta = 0°)$ with an angular velocity $\omega = 2$ rad/s when it is released from rest at $\theta = 90°$. For the calculation, treat the door as a thin plate having a mass of 70 kg.

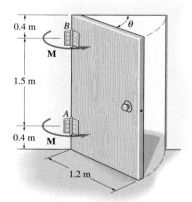

**Prob. 17–64**

**17-65.** The kinetic diagram representing the general rotational motion of a rigid body about a fixed axis at $O$ is shown in the figure. Show that $I_G\alpha$ may be eliminated by moving the vectors $m(\mathbf{a}_G)_t$ and $m(\mathbf{a}_G)_n$ to point $P$, located a distance $r_{GP} = k_G^2/r_{OG}$ from the center of mass $G$ of the body. Here $k_G$ represents the radius of gyration of the body about $G$. The point $P$ is called the *center of percussion* of the body.

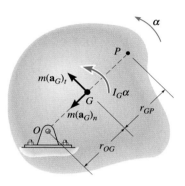

**Prob. 17–65**

**17-66.** Determine the position $r_P$ of the center of percussion $P$ of the 10-kN ($\approx$ 1-tonne) slender bar. (See Prob. 17–65.) What is the horizontal force $A_x$ at the pin when the bar is struck at $P$ with a force of $F = 20$ kN?

**Prob. 17–66**

**17-67.** The 4-kg slender rod is supported horizontally by a spring at $A$ and a cord at $B$. Determine the angular acceleration of the rod and the acceleration of the rod's mass center at the instant the cord at $B$ is cut. *Hint:* The stiffness of the spring is not needed for the calculation.

Prob. 17–67

**\*17-68.** The operation of the doorbell requires the use of the electromagnet, which attracts the iron clapper $AB$, pinned at end $A$ and consisting of a 0.2-kg slender rod to which is attached the 0.04-kg steel ball having a radius of 6 mm. If the attractive force of the magnet at $C$ is 0.5 N on the center of the ball when the button is pushed, determine the initial angular acceleration of the clapper. The spring is originally stretched 20 mm.

Prob. 17–68

**17-69.** The 5-kg disk $D$ is subjected to a counterclockwise moment of $M = (10t)$ N · m, where $t$ is in seconds. Determine the angular velocity of the disk 4 s after the moment is applied. Due to the spring the plate $P$ exerts a constant force of 500 N on the disk. The coefficients of static and kinetic friction between the disk and the plate are $\mu_s = 0.3$ and $\mu_k = 0.2$, respectively. *Hint:* First find the time needed to start the disk rotating.

Prob. 17–69

**17-70.** If the support at $B$ is suddenly removed, determine the initial reactions at the pin $A$. The plate has a weight of 30 kN.

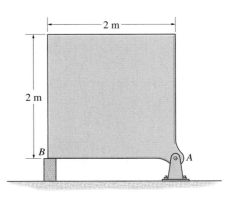

Prob. 17–70

**17-71.** If the support at $B$ is suddenly removed, determine the initial downward acceleration of point $C$. Segments $AC$ and $CB$ each have a weight of 10 N ($\approx$ 1 kg).

**Prob. 17–71**

**\*17-72.** Determine the angular acceleration of the 25-kg diving board and the horizontal and vertical components of reaction at the pin $A$ the instant the man jumps off. Assume that the board is uniform and rigid, and that at the instant he jumps off the spring is compressed a maximum amount of 200 mm, $\omega = 0$, and the board is horizontal. Take $k = 7$ kN/m.

**Prob. 17–72**

**17-73.** The disk has a mass of 20 kg and is originally spinning at the end of the strut with an angular velocity of $\omega = 60$ rad/s. If it is then placed against the wall, for which the coefficient of kinetic friction is $\mu_k = 0.3$ determine the time required for the motion to stop. What is the force in strut $BC$ during this time?

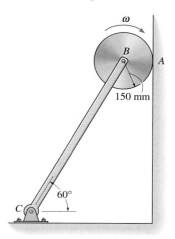

**Prob. 17–73**

**17-74.** The disk has a mass $M$ and a radius $R$. If a block of mass $m$ is attached to the cord, determine the angular acceleration of the disk when the block is released from rest. Also, what is the velocity of the block after it falls a distance $2R$ starting from rest?

**Prob. 17–74**

**17-75.** The two blocks $A$ and $B$ have a mass $m_A$ and $m_B$, respectively, where $m_B > m_A$. If the pulley can be treated as a disk of mass $M$, determine the acceleration of block $A$. Neglect the mass of the cord and any slipping on the pulley.

Prob. 17–75

**17-77.** The two-bar assembly is released from rest in the position shown. Determine the initial bending moment at the fixed joint $B$. Each bar has a mass $m$ and length $l$.

Prob. 17–77

***17-76.** The lightweight turbine consists of a rotor which is powered from a torque applied at its center. At the instant the rotor is horizontal it has an angular velocity of 15 rad/s and a clockwise angular acceleration of 8 rad/s². Determine the internal normal force, shear force, and moment at a section through $A$. Assume the rotor is a 50-m-long slender rod, having a mass of 3 kg/m.

**17-78.** The armature (slender rod) $AB$ has a mass of 0.2 kg and can pivot about the pin at $A$. Movement is controlled by the electromagnet $E$, which exerts a horizontal attractive force on the armature at $B$ of $F_B = (0.2(10^{-3})l^{-2})$ N, where $l$ in meters is the gap between the armature and the magnet at any instant. If the armature lies in the horizontal plane, and is originally at rest, determine the speed of the contact at $B$ the instant $l = 0.01$ m. Originally $l = 0.02$ m.

Prob. 17–76

Prob. 17–78

**17-79.** The wheel has a mass of 25 kg and a radius of gyration $k_B = 0.15$ m. It is originally spinning at $\omega_1 = 40$ rad/s. If it is placed on the ground, for which the coefficient of kinetic friction is $\mu_C = 0.5$, determine the time required for the motion to stop. What are the horizontal and vertical components of reaction which the pin at $A$ exerts on $AB$ during this time? Neglect the mass of $AB$.

**Prob. 17–79**

*17-80.** The cord is wrapped around the inner core of the spool. If a 0.5-kg block $B$ is suspended from the cord and released from rest, determine the spool's angular velocity when $t = 3$ s. Neglect the mass of the cord. The spool has a weight of 180 N ($\approx 18$ kg) and the radius of gyration about the axle $A$ is $k_A = 0.125$ m. Solve the problem in two ways, first by considering the "system" consisting of the block and spool, and then by considering the block and spool separately.

**Prob. 17–80**

■**17-81.** A 40-kg boy sits on top of the large wheel which has a mass of 400 kg and a radius of gyration $k_G = 5.5$ m. If the boy essentially starts from rest at $\theta = 0°$, and the wheel begins to rotate freely, determine the angle at which the boy begins to slip. The coefficient of static friction between the wheel and the boy is $\mu_s = 0.5$. Neglect the size of the boy in the calculation.

**Prob. 17–81**

**17-82.** Disk $D$ turns with a constant clockwise angular velocity of 30 rad/s. Disk $E$ has a weight of 600 N ($\approx 60$ kg) and is initially at rest when it is brought into contact with $D$. Determine the time required for disk $E$ to attain the same angular velocity as disk $D$. The coefficient of kinetic friction between the two disks is $\mu_k = 0.3$. Neglect the weight of bar $BC$.

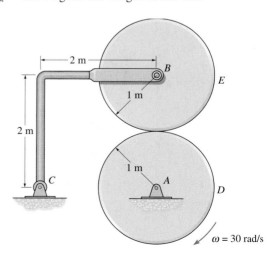

**Prob. 17–82**

**17-83.** The bar has a weight per length of w. If it is rotating in the vertical plane at a constant rate $\omega$ about point $O$, determine the internal normal force, shear force, and moment as a function of $x$ and $\theta$.

**Prob. 17–83**

**17-85.** The "Catherine wheel" is a firework that consists of a coiled tube of powder which is pinned at its center. If the powder burns at a constant rate of 20 g/s such that the exhaust gases always exert a force having a constant magnitude of 0.3 N, directed tangent to the wheel, determine the angular velocity of the wheel when 75% of the mass is burned off. Initially, the wheel is at rest and has a mass of 100 g and a radius of $r = 75$ mm. For the calculation, consider the wheel to always be a thin disk.

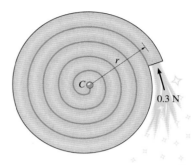

**Prob. 17–85**

***17-84.** A force $F = 20$ N is applied perpendicular to the axis of the 50-N ($\approx$ 5-kg) rod and moves from $O$ to $A$ at a constant rate of 4 m/s. If the rod is at rest when $\theta = 0°$ and **F** is at $O$ when $t = 0$, determine the rod's angular velocity at the instant the force is at $A$. Through what angle has the rod rotated when this occurs? The rod rotates in the *horizontal plane*.

**17-86.** The drum has a weight of 50 kN ($\approx$ 5000 kg) and a radius of gyration $k_A = 0.4$ m. A 35-m-long chain having a weight of 2 kN/m ($\approx$ 200 kg/m) is wrapped around the outer surface of the drum so that a chain length of $s = 3$ m is suspended as shown. If the drum is originally at rest, determine its angular velocity after the end $B$ has descended to $s = 13$ m. Neglect the thickness of the chain.

**Prob. 17–84**

**Prob. 17–86**

## 17.5 Equations of Motion: General Plane Motion

The rigid body (or slab) shown in Fig. 17–20a is subjected to general plane motion caused by the externally applied force and couple-moment system. The free-body and kinetic diagrams for the body are shown in Fig. 17–20b. If an $x$ and $y$ inertial coordinate system is chosen as shown, the three equations of motion may be written as

$$\begin{aligned} \Sigma F_x &= m(a_G)_x \\ \Sigma F_y &= m(a_G)_y \\ \Sigma M_G &= I_G\alpha \end{aligned} \tag{17–17}$$

In some problems it may be convenient to sum moments about some point $P$ other than $G$. This is usually done in order to eliminate unknown forces from the moment summation. When used in this more general sense, the three equations of motion become

$$\begin{aligned} \Sigma F_x &= m(a_G)_x \\ \Sigma F_y &= m(a_G)_y \\ \Sigma M_P &= \Sigma(\mathcal{M}_k)_P \end{aligned} \tag{17–18}$$

Here $\Sigma(\mathcal{M}_k)_P$ represents the moment sum of $I_G\boldsymbol{\alpha}$ and $m\mathbf{a}_G$ (or its components) about $P$ as determined by the data on the kinetic diagram.

(a)

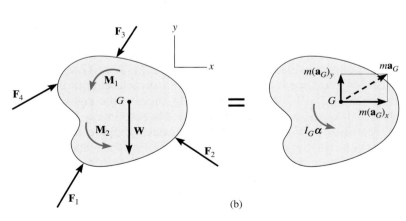

(b)

**Fig. 17–20**

**Frictional Rolling Problems.** There is a class of planar kinetics problems which deserves special mention. These problems involve wheels, cylinders, or bodies of similar shape, which roll on a *rough* plane surface. Because of the applied loadings, it may not be known if the body *rolls without slipping*, or if it *slides as it rolls*. For example, consider the homogeneous disk shown in Fig. 17–21a, which has a mass $m$ and is subjected to a known horizontal force $\mathbf{P}$. The free-body diagram is shown in Fig. 17–21b. Since $\mathbf{a}_G$ is directed to the right and $\boldsymbol{\alpha}$ is clockwise, we have

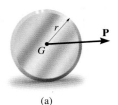

(a)

$$\xrightarrow{+} \Sigma F_x = m(a_G)_x; \qquad P - F = ma_G \qquad (17\text{–}19)$$
$$+\uparrow \Sigma F_y = m(a_G)_y; \qquad N - mg = 0 \qquad (17\text{–}20)$$
$$\zeta + \Sigma M_G = I_G\alpha; \qquad Fr = I_G\alpha \qquad (17\text{–}21)$$

A fourth equation is needed since these *three equations* contain *four unknowns: F, N, $\alpha$, and $a_G$.*

**No Slipping.** If the frictional force F is great enough to allow the disk to roll without slipping, then $a_G$ may be related to $\alpha$ by the kinematic equation,*

$$(\zeta+) \qquad\qquad a_G = \alpha r \qquad\qquad (17\text{–}22)$$

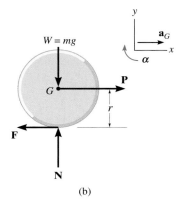

(b)

Fig. 17–21

The four unknowns are determined by *solving simultaneously* Eqs. 17–19 to 17–22. When the solution is obtained, the assumption of no slipping must be *checked*. Recall that no slipping occurs provided $F \leq \mu_s N$, where $\mu_s$ is the coefficient of static friction. If the inequality is satisfied, the problem is solved. However, if $F > \mu_s N$, the problem must be *reworked*, since then the disk slips as it rolls.

**Slipping.** In the case of slipping, $\alpha$ and $a_G$ are *independent of one another* so that Eq. 17–22 does not apply. Instead, the magnitude of the frictional force is related to the magnitude of the normal force using the coefficient of kinetic friction $\mu_k$, i.e.,

$$F = \mu_k N \qquad\qquad (17\text{–}23)$$

In this case Eqs. 17–19 to 17–21 and 17–23 are used for the solution. It is important to keep in mind that whenever Eq. 17–22 or 17–23 is applied, it is necessary to have consistency in the directional sense of the vectors. In the case of Eq. 17–22, $\mathbf{a}_G$ must be directed to the right when $\boldsymbol{\alpha}$ is clockwise, since the rolling motion requires it. And in Eq. 17–23, $\mathbf{F}$ must be directed to the left to prevent the assumed slipping motion to the right, Fig. 17–21b. On the other hand, if these equations are *not used* for the solution, these vectors can have *any* assumed directional sense. Then if the calculated numerical value of these quantities is negative, the vectors act in their opposite sense of direction. Examples 17.15 and 17.16 illustrate these concepts numerically.

*See Example 16.3 or 16.14.

As the soil compactor moves forward, the roller has general plane motion. The forces shown on the roller's free-body diagram cause the effects shown on the kinetic diagram. If moments are summed about the mass center, $G$, then $\Sigma M_G = I_G \alpha$. However, if moments are summed about point $A$ then $\zeta + \Sigma M_A = I_G \alpha + (m a_G)d$.

## PROCEDURE FOR ANALYSIS

Kinetic problems involving general plane motion of a rigid body can be solved using the following procedure.

### Free-Body Diagram.

- Establish the $x, y$ inertial coordinate system and draw the free-body diagram for the body.

- Specify the direction and sense of the acceleration of the mass center, $\mathbf{a}_G$, and the angular acceleration $\boldsymbol{\alpha}$ of the body.

- Compute the moment of inertia $I_G$.

- Identify the unknowns in the problem.

- If it is decided that the rotational equation of motion $\Sigma M_P = \Sigma (\mathcal{M}_k)_P$ is to be used, then consider drawing the kinetic diagram in order to help "visualize" the "moments" developed by the components $m(\mathbf{a}_G)_x, m(\mathbf{a}_G)_y$, and $I_G \boldsymbol{\alpha}$ when writing the terms in the moment sum $\Sigma (\mathcal{M}_k)_P$.

### Equations of Motion.

- Apply the three equations of motion in accordance with the established sign convention.

- When friction is present, there is the possibility for motion with no slipping or tipping. Each possibility for motion should be considered.

### Kinematics.

- Use kinematics if a complete solution cannot be obtained strictly from the equations of motion.

- If the body's motion is *constrained* due to its supports, additional equations may be obtained by using $\mathbf{a}_B = \mathbf{a}_A + \mathbf{a}_{B/A}$, which relates the accelerations of any two points $A$ and $B$ on the body.

- When a wheel, disk, cylinder, or ball *rolls without slipping*, then $a_G = \alpha r$.

# EXAMPLE 17.14

The spool in Fig. 17–22a has a mass of 8 kg and a radius of gyration of $k_G = 0.35$ m. If cords of negligible mass are wrapped around its inner hub and outer rim as shown, determine the spool's angular acceleration.

## Solution I

*Free-Body Diagram.* Fig. 17–22b. The 100-N force causes $\mathbf{a}_G$ to act upward. Also, $\alpha$ acts clockwise, since the spool winds around the cord at $A$.

There are three unknowns $T$, $a_G$, and $\alpha$. The moment of inertia of the spool about its mass center is

$$I_G = mk_G^2 = 8 \text{ kg}(0.35 \text{ m})^2 = 0.980 \text{ kg} \cdot \text{m}^2$$

(a)

*Equations of Motion.*

$$+\uparrow \Sigma F_y = m(a_G)_y; \qquad T + 100 \text{ N} - 78.48 \text{ N} = (8 \text{ kg})a_G \qquad (1)$$

$$\zeta + \Sigma M_G = I_G\alpha; \quad 100 \text{ N}(0.2 \text{ m}) - T(0.5 \text{ m}) = (0.980 \text{ kg} \cdot \text{m}^2)\alpha \quad (2)$$

*Kinematics.* A complete solution is obtained if kinematics is used to relate $a_G$ to $\alpha$. In this case the spool "rolls without slipping" on the cord at $A$. Hence, we can use the results of Example 16.3 or 16.14, so that

$$(\zeta+)a_G = \alpha r, \qquad a_G = 0.5\alpha \qquad (3)$$

Solving Eqs. 1 to 3, we have

$$\alpha = 10.3 \text{ rad/s}^2 \qquad \qquad Ans.$$
$$a_G = 5.16 \text{ m/s}^2$$
$$T = 19.8 \text{ N}$$

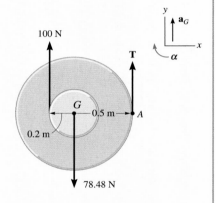

(b)

## Solution II

*Equations of Motion.* We can eliminate the unknown $T$ by summing moments about point $A$. From the free-body and kinetic diagrams Figs. 17–22b and 17–22c, we have

$$\zeta + \Sigma M_A = \Sigma(\mathcal{M}_k)_A; \qquad 100 \text{ N}(0.7 \text{ m}) - 78.48 \text{ N}(0.5 \text{ m})$$
$$= (0.980 \text{ kg} \cdot \text{m}^2)\alpha + [(8 \text{ kg})a_G](0.5 \text{ m})$$

Using Eq. (3),

$$\alpha = 10.3 \text{ rad/s}^2 \qquad \qquad Ans.$$

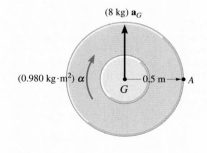

(c)

**Fig. 17–22**

EXAMPLE 17.15

The 25-kg wheel shown in Fig. 17–23a has a radius of gyration $k_G = 0.2$ m. If a 50-N · m couple moment is applied to the wheel, determine the acceleration of its mass center $G$. The coefficients of static and kinetic friction between the wheel and the plane at $A$ are $\mu_s = 0.3$ and $\mu_k = 0.25$, respectively.

**Solution**

*Free-Body Diagram.*    By inspection of Fig. 17–23b, it is seen that the couple moment causes the wheel to have a clockwise angular acceleration of $\boldsymbol{\alpha}$. As a result, the acceleration of the mass center, $\mathbf{a}_G$, is directed to the right. The moment of inertia is

$$I_G = mk_G^2 = (25 \text{ kg})(0.2 \text{ m})^2 = 1.0 \text{ kg} \cdot \text{m}^2$$

The unknowns are $N_A$, $F_A$, $a_G$, and $\alpha$.

*Equations of Motion.*

$$\xrightarrow{+} \Sigma F_x = m(a_G)_x; \qquad F_A = (25 \text{ kg})a_G \qquad (1)$$

$$+\uparrow \Sigma F_y = m(a_G)_y; \qquad N_A - 25(9.81) \text{ N} = 0 \qquad (2)$$

$$\zeta+ \Sigma M_G = I_G\alpha; \qquad 50 \text{ N} \cdot \text{m} - 0.4 \text{ m}(F_A) = (1.0 \text{ kg} \cdot \text{m}^2)\alpha \qquad (3)$$

A fourth equation is needed for a complete solution.

*Kinematics (No Slipping).*    If this assumption is made, then

$$(\zeta+) \qquad\qquad a_G = (0.4 \text{ m})\alpha \qquad (4)$$

Solving Eqs. 1 to 4,

$$N_A = 245.25 \text{ N} \qquad F_A = 100 \text{ N}$$
$$\alpha = 10.0 \text{ rad/s}^2 \qquad a_G = 4.0 \text{ m/s}^2$$

The original assumption of no slipping requires $F_A \le \mu_s N_A$. However, since 100 N > 0.3(245.25 N) = 73.6 N, the wheel slips as it rolls.

*(Slipping).*    Equation 4 is not valid, and so $F_A = \mu_k N_A$, or

$$F_A = 0.25N_A \qquad (5)$$

Solving Eqs. 1 to 3 and 5 yields

$$N_A = 245.25 \text{ N} \qquad F_A = 61.31 \text{ N}$$
$$\alpha = 25.5 \text{ rad/s}^2$$
$$a_G = 2.45 \text{ m/s}^2 \rightarrow \qquad\qquad Ans.$$

$M = 50$ N·m

$G$

0.4 m

$A$

(a)

25 (9.81) N

50 N · m

$G$

0.4 m

$\mathbf{F}_A$

$\mathbf{N}_A$

$\alpha$

$\mathbf{a}_G$

$y$

$x$

(b)

**Fig. 17–23**

# E X A M P L E  17.16

The uniform slender pole shown in Fig. 17–24$a$ has a mass of 100 kg and a moment of inertia $I_G = 75$ kg·m$^2$. If the coefficients of static and kinetic friction between the end of the pole and the surface are $\mu_s = 0.3$ and $\mu_k = 0.25$, respectively, determine the pole's angular acceleration at the instant the 400-N horizontal force is applied. The pole is originally at rest.

(a)

### Solution

*Free-Body Diagram.*    Figure 17–24$b$. The path of motion of the mass center $G$ will be along an unknown curved path having a radius of curvature $\rho$, which is initially parallel to the $y$ axis. There is no normal or $y$ component of acceleration since the pole is originally at rest, i.e., $\mathbf{v}_G = \mathbf{0}$, so that $(a_G)_y = v_G^2/\rho = 0$. We will assume the mass center accelerates to the right and that the pole has a clockwise angular acceleration of $\boldsymbol{\alpha}$. The unknowns are $N_A$, $F_A$, $a_G$, and $\alpha$.

*Equations of Motion.*

$$\xrightarrow{+} \Sigma F_x = m(a_G)_x; \qquad 400 \text{ N} - F_A = (100 \text{ kg})a_G \qquad (1)$$

$$+\uparrow\Sigma F_y = m(a_G)_y; \qquad N_A - 981 \text{ N} = 0 \qquad (2)$$

$$\zeta+\Sigma M_G = I_G\alpha; \quad F_A(1.5 \text{ m}) - 400 \text{ N}(1 \text{ m}) = (75 \text{ kg·m}^2)\alpha \qquad (3)$$

A fourth equation is needed for a complete solution.

(b)

**Fig. 17–24**

*Kinematics (No Slipping).*    In this case point $A$ acts as a "pivot" so that indeed, if $\alpha$ is clockwise, then $a_G$ is directed to the right.

$$\zeta+a_G = \alpha r_{AG}; \qquad a_G = (1.5 \text{ m})\alpha \qquad (4)$$

Solving Eqs. 1 to 4 yields

$$N_A = 981 \text{ N} \qquad F_A = 300 \text{ N}$$
$$a_G = 1 \text{ m/s}^2 \qquad \alpha = 0.667 \text{ rad/s}^2$$

Testing the original assumption of no slipping requires $F_A \leq \mu_s N_A$. However, 300 N > 0.3(981 N) = 294 N. (Slips at $A$.)

*(Slipping).*    For this case Eq. 4 does *not* apply. Instead the frictional equation $F_A = \mu_k N_A$ is used. Hence,

$$F_A = 0.25N_A \qquad (5)$$

Solving Eqs. 1 to 3 and 5 simultaneously yields

$$N_A = 981 \text{ N} \qquad F_A = 245 \text{ N} \qquad a_G = 1.55 \text{ m/s}^2$$
$$\alpha = -0.428 \text{ rad/s}^2 = 0.428 \text{ rad/s}^2 \zeta \qquad \qquad Ans.$$

E X A M P L E 17.17

(a)

(b)

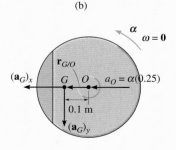

(c)

Fig. 17–25

The 30-kg wheel shown in Fig. 17–25a has a mass center at $G$ and a radius of gyration $k_G = 0.15$ m. If the wheel is originally at rest and released from the position shown, determine its angular acceleration. No slipping occurs.

**Solution**

*Free-Body and Kinetic Diagrams.* The two unknowns $F_A$ and $N_A$ shown on the free-body diagram, Fig. 17–25b, can be eliminated from the analysis by summing moments about point $A$. The kinetic diagram accompanies the solution in order to illustrate application of $\Sigma(\mathcal{M}_k)_A$. Since point $G$ moves along a curved path, the two components $m(\mathbf{a}_G)_x$ and $m(\mathbf{a}_G)_y$ are shown on the kinetic diagram, Fig. 17–25b. The moment of inertia is

$$I_G = mk_G^2 = 30(0.15)^2 = 0.675 \text{ kg} \cdot \text{m}^2$$

There are five unknowns, $N_A$, $F_A$, $(a_G)_x$, $(a_G)_y$, and $\alpha$.

*Equation of Motion.* Applying the rotational equation of motion about point $A$, to eliminate $N_A$, and $F_A$, we have

$$\zeta + \Sigma M_A = \Sigma(\mathcal{M}_k)_A; \quad 30(9.81) \text{ N}(0.1 \text{ m}) =$$
$$(0.675 \text{ kg} \cdot \text{m}^2)\alpha + (30 \text{ kg})(a_G)_x(0.25 \text{ m}) + (30 \text{ kg})(a_G)_y(0.1 \text{ m}) \quad (1)$$

There are three unknowns in this equation: $(a_G)_x$, $(a_G)_y$, and $\alpha$.

*Kinematics.* Using kinematics, $(a_G)_x$, $(a_G)_y$ will be related to $\alpha$. As shown in Fig. 17–25c, these vectors must have the same directional sense as the corresponding vectors on the kinetic diagram since we are seeking a simultaneous solution with Eq. 1. Since no slipping occurs, $a_O = \alpha r = \alpha(0.25 \text{ m})$, directed to the left, Fig. 17–25c. Also, $\omega = 0$, since the wheel is originally at rest. Applying the acceleration equation to point $O$ (base point) and point $G$, we have

$$\mathbf{a}_G = \mathbf{a}_O + \boldsymbol{\alpha} \times \mathbf{r}_{G/O} - \omega^2 \mathbf{r}_{G/O}$$
$$-(a_G)_x\mathbf{i} - (a_G)_y\mathbf{j} = -\alpha(0.25)\mathbf{i} + (\alpha\mathbf{k}) \times (-0.1\mathbf{i}) - \mathbf{0}$$

Expanding and equating the respective $\mathbf{i}$ and $\mathbf{j}$ components, we have

$$(a_G)_x = \alpha(0.25) \quad (2)$$
$$(a_G)_y = \alpha(0.1) \quad (3)$$

Solving Eqs. 1 to 3 yields

$$\alpha = 10.3 \text{ rad/s}^2 \zeta \qquad \qquad Ans.$$
$$(a_G)_x = 2.58 \text{ m/s}^2$$
$$(a_G)_y = 1.03 \text{ m/s}^2$$

As an exercise, show that $F_A = 77.4$ N and $N_A = 263$ N.

# PROBLEMS

**17-87.** If the disk in Fig. 17–21*a rolls without slipping*, show that when moments are summed about the instantaneous center of zero velocity, *IC*, it is possible to use the moment equation $\Sigma M_{IC} = I_{IC}\alpha$, where $I_{IC}$ represents the moment of inertia of the disk calculated about the instantaneous axis of zero velocity.

**\*17-88.** The 20-kg punching bag has a radius of gyration about its center of mass *G* of $k_G = 0.4$ m. If it is initially at rest and is subjected to a horizontal force $F = 30$ N, determine the initial angular acceleration of the bag and the tension in the supporting cable *AB*.

**Prob. 17–88**

**17-89.** The semicircular disk having a mass of 10 kg is rotating at $\omega = 4$ rad/s at the instant $\theta = 60°$. If the coefficient of static friction at *A* is $\mu_s = 0.5$, determine if the disk slips at this instant.

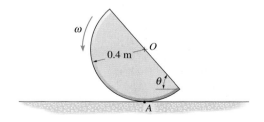

**Prob. 17–89**

**17-90.** The rocket has a weight of 100 kN ($\approx$ 10 000 kg), mass center at *G*, and radius of gyration about the mass center of $k_G = 7$ m when it is fired. Each of its two engines provides a thrust $T = 250$ kN. At a given instant, engine *A* suddenly fails to operate. Determine the angular acceleration of the rocket and the acceleration of its nose *B*.

**Prob. 17–90**

**17-91.** Two men exert constant vertical forces of 200 N and 150 N at the ends *A* and *B* of a uniform plank which has a weight of 250 N ($\approx$ 25 kg). If the plank is originally at rest, determine the acceleration of its center and its angular acceleration. Assume the plank to be a slender rod.

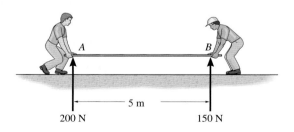

**Prob. 17–91**

**\*17-92.** The uniform 500-N ($\approx$ 50-kg) board is suspended from cords at $C$ and $D$. If these cords are subjected to constant forces of 300 N and 450 N, respectively, determine the acceleration of the board's center and the board's angular acceleration. Assume the board is a thin plate. Neglect the mass of the pulleys at $E$ and $F$.

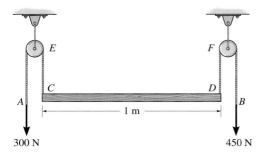

**Prob. 17–92**

**17-93.** The spool has a mass of 500 kg and a radius of gyration $k_G = 1.30$ m. It rests on the surface of a conveyor belt for which the coefficient of static friction is $\mu_s = 0.5$ and the coefficient of kinetic friction is $\mu_k = 0.4$. If the conveyor accelerates at $a_C = 1$ m/s$^2$, determine the initial tension in the wire and the angular acceleration of the spool. The spool is originally at rest.

**17-94.** The spool has a mass of 500 kg and a radius of gyration $k_G = 1.30$ m. It rests on the surface of a conveyor belt for which the coefficient of static friction is $\mu_s = 0.5$. Determine the greatest acceleration $a_C$ of the conveyor so that the spool will not slip. Also, what are the initial tension in the wire and the angular acceleration of the spool? The spool is originally at rest.

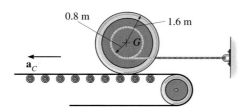

**Probs. 17–93/94**

**17-95.** The spool has a mass of 100 kg and a radius of gyration of $k_G = 0.3$ m. If the coefficients of static and kinetic friction at $A$ are $\mu_s = 0.2$ and $\mu_k = 0.15$, respectively, determine the angular acceleration of the spool if $P = 50$ N.

**\*17-96.** Solve Prob. 17–95 if the cord and force $P = 50$ N are directed vertically upwards.

**17-97.** The spool has a mass of 100 kg and a radius of gyration $k_G = 0.3$ m. If the coefficients of static and kinetic friction at $A$ are $\mu_s = 0.2$ and $\mu_k = 0.15$, respectively, determine the angular acceleration of the spool if $P = 600$ N.

**Probs. 17–95/96/97**

**17-98.** The upper body of the crash dummy has a mass of 375 N ($\approx$ 37.5 kg), a center of gravity at $G$, and a radius of gyration about $G$ of $k_G = 0.21$ m. By means of the seat belt this body segment is assumed to be pin-connected to the seat of the car at $A$. If a crash causes the car to decelerate at 15 m/s$^2$, determine the angular velocity of the body when it has rotated to $\theta = 30°$.

**Prob. 17–98**

**17-99.** The 2-kg slender bar is supported by cord $BC$ and then released from rest at $A$. Determine the initial angular acceleration of the bar and the tension in the cord.

**Prob. 17–99**

**\*17-100.** A uniform rod having a weight of 100 N ($\approx$ 10 kg) is pin-supported at $A$ from a roller which rides on a horizontal track. If the rod is originally at rest, and a horizontal force of $F = 150$ N is applied to the roller, determine the acceleration of the roller. Neglect the mass of the roller and its size $d$ in the computations.

**17-101.** Solve Prob. 17–100 assuming that the roller at $A$ is replaced by a slider block having a negligible mass. The coefficient of kinetic friction between the block and the track is $\mu_k = 0.2$. Neglect the dimension $d$ and the size of the block in the computations.

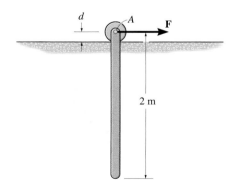

**Probs. 17–100/101**

**17-102.** The lawn roller has a mass of 80 kg and a radius of gyration $k_G = 0.175$ m. If it is pushed forward with a force of 200 N when the handle is at 45°, determine its angular acceleration. The coefficients of static and kinetic friction between the ground and the roller are $\mu_s = 0.12$ and $\mu_k = 0.1$, respectively.

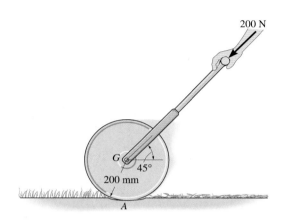

**Prob. 17–102**

**17-103.** The two pin-connected bars each have a weight of 100 N/m ($\approx$ 10 kg/m). If a moment of $M = 600$ N · m is applied to bar $AB$, determine the initial vertical reaction at $C$ and the horizontal and vertical components of reaction at $B$. Neglect the size of the roller at $C$. The bars are initially at rest.

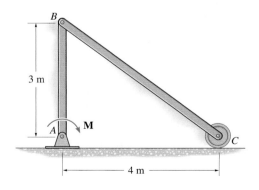

**Prob. 17–103**

**\*17-104.** A long strip of paper is wrapped into two rolls, each having a mass of 8 kg. Roll $A$ is pin supported about its center whereas roll $B$ is not centrally supported. If $B$ is brought into contact with $A$ and released from rest, determine the initial tension in the paper between the rolls and the angular acceleration of each roll. For the calculation, assume the rolls to be approximated by cylinders.

90 mm

90 mm

**Prob. 17–104**

**17-106.** The ladder has a weight $W$ and rests against the smooth wall and ground. Determine its angular acceleration as a function of $\theta$ when it is released and allowed to slide downward. For the calculation, treat the ladder as a slender rod.

**Prob. 17–106**

**17-105.** The uniform bar of mass $m$ and length $L$ is balanced in the vertical position when the horizontal force $\mathbf{P}$ is applied to the roller at $A$. Determine the bar's initial angular acceleration and the acceleration of its top point $B$.

**Prob. 17–105**

**17-107.** The 8-kg bowling ball is cast horizontally onto a lane such that initially $\omega = 0$ and its mass center has a velocity $v = 2.4$ m/s. If the coefficient of kinetic friction between the lane and the ball is $\mu_k = 0.12$, determine the distance the ball travels before it rolls without slipping. For the calculation, neglect the finger holes in the ball and assume the ball has a uniform density.

**Prob. 17–107**

**\*17-108.** The 10-N ($\approx$ 1-kg) hoop or thin ring is given an initial angular velocity of 6 rad/s when it is placed on the surface. If the coefficient of kinetic friction between the hoop and the surface is $\mu_k = 0.3$, determine the distance the hoop moves before it stops slipping.

$\omega_0 = 6$ rad/s

6 cm

O

Prob. 17–108

**17-109.** The 150-N ($\approx$ 15-kg) circular plate is suspended from a pin at $A$. If the pin is connected to a track which is given an acceleration $a_A = 3$ m/s$^2$, determine the horizontal and vertical components of reaction at $A$ and the acceleration of the plate's mass center $G$. The plate is originally at rest.

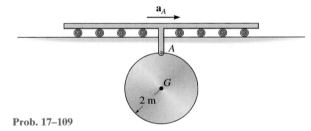

$\mathbf{a}_A$

A

G

2 m

Prob. 17–109

**17-110.** A cord $C$ is wrapped around each of the two 10-kg disks. If they are released from rest, determine the tension in the fixed cord $D$. Neglect the mass of the cord.

D

A
90 mm

C

B
90 mm

Prob. 17–110

**■17-111.** The assembly consists of an 8-kg disk and a 10-kg bar which is pin connected to the disk. If the system is released from rest, determine the angular acceleration of the disk. The coefficients of static and kinetic friction between the disk and the inclined plane are $\mu_s = 0.6$ and $\mu_k = 0.4$, respectively. Neglect friction at $B$.

**\*17-112.** Solve Prob. 17–111 if the bar is removed. The coefficients of static and kinetic friction between the disk and inclined plane are $\mu_s = 0.15$ and $\mu_k = 0.1$, respectively.

B

1 m

A

0.3 m

C

30°

Probs. 17–111/112

**17-113.** The 5-kN ($\approx$ 500-kg) beam is supported at $A$ and $B$ when it is subjected to a force of 10 kN as shown. If the pin support at $A$ suddenly fails, determine the beam's initial angular acceleration and the force of the roller support on the beam. For the calculation, assume that the beam is a slender rod so that its thickness can be neglected.

10 kN

5 | 3
4

B | A

8 m | 2 m

Prob. 17–113

# DESIGN PROJECTS

### 17-1D. DESIGN OF A DYNAMOMETER

In order to test the dynamic strength of cables, an instrument called a *dynamometer* must be used that will measure the tension in a cable when it hoists a very heavy object with accelerated motion. Design such an instrument, based on the use of single or multiple springs so that it can be used on the cable supporting the 300-kg pipe that is given an upward acceleration of $2 \text{ m/s}^2$. Submit a drawing and explain how your dynamometer operates.

**Prob. 17–1D**

### 17-2D. DESIGN OF A SMALL ELEVATOR BRAKE

A small household elevator is operated using a hoist. For safety purposes it is necessary to install a braking mechanism which will automatically engage in case the cable fails during operation. Design the braking mechanism using steel members and springs. The elevator and its contents are assumed to have a mass of 300 kg, and it travels at 2.5 m/s. The maximum allowable deceleration to stop the motion is to be $4 \text{ m/s}^2$. Assume the coefficient of kinetic friction between any steel members and the walls of the elevator shaft is $\mu_k = 0.3$. The gap between the elevator frame and each wall of the shaft is 50 mm. Submit a scale drawing of your design along with a force analysis to show that your design will arrest the motion as required. Discuss the safety and reliability of the mechanism.

**Prob. 17–2D**

### 17-3D. SAFETY PERFORMANCE OF A BICYCLE

One of the most common accidents one can have on a bicycle is to flip over the handle bars. Obtain the necessary measurements of a standard-size bicycle and its mass and center of mass. Consider yourself as the rider, with center of mass at your navel. Perform an experiment to determine the coefficient of kinetic friction between the wheels and the pavement. With this data, calculate the possibility of flipping over when (a) only the rear brakes are applied, (b) only the front brakes are applied, and (c) both front and rear brakes are applied simultaneously. What effect does the height of the seat have on these results? Suggest a way to improve the bicycle's design, and write a report on the safety of cycling based on this analysis.

**Prob. 17–3D**

# CHAPTER REVIEW

- *Moment of Inertia.* The moment of inertia is a measure of the resistance of a body to a change in its angular velocity. It is defined by $I = \int r^2 \, dm$ and will be different for each axis about which it is computed. For a body having an axial symmetry, the integration is usually performed using disk or shell elements.

  Many bodies are composed of simple shapes. If this is the case, then tabular values of $I$ can be used, such as the ones given on the inside back cover of this book. To obtain the moment of inertia of a composite body about any specified axis, the moment of inertia of each part is determined about the axis and the results are added together. Doing this often requires use of the parallel-axis theorem $I = I_G + md^2$. Handbooks may also report values of the radius of gyration $k$ for the body. If the body's mass is known, then the mass moment of inertia is determined from $I = mk^2$.

- *Planar Equations of Motion.* The equation which defines the translational motion of a rigid body is $\Sigma \mathbf{F} = m\mathbf{a}_G$. Here, $\mathbf{a}_G$ is the acceleration of the body's mass center.

  The equation which describes the rotational motion of the body is determined by taking the moments of all of the particles in the body about an axis. When the axis passes through the mass center, the result becomes $\Sigma M_G = I_G \alpha$. If moments are taken about some arbitrary point $P$, then we get $\Sigma M_P = \Sigma (\mathcal{M}_k)_P$. The sum on the right side represents the moments of the kinetic vectors $m\mathbf{a}_G$ and $I_G \boldsymbol{\alpha}$ about point $P$.

  In order to account for all of the terms in these equations, application should always be accompanied with a free-body diagram, and for some problems, it may also be convenient to draw the kinetic diagram.

- *Translation.* Here $I_G \boldsymbol{\alpha} = \mathbf{0}$ since $\boldsymbol{\alpha} = \mathbf{0}$. If the body undergoes rectilinear translation, use an inertial $x$–$y$ axis, in which case the equations of motion are

$$\Sigma F_x = m(a_G)_x$$
$$\Sigma F_y = m(a_G)_y$$
$$\Sigma M_G = 0$$

For curvilinear translation, use inertial $n$–$t$ axes so that

$$\Sigma F_n = m(a_G)_n$$
$$\Sigma F_t = m(a_G)_t$$
$$\Sigma M_G = 0$$

- *Rotation About a Fixed Axis.* For fixed axis rotation, the kinetic vector $m(\mathbf{a}_G)_n$ produces no moment about the axis of rotation, and so the rotational equation of motion reduces to a simplified form about point $O$. The equations of motion are

$$\Sigma F_n = m\omega^2 r_G \qquad \Sigma F_t = m\alpha r_G$$
$$\Sigma M_G = I_G \alpha \quad \text{or} \quad \Sigma M_O = I_O \alpha$$

- *General Plane Motion.* For general plane motion, we have

$$\Sigma F_x = m(a_G)_x \qquad \Sigma F_y = m(a_G)_y$$
$$\Sigma M_G = I_G \alpha \quad \text{or} \quad \Sigma M_P = \Sigma (\mathcal{M}_k)_P$$

If the body is constrained by its supports, then additional equations of kinematics can be obtained by using $\mathbf{a}_B = \mathbf{a}_A + \mathbf{a}_{B/A}$ to relate the accelerations of any two points $A$ and $B$ on the body.

The principle of work and energy plays an important role in the motion of the draw works used to lift pipe on this drilling rig.

# Planar Kinetics of a Rigid Body: Work and Energy

- To develop formulations for the kinetic energy of a body, and define the various ways a force and couple do work.
- To apply the principle of work and energy to solve rigid-body planar kinetic problems that involve force, velocity, and displacement.
- To show how the conservation of energy can be used to solve rigid-body planar kinetic problems.

## 18.1 Kinetic Energy

In this chapter we will apply work and energy methods to problems involving force, velocity, and displacement related to the planar motion of a rigid body. Before doing this, however, it will first be necessary to develop a means of obtaining the body's kinetic energy when the body is subjected to translation, rotation about a fixed axis, or general plane motion.

To do this we will consider the rigid body shown in Fig. 18–1, which is represented here by a *slab* moving in the inertial $x$–$y$ reference plane. An arbitrary $i$th particle of the body, having a mass $dm$, is located at $r$ from the arbitrary point $P$. If at the *instant* shown the particle has a velocity $\mathbf{v}_i$, then the particle's kinetic energy is $T_i = \frac{1}{2} dm \, v_i^2$.

Fig. 18–1

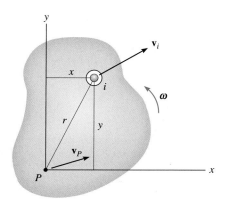

**Fig. 18–1**

The kinetic energy of the entire body is determined by writing similar expressions for each particle of the body and integrating the results, i.e.,

$$T = \frac{1}{2} \int_m dm \, v_i^2$$

This equation may also be expressed in terms of the velocity of point $P$. If the body has an angular velocity $\boldsymbol{\omega}$, then from Fig. 18–1 we have

$$\mathbf{v}_i = \mathbf{v}_P + \mathbf{v}_{i/P}$$
$$= (v_P)_x \mathbf{i} + (v_P)_y \mathbf{j} + \omega \mathbf{k} \times (x\mathbf{i} + y\mathbf{j})$$
$$= [(v_P)_x - \omega y]\mathbf{i} + [(v_P)_y + \omega x]\mathbf{j}$$

The square of the magnitude of $\mathbf{v}_i$ is thus

$$\mathbf{v}_i \cdot \mathbf{v}_i = v_i^2 = [(v_P)_x - \omega y]^2 + [(v_P)_y + \omega x]^2$$
$$= (v_P)_x^2 - 2(v_P)_x \omega y + \omega^2 y^2 + (v_P)_y^2 + 2(v_P)_y \omega x + \omega^2 x^2$$
$$= v_P^2 - 2(v_P)_x \omega y + 2(v_P)_y \omega x + \omega^2 r^2$$

Substituting into the equation of kinetic energy yields

$$T = \frac{1}{2}\left( \int_m dm \right) v_P^2 - (v_P)_x \omega \left( \int_m y \, dm \right) + (v_P)_y \omega \left( \int_m x \, dm \right) + \frac{1}{2}\omega^2 \left( \int_m r^2 \, dm \right)$$

The first integral on the right represents the entire mass $m$ of the body. Since $\bar{y}m = \int y \, dm$ and $\bar{x}m = \int x \, dm$, the second and third integrals locate the body's center of mass $G$ with respect to $P$. The last integral represents the body's moment of inertia $I_P$, computed about the $z$ axis passing through point $P$. Thus,

$$T = \frac{1}{2}mv_P^2 - (v_P)_x \omega \bar{y}m + (v_P)_y \omega \bar{x}m + \frac{1}{2}I_P \omega^2 \qquad (18\text{–}1)$$

As a special case, if point $P$ coincides with the mass center $G$ for the body, then $\bar{y} = \bar{x} = 0$, and therefore

$$T = \frac{1}{2}mv_G^2 + \frac{1}{2}I_G\omega^2 \qquad (18\text{–}2)$$

Here $I_G$ is the moment of inertia for the body about an axis which is perpendicular to the plane of motion and passes through the mass center. Both terms on the right side are *always positive*, since the velocities are squared. Furthermore, it may be verified that these terms have units of length times force, a common unit being m · N. Recall, however, that in the SI system the unit of energy is the joule (J), where 1 J = 1 m · N.

**Translation.** When a rigid body of mass $m$ is subjected to either rectilinear or curvilinear *translation*, the kinetic energy due to rotation is zero, since $\boldsymbol{\omega} = \mathbf{0}$. From Eq. 18–2, the kinetic energy of the body is therefore

$$T = \tfrac{1}{2}mv_G^2 \qquad (18\text{–}3)$$

where $v_G$ is the magnitude of the translational velocity $\mathbf{v}$ at the instant considered, Fig. 18–2.

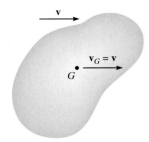

Translation

Fig. 18–2

**Rotation About a Fixed Axis.** When a rigid body is *rotating about a fixed axis* passing through point $O$, Fig. 18–3, the body has both *translational* and *rotational* kinetic energy as defined by Eq. 18–2, i.e.,

$$T = \tfrac{1}{2}mv_G^2 + \tfrac{1}{2}I_G\omega^2 \qquad (18\text{–}4)$$

The body's kinetic energy may also be formulated by noting that $v_G = r_G\omega$, in which case $T = \tfrac{1}{2}(I_G + mr_G^2)\omega^2$. By the parallel-axis theorem, the terms inside the parentheses represent the moment of inertia $I_O$ of the body about an axis perpendicular to the plane of motion and passing through point $O$. Hence,*

$$T = \tfrac{1}{2}I_O\omega^2 \qquad (18\text{–}5)$$

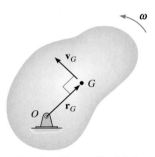

Rotation About a Fixed Axis

Fig. 18–3

From the derivation, this equation will give the same result as Eq. 18–4, since it accounts for *both* the translational and rotational kinetic energies of the body.

**General Plane Motion.** When a rigid body is subjected to general plane motion, Fig. 18–4, it has an angular velocity $\boldsymbol{\omega}$ and its mass center has a velocity $\mathbf{v}_G$. Hence, the kinetic energy is defined by Eq. 18–2, i.e.,

$$T = \tfrac{1}{2}mv_G^2 + \tfrac{1}{2}I_G\omega^2 \qquad (18\text{–}6)$$

Here it is seen that the total kinetic energy of the body consists of the *scalar* sum of the body's *translational* kinetic energy, $\tfrac{1}{2}mv_G^2$, and *rotational* kinetic energy about its mass center, $\tfrac{1}{2}I_G\omega^2$.

Because energy is a scalar quantity, the total kinetic energy for a system of *connected* rigid bodies is the sum of the kinetic energies of all its moving parts. Depending on the type of motion, the kinetic energy of *each body* is found by applying Eq. 18–2 or the alternative forms mentioned above.

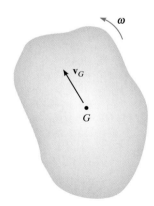

General Plane Motion

Fig. 18–4

---

*The similarity between this derivation and that of $\Sigma M_O = I_O\alpha$, Eq. 17–16, should be noted. Also note that the same result can be obtained directly from Eq. 18–1 by selecting point $P$ at $O$, realizing that $\mathbf{v}_O = \mathbf{0}$.

The total kinetic energy of this soil compactor consists of the kinetic energy of the body or frame of the machine due to its translation, and the translational and rotational kinetic energies of the roller and the wheels due to their general plane motion. Here we exclude the additional kinetic energy developed by the moving parts of the engine and drive train.

---

## EXAMPLE 18.1

(a)

(b)

**Fig. 18–5**

The system of three elements shown in Fig. 18–5a consists of a 6-kg block $B$, a 10-kg disk $D$, and a 12-kg cylinder $C$. If no slipping occurs, determine the total kinetic energy of the system at the instant shown.

### Solution

In order to compute the kinetic energy of the disk and cylinder, it is first necessary to determine $\omega_D$, $\omega_C$, and $v_G$, Fig. 18–5a. From the *kinematics* of the disk,

$$v_B = r_D\omega_D; \qquad 0.8 \text{ m/s} = (0.1 \text{ m})\omega_D \qquad \omega_D = 8 \text{ rad/s}$$

Since the cylinder rolls without slipping, the instantaneous center of zero velocity is at the point of contact with the ground, Fig. 18–5b, hence,

$$v_E = r_{E/IC}\omega_C; \qquad 0.8 \text{ m/s} = (0.2 \text{ m})\omega_C \qquad \omega_C = 4 \text{ rad/s}$$
$$v_G = r_{G/IC}\omega_C; \qquad v_G = (0.1 \text{ m})(4 \text{ rad/s}) = 0.4 \text{ m/s}$$

*Block*

$$T_B = \tfrac{1}{2}m_B v_B^2 = \tfrac{1}{2}(6 \text{ kg})(0.8 \text{ m/s})^2 = 1.92 \text{ J}$$

*Disk*

$$T_D = \tfrac{1}{2}I_D\omega_D^2 = \tfrac{1}{2}(\tfrac{1}{2}m_D r_D^2)\omega_D^2$$
$$= \tfrac{1}{2}[\tfrac{1}{2}(10 \text{ kg})(0.1 \text{ m})^2](8 \text{ rad/s})^2 = 1.60 \text{ J}$$

*Cylinder*

$$T_C = \tfrac{1}{2}mv_G^2 + \tfrac{1}{2}I_G\omega_C^2 = \tfrac{1}{2}mv_G^2 + \tfrac{1}{2}(\tfrac{1}{2}m_C r_C^2)\omega_C^2$$
$$= \tfrac{1}{2}(12 \text{ kg})(0.4 \text{ m/s})^2 + \tfrac{1}{2}[\tfrac{1}{2}(12 \text{ kg})(0.1 \text{ m})^2](4 \text{ rad/s})^2 = 1.44 \text{ J}$$

The total kinetic energy of the system is therefore

$$T = T_B + T_D + T_C$$
$$= 1.92 \text{ J} + 1.60 \text{ J} + 1.44 \text{ J} = 4.96 \text{ J} \qquad \textit{Ans.}$$

## 18.2   The Work of a Force

Several types of forces are often encountered in planar kinetics problems involving a rigid body. The work of each of these forces has been presented in Sec. 14.1 and is listed below as a summary.

**Work of a Variable Force.**   If an external force $\mathbf{F}$ acts on a rigid body, the work done by the force when it moves along the path $s$, Fig. 18–6, is defined as

$$U_F = \mathbf{F} \cdot \mathbf{r} = \int_s F \cos \theta \, ds \qquad (18\text{–}7)$$

Here $\theta$ is the angle between the "tails" of the force vector and the differential displacement. In general, the integration must account for the variation of the force's direction and magnitude.

**Fig. 18–6**

**Work of a Constant Force.**   If an external force $\mathbf{F}_c$ acts on a rigid body, Fig. 18–7, and maintains a constant magnitude $F_c$ and constant direction $\theta$, while the body undergoes a translation $s$, Eq. 18–7 can be integrated so that the work becomes

$$U_{F_c} = (F_c \cos \theta)s \qquad (18\text{–}8)$$

Here $F_c \cos \theta$ represents the magnitude of the component of force in the direction of displacement.

**Fig. 18–7**

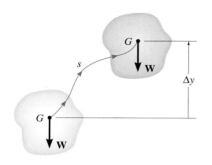

Fig. 18–8

**Work of a Weight.** The weight of a body does work only when the body's center of mass $G$ undergoes a *vertical displacement* $\Delta y$. If this displacement is *upward*, Fig. 18–8, the work is negative, since the weight and displacement are in opposite directions.

$$U_W = -W\Delta y \qquad (18\text{--}9)$$

Likewise, if the displacement is *downward* $(-\Delta y)$ the work becomes *positive*. In both cases the elevation change is considered to be small so that $\mathbf{W}$, which is caused by gravitation, is constant.

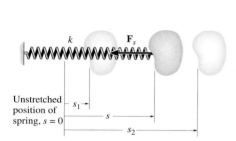

Fig. 18–9

**Work of a Spring Force.** If a linear elastic spring is attached to a body, the spring force $F_s = ks$ *acting on the body* does work when the spring either stretches or compresses from $s_1$ to a *further* position $s_2$. In both cases the work will be *negative* since the *displacement of the body* is in the opposite direction to the force, Fig. 18–9. The work done is

$$U_s = -(\tfrac{1}{2}ks_2^2 - \tfrac{1}{2}ks_1^2) \qquad (18\text{--}10)$$

where $|s_2| > |s_1|$.

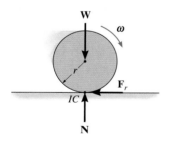

Fig. 18–10

**Forces That Do No Work.** There are some external forces that do no work when the body is displaced. These forces can act either at *fixed points* on the body, or they can have a direction *perpendicular to their displacement*. Examples include the reactions at a pin support about which a body rotates, the normal reaction acting on a body that moves along a fixed surface, and the weight of a body when the center of gravity of the body moves in a *horizontal plane*, Fig. 18–10. A rolling resistance force $\mathbf{F}_r$ acting on a round body as it *rolls without slipping* over a rough surface also does no work, Fig. 18–10.* This is because, during any *instant of time* $dt$, $\mathbf{F}_r$ acts at a point on the body which has *zero velocity* (instantaneous center, $IC$), and so the work done by the force on the point is zero. In other words, the point is not displaced in the direction of the force during this instant. Since $\mathbf{F}_r$ contacts successive points for only an instant, the work of $\mathbf{F}_r$ will be zero.

---

*The work done by the frictional force *when the body slips* has been discussed in Sec. 14.3.

## 18.3  The Work of a Couple

When a body subjected to a couple undergoes general plane motion, the two couple forces do work *only* when the body undergoes a *rotation*. To show this, consider the body in Fig. 18–11*a*, which is subjected to a couple moment $M = Fr$. Any general differential displacement of the body can be considered as a translation plus rotation. When the body *translates*, such that the *component of displacement* along the line of action of the forces is $ds_t$, Fig. 18–11*b*, clearly the "positive" work of one force *cancels* the "negative" work of the other. If the body undergoes a differential rotation $d\theta$ about an axis which is perpendicular to the plane of the couple and intersects the plane at point $O$, Fig. 18–11*c*, then each force undergoes a displacement $ds_\theta = (r/2)\, d\theta$ in the direction of the force. Hence, the total work done is

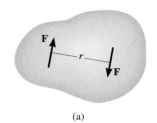

(a)

$$dU_M = F\left(\frac{r}{2}d\theta\right) + F\left(\frac{r}{2}d\theta\right) = (Fr)\, d\theta$$

$$= M\, d\theta$$

Translation
(b)

Here the line of action of $d\theta$ is parallel to the line of action of $M$. This is *always the case for general plane motion*, since $\mathbf{M}$ and $d\boldsymbol{\theta}$ are perpendicular to the plane of motion. Furthermore, the resultant work is *positive* when $\mathbf{M}$ and $d\boldsymbol{\theta}$ have the *same sense of direction* and *negative* if these vectors have an *opposite sense of direction*.

When the body rotates in the plane through a finite angle $\theta$ measured in radians, from $\theta_1$ to $\theta_2$, the work of a couple is

Rotation
(c)

**Fig. 18–11**

$$U_M = \int_{\theta_1}^{\theta_2} M\, d\theta \qquad (18\text{–}11)$$

If the couple moment $\mathbf{M}$ has a *constant magnitude*, then

$$U_M = M(\theta_2 - \theta_1) \qquad (18\text{–}12)$$

Here the work is *positive* provided $\mathbf{M}$ and $(\boldsymbol{\theta}_2 - \boldsymbol{\theta}_1)$ are in the same direction.

# EXAMPLE 18.2

(a)

(b)

Fig. 18–12

The bar shown in Fig. 18–12a has a mass of 10 kg and is subjected to a couple moment of $M = 50 \, \text{N} \cdot \text{m}$ and a force of $P = 80 \, \text{N}$, which is always applied perpendicular to the end of the bar. Also, the spring has an unstretched length of 0.5 m and remains in the vertical position due to the roller guide at $B$. Determine the total work done by all the forces acting on the bar when it has rotated downward from $\theta = 0°$ to $\theta = 90°$.

**Solution**

First the free-body diagram of the bar is drawn in order to account for all the forces that act on it, Fig. 18–12b.

*Weight W.* Since the weight $10(9.81) \, \text{N} = 98.1 \, \text{N}$ is displaced downward 1.5 m, the work is

$$U_W = 98.1 \, \text{N}(1.5 \, \text{m}) = 147.2 \, \text{J}$$

Why is the work positive?

*Couple Moment M.* The couple moment rotates through an angle of $\theta = \pi/2$ rad. Hence

$$U_M = 50 \, \text{N} \cdot \text{m}(\pi/2) = 78.5 \, \text{J}$$

*Spring Force $F_s$.* When $\theta = 0°$ the spring is stretched $(0.75 \, \text{m} - 0.5) = 0.25 \, \text{m}$, and when $\theta = 90°$, the stretch is $(2 \, \text{m} + 0.75 \text{m}) - 0.5\text{m} = 2.25 \, \text{m}$. Thus

$$U_s = -[\tfrac{1}{2}(30 \, \text{N/m})(2.25 \, \text{m})^2 - \tfrac{1}{2}(30 \, \text{N/m})(0.25 \, \text{m})^2] = -75.0 \, \text{J}$$

By inspection the spring does negative work on the bar since $F_s$ acts in the opposite direction to displacement. This checks with the result.

*Force P.* As the bar moves downward, the force is displaced through a distance of $(\pi/2)(3 \, \text{m}) = 4.712 \, \text{m}$. The work is positive. Why?

$$U_P = 80 \, \text{N}(4.712 \, \text{m}) = 377.0 \, \text{J}$$

*Pin Reactions.* Forces $\mathbf{A}_x$ and $\mathbf{A}_y$ do no work since they are not displaced.

*Total Work.* The work of all the forces when the bar is displaced is thus

$$U = 147.2 \, \text{J} + 78.5 \, \text{J} - 75.0 \, \text{J} + 377.0 \, \text{J} = 528 \, \text{J} \qquad \textit{Ans.}$$

## 18.4 Principle of Work and Energy

By applying the principle of work and energy developed in Sec. 14.2 to each of the particles of a rigid body and adding the results algebraically, since energy is a scalar, the principle of work and energy for a rigid body becomes

$$T_1 + \Sigma U_{1-2} = T_2 \qquad (18\text{–}13)$$

This equation states that the body's initial translational *and* rotational kinetic energy, plus the work done by all the external forces and couple moments acting on the body as the body moves from its initial to its final position, is equal to the body's final translational *and* rotational kinetic energy. Note that the work of the body's *internal forces* does not have to be considered since the body is rigid. These forces occur in equal but opposite collinear pairs, so that when the body moves, the work of one force cancels that of its counterpart. Furthermore, since the body is rigid, *no relative movement* between these forces occurs, so that no internal work is done.

When several rigid bodies are pin connected, connected by inextensible cables, or in mesh with one another, Eq. 18–13 may be applied to the entire system of connected bodies. In all these cases the internal forces, which hold the various members together, do no work and hence are eliminated from the analysis.

The work of the torque or moment developed by the driving gears on the two motors is transformed into kinetic energy of rotation of the drum of the mixer.

## PROCEDURE FOR ANALYSIS

The principle of work and energy is used to solve kinetic problems that involve *velocity, force*, and *displacement*, since these terms are involved in the formulation. For application, it is suggested that the following procedure be used.

### Kinetic Energy (Kinematic Diagrams).

- The kinetic energy of a body is made up of two parts. Kinetic energy of translation is referenced to the velocity of the mass center, $T = \frac{1}{2}mv_G^2$, and kinetic energy of rotation is determined from knowing the moment of inertia about the mass center, $T = \frac{1}{2}I_G\omega^2$. In the special case of rotation about a fixed axis, these two kinetic energies are combined and can be expressed as $T = \frac{1}{2}I_O\omega^2$, where $I_O$ is the moment of inertia about the axis of rotation.

- *Kinematic diagrams* for velocity may be useful for determining $v_G$ and $\omega$ or for establishing a *relationship* between $v_G$ and $\omega$.*

### Work (Free-Body Diagram).

- Draw a free-body diagram of the body when it is located at an intermediate point along the path in order to account for all the forces and couple moments which do work on the body as it moves along the path.

- A force does work when it moves through a displacement in the direction of the force.

- Forces that are functions of displacement must be integrated to obtain the work. Graphically, the work is equal to the area under the force–displacement curve.

- The work of a weight is the product of its magnitude and the vertical displacement, $U_W = Wy$. It is positive when the weight moves downwards.

- The work of a spring is of the form $U_s = \frac{1}{2}ks^2$, where $k$ is the spring stiffness and $s$ is the stretch or compression of the spring.

- The work of a couple is the product of the couple moment and the angle in radians through which it rotates.

- Since *algebraic addition* of the work terms is required, it is important that the proper sign of each term be specified. Specifically, work is *positive* when the force (couple moment) is in the *same direction* as its displacement (rotation); otherwise, it is negative.

### Principle of Work and Energy.

- Apply the principle of work and energy, $T_1 + \Sigma U_{1-2} = T_2$. Since this is a scalar equation, it can be used to solve for only one unknown when it is applied to a single rigid body.

*A brief review of Secs. 16.5 to 16.7 may prove helpful in solving problems, since computations for kinetic energy require a kinematic analysis of velocity.

# EXAMPLE 18.3

The 30-kg disk shown in Fig. 18–13a is pin supported at its center. Determine the number of revolutions it must make to attain an angular velocity of 20 rad/s starting from rest. It is acted upon by a constant force $F = 10$ N, which is applied to a cord wrapped around its periphery, and a constant couple moment $M = 5$ N·m. Neglect the mass of the cord in the calculation.

$M = 5$ N·m

0.2 m

$F = 10$ N

(a)

## Solution

*Kinetic Energy.* Since the disk rotates about a fixed axis, the kinetic energy can be computed using $T = \frac{1}{2}I_O\omega^2$, where the moment of inertia is $I_O = \frac{1}{2}mr^2$. Initially, the disk is at rest, so that

$$T_1 = 0$$
$$T_2 = \tfrac{1}{2}I_O\omega_2^2 = \tfrac{1}{2}[\tfrac{1}{2}(30\text{ kg})(0.2\text{ m})^2](20\text{ rad/s})^2 = 120\text{ J}$$

*Work (Free-Body Diagram).* As shown in Fig. 18–13b, the pin reactions $\mathbf{O}_x$ and $\mathbf{O}_y$ and the weight (294.3 N) do no work, since they are not displaced. The *couple moment*, having a constant magnitude, does positive work $U_M = M\theta$ as the disk *rotates* through a clockwise angle of $\theta$ rad, and the *constant force* $\mathbf{F}$ does positive work $U_{F_c} = Fs$ as the cord *moves* downward $s = \theta r = \theta(0.2\text{ m})$.

*Principle of Work and Energy*

$$\{T_1\} + \{\Sigma U_{1-2}\} = \{T_2\}$$
$$\{T_1\} + \{M\theta + Fs\} = \{T_2\}$$
$$\{0\} + \{(5\text{ N·m})\theta + (10\text{ N})\theta(0.2\text{ m})\} = \{120\text{ J}\}$$
$$\theta = 17.1\text{ rad} = 17.1\text{ rad}\left(\frac{1\text{ rev}}{2\pi\text{ rad}}\right) = 2.73\text{ rev} \qquad Ans.$$

This problem has also been solved in Example 17.9. Compare the two methods of solution and note that since force, velocity, and displacement $\theta$ are involved, a work-energy approach yields a more direct solution.

294.3 N

$M = 5$ N·m

$\mathbf{O}_x$

$\mathbf{O}_y$

0.2 m

$F = 10$ N

(b)

Fig. 18–13

**E X A M P L E  18.4**

The 700-kg pipe is equally suspended from the two tines of the fork lift shown in the photo. It is undergoing a swinging motion such that when $\theta = 30°$ it is momentarily at rest. Determine the normal and frictional forces acting on each tine which are needed to support the pipe at the instant $\theta = 0°$. Measurements of the pipe and the suspender are shown in Fig. 18–14a. Neglect the mass of the suspender and the thickness of the pipe.

(a)

Fig. 18–14

**Solution**

We must use the equations of motion to find the forces on the tines since these forces do no work. Before doing this, however, we will apply the principle of work and energy to determine the angular velocity of the pipe when $\theta = 0°$.

*Kinetic Energy (Kinematic Diagram).*  Since the pipe is originally at rest, then

$$T_1 = 0$$

The final kinetic energy may be computed with reference to either the fixed point $O$ or the center of mass $G$. For the calculation we will consider the pipe to be a thin ring so that $I_G = mr^2$. If point $G$ is considered, we have

$$T_2 = \tfrac{1}{2}m(v_G)_2^2 + \tfrac{1}{2}I_G\omega_2^2$$
$$= \tfrac{1}{2}(700 \text{ kg})[(0.4 \text{ m})\omega_2]^2 + \tfrac{1}{2}[700 \text{ kg}(0.15 \text{ m})^2]\omega_2^2$$
$$= 63.875\omega_2^2$$

If point $O$ is considered then the parallel-axis theorem must be used to determine $I_O$. Hence,

$$T_2 = \tfrac{1}{2}I_O\omega_2^2 = \tfrac{1}{2}[700 \text{ kg}(0.15 \text{ m})^2 + 700 \text{ kg}(0.4 \text{ m})^2]\omega_2^2$$
$$= 63.875\omega_2^2$$

*Work (Free-Body Diagram).*  Fig. 18–14*b*. The normal and frictional forces on the tines do no work since they do not move as the pipe swings. The weight, centered at $G$, does positive work since the weight moves downward through a vertical distance $\Delta y = 0.4\text{m} - 0.4 \cos 30° \text{ m} = 0.05359 \text{ m}$.

(b)

*Principle of Work and Energy*

$$\{T_1\} + \{\Sigma U_{1-2}\} = \{T_2\}$$
$$\{0\} + \{700(9.81) \text{ N}(0.05359 \text{ m})\} = \{63.875\omega_2^2\}$$
$$\omega_2 = 2.40 \text{ rad/s}$$

*Equations of Motion.*  Referring to the free-body and kinetic diagrams shown in Fig. 18–14*c*, and using the result for $\omega_2$, we have

$$\xleftarrow{+} \Sigma F_t = m(a_G)_t; \qquad F_T = 700(a_G)_t$$
$$+\uparrow \Sigma F_n = m(a_G)_n; \quad N_T - 700(9.81) \text{ N} = 700 \text{ kg}(2.40 \text{ rad/s})^2(0.4 \text{ m})$$
$$\zeta + \Sigma M_O = I_O\alpha; \quad 0 = [700 \text{ kg}(0.15 \text{ m})^2 + 700 \text{ kg}(0.4 \text{ m})^2]\alpha$$

Since $(a_G)_t = 0.4\alpha$, then

$$\alpha = 0, \ (a_G)_t = 0$$
$$F_T = 0$$
$$N_T = 8.48 \text{ kN}$$

There are two tines used to support the load, therefore

$$F'_T = 0 \qquad\qquad\qquad\qquad Ans.$$

$$N'_T = \frac{8.48 \text{ kN}}{2} = 4.24 \text{ kN} \qquad\qquad Ans.$$

Due to the swinging motion the tines are subjected to a *greater* normal force than would be the case if the load was static, in which case $N'_T = 700(9.81)\text{N}/2 = 3.43 \text{ kN}$.

$$\mathbf{F}_T \xrightarrow{\quad} \mathbf{N}_T \quad O$$

(c)

## EXAMPLE 18.5

The wheel shown in Fig. 18–15a weighs 20 kg and has a radius of gyration $k_G = 0.18$ m about its mass center $G$. If it is subjected to a clockwise couple moment of 22 N · m and rolls from rest without slipping, determine its angular velocity after its center $G$ moves 0.15 m. The spring has a stiffness $k = 160$ N/m and is initially unstretched when the couple moment is applied.

$k = 160$ N/m

(a)

(b)

(c)

**Fig. 18–15**

### Solution

*Kinetic Energy (Kinematic Diagram).* Since the wheel is initially at rest,

$$T_1 = 0$$

The kinematic diagram of the wheel when it is in the final position is shown in Fig. 18–15b. Hence, the final kinetic energy is

$$T_2 = \tfrac{1}{2}m(v_G)_2^2 + \tfrac{1}{2}I_G\omega_2^2$$

$$= \frac{1}{2}(20)(v_G)_2^2 + \frac{1}{2}[(20)(0.18 \text{ m})^2]\omega_2^2$$

The velocity of the mass center can be related to the angular velocity from the instantaneous center of zero velocity ($IC$), i.e., $(v_G)_2 = 0.24\omega_2$. Substituting into the above equation and simplifying, we have

$$T_2 = 0.9\omega_2^2$$

*Work (Free-Body Diagram).* As shown in Fig. 18–15c, only the spring force $\mathbf{F}_s$ and the couple moment do work. The normal force does not move along its line of action and the frictional force does *no work*, since the wheel does not slip as it rolls.

The work of $\mathbf{F}_s$ may be computed using $U_s = -\tfrac{1}{2}ks^2$. Here the work is negative since $\mathbf{F}_s$ is in the opposite direction to displacement. Since the wheel does not slip when the center $G$ moves 0.15 m, then the wheel rotates $\theta = s_G/r_{G/IC} = 0.15$ m/0.24 m $= 0.625$ rad, Fig. 18–15b. Hence, the spring stretches $s_A = \theta r_{A/IC} = 0.625$ rad (0.48 m) = 0.3 m.

*Principle of Work and Energy*

$$\{T_1\} + \{\Sigma U_{1-2}\} = \{T_2\}$$
$$\{T_1\} + \{M\theta - \tfrac{1}{2}ks^2\} = \{T_2\}$$

$$\{0\} + 22 \text{ N} \cdot \text{m} (0.625 \text{ rad}) - \frac{1}{2}(160 \text{ N/m})(0.3 \text{ m})^2 = (0.9)(\omega_2)^2 \text{ J}$$

$$\omega_2 = 2.70 \text{ rad/s} \downarrow \qquad\qquad \textit{Ans.}$$

# E X A M P L E 18.6

The 10-kg rod shown in Fig. 18–16a is constrained so that its ends move along the grooved slots. The rod is initially at rest when $\theta = 0°$. If the slider block at $B$ is acted upon by a horizontal force $P = 50$ N, determine the angular velocity of the rod at the instant $\theta = 45°$. Neglect friction and the mass of blocks $A$ and $B$.

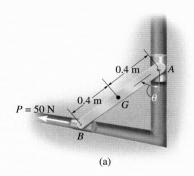

(a)

### Solution

Why can the principle of work and energy be used to solve this problem?

*Kinetic Energy (Kinematic Diagrams).* Two kinematic diagrams of the rod, when it is, in the initial position 1 and final position 2, are shown in Fig. 18–16b. When the rod is in position 1, $T_1 = 0$ since $(\mathbf{v}_G)_1 = \boldsymbol{\omega}_1 = \mathbf{0}$. In position 2 the angular velocity is $\boldsymbol{\omega}_2$ and the velocity of the mass center is $(\mathbf{v}_G)_2$. Hence, the kinetic energy is

$$T_2 = \tfrac{1}{2}m(v_G)_2^2 + \tfrac{1}{2}I_G\omega_2^2$$
$$= \tfrac{1}{2}(10 \text{ kg})(v_G)_2^2 + \tfrac{1}{2}[\tfrac{1}{12}(10 \text{ kg})(0.8 \text{ m})^2]\omega_2^2$$
$$= 5(v_G)_2^2 + 0.267(\omega_2)^2$$

The two unknowns $(v_G)_2$ and $\omega_2$ may be related from the instantaneous center of zero velocity for the rod. Fig. 18–16b. It is seen that as $A$ moves downward with a velocity $(\mathbf{v}_A)_2$, $B$ moves horizontally to the left with a velocity $(\mathbf{v}_B)_2$. Knowing these directions, the $IC$ is determined as shown in the figure. Hence,

$$(v_G)_2 = r_{G/IC}\omega_2 = (0.4 \tan 45° \text{ m})\omega_2$$
$$= 0.4\omega_2$$

Therefore,

$$T_2 = 0.8\omega_2^2 + 0.267\omega_2^2 = 1.067\omega_2^2$$

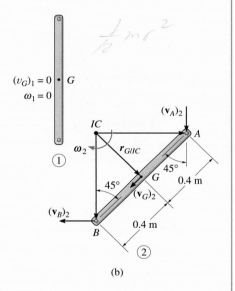

(b)

*Work (Free-Body Diagram).* Fig. 18–16c. The normal forces $\mathbf{N}_A$ and $\mathbf{N}_B$ do no work as the rod is displaced. Why? The 98.1-N weight is displaced a vertical distance of $\Delta y = (0.4 - 0.4 \cos 45°)$ m; whereas the 50-N force moves a horizontal distance of $s = (0.8 \sin 45°)$ m. Both of these forces do positive work. Why?

*Principle of Work and Energy*

$$\{T_1\} + \{\Sigma U_{1-2}\} = \{T_2\}$$
$$\{T_1\} + \{W\,\Delta y + Ps\} = \{T_2\}$$

$$\{0\} + \{98.1 \text{ N}(0.4 \text{ m} - 0.4 \cos 45° \text{ m}) + 50 \text{ N}(0.8 \sin 45° \text{ m})\}$$
$$= \{1.067\omega_2^2 \text{J}\}$$

Solving for $\omega_2$ gives

$$\omega_2 = 6.11 \text{ rad/s} \downarrow \qquad\qquad Ans.$$

(c)

**Fig. 18–16**

# PROBLEMS

**18-1.** At a given instant the body of mass $m$ has an angular velocity $\omega$ and its mass center has a velocity $\mathbf{v}_G$. Show that its kinetic energy can be represented as $T = \frac{1}{2}I_{IC}\omega^2$, where $I_{IC}$ is the moment of inertia of the body computed about the instantaneous axis of zero velocity, located a distance $r_{G/IC}$ from the mass center as shown.

Prob. 18–1

**18-2.** The wheel is made from a 5-kg thin ring and two 2-kg slender rods. If the torsional spring attached to the wheel's center has a stiffness $k = 2\,\text{N} \cdot \text{m/rad}$, so that the torque on the center of the wheel is $M = (2\theta)\,\text{N} \cdot \text{m}$, where $\theta$ is in radians, determine the maximum angular velocity of the wheel if it is rotated two revolutions and then released from rest.

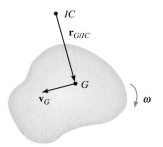

Prob. 18–2

**18-3.** At the instant shown, the 30-kg disk has a counterclockwise angular velocity of 5 rad/s when its center has a velocity of 10 m/s. Determine the kinetic energy of the disk at this instant.

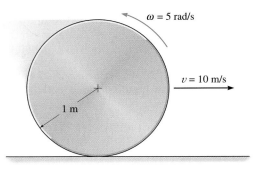

Prob. 18–3

**\*18-4.** The double pulley consists of two parts that are attached to one another. It has a mass of 50 kg and a centroidal radius of gyration of $k_O = 0.6$ m and is turning with an angular velocity of 20 rad/s clockwise. Determine the kinetic energy of the system. Assume that neither cable slips on the pulley.

Prob. 18–4

**18-5.** At the instant shown, link $AB$ has an angular velocity $\omega_{AB} = 2$ rad/s. If each link is considered as a uniform slender bar with a mass of 0.5 kg/cm, determine the total kinetic energy of the system.

**Prob. 18–5**

**18-6.** Solve Prob. 17–58 using the principle of work and energy.

**18-7.** Solve Prob. 17–59 using the principle of work and energy.

**\*18-8.** Solve Prob. 17–63 using the principle of work and energy.

**18-9.** A force of $P = 20$ N is applied to the cable, which causes the 175-kg reel to turn since it is resting on the two rollers $A$ and $B$ of the dispenser. Determine the angular velocity of the reel after it has made two revolutions starting from rest. Neglect the mass of the rollers and the mass of the cable. The radius of gyration of the reel about its center axis is $k_G = 0.42$ m.

**18-10.** The tub of the mixer has a weight of 350 N ($\approx 35$ kg) and a radius of gyration $k_G = 0.65$ m about its center of gravity. If a constant torque $M = 300$ N $\cdot$ m is applied to the dumping wheel, determine the angular velocity of the tub when it has rotated $\theta = 90°$. Originally the tub is at rest when $\theta = 0°$.

**Prob. 18–10**

**18-11.** A yo-yo has a weight of 3 N ($\approx 0.3$ kg) and a radius of gyration $k_O = 0.03$ m. If it is released from rest, determine how far it must descend in order to attain an angular velocity $\omega = 70$ rad/s. Neglect the mass of the string and assume that the string is wound around the central peg such that the mean radius at which it unravels is $r = 0.01$ m.

**Prob. 18–9**

**Prob. 18–11**

**\*18-12.** The soap-box car has a weight of 550 N ($\approx$ 55 kg), including the passenger but *excluding* its four wheels. Each wheel has a weight of 25 N ($\approx$ 2.5 kg), radius of 0.15 m, and a radius of gyration $k = 0.09$ m, computed about an axis passing through the wheel's axle. Determine the car's speed after it has traveled 30 m starting from rest. The wheels roll without slipping. Neglect air resistance.

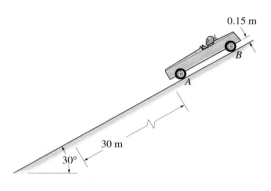

**Prob. 18–12**

**18-13.** The pendulum of the Charpy impact machine has a mass of 50 kg and a radius of gyration of $k_A = 1.75$ m. If it is released from rest when $\theta = 0°$, determine its angular velocity just before it strikes the specimen $S$, $\theta = 90°$.

**Prob. 18–13**

**18-14.** A motor supplies a constant torque or twist of $M = 120$ kN $\cdot$ m to the drum. If the drum has a weight of 30 kN ($\approx$ 3 tonnes) and a radius of gyration of $k_O = 0.8$ m, determine the speed of the 15-kN ($\approx$ 1500-kg) crate $A$ after it rises $s = 4$ m starting from rest. Neglect the mass of the cord.

**Prob. 18–14**

**18-15.** The hand winch is used to lift the 50-kg load. Determine the work required to rotate the handle five revolutions. The gear at $A$ has a radius of 20 mm.

**Prob. 18–15**

**\*18-16.** The 4-kg slender rod is subjected to the force and couple moment. When it is in the position shown it has an angular velocity $\omega_1 = 6$ rad/s. Determine its angular velocity at the instant it has rotated downward 90°. The force is always applied perpendicular to the axis of the rod. Motion occurs in the vertical plane.

**18-17.** The 4-kg slender rod is subjected to the force and couple moment. When the rod is in the position shown it has a angular velocity $\omega_1 = 6$ rad/s. Determine its angular velocity at the instant it has rotated 360°. The force is always applied perpendicular to the axis of the rod and motion occurs in the vertical plane.

Probs. 18–16/17

**18-18.** The elevator car $E$ has a mass of 1.80 Mg and the counterweight $C$ has a mass of 2.30 Mg. If a motor turns the driving sheave $A$ with a constant torque of $M = 100$ N · m, determine the speed of the elevator when it has ascended 10 m starting from rest. Each sheave $A$ and $B$ has a mass of 150 kg and a radius of gyration of $k = 0.2$ m about its mass center or pinned axis. Neglect the mass of the cable and assume the cable does not slip on the sheaves.

**18-19.** The elevator car $E$ has a mass of 1.80 Mg and the counterweight $C$ has a mass of 2.30 Mg. If a motor turns the driving sheave $A$ with a torque of $M = (0.06\theta^2 + 7.5)$ N · m, where $\theta$ is in radians, determine the speed of the elevator when it has ascended 12 m starting from rest. Each sheave $A$ and $B$ has a mass of 150 kg and a radius of gyration of $k = 0.2$ m about its mass center or pinned axis. Neglect the mass of the cable and assume the cable does not slip on the sheaves.

Probs. 18–18/19

**\*18-20.** The pendulum consists of two slender rods each having a mass of 4 kg/m. If it is acted upon by a moment $M = 50$ N · m and released from the position shown, determine its angular velocity when it has rotated (a) 90° and (b) 180°. Motion occurs in the vertical plane.

Prob. 18–20

**18-21.** A motor supplies a constant torque $M = 6$ kN·m to the winding drum that operates the elevator. If the elevator has a mass of 900 kg, the counterweight $C$ has a mass of 200 kg, and the winding drum has a mass of 600 kg and radius of gyration about its axis of $k = 0.6$ m, determine the speed of the elevator after it rises 5 m starting from rest. Neglect the mass of the pulleys.

**Prob. 18–21**

**18-22.** The 20-kg disk is originally at rest, and the spring holds it in equilibrium. A couple moment of $M = 30$ N·m is then applied to the disk as shown. Determine its angular velocity at the instant its mass center $G$ has moved 0.8 m down along the inclined plane. The disk rolls without slipping.

**18-23.** The 20-kg disk is originally at rest, and the spring holds it in equilibrium. A couple moment of $M = 30$ N·m is then applied to the disk as shown. Determine how far the center of mass of the disk travels down along the incline, measured from the equilibrium position, before it stops. The disk rolls without slipping.

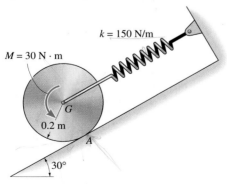

**Probs. 18–22/23**

**\*18-24.** The linkage consists of two 8-kg rods $AB$ and $CD$ and a 10-kg bar $AD$. When $\theta = 0°$, rod $AB$ is rotating with an angular velocity $\omega_{AB} = 2$ rad/s. If rod $CD$ is subjected to a couple moment $M = 150$ N·m and bar $AD$ is subjected to a horizontal force $P = 200$ N as shown, determine $\omega_{AB}$ at the instant $\theta = 90°$.

**18-25.** The linkage consists of two 8-kg rods $AB$ and $CD$ and a 10-kg bar $AD$. When $\theta = 0°$, rod $AB$ is rotating with an angular velocity $\omega_{AB} = 2$ rad/s. If rod $CD$ is subjected to a couple moment $M = 150$ N·m and bar $AD$ is subjected to a horizontal force $P = 200$ N as shown, determine $\omega_{AB}$ at the instant $\theta = 45°$.

**Probs. 18–24/25**

**18-26.** The spool has a weight of 5000 N ($\approx 500$ kg) and a radius of gyration of $k_G = 1.75$ m. A horizontal force of $P = 150$ N is applied to a cable wrapped around its inner core. If the spool is originally at rest, determine its angular velocity after the mass center $G$ has moved 6 m to the left. The spool rolls without slipping. Neglect the mass of the cable.

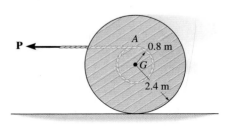

**Prob. 18–26**

**18-27.** The uniform bar has a mass $m$ and length $l$. If it is released from rest when $\theta = 0°$, determine the angle $\theta$ at which it first begins to slip. The coefficient of static friction at $O$ is $\mu_s = 0.3$.

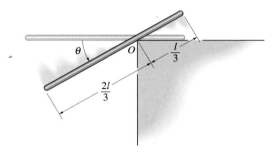

Prob. 18–27

**18-29.** The two 2-kg gears $A$ and $B$ are attached to the ends of a 3-kg slender bar. The gears roll within the fixed ring gear $C$, which lies in the horizontal plane. If a 10-N · m torque is applied to the center of the bar as shown, determine the number of revolutions the bar must rotate starting from rest in order for it to have an angular velocity of $\omega_{AB} = 20$ rad/s. For the calculation, assume the gears can be approximated by thin disks. What is the result if the gears lie in the vertical plane?

Prob. 18–29

**\*18-28.** The system consists of a 20-kg disk $A$, 4-kg slender rod $BC$, and a 1-kg smooth collar $C$. If the disk rolls without slipping, determine the velocity of the collar at the instant the rod becomes horizontal, i.e., $\theta = 0°$. The system is released from rest when $\theta = 45°$.

**18-30.** The assembly consists of two 150-N ($\approx$ 15-kg) slender rods and a 200-N ($\approx$ 20-kg) disk. If the spring is unstretched when $\theta = 45°$ and the assembly is released from rest at this position, determine the angular velocity of rod $AB$ at the instant $\theta = 0°$. The disk rolls without slipping.

Prob. 18–28

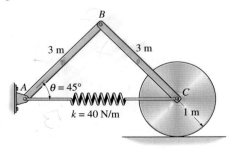

Prob. 18–30

**18-31.** The uniform door has a mass of 20 kg and can be treated as a thin plate having the dimensions shown. If it is connected to a torsional spring at $A$, which has a stiffness of $k = 80 \text{ N} \cdot \text{m/rad}$, determine the required initial twist of the spring in radians so that the door has an angular velocity of 12 rad/s when it closes at $\theta = 0°$ after being opened at $\theta = 90°$ and released from rest. *Hint:* For a torsional spring $M = k\theta$, when $k$ is the stiffness and $\theta$ is the angle of twist.

Prob. 18–31

**18-33.** A ball of mass $m$ and radius $r$ is cast onto the horizontal surface such that it rolls without slipping. Determine the minimum speed $v_G$ of its mass center $G$ so that it rolls completely around the loop of radius $R + r$ without leaving the track.

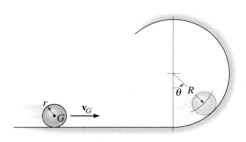

Prob. 18–33

**\*18-32.** Pulley $A$ weighs 15 kN ($\approx 1500$ kg) and has a radius of gyration of $k_O = 0.8$ m. If the system is released from rest, determine the velocity of the center $O$ of the pulley after the 10-kN ($\approx 1000$-kg) block moves downward 4 m. Neglect the mass of the pulley at $B$.

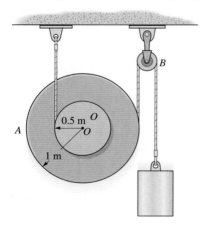

Prob. 18–32

**18-34.** The beam has a weight of 7500 N ($\approx 750$ kg) and is being raised to a vertical position by pulling very slowly on its bottom end $A$. If the cord fails when $\theta = 60°$ and the beam is essentially at rest, determine the speed of $A$ at the instant cord $BC$ becomes vertical. Neglect friction and the mass of the cords, and treat the beam as a slender rod.

Prob. 18–34

## 18.5 Conservation of Energy

When a force system acting on a rigid body consists only of *conservative forces*, the conservation of energy theorem may be used to solve a problem which otherwise would be solved using the principle of work and energy. This theorem is often easier to apply since the work of a conservative force is *independent of the path* and depends only on the initial and final positions of the body. It was shown in Sec. 14.5 that the work of a conservative force may be expressed as the difference in the body's potential energy measured from an arbitrarily selected reference or datum.

**Gravitational Potential Energy.** Since the total weight of a body can be considered concentrated at its center of gravity, the *gravitational potential energy* of the body is determined by knowing the height of the body's center of gravity above or below a horizontal datum. Measuring $y_G$ as *positive upward*, the gravitational potential energy of the body is thus

$$V_g = W y_G \qquad (18-14)$$

Here the potential energy is *positive* when $y_G$ is positive, since the weight has the ability to do *positive work* when the body is moved back to the datum, Fig. 18–17. Likewise, if the body is located *below* the datum $(-y_G)$, the gravitational potential energy is *negative*, since the weight does *negative work* when the body is returned to the datum.

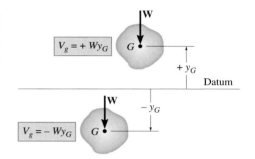

Gravitational potential energy

**Fig. 18–17**

**Elastic Potential Energy.** The force developed by an elastic spring is also a conservative force. The *elastic potential energy* which a spring imparts to an attached body when the spring is elongated or compressed from an initial undeformed position ($s = 0$) to a final position $s$, Fig. 18–18, is

$$V_e = +\tfrac{1}{2}ks^2 \qquad (18-15)$$

In the deformed position, the spring force acting *on the body* always has the capacity for doing positive work when the spring is returned back to its original undeformed position (see Sec. 14.5).

Elastic potential energy

**Fig. 18–18**

**Conservation of Energy.** In general, if a body is subjected to both gravitational and elastic forces, the total *potential energy* is expressed as a potential function $V$ represented as the algebraic sum

$$V = V_g + V_e \qquad (18\text{–}16)$$

Here measurement of $V$ depends on the location of the body with respect to the selected datum.

Realizing that the work of conservative forces can be written as a difference in their potential energies, i.e., $(\Sigma U_{1-2})_{\text{cons}} = V_1 - V_2$, Eq. 14–16, we can rewrite the principle of work and energy for a rigid body as

$$T_1 + V_1 + (\Sigma U_{1-2})_{\text{noncons}} = T_2 + V_2 \qquad (18\text{–}17)$$

Here $(\Sigma U_{1-2})_{\text{noncons}}$ represents the work of the nonconservative forces such as friction. If this term is zero, then

$$T_1 + V_1 = T_2 + V_2 \qquad (18\text{–}18)$$

This equation is referred to as the conservation of mechanical energy. It states that the *sum* of the potential and kinetic energies of the body remains *constant* when the body moves from one position to another. It also applies to a system of smooth, pin-connected rigid bodies, bodies connected by inextensible cords, and bodies in mesh with other bodies. In all these cases the forces acting at the points of contact are *eliminated* from the analysis, since they occur in equal but opposite collinear pairs and each pair of forces moves through an equal distance when the system undergoes a displacement.

It is important to remember that only problems involving conservative force systems may be solved by using Eq. 18–18. As stated in Sec. 14.5, friction or other drag-resistant forces, which depend on velocity or acceleration, are nonconservative. The work of such forces is transformed into thermal energy used to heat up the surfaces of contact, and consequently this energy is dissipated into the surroundings and may not be recovered. Therefore, problems involving frictional forces can be solved by using either the principle of work and energy written in the form of Eq. 18–17, if it applies, or the equations of motion.

The torsional springs located at the top of the garage door wind up as the door is lowered. When the door is raised, the potential energy stored in the springs is then transferred into gravitational potential energy of the door's weight, thereby making it easy to open.

## PROCEDURE FOR ANALYSIS

The conservation of energy equation is used to solve problems involving *velocity, displacement*, and *conservative force systems*. For application it is suggested that the following procedure be used.

*Potential Energy.*

- Draw two diagrams showing the body located at its initial and final positions along the path.

- If the center of gravity, $G$, is subjected to a *vertical displacement*, establish a fixed horizontal datum from which to measure the body's gravitational potential energy $V_g$.

- Data pertaining to the elevation $y_G$ of the body's center of gravity from the datum and the extension or compression of any connecting springs can be determined from the problem geometry and listed on the two diagrams.

- Recall that the potential energy $V = V_g + V_e$. Here $V_g = W y_G$, which can be positive or negative, and $V_e = \frac{1}{2} k s^2$, which is always positive.

*Kinetic Energy.*

- The kinetic energy of the body consists of two parts, namely translational kinetic energy, $T = \frac{1}{2} m v_G^2$, and rotational kinetic energy, $T = \frac{1}{2} I_G \omega^2$.

- Kinematic diagrams for velocity may be useful for determining $v_G$ and $\omega$ for establishing a *relationship* between these quantities.

*Conservation of Energy.*

- Apply the conservation of energy equation $T_1 + V_1 = T_2 + V_2$.

# EXAMPLE 18.7

(a)

(b)

(c)

**Fig. 18–19**

The 10-kg rod $AB$ shown in Fig. 18–19a is confined so that its ends move in the horizontal and vertical slots. The spring has a stiffness of $k = 800 \text{ N/m}$ and is unstretched when $\theta = 0°$. Determine the angular velocity of $AB$ when $\theta = 0°$, if the rod is released from rest when $\theta = 30°$. Neglect the mass of the slider blocks.

### Solution

*Potential Energy.* The two diagrams of the rod, when it is located at its initial and final positions, are shown in Fig. 18–19b. The datum, used to measure the gravitational potential energy, is placed in line with the rod when $\theta = 0°$.

When the rod is in position 1, the center of gravity $G$ is located *below the datum* so that the gravitational potential energy is *negative*. Furthermore, (positive) elastic potential energy is stored in the spring, since it is stretched a distance of $s_1 = (0.4 \sin 30°)$ m. Thus,

$$V_1 = -Wy_1 + \tfrac{1}{2}ks_1^2$$
$$= -98.1 \text{ N}(0.2 \sin 30° \text{ m}) + \tfrac{1}{2}(800 \text{ N/m})(0.4 \sin 30° \text{ m})^2 = 6.19 \text{ J}$$

When the rod is in position 2, the potential energy of the rod is zero, since the spring is unstretched, $s_2 = 0$, and the center of gravity $G$ is located at the datum. Thus,

$$V_2 = 0$$

*Kinetic Energy.* The rod is released from rest from position 1, thus $(\mathbf{v}_G)_1 = \mathbf{0}$ and $\boldsymbol{\omega}_1 = \mathbf{0}$, and

$$T_1 = 0$$

In position 2, the angular velocity is $\boldsymbol{\omega}_2$ and the rod's mass center has a velocity of $(\mathbf{v}_G)_2$. Thus,

$$T_2 = \tfrac{1}{2}m(v_G)_2^2 + \tfrac{1}{2}I_G\omega_2^2$$
$$= \tfrac{1}{2}(10 \text{ kg})(v_G)_2^2 + \tfrac{1}{2}[\tfrac{1}{12}(10 \text{ kg})(0.4 \text{ m})^2]\omega_2^2$$

Using *kinematics*, $(\mathbf{v}_G)_2$ can be related to $\boldsymbol{\omega}_2$ as shown in Fig. 18–19c. At the instant considered, the instantaneous center of zero velocity (IC) for the rod is at point $A$; hence, $(v_G)_2 = (r_{G/IC})\omega_2 = (0.2)\omega_2$. Substituting into the above expression and simplifying, we get

$$T_2 = 0.267\omega_2^2$$

*Conservation of Energy*

$$\{T_1\} + \{V_1\} = \{T_2\} + \{V_2\}$$
$$\{0\} + \{6.19\} = \{0.267\omega_2^2\} + \{0\}$$
$$\omega_2 = 4.82 \text{ rad/s} \qquad\qquad Ans.$$

# E X A M P L E  18.8

The disk shown in Fig. 18–20a has a mass of 15 kg and a radius of gyration of $k_G = 0.18$ m, and it is attached to a spring which has a stiffness $k = 30$ N/m and an unstretched length of 0.3 m. If the disk is released from rest in the position shown and rolls without slipping, determine its angular velocity at the instant $G$ moves 0.9 m to the left.

$k = 30$ N/m

1.2 m

0.225 m

0.9 m

(a)

## Solution

*Potential Energy.* Two diagrams of the disk, when it is located in its initial and final positions, are shown in Fig. 18–20b. A gravitational datum is not needed here since the weight is not displaced vertically. From the problem geometry the spring is stretched $s_1 = (\sqrt{0.9^2 + 1.2^2} - 0.3) = 1.2$ m and $s_2 = (1.2 - 0.3) = 0.9$ m in the initial and final positions, respectively. Hence,

$$V_1 = \tfrac{1}{2}ks_1^2 = \tfrac{1}{2}(30 \text{ N/m})(1.2 \text{ m})^2 = 21.6 \text{ J}$$
$$V_2 = \tfrac{1}{2}ks_2^2 = \tfrac{1}{2}(30 \text{ N/m})(0.9 \text{ m})^2 = 12.15 \text{ J}$$

*Kinetic Energy.* The disk is released from rest so that $(\mathbf{v}_G)_1 = \mathbf{0}$, $\boldsymbol{\omega}_1 = \mathbf{0}$, and

$$T_1 = 0$$

In the final position,

$s_2 = 0.9$ m

$s_1 = 1.2$ m

15(9.81) N

15(9.81) N

② ①

(b)

$$T_2 = \frac{1}{2}m(v_G)_2^2 + \frac{1}{2}I_G\omega_2^2$$
$$= \frac{1}{2}(15 \text{ kg})(v_G)_2^2 + \frac{1}{2}[(15 \text{ kg})(0.18 \text{ m})^2]\omega_2^2$$

Since the disk rolls without slipping, $(\mathbf{v}_G)_2$ can be related to $\boldsymbol{\omega}_2$ from the instantaneous center of zero velocity, Fig. 18–20c, i.e., $(v_G)_2 = (0.225 \text{ m})\omega_2$. Substituting and simplifying yields

$$T_2 = 0.6227\omega_2^2$$

$\omega_2$

$(v_G)_2$

0.225 m

IC

(c)

## Conservation of Energy

$$\{T_1\} + \{V_1\} = \{T_2\} + \{V_2\}$$
$$\{0\} + \{21.6\} = \{0.6227\omega_2^2\} + \{12.15\}$$
$$\omega_2 = 3.90 \text{ rad/s} \uparrow \qquad\qquad Ans.$$

**Fig. 18–20**

E X A M P L E 18.9

(a)

(b)

(c)

Fig. 18–21

The 10-kg homogeneous disk shown in Fig. 18–21a is attached to a uniform 5-kg rod $AB$. If the assembly is released from rest when $\theta = 60°$, determine the angular velocity of the rod when $\theta = 0°$. Assume that the disk rolls without slipping. Neglect friction along the guide and the mass of the collar at $B$.

**Solution**

*Potential Energy.* Two diagrams for the rod and disk, when they are located at their initial and final positions, are shown in Fig. 18–21b. For convenience the datum passes through point $A$.

When the system is in position 1, the rod's weight has positive potential energy. Thus,

$$V_1 = W_R y_1 = 49.05 \text{ N}(0.3 \sin 60° \text{ m}) = 12.74 \text{ J}$$

When the system is in position 2, both the weight of the rod and the weight of the disk have zero potential energy. Why? Thus,

$$V_2 = 0$$

*Kinetic Energy.* Since the entire system is at rest at the initial position,

$$T_1 = 0$$

In the final position the rod has an angular velocity $(\boldsymbol{\omega}_R)_2$ and its mass center has a velocity $(\mathbf{v}_G)_2$, Fig. 18–21c. Since the rod is *fully extended* in this position, the disk is momentarily at rest, so $(\boldsymbol{\omega}_D)_2 = \mathbf{0}$ and $(\mathbf{v}_A)_2 = \mathbf{0}$. For the rod $(\mathbf{v}_G)_2$ can be related to $(\boldsymbol{\omega}_R)_2$ from the instantaneous center of zero velocity, which is located at point $A$, Fig. 18–21c. Hence, $(v_G)_2 = r_{G/IC}(\omega_R)_2$ or $(v_G)_2 = 0.3(\omega_R)_2$. Thus,

$$T_2 = \frac{1}{2}m_R(v_G)_2^2 + \frac{1}{2}I_G(\omega_R)_2^2 + \frac{1}{2}m_D(v_A)_2^2 + \frac{1}{2}I_A(\omega_D)_2^2$$

$$= \frac{1}{2}(5 \text{ kg})[0.3 \text{ m}(\omega_R)_2]^2 + \frac{1}{2}\left[\frac{1}{12}(5 \text{ kg})(0.6 \text{ m})^2\right](\omega_R)_2^2 + 0 + 0$$

$$= 0.3(\omega_R)_2^2$$

*Conservation of Energy*

$$\{T_1\} + \{V_1\} = \{T_2\} + \{V_2\}$$
$$\{0\} + \{12.74\} = \{0.3(\omega_R)_2^2\} + \{0\}$$
$$(\omega_R)_2 = 6.52 \text{ rad/s}\downarrow \qquad \textit{Ans.}$$

# PROBLEMS

**18-35.** Solve Prob. 18–13 using the conservation of energy equation.

**\*18-36.** Solve Prob. 18–12 using the conservation of energy equation.

**18-37.** Solve Prob. 18–30 using the conservation of energy equation.

**18-38.** Solve Prob. 18–11 using the conservation of energy equation.

**18-39.** Solve Prob. 18–34 using the conservation of energy equation.

**\*18-40.** Solve Prob. 18–28 using the conservation of energy equation.

**18-41.** The spool has a mass of 50 kg and a radius of gyration $k_O = 0.280$ m. If the 20-kg block $A$ is released from rest, determine the distance the block must fall in order for the spool to have an angular velocity $\omega = 5$ rad/s. Also, what is the tension in the cord while the block is in motion? Neglect the mass of the cord.

**18-42.** When the slender 10-kg bar $AB$ is horizontal it is at rest and the spring is unstretched. Determine the stiffness $k$ of the spring so that the motion of the bar is momentarily stopped when it has rotated downward 90°.

Prob. 18–42

**18-43.** The 50-kg wheel has a radius of gyration about its center of gravity $G$ of $k_G = 0.7$ m. If it rolls without slipping, determine its angular velocity when it has rotated clockwise 90° from the position shown. The spring $AB$ has a stiffness $k = 12$ N/m and an unstretched length of 0.5 m. The wheel is released from rest.

Prob. 18–41

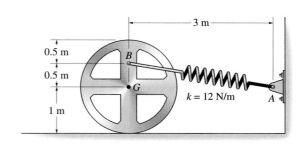

Prob. 18–43

**\*18-44.** The door is made from one piece, whose ends move along the horizontal and vertical tracks. If the door is in the open position, $\theta = 0°$, and then released, determine the speed at which its end $A$ strikes the stop at $C$. Assume the door is a 90-kg thin plate having a width of 3 m.

**Prob. 18–44**

**18-46.** An automobile tire has a mass of 7 kg and radius of gyration $k_G = 0.3$ m. If it is released from rest at $A$ on the incline, determine its angular velocity when it reaches the horizontal plane. The tire rolls without slipping.

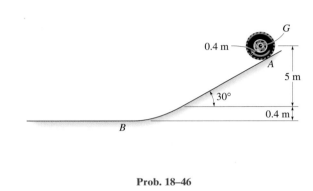

**Prob. 18–46**

**18-45.** The two bars are released from rest at the position $\theta$. Determine their angular velocities at the instant they become horizontal. Neglect the mass of the roller at $C$. Each bar has a mass $m$ and length $L$.

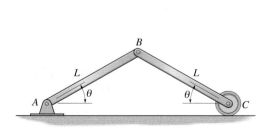

**Prob. 18–45**

**18-47.** The compound disk pulley consists of a hub and attached outer rim. If it has a mass of 3 kg and a radius of gyration $k_G = 45$ mm, determine the speed of block $A$ after $A$ descends 0.2 m from rest. Blocks $A$ and $B$ each have a mass of 2 kg. Neglect the mass of the cords.

**Prob. 18–47**

**\*18-48.** At the instant the spring becomes undeformed, the center of the 40-kg disk has a speed of 4 m/s. From this point determine the distance $d$ the disk moves down the plane before momentarily stopping. The disk rolls without slipping.

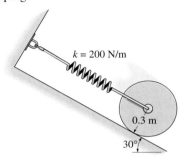

Prob. 18–48

**18-49.** The pendulum consists of a 2-kN ($\approx$ 200-kg) rod $BA$ and a 6-kN ($\approx$ 600-kg) disk. The spring is stretched 0.3 m when the rod is horizontal as shown. If the pendulum is released from rest and rotates about point $D$, determine its angular velocity at the instant the rod becomes vertical. The roller at $C$ allows the spring to remain vertical as the rod falls.

Prob. 18–49

**18-50.** The assembly consists of a 3-kg pulley $A$ and 10-kg pulley $B$. If a 2-kg block is suspended from the cord, determine the block's speed after it descends 0.5 m starting from rest. Neglect the mass of the cord and treat the pulleys as thin disks. No slipping occurs.

Prob. 18–50

**18-51.** A uniform ladder having a weight of 150 N ($\approx$ 15 kg) is released from rest when it is in the vertical position. If it is allowed to fall freely, determine the angle $\theta$ at which the bottom end $A$ starts to lift off the ground. For the calculation, assume the ladder to be a slender rod and neglect friction at $A$.

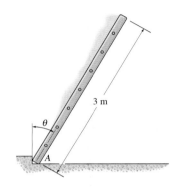

Prob. 18–51

**\*18-52.** The 25-kg slender rod $AB$ is attached to a spring $BC$ which, has an unstretched length of 0.4 m. If the rod is released from rest when $\theta = 30°$, determine its angular velocity at the instant $\theta = 90°$.

**18-53.** The 25-kg slender rod $AB$ is attached to a spring $BC$ which has an unstretched length of 0.4 m. If the rod is released from rest when $\theta = 30°$, determine the angular velocity of the rod the instant the spring becomes unstretched.

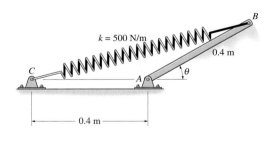

Probs. 18–52/53

**18-54.** A chain that has a negligible mass is draped over the sprocket which has a mass of 2 kg and a radius of gyration of $k_O = 50$ mm. If the 4-kg block $A$ is released from rest in the position $s = 1$ m, determine the angular velocity of the sprocket at the instant $s = 2$ m.

**18-55.** Solve Prob. 18–54 if the chain has a mass of 0.8 kg/m. For the calculation neglect the portion of the chain that wraps over the sprocket.

Probs. 18–54/55

**18-57.** At the instant shown, the 50-kg bar is rotating downwards at 2 rad/s. The spring attached to its end always remains vertical due to the roller guide at $C$. If the spring has an unstretched length of 1 m and a stiffness of $k = 120$ N/m, determine the angular velocity of the bar the instant it has rotated downward 30° below the horizontal.

**18-58.** At the instant shown, the 50-kg bar is rotating downwards at 2 rad/s. The spring attached to its end always remains vertical due to the roller guide at $C$. If the spring has an unstretched length of 1 m and a stiffness of $k = 240$ N/m, determine the angle $\theta$, measured below the horizontal, to which the bar rotates before it momentarily stops.

Probs. 18–57/58

*18-56.** The disk $A$ is pinned at $O$ and weighs 150 N ($\approx$ 15 kg). A 1-m rod weighing 20 N ($\approx$ 2 kg) and a 1-m-diameter sphere weighing 100 N ($\approx$ 10 kg) are welded to the disk, as shown. If the spring is orginally stretched 1 m and the sphere is released from the position shown, determine the angular velocity of the disk when it has rotated 90°.

**18-59.** The end $A$ of the garage door $AB$ travels along the horizontal track, and the end of member $BC$ is attached to a spring at $C$. If the spring is originally unstretched, determine the stiffness $k$ so that when the door falls downward from rest in the position shown, it will have zero angular velocity the moment it closes, i.e., when it and $BC$ become vertical. Neglect the mass of member $BC$ and assume the door is a thin plate having a weight of 1000 N ($\approx$ 100 kg) and a width and height of 3.6 m. There is similar connection and spring on the other side of the door.

Prob. 18–56

Prob. 18–59

# CHAPTER REVIEW

- *Kinetic Energy.* The kinetic energy of a rigid body that undergoes planar motion can be referenced to its mass center. For a translating body $T = \frac{1}{2}mv_G^2$. If the body is rotating about a fixed axis through point $O$, then its mass center has a velocity, and the body also has an angular velocity. Therefore $T = \frac{1}{2}mv_G^2 + \frac{1}{2}I_G\omega^2$. Using $v_G = \omega r$ and the parallel-axis theorem, we can also determine the kinetic energy relative to point $O$. We have $T = \frac{1}{2}I_O\omega^2$.

  For general plane motion, the kinetic energy is simply $T = \frac{1}{2}mv_G^2 + \frac{1}{2}I_G\omega^2$, the scalar sum of its translational and rotational kinetic energies.

- *Work of a Force and a Couple Moment.* A force does work when it undergoes a displacement $ds$ in the direction of the force. The work is $U = \int F\,ds$. If the force is constant and is in the direction of its displacement $\Delta s$, then $U = F\Delta s$. If a weight $\mathbf{W}$ is displaced downward by $\Delta y$, then $U = W\Delta y$. If a force $\mathbf{F}$ stretches a spring a distance $s$, then $U = \frac{1}{2}ks^2$. The frictional and normal forces that act on a cylinder or sphere that rolls without slipping will do no work, since the normal force does not displace and the fictional force acts on successive points on the surface of the body. A couple moment will do work when it undergoes a rotation $\theta$ in the direction of the couple moment. If this moment is constant, then $U = M\theta$.

- *Principle of Work and Energy.* Problems that involve velocity, force, and displacement can be solved using the principle of work and energy.

$$T_1 + \Sigma U_{1-2} = T_2$$

Here, the kinetic energy is the sum of both its rotational and translational parts. For application, a free-body diagram should be drawn in order to account for the work of all of the forces and couple moments that act on the body as it moves along the path.

- *Conservation of Energy.* If a rigid body is subjected only to conservative forces, then the conservation of energy equation can be used to solve the problem. This equation requires that the sum of the potential and kinetic energies of the body remains the same at any two points along the path, that is,

$$T_1 + V_1 = T_2 + V_2$$

Here, the potential energy is the sum of its gravitational and elastic potential energies.

$$V = V_g + V_e$$

In particular, the gravitational potential energy will be positive if the body's center of mass is located above a datum. If it is below the datum, then it will be negative. The elastic potential energy is always positive, regardless if the spring is stretched or compressed.

The launching of this weather satellite requires application of impulse and momentum principles to accurately predict its orbital angular motion and proper orientation.

# CHAPTER 19

# Planar Kinetics of a Rigid Body: Impulse and Momentum

**CHAPTER OBJECTIVES**

- To develop formulations for the linear and angular momentum of a body.
- To apply the principles of linear and angular impulse and momentum to solve rigid-body planar kinetic problems that involve force, velocity, and time.
- To discuss application of the conservation of momentum.
- To analyze the mechanics of eccentric impact.

## 19.1 Linear and Angular Momentum

In this chapter we will use the principles of linear and angular impulse and momentum to solve problems involving force, velocity, and time as related to the planar motion of a rigid body. Before doing this, however, it will first be necessary to formalize the methods for obtaining the body's linear and angular momentum when the body is subjected to translation, rotation about a fixed axis, and general plane motion. Here we will assume the body is symmetric with respect to an inertial $x$–$y$ reference plane.

Particle momentum
diagram

(a)

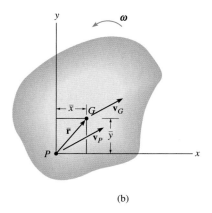

(b)

Fig. 19–1

**Linear Momentum.** The linear momentum of a rigid body is determined by summing vectorially the linear momenta of all the particles of the body, i.e., $\mathbf{L} = \Sigma m_i \mathbf{v}_i$. Since $\Sigma m_i \mathbf{v}_i = m\mathbf{v}_G$ (see Sec. 15.2) we can also write

$$\mathbf{L} = m\mathbf{v}_G \tag{19–1}$$

This equation states that the body's linear momentum is a vector quantity having a *magnitude* $mv_G$, which is commonly measured in unit of kg · m/s, and a *direction* defined by $\mathbf{v}_G$, the velocity of the body's mass center.

**Angular Momentum.** Consider the body in Fig. 19–1a, which is subjected to general plane motion. At the instant shown, the arbitrary point $P$ has a velocity $\mathbf{v}_P$, and the body has an angular velocity $\boldsymbol{\omega}$. If the velocity of the *i*th particle of the body is to be determined, Fig. 19–1a, then

$$\mathbf{v}_i = \mathbf{v}_P + \mathbf{v}_{i/P} = \mathbf{v}_P + \boldsymbol{\omega} \times \mathbf{r}$$

The angular momentum of particle $i$ about point $P$ is equal to the "moment" of the particle's linear momentum about $P$, Fig. 19–1a. Thus,

$$(\mathbf{H}_P)_i = \mathbf{r} \times m_i \mathbf{v}_i$$

Expressing $\mathbf{v}_i$ in terms of $\mathbf{v}_P$ and using Cartesian vectors, we have

$$(H_P)_i\mathbf{k} = m_i(x\mathbf{i} + y\mathbf{j}) \times [(v_P)_x\mathbf{i} + (v_P)_y\mathbf{j} + \omega\mathbf{k} \times (x\mathbf{i} + y\mathbf{j})]$$
$$(H_P)_i = -m_i y(v_P)_x + m_i x(v_P)_y + m_i \omega r^2$$

Letting $m_i \to dm$ and integrating over the entire mass $m$ of the body, we obtain

$$H_P = -\left(\int_m y\, dm\right)(v_P)_x + \left(\int_m x\, dm\right)(v_P)_y + \left(\int_m r^2\, dm\right)\omega$$

Here $H_P$ represents the angular momentum of the body about an axis (the $z$ axis) perpendicular to the plane of motion and passing through point $P$. Since $\bar{y}m = \int y\, dm$ and $\bar{x}m = \int x\, dm$, the integrals for the first and second terms on the right are used to locate the body's center of mass $G$ with respect to $P$, Fig. 19–1b. Also, the last integral represents the body's moment of inertia computed about the $z$ axis, i.e., $I_P = \int r^2\, dm$. Thus,

$$H_P = -\bar{y}m(v_P)_x + \bar{x}m(v_P)_y + I_P\omega \tag{19–2}$$

This equation reduces to a simpler form if point $P$ coincides with the mass center $G$ for the body,* in which case $\bar{x} = \bar{y} = 0$. Hence,

*It also reduces to the same simple form, $H_P = I_P\omega$, if point $P$ is a *fixed point* (see Eq. 19–9) or the velocity of point $P$ is directed along the line $PG$.

$$H_G = I_G\omega \qquad (19\text{–}3)$$

*This equation states that the angular momentum of the body computed about G is equal to the product of the moment of inertia of the body about an axis passing through G and the body's angular velocity.* It is important to realize that $\mathbf{H}_G$ is a vector quantity having a *magnitude* $I_G\omega$, which is commonly measured in unit of kg · m²/s, and a *direction* defined by $\boldsymbol{\omega}$, which is always perpendicular to the plane of motion.

Equation 19–2 can also be rewritten in terms of the $x$ and $y$ components of the velocity of the body's mass center, $(v_G)_x$ and $(v_G)_y$, and the body's moment of inertia $I_G$. Since point $G$ is located at coordinates $(\bar{x}, \bar{y})$, then by the parallel-axis theorem, $I_P = I_G + m(\bar{x}^2 + \bar{y}^2)$. Substituting into Eq. 19–2 and rearranging terms, we have

$$H_P = \bar{y}m[-(v_P)_x + \bar{y}\omega] + \bar{x}m[(v_P)_y + \bar{x}\omega] + I_G\omega \qquad (19\text{–}4)$$

From the kinematic diagram of Fig. 19–1*b*, $\mathbf{v}_G$ can be expressed in terms of $\mathbf{v}_P$ as

$$\mathbf{v}_G = \mathbf{v}_p + \boldsymbol{\omega} \times \bar{\mathbf{r}}$$
$$(v_G)_x\mathbf{i} + (v_G)_y\mathbf{j} = (v_p)_x\mathbf{i} + (v_p)_y\mathbf{j} + \omega\mathbf{k} \times (\bar{x}\mathbf{i} + \bar{y}\mathbf{j})$$

Carrying out the cross product and equating the respective $\mathbf{i}$ and $\mathbf{j}$ components yields the two scalar equations

$$(v_G)_x = (v_P)_x - \bar{y}\omega$$
$$(v_G)_y = (v_P)_y + \bar{x}\omega$$

Substituting these results into Eq. 19–4 yields

$$H_P = -\bar{y}m(v_G)_x + \bar{x}m(v_G)_y + I_G\omega \qquad (19\text{–}5)$$

With reference to Fig. 19–1*c*, *this result indicates that when the angular momentum of the body is computed about point P, it is equivalent to the moment of the linear momentum* $m\mathbf{v}_G$ *or its components* $m(\mathbf{v}_G)_x$ *and* $m(\mathbf{v}_G)_y$ *about P plus the angular momentum* $I_G\boldsymbol{\omega}$. Note that since $\boldsymbol{\omega}$ is a free vector, $\mathbf{H}_G$ *can act at any point on the body* provided it preserves its same magnitude and direction. Furthermore, since angular momentum is equal to the "moment" of the linear momentum, the *line of action of* $\mathbf{L}$ *must pass through the body's mass center G* in order to preserve the correct magnitude of $\mathbf{H}_P$ when "moments" are computed about $P$, Fig. 19–1*c*. As a result of this analysis, we will now consider three types of motion.

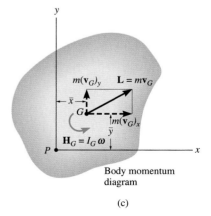

Body momentum diagram

(c)

Fig. 19–1

**Translation.**   When a rigid body of mass $m$ is subjected to either rectilinear or curvilinear *translation*, Fig. 19–2a, its mass center has a velocity of $\mathbf{v}_G = \mathbf{v}$ and $\boldsymbol{\omega} = \mathbf{0}$ for the body. Hence, the linear momentum and the angular momentum computed about $G$ become

$$\boxed{\begin{aligned} L &= mv_G \\ H_G &= 0 \end{aligned}} \tag{19–6}$$

If the angular momentum is computed about any other point $A$ on or off the body, Fig. 19–2a, the "moment" of the linear momentum $\mathbf{L}$ must be computed about the point. Since $d$ is the "moment arm" as shown in the figure, then in accordance with Eq. 19–5, $H_A = (d)(mv_G)\,\zeta$.

**Rotation About a Fixed Axis.**   When a rigid body is *rotating about a fixed axis* passing through point $O$, Fig. 19–2b, the linear momentum and the angular momentum computed about $G$ are

$$\boxed{\begin{aligned} L &= mv_G \\ H_G &= I_G\omega \end{aligned}} \tag{19–7}$$

It is sometimes convenient to compute the angular momentum of the body about point $O$. In this case it is necessary to account for the "moment" of *both* $\mathbf{L}$ and $\mathbf{H}_G$ about $O$. Noting that $\mathbf{L}$ (or $\mathbf{v}_G$) is always *perpendicular to* $\mathbf{r}_G$, we have

$$\zeta+ \qquad\qquad H_O = I_G\omega + r_G(mv_G) \tag{19–8}$$

This equation may be *simplified* by first substituting $v_G = r_G\omega$, in which case $H_O = (I_G + mr_G^2)\omega$, and, by the parallel-axis theorem, noting that the terms inside the parentheses represent the moment of inertia $I_O$ of the body about an axis perpendicular to the plane of motion and passing through point $O$. Hence,*

$$\boxed{H_O = I_O\boldsymbol{\omega}} \tag{19–9}$$

For the calculation, then, either Eq. 19–8 or 19–9 can be used.

---

*The similarity between this derivation and that of Eq. 17–16 ($\Sigma M_O = I_O\alpha$) and Eq. 18–5 ($T = \frac{1}{2}I_O\omega^2$) should be noted. Also note that the same result can be obtained from Eq. 19–2 by selecting point $P$ at $O$, realizing that $(v_O)_x = (v_O)_y = 0$.

Translation

(a)

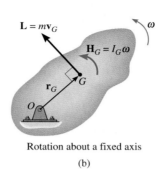

Rotation about a fixed axis

(b)

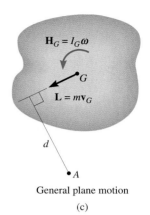

General plane motion

(c)

**Fig. 19–2**

**General Plane Motion.**   When a rigid body is subjected to general plane motion, Fig. 19–2c, the linear momentum and the angular momentum computed about $G$ become

$$\boxed{\begin{array}{c} L = mv_G \\ H_G = I_G\boldsymbol{\omega} \end{array}}$$

(19–10)

   If the angular momentum is computed about a point $A$ located either on or off the body, Fig. 19–2c, it is necessary to find the moments of *both* **L** and **H**$_G$ about this point. In this case,

$\zeta+$ $\qquad\qquad\qquad H_A = I_G\omega + (d)(mv_G)$

Here $d$ is the moment arm, as shown in the figure.

As the pendulum swings downward, its angular momentum about point $O$ can be determined by computing the moment of $I_G\boldsymbol{\omega}$ and $mv_G$ about $O$. This is $H_O = I_G\omega + (mv_G)d$. Since $v_G = \omega d$, then $H_O = I_G\omega + m(\omega d)d = (I_G + md^2)\omega = I_O\omega$.

**EXAMPLE 19.1**

At a given instant the 10-kg disk and 5-kg bar have the motions shown in Fig. 19–3a. Determine their angular momenta about point $G$ and about point $B$ for the disk and about $G$ and about the $IC$ for the bar at this instant.

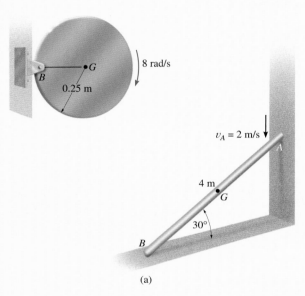

(a)

**Solution**

*Disk.*  Since the disk is *rotating about a fixed axis* (through point $B$), then $v_G = (8 \text{ rad/s})(0.25 \text{ m}) = 2 \text{ m/s}$, Fig. 19–3b. Hence

$$\zeta + H_G = I_G\omega = [\tfrac{1}{2}(10 \text{ kg})(0.25 \text{ m})^2](8 \text{ rad/s}) = 2.50 \text{ kg} \cdot \text{m}^2/\text{s} \quad Ans.$$

$$\zeta + H_B = I_G\omega + (mv_G)r_G = 2.50 \text{ kg} \cdot \text{m}^2/\text{s} + (10 \text{ kg})(2 \text{ m/s})(0.25 \text{ m})$$
$$= 7.50 \text{ kg} \cdot \text{m}^2/\text{s} \qquad\qquad Ans.$$

Also, from the table on the inside back cover, $I_B = (3/2)mr^2$, so that

$$\zeta + H_B = I_B\omega = [\tfrac{3}{2}(10 \text{ kg})(0.25 \text{ m})^2](8 \text{ rad/s}) = 7.50 \text{ kg} \cdot \text{m}^2/\text{s} \quad Ans.$$

*Bar.*  The bar undergoes *general plane motion*. The $IC$ is established in Fig. 19–3c, so that $\omega = (2 \text{ m/s})/(3.464 \text{ m}) = 0.5774 \text{ rad/s}$ and $v_G = (0.5774 \text{ rad/s})(2 \text{ m}) = 1.155 \text{ m/s}$. Thus,

$$\zeta + H_G = I_G\omega = [\tfrac{1}{12}(5 \text{ kg})(4 \text{ m})^2](0.5774 \text{ rad/s}) = 3.85 \text{ kg} \cdot \text{m}^2/\text{s} \quad Ans.$$

Moments of $I_G\omega$ and $mv_G$ about the $IC$ yield

$$\zeta + H_{IC} = I_G\omega + d(mv_G) = 3.85 \text{ kg} \cdot \text{m}^2/\text{s} + (2 \text{ m})(5 \text{ kg})(1.155 \text{ m/s})$$
$$= 15.4 \text{ kg} \cdot \text{m}^2/\text{s} \qquad\qquad Ans.$$

(b)

(c)

**Fig. 19–3**

## 19.2 Principle of Impulse and Momentum

Like the case for particle motion, the principle of impulse and momentum for a rigid body is developed by *combining* the equation of motion with kinematics. The resulting equation will allow a *direct solution* to problems involving force, velocity, and time.

**Principle of Linear Impulse and Momentum.** The equation of translational motion for a rigid body can be written as $\Sigma \mathbf{F} = m\mathbf{a}_G = m\,(d\mathbf{v}_G/dt)$. Since the mass of the body is constant,

$$\Sigma \mathbf{F} = \frac{d}{dt}(m\mathbf{v}_G)$$

Multiplying both sides by $dt$ and integrating from $t = t_1$, $\mathbf{v}_G = (\mathbf{v}_G)_1$ to $t = t_2$, $\mathbf{v}_G = (\mathbf{v}_G)_2$ yields

$$\Sigma \int_{t_1}^{t_2} \mathbf{F}\,dt = m(\mathbf{v}_G)_2 - m(\mathbf{v}_G)_1 \qquad (19\text{–}11)$$

This equation is referred to as the *principle of linear impulse and momentum*. It states that the sum of all the impulses created by the *external force system* which acts on the body during the time interval $t_1$ to $t_2$ is equal to the change in the linear momentum of the body during the time interval, Fig. 19–4.

**Principle of Angular Impulse and Momentum.** If the body has *general plane motion* we can write $\Sigma M_G = I_G\alpha = I_G(d\omega/dt)$. Since the moment of inertia is constant,

$$\Sigma M_G = \frac{d}{dt}(I_G\omega)$$

Multiplying both sides by $dt$ and integrating from $t = t_1$, $\omega = \omega_1$ to $t = t_2$, $\omega = \omega_2$ gives

$$\Sigma \int_{t_1}^{t_2} M_G\,dt = I_G\omega_2 - I_G\omega_1 \qquad (19\text{–}12)$$

In a similar manner, for *rotation about a fixed axis* passing through point $O$, Eq. 17–16 ($\Sigma M_O = I_O\alpha$) when integrated becomes

$$\Sigma \int_{t_1}^{t_2} M_O\,dt = I_O\omega_2 - I_O\omega_1 \qquad (19\text{–}13)$$

Equations 19–12 and 19–13 are referred to as the *principle of angular impulse and momentum*. Both equations state that the sum of the angular impulses acting on the body during the time interval $t_1$ to $t_2$ is equal to the change in the body's angular momentum during this time interval. In particular, the angular impulse considered is determined by integrating the moments about point $G$ or $O$ of all the external forces and couple moments applied to the body.

Fig. 19–4

Initial
momentum
diagram

(a)

Impulse
diagram

(b)

$\|$

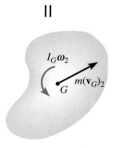

Final
momentum
diagram

(c)

**Fig. 19–4**

To summarize the preceding concepts, if motion is occurring in the $x$–$y$ plane, using impulse and momentum principles the following *three scalar equations* may be written which describe the *planar motion* of the body:

$$
m(v_{Gx})_1 + \Sigma \int_{t_1}^{t_2} F_x \, dt = m(v_{Gx})_2
$$

$$
m(v_{Gy})_1 + \Sigma \int_{t_1}^{t_2} F_y \, dt = m(v_{Gy})_2 \tag{19–14}
$$

$$
I_G \omega_1 + \Sigma \int_{t_1}^{t_2} M_G \, dt = I_G \omega_2
$$

The first two of these equations represent the principle of linear impulse and momentum in the $x$–$y$ plane, Eq. 19–11, and the third equation represents the principle of angular impulse and momentum about the $z$ axis, which passes through the body's mass center $G$, Eq. 19–12.

The terms in Eqs. 19–14 can be graphically accounted for by drawing a set of impulse and momentum diagrams for the body, Fig. 19–4. Note that the linear momenta $m\mathbf{v}_G$ are applied at the body's mass center, Figs. 19–4a and 19–4c; whereas the angular momenta $I_G\boldsymbol{\omega}$ are free vectors, and therefore, like a couple moment, they may be applied at any point on the body. When the impulse diagram is constructed, Fig. 19–4b, the forces $\mathbf{F}$ and moment $\mathbf{M}$ vary with time, and are indicated by the integrals. However, if $\mathbf{F}$ and $\mathbf{M}$ are *constant* from $t_1$ to $t_2$, integration of the impulses yields $\mathbf{F}(t_2 - t_1)$ and $\mathbf{M}(t_2 - t_1)$, respectively. Such is the case for the body's weight $\mathbf{W}$, Fig. 19–4b.

Equations 19–14 may also be applied to an entire system of connected bodies rather than to each body separately. Doing this eliminates the need to include reactive impulses which occur at the connections since they are *internal* to the system. The resultant equations may be written in symbolic form as

$$
\left( \Sigma \begin{matrix} \text{syst. linear} \\ \text{momentum} \end{matrix} \right)_{x1} + \left( \Sigma \begin{matrix} \text{syst. linear} \\ \text{impulse} \end{matrix} \right)_{x(1-2)} = \left( \Sigma \begin{matrix} \text{syst. linear} \\ \text{momentum} \end{matrix} \right)_{x2}
$$

$$
\left( \Sigma \begin{matrix} \text{syst. linear} \\ \text{momentum} \end{matrix} \right)_{y1} + \left( \Sigma \begin{matrix} \text{syst. linear} \\ \text{impulse} \end{matrix} \right)_{y(1-2)} = \left( \Sigma \begin{matrix} \text{syst. linear} \\ \text{momentum} \end{matrix} \right)_{y2}
$$

$$
\left( \Sigma \begin{matrix} \text{syst. angular} \\ \text{momentum} \end{matrix} \right)_{O1} + \left( \Sigma \begin{matrix} \text{syst. angular} \\ \text{impulse} \end{matrix} \right)_{O(1-2)} = \left( \Sigma \begin{matrix} \text{syst. angular} \\ \text{momentum} \end{matrix} \right)_{O2}
$$

$$(19–15)$$

As indicated, the system's angular momentum and angular impulse must be computed with respect to the *same fixed reference point O* for all the bodies of the system.

# PROCEDURE FOR ANALYSIS

Impulse and momentum principles are used to solve kinetic problems that involve *velocity, force*, and *time* since these terms are involved in the formulation.

*Free-Body Diagram.*

- Establish the $x, y, z$ inertial frame of reference and draw the free-body diagram in order to account for all the forces and couple moments that produce impulses on the body.

- The direction and sense of the initial and final velocity of the body's mass center, $\mathbf{v}_G$, and the body's angular velocity $\boldsymbol{\omega}$ should be established. If any of these motions is unknown, assume that the sense of its components is in the direction of the positive inertial coordinates.

- Compute the moment of inertia $I_G$ or $I_O$.

- As an alternative procedure, draw the impulse and momentum diagrams for the body or system of bodies. Each of these diagrams represents an outlined shape of the body which graphically accounts for the data required for each of the three terms in Eqs. 19–14 or 19–15, Fig. 19–4. These diagrams are particularly helpful in order to visualize the "moment" terms used in the principle of angular impulse and momentum, if application is about a point other than the body's mass center $G$ or a fixed point $O$.

*Principle of Impulse and Momentum.*

- Apply the three scalar equations of impulse and momentum.

- The angular momentum of a rigid body rotating about a fixed axis is the moment of $m\mathbf{v}_G$ plus $I_G\boldsymbol{\omega}$ about the axis. This can be shown to be equal to $H_O = I_O\boldsymbol{\omega}$, where $I_O$ is the moment of inertia of the body about the axis.

- All the forces acting on the body's free-body diagram will create an impulse; however, some of these forces will do no work.

- Forces that are functions of time must be integrated to obtain the impulse. Graphically, the impulse is equal to the area under the force-time curve.

- The principle of angular impulse and momentum is often used to eliminate unknown impulsive forces that are parallel or pass through a common axis, since the moment of these forces is zero about this axis.

*Kinematics.*

- If more than three equations are needed for a complete solution, it may be possible to relate the velocity of the body's mass center to the body's angular velocity using *kinematics*. If the motion appears to be complicated, kinematic (velocity) diagrams may be helpful in obtaining the necessary relation.

E X A M P L E  **19.2**

$M = 6\,N \cdot m$

0.25 m

A

$F = 50\,N$

(a)

$y$

$\omega$

$x$

6 N · m

100 N

$A_x$  A  0.25 m

$A_y$

50 N

(b)

**Fig. 19–5**

The 100-N ($\approx$ 10-kg) disk shown in Fig. 19–5a is assumed to be uniform and is pin supported at its center. If it is acted upon by a constant couple moment of 6 N · m and a force of 50 N which is applied to a cord wrapped around its periphery, determine the angular velocity of the disk two seconds after starting from rest. Also, what are the force components of reaction at the pin?

**Solution**

Since angular velocity, force, and time are involved in the problems we will apply the principles of impulse and momentum to the solution.

*Free-Body Diagram.* Fig. 19–5b. The disk's mass center does not move; however, the loading causes the disk to rotate clockwise.

The moment of inertia of the disk about its fixed axis of rotation is

$$I_A = \frac{1}{2}\,mr^2 = \frac{1}{2}\left(\frac{100\,N}{9.81\,m/s^2}\right)(0.25\,m)^2 = 0.31855\,kg \cdot m^2$$

*Principle of Impulse and Momentum.*

$(\overset{+}{\rightarrow})$  $\qquad m(v_{Ax})_1 + \Sigma \int_{t_1}^{t_2} F_x\,dt = m(v_{Ax})_2$

$$0 + A_x(2\,s) = 0$$

$(+\uparrow)$  $\qquad m(v_{Ay})_1 + \Sigma \int_{t_1}^{t_2} F_y\,dt = m(v_{Ay})_2$

$$0 + A_y(2\,s) - 100\,N(2\,s) - 50\,N\,(2\,s) = 0$$

$(\curvearrowright+)$  $\qquad I_A\omega_1 + \Sigma \int_{t_1}^{t_2} M_A\,dt = I_A\omega_2$

$$0 + 6\,N \cdot m\,(2\,s) + [50\,N(2\,s)](0.25\,m) = 0.31855\omega_2$$

Solving these equations yields

$$A_x = 0 \qquad\qquad\qquad Ans.$$
$$A_y = 30\,lb \qquad\qquad\qquad Ans.$$
$$\omega_2 = 116.2\,rad/s \;\downarrow \qquad\qquad Ans.$$

**EXAMPLE** 19.3

The 100-kg spool shown in Fig. 19–6a has a radius of gyration $k_G = 0.35$ m. A cable is wrapped around the central hub of the spool, and a horizontal force having a variable magnitude of $P = (t + 10)$ N is applied, where $t$ is in seconds. If the spool is initially at rest, determine its angular velocity in 5 s. Assume that the spool rolls without slipping at $A$.

(a)

**Solution**

*Free-Body Diagram.*  By inspection of the free-body diagram, Fig. 19–6b, the *variable* force $P$ will cause the friction force $F_A$ to be variable, and thus the impulses created by both $P$ and $F_A$ must be determined by integration. The force **P** causes the mass center to have a velocity $\mathbf{v}_G$ to the right, and the spool has a clockwise angular velocity $\boldsymbol{\omega}$.

The moment of inertia of the spool about its mass center is

$$I_G = mk_G^2 = 100 \text{ kg}(0.35 \text{ m})^2 = 12.25 \text{ kg} \cdot \text{m}^2$$

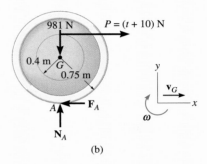

(b)

*Principle of Impulse and Momentum.*

$(\xrightarrow{+})$  $$m(v_G)_1 + \Sigma \int F_x \, dt = m(v_G)_2$$

$$0 + \int_0^{5 \text{ s}} (t + 10) \text{ N } dt - \int F_A \, dt = 100 \text{ kg}(v_G)_2$$

$$62.5 - \int F_A \, dt = 100(v_G)_2 \qquad (1)$$

$(\curvearrowright +)$  $$I_G\omega_1 + \Sigma \int M_G \, dt = I_G\omega_2$$

$$0 + \left[ \int_0^{5 \text{ s}} (t + 10) \text{ N } dt \right](0.4 \text{ m}) + \left( \int F_A \, dt \right)(0.75 \text{ m}) = (12.25 \text{ kg} \cdot \text{m}^2)\omega_2$$

$$25 + \left( \int F_A \, dt \right)(0.75) = 12.25\omega_2 \qquad (2)$$

*Kinematics.*  Since the spool does not slip, the instantaneous center of zero velocity is at point $A$, Fig. 19–6c. Hence, the velocity of $G$ can be expressed in terms of the spool's angular velocity as $(v_G)_2 = (0.75 \text{ m})\omega_2$. Substituting this into Eq. 1 and eliminating the unknown impulse $\int F_A \, dt$ between Eqs. 1 and 2, we obtain

$$\omega_2 = 1.05 \text{ rad/s } \downarrow \qquad \qquad Ans.$$

(c)

*Note:* A more direct solution can be obtained by applying the principle of angular impulse and momentum about point $A$. As an exercise, do this and show that one obtains the same result.

**Fig. 19–6**

E X A M P L E  **19.4**

The block shown in Fig. 19–7a has a mass of 6 kg. It is attached to a cord which is wrapped around the periphery of a 20-kg disk that has a moment of inertia $I_A = 0.40 \text{ kg} \cdot \text{m}^2$. If the block is initially moving downward with a speed of 2 m/s, determine its speed in 3 s. Neglect the mass of the cord in the calculation.

(a)

**Solution I**

*Free-Body Diagram.* The free-body diagrams of the block and disk are shown in Fig. 19–7b. All the forces are *constant* since the weight of the block causes the motion. The downward motion of the block, $v_B$, causes $\boldsymbol{\omega}$ of the disk to be clockwise.

*Principle of Impulse and Momentum.* We can eliminate $\mathbf{A}_x$ and $\mathbf{A}_y$ from the analysis by applying the principle of angular impulse and momentum about point $A$. Hence

Disk

$$(\curvearrowright+) \qquad I_A\omega_1 + \Sigma \int M_A \, dt = I_A\omega_2$$

$$0.40 \text{ kg} \cdot \text{m}^2(\omega_1) + T(3 \text{ s})(0.2 \text{ m}) = (0.4 \text{ kg} \cdot \text{m}^2)\omega_2$$

Block

$$(+\uparrow) \qquad m_B(v_B)_1 + \Sigma \int F_y \, dt = m_B(v_B)_2$$

$$-6 \text{ kg}(2 \text{ m/s}) + T(3 \text{ s}) - 58.86 \text{ N}(3 \text{ s}) = -6 \text{ kg}(v_B)_2$$

*Kinematics.* Since $\omega = v_B/r$, then $\omega_1 = (2 \text{ m/s})/(0.2 \text{ m}) = 10 \text{ rad/s}$ and $\omega_2 = (v_B)_2/0.2 \text{ m} = 5(v_B)_2$. Substituting and solving the equations simultaneously for $(v_B)_2$ yields

$$(v_B)_2 = 13.0 \text{ m/s} \downarrow \qquad \textit{Ans.}$$

(b)

**Fig. 19–7**

Solution II

*Impulse and Momentum Diagrams.* We can obtain $(v_B)_2$ *directly* by considering the *system* consisting of the block, the cord, and the disk. The impulse and momentum diagrams have been drawn to clarify application of the principle of angular impulse and momentum about point $A$, Fig. 19–7c.

*Principle of Angular Impulse and Momentum.* Realizing that $\omega_1 = 10$ rad/s and $\omega_2 = 5(v_B)_2$, we have

$$(\circlearrowright+) \quad \left(\sum \begin{array}{c} \text{syst. angular} \\ \text{momentum} \end{array}\right)_{A1} + \left(\sum \begin{array}{c} \text{syst. angular} \\ \text{impulse} \end{array}\right)_{A(1-2)} = \left(\sum \begin{array}{c} \text{syst. angular} \\ \text{momentum} \end{array}\right)_{A2}$$

$$6 \text{ kg}(2 \text{ m/s})(0.2 \text{ m}) + 0.4 \text{ kg} \cdot \text{m}^2(10 \text{ rad/s}) + 58.86 \text{ N}(3 \text{ s})(0.2 \text{ m})$$
$$= 6 \text{ kg}(v_B)_2(0.2 \text{ m}) + 0.40 \text{ kg} \cdot \text{m}^2[5(v_B)_2(0.2 \text{ m})]$$
$$(v_B)_2 = 13.0 \text{ m/s} \downarrow \qquad\qquad Ans.$$

(c)

**Fig. 19–7**

E X A M P L E **19.5**

(a)

(b)

Fig. 19–8

The Charpy impact test is used in materials testing to determine the energy absorption characteristics of a material during impact. The test is performed using the pendulum shown in Fig. 19–8a, which has a mass $m$, mass center at $G$, and a radius of gyration $k_G$ about $G$. Determine the distance $r_P$ from the pin at $A$ to the point $P$ where the impact with the specimen $S$ should occur so that the horizontal force at the pin is essentially zero during the impact. For the calculation, assume the specimen absorbs all the pendulum's kinetic energy gained during the time it falls and thereby stops the pendulum from swinging when $\theta = 0°$.

**Solution**

*Free-Body Diagram.* As shown on the free-body diagram, Fig. 19–8b, the conditions of the problem require the horizontal impulse at $A$ to be zero. Just before impact, the pendulum has a clockwise angular velocity $\omega_1$, and the mass center of the pendulum is moving to the left at $(v_G)_1 = \bar{r}\omega_1$.

*Principle of Impulse and Momentum.* We will apply the principle of angular impulse and momentum about point $A$. Thus,

$$(\curvearrowright +) \qquad\qquad I_A\omega_1 + \Sigma M_A\, dt = I_A\omega_2$$

$$I_A\omega_1 - \left(\int F\, dt\right) r_p = 0$$

$$(\xrightarrow{+}) \qquad\qquad m(v_G)_1 + \Sigma F\, dt = m(v_G)_2$$

$$-m(\bar{r}\omega_1) + \int F\, dt = 0$$

Eliminating the impulse $\int F\, dt$ and substituting $I_A = mk_G^2 + m\bar{r}^2$ yields

$$[mk_G^2 + m\bar{r}^2]\omega_1 - m(\bar{r}\omega_1)r_P = 0$$

Factoring out $m\omega_1$ and solving for $r_P$, we obtain

$$r_P = \bar{r} + \frac{k_G^2}{\bar{r}} \qquad\qquad\qquad Ans.$$

The point $P$, so defined, is called the *center of percussion*. By placing the striking point at $P$, the force developed at the pin will be minimized. Many sports rackets, clubs, etc. are designed so that collision with the object being struck occurs at the center of percussion. As a consequence, no "sting" or little sensation occurs in the hand of the player. (Also see Probs. 17–65 and 19–1.)

# PROBLEMS

**19-1.** The rigid body (slab) has a mass $m$ and is rotating with an angular velocity $\omega$ about an axis passing through the fixed point $O$. Show that the momenta of all the particles composing the body can be represented by a single vector having a magnitude $mv_G$ and acting through point $P$, called the *center of percussion*, which lies at a distance $r_{P/G} = k_G^2/r_{G/O}$ from the mass center $G$. Here $k_G$ is the radius of gyration of the body, computed about an axis perpendicular to the plane of motion and passing through $G$.

**Prob. 19–1**

**19-2.** At a given instant, the body has a linear momentum $\mathbf{L} = m\mathbf{v}_G$ and an angular momentum $\mathbf{H}_G = I_G\boldsymbol{\omega}$ computed about its mass center. Show that the angular momentum of the body computed about the instantaneous center of zero velocity $IC$ can be expressed as $\mathbf{H}_{IC} = I_{IC}\boldsymbol{\omega}$, where $I_{IC}$ represents the body's moment of inertia computed about the instantaneous axis of zero velocity. As shown, the $IC$ is located at a distance $r_{G/IC}$ away from the mass center $G$.

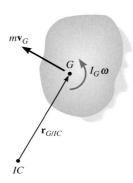

**Prob. 19–2**

**19-3.** Show that if a slab is rotating about a fixed axis perpendicular to the slab and passing through its mass center $G$, the angular momentum is the same when computed about any other point $P$ on the slab.

**Prob. 19–3**

**\*19-4.** The space capsule has a mass of 1200 kg and a moment of inertia $I_G = 900$ kg·m² about an axis passing through $G$ and directed perpendicular to the page. If it is traveling forward with a speed $v_G = 800$ m/s and executes a turn by means of two jets, which provide a constant thrust of 400 N for 0.3 s, determine the capsule's angular velocity just after the jets are turned off.

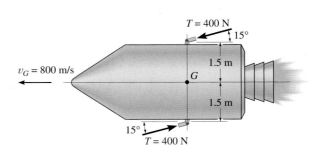

**Prob. 19–4**

**19-5.** Solve Prob. 17–55 using the principle of impulse and momentum.

**19-6.** Solve Prob. 17–54 using the principle of impulse and momentum.

**19-7.** Solve Prob. 17–69 using the principle of impulse and momentum.

*****19-8.** Solve Prob. 17–80 using the principle of impulse and momentum.

**19-9.** Solve Prob. 17–73 using the principle of impulse and momentum.

**19-10.** A flywheel has a mass of 60 kg and a radius of gyration of $k_G = 150$ mm about an axis of rotation passing through its mass center. If a motor supplies a clockwise torque having a magnitude of $M = (5t)$ N · m, where $t$ is in seconds, determine the flywheel's angular velocity in $t = 3$ s. Initially the flywheel is rotating clockwise at $\omega_1 = 2$ rad/s.

**19-11.** The pilot of a crippled F-15 fighter was able to control his plane by throttling the two engines. If the plane has a weight of 85 000 ($\approx$ 8500 kg) and a radius of gyration of $k_G = 1.4$ m about the mass center $G$, determine the angular velocity of the plane and the velocity of its mass center $G$ in $t = 5$ s if the thrust in each engine is altered to $T_1 = 25\,000$ N and $T_2 = 4000$ N as shown. Originally the plane is flying straight at 360 m/s. Neglect the effects of drag and the loss of fuel.

*****19-12.** The spool has a mass of 30 kg and a radius of gyration $k_O = 0.25$ m. Block $A$ has a mass of 25 kg, and block $B$ has a mass of 10 kg. If they are released from rest, determine the time required for block $A$ to attain a speed of 2 m/s. Neglect the mass of the ropes.

**Prob. 19–12**

**19-13.** The man pulls the rope off the reel with a constant force of 40 N in the direction shown. If the reel has a weight of 1250 N ($\approx$ 125 kg) and radius of gyration $k_G = 0.24$ m about the trunnion (pin) at $A$, determine the angular velocity of the reel in 3 s starting from rest. Neglect friction and the weight of rope that is removed.

**Prob. 19–13**

**Prob. 19–11**

**19-14.** Angular motion is transmitted from a driver wheel $A$ to the driven wheel $B$ by friction between the wheels at $C$. If $A$ always rotates at a constant rate of 16 rad/s, and the coefficient of kinetic friction between the wheels is $\mu_k = 0.2$, determine the time required for $B$ to reach a constant angular velocity once the wheels make contact with a normal force of 50 N. What is the final angular velocity of wheel $B$? Wheel $B$ has a mass of 90 kg and a radius of gyration about its axis of rotation of $k_G = 120$ mm.

**Prob. 19–14**

**19-15.** The impact wrench consists of a slender 1-kg rod $AB$ which is 580 mm long, and cylindrical end weights at $A$ and $B$ that each have a diameter of 20 mm and a mass of 1 kg. This assembly is free to turn about the handle and socket, which are attached to the lug nut on the wheel of a car. If the rod $AB$ is given an angular velocity of 4 rad/s and it strikes the bracket $C$ on the handle without rebounding, determine the angular impulse imparted to the lug nut.

**Prob. 19–15**

*19-16.** The space shuttle is located in "deep space," where the effects of gravity can be neglected. It has a mass of 120 Mg, a center of mass at $G$, and a radius of gyration $(k_G)_x = 14$ m about the $x$ axis. It is originally traveling forward at $v = 3$ km/s when the pilot turns on the engine at $A$, creating a thrust $T = 600(1 - e^{-0.3t})$ kN, where $t$ is in seconds. Determine the shuttle's angular velocity 2 s later.

**Prob. 19–16**

**19-17.** The drum has a mass of 70 kg, a radius of 300 mm, and radius of gyration $k_O = 125$ mm. If the coefficients of static and kinetic friction at $A$ are $\mu_s = 0.4$ and $\mu_k = 0.3$, respectively, determine the drum's angular velocity 2 s after it is released from rest. Take $\theta = 30°$.

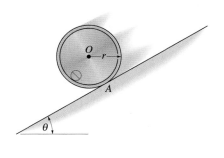

**Prob. 19–17**

**19-18.** The double pulley consists of two wheels which are attached to one another and turn at the same rate. The pulley has a mass of 15 kg and a radius of gyration $k_O = 110$ mm. If the block at $A$ has a mass of 40 kg, determine the speed of the block in 3 s after a constant force $F = 2$ kN is applied to the rope wrapped around the inner hub of the pulley. The block is originally at rest. Neglect the mass of the rope.

200 mm  $O$  75 mm

$F$

$A$

Prob. 19–18

**19-19.** The spool has a weight of 300 N ($\approx 30$ kg) and a radius of gyration $k_O = 0.45$ m. A cord is wrapped around its inner hub and the end subjected to a horizontal force $P = 50$ N. Determine the spool's angular velocity in 4 s starting from rest. Assume the spool rolls without slipping.

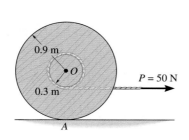

0.9 m

$O$

$P = 50$ N

0.3 m

$A$

Prob. 19–19

**\*19-20.** The drum of mass $m$, radius $r$, and radius of gyration $k_O$ rolls along an inclined plane for which the coefficient of static friction is $\mu_s$. If the drum is released from rest, determine the maximum angle $\theta$ for the incline so that it rolls without slipping.

$\theta$  $A$

Prob. 19–20

**19-21.** The 12-kg disk has an angular velocity of $\omega = 20$ rad/s. If the brake $ABC$ is applied such that the magnitude of force **P** varies with time as shown, determine the time needed to stop the disk. The coefficient of kinetic friction at $B$ is $\mu_k = 0.4$.

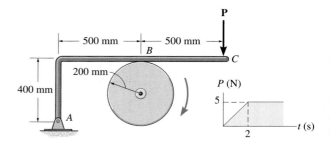

**P**

500 mm  500 mm

$B$  $C$

200 mm

400 mm

$A$

$P$ (N)

5

2  $t$ (s)

Prob. 19–21

**19-22.** The pulley has a weight of 8 kN ($\approx$ 800 kg) and may be treated as a thin disk. A cord wrapped over its surface is subjected to forces $T_A = 4$ kN and $T_B = 5$ kN. Determine the angular velocity of the pulley when $t = 4$ s if it starts from rest when $t = 0$. Neglect the mass of the cord.

Prob. 19–22

**19-23.** The inner hub of the wheel rests on the horizontal track. If it does not slip at $A$, determine the speed of the 10-kg block in 2 s after the block is released from rest. The wheel has a weight of 300 N ($\approx$ 30 kg) and a radius of gyration $k_G = 0.13$ m. Neglect the mass of the pulley and cord.

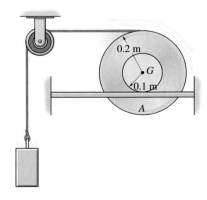

Prob. 19–23

**\*19-24.** For safety reasons, the 20-kg supporting leg of a sign is designed to break away with negligible resistance at $B$ when the leg is subjected to the impact of a car. Assuming that the leg is pin supported at $A$ and approximates a thin rod, determine the impulse the car bumper exerts on it, if after the impact the leg appears to rotate upward to an angle of $\theta_{max} = 150°$.

Prob. 19–24

**19-25.** The 10-kg rectangular plate is at rest on a smooth *horizontal* floor. If it is given the horizontal impulses shown, determine its angular velocity and the velocity of the mass center.

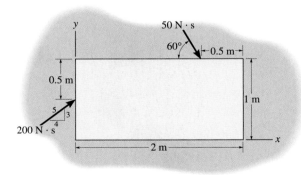

Prob. 19–25

**19-26.** The ball of mass $m$ and radius $r$ rolls along an inclined plane for which the coefficient of static friction is $\mu$. If the ball is released from rest, determine the maximum angle $\theta$ for the incline so that it rolls without slipping at $A$.

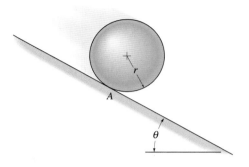

Prob. 19–26

**19-27.** The spool has a weight of 750 N ($\approx$ 75 kg) and a radius of gyration $k_O = 0.6$ m. If the block $B$ weighs 600 N ($\approx$ 60 kg), and a force $P = 250$ N is applied to the cord, determine the speed of the block in 5 s starting from rest. Neglect the mass of the cord.

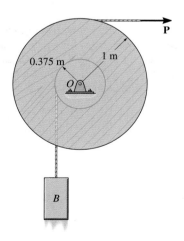

Prob. 19–27

**\*19-28.** The hoop (thin ring) has a mass of 5 kg and is released down the inclined plane such that it has a backspin $\omega = 8$ rad/s and its center has a velocity $v_G = 3$ m/s as shown. If the coefficient of kinetic friction between the hoop and the plane is $\mu_k = 0.6$, determine how long the hoop rolls before it stops slipping.

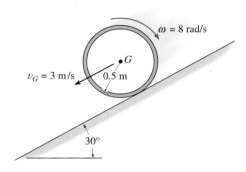

Prob. 19–28

**19-29.** If the ball has a weight $W$ and radius $r$ and is thrown onto a *rough surface* with a velocity $\mathbf{v}_0$ parallel to the surface, determine the amount of backspin, $\boldsymbol{\omega}_0$, it must be given so that it stops spinning at the same instant that its forward velocity is zero. It is not necessary to know the coefficient of friction at $A$ for the calculation.

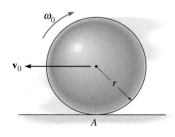

Prob. 19–29

**19-30.** The square plate has a mass $m$ and is suspended at its corner $A$ by a cord. If it receives a horizontal impulse **I** at corner $B$, determine the location $y$ of the point $P$ about which the plate appears to rotate during the impact.

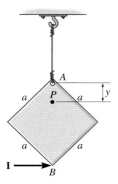

Prob. 19–30

**19-31.** The car strikes the side of a light standard, which is designed to break away from its base with negligible resistance. From a video taken of the collision it is observed that the pole was given an angular velocity of 60 rad/s when $AC$ was vertical. The pole has a mass of 175 kg, a center of mass at $G$, and a radius of gyration about an axis perpendicular to the plane of the pole assembly and passing through $G$ of $k_G = 2.25$ m. Determine the horizontal impulse which the car exerts on the pole while $AC$ is essentially vertical.

Prob. 19–31

*19-32.** The double pulley consists of two wheels which are attached to one another and turn at the same rate. The pulley has a mass of 30 kg and a radius of gyration $k_O = 250$ mm. If two men $A$ and $B$ grab the suspended ropes and step off the ledges at the same time, determine their speeds in 4 s starting from rest. The men $A$ and $B$ have a mass of 60 kg and 70 kg, respectively. Assume they do not move relative to the rope during the motion. Neglect the mass of the rope.

Prob. 19–32

**19-33.** The crate has a mass $m_c$. Determine the constant speed $v_0$ it acquires as it moves down the conveyor. The rollers each have a radius of $r$, mass $m$, and are spaced $d$ apart. Note that friction causes each roller to rotate when the crate comes in contact with it.

Prob. 19–33

## 19.3 Conservation of Momentum

**Conservation of Linear Momentum.** If the sum of all the *linear impulses* acting on a system of connected rigid bodies is *zero*, the linear momentum of the system is constant, or conserved. Consequently, the first two of Eqs. 19–15 reduce to the form

$$\left( \Sigma \begin{matrix} \text{syst. linear} \\ \text{momentum} \end{matrix} \right)_1 = \left( \Sigma \begin{matrix} \text{syst. linear} \\ \text{momentum} \end{matrix} \right)_2 \qquad (19\text{–}16)$$

This equation is referred to as the *conservation of linear momentum*.

Without inducing appreciable errors in the calculations, it may be possible to apply Eq. 19–16 in a specified direction for which the linear impulses are small or *nonimpulsive*. Specifically, nonimpulsive forces occur when small forces act over very short periods of time. Typical examples include the force of a slightly deformed spring, the initial contact with soft ground, and in some cases the weight of the body.

**Conservation of Angular Momentum.** The angular momentum of a system of connected rigid bodies is conserved about the system's center of mass $G$, or a fixed point $O$, when the sum of all the angular impulses created by the external forces acting on the system is zero or appreciably small (nonimpulsive) when computed about these points. The third of Eqs. 19–15 then becomes

$$\left( \Sigma \begin{matrix} \text{syst. angular} \\ \text{momentum} \end{matrix} \right)_{O1} = \left( \Sigma \begin{matrix} \text{syst. angular} \\ \text{momentum} \end{matrix} \right)_{O2} \qquad (19\text{–}17)$$

This equation is referred to as the *conservation of angular momentum*. In the case of a single rigid body, Eq. 19–17 applied to point $G$ becomes $(I_G\omega)_1 = (I_G\omega)_2$. To illustrate an application of this equation, consider a swimmer who executes a somersault after jumping off a diving board. By tucking his arms and legs in close to his chest, he *decreases* his body's moment of inertia and thus *increases* his angular velocity ($I_G\omega$ must be constant). If he straightens out just before entering the water, his body's moment of inertia is *increased*, and his angular velocity *decreases*. Since the weight of his body creates a linear impulse during the time of motion, this example also illustrates how the angular momentum of a body can be conserved and yet the linear momentum is *not*. Such cases occur whenever the external forces creating the linear impulse pass through either the center of mass of the body or a fixed axis of rotation.

Provided the initial linear or angular velocity of the body is known, the conservation of linear or angular momentum is used to determine the respective final linear or angular velocity of the body *just after the* time period considered. Furthermore, by applying these equations to a *system* of bodies, the internal impulses acting within the system, which may be unknown, are eliminated from the analysis, since they occur in equal but opposite collinear pairs. If it is necessary to determine an *internal impulsive force* acting on only one body of a system of connected bodies, the body must be *isolated* (free-body diagram) and the principle of linear or angular impulse and momentum applied *to the body*. After the impulse $\int F \, dt$ is calculated; then, provided the time $\Delta t$ for which the impulse acts is known, the *average impulsive force* $F_{avg}$ can be determined from $F_{avg} = (\int F \, dt)/\Delta t$.

---

## PROCEDURE FOR ANALYSIS

The conservation of linear or angular momentum should be applied using the following procedure.

*Free-Body Diagram.*

- Establish the $x, y$ inertial frame of reference and draw the free-body diagram for the body or system of bodies during the time of impact. From this diagram classify each of the applied forces as being either "impulsive" or "nonimpulsive."

- By inspection of the free-body diagram, the *conservation of linear momentum* applies in a given direction when *no* external impulsive forces act on the body or system in that direction; whereas the *conservation of angular momentum* applies about a fixed point $O$ or at the mass center $G$ of a body or system of bodies when all the external impulsive forces acting on the body or system create zero moment (or zero angular impulse) about $O$ or $G$.

- As an alternative procedure, draw the impulse and momentum diagrams for the body or system of bodies. These diagrams are particularly helpful in order to visualize the "moment" terms used in the conservation of angular momentum equation, when it has been decided that angular momenta are to be computed about a point other than the body's mass center $G$.

*Conservation of Momentum.*

- Apply the conservation of linear or angular momentum in the appropriate directions.

*Kinematics.*

- If the motion appears to be complicated, kinematic (velocity) diagrams may be helpful in obtaining the necessary kinematic relations.

E X A M P L E **19.6**

(a)

$r' = (0.2 - 0.03)$ m

**+**

**||**

(b)

(c)

**Fig. 19–9**

The 10-kg wheel shown in Fig. 19–9a has a moment of inertia $I_G = 0.156$ kg · m². Assuming that the wheel does not slip or rebound, determine the minimum velocity $\mathbf{v}_G$ it must have to just roll over the obstruction at $A$.

### Solution

*Impulse and Momentum Diagrams.* Since no slipping or rebounding occurs, the wheel essentially *pivots* about point $A$ during contact. This condition is shown in Fig. 19–9b, which indicates, respectively, the momentum of the wheel *just before impact*, the impulses given to the wheel *during impact*, and the momentum of the wheel *just after impact*. Only two impulses (forces) act on the wheel. By comparison, the force at $A$ is much greater than that of the weight, and since the time of impact is very short, the weight can be considered nonimpulsive. The impulsive force $\mathbf{F}$ at $A$ has both an unknown magnitude and an unknown direction $\theta$. To eliminate this force from the analysis, note that angular momentum about $A$ is essentially *conserved* since $(98.1\Delta t)d \approx 0$.

*Conservation of Angular Momentum.* With reference to Fig. 19–9b,

$(\curvearrowleft+)$
$$(H_A)_1 = (H_A)_2$$
$$r'm(v_G)_1 + I_G\omega_1 = rm(v_G)_2 + I_G\omega_2$$
$$(0.2 \text{ m} - 0.03 \text{ m})(10 \text{ kg})(v_G)_1 + (0.156 \text{ kg}\cdot\text{m}^2)(\omega_1) =$$
$$(0.2 \text{ m})(10 \text{ kg})(v_G)_2 + (0.156 \text{ kg}\cdot\text{m}^2)(\omega_2)$$

*Kinematics.* Since no slipping occurs, in general $\omega = v_G/r = v_G/0.2 \text{ m} = 5v_G$. Substituting this into the above equation and simplifying yields

$$(v_G)_2 = 0.892(v_G)_1 \qquad (1)$$

*Conservation of Energy.** In order to roll over the obstruction, the wheel must pass position 3 shown in Fig. 19–9c. Hence, if $(v_G)_2$ [or $(v_G)_1$] is to be a minimum, it is necessary that the kinetic energy of the wheel at position 2 be equal to the potential energy at position 3. Constructing the datum through the center of gravity, as shown in the figure, and applying the conservation of energy equation, we have

$$\{T_2\} + \{V_2\} = \{T_3\} + \{V_3\}$$
$$\{\tfrac{1}{2}(10 \text{ kg})(v_G)_2^2 + \tfrac{1}{2}(0.156 \text{ kg}\cdot\text{m}^2)\omega_2^2\} + \{0\} =$$
$$\{0\} + \{(98.1 \text{ N})(0.03 \text{ m})\}$$

Substituting $\omega_2 = 5(v_G)_2$ and Eq. 1 into this equation, and solving,

$$(v_G)_1 = 0.729 \text{ m/s} \rightarrow \qquad\qquad Ans.$$

*This principle *does not* apply during *impact*, since energy is *lost* during the collision; however, just after impact, position 2, it can be used.

## E X A M P L E 19.7

The 5-kg slender rod shown in Fig. 19–10a is pinned at $O$ and is initially at rest. If a 4-g bullet is fired into the rod with a velocity of 400 m/s, as shown in the figure, determine the angular velocity of the rod just after the bullet becomes embedded in it.

(a)

### Solution

*Impulse and Momentum Diagrams.* The impulse which the bullet exerts on the rod can be eliminated from the analysis, and the angular velocity of the rod just after impact can be determined by considering the bullet and rod as a single system. To clarify the principles involved, the impulse and momentum diagrams are shown in Fig. 19–10b. The momentum diagrams are drawn *just before and just after impact.* During impact, the bullet and rod exchange equal but *opposite internal impulses* at $A$. As shown on the impulse diagram, the impulses that are external to the system are due to the reactions at $O$ and the weights of the bullet and rod. Since the time of impact, $\Delta t$, is very short, the rod moves only a slight amount, and so the "moments" of the weight impulses about point $O$ are essentially zero. Therefore angular momentum is conserved about this point.

(b)

*Conservation of Angular Momentum.* From Fig. 19–10b, we have

$$(\downarrow+) \qquad \Sigma(H_O)_1 = \Sigma(H_O)_2$$

$$m_B(v_B)_1 \cos 30°(0.75 \text{ m}) = m_B(v_B)_2(0.75 \text{ m}) + m_R(v_G)_2(0.5 \text{ m}) + I_G\omega_2$$

$$(0.004 \text{ kg})(400 \cos 30°\text{m/s})(0.75 \text{ m}) =$$

$$(0.004 \text{ kg})(v_B)_2(0.75 \text{ m}) + (5 \text{ kg})(v_G)_2(0.5 \text{ m}) + [\tfrac{1}{12}(5 \text{ kg})(1 \text{ m})^2]\omega_2$$

or

$$1.039 = 0.003(v_B)_2 + 2.50(v_G)_2 + 0.417\omega_2 \qquad (1)$$

*Kinematics.* Since the rod is pinned at $O$, from Fig. 19–10c we have

$$(v_G)_2 = (0.5 \text{ m})\omega_2 \qquad (v_B)_2 = (0.75 \text{ m})\omega_2$$

Substituting into Eq. 1 and solving yields

$$\omega_2 = 0.623 \text{ rad/s} \nwarrow \qquad\qquad Ans.$$

(c)

**Fig. 19–10**

## 19.4 Eccentric Impact

An example of eccentric impact occurring between this bowling ball and pin.

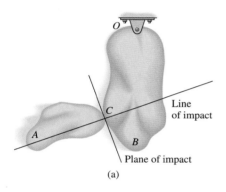

Fig. 19–11

The concepts involving central and oblique impact of particles have been presented in Sec. 15.4. We will now expand this treatment and discuss the eccentric impact of two bodies. *Eccentric impact* occurs when the line connecting the *mass centers* of the two bodies *does not* coincide with the line of impact.* This type of impact often occurs when one or both of the bodies are constrained to rotate about a fixed axis. Consider, for example, the collision at $C$ between the two bodies $A$ and $B$, shown in Fig. 19–11a. It is assumed that just before collision $B$ is rotating counterclockwise with an angular velocity $(\boldsymbol{\omega}_B)_1$, and the velocity of the contact point $C$ located on $A$ is $(\mathbf{u}_A)_1$. Kinematic diagrams for both bodies just before collision are shown in Fig. 19–11b. Provided the bodies are smooth, the *impulsive forces* they exert on each other *are directed along the line of impact*. Hence, the component of velocity of point $C$ on body. $B$, which is directed along the line of impact, is $(v_B)_1 = (\omega_B)_1 r$, Fig. 19–11b. Likewise, on body $A$ the component of velocity $(\mathbf{u}_A)_1$ along the line of impact is $(\mathbf{v}_A)_1$. In order for a collision to occur, $(v_A)_1 > (v_B)_1$.

During the impact an equal but opposite impulsive force **P** is exerted between the bodies which *deforms* their shapes at the point of contact. The resulting impulse is shown on the impulse diagrams for both bodies, Fig. 19–11c. Note that the impulsive force created at point $C$ on the rotating body creates impulsive pin reactions at $O$. On these diagrams it is assumed that the impact creates forces which are much larger than the nonimpulsive weights of the bodies, which are not shown. When the deformation at point $C$ is a maximum, $C$ on both the bodies moves with a common velocity **v** along the line of impact, Fig. 19–11d. A period of *restitution* then occurs in which the bodies tend to regain their original shapes. The restitution phase creates an equal but opposite impulsive force **R** acting between the bodies as shown on the impulse diagram, Fig. 19–11e. After restitution the bodies move apart such that point $C$ on body $B$ has a velocity $(\mathbf{v}_B)_2$ and point $C$ on body $A$ has a velocity $(\mathbf{u}_A)_2$, Fig. 19–11f, where $(v_B)_2 > (v_A)_2$.

In general, a problem involving the impact of two bodies requires determining the *two unknowns* $(v_A)_2$ and $(v_B)_2$, assuming $(v_A)_1$ and $(v_B)_1$ are known (or can be determined using kinematics, energy methods, the equations of motion, etc.). To solve this problem, two equations must be written. The *first equation* generally involves application of *the conservation of angular momentum to the two bodies*. In the case of both bodies $A$ and $B$, we can state that angular momentum is conserved about point $O$ since the impulses at $C$ are internal to the system and the impulses at $O$ create zero moment (or zero angular impulse) about point

---

*When these lines coincide, central impact occurs and the problem can be analyzed as discussed in Sec. 15.4.

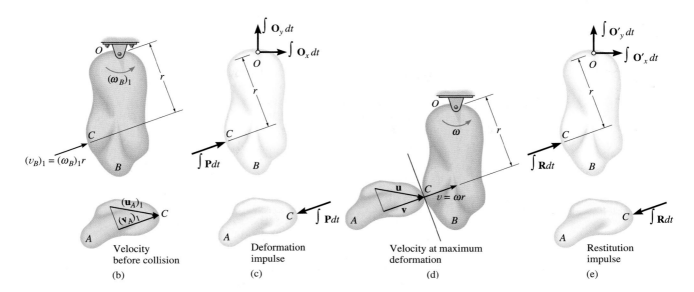

Velocity before collision (b)

Deformation impulse (c)

Velocity at maximum deformation (d)

Restitution impulse (e)

$O$. The *second equation* is obtained using the definition of the *coefficient of restitution, e*, which is a ratio of the restitution impulse to the deformation impulse. To establish a useful form of this equation we must first apply the principle of angular impulse and momentum about point $O$ to bodies $B$ and $A$ separately. Combining the results, we then obtain the necessary equation. Proceeding in this manner, the principle of impulse and momentum applied to body $B$ from the time just before the collision to the instant of maximum deformation, Figs. 19–11$b$, 19–11$c$, and 19–11$d$, becomes

$$(\downarrow+) \qquad I_O(\omega_B)_1 + r\int P\, dt = I_O\omega \qquad (19\text{–}18)$$

Here $I_O$ is the moment of inertia of body $B$ about point $O$. Similarly, applying the principle of angular impulse and momentum from the instant of maximum deformation to the time just after the impact, Figs. 19–11$d$, 19–11$e$, and 19–11$f$, yields

$$(\downarrow+) \qquad I_O\omega + r\int R\, dt = I_O(\omega_B)_2 \qquad (19\text{–}19)$$

Solving Eqs. 19–18 and 19–19 for $\int P\, dt$ and $\int R\, dt$, respectively, and formulating $e$, we have

$$e = \frac{\displaystyle\int R\, dt}{\displaystyle\int P\, dt} = \frac{r(\omega_B)_2 - r\omega}{r\omega - r(\omega_B)_1} = \frac{(v_B)_2 - v}{v - (v_B)_1}$$

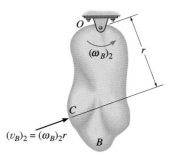

Velocity after collision (f)

Fig. 19–11

In the same manner, we may write an equation which relates the magnitudes of velocity $(v_A)_1$ and $(v_A)_2$ of body $A$. The result is

$$e = \frac{v - (v_A)_2}{(v_A)_1 - v}$$

Combining the above equations by eliminating the common velocity $v$ yields the desired result, i.e.,

$(+\nearrow)$

$$e = \frac{(v_B)_2 - (v_A)_2}{(v_A)_1 - (v_B)_1} \qquad (19\text{–}20)$$

This equation is identical to Eq. 15–11, which was derived for the central impact between two particles. Equation 19–20 states that the coefficient of restitution is equal to the ratio of the relative velocity of *separation* of the points of contact $(C)$ *just after impact* to the relative velocity at which the points *approach* one another *just* before impact. In deriving this equation, we assumed that the points of contact for both bodies move up and to the right *both* before and after impact. If motion of any one of the contacting points occurs down and to the left, the velocity of this point is considered a negative quantity in Eq. 19–20.

As stated previously, when Eq. 19–20 is used in conjunction with the conservation of angular momentum for the bodies, it provides a useful means of obtaining the velocities of two colliding bodies just after collision.

During impact the columns on many highway signs are intended to break out of their supports and easily collapse at their joints. This is shown by the slotted connections at their base and the breaks at the column's midsection. The mechanics of eccentric impact is used in the design of these structures.

# E X A M P L E  19.8

The 5-kg slender rod is suspended from the pin at $A$, Fig. 19–12a. If a 1-kg ball $B$ is thrown at the rod and strikes its center with a horizontal velocity of 9 m/s, determine the angular velocity of the rod just after impact. The coefficient of restitution is $e = 0.4$.

(a)

## Solution

*Conservation of Angular Momentum.*   Consider the ball and rod as a system, Fig. 19–12b. Angular momentum is conserved about point $A$ since the impulsive force between the rod and ball is *internal*. Also, the *weights* of the ball and rod are *nonimpulsive*. Noting the directions of the velocities of the ball and rod just after impact as shown on the kinematic diagram, Fig. 19–12c, we require

(b)

$$(\downarrow +) \qquad (H_A)_1 = (H_A)_2$$
$$m_B(v_B)_1(0.5 \text{ m}) = m_B(v_B)_2(0.5 \text{ m}) + m_R(v_G)_2(0.5 \text{ m}) + I_G\omega_2$$

$$(1 \text{ kg})(9 \text{ m/s})(0.5 \text{ m}) = (1 \text{ kg})(v_B)_2(0.5 \text{ m}) +$$

$$(5 \text{ kg})(v_G)_2(0.5 \text{ m}) + \left[\frac{1}{12}(5 \text{ kg})(1 \text{ m})^2\right]\omega_2$$

Since $(v_G)_2 = 0.5\omega_2$ then

$$4.5 = 0.5(v_B)_2 + 1.6667\omega_2 \qquad (1)$$

*Coefficient of Restitution.*   With reference to Fig. 19–12c, we have

$$(\xrightarrow{+}) \qquad e = \frac{(v_G)_2 - (v_B)_2}{(v_B)_1 - (v_G)_1} \qquad 0.4 = \frac{(0.5 \text{ m})\omega_2 - (v_B)_2}{9 \text{ m/s} - 0}$$

$$3.6 = 0.5\omega_2 - (v_B)_2$$

(c)

**Fig. 19–12**

Solving,

$$(v_B)_2 = -1.96 \text{ m/s} = 1.96 \text{ m/s} \leftarrow$$

$$\omega_2 = 3.287 \text{ rad/s} \, \mathord{\Upsilon} \qquad\qquad\qquad Ans.$$

## PROBLEMS

**19-34.** Two wheels $A$ and $B$ have masses $m_A$ and $m_B$, and radii of gyration about their central vertical axes of $k_A$ and $k_B$, respectively. If they are freely rotating in the same direction at $\boldsymbol{\omega}_A$ and $\boldsymbol{\omega}_B$ about the same vertical axis, determine their common angular velocity after they are brought into contact and slipping between them stops.

**19-35.** A horizontal circular platform has a weight of 1500 N ($\approx$ 150 kg) and a radius of gyration $k_z = 2.4$ m about the $z$ axis passing through its center $O$. The platform is free to rotate about the $z$ axis and is initially at rest. A man having a weight of 750 N ($\approx$ 75 kg) begins to run along the edge in a circular path of radius 3 m. If he has a speed of 1.2 m/s and maintains this speed relative to the platform, determine the angular velocity of the platform. Neglect friction.

**Prob. 19–36**

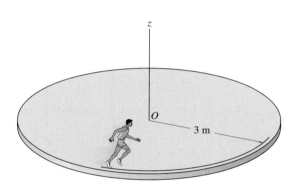

**Prob. 19–35**

**19-37.** Each of the two slender rods and the disk have the same mass $m$. Also, the length of each rod is equal to the diameter $d$ of the disk. If the assembly is rotating with an angular velocity $\boldsymbol{\omega}_1$ when the rods are directed outward, determine the angular velocity of the assembly if by internal means the rods are brought to an upright vertical position.

**\*19-36.** A horizontal circular platform has a weight of 1500 N ($\approx$ 150 kg) and a radius of gyration $k_z = 2.4$ m about the $z$ axis passing through its center $O$. The platform is free to rotate about the $z$ axis and is initially at rest. A man having a weight of 750 N ($\approx$ 75 kg) throws a 75-N ($\approx$ 7.5-kg) block off the edge of the platform with a horizontal velocity of 1.5 m/s, *measured relative to the platform*. Determine the angular velocity of the platform if the block is thrown (a) tangent to the platform, along the $+t$ axis, and (b) outward along a radial line, or $+n$ axis. Neglect the size of the man.

**Prob. 19–37**

**19-38.** The man sits on the swivel chair holding two 25-N ($\approx$ 2.5-kg) weights with his arms outstretched. If he is turning at 3 rad/s in this position, determine his angular velocity when the weights are drawn in and held 0.09 m from the axis of rotation. Assume he weighs 800 N ($\approx$ 80 kg) and has a radius of gyration $k_z = 0.165$ m about the $z$ axis. Neglect the mass of his arms and the size of the weights for the calculation.

Prob. 19–38

**19-39.** A man has a moment of inertia $I_z$ about the $z$ axis. He is originally at rest and standing on a small platform which can turn freely. If he is handed a wheel which is rotating at $\omega$ and has a moment of inertia $I$ about its spinning axis, determine his angular velocity if (a) he holds the wheel upright as shown, (b) turns the wheel out, $\theta = 90°$, and (c) turns the wheel downward, $\theta = 180°$.

Prob. 19–39

*19-40.** The space satellite has a mass of 125 kg and a moment of inertia $I_z = 0.940$ kg $\cdot$ m$^2$, excluding the four solar panels A, B, C, and D. Each solar panel has a mass of 20 kg and can be approximated as a thin plate. If the satellite is originally spinning about the $z$ axis at a constant rate $\omega_z = 0.5$ rad/s when $\theta = 90°$, determine the rate of spin if all the panels are raised and reach the upward position, $\theta = 0°$, at the same instant.

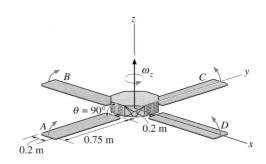

Prob. 19–40

**19-41.** The 2-kg rod $ACB$ supports the two 4-kg disks at its ends. If both disks are given a clockwise angular velocity $(\omega_A)_1 = (\omega_B)_1 = 5$ rad/s while the rod is held stationary and then released, determine the angular velocity of the rod after both disks have stopped spinning relative to the rod due to frictional resistance at the pins A and B. Motion is in the *horizontal plane*. Neglect friction at pin C.

Prob. 19–41

**19-42.** The 50-kg rod $AB$ supports the 30-kg disk at its end. If the disk is given an angular velocity $\omega_D = 8$ rad/s while the rod is held stationary and then released, determine the angular velocity of the rod after the disk has stopped spinning relative to the rod due to frictional resistance at the bearing $A$. Motion is in the *horizontal plane*. Neglect friction at the fixed bearing $B$.

**Prob. 19-42**

**19-43.** A thin disk of mass $m$ has an angular velocity $\omega_r$ while rotating on a smooth surface. Determine its new angular velocity just after the hook at its edge strikes the peg $P$ and the disk starts to rotate about $P$ without rebounding.

**Prob. 19-43**

**\*19-44.** The pendulum consists of a 25-N ($\approx$ 2.5-kg) slender rod $AB$ and a 50-N ($\approx$ 5-kg) wooden block. A projectile weighing 1 N ($\approx$ 0.1 kg) is fired into the center of the block with a velocity of 300 m/s. If the pendulum is initially at rest, and the projectile embeds itself into the block, determine the angular velocity of the pendulum just after the impact.

**Prob. 19-44**

**19-45.** A thin ring having a mass of 15 kg strikes the 20-mm-high step. Determine the largest angular velocity $\omega_1$ the ring can have so that it will not rebound off the step at $A$ when it strikes it.

**Prob. 19-45**

**19-46.** Determine the height $h$ at which a billiard ball of mass $m$ must be struck so that no frictional force develops between it and the table at $A$. Assume that the cue $C$ only exerts a horizontal force $\mathbf{P}$ on the ball.

Prob. 19–46

**19-47.** The disk has a mass of 15 kg. If it is released from rest when $\theta = 30°$, determine the maximum angle $\theta$ of rebound after it collides with the wall. The coefficient of restitution between the disk and the wall is $e = 0.6$. When $\theta = 0°$, the disk hangs such that it just touches the wall. Neglect friction at the pin $C$.

Prob. 19–47

**\*19-48.** The 10-kN ($\approx$ 1000-kg) block is sliding on the smooth surface when the corner $D$ hits a stop block $S$. Determine the minimum velocity $\mathbf{v}$ the block should have which would allow it to tip over on its side and land in the position shown. Neglect the size of $S$. *Hint:* During impact consider the weight of the block to be nonimpulsive.

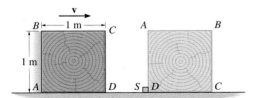

Prob. 19–48

**19-49.** A 7-g bullet having a velocity of 800 m/s is fired into the edge of the 5-kg disk as shown. Determine the angular velocity of the disk just after the bullet becomes embedded in it. Also, calculate how far $\theta$ the disk will swing until it stops. The disk is originally at rest.

Prob. 19–49

**19-50.** The two disks each weigh 10 kN ($\approx$ 1000 kg). If they are released from rest when $\theta = 30°$, determine $\theta$ after they collide and rebound from each other. The coefficient of restitution is $e = 0.75$. When $\theta = 0°$, the disks hang so that they just touch one another.

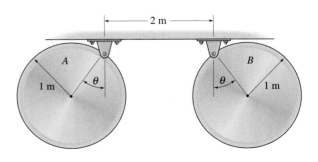

Prob. 19–50

**19-51.** The 40-kg rod $AB$ is hanging in the vertical position. A 20-kg block, sliding on a smooth horizontal surface with a velocity of 12 m/s, strikes the rod at its end $B$. Determine the velocity of the block immediately after the collision. The coefficient of restitution between the block and the rod at $B$ is $e = 0.8$.

Prob. 19–51

***19-52.** The pendulum consists of a 500-N ($\approx$ 50-kg) solid ball and 200-N ($\approx$ 20-kg) rod. If it is released from rest when $\theta_1 = 0°$, determine the angle $\theta_2$ after the ball strikes the wall, rebounds, and the pendulum swings up to the point of momentary rest. Take $e = 0.6$.

Prob. 19–52

**19-53.** The 6-kg slender rod $AB$ is originally at rest, suspended in the vertical position. A 1-kg ball is thrown at the rod with a velocity $v = 50$ m/s and strikes the rod at $C$. Determine the angular velocity of the rod just after the impact. Take $e = 0.7$ and $d = 2$ m.

Prob. 19–53

**19-54.** The disk has a mass $m$ and radius $r$. If it strikes the rough step having a height $\frac{1}{8}r$ as shown, determine the largest angular velocity $\omega_1$ the disk can have and not rebound off the step when it strikes it.

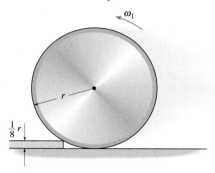

Prob. 19–54

**19-55.** The solid ball of mass $m$ is dropped with a velocity $v_1$ onto the edge of the rough step. If it rebounds horizontally off the step with a velocity $v_2$, determine the angle $\theta$ at which contact occurs. Assume no slipping when the ball strikes the step. The coefficient of restitution is $e$.

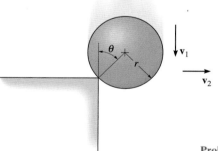

Prob. 19–55

***19-56.** A solid ball with a mass $m$ is thrown on the ground such that at the instant of contact it has an angular velocity $\omega_1$ and velocity components $(v_G)_{x1}$ and $(v_G)_{y1}$ as shown. If the ground is rough so no slipping occurs, determine the components of the velocity of its mass center just after impact. The coefficient of restitution is $e$.

Prob. 19–56

# CHAPTER REVIEW

- **Linear and Angular Momentum.** The linear momentum of a rigid body can be referenced to the velocity of its mass center $G$. The result is $\mathbf{L} = m\mathbf{v}_G$. By summing the moments of the linear momenta of all of the particles of the body about an axis passing through $G$, it can be shown that the angular momentum for the body about $G$ is $\mathbf{H}_G = I_G\boldsymbol{\omega}$. If the angular momentum is to be determined about an axis other than the one passing through the mass center, then the angular momentum is determined by summing vector $\mathbf{H}_G$ and the moment of vector $\mathbf{L}_G$ about this axis.

*Translation.* If the body is translating, then $\omega = 0$, and so

$$L = mv_G \qquad H_G = 0$$

*Rotation About a Fixed Axis.* Here

$$L = mv_G \qquad H_G = I_G\omega$$

Since $v_G = \omega r$, then, using the parallel-axis theorem, the angular momentum about the axis of rotation becomes

$$H_O = I_O\omega$$

*General Plane Motion.* The linear momentum and the angular momentum about point $G$ for this case are

$$L = mv_G \qquad H_G = I_G\omega$$

- **Principle of Impulse and Momentum.** The principles of linear and angular impulse and momentum for a rigid body are

$$m(\mathbf{v}_G)_1 + \Sigma \int_{t_1}^{t_2} \mathbf{F}\, dt = m(\mathbf{v}_G)_2$$

$$I_G\omega_1 + \Sigma \int_{t_1}^{t_2} M_G\, dt = I_G\omega_2$$

Before applying these equations, it is important to establish the $x$, $y$, $z$ inertial coordinate system. The free-body diagram for the body should also be drawn in order to account for all of the forces and couple moments that produce impulses on the body.

- **Conservation of Momentum.** Provided the sum of the linear impulses acting on a system of connected rigid bodies is zero in a particular direction, then the linear momentum for the system is conserved in this direction. Conservation of angular momentum occurs if the impulses pass through an axis or are parallel to it. Momentum is also conserved if the external forces are small and thereby create nonimpulsive forces on the system.

  A free-body diagram should accompany any application in order to classify the forces as impulsive or nonimpulsive and to determine an axis about which the angular momentum may be conserved.

- **Eccentric Impact.** If the line of impact does not coincide with the line connecting the mass centers of two colliding bodies, then eccentric impact will occur. If the motion of the bodies just after the impact is to be determined, then it is necessary to consider a conservation of momentum equation for the system and use the coefficient of restitution equation.

# Planar Kinematics and Kinetics of a Rigid Body

Having presented the various topics in planar kinematics and kinetics in Chapters 16 through 19, we will now summarize these principles and provide an opportunity for applying them to the solution of various types of problems.

**Kinematics.** Here we are interested in studying the geometry of motion, without concern for the forces which cause the motion. Before solving a planar kinematics problem, it is *first* necessary to *classify the motion* as being either rectilinear or curvilinear translation, rotation about a fixed axis, or general plane motion. In particular, problems involving general plane motion can be solved either with reference to a fixed axis (absolute motion analysis) or using translating or rotating frames of reference (relative motion analysis). The choice generally depends upon the type of constraints and the problem's geometry. In all cases, application of the necessary equations may be clarified by drawing a kinematic diagram. Remember that the *velocity* of a point is always *tangent* to its path of motion, and the *acceleration* of a point can have *components* in the *n-t* directions when the path is *curved*.

**Translation.** When the body moves with rectilinear or curvilinear translation, *all* the points on the body have the *same motion*.

$$\mathbf{v}_B = \mathbf{v}_A \qquad \mathbf{a}_B = \mathbf{a}_A$$

## Rotation About a Fixed Axis.

### Angular Motion.

*Variable Angular Acceleration.* Provided a mathematical relationship is given between *any two* of the *four* variables $\theta$, $\omega$, $\alpha$, and $t$, then a *third* variable can be determined by solving one of the following equations which relate all three variables.

$$\omega = \frac{d\theta}{dt} \qquad \alpha = \frac{d\omega}{dt} \qquad \alpha \, d\theta = \omega \, d\omega$$

*Constant Angular Acceleration.* The following equations apply when it is *absolutely certain* that the angular acceleration is constant.

$$\theta = \theta_0 + \omega_0 t + \tfrac{1}{2}\alpha_c t^2 \qquad \omega = \omega_0 + \alpha_c t \qquad \omega^2 = \omega_0^2 + 2\alpha_c(\theta - \theta_0)$$

### Motion of Point P.

Once $\omega$ and $\alpha$ have been determined, then the circular motion of point $P$ can be specified using the following scalar or vector equations.

$$v = \omega r \qquad\qquad \mathbf{v} = \boldsymbol{\omega} \times \mathbf{r}$$
$$a_t = \alpha r \quad a_n = \omega^2 r \qquad \mathbf{a} = \boldsymbol{\alpha} \times \mathbf{r} + \boldsymbol{\omega} \times (\boldsymbol{\omega} \times \mathbf{r})$$

**General Plane Motion—Relative-Motion Analysis.** Recall that when *translating axes* are placed at the "base point" $A$, the *relative motion* of point $B$ with respect to $A$ is simply *circular motion of B about A*. The following equations apply to two points $A$ and $B$ located on the *same* rigid body.

$$\mathbf{v}_B = \mathbf{v}_A + \mathbf{v}_{B/A} = \mathbf{v}_A + (\boldsymbol{\omega} \times \mathbf{r}_{B/A})$$
$$\mathbf{a}_B = \mathbf{a}_A + \mathbf{a}_{B/A} = \mathbf{a}_A + \boldsymbol{\alpha} \times \mathbf{r}_{B/A} + \boldsymbol{\omega} \times (\boldsymbol{\omega} \times \mathbf{r}_{B/A})$$

*Rotating and translating axes* are often used to analyze the motion of rigid bodies which are connected together by collars or slider blocks.

$$\mathbf{v}_B = \mathbf{v}_A + \boldsymbol{\Omega} \times \mathbf{r}_{B/A} + (\mathbf{v}_{B/A})_{xyz}$$
$$\mathbf{a}_B = \mathbf{a}_A + \dot{\boldsymbol{\Omega}} \times \mathbf{r}_{B/A} + \boldsymbol{\Omega} \times (\boldsymbol{\Omega} \times \mathbf{r}_{B/A}) + 2\boldsymbol{\Omega} \times (\mathbf{v}_{B/A})_{xyz} + (\mathbf{a}_{B/A})_{xyz}$$

**Kinetics.** To analyze the forces which cause the motion we must use the principles of kinetics. When applying the necessary equations, it is important to first establish the inertial coordinate system and define the positive directions of the axes. The *directions* should be the *same* as those selected when writing any equations of kinematics provided *simultaneous solution* of equations becomes necessary.

**Equations of Motion.** These equations are used to determine accelerated motions or forces causing the motion. If used to determine position, velocity, or time of motion, then kinematics will have to be considered for part of the solution. Before applying the equations of motion, *always draw a free-body diagram* in order to identify all the forces acting on the body. Also, establish the directions of the acceleration of the mass center and the angular acceleration of the body. (A kinetic diagram may also be drawn in order to represent $m\mathbf{a}_G$ and $I_G\boldsymbol{\alpha}$ graphically. This diagram is particularly convenient for resolving $m\mathbf{a}_G$ into components and for identifying the terms in the moment sum $\Sigma(\mathcal{M}_k)_P$.)

The three equations of motion are

$$\Sigma F_x = m(a_G)_x$$
$$\Sigma F_y = m(a_G)_y$$
$$\Sigma M_G = I_G\alpha \quad \text{or} \quad \Sigma M_P = \Sigma(\mathcal{M}_k)_P$$

In particular, if the body is *rotating about a fixed axis*, moments may also be summed about point $O$ on the axis, in which case

$$\Sigma M_O = \Sigma(\mathcal{M}_k)_O = I_O\alpha$$

**Work and Energy.** *The equation of work and energy is used to solve problems involving force, velocity, and displacement.* Before applying this equation, *always draw a free-body diagram* of the body in order to identify the forces which do work. Recall that the kinetic energy of the body is due to translational motion of the mass center, $\mathbf{v}_G$, *and* rotational motion of the body, $\boldsymbol{\omega}$.

$$T_1 + \Sigma U_{1-2} = T_2$$

where

$$T = \tfrac{1}{2}mv_G^2 + \tfrac{1}{2}I_G\omega^2$$

$$U_F = \int F\cos\theta\,ds \qquad \text{(variable force)}$$

$$U_{F_c} = F_c\cos\theta(s_2 - s_1) \quad \text{(constant force)}$$
$$U_W = -W\,\Delta y \qquad\qquad \text{(weight)}$$
$$U_s = -(\tfrac{1}{2}ks_2^2 - \tfrac{1}{2}ks_1^2) \quad \text{(spring)}$$
$$U_M = M\theta \qquad\qquad\quad \text{(constant couple moment)}$$

If the forces acting on the body are *conservative forces*, then apply the *conservation of energy equation*. This equation is easier to use than the equation of work and energy, since it applies only at *two points* on the path and *does not* require calculation of the work done by a force as the body moves along the path.

$$T_1 + V_1 = T_2 + V_2$$

where

$$V_g = Wy \quad \text{(gravitational potential energy)}$$
$$V_e = \tfrac{1}{2}ks^2 \quad \text{(elastic potential energy)}$$

**Impulse and Momentum.**   *The principles of linear and angular impulse and momentum are used to solve problems involving force, velocity, and time.* Before applying the equations, *draw a free-body diagram* in order to identify all the forces which cause linear and angular impulses on the body. Also, establish the directions of the velocity of the mass center and the angular velocity of the body just before and just after the impulses are applied. (As an alternative procedure, the impulse and momentum diagrams may accompany the solution in order to graphically account for the terms in the equations. These diagrams are particularly advantageous when computing the angular impulses and angular momenta about a point other than the body's mass center.)

$$m(\mathbf{v}_G)_1 + \Sigma \int \mathbf{F}\, dt = m(\mathbf{v}_G)_2$$

$$(\mathbf{H}_G)_1 + \Sigma \int \mathbf{M}_G\, dt = (\mathbf{H}_G)_2$$

or

$$(\mathbf{H}_O)_1 + \Sigma \int \mathbf{M}_O\, dt = (\mathbf{H}_O)_2$$

**Conservation of Momentum.**   If nonimpulsive forces or no impulsive forces act on the body in a particular direction, or if the motions of several bodies are involved in the problem, then consider applying the conservation of linear or angular momentum for the solution. Investigation of the free-body diagram (or the impulse diagram) will aid in determining the directions for which the impulsive forces are zero, or axes about which the impulsive forces cause zero angular momentum. For these cases,

$$m(\mathbf{v}_G)_1 = m(\mathbf{v}_G)_2$$
$$(\mathbf{H}_O)_1 = (\mathbf{H}_O)_2$$

The problems that follow involve application of all the above concepts. They are presented in *random order* so that practice may be gained at identifying the various types of problems and developing the skills necessary for their solution.

# REVIEW PROBLEMS

**R2-1.** At a given instant, the wheel is rotating with the angular motions shown. Determine the acceleration of the collar at $A$ at this instant.

**Prob. R2–1**

**R2-2.** The hoisting gear $A$ has an initial angular velocity of 60 rad/s and a constant deceleration of 1 rad/s². Determine the velocity and deceleration of the block which is being hoisted by the hub on gear $B$ when $t = 3$ s.

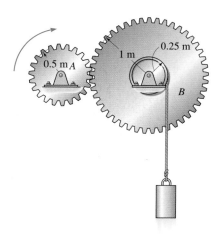

**Prob. R2–2**

**R2-3.** The rod is bent into the shape of a sine curve and is forced to rotate about the $y$ axis by connecting the spindle $S$ to a motor. If the rod starts from rest in the position shown and a motor drives it for a short time with an angular acceleration $\alpha = (1.5e^t)$ rad/s², where $t$ is in seconds, determine the magnitudes of the angular velocity and angular displacement of the rod when $t = 3$ s. Locate the point on the rod which has the greatest velocity and acceleration, and compute the magnitudes of the velocity and acceleration of this point when $t = 3$ s. The curve defining the rod is $z = 0.25 \sin(\pi y)$, where the argument for the sine is given in radians when $y$ is in meters.

**Prob. R2–3**

**\*R2-4.** A cord is wrapped around the inner spool of the gear. If it is pulled with a constant velocity $v$, determine the velocity and acceleration of points $A$ and $B$. The gear rolls on the fixed gear rack.

**Prob. R2–4**

**R2-5.** A 7-kg automobile tire is released from rest at $A$ on the incline and rolls without slipping to point $B$, where it then travels in free flight. Determine the maximum height $h$ the tire attains. The radius of gyration of the tire about its mass center is $k_G = 0.3$ m.

**R2-7.** The uniform connecting rod $BC$ has a mass of 3 kg and is pin-connected at its end points. Determine the vertical forces which the pins exert on the ends $B$ and $C$ of the rod at the instant (a) $\theta = 0°$, and (b) $\theta = 90°$. The crank $AB$ is turning with a constant angular velocity $\omega_{AB} = 5$ rad/s.

Prob. R2–5

Prob. R2–7

**R2-6.** The link $OA$ is pinned at $O$ and rotates because of the sliding action of rod $R$ along the horizontal groove. If $R$ starts from rest. when $\theta = 0°$ and has a constant acceleration $a_R = 60$ mm/s$^2$ to the right, determine the angular velocity and angular acceleration of $OA$ when $t = 2$ s.

**\*R2-8.** The tire has a mass of 9 kg and a radius of gyration $k_O = 225$ mm. If it is released from rest and rolls down the plane without slipping, determine the speed of its center $O$ when $t = 3$ s.

Prob. R2–6

Prob. R2–8

**R2-9.** The double pendulum consists of two rods. Rod *AB* has a constant angular velocity of 3 rad/s, and rod *BC* has a constant angular velocity of 2 rad/s. Both of these absolute motions are measured counterclockwise. Determine the velocity and acceleration of point *C* at the instant shown.

**R2-11.** If the ball has a weight of 150 N ($\approx$ 15 kg) and is thrown onto a *rough surface* so that its center has a velocity of 6 m/s parallel to the surface, determine the amount of backspin, $\omega$, the ball must be given so that it stops spinning at the same instant that its forward velocity is zero. It is not necessary to know the coefficient of kinetic friction at *A* for the calculation.

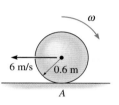

Prob. R2–11

Prob. R2–9

**R2-10.** The spool and wire wrapped around its core have a mass of 20 kg and a centroidal radius of gyration $k_G = 250$ mm. If the coefficient of kinetic friction at the ground is $\mu_B = 0.1$, determine the angular acceleration of the spool when the 30-N · m couple moment is applied.

**\*R2-12.** Blocks *A* and *B* weigh 50 and 10 N ($\approx$ 5 and 1 kg), respectively. If *P* = 100 N, determine the normal force exerted by block *A* on block *B*. Neglect friction and the weights of the pulleys, cord, and bars of the triangular frame.

Prob. R2–10

Prob. R2–12

**R2-13.** Determine the velocity and acceleration of rod $R$ for any angle $\theta$ of cam $C$ if the cam rotates with a constant angular velocity $\omega$. The pin connection at $O$ does not cause an interference with the motion of $A$ on $C$.

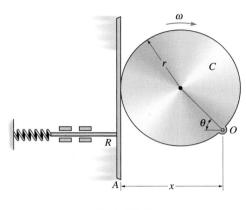

Prob. R2–13

**R2-15.** A tape having a thickness $s$ wraps around the wheel which is turning at a constant rate $\omega$. Assuming the unwrapped portion of tape remains horizontal, determine the acceleration of point $P$ on the tape when the radius is $r$. *Hint:* Since $v_p = \omega r$, take the time derivative and note that $dr/dt = \omega(s/2\pi)$.

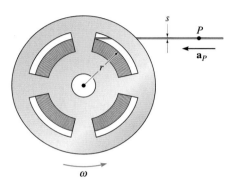

Prob. R2–15

**R2-14.** The uniform plate weighs 40 N ($\approx$ 4 kg) and is supported by a roller at $A$. If a horizontal force $F = 70$ N is suddenly applied to the roller, determine the acceleration of the center of the roller at the instant the force is applied. The plate has a moment of inertia about its center of mass of $I_G = 1.36$ kg · m². Neglect the weight of the roller.

**\*R2-16.** The 150-kg cylinder is initially at rest on a 50-kg plate. If a couple moment $M = 400$ N · m is applied to the cylinder, determine the angular acceleration of the cylinder and the time needed for the end $B$ of the plate to travel 3 m and strike the wall. Assume the cylinder does not slip on the plate, and neglect the mass of the rollers under the plate.

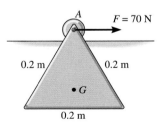

Prob. R2–14

Prob. R2–16

**R2-17.** The wheel barrow and its contents have a mass of 40 kg and a mass center at $G$, excluding the wheel. The wheel has a mass of 2 kg and a radius of gyration $k_O = 0.120$ m. If the wheelbarrow is released from rest from the position shown, determine its speed after it travels 4 m down the incline. The coefficient of kinetic friction between the incline and $A$ is $\mu_A = 0.3$. The wheels roll without slipping at $B$.

**Prob. R2–17**

**R2-18.** The drum of mass $m$, radius $r$, and radius of gyration $k_O$ rolls along an inclined plane for which the coefficient of static friction is $\mu$. If the drum is released from rest, determine the maximum angle $\theta$ for the incline so that it rolls without slipping.

**Prob. R2–18**

**R2-19.** The 20-kg solid ball is cast on the floor such that it has a backspin $\omega = 15$ rad/s and its center has an initial horizontal velocity $v_G = 20$ m/s. If the coefficient of kinetic friction between the floor and the ball is $\mu_A = 0.3$, determine the distance it travels before it stops spinning.

**\*R2-20.** Determine the backspin $\omega$ which should be given to the 20-kg ball so that when its center is given an initial horizontal velocity $v_G = 20$ m/s it stops spinning and translating at the same instant. The coefficient of kinetic friction is $\mu_A = 0.3$.

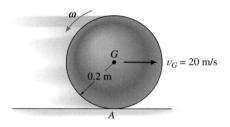

**Probs. R2–19/20**

**R2-21.** A 20-kg roll of paper, originally at rest, is pin-supported at its ends to bracket $AB$. The roll rests against a wall for which the coefficient of kinetic friction at $C$ is $\mu_C = 0.3$. If a force of 40 N is applied uniformly to the end of the sheet, determine the initial angular acceleration of the roll and the tension in the bracket as the paper unwraps. For the calculation, treat the roll as a cylinder.

**Prob. R2–21**

**R2-22.** Compute the velocity of rod $R$ for any angle $\theta$ of the cam $C$ if the cam rotates with a constant angular velocity $\boldsymbol{\omega}$. The pin connection at $O$ does not cause an interference with the motion of $A$ on $C$.

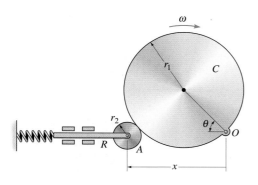

Prob. R2–22

**R2-23.** The assembly weighs 10 kN ($\approx$ 1000 kg) and has a radius of gyration $k_G = 0.6$ m about its center of mass $G$. The kinetic energy of the assembly is 31 kN · m when it is in the position shown. If it is rolling counterclockwise on the surface without slipping, determine its linear momentum at this instant.

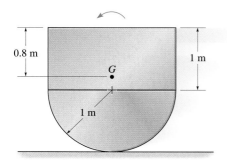

Prob. R2–23

**\*R2-24.** The pendulum consists of a 30-kg sphere and a 10-kg slender rod. Compute the reaction at the pin $O$ just after the cord $AB$ is cut.

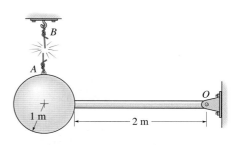

Prob. R2–24

**R2-25.** The board rests on the surface of two drums. At the instant shown, it has an acceleration of 0.5 m/s² to the right, while at the same instant points on the outer rim of each drum have an acceleration with a magnitude of 3 m/s². If the board does not slip on the drums, determine its speed due to the motion.

Prob. R2–25

**R2-26.** The center of the pulley is being lifted vertically with an acceleration of $4 \text{ m/s}^2$ at the instant it has a velocity of 2 m/s. If the cable does not slip on the pulley's surface, determine the accelerations of the cylinder $B$ and point $C$ on the pulley.

Prob. R2–26

**R2-27.** At the instant shown, two forces act on the 30-kg slender rod which is pinned at $O$. Determine the magnitude of force **F** and the initial angular acceleration of the rod so that the horizontal reaction which the *pin exerts on the rod* is 50 N directed to the right.

Prob. R2–27

**\*R-28.** The tub of the mixer has a weight of 350 N ($\approx 35$ kg) and a radius of gyration $k_G = 0.65$ m about its center of gravity. If a constant torque $M = 300 \text{ N} \cdot \text{m}$ is applied to the dumping wheel, determine the angular velocity of the tub when it has rotated $\theta = 90°$. Originally the tub is at rest when $\theta = 0°$.

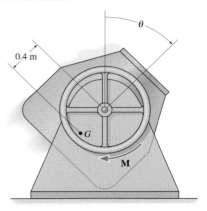

Prob. R2–28

**R2-29.** The spool has a weight of 300 N ($\approx 30$ kg) and a radius of gyration $k_O = 0.065$ m. If a force of 400 N is applied to the cord at $A$, determine the angular velocity of the spool in $t = 3$ s starting from rest. Neglect the mass of the pulley and cord.

**R2-30.** Solve Prob. R2–29 if a 400-N ($\approx 40$-kg) block is suspended from the cord at $A$, rather than applying the 400-N force.

Probs. R2–29/30

**R2-31.** The dresser has a weight of 800 N ($\approx$ 80 kg) and is pushed along the floor. If the coefficient of static friction at $A$ and $B$ is $\mu_s = 0.3$ and the coefficient of kinetic friction is $\mu_k = 0.2$, determine the smallest horizontal force $P$ needed to cause motion. If this force is increased slightly, determine the acceleration of the dresser. Also, what are the normal reactions at $A$ and $B$ when it begins to move?

**Prob. R2–31**

**\*R2-32.** When the crank on the Chinese windlass is turning, the rope on shaft $A$ unwinds while that on shaft $B$ winds up. Determine the speed at which the block lowers if the crank is turning with an angular velocity $\omega = 4$ rad/s. What is the angular velocity of the pulley at $C$? The rope segments on each side of the pulley are both parallel and vertical, and the rope does not slip on the pulley.

**Prob. R2–32**

**R2-33.** The semicircular disk has a mass of 50 kg and is released from rest from the position shown. The coefficients of static and kinetic friction between the disk and the beam are $\mu_s = 0.5$ and $\mu_k = 0.3$, respectively. Determine the initial reactions at the pin $A$ and roller $B$, used to support the beam. Neglect the mass of the beam for the calculation.

**R2-34.** The semicircular disk has a mass of 50 kg and is released from rest from the position shown. The coefficients of static and kinetic friction between the disk and the beam are $\mu_s = 0.2$ and $\mu_k = 0.1$, respectively. Determine the initial reactions at the pin $A$ and roller $B$ used to support the beam. Neglect the mass of the beam for the calculation.

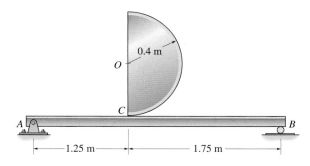

**Probs. R2–33/34**

**R2-35.** The cylinder having a mass of 5 kg is initially at rest when it is placed in contact with the wall $B$ and the rotor at $A$. If the rotor always maintains a constant clockwise angular velocity $\omega = 6$ rad/s, determine the initial angular acceleration of the cylinder. The coefficient of kinetic friction at the contacting surfaces $B$ and $C$ is $\mu_k = 0.2$.

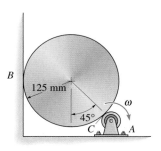

**Prob. R2–35**

**\*R2-36.** The truck carries the 4000-N ($\approx$ 400-kg) crate which has a center of gravity at $G_c$. Determine the largest acceleration of the truck so that the crate will not slip or tip on the truck bed. The coefficient of static friction between the crate and the truck is $\mu_s = 0.6$.

Prob. R2–36

**R2-37.** The truck has a weight of 40 000 N ($\approx$ 4000 kg) and center of gravity at $G_t$. It carries the 4000-N ($\approx$ 400-kg) crate, which has a center of gravity at $G_c$. Determine the normal reaction at *each* of its four tires if it accelerates at $a = 0.15$ m/s$^2$. Also, what is the frictional force acting between the crate and the truck, and between *each* of the rear tires and the road? Assume that power is delivered only to the rear tires. The front tires are free to roll. Neglect the mass of the tires. The crate does not slip or tip on the truck.

Prob. R2–37

**R2-38.** Spool $B$ is at rest and spool $A$ is rotating at 6 rad/s when the slack in the cord connecting them is taken up. Determine the angular velocity of each spool immediately after the cord is jerked tight. The spools $A$ and $B$ have weights and radii of gyration $W_A = 300$ N ($\approx$ 30 kg), $k_A = 0.2$ m and $W_B = 150$ N ($\approx$ 15 kg), $k_B = 0.15$ m, respectively.

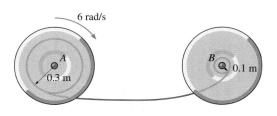

Prob. R2–38

**R2-39.** The two 30-kg rods $EF$ and $HI$ are fixed (welded) to the link $AC$ at $E$. Determine the internal axial force $E_x$, shear force $E_y$, and moment $M_E$, which the bar $AC$ exerts on $FE$ at $E$ if at the instant $\theta = 30°$ link $AB$ has an angular velocity $\omega = 5$ rad/s and an angular acceleration $\alpha = 8$ rad/s$^2$ as shown.

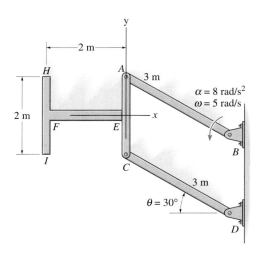

Prob. R2–39

***R2-40.*** The dragster has a mass of 1500 kg and a center of mass at $G$. If the coefficient of kinetic friction between the rear wheels and the pavement is $\mu_k = 0.6$, determine if it is possible for the driver to lift the front wheels, $A$, off the ground while the rear wheels are slipping. If so, what acceleration is necessary to do this? Neglect the mass of the wheels and assume that the front wheels are free to roll.

**Prob. R2–40**

**R2-42.** The 1.6-Mg car shown has been "raked" by increasing the height $h = 0.2$ m of its center of mass. This was done by raising the springs on the rear axle. If the coefficient of kinetic friction between the rear wheels and the ground is $\mu_k = 0.3$, show that the car can accelerate slightly faster than its counterpart for which $h = 0$. Neglect the mass of the wheels and driver and assume the front wheels at $B$ are free to roll while the rear wheels slip.

**Prob. R2–42**

**R2-41.** The dragster has a mass of 1500 kg and a center of mass at $G$. If no slipping occurs, determine the friction force $F_B$ which must be applied to *each* of the rear wheels $B$ in order to develop an acceleration $a = 6$ m/s$^2$. What are the normal reactions of *each* wheel on the ground? Neglect the mass of the wheels and assume that the front wheels are free to roll.

**Prob. R2–41**

**R2-43.** The handcart has a mass of 200 kg and center of mass at $G$. Determine the normal reactions at *each* of the wheels at $A$ and $B$ if a force $P = 50$ N is applied to the handle. Neglect the mass and rolling resistance of the wheels.

**Prob. R2–43**

**\*R2-44.** If bar $AB$ has an angular velocity $\omega_{AB} = 6$ rad/s, determine the velocity of the slider block $C$ at the instant shown.

**R2-46.** The 800-kg cylinder is attached to the 100-kg slender rod which is pinned from point $A$. At the instant $\theta = 30°$ it has an angular velocity $\omega_1 = 1$ rad/s as shown. Determine the largest angle $\theta$ to which the rod swings before it momentarily stops.

**Prob. R2–44**

**Prob. R2–46**

**R2-45.** The disk is rotating at a constant rate $\omega = 4$ rad/s, and as it falls freely, its center has an acceleration of 9.81 m/s². Determine the acceleration of points $A$ and $B$ on the rim of the disk at the instant shown.

**R2-47.** The bicycle and rider have a mass of 80 kg with center of mass located at $G$. If the coefficient of kinetic friction at the rear tire is $\mu_B = 0.8$, determine the normal reactions at the tires $A$ and $B$, and the deceleration of the rider, when the rear wheel locks for braking. What is the normal reaction at the rear wheel when the bicycle is traveling at constant velocity and the brakes are not applied? Neglect the mass of the wheels.

**Prob. R2–45**

**Prob. R2–47**

**\*R2-48.** At the instant shown, link $AB$ has an angular velocity $\omega_{AB} = 2$ rad/s and an angular acceleration $\alpha_{AB} = 6$ rad/s². Determine the acceleration of the pin at $C$ and the angular acceleration of link $CB$ at this instant, when $\theta = 60°$.

Prob. R2–48

**R2-49.** The spool has a mass of 60 kg and a radius of gyration $k_G = 0.3$ m. If it is released from rest, determine how far it descends down the smooth plane before it attains an angular velocity $\omega = 6$ rad/s. Neglect friction and the mass of the cord which is wound around the central core.

**R2-50.** Solve Prob. R2–49 if the plane is rough, such that the coefficient of kinetic friction at $A$ is $\mu_A = 0.2$.

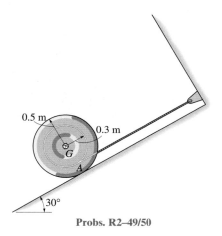

Probs. R2–49/50

**R2-51.** The gear rack has a mass of 6 kg, and the gears each have a mass of 4 kg and a radius of gyration $k = 30$ mm at their centers. If the rack is originally moving downward at 2 m/s, when $s = 0$, determine the speed of the rack when $s = 600$ mm. The gears are free to turn about their centers, $A$ and $B$.

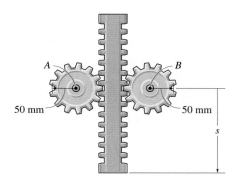

Prob. R2–51

**\*R2-52.** The car has a mass of 1.50 Mg and a mass center at $G$. Determine the maximum acceleration it can have if (a) power is supplied only to the rear wheels, (b) power is supplied only to the front wheels. Neglect the mass of the wheels in the calculation, and assume that the wheels that do not receive power are free to roll. Also, assume that slipping of the powered wheels occurs, where the coefficient of kinetic friction is $\mu_k = 0.3$.

Prob. R2–52

The three-dimensional motion of these industrial robots used in the manufacturing of automobiles must be accurately specified.

# Three-Dimensional Kinematics of a Rigid Body

- To analyze the kinematics of a body subjected to rotation about a fixed axis and general plane motion.
- To provide a relative-motion analysis of a rigid body using translating and rotating axes.

## 20.1 Rotation About a Fixed Point

When a rigid body rotates about a fixed point, the distance $r$ from the point to a particle $P$ located on the body is the *same* for *any position* of the body. Thus, the path of motion for the particle lies on the *surface of a sphere* having a radius $r$ and centered at the fixed point. Since motion along this path occurs only from a series of rotations made during a finite time interval, we will first develop a familiarity with some of the properties of rotational displacements.

The boom can rotate up and down, and because it is hinged at a point on the vertical axis about which it turns it is subjected to rotation about a fixed point.

**Euler's Theorem.** Euler's theorem states that two "component" rotations about different axes passing through a point are equivalent to a single resultant rotation about an axis passing through the point. If more than two rotations are applied, they can be combined into pairs, and each pair can be further reduced to combine into one rotation.

**Finite Rotations.** If component rotations used in Euler's theorem are *finite*, it is important that the *order* in which they are applied be maintained. This is because finite rotations do *not* obey the law of vector addition, and hence they cannot be classified as vector quantities. To show this, consider the two finite rotations $\theta_1 + \theta_2$ applied to the block in Fig. 20–1a. Each rotation has a magnitude of 90° and a direction defined by the right-hand rule, as indicated by the arrow. The resultant orientation of the block is shown at the right. When these two rotations are applied in the order $\theta_2 + \theta_1$, as shown in Fig. 20–1b, the resultant position of the block is *not* the same as it is in Fig. 20–1a. Consequently, *finite rotations* do not obey the commutative law of addition ($\theta_1 + \theta_2 \neq \theta_2 + \theta_1$), and therefore *they cannot be classified as vectors*. If smaller, yet finite, rotations had been used to illustrate this point, e.g., 10° instead of 90°, the *resultant* orientation of the block after each combination of rotations would also be different; however, in this case, the difference is only a small amount.

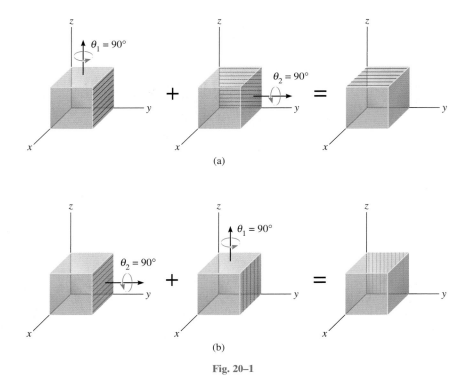

**Fig. 20–1**

**Infinitesimal Rotations.** When defining the angular motions of a body subjected to three-dimensional motion, only rotations which are *infinitesimally small* will be considered. *Such rotations may be classified as vectors, since they can be added vectorially in any manner.* To show this, let us for purposes of simplicity consider the rigid body itself to be a sphere which is allowed to rotate about its central fixed point $O$, Fig. 20–2a. If we impose two infinitesimal rotations $d\boldsymbol{\theta}_1 + d\boldsymbol{\theta}_2$ on the body, it is seen that point $P$ moves along the path $d\boldsymbol{\theta}_1 \times \mathbf{r} + d\boldsymbol{\theta}_2 \times \mathbf{r}$ and ends up at $P'$. Had the two successive rotations occurred in the order $d\boldsymbol{\theta}_2 + d\boldsymbol{\theta}_1$, then the resultant displacements of $P$ would have been $d\boldsymbol{\theta}_2 \times \mathbf{r} + d\boldsymbol{\theta}_1 \times \mathbf{r}$. Since the vector cross product obeys the distributive law, by comparison $(d\boldsymbol{\theta}_1 + d\boldsymbol{\theta}_2) \times \mathbf{r} = (d\boldsymbol{\theta}_2 + d\boldsymbol{\theta}_1) \times \mathbf{r}$. Here infinitesimal rotations $d\boldsymbol{\theta}$ are vectors, since these quantities have both a magnitude and direction for which the order of (vector) addition is not important, i.e., $d\boldsymbol{\theta}_1 + d\boldsymbol{\theta}_2 = d\boldsymbol{\theta}_2 + d\boldsymbol{\theta}_1$. Furthermore, as shown in Fig. 20–2a, the two "component" rotations $d\boldsymbol{\theta}_1$ and $d\boldsymbol{\theta}_2$ are equivalent to a single resultant rotation $d\boldsymbol{\theta} = d\boldsymbol{\theta}_1 + d\boldsymbol{\theta}_2$, a consequence of Euler's theorem.

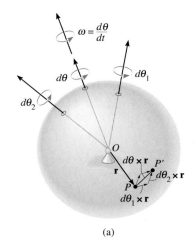

(a)

**Angular Velocity.** If the body is subjected to an angular rotation $d\boldsymbol{\theta}$ about a fixed point, the angular velocity of the body is defined by the time derivative,

$$\boldsymbol{\omega} = \dot{\boldsymbol{\theta}} \qquad (20\text{–}1)$$

The line specifying the direction of $\boldsymbol{\omega}$, which is collinear with $d\boldsymbol{\theta}$, is referred to as the *instantaneous axis of rotation*, Fig. 20–2b. In general, this axis changes direction during each instant of time. Since $d\boldsymbol{\theta}$ is a vector quantity, so too is $\boldsymbol{\omega}$, and it follows from vector addition that if the body is subjected to two component angular motions, $\boldsymbol{\omega}_1 = \dot{\boldsymbol{\theta}}_1$ and $\boldsymbol{\omega}_2 = \dot{\boldsymbol{\theta}}_2$, the resultant angular velocity is $\boldsymbol{\omega} = \boldsymbol{\omega}_1 + \boldsymbol{\omega}_2$.

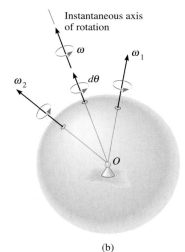

(b)

**Fig. 20–2**

**Angular Acceleration.** The body's angular acceleration is determined from the time derivative of the angular velocity, i.e.,

$$\boldsymbol{\alpha} = \dot{\boldsymbol{\omega}} \qquad (20\text{–}2)$$

For motion about a fixed point, $\boldsymbol{\alpha}$ must account for a change in *both* the magnitude and direction of $\boldsymbol{\omega}$, so that, in general, $\boldsymbol{\alpha}$ is not directed along the instantaneous axis of rotation, Fig. 20–3.

As the direction of the instantaneous axis of rotation (or the line of action of $\boldsymbol{\omega}$) changes in space, the locus of points defined by the axis generates a fixed *space cone*. If the change in this axis is viewed with respect to the rotating body, the locus of the axis generates a *body cone*,

**Fig. 20–3**

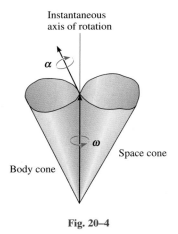

Fig. 20–4

Fig. 20–4. At any given instant, these cones are tangent along the instantaneous axis of rotation, and when the body is in motion, the body cone appears to roll either on the inside or the outside surface of the fixed space cone. Provided the paths defined by the open ends of the cones are described by the head of the $\boldsymbol{\omega}$ vector, $\boldsymbol{\alpha}$ must act tangent to these paths at any given instant, since the time rate of change of $\boldsymbol{\omega}$ is equal to $\boldsymbol{\alpha}$. Fig. 20–4.

**Velocity.**   Once $\boldsymbol{\omega}$ is specified, the velocity of any point $P$ on a body rotating about a fixed point can be determined using the same methods as for a body rotating about a fixed axis (Sec. 16.3). Hence, by the cross product,

$$\mathbf{v} = \boldsymbol{\omega} \times \mathbf{r} \tag{20–3}$$

Here $\mathbf{r}$ defines the position of $P$ measured from the fixed point $O$, Fig. 20–3.

**Acceleration.**   If $\boldsymbol{\omega}$ and $\boldsymbol{\alpha}$ are known at a given instant, the acceleration of any point $P$ on the body can be obtained by time differentiation of Eq. 20–3, which yields

$$\mathbf{a} = \boldsymbol{\alpha} \times \mathbf{r} + \boldsymbol{\omega} \times (\boldsymbol{\omega} \times \mathbf{r}) \tag{20–4}$$

The form of this equation is the same as that developed in Sec. 16.3, which defines the acceleration of a point located on a body subjected to rotation about a fixed axis.

## *20.2   The Time Derivative of a Vector Measured from Either a Fixed or Translating-Rotating System

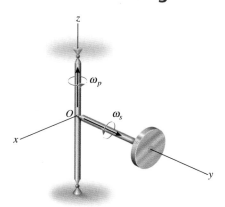

Fig. 20–5

In many types of problems involving the motion of a body about a fixed point, the angular velocity $\boldsymbol{\omega}$ is specified in terms of its component angular motions. For example, the disk in Fig. 20–5 spins about the horizontal $y$ axis at $\boldsymbol{\omega}_s$ while it rotates or precesses about the vertical $z$ axis at $\boldsymbol{\omega}_p$. Therefore, its resultant angular velocity is $\boldsymbol{\omega} = \boldsymbol{\omega}_s + \boldsymbol{\omega}_p$. If the angular acceleration $\boldsymbol{\alpha} = \dot{\boldsymbol{\omega}}$ of such a body is to be determined, it is sometimes easier to compute the time derivative of $\boldsymbol{\omega}$ by using a coordinate system which has a *rotation* defined by one or more of the components of $\boldsymbol{\omega}$.* For this reason, and for other uses later, an equation will presently be derived that relates the time derivative of any vector $\mathbf{A}$ defined from a translating-rotating reference to its time derivative defined from a fixed reference.

---

*In the case of the spinning disk, Fig. 20–5, the $x, y, z$ axes may be given an angular velocity of $\boldsymbol{\omega}_p$.

Consider the $x, y, z$ axes of the moving frame of reference to have an angular velocity $\boldsymbol{\Omega}$ which is measured from the fixed $X, Y, Z$ axes, Fig. 20–6a. In the following discussion, it will be convenient to express vector $\mathbf{A}$ in terms of its $\mathbf{i}, \mathbf{j}, \mathbf{k}$ components, which define the directions of the moving axes. Hence,

$$\mathbf{A} = A_x\mathbf{i} + A_y\mathbf{j} + A_z\mathbf{k}$$

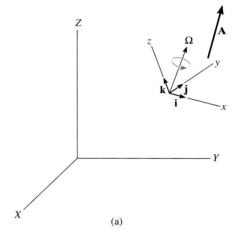

In general, the time derivative of $\mathbf{A}$ must account for the change in both the vector's magnitude and direction. However, if this derivative is taken *with respect to the moving frame of reference*, only a change in the magnitudes of the components of $\mathbf{A}$ must be accounted for, since the directions of the components do not change with respect to the moving reference. Hence,

$$(\dot{\mathbf{A}})_{xyz} = \dot{A}_x\mathbf{i} + \dot{A}_y\mathbf{j} + \dot{A}_z\mathbf{k} \qquad (20\text{–}5)$$

When the time derivative of $\mathbf{A}$ is taken *with respect to the fixed frame of reference*, the *directions* of $\mathbf{i}, \mathbf{j},$ and $\mathbf{k}$ change only on account of the *rotation* $\boldsymbol{\Omega}$ of the axes and not their translation. Hence, in general,

$$\dot{\mathbf{A}} = \dot{A}_x\mathbf{i} + \dot{A}_y\mathbf{j} + \dot{A}_z\mathbf{k} + A_x\dot{\mathbf{i}} + A_y\dot{\mathbf{j}} + A_z\dot{\mathbf{k}}$$

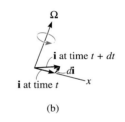

(b)

Fig. 20–6

The time derivatives of the unit vectors will now be considered. For example, $\dot{\mathbf{i}} = d\mathbf{i}/dt$ represents only a change in the *direction* of $\mathbf{i}$ with respect to time, since $\mathbf{i}$ has a fixed magnitude of 1 unit. As shown in Fig. 20–6b, the change, $d\mathbf{i}$, is *tangent to the path* described by the arrowhead of $\mathbf{i}$ as $\mathbf{i}$ moves due to the rotation $\boldsymbol{\Omega}$. Accounting for both the magnitude and direction of $d\mathbf{i}$, we can therefore define $\dot{\mathbf{i}}$ using the cross product, $\dot{\mathbf{i}} = \boldsymbol{\Omega} \times \mathbf{i}$. In general,

$$\dot{\mathbf{i}} = \boldsymbol{\Omega} \times \mathbf{i} \qquad \dot{\mathbf{j}} = \boldsymbol{\Omega} \times \mathbf{j} \qquad \dot{\mathbf{k}} = \boldsymbol{\Omega} \times \mathbf{k}$$

These formulations were also developed in Sec. 16.8, regarding planar motion of the axes. Substituting the results into the above equation and using Eq. 20–5 yields

$$\boxed{\dot{\mathbf{A}} = (\dot{\mathbf{A}})_{xyz} + \boldsymbol{\Omega} \times \mathbf{A}} \qquad (20\text{–}6)$$

This result is rather important, and it will be used throughout Sec. 20.4 and Chapter 21. It states that the time derivative of *any vector* $\mathbf{A}$ as observed from the fixed $X, Y, Z$ frame of reference is equal to the time rate of change of $\mathbf{A}$ as observed from the $x, y, z$ translating-rotating frame of reference, Eq. 20–5, plus $\boldsymbol{\Omega} \times \mathbf{A}$, the change of $\mathbf{A}$ caused by the rotation of the $x, y, z$ frame. As a result, Eq. 20–6 should always be used whenever $\boldsymbol{\Omega}$ produces a change in the direction of $\mathbf{A}$ as seen from the $X, Y, Z$ reference. If this change does not occur, i.e., $\boldsymbol{\Omega} = \mathbf{0}$, then $\dot{\mathbf{A}} = (\dot{\mathbf{A}})_{xyz}$, and so the time rate of change of $\mathbf{A}$ as observed from both coordinate systems will be the *same*.

**E X A M P L E  20.1**

The disk shown in Fig. 20–7a is spinning about its horizontal axis with a constant angular velocity $\omega_s = 3$ rad/s, while the horizontal platform on which the disk is mounted is rotating about the vertical axis at a constant rate $\omega_p = 1$ rad/s. Determine the angular acceleration of the disk and the velocity and acceleration of point $A$ on the disk when it is in the position shown.

(a)

**Fig. 20–7**

**Solution**

Point $O$ represents a fixed point of rotation for the disk if one considers a hypothetical extension of the disk to this point. To determine the velocity and acceleration of point $A$, it is first necessary to determine the resultant angular velocity $\boldsymbol{\omega}$ and angular acceleration $\boldsymbol{\alpha}$ of the disk, since these vectors are used in Eqs. 20–3 and 20–4.

*Angular Velocity.* The angular velocity, which is measured from $X, Y, Z$, is simply the vector addition of the two component motions. Thus,

$$\boldsymbol{\omega} = \boldsymbol{\omega}_s + \boldsymbol{\omega}_p = \{3\mathbf{j} - 1\mathbf{k}\} \text{ rad/s}$$

At first glance, it may not appear that the disk is actually rotating with this angular velocity, since it is generally more difficult to imagine the resultant of angular motions in comparison with linear motions. To further understand the angular motion, consider the disk as being replaced by a cone (a body cone), which is rolling over the stationary space cone, Fig. 20–7b. The instantaneous axis of rotation is along the line of contact of the cones. This axis defines the direction of the resultant $\boldsymbol{\omega}$, which has components $\boldsymbol{\omega}_s$ and $\boldsymbol{\omega}_p$.

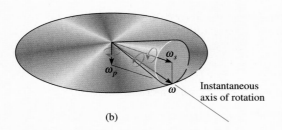

(b)

*Angular Acceleration.*  Since the magnitude of $\boldsymbol{\omega}$ is constant, only a change in its direction, as seen from a fixed reference, creates the angular acceleration $\boldsymbol{\alpha}$ of the disk. One way to obtain $\boldsymbol{\alpha}$ is to compute the time derivative of *each of the two components* of $\boldsymbol{\omega}$ using Eq. 20–6. At the instant shown in Fig. 20–7a, imagine the fixed $X, Y, Z$ and a rotating $x, y, z$ frame to be coincident. If the rotating $x, y, z$ frame is chosen to have an angular velocity of $\Omega = \boldsymbol{\omega}_p = \{-1\mathbf{k}\}$ rad/s, then $\boldsymbol{\omega}_s$ will *always* be directed along the $y$ (not $Y$) axis, and the time rate of change of $\boldsymbol{\omega}_s$ as seen from $x, y, z$ is *zero*; i.e., $(\dot{\boldsymbol{\omega}}_s)_{xyz} = \mathbf{0}$ (the magnitude and direction of $\boldsymbol{\omega}_s$ is constant). Thus, by Eq. 20–6,

$$\dot{\boldsymbol{\omega}}_s = (\dot{\boldsymbol{\omega}}_s)_{xyz} + \boldsymbol{\omega}_p \times \boldsymbol{\omega}_s = \mathbf{0} + (-1\mathbf{k}) \times (3\mathbf{j}) = \{3\mathbf{i}\} \text{ rad/s}^2$$

By the same choice of axes rotation, $\Omega = \boldsymbol{\omega}_p$, or even with $\Omega = \mathbf{0}$, the time derivative $(\dot{\boldsymbol{\omega}}_p)_{xyz} = \mathbf{0}$, since $\boldsymbol{\omega}_p$ has a constant magnitude and direction. Hence,

$$\dot{\boldsymbol{\omega}}_p = (\dot{\boldsymbol{\omega}}_p)_{xyz} + \boldsymbol{\omega}_p \times \boldsymbol{\omega}_p = \mathbf{0} + \mathbf{0} = \mathbf{0}$$

The angular acceleration of the disk is therefore

$$\boldsymbol{\alpha} = \dot{\boldsymbol{\omega}} = \dot{\boldsymbol{\omega}}_s + \dot{\boldsymbol{\omega}}_p = \{3\mathbf{i}\} \text{ rad/s}^2 \qquad \text{*Ans.*}$$

*Velocity and Acceleration.*  Since $\boldsymbol{\omega}$ and $\boldsymbol{\alpha}$ have been determined, the velocity and acceleration of point $A$ can be computed using Eqs. 20–3 and 20–4. Realizing that $\mathbf{r}_A = \{1\mathbf{j} + 0.25\mathbf{k}\}$ m, Fig. 20–7a, we have

$$\mathbf{v}_A = \boldsymbol{\omega} \times \mathbf{r}_A = (3\mathbf{j} - 1\mathbf{k}) \times (1\mathbf{j} + 0.25\mathbf{k}) = \{1.75\mathbf{i}\} \text{ m/s} \qquad \text{*Ans.*}$$

$$\mathbf{a}_A = \boldsymbol{\alpha} \times \mathbf{r}_A + \boldsymbol{\omega} \times (\boldsymbol{\omega} \times \mathbf{r}_A)$$
$$= (3\mathbf{i}) \times (1\mathbf{j} + 0.25\mathbf{k}) + (3\mathbf{j} - 1\mathbf{k}) \times [(3\mathbf{j} - 1\mathbf{k}) \times (1\mathbf{j} + 0.25\mathbf{k})]$$
$$= \{-2.50\mathbf{j} - 2.25\mathbf{k}\} \text{ m/s}^2 \qquad \text{*Ans.*}$$

**E X A M P L E  20.2**

At the instant $\theta = 60°$, the gyrotop in Fig. 20–8 has three components of angular motion directed as shown and having magnitudes defined as:

*spin:* $\omega_s = 10$ rad/s, increasing at the rate of 6 rad/s²

*nutation:* $\omega_n = 3$ rad/s, increasing at the rate of 2 rad/s²

*precession:* $\omega_p = 5$ rad/s, increasing at the rate of 4 rad/s²

Determine the angular velocity and angular acceleration of the top.

**Solution**

*Angular Velocity.* The top is rotating about the fixed point $O$. If the fixed and rotating frames are coincident at the instant shown, then the angular velocity can be expressed in terms of $\mathbf{i}$, $\mathbf{j}$, $\mathbf{k}$ components, appropriate to the $x$, $y$, $z$ frame; i.e.,

$$\boldsymbol{\omega} = -\omega_n \mathbf{i} + \omega_s \sin\theta \mathbf{j} + (\omega_p + \omega_s \cos\theta)\mathbf{k}$$
$$= -3\mathbf{i} + 10\sin 60°\mathbf{j} + (5 + 10\cos 60°)\mathbf{k}$$
$$= \{-3\mathbf{i} + 8.66\mathbf{j} + 10\mathbf{k}\} \text{ rad/s} \qquad \textit{Ans.}$$

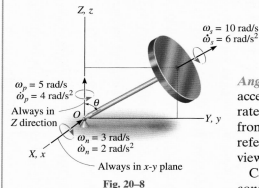

$\omega_s = 10$ rad/s
$\dot{\omega}_s = 6$ rad/s²

$\omega_p = 5$ rad/s
$\dot{\omega}_p = 4$ rad/s²
Always in Z direction

$\omega_n = 3$ rad/s
$\dot{\omega}_n = 2$ rad/s²

Always in $x$-$y$ plane

**Fig. 20–8**

*Angular Acceleration.* As in the solution of Example 20.1, the angular acceleration $\boldsymbol{\alpha}$ will be determined by investigating separately the time rate of change of *each of the angular velocity components* as observed from the fixed $X$, $Y$, $Z$ reference. We will choose an $\boldsymbol{\Omega}$ for the $x$, $y$, $z$ reference so that the component of $\boldsymbol{\omega}$ which is being considered is viewed as having a *constant direction* when observed from $x$, $y$, $z$.

Careful examination of the motion of the top reveals that $\boldsymbol{\omega}_s$ has a *constant direction* relative to $x$, $y$, $z$ if these axes rotate at $\boldsymbol{\Omega} = \boldsymbol{\omega}_n + \boldsymbol{\omega}_p$. Thus,

$$\dot{\boldsymbol{\omega}}_s = (\dot{\boldsymbol{\omega}}_s)_{xyz} + (\boldsymbol{\omega}_n + \boldsymbol{\omega}_p) \times \boldsymbol{\omega}_s$$
$$= (6\sin 60°\mathbf{j}+6\cos 60°\mathbf{k})+(-3\mathbf{i}+5\mathbf{k})\times(10\sin 60°\mathbf{j}+10\cos 60°\mathbf{k})$$
$$= \{-43.30\mathbf{i} + 20.20\mathbf{j} - 22.98\mathbf{k}\} \text{ rad/s}²$$

Since $\boldsymbol{\omega}_n$ *always* lies in the fixed $X$-$Y$ plane, this vector has a *constant direction* if the motion is viewed from axes $x$, $y$, $z$ having a rotation of $\boldsymbol{\Omega} = \boldsymbol{\omega}_p$ (not $\boldsymbol{\Omega} = \boldsymbol{\omega}_s + \boldsymbol{\omega}_p$). Thus,

$$\dot{\boldsymbol{\omega}}_n = (\dot{\boldsymbol{\omega}}_n)_{xyz}+\boldsymbol{\omega}_p \times \boldsymbol{\omega}_n = -2\mathbf{i}+(5\mathbf{k}) \times (-3\mathbf{i}) = \{-2\mathbf{i}-15\mathbf{j}\} \text{ rad/s}²$$

Finally, the component $\boldsymbol{\omega}_p$ is *always directed* along the $Z$ axis so that here it is not necessary to think of $x$, $y$, $z$ as rotating, i.e., $\boldsymbol{\Omega} = \mathbf{0}$. Expressing the data in terms of the $\mathbf{i}$, $\mathbf{j}$, $\mathbf{k}$ components, we therefore have

$$\dot{\boldsymbol{\omega}}_p = (\dot{\boldsymbol{\omega}}_p)_{xyz} + \mathbf{0} \times \boldsymbol{\omega}_p = \{4\mathbf{k}\} \text{ rad/s}²$$

Thus, the angular acceleration of the top is

$$\boldsymbol{\alpha} = \dot{\boldsymbol{\omega}}_s + \dot{\boldsymbol{\omega}}_n + \dot{\boldsymbol{\omega}}_p = \{-45.3\mathbf{i} + 5.20\mathbf{j} - 19.0\mathbf{k}\} \text{ rad/s}² \quad \textit{Ans.}$$

## 20.3  General Motion

Shown in Fig. 20–9 is a rigid body subjected to general motion in three dimensions for which the angular velocity is $\omega$ and the angular acceleration is $\alpha$. If point $A$ has a known motion of $\mathbf{v}_A$ and $\mathbf{a}_A$, the motion of any other point $B$ may be determined by using a relative-motion analysis. In this section a *translating coordinate system* will be used to define the relative motion, and in the next section a reference that is both rotating and translating will be considered.

If the origin of the translating coordinate system $x, y, z$ ($\Omega = 0$) is located at the "base point" $A$, then, at the instant shown, the motion of the body may be regarded as the sum of an instantaneous translation of the body having a motion of $\mathbf{v}_A$ and $\mathbf{a}_A$ and a rotation of the body about an instantaneous axis passing through the base point. Since the body is rigid, the motion of point $B$ measured by an observer located at $A$ is the same as *motion of the body about a fixed point*. This relative motion occurs about the instantaneous axis of rotation and is defined by $\mathbf{v}_{B/A} = \omega \times \mathbf{r}_{B/A}$, Eq. 20–3, and $\mathbf{a}_{B/A} = \alpha \times \mathbf{r}_{B/A} + \omega \times (\omega \times \mathbf{r}_{B/A})$, Eq. 20–4. For translating axes the relative motions are related to absolute motions by $\mathbf{v}_B = \mathbf{v}_A + \mathbf{v}_{B/A}$ and $\mathbf{a}_B = \mathbf{a}_A + \mathbf{a}_{B/A}$, Eqs. 16–15 and 16–17, so that the absolute velocity and acceleration of point $B$ can be determined from the equations

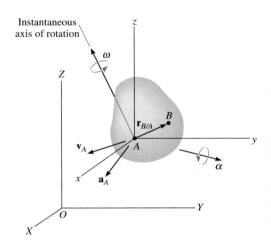

Fig. 20–9

$$\mathbf{v}_B = \mathbf{v}_A + \omega \times \mathbf{r}_{B/A} \qquad (20\text{–}7)$$

and

$$\mathbf{a}_B = \mathbf{a}_A + \alpha \times \mathbf{r}_{B/A} + \omega \times (\omega \times \mathbf{r}_{B/A}) \qquad (20\text{–}8)$$

These two equations are identical to those describing the general plane motion of a rigid body, Eqs. 16–16 and 16–18. However, difficulty in application arises for three-dimensional motion, because $\alpha$ measures the change in *both* the magnitude and direction of $\omega$. (Recall that, for general plane motion, $\alpha$ and $\omega$ are always parallel or perpendicular to the plane of motion, and therefore $\alpha$ measures only a change in the magnitude of $\omega$.) In some problems the constraints or connections of a body will require that the directions of the angular motions or displacement paths of points on the body be defined. As illustrated in the following example, this information is useful for obtaining some of the terms in the above equations.

# E X A M P L E 20.3

(a)

(b)

**Fig. 20–10**

One end of the rigid bar $CD$ shown in Fig. 20–10$a$ slides along the horizontal member $AB$, and the other end slides along the vertical member $EF$. If the collar at $C$ is moving towards $B$ at a speed of 3 m/s, determine the velocity of the collar at $D$ and the angular velocity of the bar at the instant shown. The bar is connected to the collars at its end points by ball-and-socket joints.

## Solution

Bar $CD$ is subjected to general motion. Why? The velocity of point $D$ on the bar may be related to the velocity of point $C$ by the equation

$$\mathbf{v}_D = \mathbf{v}_C + \boldsymbol{\omega} \times \mathbf{r}_{D/C}$$

The fixed and translating frames of reference are assumed to coincide at the instant considered, Fig. 20–10$b$. We have

$$\mathbf{v}_D = -v_D\mathbf{k} \qquad \mathbf{v}_C = \{3\mathbf{j}\} \text{ m/s}$$
$$\mathbf{r}_{D/C} = \{1\mathbf{i} + 2\mathbf{j} - 0.5\mathbf{k}\} \text{ m} \qquad \boldsymbol{\omega} = \omega_x\mathbf{i} + \omega_y\mathbf{j} + \omega_z\mathbf{k}$$

Substituting these quantities into the above equation gives

$$-v_D\mathbf{k} = 3\mathbf{j} + \begin{vmatrix} \mathbf{i} & \mathbf{j} & \mathbf{k} \\ \omega_x & \omega_y & \omega_z \\ 1 & 2 & -0.5 \end{vmatrix}$$

Expanding and equating the respective $\mathbf{i}$, $\mathbf{j}$, $\mathbf{k}$ components yields

$$-0.5\omega_y - 2\omega_z = 0 \qquad (1)$$
$$0.5\omega_x + 1\omega_z + 3 = 0 \qquad (2)$$
$$2\omega_x - 1\omega_y + v_D = 0 \qquad (3)$$

These equations contain four unknowns.* A fourth equation can be written if the direction of $\boldsymbol{\omega}$ is specified. In particular, any component of $\boldsymbol{\omega}$ acting along the bar's axis has no effect on moving the collars. This is because the bar is *free to rotate* about its axis. Therefore, if $\boldsymbol{\omega}$ is specified as acting *perpendicular* to the axis of the bar, then $\boldsymbol{\omega}$ must have a unique magnitude to satisfy the above equations. Perpendicularity is guaranteed provided the dot product of $\boldsymbol{\omega}$ and $\mathbf{r}_{D/C}$ is zero (see Eq. C–14 of Appendix C). Hence,

$$\boldsymbol{\omega} \cdot \mathbf{r}_{D/C} = (\omega_x\mathbf{i} + \omega_y\mathbf{j} + \omega_z\mathbf{k}) \cdot (1\mathbf{i} + 2\mathbf{j} - 0.5\mathbf{k}) = 0$$
$$1\omega_x + 2\omega_y - 0.5\omega_z = 0 \qquad (4)$$

Solving Eqs. 1 through 4 simultaneously yields

$$\omega_x = -4.86 \text{ rad/s} \quad \omega_y = 2.29 \text{ rad/s} \quad \omega_z = -0.571 \text{ rad/s} \quad \textit{Ans.}$$
$$v_D = 12.0 \text{ m/s} \downarrow \qquad \qquad \textit{Ans.}$$

*Although this is the case, the magnitude of $\mathbf{v}_D$ can be obtained. For example, solve Eqs. 1 and 2 for $\omega_y$ and $\omega_x$ in terms of $\omega_z$ and substitute into Eq. 3. It will be noted that $\omega_z$ will *cancel out*, which will allow a solution for $v_D$.

# PROBLEMS

**20-1.** The ladder of the fire truck rotates around the $z$ axis with an angular velocity $\omega_1 = 0.15$ rad/s, which is increasing at $0.8$ rad/s². At the same instant it is rotating upward at a constant rate $\omega_2 = 0.6$ rad/s. Determine the velocity and acceleration of point $A$ located at the top of the ladder at this instant.

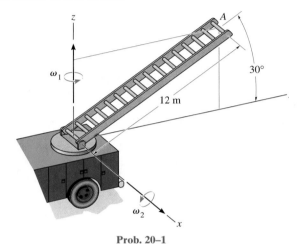

**Prob. 20–1**

**20-2.** The ladder of the fire truck rotates around the $z$ axis with an angular velocity of $\omega_1 = 0.15$ rad/s, which is increasing at $0.2$ rad/s². At the same instant it is rotating upwards at $\omega_2 = 0.6$ rad/s while increasing at $0.4$ rad/s². Determine the velocity and acceleration of point $A$ located at the top of the ladder at this instant.

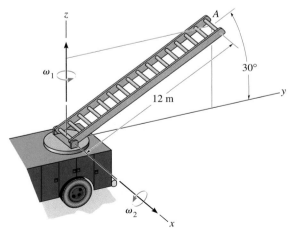

**Prob. 20–2**

**20-3.** The motion of the top is such that at the instant shown it is rotating about the $z$ axis at $\omega_1 = 0.6$ rad/s, while it is spinning at $\omega_2 = 8$ rad/s. Determine the angular velocity and angular acceleration of the top at this instant. Express the result as a Cartesian vector.

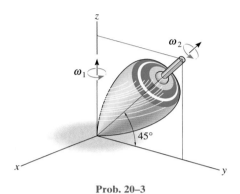

**Prob. 20–3**

**\*20-4.** At a given instant, the satellite dish has an angular motion $\omega_1 = 6$ rad/s and $\dot{\omega}_1 = 3$ rad/s² about the $z$ axis. At this same instant $\theta = 25°$, the angular motion about the $x$ axis is $\omega_2 = 2$ rad/s, and $\dot{\omega}_2 = 1.5$ rad/s². Determine the velocity and acceleration of the signal horn $A$ at this instant.

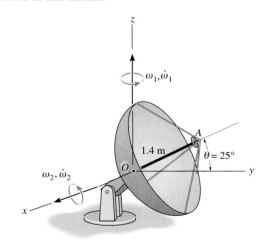

**Prob. 20–4**

**20-5.** Gear $A$ is fixed while gear $B$ is free to rotate on the shaft $S$. If the shaft is turning about the $z$ axis at $\omega_z = 5$ rad/s, while increasing at 2 rad/s$^2$, determine the velocity and acceleration of point $C$ at the instant shown. The face of gear $B$ lies in a vertical plane.

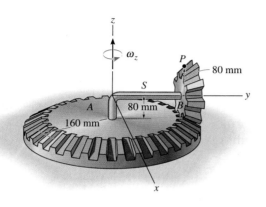

**Prob. 20–5**

**20-6.** Gear $B$ is connected to the rotating shaft, while the plate gear $A$ is fixed. If the shaft is turning at a constant rate of $\omega_z = 10$ rad/s about the $z$ axis, determine the magnitudes of the angular velocity and the angular acceleration of gear $B$. Also, determine the magnitudes of the velocity and acceleration of point $P$.

**Prob. 20–6**

**20-7.** At a given instant, the antenna has an angular motion $\omega_1 = 3$ rad/s and $\dot{\omega}_1 = 2$ rad/s$^2$ about the $z$ axis. At this same instant $\theta = 30°$, the angular motion about the $x$ axis is $\omega_2 = 1.5$ rad/s, and $\dot{\omega}_2 = 4$ rad/s$^2$. Determine the velocity and acceleration of the signal horn $A$ at this instant. The distance from $O$ to $A$ is $d = 1$ m.

**Prob. 20–7**

*20-8.** The cone rolls without slipping such that at the instant shown $\omega_z = 4$ rad/s and $\dot{\omega}_z = 3$ rad/s$^2$. Determine the velocity and acceleration of point $A$ at this instant.

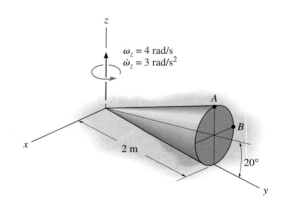

**Prob. 20–8**

**20-9.** The cone rolls without slipping such that at the instant shown $\omega_z = 4$ rad/s and $\dot{\omega}_z = 3$ rad/s². Determine the velocity and acceleration of point $B$ at this instant.

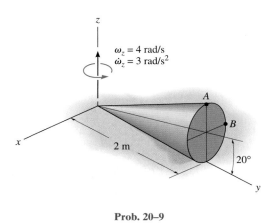

$\omega_z = 4$ rad/s
$\dot{\omega}_z = 3$ rad/s²

$A$

$B$

2 m

20°

**Prob. 20–9**

**20-10.** If the top gear $B$ is rotating at a constant rate of $\boldsymbol{\omega}$, determine the angular velocity of gear $A$, which is free to turn about the shaft and rolls on the bottom fixed gear $C$.

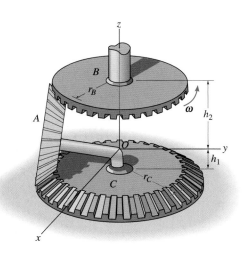

**Prob. 20–10**

**20-11.** Gear $A$ is fixed to the crankshaft $S$, while gear $C$ is fixed and $B$ are free to rotate. The crankshaft is turning at 80 rad/s about its axis. Determine the magnitudes of the angular velocity of the propeller and the angular acceleration of gear $B$.

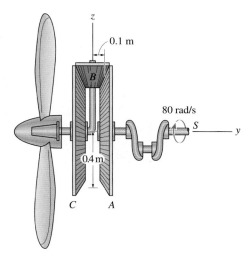

0.1 m

$B$

80 rad/s

$S$

$y$

0.4 m

$C$   $A$

**Prob. 20–11**

*20-12.** The disk $B$ is free to rotate on the shaft $S$. If the shaft is turning about the $z$ axis at $\omega_z = 2$ rad/s, while increasing at 8 rad/s², determine the velocity and acceleration of point $A$ at the instant shown.

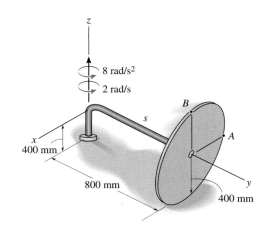

8 rad/s²

2 rad/s

$B$

$s$

$A$

$x$

400 mm

800 mm

$y$

400 mm

**Prob. 20–12**

**20-13.** Shaft $BD$ is connected to a ball-and-socket joint at $B$, and a beveled gear $A$ is attached to its other end. The gear is in mesh with a fixed gear $C$. If the shaft and gear $A$ are *spinning* with a constant angular velocity $\omega_1 = 8$ rad/s, determine the angular velocity and angular acceleration of gear $A$.

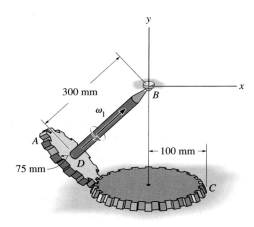

Prob. 20–13

**20-14.** The truncated cone rotates about the $z$ axis at a constant rate $\omega_z = 0.4$ rad/s without slipping on the horizontal plane. Determine the velocity and acceleration of point $A$ on the cone.

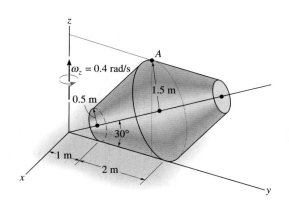

Prob. 20–14

**20-15.** At the instant shown, the tower crane is rotating about the $z$ axis with an angular velocity $\omega_1 = 0.25$ rad/s, which is increasing at $0.6$ rad/s². The boom $OA$ is rotating downward with an angular velocity $\omega_2 = 0.4$ rad/s, which is increasing at $0.8$ rad/s². Determine the velocity and acceleration of point $A$ located at the top of the boom at this instant.

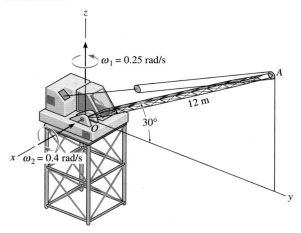

Prob. 20–15

**\*20-16.** The construction boom $OA$ is rotating about the $z$ axis with a constant angular velocity of $\omega_1 = 0.15$ rad/s, while it is rotating downward with a constant angular velocity of $\omega_2 = 0.2$ rad/s. Determine the velocity and acceleration of point $A$ located at the tip of the boom at the instant shown.

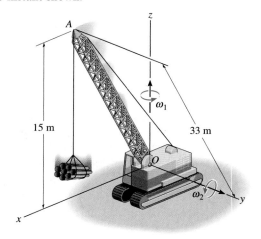

Prob. 20–16

**20-17.** The differential of an automobile allows the two rear wheels to rotate at different speeds when the automobile travels along a curve. For operation, the rear axles are attached to the wheels at one end and have beveled gears $A$ and $B$ on their other ends. The differential case $D$ is placed over the left axle but can rotate about $C$ independent of the axle. The case supports a pinion gear $E$ on a shaft, which meshes with gears $A$ and $B$. Finally, a ring gear $G$ is *fixed* to the differential case so that the case rotates with the ring gear when the latter is driven by the drive pinion $H$. This gear, like the differential case, is free to rotate about the left wheel axle. If the drive pinion is turning at $\omega_H = 100$ rad/s and the pinion gear $E$ is spinning about its shaft at $\omega_E = 30$ rad/s, determine the angular velocity, $\omega_A$ and $\omega_B$, of each axle.

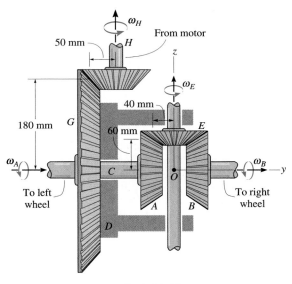

**Prob. 20–17**

**20-18.** Rod $AB$ is attached to the rotating arm using ball-and-socket joints. If $AC$ is rotating with a constant angular velocity of 8 rad/s about the pin at $C$, determine the angular velocity of link $BD$ at the instant shown.

**20-19.** Rod $AB$ is attached to the rotating arm using ball-and-socket joints. If $AC$ is rotating about point $C$ with an angular velocity of 8 rad/s and has an angular acceleration of 6 rad/s² at the instant shown, determine the angular velocity and angular acceleration of link $BD$ at this instant.

**Probs. 20–18/19**

**\*20-20.** If the rod is attached with ball-and-socket joints to smooth collars $A$ and $B$ at its end points, determine the speed of $B$ at the instant shown if $A$ is moving downward at a constant speed of $v_A = 8$ cm/s. Also, determine the angular velocity of the rod if it is directed perpendicular to the axis of the rod.

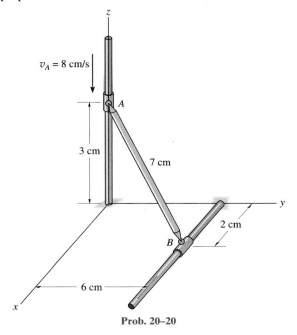

**Prob. 20–20**

**20-21.** If the collar at $A$ is moving downward with an acceleration $\mathbf{a}_A = \{-5\mathbf{k}\}$ cm/s$^2$, at the instant its speed is $v_A = 8$ cm/s, determine the acceleration of the collar at $B$ at this instant.

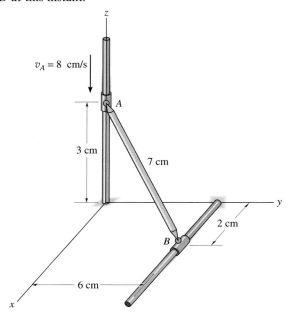

**Prob. 20–21**

**20-22.** The rod $AB$ is attached to collars at its ends by ball-and-socket joints. If collar $A$ has a speed $v_A = 3$ m/s, determine the speed of collar $B$ at the instant shown.

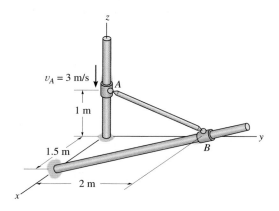

**Prob. 20–22**

**20-23.** If the collar at $A$ has an acceleration of $\mathbf{a}_A = \{-2\mathbf{k}\}$ m/s$^2$ at the instant its speed is $v_A = 3$ m/s, determine the magnitude of the acceleration of the collar at $B$ at this instant.

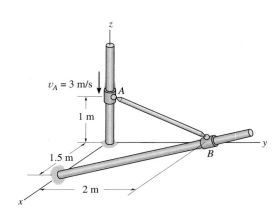

**Prob. 20–23**

**20-24.** The rod $AB$ is attached to collars at its ends by ball-and-socket joints. If collar $A$ has a velocity of $v_A = 5$ m/s, determine the angular velocity of the rod and the velocity of collar $B$ at the instant shown. Assume the angular velocity of the rod is directed perpendicular to the rod.

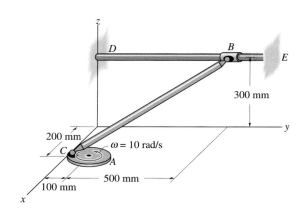

**Prob. 20–24**

**20-25.** Solve Prob. 20–24 if the connection at $B$ consists of a pin as shown in the figure below, rather than a ball-and-socket joint. *Hint:* The constraint allows rotation of the rod both along the bar ($\mathbf{j}$ direction) and along the axis of the pin ($\mathbf{n}$ direction). Since there is no rotational component in the $\mathbf{u}$ direction, i.e., perpendicular to $\mathbf{n}$ and $\mathbf{j}$ where $\mathbf{u} = \mathbf{j} \times \mathbf{n}$, an additional equation for solution can be obtained from $\boldsymbol{\omega} \cdot \mathbf{u} = 0$. The vector $\mathbf{n}$ is in the same direction as $\mathbf{r}_{B/C} \times \mathbf{r}_{D/C}$.

**Prob. 20–25**

**20-26.** The rod assembly is supported at $B$ by a ball-and-socket joint and at $A$ by a clevis. If the collar at $B$ moves in the $x$–$z$ plane with a speed $v_B = 5$ cm/s, determine the velocity of points $A$ and $C$ on the rod assembly at the instant shown. *Hint:* See Prob. 20–25.

**Prob. 20–26**

**20-27.** Rod $AB$ is attached to collars at its ends by ball-and-socket joints. If collar $A$ moves upward with a velocity of 8 cm/s, determine the angular velocity of the rod and the speed of collar $B$ at the instant shown. Assume that the rod's angular velocity is directed perpendicular to the rod.

**\*20-28.** Rod $AB$ is attached to collars at its ends by ball-and-socket joints. If collar $A$ moves upward with an acceleration of $a_A = 4$ cm/s$^2$, determine the angular acceleration of rod $AB$ and the magnitude of acceleration of collar $B$. Assume that the rod's angular acceleration is directed perpendicular to the rod.

**Probs. 20–27/28**

**20-29.** The triangular plate $ABC$ is supported at $A$ by a ball-and-socket joint and at $C$ by the $x$–$z$ plane. The side $AB$ lies in the $x$–$y$ plane. At the instant $\theta = 60°$, $\dot{\theta} = 2$ rad/s and point $C$ has the coordinates shown. Determine the angular velocity of the plate and the velocity of point $C$ at this instant.

**20-30.** The triangular plate $ABC$ is supported at $A$ by a ball-and-socket joint and at $C$ by the $x$–$z$ plane. The side $AB$ lies in the $x$–$y$ plane. At the instant $\theta = 60°$, $\dot{\theta} = 2$ rad/s, $\ddot{\theta} = 3$ rad/s$^2$, and point $C$ has the coordinates shown. Determine the angular acceleration of the plate and the acceleration of point $C$ at this instant.

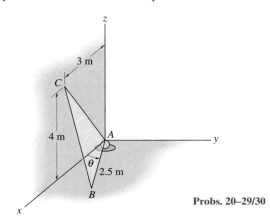

**Probs. 20–29/30**

## *20.4 Relative-Motion Analysis Using Translating and Rotating Axes

The most general way to analyze the three-dimensional motion of a rigid body requires the use of $x, y, z$ axes that both translate and rotate relative to a second frame $X, Y, Z$. This analysis will also provide a means for determining the motions of two points $A$ and $B$ located on separate members of a mechanism, and for determining the relative motion of one particle with respect to another when one or both particles are moving along *rotating paths*.

As shown in Fig. 20–11, the locations of points $A$ and $B$ are specified relative to the $X, Y, Z$ frame of reference by position vectors $\mathbf{r}_A$ and $\mathbf{r}_B$. The base point $A$ represents the origin of the $x, y, z$ coordinate system, which is translating and rotating with respect to $X, Y, Z$. At the instant considered, the velocity and acceleration of point $A$ are $\mathbf{v}_A$ and $\mathbf{a}_A$, respectively, and the angular velocity and angular acceleration of the $x, y, z$ axes are $\mathbf{\Omega}$ and $\dot{\mathbf{\Omega}} = d\mathbf{\Omega}/dt$, respectively. All these vectors are *measured* with respect to the $X, Y, Z$ frame of reference, although they may be expressed in Cartesian component form along either set of axes.

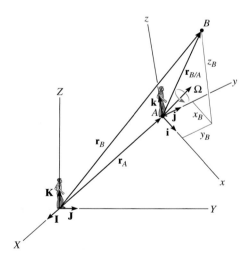

**Fig. 20–11**

**Position.**  If the position of "$B$ with respect to $A$" is specified by the *relative-position vector* $\mathbf{r}_{B/A}$, Fig. 20–11, then, by vector addition,

$$\boxed{\mathbf{r}_B = \mathbf{r}_A + \mathbf{r}_{B/A}} \qquad (20\text{–}9)$$

where

$\mathbf{r}_B$ = position of $B$

$\mathbf{r}_A$ = position of the origin $A$

$\mathbf{r}_{B/A}$ = relative position of "$B$ with respect to $A$"

**Velocity.**  The velocity of point $B$ measured from $X, Y, Z$ is determined by taking the time derivative of Eq. 20–9, which yields

$$\dot{\mathbf{r}}_B = \dot{\mathbf{r}}_A + \dot{\mathbf{r}}_{B/A}$$

The first two terms represent $\mathbf{v}_B$ and $\mathbf{v}_A$. The last term is evaluated by applying Eq. 20–6, since $\mathbf{r}_{B/A}$ is measured between two points in a rotating reference. Hence,

$$\dot{\mathbf{r}}_{B/A} = (\dot{\mathbf{r}}_{B/A})_{xyz} + \boldsymbol{\Omega} \times \mathbf{r}_{B/A} = (\mathbf{v}_{B/A})_{xyz} + \boldsymbol{\Omega} \times \mathbf{r}_{B/A} \quad (20\text{–}10)$$

Here $(\mathbf{v}_{B/A})_{xyz}$ is the relative velocity of $B$ with respect to $A$ measured from $x, y, z$. Thus,

$$\boxed{\mathbf{v}_B = \mathbf{v}_A + \boldsymbol{\Omega} \times \mathbf{r}_{B/A} + (\mathbf{v}_{B/A})_{xyz}} \qquad (20\text{–}11)$$

where

$\mathbf{v}_B$ = velocity of $B$

$\mathbf{v}_A$ = velocity of the origin $A$ of the $x, y, z$ frame of reference

$(\mathbf{v}_{B/A})_{xyz}$ = relative velocity of "$B$ with respect to $A$" as measured by an observer attached to the rotating $x, y, z$ frame of referenc

$\boldsymbol{\Omega}$ = angular velocity of the $x, y, z$ frame of reference

$\mathbf{r}_{B/A}$ = relative position of "$B$ with respect to $A$"

**Acceleration.** The acceleration of point $B$ measured from $X, Y, Z$ is determined by taking the time derivative of Eq. 20–11, which yields

$$\dot{\mathbf{v}}_B = \dot{\mathbf{v}}_A + \dot{\boldsymbol{\Omega}} \times \mathbf{r}_{B/A} + \boldsymbol{\Omega} \times \dot{\mathbf{r}}_{B/A} + \frac{d}{dt}(\mathbf{v}_{B/A})_{xyz}$$

The time derivatives defined in the first and second terms represent $\mathbf{a}_B$ and $\mathbf{a}_A$ respectively. The fourth term is evaluated using Eq. 20–10, and the last term is evaluated by applying Eq. 20–6, which yields

$$\frac{d}{dt}(\mathbf{v}_{B/A})_{xyz} = (\ \dot{\mathbf{v}}_{B/A})_{xyz} + \boldsymbol{\Omega} \times (\mathbf{v}_{B/A})_{xyz}$$
$$= (\mathbf{a}_{B/A})_{xyz} + \boldsymbol{\Omega} \times (\mathbf{v}_{B/A})_{xyz}$$

Here $(\mathbf{a}_{B/A})_{xyz}$ is the relative acceleration of $B$ with respect to $A$ measured from $x, y, z$. Substituting this result and Eq. 20–10 into the above equation and simplifying, we have

$$\mathbf{a}_B = \mathbf{a}_A + \dot{\boldsymbol{\Omega}} \times \mathbf{r}_{B/A} + \boldsymbol{\Omega} \times (\boldsymbol{\Omega} \times \mathbf{r}_{B/A}) + 2\boldsymbol{\Omega} \times (\mathbf{v}_{B/A})_{xyz} + (\mathbf{a}_{B/A})_{xyz}$$

(20–12)

where

$$\mathbf{a}_B = \text{acceleration of } B$$

$$\mathbf{a}_A = \text{acceleration of the origin } A \text{ of the } x, y, z \text{ frame of reference}$$

$$(\mathbf{a}_{B/A})_{xyz}, (\mathbf{v}_{B/A})_{xyz} = \text{relative acceleration and relative velocity of "}B \text{ with respect to } A\text{" as measured by an observer attached to the rotating } x, y, z \text{ frame of reference}$$

$$\dot{\boldsymbol{\Omega}}, \boldsymbol{\Omega} = \text{angular acceleration and angular velocity of the } x, y, z \text{ frame of reference}$$

$$\mathbf{r}_{B/A} = \text{relative position of "}B \text{ with respect to } A\text{"}$$

Complicated spatial motion of the concrete bucket $B$ occurs due to the rotation of the boom about the $Z$ axis, motion of the carriage $A$ along the boom, and extension and swinging of the cable $AB$. A translating-rotating $x, y, z$ coordinate system can be established on the carriage, and a relative-motion analysis can then be applied to study this motion.

Equations 20–11 and 20–12 are identical to those used in Sec. 16.8 for analyzing relative plane motion.* In that case, however, application is simplified since $\boldsymbol{\Omega}$ and $\dot{\boldsymbol{\Omega}}$ have a *constant direction* which is always perpendicular to the plane of motion. For three-dimensional motion, $\dot{\boldsymbol{\Omega}}$ must be computed by using Eq. 20–6, since $\dot{\boldsymbol{\Omega}}$ depends on the change in *both* the magnitude and direction of $\boldsymbol{\Omega}$.

*Refer to Sec. 16.8 for an interpretation of the terms.

## PROCEDURE FOR ANALYSIS

Three-dimensional motion of particles or rigid bodies can be analyzed with Eqs. 20–11 and 20–12 by using the following procedure.

*Coordinate Axes.*

- Select the location and orientation of the $X, Y, Z$ and $x, y, z$ coordinate axes. Most often solutions are easily obtained if at the instant considered:

  (1) the origins are *coincident*
  (2) the axes are collinear
  (3) the axes are parallel

- If several components of angular velocity are involved in a problem, the calculations will be reduced if the $x, y, z$ axes are selected such that only one component of angular velocity is observed in this frame $(\Omega_{xyz})$ and the frame rotates with $\Omega$ defined by the other components of angular velocity.

*Kinematic Equations.*

- After the origin of the moving reference, $A$, is defined and the moving point $B$ is specified, Eqs. 20–11 and 20–12 should be written in symbolic form as

$$\mathbf{v}_B = \mathbf{v}_A + \mathbf{\Omega} \times \mathbf{r}_{B/A} + (\mathbf{v}_{B/A})_{xyz}$$

$$\mathbf{a}_B = \mathbf{a}_A + \dot{\mathbf{\Omega}} \times \mathbf{r}_{B/A} + \mathbf{\Omega} \times (\mathbf{\Omega} \times \mathbf{r}_{B/A}) + 2\mathbf{\Omega} \times (\mathbf{v}_{B/A})_{xyz} + (\mathbf{a}_{B/A})_{xyz}$$

- If $\mathbf{r}_A$ and $\mathbf{\Omega}$ appear to *change direction* when observed from the fixed $X, Y, Z$ reference use a set of primed reference axes, $x', y', z'$ having $\mathbf{\Omega}' = \mathbf{\Omega}$ and Eq. 20–6 to determine $\dot{\mathbf{\Omega}}$ and the motion $\mathbf{v}_A$ and $\mathbf{a}_A$ of the origin of the moving $x, y, z$ axes.

- If $(\mathbf{r}_{B/A})_{xyz}$ and $\mathbf{\Omega}_{xyz}$ appear to *change direction* as observed from $x, y, z$, then use a set of primed reference axes $x', y', z'$ having $\mathbf{\Omega}' = \mathbf{\Omega}_{xyz}$ and Eq. 20–6 to determine $\dot{\mathbf{\Omega}}_{xyz}$ and the relative motion $(\mathbf{v}_{B/A})_{xyz}$ and $(\mathbf{a}_{B/A})_{xyz}$.

- After the final forms of $\dot{\mathbf{\Omega}}$, $\mathbf{v}_A$, $\mathbf{a}_A$, $\dot{\mathbf{\Omega}}_{xyz}$, $(\mathbf{v}_{B/A})_{xyz}$, and $(\mathbf{a}_{B/A})_{xyz}$ are obtained, numerical problem data may be substituted and the kinematic terms evaluated. The components of all these vectors may be selected either along the $X, Y, Z$ axes or along $x, y, z$. The choice is arbitrary, provided a consistent set of unit vectors is used.

**EXAMPLE 20.4**

A motor and attached rod $AB$ have the angular motions shown in Fig. 20–12. A collar $C$ on the rod is located 0.25 m from $A$ and is moving downward along the rod with a velocity of 3 m/s and an acceleration of 2 m/s². Determine the velocity and acceleration of $C$ at this instant.

**Solution**

*Coordinate Axes.* The origin of the fixed $X, Y, Z$ reference is chosen at the center of the platform, and the origin of the moving, $x, y, z$ frame at point $A$, Fig. 20–12. Since the collar is subjected to two components of angular motion, $\boldsymbol{\omega}_p$ and $\boldsymbol{\omega}_M$, it will be viewed as having an angular velocity of $\boldsymbol{\Omega}_{xyz} = \boldsymbol{\omega}_M$ in $x, y, z$. The $x, y, z$ axes will be attached to the platform so that $\boldsymbol{\Omega} = \boldsymbol{\omega}_p$.

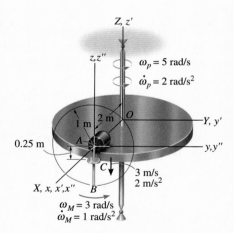

**Fig. 20–12**

*Kinematic Equations.* Equations 20–11 and 20–12, applied to points $C$ and $A$, become

$$\mathbf{v}_C = \mathbf{v}_A + \boldsymbol{\Omega} \times \mathbf{r}_{C/A} + (\mathbf{v}_{C/A})_{xyz}$$
$$\mathbf{a}_C = \mathbf{a}_A + \dot{\boldsymbol{\Omega}} \times \mathbf{r}_{C/A} + \boldsymbol{\Omega} \times (\boldsymbol{\Omega} \times \mathbf{r}_{C/A}) + 2\boldsymbol{\Omega} \times (\mathbf{v}_{C/A})_{xyz} + (\mathbf{a}_{C/A})_{xyz}$$

*Motion of A.*

Here $\mathbf{r}_A$ changes direction relative to $XYZ$.

To find the time derivatives of $\mathbf{r}_A$ we will use a set of $x'$, $y'$, $z'$ axes coincident with the $X$, $Y$, $Z$ axes that rotate at $\boldsymbol{\Omega}' = \boldsymbol{\Omega} = \boldsymbol{\omega}_p$. Thus

$\boldsymbol{\Omega} = \boldsymbol{\omega}_p = \{5\mathbf{k}\}$ rad/s ($\boldsymbol{\Omega}$ does not change direction relative to $XYZ$.)

$\dot{\boldsymbol{\Omega}} = \dot{\boldsymbol{\omega}}_p = \{2\mathbf{k}\}$ rad/s$^2$

$\mathbf{r}_A = \{2\mathbf{i}\}$ m

$\mathbf{v}_A = \dot{\mathbf{r}}_A = (\dot{\mathbf{r}}_A)_{x'y'z'} + \boldsymbol{\omega}_p \times \mathbf{r}_A = \mathbf{0} + 5\mathbf{k} \times 2\mathbf{i} = \{10\mathbf{j}\}$ m/s

$\mathbf{a}_A = \ddot{\mathbf{r}}_A = [(\ddot{\mathbf{r}}_A)_{x'y'z'} + \boldsymbol{\omega}_p \times (\dot{\mathbf{r}}_A)_{x'y'z'}] + \dot{\boldsymbol{\omega}}_p \times \mathbf{r}_A + \boldsymbol{\omega}_p \times \dot{\mathbf{r}}_A$

$\quad = [0 + 0] + 2\mathbf{k} \times 2\mathbf{i} + 5\mathbf{k} \times 10\mathbf{j} = \{-50\mathbf{i} + 4\mathbf{j}\}$ m/s$^2$

*Motion of C with Respect to A.*

Here $(\mathbf{r}_{C/A})_{xyz}$ changes direction relative to $x\,y\,z$. To find the time derivatives of $(\mathbf{r}_{C/A})_{xyz}$ use a set of $x''$, $y''$, $z''$ axes that rotate at $\boldsymbol{\Omega}'' = \boldsymbol{\Omega}_{xyz} = \boldsymbol{\omega}_M$. Thus

$\boldsymbol{\Omega}_{xyz} = \boldsymbol{\omega}_M = \{3\mathbf{i}\}$ rad/s ($\boldsymbol{\Omega}_{xyz}$ does not change direction relative to $xyz$.)

$\dot{\boldsymbol{\Omega}}_{xyz} = \dot{\boldsymbol{\omega}}_M = \{1\mathbf{i}\}$ rad/s$^2$

$(\mathbf{r}_{C/A})_{xyz} = \{-0.25\mathbf{k}\}$ m

$(\mathbf{v}_{C/A})_{xyz} = (\dot{\mathbf{r}}_{C/A})_{xyz} = (\dot{\mathbf{r}}_{C/A})_{xyz} + \boldsymbol{\omega}_M \times (\mathbf{r}_{C/A})_{xyz}$

$\quad = -3\mathbf{k} + [3\mathbf{i} \times (-0.25\mathbf{k})] = \{0.75\mathbf{j} - 3\mathbf{k}\}$ m/s

$(\mathbf{a}_{C/A})_{xyz} = (\ddot{\mathbf{r}}_{C/A})_{xyz} = [(\ddot{\mathbf{r}}_{C/A})_{xyz} + \boldsymbol{\omega}_M \times (\dot{\mathbf{r}}_{C/A})_{xyz}] + \dot{\boldsymbol{\omega}}_M \times (\mathbf{r}_{C/A})_{xyz} + \boldsymbol{\omega}_M \times (\mathbf{r}_{C/A})_{xyz}$

$\quad = [-2\mathbf{k} + 3\mathbf{i} \times (-3\mathbf{k})] + (1\mathbf{i}) \times (-0.25\mathbf{k}) + (3\mathbf{i}) \times (0.75\mathbf{j} - 3\mathbf{k})$

$\quad = \{18.25\mathbf{j} + 0.25\mathbf{k}\}$ m/s$^2$

*Motion of C.*

$\mathbf{v}_C = \mathbf{v}_A + \boldsymbol{\Omega} \times \mathbf{r}_{C/A} + (\mathbf{v}_{C/A})_{xyz}$

$\quad = 10\mathbf{j} + [5\mathbf{k} \times (-0.25\mathbf{k})] + (0.75\mathbf{j} - 3\mathbf{k})$

$\quad = \{10.8\mathbf{j} - 3\mathbf{k}\}$ m/s                    *Ans.*

$\mathbf{a}_C = \mathbf{a}_A + \dot{\boldsymbol{\Omega}} \times \mathbf{r}_{C/A} + \boldsymbol{\Omega} \times (\boldsymbol{\Omega} \times \mathbf{r}_{C/A}) + 2\boldsymbol{\Omega} \times (\mathbf{v}_{C/A})_{xyz} + (\mathbf{a}_{C/A})_{xyz}$

$\quad = (-50\mathbf{i} + 4\mathbf{j}) + [2\mathbf{k} \times (-0.25\mathbf{k})] + 5\mathbf{k} \times [5\mathbf{k} \times (-0.25\mathbf{k})]$

$\quad + 2[5\mathbf{k} \times (0.75\mathbf{j} - 3\mathbf{k})] + (18.25\mathbf{j} + 0.25\mathbf{k})$

$\quad = \{-57.5\mathbf{i} + 22.2\mathbf{j} + 0.25\mathbf{k}\}$ m/s$^2$                    *Ans.*

## EXAMPLE 20.5

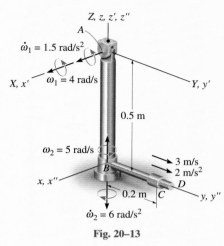

**Fig. 20–13**

The pendulum shown in Fig. 20–13 consists of two rods; $AB$ is pin supported at $A$ and swings only in the $Y$–$Z$ plane, whereas a bearing at $B$ allows the attached rod $BD$ to spin about rod $AB$. At a given instant, the rods have the angular motions shown. Also, a collar $C$, located 0.2 m from $B$, has a velocity of 3 m/s and an acceleration of 2 m/s² along the rod. Determine the velocity and acceleration of the collar at this instant.

### Solution I

*Coordinate Axes.* The origin of the fixed $X, Y, Z$ frame will be chosen at $A$. Motion of the collar is conveniently observed from $B$, so the origin of the $x, y, z$ frame is located at this point. We will choose $\mathbf{\Omega} = \boldsymbol{\omega}_1$ and $\mathbf{\Omega}_{xyz} = \boldsymbol{\omega}_2$.

*Kinematic Equations.*

$$\mathbf{v}_C = \mathbf{v}_B + \mathbf{\Omega} \times \mathbf{r}_{C/B} + (\mathbf{v}_{C/B})_{xyz}$$

$$\mathbf{a}_C = \mathbf{a}_B + \dot{\mathbf{\Omega}} \times \mathbf{r}_{C/B} + \mathbf{\Omega} \times (\mathbf{\Omega} \times \mathbf{r}_{C/B}) + 2\mathbf{\Omega} \times (\mathbf{v}_{C/B})_{xyz} + (\mathbf{a}_{C/B})_{xyz}$$

*Motion of B.* To find the time derivatives of $\mathbf{r}_B$ let the $x', y', z'$ axes rotate with $\mathbf{\Omega} = \boldsymbol{\omega}_1$. Then

$$\mathbf{\Omega} = \boldsymbol{\omega}_1 = \{4\mathbf{i}\} \text{ rad/s} \qquad \dot{\mathbf{\Omega}} = \dot{\boldsymbol{\omega}}_1 = \{1.5\mathbf{i}\} \text{ rad/s}^2$$

$$\mathbf{r}_B = \{-0.5\mathbf{k}\} \text{ m}$$

$$\mathbf{v}_B = \dot{\mathbf{r}}_B = (\dot{\mathbf{r}}_B)_{x'y'z'} + \boldsymbol{\omega}_1 \times \mathbf{r}_B = 0 + 4\mathbf{i} \times (-0.5\mathbf{k}) = \{2\mathbf{j}\} \text{ m/s}$$

$$\mathbf{a}_B = \ddot{\mathbf{r}}_B = [(\ddot{\mathbf{r}}_B)_{x'y'z'} + \boldsymbol{\omega}_1 \times (\dot{\mathbf{r}}_B)_{x'y'z'}] + \dot{\boldsymbol{\omega}}_1 \times \mathbf{r}_B + \boldsymbol{\omega}_1 \times \dot{\mathbf{r}}_B$$
$$= [0 + 0] + 1.5\mathbf{i} \times (-0.5\mathbf{k}) + 4\mathbf{i} \times 2\mathbf{j} = \{0.75\mathbf{j} + 8\mathbf{k}\} \text{ m/s}^2$$

*Motion of C with Respect to B.*

To find the time derivatives of $(\mathbf{r}_{C/B})_{xyz}$, let the $x'', y'', z''$ axes rotate with $\mathbf{\Omega}_{xyz} = \boldsymbol{\omega}_2$. Then

$$\mathbf{\Omega}_{xyz} = \boldsymbol{\omega}_2 = \{5\mathbf{k}\} \text{ rad/s} \qquad \dot{\mathbf{\Omega}}_{xyx} = \dot{\boldsymbol{\omega}}_2 = \{-6\mathbf{k}\} \text{ rad/s}^2$$

$$(\mathbf{r}_{C/B})_{xyz} = \{0.2\mathbf{j}\} \text{ m}$$

$$(\mathbf{v}_{C/B})_{xyz} = (\dot{\mathbf{r}}_{C/B})_{xyz} = (\dot{\mathbf{r}}_{C/B})_{x''y''z''} + \boldsymbol{\omega}_2 \times (\mathbf{r}_{C/B})_{xyz} = 3\mathbf{j} + 5\mathbf{k} \times 0.2\mathbf{j} = \{-1\mathbf{i} + 3\mathbf{j}\} \text{ m/s}$$

$$(\mathbf{a}_{C/B})_{xyz} = (\ddot{\mathbf{r}}_{C/B})_{xyz} = [(\ddot{\mathbf{r}}_{C/B})_{x''y''z''} + \boldsymbol{\omega}_2 \times (\dot{\mathbf{r}}_{C/B})_{x''y''z''}] + \dot{\boldsymbol{\omega}}_2 \times (\mathbf{r}_{C/B})_{xyz} + \boldsymbol{\omega}_2 \times (\dot{\mathbf{r}}_{C/B})_{xyz}$$
$$= (2\mathbf{j} + 5\mathbf{k} \times 3\mathbf{j}) + (-6\mathbf{k} \times 0.2\mathbf{j}) + [5\mathbf{k} \times (-1\mathbf{i} + 3\mathbf{j})]$$
$$= \{-28.8\mathbf{i} - 3\mathbf{j}\} \text{ m/s}^2$$

*Motion of C.*

$$\mathbf{v}_C = \mathbf{v}_B + \mathbf{\Omega} \times \mathbf{r}_{C/B} + (\mathbf{v}_{C/B})_{xyz} = 2\mathbf{j} + 4\mathbf{i} \times 0.2\mathbf{j} + (-1\mathbf{i} + 3\mathbf{j})$$
$$= \{-1\mathbf{i} + 5\mathbf{j} + 0.8\mathbf{k}\} \text{ m/s} \qquad\qquad Ans.$$

$$\mathbf{a}_C = \mathbf{a}_B + \dot{\mathbf{\Omega}} \times \mathbf{r}_{C/B} + \mathbf{\Omega} \times (\mathbf{\Omega} \times \mathbf{r}_{C/B}) + 2\mathbf{\Omega} \times (\mathbf{v}_{C/B})_{xyz} + (\mathbf{a}_{C/B})_{xyz}$$
$$= (0.75\mathbf{j} + 8\mathbf{k}) + (1.5\mathbf{i} \times 0.2\mathbf{j}) + [4\mathbf{i} \times (4\mathbf{i} \times 0.2\mathbf{j})]$$
$$+ 2[4\mathbf{i} \times (-1\mathbf{i} + 3\mathbf{j})] + (-28.8\mathbf{i} - 3\mathbf{j})$$
$$= \{-28.8\mathbf{i} - 5.45\mathbf{j} + 32.3\mathbf{k}\} \text{ m/s}^2 \qquad\qquad Ans.$$

**Solution II**

*Coordinate Axes.* Here we will let the $x$, $y$, $z$ axes rotate at

$$\Omega = \omega_1 + \omega_2 = \{4\mathbf{i} + 5\mathbf{k}\} \text{ rad/s}$$

Then $\Omega_{xyz} = 0$.

*Motion of B.*

From the constraints of the problem $\omega_1$ does not change direction relative to $X$, $Y$, $Z$; however, the direction of $\omega_2$ is changed by $\omega_1$. Thus, to obtain $\dot{\Omega}$ consider $x'$, $y'$, $z'$ axes coincident with the $X$, $Y$, $Z$ axes at $A$, such that $\dot{\Omega} = \omega_1$. Then taking the derivative of its components,

$$\dot{\Omega} = \dot{\omega}_1 + \dot{\omega}_2 = [(\dot{\omega}_1)_{x'y'z'} + \omega_1 \times \omega_1] + [(\dot{\omega}_2)_{x'y'z'} + \omega_1 \times \omega_2]$$

$$= [1.5\mathbf{i} + 0] + [-6\mathbf{k} + 4\mathbf{i} \times 5\mathbf{k}] = \{1.5\mathbf{i} - 20\mathbf{j} - 6\mathbf{k}\} \text{ rad/s}^2$$

Also, $\omega_1$ changes the direction of $\mathbf{r}_B$ so that the time derivatives of $\mathbf{r}_B$ can be computed using the primed axes defined above. Hence,

$$\mathbf{v}_B = \dot{\mathbf{r}}_B = (\dot{\mathbf{r}}_B)_{x'y'z'} + \omega_1 \times \mathbf{r}_B$$

$$= 0 + 4\mathbf{i} \times (-0.5\mathbf{k}) = \{2\mathbf{j}\} \text{ m/s}$$

$$\mathbf{a}_B = \ddot{\mathbf{r}}_B = [(\ddot{\mathbf{r}}_B)_{x'y'z'} + \omega_1 \times (\dot{\mathbf{r}}_B)_{x'y'z'}] + \dot{\omega}_1 \times \mathbf{r}_B + \omega_1 \times \dot{\mathbf{r}}_B$$

$$= [0 + 0] + 1.5\mathbf{i} \times (-0.5\mathbf{k}) + 4\mathbf{i} \times 2\mathbf{j} = \{0.75\mathbf{j} + 8\mathbf{k}\} \text{ m/s}^2$$

*Motion of C with Respect to B.*

$$\Omega_{xyz} = 0$$

$$\dot{\Omega}_{xyz} = 0$$

$$(\mathbf{r}_{C/B})_{xyz} = \{0.2\mathbf{j}\} \text{ m}$$

$$(\mathbf{v}_{C/B})_{xyz} = \{3\mathbf{j}\} \text{ m/s}$$

$$(\mathbf{a}_{C/B})_{xyz} = \{2\mathbf{j}\} \text{ m/s}^2$$

*Motion of C.*

$$\mathbf{v}_C = \mathbf{v}_B + \Omega \times \mathbf{r}_{C/B} + (\mathbf{v}_{C/B})_{xyz}$$

$$= 2\mathbf{j} + [(4\mathbf{i} + 5\mathbf{k}) \times (0.2\mathbf{j})] + 3\mathbf{j}$$

$$= \{-1\mathbf{i} + 5\mathbf{j} + 0.8\mathbf{k}\} \text{ m/s} \qquad\qquad Ans.$$

$$\mathbf{a}_C = \mathbf{a}_B + \dot{\Omega} \times \mathbf{r}_{C/B} + \Omega \times (\Omega \times \mathbf{r}_{C/B}) + 2\Omega \times (\mathbf{v}_{C/B})_{xyz} + (\mathbf{a}_{C/B})_{xyz}$$

$$= (0.75\mathbf{j} + 8\mathbf{k}) + [(1.5\mathbf{i} - 20\mathbf{j} - 6\mathbf{k}) \times (0.2\mathbf{j})]$$

$$+ (4\mathbf{i} + 5\mathbf{k}) \times [(4\mathbf{i} + 5\mathbf{k}) \times 0.2\mathbf{j}] + 2[(4\mathbf{i} + 5\mathbf{k}) \times 3\mathbf{j}] + 2\mathbf{j}$$

$$= \{-28.8\mathbf{i} - 5.45\mathbf{j} + 32.3\mathbf{k}\} \text{ m/s}^2 \qquad\qquad Ans.$$

# PROBLEMS

**20-31.** Solve Example 20–5 such that the $x$, $y$, $z$ axes move with curvilinear translation, $\Omega = 0$, in which case the collar appears to have both an angular velocity $\Omega_{xyz} = \omega_1 + \omega_2$ and radial motion.

*20-32.* Solve Example 20–5 by fixing $x$, $y$, $z$ axes to rod $BD$ so that $\Omega = \omega_1 + \omega_2$. In this case the collar appears only to move radially outward along $BD$; hence $\Omega_{xyz} = 0$.

**20-33.** At a given instant, rod $BD$ is rotating about the $y$ axis with an angular velocity $\omega_{BD} = 2$ rad/s and an angular acceleration $\dot{\omega}_{BD} = 5$ rad/s$^2$. Also, when $\theta = 60°$ link $AC$ is rotating downward such that $\dot{\theta} = 2$ rad/s and $\ddot{\theta} = 8$ rad/s$^2$. Determine the velocity and acceleration of point $A$ on the link at this instant.

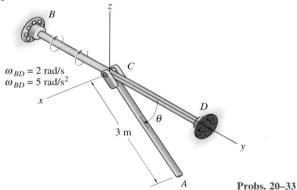

$\omega_{BD} = 2$ rad/s
$\omega_{BD} = 5$ rad/s$^2$

3 m

**Probs. 20–33**

**20-34.** During the instant shown the frame of the X-ray camera is rotating about the vertical axis at $\omega_z = 5$ rad/s and $\dot{\omega}_z = 2$ rad/s$^2$. Relative to the frame the arm is rotating at $\omega_{rel} = 2$ rad/s and $\dot{\omega}_{rel} = 1$ rad/s$^2$. Determine the velocity and acceleration of the center of the camera $C$ at this instant.

1.25 m    1.75 m

$\omega_z = 5$ rad/s
$\dot{\omega}_z = 2$ rad/s$^2$

$\omega_{rel} = 2$ rad/s
$\dot{\omega}_{rel} = 1$ rad/s$^2$

1 m

1.25 m

**Prob. 20–34**

**20-35.** The boom $AB$ of the crane is rotating about the $z$ axis with an angular velocity $\omega_z = 0.75$ rad/s, which is increasing at $\dot{\omega}_z = 2$ rad/s$^2$. At the same instant, $\theta = 60°$ and the boom is rotating upward at a constant rate $\dot{\theta} = 0.5$ rad/s$^2$. Determine the velocity and acceleration of the tip $B$ of the boom at this instant.

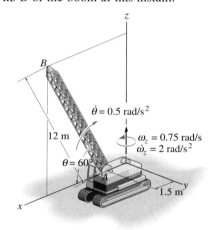

$\dot{\theta} = 0.5$ rad/s$^2$

12 m

$\omega_z = 0.75$ rad/s
$\dot{\omega}_z = 2$ rad/s$^2$

$\theta = 60°$

1.5 m

**Prob. 20–35**

*20-36.* The boom $AB$ of the crane is rotating about the $z$ axis with an angular velocity of $\omega_z = 0.75$ rad/s, which is increasing at $\dot{\omega}_z = 2$ rad/s$^2$. At the same instant, $\theta = 60°$ and the boom is rotating upward at $\dot{\theta} = 0.5$ rad/s$^2$, which is increasing at $\ddot{\theta} = 0.75$ rad/s$^2$. Determine the velocity and acceleration of the tip $B$ of the boom at this instant.

$\dot{\theta} = 0.5$ rad/s$^2$

12 m

$\omega_z = 0.75$ rad/s
$\dot{\omega}_z = 2$ rad/s$^2$

$\theta = 60°$

1.5 m

**Prob. 20–36**

**20-37.** At the instant shown, the boom is rotating about the z axis with an angular velocity $\omega_1 = 2$ rad/s and angular acceleration $\dot{\omega}_1 = 0.8$ rad/s². At this same instant the swivel is rotating at $\omega_2 = 3$ rad/s when $\dot{\omega}_2 = 2$ rad/s², both measured relative to the boom. Determine the velocity and acceleration of point $P$ on the pipe at this instant.

Prob. 20–37

**20-38.** The boom $AB$ of the locomotive crane is rotating about the Z axis with an angular velocity $\omega_1 = 0.5$ rad/s, which is increasing at $\dot{\omega}_1 = 3$ rad/s². At this same instant, $\theta = 30°$ and the boom is rotating upward at a constant rate of $\dot{\theta} = 3$ rad/s. Determine the velocity and acceleration of the tip $B$ of the boom at this instant.

**20-39.** The locomotive crane is traveling to the right at 2 m/s and has an acceleration of 1.5 m/s², while the boom is rotating about the Z axis with an angular velocity $\omega_1 = 0.5$ rad/s, which is increasing at $\dot{\omega}_1 = 3$ rad/s². At this same instant, $\theta = 30°$ and the boom is rotating upward at a constant rate $\dot{\theta} = 3$ rad/s. Determine the velocity and acceleration of the tip $B$ of the boom at this instant.

Probs. 20–38/39

*20-40.** At the instant shown, the helicopter is moving upwards with a velocity $v_H = 1.2$ m/s, and has an acceleration $a_H = 0.6$ m/s². At the same instant the frame $H$, *not* the horizontal blade, is rotating about a vertical axis with a constant angular velocity $\omega_H = 0.9$ rad/s. If the tail blade $B$ is rotating with a constant angular velocity $\omega_{B/H} = 180$ rad/s, measured relative to $H$, determine the velocity and acceleration of point $P$, located on the tip of the blade, at the instant the blade is in the vertical position.

Prob. 20–40

**20-41.** At the instant shown, the arm $OA$ of the conveyor belt is rotating about the z axis with a constant angular velocity $\omega_1 = 6$ rad/s, while at the same instant the arm is rotating upward at a constant rate $\omega_2 = 4$ rad/s. If the conveyor is running at a constant rate $\dot{r} = 5$ m/s, determine the velocity and acceleration of the package $P$ at the instant shown. Neglect the size of the package.

**20-42.** At the instant shown, the arm $OA$ of the conveyor belt is rotating about the z axis with a constant angular velocity $\omega_1 = 6$ rad/s, while at the same instant the arm is rotating upward at a constant rate $\omega_2 = 4$ rad/s. If the conveyor is running at a rate $\dot{r} = 5$ m/s, which is increasing at $\ddot{r} = 8$ m/s², determine the velocity and acceleration of the package $P$ at the instant shown. Neglect the size of the package.

Probs. 20–41/42

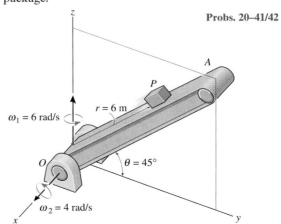

**20-43.** The particle $P$ slides around the circular hoop with a constant angular velocity of $\dot{\theta} = 6$ rad/s, while the hoop rotates about the $x$ axis at a constant rate of $\omega = 4$ rad/s. If at the instant shown the hoop is in the x–y plane and the angle $\theta = 45°$, determine the velocity and acceleration of the particle at this instant.

**Prob. 20–43**

*20-44.** At the given instant, the rod is spinning about the $z$ axis with an angular velocity $\omega_1 = 8$ rad/s and angular acceleration $\dot{\omega}_1 = 2$ rad/s². At this same instant, the disk is spinning at a constant rate $\omega_2 = 4$ rad/s, measured *relative* to the rod. Determine the velocity and acceleration of point $P$ on the disk at this instant.

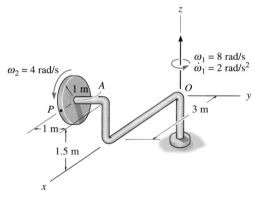

**Prob. 20–44**

**20-45.** At the instant shown, the base of the robotic arm is turning about the $z$ axis with an angular velocity of $\omega_1 = 4$ rad/s, which is increasing at $\dot{\omega}_1 = 3$ rad/s². Also, the boom segment $BC$ is rotating at a constant rate of $\omega_{BC} = 8$ rad/s. Determine the velocity and acceleration of the part $C$ held in its grip at this instant.

**20-46.** At the instant shown, the base of the robotic arm is turning about the $z$ axis with an angular velocity of $\omega_1 = 4$ rad/s, which is increasing at $\dot{\omega}_1 = 3$ rad/s². Also, the boom segment $BC$ is rotating at $\omega_{BC} = 8$ rad/s, which is increasing at $\dot{\omega}_{BC} = 2$ rad/s². Determine the velocity and acceleration of the part $C$ held in its grip at this instant.

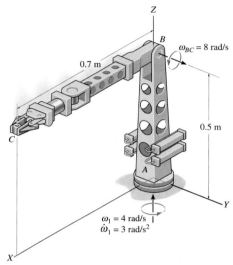

**Probs. 20–45/46**

**20-47.** At the instant shown, the industrial manipulator is rotating about the $z$ axis at $\omega_1 = 5$ rad/s, and about joint $B$ at $\omega_2 = 2$ rad/s. Determine the velocity and acceleration of the grip $A$ at this instant, when $\phi = 30°$, $\theta = 45°$, and $r = 1.6$ m.

**Prob. 20–47**

# CHAPTER REVIEW

- *Rotation About a Fixed Point.* When a body rotates about a fixed point $O$, then points on the body follow a path that lies on the surface of a sphere. Infinitesimal rotations are vector quantities, whereas finite rotations are not.

Since the angular acceleration is a time rate of change in the angular velocity, then we must account for both the magnitude and directional changes of $\boldsymbol{\omega}$ when finding its derivative. To do this, the angular velocity is often specified in terms of its component motions, such that some of these components will remain constant relative to rotating $x$, $y$, $z$ axes. If this is the case, then the time derivative relative to the fixed axis can be determined from Eq. 20–6, that is,

$$\dot{\mathbf{A}} = (\dot{\mathbf{A}})_{xyz} + \boldsymbol{\Omega} \times \mathbf{A}$$

Once $\boldsymbol{\omega}$ and $\boldsymbol{\alpha}$ are known, then the velocity and acceleration of point $P$ can be determined from

$$\mathbf{a} = \boldsymbol{\alpha} \times \mathbf{r} + \boldsymbol{\omega} \times (\boldsymbol{\omega} \times \mathbf{r})$$

$$\mathbf{v} = \boldsymbol{\omega} \times \mathbf{r}$$

- *General Motion.* If the body undergoes general motion, then the motion of a point $B$ in the body can be related to the motion of another point $A$ using a relative motion analysis, along with translating axes at $A$. The relationships are

$$\mathbf{v}_B = \mathbf{v}_A + \boldsymbol{\omega} \times \mathbf{r}_{B/A}$$

$$\mathbf{a}_B = \mathbf{a}_A + \boldsymbol{\alpha} \times \mathbf{r}_{B/A} + \boldsymbol{\omega} \times (\boldsymbol{\omega} \times \mathbf{r}_{B/A})$$

- *Relative Motion Analysis Using Translating and Rotating Axes.* The motion of two points $A$ and $B$ on a body, a series of connected bodies, or located on two different paths, can be related using a relative motion analysis with rotating and translating axes at $A$. The relationships are

$$\mathbf{v}_B = \mathbf{v}_A + \boldsymbol{\Omega} \times \mathbf{r}_{B/A} + (\mathbf{v}_{B/A})_{xyz}$$

$$\mathbf{a}_B = \mathbf{a}_A + \dot{\boldsymbol{\Omega}} \times \mathbf{r}_{B/A} + \boldsymbol{\Omega} \times (\boldsymbol{\Omega} \times \mathbf{r}_{B/A}) + 2\boldsymbol{\Omega} \times (\mathbf{v}_{B/A})_{xyz} + (\mathbf{a}_{B/A})_{xyz}$$

When applying these equations, it is important to account for both the magnitude and directional changes of $\mathbf{r}_A$, $(\mathbf{r}_{B/A})_{xyz}$, $\boldsymbol{\Omega}$, and $\boldsymbol{\Omega}_{xyz}$ when taking their time derivatives to find $\mathbf{v}_A$, $\mathbf{a}_A$, $(\mathbf{v}_{B/A})_{xyz}$, $(\mathbf{a}_{B/A})_{xyz}$, and $\dot{\boldsymbol{\Omega}}$, and $\dot{\boldsymbol{\Omega}}_{xyz}$. To do this properly, one must use Eq. 20–6.

The design of amusement-park rides requires a force analysis that depends on their three-dimensional motion.

# Three-Dimensional Kinetics of a Rigid Body

- To introduce the methods for finding the moments of inertia and products of inertia of a body about various axes.
- To show how to apply the principles of work and energy and linear and angular momentum to a rigid body having three-dimensional motion.
- To develop and apply the equations of motion in three dimensions.
- To study the motion of a gyroscope and torque-free motion.

## *21.1   Moments and Products of Inertia

When studying the planar kinetics of a body, it was necessary to introduce the moment of inertia $I_G$, which was computed about an axis perpendicular to the plane of motion and passing through the body's mass center $G$. For the kinetic analysis of three-dimensional motion it will sometimes be necessary to calculate six inertial quantities. These terms, called the moments and products of inertia, describe in a particular way the distribution of mass for a body relative to a given coordinate system that has a specified orientation and point of origin.

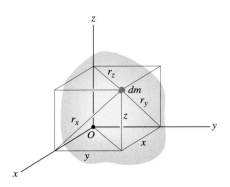

**Fig. 21–1**

**Moment of Inertia.** Consider the rigid body shown in Fig. 21–1. The *moment of inertia* for a differential element $dm$ of the body about any one of the three coordinate axes is defined as the product of the mass of the element and the square of the shortest distance from the axis to the element. For example, as noted in the figure, $r_x = \sqrt{y^2 + z^2}$, so that the mass moment of inertia of $dm$ about the $x$ axis is

$$dI_{xx} = r_x^2 \, dm = (y^2 + z^2) \, dm$$

The moment of inertia $I_{xx}$ for the body is determined by integrating this expression over the entire mass of the body. Hence, for each of the axes, we may write

$$
\begin{aligned}
I_{xx} &= \int_m r_x^2 \, dm = \int_m (y^2 + z^2) \, dm \\
I_{yy} &= \int_m r_y^2 \, dm = \int_m (x^2 + z^2) \, dm \\
I_{zz} &= \int_m r_z^2 \, dm = \int_m (x^2 + y^2) \, dm
\end{aligned}
\tag{21–1}
$$

Here it is seen that the moment of inertia is *always a positive quantity*, since it is the summation of the product of the mass $dm$, which is always positive, and the distances squared.

**Product of Inertia.** The *product of inertia* for a differential element $dm$ is defined with respect to a set of *two orthogonal planes* as the product of the mass of the element and the perpendicular (or shortest) distances from the planes to the element. For example, this distance is $x$ to the $y$–$z$ plane and it is $y$ to the $x$–$z$ plane, Fig. 21–1. The product of inertia $dI_{xy}$ for the element $dm$ is therefore

$$dI_{xy} = xy \, dm$$

Note also that $dI_{yx} = dI_{xy}$. By integrating over the entire mass, the product of inertia of the body for each combination of planes may be expressed as

$$
\begin{aligned}
I_{xy} &= I_{yx} = \int_m xy \, dm \\
I_{yz} &= I_{zy} = \int_m yz \, dm \\
I_{xz} &= I_{zx} = \int_m xz \, dm
\end{aligned}
\tag{21–2}
$$

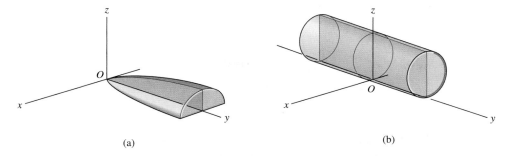

(a)                          (b)

**Fig. 21–2**

Unlike the moment of inertia, which is always positive, the product of inertia may be positive, negative, or zero. The result depends on the signs of the two defining coordinates, which vary independently from one another. In particular, if either one or both of the orthogonal planes are *planes of symmetry* for the mass, the *product of inertia* with respect to these planes will be *zero*. In such cases, elements of mass will occur in *pairs* located on each side of the plane of symmetry. On one side of the plane the product of inertia for the element will be positive, while on the other side the product of inertia for the corresponding element will be negative, the sum therefore yielding zero. Examples of this are shown in Fig. 21–2. In the first case, Fig. 21–2a, the $y$–$z$ plane is a plane of symmetry, and hence $I_{xy} = I_{xz} = 0$. Calculation of $I_{yz}$ will yield a *positive* result, since all elements of mass are located using only positive $y$ and $z$ coordinates. For the cylinder, with the coordinate axes located as shown in Fig. 21–2b, the $x$–$z$ and $y$–$z$ planes are both planes of symmetry. Thus, $I_{xy} = I_{yz} = I_{zx} = 0$.

**Parallel-Axis and Parallel-Plane Theorems.**   The techniques of integration which are used to determine the moment of inertia of a body were described in Sec. 17.1. Also discussed were methods to determine the moment of inertia of a composite body, i.e., a body that is composed of simpler segments, as tabulated on the inside back cover. In both of these cases the *parallel-axis theorem* is often used for the calculations. This theorem, which was developed in Sec. 17.1, is used to transfer the moment of inertia of a body from an axis passing through its mass center $G$ to a parallel axis passing through some other point. In this regard, if $G$ has coordinates $x_G, y_G, z_G$ defined from the $x, y, z$ axes, Fig. 21–3, then

**Fig. 21–3**

The dynamics of the space shuttle as it orbits the earth can be predicted only if its moments and products of inertia are known.

the parallel-axis equations used to calculate the moments of inertia about the $x, y, z$ axes are

$$
\begin{aligned}
I_{xx} &= (I_{x'x'})_G + m(y_G^2 + z_G^2) \\
I_{yy} &= (I_{y'y'})_G + m(x_G^2 + z_G^2) \\
I_{zz} &= (I_{z'z'})_G + m(x_G^2 + y_G^2)
\end{aligned}
\tag{21–3}
$$

The products of inertia of a composite body are computed in the same manner as the body's moments of inertia. Here, however, the *parallel-plane theorem* is important. This theorem is used to transfer the products of inertia of the body from a set of three orthogonal planes passing through the body's mass center to a corresponding set of three parallel planes passing through some other point $O$. Defining the perpendicular distances between the planes as $x_G$, $y_G$ and $z_G$, Fig. 21–3, the parallel-plane equations can be written as

$$
\begin{aligned}
I_{xy} &= (I_{x'y'})_G + m x_G y_G \\
I_{yz} &= (I_{y'z'})_G + m y_G z_G \\
I_{zx} &= (I_{z'x'})_G + m z_G x_G
\end{aligned}
\tag{21–4}
$$

The derivation of these formulas is similar to that given for the parallel-axis equation, Sec. 17.1.

**Inertia Tensor.** The inertial properties of a body are completely characterized by nine terms, six of which are independent of one another. This set of terms is defined using Eqs. 21–1 and 21–2 and can be written as

$$
\begin{pmatrix}
I_{xx} & -I_{xy} & -I_{xz} \\
-I_{yx} & I_{yy} & -I_{yz} \\
-I_{zx} & -I_{zy} & I_{zz}
\end{pmatrix}
$$

This array is called an *inertia tensor*. It has a unique set of values for a body when it is computed for each location of the origin $O$ and orientation of the coordinate axes.

In general, for point $O$ we can specify a unique axes inclination for which the products of inertia for the body are zero when computed with respect to these axes. When this is done, the inertia tensor is said to be "diagonalized" and may be written in the simplified form

$$
\begin{pmatrix}
I_x & 0 & 0 \\
0 & I_y & 0 \\
0 & 0 & I_z
\end{pmatrix}
$$

Here $I_x = I_{xx}$, $I_y = I_{yy}$, and $I_z = I_{zz}$ are termed the *principal moments of inertia* for the body, which are computed from the *principal axes of inertia*. Of these three principal moments of inertia, one will be a maximum and another a minimum of the body's moment of inertia.

Mathematical determination of the directions of principal axes of inertia will not be discussed here (see Prob. 21–21). There are many cases, however, in which the principal axes may be determined by inspection. From the previous discussion it was noted that if the coordinate axes are oriented such that *two* of the three orthogonal planes containing the axes are planes of *symmetry* for the body, then all the products of inertia for the body are zero with respect to the coordinate planes, and hence the coordinate axes are principal axes of inertia. For example, the $x$, $y$, $z$ axes shown in Fig. 21–2$b$ represent the principal axes of inertia for the cylinder at point $O$.

### Moment of Inertia About an Arbitrary Axis.

Consider the body shown in Fig. 21–4, where the nine elements of the inertia tensor have been computed for the $x$, $y$, $z$ axes having an origin at $O$. Here we wish to determine the moment of inertia of the body about the $Oa$ axis, for which the direction is defined by the unit vector $\mathbf{u}_a$. By definition $I_{Oa} = \int b^2 \, dm$, where $b$ is the *perpendicular distance* from $dm$ to $Oa$. If the position of $dm$ is located using $\mathbf{r}$, then $b = r \sin \theta$, which represents the *magnitude* of the cross product $\mathbf{u}_a \times \mathbf{r}$. Hence, the moment of inertia can be expressed as

$$I_{Oa} = \int_m |(\mathbf{u}_a \times \mathbf{r})|^2 \, dm = \int_m (\mathbf{u}_a \times \mathbf{r}) \cdot (\mathbf{u}_a \times \mathbf{r}) \, dm$$

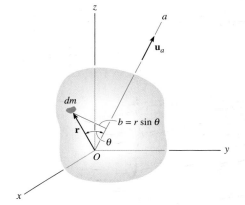

Provided $\mathbf{u}_a = u_x \mathbf{i} + u_y \mathbf{j} + u_z \mathbf{k}$ and $\mathbf{r} = x\mathbf{i} + y\mathbf{j} + z\mathbf{k}$, so that $\mathbf{u}_a \times \mathbf{r} = (u_y z - u_z y)\mathbf{i} + (u_z x - u_x z)\mathbf{j} + (u_x y - u_y x)\mathbf{k}$, then, after substituting and performing the dot-product operation, we can write the moment of inertia as

$$I_{Oa} = \int_m [(u_y z - u_z y)^2 + (u_z x - u_x z)^2 + (u_x y - u_y x)^2] \, dm$$

$$= u_x^2 \int_m (y^2 + z^2) \, dm + u_y^2 \int_m (z^2 + x^2) \, dm + u_z^2 \int_m (x^2 + y^2) \, dm$$

$$- 2u_x u_y \int_m xy \, dm - 2u_y u_z \int_m yz \, dm - 2u_z u_x \int_m zx \, dm$$

**Fig. 21–4**

Recognizing the integrals to be the moments and products of inertia of the body, Eqs. 21–1 and 21–2, we have

$$\boxed{I_{Oa} = I_{xx} u_x^2 + I_{yy} u_y^2 + I_{zz} u_z^2 - 2I_{xy} u_x u_y - 2I_{yz} u_y u_z - 2I_{zx} u_z u_x} \quad (21\text{–}5)$$

Thus, if the inertia tensor is specified for the $x$, $y$, $z$ axes, the moment of inertia of the body about the inclined $Oa$ axis can be found by using Eq. 21–5. For the calculation, the direction cosines $u_x$, $u_y$, $u_z$ of the axes must be determined. These terms specify the cosines of the coordinate direction angles $\alpha$, $\beta$, $\gamma$ made between the positive $Oa$ axis and the positive $x$, $y$, $z$ axes, respectively (see Appendix C).

# E X A M P L E | 21.1

(a)

Determine the moment of inertia of the bent rod shown in Fig. 21–5a about the $Aa$ axis. The mass of each of the three segments is shown in the figure.

### Solution

Before applying Eq. 21–5, it is first necessary to determine the moments and products of inertia of the rod about the $x, y, z$ axes. This is done using the formula for the moment of inertia of a slender rod, $I = \frac{1}{12}ml^2$, and the parallel-axis and parallel-plane theorems, Eqs. 21–3 and 21–4. Dividing the rod into three parts and locating the mass center of each segment, Fig. 21–5b, we have

$$I_{xx} = [\tfrac{1}{12}(2)(0.2)^2 + 2(0.1)^2] + [0 + 2(0.2)^2]$$
$$+ [\tfrac{1}{12}(4)(0.4)^2 + 4((0.2)^2 + (0.2)^2)] = 0.480 \text{ kg} \cdot \text{m}^2$$
$$I_{yy} = [\tfrac{1}{12}(2)(0.2)^2 + 2(0.1)^2] + [\tfrac{1}{12}(2)(0.2)^2 + 2((-0.1)^2 + (0.2)^2)]$$
$$+ [0 + 4((-0.2)^2 + (0.2)^2)] = 0.453 \text{ kg} \cdot \text{m}^2$$
$$I_{zz} = [0 + 0] + [\tfrac{1}{12}(2)(0.2)^2 + 2(0.1)^2] + [\tfrac{1}{12}(4)(0.4)^2 + 4((-0.2)^2$$
$$+ (0.2)^2)] = 0.400 \text{ kg} \cdot \text{m}^2$$
$$I_{xy} = [0 + 0] + [0 + 0] + [0 + 4(-0.2)(0.2)] = -0.160 \text{ kg} \cdot \text{m}^2$$
$$I_{yz} = [0 + 0] + [0 + 0] + [0 + 4(0.2)(0.2)] = 0.160 \text{ kg} \cdot \text{m}^2$$
$$I_{zx} = [0 + 0] + [0 + 2(0.2)(-0.1)] + [0 + 4(0.2)(-0.2)] = -0.200 \text{ kg} \cdot \text{m}^2$$

The $Aa$ axis is defined by the unit vector

$$\mathbf{u}_{Aa} = \frac{\mathbf{r}_D}{r_D} = \frac{-0.2\mathbf{i} + 0.4\mathbf{j} + 0.2\mathbf{k}}{\sqrt{(-0.2)^2 + (0.4)^2 + (0.2)^2}} = -0.408\mathbf{i} + 0.816\mathbf{j} + 0.408\mathbf{k}$$

Thus,

$$u_x = -0.408 \qquad u_y = 0.816 \qquad u_z = 0.408$$

Substituting these results into Eq. 21–5 yields

$$I_{Aa} = I_{xx}u_x^2 + I_{yy}u_y^2 + I_{zz}u_z^2 - 2I_{xy}u_xu_y - 2I_{yz}u_yu_z - 2I_{zx}u_zu_x$$
$$= 0.480(-0.408)^2 + (0.453)(0.816)^2 + 0.400(0.408)^2$$
$$- 2(-0.160)(-0.408)(0.816) - 2(0.160)(0.816)(0.408)$$
$$- 2(-0.200)(0.408)(-0.408)$$
$$= 0.169 \text{ kg} \cdot \text{m}^2 \qquad\qquad\qquad Ans.$$

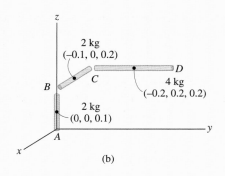

(b)

**Fig. 21–5**

# PROBLEMS

**21-1.** Show that the sum of the moments of inertia of a body, $I_{xx} + I_{yy} + I_{zz}$, is independent of the orientation of the $x$, $y$, $z$ axes and thus depends only on the location of the origin.

**21-2.** Determine the moment of inertia of the cylinder with respect to the $a$–$a$ axis of the cylinder. The cylinder has a mass $m$.

**Prob. 21–2**

**21-3.** Determine moment of inertia $I_y$ of the solid formed by revolving the shaded area around the $x$ axis. The density of the material is $\rho = 5000$ kg/m³.

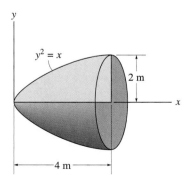

**Prob. 21–3**

**\*21-4.** Determine the product of inertia $I_{xy}$ of the body formed by revolving the shaded area about the line $x = 5$ m. Express the result in terms of the density of the maerial, $\rho$.

**21-5.** Determine the moment of inertia $I_y$ of the body formed by revolving the shaded area about the line $x = 5$ m. Express the result in terms of the density of the material, $\rho$.

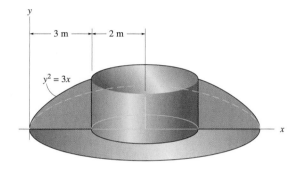

**Probs. 21–4/5**

**21-6.** Determine by direct integration the product of inertia $I_{yz}$ for the homogeneous prism. The density of the material is $\rho$. Express the result in terms of the mass $m$ of the prism.

**21-7.** Determine by direct integration the product of inertia $I_{xy}$ for the homogeneous prism. The density of the material is $\rho$. Express the result in terms of the mass $m$ of the prism.

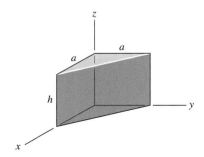

**Probs. 21–6/7**

**\*21-8.** Determine the radii of gyration $k_x$ and $k_y$ for the solid formed by revolving the shaded area about the $y$ axis. The density of the material is $\rho$.

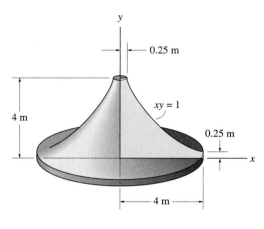

0.25 m

$xy = 1$

4 m

0.25 m

4 m

**Prob. 21–8**

**21-10.** Determine the elements of the inertia tensor for the cube with respect to the $x, y, z$ coordinate system. The mass of the cube is $m$.

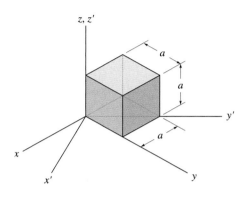

$z, z'$

$a$

$a$

$y'$

$x$

$a$

$x'$

$y$

**Prob. 21–10**

**21-9.** Determine the mass moment of inertia of the homogeneous block with respect to its centroidal $x'$ axis. The mass of the block is $m$.

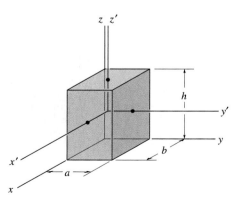

$z \ z'$

$h$

$y'$

$y$

$b$

$x'$

$a$

$x$

**Prob. 21–9**

**21-11.** Determine the moments of inertia about the $x$, $y$, $z$ axes of the rod assembly. The rods have a mass of 0.75 kg/m.

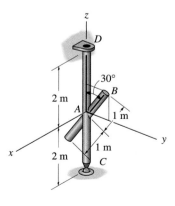

$z$

$D$

$30°$

$B$

2 m

$A$

1 m

$y$

1 m

$x$

2 m

$C$

**Prob. 21–11**

***21-12.** Determine the moment of inertia of the cone about the $z'$ axis. The mass of the cone is 15 kg, the *height* is $h = 1.5$ m, and the radius is $r = 0.5$ m.

Prob. 21–12

**21-14.** Determine the moment of inertia of both the 1.5 kg rod and 4 kg disk about the $z'$ axis.

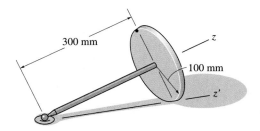

300 mm

100 mm

Prob. 21–14

**21-13.** The bent rod has a weight of 25 N/m ($\approx 2.5$ kg/m). Locate the center of gravity $G(\bar{x}, \bar{y})$ and determine the principal moments of inertia $I_{x'}$, $I_{y'}$, and $I_{z'}$ of the rod with respect to the $x'$, $y'$, $z'$ axes.

**21-15.** Determine the moment of inertia $I_x$ of the composite plate assembly. The plates have a mass of 30 kg/m².

***21-16.** Determine the product of inertia $I_{yz}$ of the composite plate assembly. The plates have a mass of 30 kg/m².

Prob. 21–13

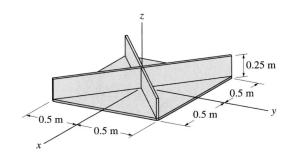

Probs. 21–15/16

**21-17.** Determine the moment of inertia of the composite body about the *aa* axis. The cylinder weighs 20 kN ($\approx$ 2000 kg), and each hemisphere weighs 10 kN ($\approx$ 1000 kg).

**Prob. 21–17**

**21-19.** The assembly consists of a 150-kg plate *A*, 40-kg plate *B*, and four 70-kg rods. Determine the moments of inertia of the assembly with respect to the principal *x*, *y*, *z* axes.

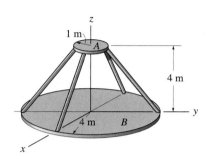

**Prob. 21–19**

**21-18.** Determine the moment of inertia of the rod-and-thin-ring assembly about the *z* axis. The rods and ring have a mass of 2 kg/m.

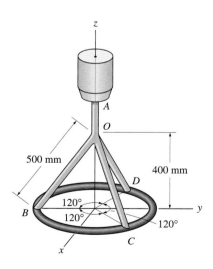

**Prob. 21–18**

**\*21-20.** The bent rod has a mass of 4 kg/m. Determine the moment of inertia of the rod about the *Oa* axis.

**Prob. 21–20**

## *21.2 Angular Momentum

In this section we will develop the necessary equations used to determine the angular momentum of a rigid body about an arbitrary point. This formulation will provide a means for developing both the principle of impulse and momentum and the equations of rotational motion for a rigid body.

Consider the rigid body in Fig. 21–6, which has a mass $m$ and center of mass at $G$. The $X, Y, Z$ coordinate system represents an inertial frame of reference, and hence, its axes are fixed or translate with a constant velocity. The angular momentum as measured from this reference will be computed relative to the arbitrary point $A$. The position vectors $\mathbf{r}_A$ and $\boldsymbol{\rho}_A$ are drawn from the origin of coordinates to point $A$ and from $A$ to the $i$th particle of the body. If the particle's mass is $m_i$, the angular momentum about point $A$ is

$$(\mathbf{H}_A)_i = \boldsymbol{\rho}_A \times m_i \mathbf{v}_i$$

where $\mathbf{v}_i$ represents the particle's velocity measured from the $X, Y, Z$ coordinate system. If the body has an angular velocity $\boldsymbol{\omega}$ at the instant considered, $\mathbf{v}_i$ may be related to the velocity of $A$ by applying Eq. 20–7, i.e.,

$$\mathbf{v}_i = \mathbf{v}_A + \boldsymbol{\omega} \times \boldsymbol{\rho}_A$$

Thus,

$$(\mathbf{H}_A)_i = \boldsymbol{\rho}_A \times m_i(\mathbf{v}_A + \boldsymbol{\omega} \times \boldsymbol{\rho}_A)$$
$$= (\boldsymbol{\rho}_A m_i) \times \mathbf{v}_A + \boldsymbol{\rho}_A \times (\boldsymbol{\omega} \times \boldsymbol{\rho}_A) m_i$$

Summing all the particles of the body requires an integration, and since $m_i \to dm$, we have

$$\mathbf{H}_A = \left( \int_m \boldsymbol{\rho}_A \, dm \right) \times \mathbf{v}_A + \int_m \boldsymbol{\rho}_A \times (\boldsymbol{\omega} \times \boldsymbol{\rho}_A) \, dm \qquad (21\text{–}6)$$

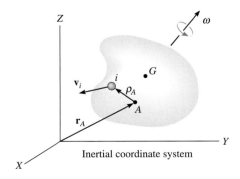

Inertial coordinate system

**Fig. 21–6**

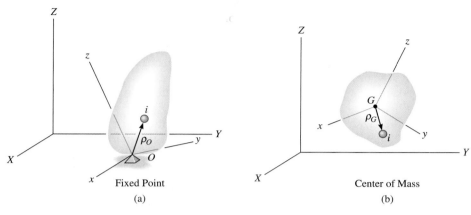

Fixed Point
(a)

Center of Mass
(b)

**Fig. 21–7**

**Fixed Point O.** If $A$ becomes a *fixed point* $O$ in the body, Fig. 21–7a, then $\mathbf{v}_A = \mathbf{0}$ and Eq. 21–6 reduces to

$$\mathbf{H}_O = \int_m \boldsymbol{\rho}_O \times (\boldsymbol{\omega} \times \boldsymbol{\rho}_O) \, dm \qquad (21\text{–}7)$$

**Center of Mass G.** If $A$ is located at the *center of mass* $G$ of the body, Fig. 21–7b, then $\int_m \boldsymbol{\rho}_A \, dm = \mathbf{0}$ and

$$\mathbf{H}_G = \int_m \boldsymbol{\rho}_G \times (\boldsymbol{\omega} \times \boldsymbol{\rho}_G) \, dm \qquad (21\text{–}8)$$

**Arbitrary Point A.** In general, $A$ may be some point other than $O$ or $G$, Fig. 21–7c, in which case Eq. 21–6 may nevertheless be simplified to the following form (see Prob. 21–22).

$$\mathbf{H}_A = \boldsymbol{\rho}_{G/A} \times m\mathbf{v}_G + \mathbf{H}_G \qquad (21\text{–}9)$$

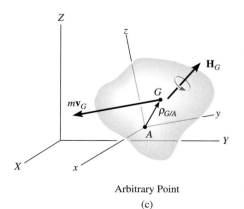

Arbitrary Point
(c)

Here the angular momentum consists of two parts—the moment of the linear momentum $m\mathbf{v}_G$ of the body about point $A$ added (vectorially) to the angular momentum $\mathbf{H}_G$. Equation 21–9 may also be used for computing the angular momentum of the body about a fixed point $O$; the results, of course, will be the same as those computed using the more convenient Eq. 21–7.

**Rectangular Components of H.** To make practical use of Eqs. 21–7 through 21–9, the angular momentum must be expressed in terms of its scalar components. For this purpose, it is convenient to choose a second set of $x$, $y$, $z$ axes having an arbitrary orientation relative to the $X$, $Y$, $Z$ axes, Fig. 21–7, and for a general formulation, note that Eqs. 21–7 and 21–8 are both of the form

$$\mathbf{H} = \int_m \boldsymbol{\rho} \times (\boldsymbol{\omega} \times \boldsymbol{\rho}) \, dm$$

Expressing $\mathbf{H}$, $\boldsymbol{\rho}$, and $\boldsymbol{\omega}$ in terms of $x$, $y$, and $z$ components, we have

$$H_x\mathbf{i} + H_y\mathbf{j} + H_z\mathbf{k} = \int_m (x\mathbf{i} + y\mathbf{j} + z\mathbf{k}) \times [(\omega_x\mathbf{i} + \omega_y\mathbf{j} + \omega_z\mathbf{k})$$
$$\times (x\mathbf{i} + y\mathbf{j} + z\mathbf{k})] \, dm$$

Expanding the cross products and combining terms yields

$$H_x\mathbf{i} + H_y\mathbf{j} + H_z\mathbf{k} = \left[\omega_x \int_m (y^2 + z^2) \, dm - \omega_y \int_m xy \, dm - \omega_z \int_m xz \, dm\right]\mathbf{i}$$
$$+ \left[-\omega_x \int_m xy \, dm + \omega_y \int_m (x^2 + z^2) \, dm - \omega_z \int_m yz \, dm\right]\mathbf{j}$$
$$+ \left[-\omega_x \int_m zx \, dm - \omega_y \int_m yz \, dm + \omega_z \int_m (x^2 + y^2) \, dm\right]\mathbf{k}$$

Equating the respective $\mathbf{i}$, $\mathbf{j}$, $\mathbf{k}$ components and recognizing that the integrals represent the moments and products of inertia, we obtain

$$\boxed{\begin{aligned} H_x &= I_{xx}\omega_x - I_{xy}\omega_y - I_{xz}\omega_z \\ H_y &= -I_{yx}\omega_x + I_{yy}\omega_y - I_{yz}\omega_z \\ H_z &= -I_{zx}\omega_x - I_{zy}\omega_y + I_{zz}\omega_z \end{aligned}} \qquad (21\text{–}10)$$

These three equations represent the scalar form of the $\mathbf{i}$, $\mathbf{j}$, $\mathbf{k}$ components of $\mathbf{H}_O$ or $\mathbf{H}_G$ (given in vector form by Eqs. 21–7 and 21–8). The angular momentum of the body about the arbitrary point $A$, other than the fixed point $O$ or the center of mass $G$, may also be expressed in scalar form. Here it is necessary to use Eq. 21–9 to represent $\boldsymbol{\rho}_{G/A}$ and $\mathbf{v}_G$ as Cartesian vectors, carry out the cross-product operation, and substitute the components, Eqs. 21–10, for $\mathbf{H}_G$.

Equations 21–10 may be simplified further if the $x$, $y$, $z$ coordinate axes are oriented such that they become *principal axes of inertia* for the body at the point. When these axes are used, the products of inertia $I_{xy} = I_{yz} = I_{zx} = 0$, and if the principal moments of inertia about the $x$, $y$, $z$ axes are represented as $I_x = I_{xx}$, $I_y = I_{yy}$, and $I_z = I_{zz}$, the three components of angular momentum become

$$\boxed{H_x = I_x\omega_x \qquad H_y = I_y\omega_y \qquad H_z = I_z\omega_z} \qquad (21\text{–}11)$$

The motion of the astronaut is controlled by use of small directional jets attached to his or her space suit. The impulses these jets provide must be carefully specified in order to prevent tumbling and loss of orientation.

**Principle of Impulse and Momentum.** Now that the formulation of the angular momentum for a body has been developed, the *principle of impulse and momentum*, as discussed in Sec. 19.2, may be used to solve kinetic problems which involve *force, velocity, and time.* For this case, the following two vector equations are available:

$$m(\mathbf{v}_G)_1 + \Sigma \int_{t_1}^{t_2} \mathbf{F}\, dt = m(\mathbf{v}_G)_2 \tag{21–12}$$

$$(\mathbf{H}_O)_1 + \Sigma \int_{t_1}^{t_2} \mathbf{M}_O\, dt = (\mathbf{H}_O)_2 \tag{21–13}$$

In three dimensions each vector term can be represented by three scalar components, and therefore a total of *six scalar equations* can be written. Three equations relate the linear impulse and momentum in the *x, y, z* directions, and the other three equations relate the body's angular impulse and momentum about the *x, y, z* axes. Before applying Eqs. 21–12 and 21–13 to the solution of problems, the material in Secs. 19.2 and 19.3 should be reviewed.

## *21.3   Kinetic Energy

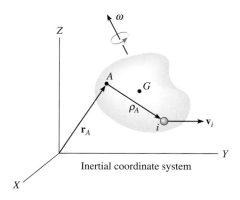

Inertial coordinate system

**Fig. 21–8**

In order to apply the principle of work and energy to the solution of problems involving general rigid body motion, it is first necessary to formulate expressions for the kinetic energy of the body. In this regard, consider the rigid body shown in Fig. 21–8, which has a mass $m$ and center of mass at $G$. The kinetic energy of the $i$th particle of the body having a mass $m_i$ and velocity $\mathbf{v}_i$, measured relative to the inertial $X, Y, Z$ frame of reference, is

$$T_i = \tfrac{1}{2} m_i v_i^2 = \tfrac{1}{2} m_i (\mathbf{v}_i \cdot \mathbf{v}_i)$$

Provided the velocity of an arbitrary point $A$ in the body is known, $\mathbf{v}_i$ may be related to $\mathbf{v}_A$ by the equation $\mathbf{v}_i = \mathbf{v}_A + \boldsymbol{\omega} \times \boldsymbol{\rho}_A$, where $\boldsymbol{\omega}$ is the angular velocity of the body, measured from the $X, Y, Z$ coordinate system, and $\boldsymbol{\rho}_A$ is a position vector drawn from $A$ to $i$. Using this expression for $\mathbf{v}_i$, the kinetic energy for the particle may be written as

$$T_i = \tfrac{1}{2} m_i (\mathbf{v}_A + \boldsymbol{\omega} \times \boldsymbol{\rho}_A) \cdot (\mathbf{v}_A + \boldsymbol{\omega} \times \boldsymbol{\rho}_A)$$
$$= \tfrac{1}{2} (\mathbf{v}_A \cdot \mathbf{v}_A) m_i + \mathbf{v}_A \cdot (\boldsymbol{\omega} \times \boldsymbol{\rho}_A) m_i + \tfrac{1}{2} (\boldsymbol{\omega} \times \boldsymbol{\rho}_A) \cdot (\boldsymbol{\omega} \times \boldsymbol{\rho}_A) m_i$$

The kinetic energy for the entire body is obtained by summing the kinetic energies of all the particles of the body. This requires an integration, and since $m_i \rightarrow dm$, we get

$$T = \tfrac{1}{2} m (\mathbf{v}_A \cdot \mathbf{v}_A) + \mathbf{v}_A \cdot \left( \boldsymbol{\omega} \times \int_m \boldsymbol{\rho}_A\, dm \right) + \tfrac{1}{2} \int_m (\boldsymbol{\omega} \times \boldsymbol{\rho}_A) \cdot (\boldsymbol{\omega} \times \boldsymbol{\rho}_A)\, dm$$

The last term on the right may be rewritten using the vector identity $\mathbf{a} \times \mathbf{b} \cdot \mathbf{c} = \mathbf{a} \cdot \mathbf{b} \times \mathbf{c}$, where $\mathbf{a} = \boldsymbol{\omega}$, $\mathbf{b} = \boldsymbol{\rho}_A$, and $\mathbf{c} = \boldsymbol{\omega} \times \boldsymbol{\rho}_A$. The final result is

$$T = \tfrac{1}{2}m(\mathbf{v}_A \cdot \mathbf{v}_A) + \mathbf{v}_A \cdot \left(\boldsymbol{\omega} \times \int_m \boldsymbol{\rho}_A \, dm\right)$$

$$+ \tfrac{1}{2}\boldsymbol{\omega} \cdot \int_m \boldsymbol{\rho}_A \times (\boldsymbol{\omega} \times \boldsymbol{\rho}_A) \, dm \quad (21\text{--}14)$$

This equation is rarely used because of the computations involving the integrals. Simplification occurs, however, if the reference point $A$ is either a fixed point $O$ or the center of mass $G$.

**Fixed Point O.**   If $A$ is a *fixed point* $O$ in the body, Fig. 21–7a, then $\mathbf{v}_A = \mathbf{0}$, and using Eq. 21–7, we can express Eq. 21–14 as

$$T = \tfrac{1}{2}\boldsymbol{\omega} \cdot \mathbf{H}_O$$

If the $x$, $y$, $z$ axes represent the principal axes of inertia for the body, then $\boldsymbol{\omega} = \omega_x \mathbf{i} + \omega_y \mathbf{j} + \omega_z \mathbf{k}$ and $\mathbf{H}_O = I_x \omega_x \mathbf{i} + I_y \omega_y \mathbf{j} + I_z \omega_z \mathbf{k}$. Substituting into the above equation and performing the dot product operations yields

$$T = \tfrac{1}{2}I_x \omega_x^2 + \tfrac{1}{2}I_y \omega_y^2 + \tfrac{1}{2}I_z \omega_z^2 \quad (21\text{--}15)$$

**Center of Mass G.**   If $A$ is located at the *center of mass $G$* of the body, Fig. 21–7b, then $\int \boldsymbol{\rho}_A \, dm = \mathbf{0}$ and, using Eq. 21–8, we can write Eq. 21–14 as

$$T = \tfrac{1}{2}mv_G^2 + \tfrac{1}{2}\boldsymbol{\omega} \cdot \mathbf{H}_G$$

In a manner similar to that for a fixed point, the last term on the right side may be represented in scalar form, in which case

$$T = \tfrac{1}{2}mv_G^2 + \tfrac{1}{2}I_x \omega_x^2 + \tfrac{1}{2}I_y \omega_y^2 + \tfrac{1}{2}I_z \omega_z^2 \quad (21\text{--}16)$$

Here it is seen that the kinetic energy consists of two parts; namely, the translational kinetic energy of the mass center, $\tfrac{1}{2}mv_G^2$, and the body's rotational kinetic energy.

**Principle of Work and Energy.**   Having formulated the kinetic energy for a body, the *principle of work and energy* may be applied to solve kinetics problems which involve *force, velocity, and displacement.* For this case only one scalar equation can be written for each body, namely,

$$T_1 + \Sigma U_{1\text{-}2} = T_2 \quad (21\text{--}17)$$

Before applying this equation, the material in Chapter 18 should be reviewed.

EXAMPLE 21.2

(a)

(b)

Fig. 21–9

The rod in Fig. 21–9a has a weight of 25 N/m ($\approx$ 2.5 kg/m). Determine its angular velocity just after the end $A$ falls onto the hook at $E$. The hook provides a permanent connection for the rod due to the spring-lock mechanism $S$. Just before striking the hook the rod is falling downward with a speed $(v_G)_1 = 3$ m/s.

**Solution**

The principle of impulse and momentum will be used since impact occurs.

*Impulse and Momentum Diagrams.* Fig. 21–9b. During the short time $\Delta t$, the impulsive force $\mathbf{F}$ acting at $A$ changes the momentum of the rod. (The impulse created by the rod's weight $\mathbf{W}$ during this time is small compared to $\int \mathbf{F}\, dt$, so that it is neglected, i.e., the weight is a nonimpulsive force.) Hence, the angular momentum of the rod is *conserved* about point $A$ since the moment of $\int \mathbf{F}\, dt$ about $A$ is zero.

*Conservation of Angular Momentum.* Equation 21–9 must be used for computing the angular momentum of the rod, since $A$ does not become a *fixed point* until *after* the impulsive interaction with the hook. Thus, with reference to Fig. 21–9b, $(\mathbf{H}_A)_1 = (\mathbf{H}_A)_2$, or

$$\mathbf{r}_{G/A} \times m(\mathbf{v}_G)_1 = \mathbf{r}_{G/A} \times m(\mathbf{v}_G)_2 + (\mathbf{H}_G)_2 \qquad (1)$$

From Fig. 21–9a, $\mathbf{r}_{G/A} = \{-0.2\mathbf{i} + 0.15\mathbf{j}\}$ m. Furthermore, the primed axes are principal axes of inertia for the rod because $I_{x'y'} = I_{x'z'} = I_{z'y'} = 0$. Hence, from Eqs. 21–11, $(\mathbf{H}_G)_2 = I_{x'}\omega_x\mathbf{i} + I_{y'}\omega_y\mathbf{j} + I_{z'}\omega_z\mathbf{k}$. The principal moments of inertia are $I_{x'} = 0.1338$ kg $\cdot$ m$^2$, $I_{y'} = 0.0765$ kg $\cdot$ m$^2$, $I_{z'} = 0.2102$ kg $\cdot$ m$^2$ (see Prob. 21–13). Substituting into Eq. 1, we have

$$(-0.2\mathbf{i} + 0.15\mathbf{j}) \times \left[\left(\frac{22.5}{9.81}\right)(-3\mathbf{k})\right] = (-0.2\mathbf{i} + 0.15\mathbf{j}) \times \left[\left(\frac{22.5}{9.81}\right)(-v_G)_2\mathbf{k}\right]$$

$$+ 0.1338\omega_x\mathbf{i} + 0.0765\omega_y\mathbf{j} + 0.2102\omega_z\mathbf{k}$$

Expanding and equating the respective $\mathbf{i}$, $\mathbf{j}$, and $\mathbf{k}$ components yields

$$-1.0321 = -0.3440(v_G)_2 + 0.1338\omega_x \qquad (2)$$
$$-1.3761 = -0.4587(v_G)_2 + 0.0765\omega_y \qquad (3)$$
$$0 = 0.2102\omega_z \qquad (4)$$

*Kinematics.* There are four unknowns in the above equations; however, another equation may be obtained by relating $\boldsymbol{\omega}$ to $(\mathbf{v}_G)_2$ using *kinematics*. Since $\omega_z = 0$ (Eq. 4) and after impact the rod rotates about the fixed point $A$, Eq. 20–3 may be applied, in which case $(\mathbf{v}_G)_2 = \boldsymbol{\omega} \times \mathbf{r}_{G/A}$, or

$$-(v_G)_2\mathbf{k} = (\omega_x\mathbf{i} + \omega_y\mathbf{j}) \times (-0.2\mathbf{i} + 0.15\mathbf{j})$$

$$-(v_G)_2 = 0.15\omega_x + 0.2\omega_y \qquad (5)$$

Solving Eqs. 2 through 5 simultaneously yields

$$(\mathbf{v}_G)_2 = \{-1.84\mathbf{k}\} \text{ m/s} \qquad \boldsymbol{\omega} = \{-2.98\mathbf{i} - 6.96\mathbf{j}\} \text{ rad/s} \qquad \textit{Ans.}$$

# EXAMPLE 21.3

A 5-N · m torque is applied to the vertical shaft $CD$ shown in Fig. 21–10a, which allows the 10-kg gear $A$ to turn freely about $CE$. Assuming that gear $A$ starts from rest, determine the angular velocity of $CD$ after it has turned two revolutions. Neglect the mass of shaft $CD$ and axle $CE$ and assume that gear $A$ can be approximated by a thin disk. Gear $B$ is fixed.

(a)

### Solution

The principle of work and energy may be used for the solution. Why?

*Work.*   If shaft $CD$, the axle $CE$, and gear $A$ are considered as a system of connected bodies, only the applied torque $\mathbf{M}$ does work. For two revolutions of $CD$, this work is $\Sigma U_{1-2} = (5\,\text{N} \cdot \text{m})(4\pi\,\text{rad}) = 62.83$ J.

*Kinetic Energy.*   Since the gear is initially at rest, its initial kinetic energy is zero. A kinematic diagram for the gear is shown in Fig. 21–10b. If the angular velocity of $CD$ is taken as $\boldsymbol{\omega}_{CD}$, then the angular velocity of gear $A$ is $\boldsymbol{\omega}_A = \boldsymbol{\omega}_{CD} + \boldsymbol{\omega}_{CE}$. The gear may be imagined as a portion of a massless extended body which is rotating about the *fixed point* $C$. The instantaneous axis of rotation for this body is along line $CH$, because both points $C$ and $H$ on the body (gear) have zero velocity and must therefore lie on this axis. This requires that the components $\omega_{CD}$ and $\omega_{CE}$ be related by the equation $\omega_{CD}/0.1$ m $= \omega_{CE}/0.3$ m or $\omega_{CE} = 3\omega_{CD}$. Thus,

$$\boldsymbol{\omega}_A = -\omega_{CE}\mathbf{i} + \omega_{CD}\mathbf{k} = -3\omega_{CD}\mathbf{i} + \omega_{CD}\mathbf{k} \qquad (1)$$

(b)

**Fig. 21–10**

The $x$, $y$, $z$ axes in Fig. 21–10a represent *principal axes of inertia* at $C$ for the gear. Since point $C$ is a fixed point of rotation, Eq. 21–15 may be applied to determine the kinetic energy, i.e.,

$$T = \tfrac{1}{2}I_x\omega_x^2 + \tfrac{1}{2}I_y\omega_y^2 + \tfrac{1}{2}I_z\omega_z^2 \qquad (2)$$

Using the parallel-axis theorem, the moments of inertia of the gear about point $C$ are as follows:

$$I_x = \tfrac{1}{2}(10\,\text{kg})(0.1\,\text{m})^2 = 0.05\,\text{kg} \cdot \text{m}^2$$

$$I_y = I_z = \tfrac{1}{4}(10\,\text{kg})(0.1\,\text{m})^2 + 10\,\text{kg}(0.3\,\text{m})^2 = 0.925\,\text{kg} \cdot \text{m}^2$$

Since $\omega_x = -3\omega_{CD}$, $\omega_y = 0$, $\omega_z = \omega_{CD}$, Eq. 2 becomes

$$T_A = \tfrac{1}{2}(0.05)(-3\omega_{CD})^2 + 0 + \tfrac{1}{2}(0.925)(\omega_{CD})^2 = 0.6875\omega_{CD}^2$$

*Principle of Work and Energy.*   Applying the principle of work and energy, we obtain

$$T_1 + \Sigma U_{1-2} = T_2$$
$$0 + 62.83 = 0.6875\omega_{CD}^2$$
$$\omega_{CD} = 9.56\,\text{rad/s} \qquad\qquad Ans.$$

# PROBLEMS

**21-21.** If a body contains *no planes of symmetry*, the principal moments of inertia can be determined mathematically. To show how this is done, consider the rigid body which is spinning with an angular velocity $\boldsymbol{\omega}$, directed along one of its principal axes of inertia. If the principal moment of inertia about this axis is $I$, the angular momentum can be expressed as $\mathbf{H} = I\boldsymbol{\omega} = I\omega_x\mathbf{i} + I\omega_y\mathbf{j} + I\omega_z\mathbf{k}$. The components of $\mathbf{H}$ may also be expressed by Eqs. 21–10, where the inertia tensor is assumed to be known. Equate the $\mathbf{i}$, $\mathbf{j}$, and $\mathbf{k}$ components of both expressions for $\mathbf{H}$ and consider $\omega_x$, $\omega_y$, and $\omega_z$ to be unknown. The solution of these three equations is obtained provided the determinant of the coefficients is zero. Show that this determinant, when expanded, yields the cubic equation

$$I^3 - (I_{xx} + I_{yy} + I_{zz})I^2 + (I_{xx}I_{yy} + I_{yy}I_{zz} + I_{zz}I_{xx}$$
$$- I_{xy}^2 - I_{yz}^2 - I_{zx}^2)I - (I_{xx}I_{yy}I_{zz} - 2I_{xy}I_{yz}I_{zx}$$
$$- I_{xx}I_{yz}^2 - I_{yy}I_{zx}^2 - I_{zz}I_{xy}^2) = 0$$

The three positive roots of $I$, obtained from the solution of this equation, represent the principal moments of inertia $I_x$, $I_y$, and $I_z$.

**21-22.** Show that if the angular momentum of a body is determined with respect to an arbitrary point $A$, then $\mathbf{H}_A$ can be expressed by Eq. 21–9. This requires substituting $\boldsymbol{\rho}_A = \boldsymbol{\rho}_G + \boldsymbol{\rho}_{G/A}$ into Eq. 21–6 and expanding, noting that $\int \boldsymbol{\rho}_G \, dm = \mathbf{0}$ by definition of the mass center and $\mathbf{v}_G = \mathbf{v}_A + \boldsymbol{\omega} \times \boldsymbol{\rho}_{G/A}$.

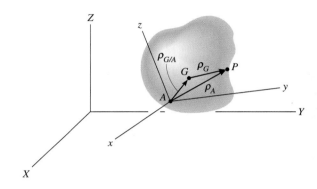

**Prob. 21–22**

**21-23.** The 2-kg gear $A$ rolls on the fixed plate gear $C$. Determine the angular velocity of rod $OB$ about the $z$ axis after it rotates one revolution about the $z$ axis, starting from rest. The rod is acted upon by the constant moment $M = 5 \text{ N} \cdot \text{m}$. Neglect the mass of rod $OB$. Assume that gear $A$ is a uniform disk having a radius of 100 mm.

**Prob. 21–21**

**Prob. 21–23**

**\*21-24.** Rod $AB$ has a mass of 6 kg and is attached to two smooth collars at its end points by ball-and-socket joints. If collar $A$ is moving downward at a speed of 8 cm/s, determine the kinetic energy of the rod at the instant shown. Assume that at this instant the angular velocity of the rod is directed perpendicular to the rod's axis.

**21-25.** At the instant shown the collar at $A$ on the 6-kg rod $AB$ has a velocity of $v_A = 8$ cm/s. Determine the kinetic energy of the rod after the collar has descended 3 cm. Neglect friction and the thickness of the rod. Neglect the mass of the collar and the collar is attached to the rod using ball-and-socket joints.

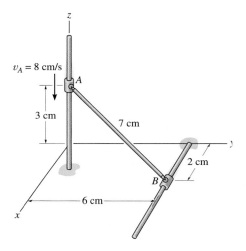

**Probs. 21–24/25**

**21-26.** The cone has a mass $m$ and rolls without slipping on the conical surface so that it has an angular velocity about the vertical axis of $\boldsymbol{\omega}$. Determine the kinetic energy of the cone due to this motion.

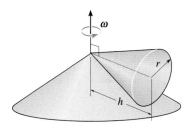

**Prob. 21–26**

**21-27.** The rod has a mass of 9 kg/m and is suspended from parallel cords at $A$ and $B$. If the rod has an angular velocity of 2 rad/s about the $z$ axis at the instant shown, determine how high the center of the rod rises at the instant the rod momentarily stops swinging.

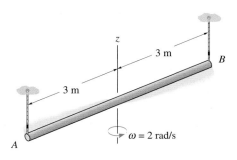

**Prob. 21–27**

**\*21-28.** The 5-kg disk is connected to the 3-kg slender rod. If the assembly is attached to a ball-and-socket joint at $A$ and the 5-N $\cdot$ m couple moment is applied, determine the angular velocity of the rod about the $z$ axis after the assembly has made two revolutions about the $z$ axis starting from rest. The disk rolls without slipping.

**21-29.** The 5-kg disk is connected to the 3-kg slender rod. If the assembly is attached to a ball-and-socket joint at $A$ and the 5-N $\cdot$ m couple moment gives it an angular velocity about the $z$ axis of $\omega_z = 2$ rad/s, determine the magnitude of the angular momentum of the assembly about $A$.

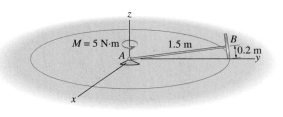

**Probs. 21–28/29**

**21-30.** The circular plate has a mass of 19 kg and a diameter of 1.5 m. If it is released from rest and falls horizontally 2.5 m onto the hook at $S$, which provides a permanent connection, determine the velocity of the mass center of the plate just after the connection with the hook is made.

**Prob. 21–30**

**21-31.** The 2-kg thin disk is connected to the slender rod which is fixed to the ball-and-socket joint at $A$. If it is released from rest in the position shown, determine the spin of the disk about the rod when the disk reaches its lowest position. Neglect the mass of the rod. The disk rolls without slipping.

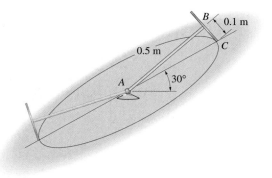

**Prob. 21–31**

**\*21-32.** Rod $AB$ has a mass of 6 kg and is attached to two smooth collars at its ends by ball-and-socket joints. If collar $A$ is moving downward with a speed of 8 cm/s when $z = 3$ cm, determine the speed of $A$ at the instant $z = 0$. The spring has an unstretched length of 2 cm. Neglect the mass of the collars. Assume the angular velocity of rod $AB$ is perpendicular to its axis.

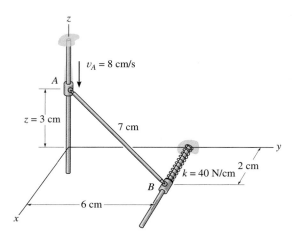

**Prob. 21–32**

**21-33.** The circular disk has a mass of 15 kg and is mounted on the shaft $AB$ at an angle of 45° with the horizontal. Determine the angular velocity of the shaft when $t = 3$ s if a constant torque $M = 2$ N · m is applied to the shaft. The shaft is originally spinning at $\omega_1 = 8$ rad/s when the torque is applied.

**21-34.** The circular disk has a mass of 15 kg and is mounted on the shaft $AB$ at an angle of 45° with the horizontal. Determine the angular velocity of the shaft when $t = 2$ s if a torque $M = (4e^{0.1t})$ N · m, where $t$ is in seconds, is applied to the shaft. The shaft is originally spinning at $\omega_1 = 8$ rad/s when the torque is applied.

**Probs. 21–33/34**

**21-35.** The 15-kg rectangular plate is free to rotate about the $y$ axis because of the bearing supports at $A$ and $B$. When the plate is balanced in the vertical plane, a 3-g bullet is fired into it, perpendicular to its surface, with a velocity $\mathbf{v} = \{-2000\mathbf{i}\}$ m/s. Compute the angular velocity of the plate at the instant it has rotated 180°. If the bullet strikes corner $D$ with the same velocity $\mathbf{v}$, instead of at $C$, does the angular velocity remain the same? Why or why not?

Prob. 21–35

**21-37.** The 150-kg plate is subjected to a force $F = 0.8$ kN which is always directed perpendicular to the face of the plate. If the plate is originally at rest, determine its angular velocity after it has rotated one revolution (360°). The plate is supported by ball-and-socket joints at $A$ and $B$.

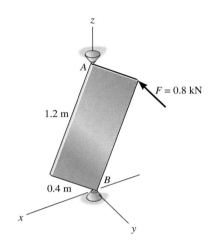

Prob. 21–37

**\*21-36.** The rod assembly is supported at $G$ by a ball-and-socket joint. Each segment has a mass of 0.5 kg/m. If the assembly is originally at rest and an impulse of $\mathbf{I} = \{-8\mathbf{k}\}$ N·s is applied at $D$, determine the angular velocity of the assembly just after the impact.

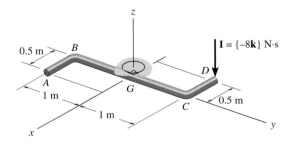

Prob. 21–36

**21-38.** The space capsule has a mass of 3.5 Mg and the radii of gyration are $k_x = k_z = 0.8$ m and $k_y = 0.5$ m. If it is traveling with a velocity $\mathbf{v}_G = \{600\mathbf{j}\}$ m/s, compute its angular velocity just after it is struck by a meteoroid having a mass of 0.60 kg and a velocity $\mathbf{V}_m = \{-200\mathbf{i} - 400\mathbf{j} + 200\mathbf{k}\}$ m/s. Assume that the meteoroid embeds itself into the capsule at point $A$ and that the capsule initially has no angular velocity.

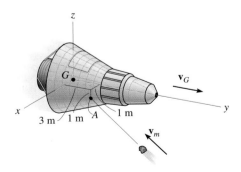

Prob. 21–38

## *21.4 Equations of Motion

Having become familiar with the techniques used to describe both the inertial properties and the angular momentum of a body, we can now write the equations which describe the motion of the body in their most useful forms.

**Equations of Translational Motion.** The *translational motion* of a body is defined in terms of the acceleration of the body's mass center, which is measured from an inertial $X, Y, Z$ reference. The equation of translational motion for the body can be written in vector form as

$$\Sigma \mathbf{F} = m\mathbf{a}_G \qquad (21\text{–}18)$$

or by the three scalar equations

$$\boxed{\begin{aligned} \Sigma F_x &= m(a_G)_x \\ \Sigma F_y &= m(a_G)_y \\ \Sigma F_z &= m(a_G)_z \end{aligned}} \qquad (21\text{–}19)$$

Here, $\Sigma \mathbf{F} = \Sigma F_x \mathbf{i} + \Sigma F_y \mathbf{j} + \Sigma F_z \mathbf{k}$ represents the sum of all the external forces acting on the body.

**Equations of Rotational Motion.** In Sec. 15.6, we developed Eq. 15–17, namely,

$$\Sigma \mathbf{M}_O = \dot{\mathbf{H}}_O \qquad (21\text{–}20)$$

which states that the sum of the moments about a fixed point $O$ of all the external forces acting on a system of particles (contained in a rigid body) is equal to the time rate of change of the total angular momentum of the body about point $O$. When moments of the external forces acting on the particles are summed about the system's *mass center G*, one again obtains the same simple form of Eq. 21–20, relating the moment summation $\Sigma \mathbf{M}_G$ to the angular momentum $\mathbf{H}_G$. To show this, consider the system of particles in Fig. 21–11, where $X, Y, Z$ represents an inertial frame of reference and the $x, y, z$ axes, with origin at $G$, *translate* with respect to this frame. In general, $G$ is *accelerating*, so by definition the translating frame is *not* an inertial reference. The angular momentum of the *i*th particle with respect to this frame is, however,

$$(\mathbf{H}_i)_G = \mathbf{r}_{i/G} \times m_i \mathbf{v}_{i/G}$$

where $\mathbf{r}_{i/G}$ and $\mathbf{v}_{i/G}$ represent the relative position and relative velocity of the *i*th particle with respect to $G$. Taking the time derivative we have

$$(\dot{\mathbf{H}}_i)_G = \dot{\mathbf{r}}_{i/G} \times m_i \mathbf{v}_{i/G} + \mathbf{r}_{i/G} \times m_i \dot{\mathbf{v}}_{i/G}$$

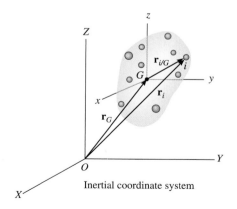

Inertial coordinate system

**Fig. 21–11**

By definition, $\mathbf{v}_{i/G} = \dot{\mathbf{r}}_{i/G}$. Thus, the first term on the right side is zero since the cross product of equal vectors is zero. Also, $\mathbf{a}_{i/G} = \dot{\mathbf{v}}_{i/G}$, so that

$$(\dot{\mathbf{H}}_i)_G = (\mathbf{r}_{i/G} \times m_i \mathbf{a}_{i/G})$$

Similar expressions can be written for the other particles of the body. When the results are summed, we get

$$\dot{\mathbf{H}}_G = \Sigma(\mathbf{r}_{i/G} \times m_i \mathbf{a}_{i/G})$$

Here $\dot{\mathbf{H}}_G$ is the time rate of change of the total angular momentum of the body computed relative to point $G$.

The relative acceleration for the $i$th particle is defined by the equation $\mathbf{a}_{i/G} = \mathbf{a}_i - \mathbf{a}_G$, where $\mathbf{a}_i$ and $\mathbf{a}_G$ represent, respectively, the accelerations of the $i$th particle and point $G$ measured with respect to the *inertial frame of reference*. Substituting and expanding, using the distributive property of the vector cross product, yields

$$\dot{\mathbf{H}}_G = \Sigma(\mathbf{r}_{i/G} \times m_i \mathbf{a}_i) - (\Sigma m_i \mathbf{r}_{i/G}) \times \mathbf{a}_G$$

By definition of the mass center, the sum $(\Sigma m_i \mathbf{r}_{i/G}) = (\Sigma m_i)\bar{\mathbf{r}}$ is equal to zero, since the position vector $\bar{\mathbf{r}}$ relative to $G$ is zero. Hence, the last term in the above equation is zero. Using the equation of motion, the product $m_i \mathbf{a}_i$ may be replaced by the resultant *external force* $\mathbf{F}_i$ acting on the $i$th particle. Denoting $\Sigma \mathbf{M}_G = (\Sigma \mathbf{r}_{i/G} \times \mathbf{F}_i)$, the final result may be written as

$$\Sigma \mathbf{M}_G = \dot{\mathbf{H}}_G \qquad (21\text{–}21)$$

The rotational equation of motion for the body will now be developed from either Eq. 21–20 or 21–21. In this regard, the scalar components of the angular momentum $\mathbf{H}_O$ or $\mathbf{H}_G$ are defined by Eqs. 21–10 or, if principal axes of inertia are used either at point $O$ or $G$, by Eqs. 21–11. If these components are computed about $x, y, z$ axes that are *rotating* with an angular velocity $\mathbf{\Omega}$, which may be *different* from the body's angular velocity $\boldsymbol{\omega}$, then the time derivative $\dot{\mathbf{H}} = d\mathbf{H}/dt$, as used in Eqs. 21–20 and 21–21, must account for the rotation of the $x, y, z$ axes as measured from the inertial $X, Y, Z$ axes. Hence, the time derivative of $\mathbf{H}$ must be determined from Eq. 20-6, in which case Eqs. 21–20 and 21–21 become

$$\Sigma \mathbf{M}_O = (\dot{\mathbf{H}}_O)_{xyz} + \mathbf{\Omega} \times \mathbf{H}_O$$
$$\Sigma \mathbf{M}_G = (\dot{\mathbf{H}}_G)_{xyz} + \mathbf{\Omega} \times \mathbf{H}_G \qquad (21\text{–}22)$$

Here $(\dot{\mathbf{H}})_{xyz}$ is the time rate of change of $\mathbf{H}$ measured from the $x, y, z$ reference.

There are three ways in which one can define the motion of the $x, y, z$ axes. Obviously, motion of this reference should be chosen to yield the simplest set of moment equations for the solution of a particular problem.

*x, y, z* **Axes Having Motion** $\Omega = 0$. If the body has general motion, the *x, y, z* axes may be chosen with origin at *G*, such that the axes only *translate* relative to the inertial *X, Y, Z* frame of reference. Doing this would certainly simplify Eq. 21–22, since $\Omega = 0$. However, the body may have a rotation $\boldsymbol{\omega}$ about these axes, and therefore the moments and products of inertia of the body would have to be expressed as *functions of time*. In most cases this would be a difficult task, so that such a choice of axes has restricted value.

*x, y, z* **Axes Having Motion** $\Omega = \omega$. The *x, y, z* axes may be chosen such that they are *fixed in and move with the body*. The moments and products of inertia of the body relative to these axes will be *constant* during the motion. Since $\Omega = \boldsymbol{\omega}$, Eqs. 21–22 become

$$\Sigma \mathbf{M}_O = (\dot{\mathbf{H}}_O)_{xyz} + \boldsymbol{\omega} \times \mathbf{H}_O$$
$$\Sigma \mathbf{M}_G = (\dot{\mathbf{H}}_G)_{xyz} + \boldsymbol{\omega} \times \mathbf{H}_G \qquad (21\text{–}23)$$

We may express each of these vector equations as three scalar equations using Eqs. 21–10. Neglecting the subscripts *O* and *G* yields

$$\Sigma M_x = I_{xx}\dot{\omega}_x - (I_{yy} - I_{zz})\omega_y\omega_z - I_{xy}(\dot{\omega}_y - \omega_z\omega_x) - I_{yz}(\omega_y^2 - \omega_z^2)$$
$$- I_{zx}(\dot{\omega}_z + \omega_x\omega_y)$$
$$\Sigma M_y = I_{yy}\dot{\omega}_y - (I_{zz} - I_{xx})\omega_z\omega_x - I_{yz}(\dot{\omega}_z - \omega_x\omega_y) - I_{zx}(\omega_z^2 - \omega_x^2)$$
$$- I_{xy}(\dot{\omega}_x + \omega_y\omega_z) \qquad (21\text{–}24)$$
$$\Sigma M_z = I_{zz}\dot{\omega}_z - (I_{xx} - I_{yy})\omega_x\omega_y - I_{zx}(\dot{\omega}_x - \omega_y\omega_z) - I_{xy}(\omega_x^2 - \omega_y^2)$$
$$- I_{yz}(\dot{\omega}_y + \omega_z\omega_x)$$

Notice that for a rigid body symmetric with respect to the x-y reference plane, and undergoing general plane motion in this plane, $I_{xz} = I_{yz} = 0$, and $\omega_x = \omega_y = d\omega_x/dt = d\omega_y/dt = 0$. Equations 21–24 reduce to the form $\Sigma M_x = \Sigma M_y = 0$, and $\Sigma M_z = I_{zz}\alpha_z$ (where $\alpha_z = \dot{\omega}_z$), which is essentially the third of Eqs. 17–16 or 17–17 depending on the choice of point *O* or *G* for summing moments.

If the *x, y,* and *z* axes are chosen as *principal axes of inertia*, the products of inertia are zero, $I_{xx} = I_x$, etc., and Eqs. 21–24 reduce to the from

$$\Sigma M_x = I_x\dot{\omega}_x - (I_y - I_z)\omega_y\omega_z$$
$$\Sigma M_y = I_y\dot{\omega}_y - (I_z - I_x)\omega_z\omega_x \qquad (21\text{–}25)$$
$$\Sigma M_z = I_z\dot{\omega}_z - (I_x - I_y)\omega_x\omega_y$$

This set of equations is known historically as the *Euler equations of motion*, named after the Swiss mathematician Leonhard Euler, who first developed them. They apply *only* for moments summed about either point *O* or *G*.

When applying these equations it should be realized that $\dot{\omega}_x$, $\dot{\omega}_y$, $\dot{\omega}_z$ represent the time derivatives of the magnitudes of the $x, y, z$ components of $\boldsymbol{\omega}$ as observed from $x, y, z$. Since the $x, y, z$ axes are rotating at $\boldsymbol{\Omega} = \boldsymbol{\omega}$, then, from Eq. 20–6, it should be noted that $\dot{\boldsymbol{\omega}} = (\dot{\boldsymbol{\omega}})_{xyz} + \boldsymbol{\omega} \times \boldsymbol{\omega}$. Since $\boldsymbol{\omega} \times \boldsymbol{\omega} = \mathbf{0}$, $\dot{\boldsymbol{\omega}} = (\dot{\boldsymbol{\omega}})_{xyz}$. This important result indicates that the required time derivative of $\boldsymbol{\omega}$ can be obtained either by first finding the components of $\boldsymbol{\omega}$ along the $x, y, z$ axes when these axes are oriented in a general position *and then* taking the time derivative of the magnitudes of these components, i.e., $(\dot{\boldsymbol{\omega}})_{xyz}$, or by finding the time derivative of $\boldsymbol{\omega}$ with respect to the $X, Y, Z$ axes, i.e., $\dot{\boldsymbol{\omega}}$, and then determining the components $\dot{\omega}_x$, $\dot{\omega}_y$, $\dot{\omega}_z$. In practice, it is generally easier to compute $\dot{\omega}_x$, $\dot{\omega}_y$, $\dot{\omega}_z$ on the basis of finding $\dot{\boldsymbol{\omega}}$. See Example 21–5.

$x, y, z$ **Axes Having Motion $\Omega \neq \omega$.**  To simplify the calculations for the time derivative of $\boldsymbol{\omega}$, it is often convenient to choose the $x, y, z$ axes having an angular velocity $\boldsymbol{\Omega}$ which is different from the angular velocity $\boldsymbol{\omega}$ of the body. This is particularly suitable for the analysis of spinning tops and gyroscopes which are *symmetrical* about their spinning axes.* When this is the case, the moments and products of inertia remain constant during the motion.

Equations 21–22 are applicable for such a set of chosen axes. Each of these two vector equations may be reduced to a set of three scalar equations which are derived in a manner similar to Eqs. 21–25,† i.e.,

$$
\begin{aligned}
\Sigma M_x &= I_x \dot{\omega}_x - I_y \Omega_z \omega_y + I_z \Omega_y \omega_z \\
\Sigma M_y &= I_y \dot{\omega}_y - I_z \Omega_x \omega_z + I_x \Omega_z \omega_x \\
\Sigma M_z &= I_z \dot{\omega}_z - I_x \Omega_y \omega_x + I_y \Omega_x \omega_y
\end{aligned}
\qquad (21\text{–}26)
$$

Here $\Omega_x$, $\Omega_y$, $\Omega_z$ represent the $x, y, z$ components of $\boldsymbol{\Omega}$, measured from the inertial frame of reference, and $\dot{\omega}_x$, $\dot{\omega}_y$, $\dot{\omega}_z$ must be determined relative to the $x, y, z$ axes that have the rotation $\boldsymbol{\Omega}$. See Example 21–6.

Any one of these sets of moment equations, Eqs. 21–24, 21–25, or 21–26, represents a series of three first-order nonlinear differential equations. These equations are "coupled," since the angular-velocity components are present in all the terms. Success in determining the solution for a particular problem therefore depends upon what is unknown in these equations. Difficulty certainly arises when one attempts to solve for the unknown components of $\boldsymbol{\omega}$, given the external moments as functions of time. Further complications can arise if the moment equations are coupled to the three scalar equations of translational motion, Eqs. 21–19. This can happen because of the existence of kinematic constraints which

*A detailed discussion of such devices is given in Sec. 21.5.
†See Prob. 21–41.

relate the rotation of the body to the translation of its mass center, as in the case of a hoop which rolls without slipping. Problems necessitating the simultaneous solution of differential equations generally require application of numerical methods with the aid of a computer. In many engineering problems, however, one is required to determine the applied moments acting on the body, given information about the motion of the body. Fortunately, many of these types of problems have direct solutions, so that there is no need to resort to computer techniques.

## PROCEDURE FOR ANALYSIS

Problems involving the three-dimensional motion of a rigid body can be solved using the following procedure.

*Free-Body Diagram*

- Draw a *free-body diagram* of the body at the instant considered and specify the $x, y, z$ coordinate system. The origin of this reference must be located either at the body's mass center $G$, or at point $O$, considered fixed in an inertial reference frame and located either in the body or on a massless extension of the body.

- Unknown reactive forces can be shown having a positive sense of direction.

- Depending on the nature of the problem, decide what type of rotational motion $\Omega$ the $x, y, z$ coordinate system should have, i.e., $\Omega = 0$, $\Omega = \omega$, or $\Omega \neq \omega$. When choosing, one should keep in mind that the moment equations are simplified when the axes move in such a manner that they represent principal axes of inertia for the body at all times.

- Compute the necessary moments and products of inertia for the body relative to the $x, y, z$ axes.

*Kinematics*

- Determine the $x, y, z$ components of the body's angular velocity and compute the time derivatives of $\boldsymbol{\omega}$.

- Note that if $\Omega = \omega$ then, $\dot{\boldsymbol{\omega}} = (\dot{\boldsymbol{\omega}})_{xyz}$, and we can either find the components of $\boldsymbol{\omega}$ along the $x, y, z$ axes when the axes are oriented in a general position, and then take the time derivative of the magnitudes of these components, $(\dot{\boldsymbol{\omega}})_{xyz}$; or we can find the time derivative of $\boldsymbol{\omega}$ with respect to the $X, Y, Z$ axes, $\dot{\boldsymbol{\omega}}$, and then determine the components $\dot{\omega}_x, \dot{\omega}_y, \dot{\omega}_z$.

*Equations of Motion*

- Apply either the two vector equations 21–18 and 21–22, or the six scalar component equations appropriate for the $x, y, z$ coordinate axes chosen for the problem.

# E X A M P L E 21.4

The gear shown in Fig. 21–12a has a mass of 10 kg and is mounted at an angle of 10° with a rotating shaft having negligible mass. If $I_z = 0.1$ kg·m², $I_x = I_y = 0.05$ kg·m², and the shaft is rotating with a constant angular velocity of $\omega = 30$ rad/s, determine the reactions that the bearing supports $A$ and $B$ exert on the shaft at the instant shown.

(a)

## Solution

*Free-Body Diagram.* Fig. 21–12b. The origin of the $x, y, z$ coordinate system is located at the gear's center of mass $G$, which is also a fixed point. The axes are fixed in and rotate with the gear, since these axes will then always represent the principal axes of inertia for the gear. Hence $\Omega = \omega$.

*Kinematics.* As shown in Fig. 21–12c, the angular velocity $\omega$ of the gear is constant in magnitude and is always directed along the axis of the shaft $AB$. Since this vector is measured from the $X, Y, Z$ inertial frame of reference, for any position of the $x, y, z$ axes,

$$\omega_x = 0 \qquad \omega_y = -30 \sin 10° \qquad \omega_z = 30 \cos 10°$$

These components remain constant for any general orientation of the $x, y, z$ axes, and so $\dot{\omega}_x = \dot{\omega}_y = \dot{\omega}_z = 0$. Also note that since $\Omega = \omega$, then $\dot{\omega} = (\dot{\omega})_{xyz}$ and we can find these time derivatives relative to the $X, Y, Z$ axes. In this regard $\omega$ has a constant magnitude and direction $(+Z)$ and so $\dot{\omega} = 0$, and so $\dot{\omega}_x = \dot{\omega}_y = \dot{\omega}_z = 0$. Furthermore, since $G$ is a fixed point, $(a_G)_x = (a_G)_y = (a_G)_z = 0$.

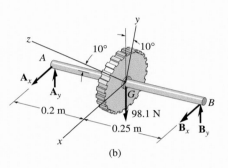

(b)

*Equations of Motion.* Applying Eqs. 21–25 ($\Omega = \omega$) yields

$$\Sigma M_x = I_x \dot{\omega}_x - (I_y - I_z)\omega_y \omega_z$$
$$-(A_Y)(0.2) + (B_Y)(0.25) = 0 - (0.05 - 0.1)(-30 \sin 10°)(30 \cos 10°)$$
$$-0.2A_Y + 0.25B_Y = -7.70 \qquad (1)$$

$$\Sigma M_y = I_y \dot{\omega}_y - (I_z - I_x)\omega_z \omega_x$$
$$A_X(0.2) \cos 10° - B_X(0.25) \cos 10° = 0 + 0$$
$$A_X = 1.25B_X \qquad (2)$$

$$\Sigma M_z = I_z \dot{\omega}_z - (I_x - I_y)\omega_x \omega_y$$
$$A_X(0.2) \sin 10° - B_X(0.25) \sin 10° = 0 + 0$$
$$A_X = 1.25B_X$$

(c)

**Fig. 21–12**

Applying Eqs. 21–19, we have

$$\Sigma F_X = m(a_G)_X; \qquad A_X + B_X = 0 \qquad (3)$$
$$\Sigma F_Y = m(a_G)_Y; \qquad A_Y + B_Y - 98.1 = 0 \qquad (4)$$
$$\Sigma F_Z = m(a_G)_Z; \qquad 0 = 0$$

Solving Eqs. 1 through 4 simultaneously gives

$$A_X = B_X = 0 \qquad A_Y = 71.6 \text{ N} \qquad B_Y = 26.5 \text{ N} \qquad \textit{Ans.}$$

E X A M P L E **21.5**

The airplane shown in Fig. 21–13a is in the process of making a steady *horizontal* turn at the rate of $\omega_p$. During this motion, the airplane's propeller is spinning at the rate of $\omega_s$. If the propeller has two blades, determine the moments which the propeller shaft exerts on the propeller at the instant the blades are in the vertical position. For simplicity, assume the blades to be a uniform slender bar having a moment of inertia $I$ about an axis perpendicular to the blades and passing through their center, and having zero moment of inertia about a longitudinal axis.

(a)

### Solution

*Free-Body Diagram.* Fig. 21–13b. The effect of the connecting shaft on the propeller is indicated by the resultants $\mathbf{F}_R$ and $\mathbf{M}_R$. (The propeller's weight is assumed to be negligible.) The x, y, z axes will be taken fixed to the propeller, since these axes always represent the principal axes of inertia for the propeller. Thus, $\mathbf{\Omega} = \boldsymbol{\omega}$. The moments of inertia $I_x$ and $I_y$ are equal ($I_x = I_y = I$) and $I_z = 0$.

*Kinematics.* The angular velocity of the propeller observed from the X, Y, Z axes, coincident with the x, y, z axes, Fig. 21–13c, is $\boldsymbol{\omega} = \boldsymbol{\omega}_s + \boldsymbol{\omega}_p = \omega_s\mathbf{i} + \omega_p\mathbf{k}$, so that the x, y, z components of $\boldsymbol{\omega}$ are

$$\omega_x = \omega_s \qquad \omega_y = 0 \qquad \omega_z = \omega_p$$

Since $\mathbf{\Omega} = \boldsymbol{\omega}$, then $\dot{\boldsymbol{\omega}} = (\dot{\boldsymbol{\omega}})_{xyz}$. The time derivative of $\dot{\boldsymbol{\omega}}$ can be determined with respect to the fixed X, Y, Z axes. To do this, Eq. 20–6 must be used since $\boldsymbol{\omega}$ is changing direction relative to X, Y, Z. Since $\boldsymbol{\omega} = \boldsymbol{\omega}_s + \boldsymbol{\omega}_p$, then $\dot{\boldsymbol{\omega}} = \dot{\boldsymbol{\omega}}_s + \dot{\boldsymbol{\omega}}_p$. The time rate of change of each of these components relative to the X, Y, Z axes can be obtained by using a third coordinate system x', y', z', which has an angular velocity $\mathbf{\Omega}' = \boldsymbol{\omega}_p$ and is coincident with the X, Y, Z axes at the instant shown. Thus

(b)

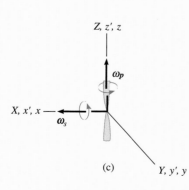

(c)

**Fig. 21–13**

$$\dot{\boldsymbol{\omega}} = (\dot{\boldsymbol{\omega}})_{x'y'z'} + \boldsymbol{\omega}_p \times \boldsymbol{\omega}$$
$$= (\dot{\boldsymbol{\omega}}_s)_{x'y'z'} + (\dot{\boldsymbol{\omega}}_p)_{x'y'z'} + \boldsymbol{\omega}_p \times (\boldsymbol{\omega}_s + \boldsymbol{\omega}_p)$$
$$= \mathbf{0} + \mathbf{0} + \boldsymbol{\omega}_p \times \boldsymbol{\omega}_s + \boldsymbol{\omega}_p \times \boldsymbol{\omega}_p$$
$$= \mathbf{0} + \mathbf{0} + \omega_p \mathbf{k} \times \omega_s \mathbf{i} + \mathbf{0} = \omega_p \omega_s \mathbf{j}$$

Since the $X, Y, Z$ axes are coincident with the $x, y, z$ axes at the instant shown, the components of $\dot{\boldsymbol{\omega}}$ along $x\ y\ z$ are therefore

$$\dot{\omega}_x = 0 \qquad \dot{\omega}_y = \omega_p \omega_s \qquad \dot{\omega}_z = 0$$

These same results can also be determined by direct calculation of $(\dot{\boldsymbol{\omega}})_{xyz}$; however, this will involve a bit more work. To do this, it will be necessary to view the propeller (or the $x, y, z$ axes) in some *general position* such as shown in Fig. 21–13d. Here the plane has turned through an angle $\phi$ (phi) and the propeller has turned through an angle $\psi$ (psi) relative to the plane. Notice that $\boldsymbol{\omega}_p$ is always directed along the fixed $Z$ axis and $\boldsymbol{\omega}_s$ follows the $x$ axis. Thus the general components of $\boldsymbol{\omega}$ are

(d)

$$\omega_x = \omega_s \qquad \omega_y = \omega_p \sin \psi \qquad \omega_z = \omega_p \cos \psi$$

Since $\omega_s$ and $\omega_p$ are constant, the time derivatives of these components become

$$\dot{\omega}_x = 0 \qquad \dot{\omega}_y = \omega_p \cos \psi\, \dot{\psi} \qquad \dot{\omega}_z = -\omega_p \sin \psi\, \dot{\psi}$$

But $\phi = \psi = 0°$ and $\dot{\psi} = \omega_s$ at the instant considered. Thus,

$$\omega_x = \omega_s \qquad \omega_y = 0 \qquad \omega_z = \omega_p$$
$$\dot{\omega}_x = 0 \qquad \dot{\omega}_y = \omega_p \omega_s \qquad \dot{\omega}_z = 0$$

which are the same results as those obtained previously.

*Equations of Motion.* Using Eqs. 21–25, we have

$$\Sigma M_x = I_x \dot{\omega}_x - (I_y - I_z)\omega_y \omega_z = I(0) - (I - 0)(0)\omega_p$$
$$M_x = 0 \qquad\qquad\qquad\qquad Ans.$$
$$\Sigma M_y = I_y \dot{\omega}_y - (I_z - I_x)\omega_z \omega_x = I(\omega_p \omega_s) - (0 - I)\omega_p \omega_s$$
$$M_y = 2I\omega_p \omega_s \qquad\qquad\qquad Ans.$$
$$\Sigma M_z = I_z \dot{\omega}_z - (I_x - I_y)\omega_x \omega_y = 0(0) - (I - I)\omega_s(0)$$
$$M_z = 0 \qquad\qquad\qquad\qquad Ans.$$

**E X A M P L E 21.6**

(a)

(b)

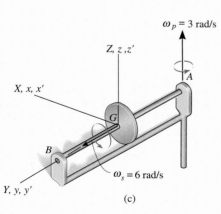

Fig. 21–14

The 10-kg flywheel (or thin disk) shown in Fig. 21–14$a$ rotates (spins) about the shaft at a constant angular velocity of $\omega_s = 6$ rad/s. At the same time, the shaft is rotating (precessing) about the bearing at $A$ with an angular velocity of $\omega_p = 3$ rad/s. If $A$ is a thrust bearing and $B$ is a journal bearing, determine the components of force reaction at each of these supports due to the motion.

**Solution I**

*Free-Body Diagram.* Fig. 21–14$b$. The origin of the $x$, $y$, $z$ coordinate system is located at the center of mass $G$ of the flywheel. Here we will let these coordinates have an angular velocity of $\mathbf{\Omega} = \boldsymbol{\omega}_p = \{3\mathbf{k}\}$ rad/s. Although the wheel spins relative to these axes, the moments of inertia *remain constant,* *i.e.,

$$I_x = I_z = \tfrac{1}{4}(10 \text{ kg})(0.2 \text{ m})^2 = 0.1 \text{ kg} \cdot \text{m}^2$$
$$I_y = \tfrac{1}{2}(10 \text{ kg})(0.2 \text{ m})^2 = 0.2 \text{ kg} \cdot \text{m}^2$$

*Kinematics.* From the coincident inertial $X$, $Y$, $Z$ frame of reference, Fig. 21–41$c$, the flywheel has an angular velocity of $\boldsymbol{\omega} = \{6\mathbf{j} + 3\mathbf{k}\}$ rad/s, so that

$$\omega_x = 0, \quad \omega_y = 6 \text{ rad/s}, \quad \omega_z = 3 \text{ rad/s}$$

The time derivative of $\boldsymbol{\omega}$ must be determined relative to the $x$, $y$, $z$ axes. In this case both $\boldsymbol{\omega}_p$ and $\boldsymbol{\omega}_s$ do not change and so

$$\dot{\omega}_x = 0, \quad \dot{\omega}_y = 0, \quad \dot{\omega}_z = 0$$

*Equations of Motion.* Applying Eqs. 21–26 ($\mathbf{\Omega} \neq \boldsymbol{\omega}$) yields

$$\Sigma M_x = I_x \dot{\omega}_x - I_y \Omega_z \omega_y + I_z \Omega_y \omega_z$$
$$-A_z(0.5) + B_z(0.5) = 0 - (0.2)(3)(6) + 0 = -3.6$$
$$\Sigma M_y = I_y \dot{\omega}_y - I_z \Omega_x \omega_z + I_x \Omega_z \omega_x$$
$$0 = 0 - 0 + 0$$
$$\Sigma M_z = I_z \dot{\omega}_z - I_x \Omega_y \omega_x + I_y \Omega_x \omega_y$$
$$A_x(0.5) - B_x(0.5) = 0 - 0 + 0$$

Applying Eqs. 21–19, we have

$$\Sigma F_X = m(a_G)_X; \qquad A_x + B_x = 0$$
$$\Sigma F_Y = m(a_G)_Y; \qquad A_y = -10(0.5)(3)^2$$
$$\Sigma F_Z = m(a_G)_Z; \qquad A_z + B_z - 10(9.81) = 0$$

Solving these equations, we obtain

$$A_x = 0 \quad A_y = -45.0 \text{ N} \quad A_z = 52.6 \text{ N} \qquad \textit{Ans.}$$
$$B_x = 0 \qquad\qquad\qquad\qquad B_z = 45.4 \text{ N} \qquad \textit{Ans.}$$

Note that if the precession $\boldsymbol{\omega}_p$ had not occurred, the reactions at $A$ and $B$ would be equal to 49.05 N. In this case, however, the difference in the reactions is caused by the "gyroscopic moment" created whenever a spinning body precesses about another axis. We will study this effect in detail in the next section.

*This would not be true for the propeller in Example 21–5.

### Solution II

This example can also be solved using Euler's equations of motion, Eqs. 21–25. In this case $\Omega = \omega = \{6\mathbf{j} + 3\mathbf{k}\}$ rad/s, and the time derivative $(\dot{\boldsymbol{\omega}})_{xyz}$ can be conveniently obtained with reference to the fixed $X, Y, Z$ axes since $\dot{\boldsymbol{\omega}} = (\dot{\boldsymbol{\omega}})_{xyz}$. This calculation can be performed by choosing $x', y', z'$ axes to have an angular velocity of $\Omega' = \boldsymbol{\omega}_p$, Fig. 21–14c, so that

$$\dot{\boldsymbol{\omega}} = (\dot{\boldsymbol{\omega}})_{x'y'z'} + \boldsymbol{\omega}_p \times \boldsymbol{\omega} = \mathbf{0} + 3\mathbf{k} \times (6\mathbf{j} + 3\mathbf{k}) = \{-18\mathbf{i}\} \text{ rad/s}^2$$

$$\dot{\omega}_x = -18 \text{ rad/s} \quad \dot{\omega}_y = 0 \quad \dot{\omega}_z = 0$$

The moment equations then become

$$\Sigma M_x = I_x\dot{\omega}_x - (I_y - I_z)\omega_y\omega_z$$
$$-A_x(0.5) + B_z(0.5) = 0.1(-18) - (0.2 - 0.1)(6)(3) = -3.6$$
$$\Sigma M_y = I_y\dot{\omega}_y - (I_z - I_x)\omega_z\omega_x$$
$$0 = 0 - 0$$
$$\Sigma M_z = I_z\dot{\omega}_z - (I_x - I_y)\omega_x\omega_y$$
$$A_x(0.5) - B_x(0.5) = 0 - 0$$

The solution then proceeds as before.

## PROBLEMS

**21-39.** Derive the scalar form of the rotational equation of motion along the $x$ axis when $\Omega \neq \omega$ and the moments and products of inertia of the body are *not constant* with respect to time.

**\*21-40.** Derive the scalar form of the rotational equation of motion along the $x$ axis when $\Omega \neq \omega$ and the moments and products of inertia of the body are *constant* with respect to time.

**21-41.** Derive the Euler equations of motion for $\Omega \neq \omega$, i.e., Eqs. 21–26.

**21-42.** The 40-kg flywheel (disk) is mounted 20 mm off its true center at $G$. If the shaft is rotating at a constant speed $\omega = 8$ rad/s, determine the maximum reactions exerted on the journal bearings at $A$ and $B$.

**Prob. 21–42**

**21-43.** The 40-kg flywheel (disk) is mounted 20 mm off its true center at $G$. If the shaft is rotating at a constant speed $\omega = 8$ rad/s, determine the minimum reactions exerted on the journal bearings at $A$ and $B$ during the motion.

**Prob. 21–43**

**\*21-44.** The 20-kg disk is mounted on the horizontal shaft $AB$ such that its plane forms an angle of 10° with the vertical. If the shaft rotates with an angular velocity of 3 rad/s, determine the vertical reactions developed at the bearings when the disk is in the position shown.

**21-46.** The conical pendulum consists of a bar of mass $m$ and length $L$ that is supported by the pin at its end $A$. If the pin is subjected to a rotation $\omega$, determine the angle $\theta$ that the bar makes with the vertical as it rotates. Also, determine the components of reaction at the pin.

Prob. 21–44

Prob. 21–46

**21-45.** The 4-kg bar rests along the smooth corners of an open box. At the instant shown, the box has a velocity $\mathbf{v} = \{3\mathbf{j}\}$ m/s and an acceleration $\mathbf{a} = \{-6\mathbf{j}\}$ m/s². Determine the $x$, $y$, $z$ components of force which the corners exert on the bar.

**21-47.** The 20-kg plate is mounted on the shaft $AB$ so that the plane of the plate makes an angle $\theta = 30°$ with the vertical. If the shaft is turning in the direction shown with an angular velocity of 25 rad/s, determine the vertical reactions at the bearing supports $A$ and $B$ when the plate is in the position shown.

Prob. 21–45

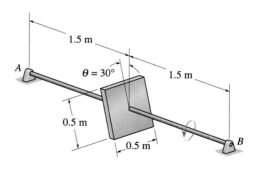

Prob. 21–47

**\*21-48.** The car is traveling around the curved road of radius $\rho$ such that its mass center has a constant speed $v_G$. Write the equations of rotational motion with respect to the $x, y, z$ axes. Assume that the car's six moments and products of inertia with respect to these axes are known.

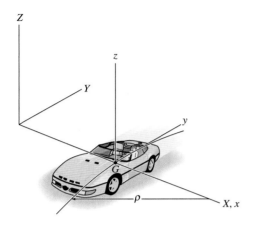

Prob. 21–48

**21-49.** The rod assembly is supported by a ball-and-socket joint at $C$ and a journal bearing at $D$, which develops only $x$ and $y$ force reactions. The rods have a mass of 0.75 kg/m. Determine the angular acceleration of the rods and the components of reaction at the supports at the instant $\omega = 8$ rad/s as shown.

Prob. 21–49

**21-50.** The rod assembly is supported by journal bearings at $A$ and $B$, which develops only $x$ and $y$ force reactions on the shaft. If the shaft $AB$ is rotating in the direction shown at $\boldsymbol{\omega} = \{-5\mathbf{j}\}$ rad/s, determine the reactions at the bearings when the assembly is in the position shown. Also, what is the shaft's angular acceleration? The mass of each rod is 1.5 kg/m.

Prob. 21–50

**21-51.** The rod assembly has a mass of 5 kg/m. It is supported at $B$ by a smooth journal bearing, which develops $x$ and $y$ force reactions, and at $A$ by a smooth thrust bearing, which develops $x$, $y$, and $z$ force reactions. If a 50-N · m torque is applied along rod $AB$, determine the components of reaction at the bearings when the assembly has an angular velocity $\omega = 10$ rad/s at the instant shown.

Prob. 21–51

**\*21-52.** The 250-kg disk is *fixed* to rod *BCD*, which has negligible mass. Determine the torque *T* which must be applied to the vertical shaft so that the shaft has an angular acceleration of $\alpha = 6$ rad/s². The shaft is free to turn in its bearings.

**21-53.** Solve Prob. 21–52, assuming rod *BCD* has a mass of 20 kg/m.

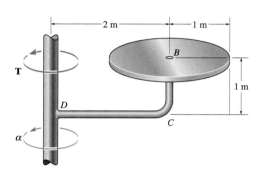

**Probs. 21–52/53**

**21-54.** The *thin rod* has a mass of 0.8 kg and a total length of 150 mm. It is rotating about its midpoint at a constant rate $\dot{\theta} = 6$ rad/s, while the table to which its axle *A* is fastened is rotating at 2 rad/s. Determine the *x, y, z* moment components which the axle exerts on the rod when the rod is in any position $\theta$.

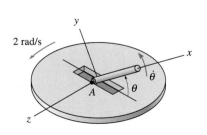

**Prob. 21–54**

**21-55.** A thin uniform plate having a mass of 0.4 kg is spinning with a constant angular velocity $\boldsymbol{\omega}$ about its diagonal *AB*. If the person holding the corner of the plate at *B* releases his finger, the plate will fall downward on its side *AC*. Determine the necessary couple moment *M* which if applied to the plate would prevent this from happening.

**Prob. 21–55**

**\*21-56.** The cylinder has a mass of 30 kg and is mounted on an axle that is supported by bearings at *A* and *B*. If the axle is turning at $\boldsymbol{\omega} = \{-40\mathbf{j}\}$ rad/s, determine the vertical components of force acting at the bearings at this instant.

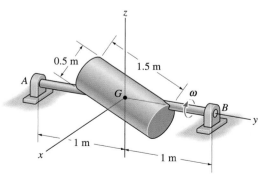

**Prob. 21–56**

**21-57.** The uniform hatch door, having a mass of 15 kg and a mass center at $G$, is supported in the horizontal plane by bearings at $A$ and $B$. If a vertical force $F = 300$ N is applied to the door as shown, determine the components of reaction at the bearings and the angular acceleration of the door. The bearing at $A$ will resist a component of force in the $y$ direction, whereas the bearing at $B$ will not. For the calculation, assume the door to be a thin plate and neglect the size of each bearing. The door is originally at rest.

**Prob. 21–57**

**21-58.** The man sits on a swivel chair which is rotating with a constant angular velocity of 3 rad/s. He holds the uniform 2.5-kg rod $AB$ horizontal. He suddenly gives it an angular acceleration of 2 rad/s², measured relative to him, as shown. Determine the required force and moment components at the grip, $A$, necessary to do this. Establish axes at the rod's center of mass $G$, with $+z$ upward, and $+y$ directed along the axis of the rod towards $A$.

**Prob. 21–58**

**21-59.** Four spheres are connected to shaft $AB$. If $m_C = 1$ kg and $m_E = 2$ kg, determine the mass of $D$ and $F$ and the angles of the rods, $\theta_D$ and $\theta_F$, so that the shaft is dynamically balanced, that is, so that the bearings at $A$ and $B$ exert only vertical reactions on the shaft as it rotates. Neglect the mass of the rods.

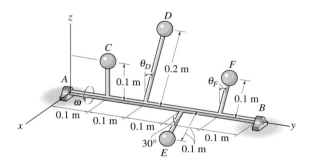

**Prob. 21–59**

**\*21-60.** The bent uniform rod $ACD$ has a mass of 5 kg/m and is supported at $A$ by a pin and at $B$ by a cord. If the vertical shaft rotates with a constant angular velocity $\omega = 20$ rad/s, determine the $x, y, z$ components of force and moment developed at $A$ and the tension in the cord.

**Prob. 21–60**

## *21.5 Gyroscopic Motion

(a)

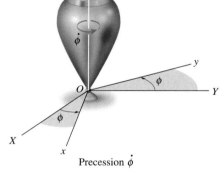

Precession $\dot{\phi}$

(b)

In this section the equations defining the motion of a body (top) which is symmetrical with respect to an axis and moving about a fixed point lying on the axis will be developed. These equations will then be applied to study the motion of a particularly interesting device, the gyroscope.

The body's motion will be analyzed using *Euler angles* $\phi$, $\theta$, $\psi$ (phi, theta, psi). To illustrate how these angles define the position of a body, reference is made to the top shown in Fig. 21–15a. The top is attached to point $O$ and has an orientation relative to the fixed $X$, $Y$, $Z$ axes at some instant of time as shown in Fig. 21–15d. To define this final position, a second set of $x$, $y$, $z$ axes will be needed. For purposes of discussion, assume that this reference is fixed in the top. Starting with the $X$, $Y$, $Z$ and $x$, $y$, $z$ axes in coincidence, Fig. 21–15a, the final position of the top is determined using the following three steps:

1. Rotate the top about the $Z$ (or $z$) axis through an angle $\phi$ $(0 \leq \phi < 2\pi)$, Fig. 21–15b.

2. Rotate the top about the $x$ axis through an angle $\theta$ $(0 \leq \theta \leq \pi)$, Fig. 21–15c.

3. Rotate the top about the $z$ axis through an angle $\psi$ $(0 \leq \psi < 2\pi)$ to obtain the final position, Fig. 20-15d.

The sequence of these three angles, $\phi$, $\theta$, then $\psi$, must be maintained, since finite rotations are *not vectors* (see Fig. 20–1). Although this is the case, the differential rotations $d\boldsymbol{\phi}$, $d\boldsymbol{\theta}$, and $d\boldsymbol{\psi}$ are vectors, and thus the angular velocity $\boldsymbol{\omega}$ of the top can be expressed in terms of the time derivatives of the Euler angles. The angular-velocity components $\dot{\phi}$, $\dot{\theta}$, and $\dot{\psi}$ are known as the *precession*, *nutation*, and *spin*, respectively. Their

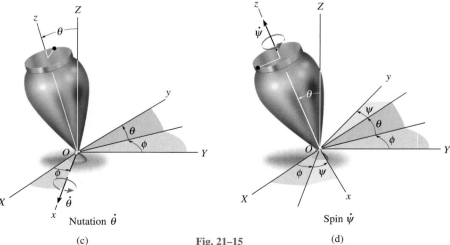

Nutation $\dot{\theta}$

(c)

Spin $\dot{\psi}$

(d)

**Fig. 21–15**

positive directions are shown in Fig. 21–16. It is seen that these vectors are not all perpendicular to one another; however, $\boldsymbol{\omega}$ of the top can still be expressed in terms of these three components.

In our case the body (top) is symmetric with respect to the $z$ or spin axis. If we consider the top to be oriented so that at the instant considered the spin angle $\psi = 0$ and *the x, y, z axes follow the motion of the body only in nutation and precession*, i.e., $\boldsymbol{\Omega} = \boldsymbol{\omega}_p + \boldsymbol{\omega}_n$, then the nutation and spin are always directed along the $x$ and $z$ axes, respectively, Fig. 21–16. Hence, the angular velocity of the body is specified only in terms of the Euler angle $\theta$, i.e.,

$$\boldsymbol{\omega} = \omega_x \mathbf{i} + \omega_y \mathbf{j} + \omega_z \mathbf{k}$$
$$= \dot{\theta}\mathbf{i} + (\dot{\phi}\sin\theta)\mathbf{j} + (\dot{\phi}\cos\theta + \dot{\psi})\mathbf{k} \qquad (21\text{–}27)$$

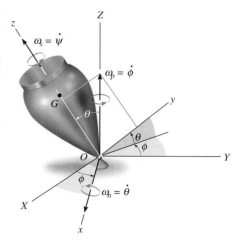

**Fig. 21–16**

Since motion of the axes is not affected by the spin component,

$$\boldsymbol{\Omega} = \Omega_x \mathbf{i} + \Omega_y \mathbf{j} + \Omega_z \mathbf{k}$$
$$= \dot{\theta}\mathbf{i} + (\dot{\phi}\sin\theta)\mathbf{j} + (\dot{\phi}\cos\theta)\mathbf{k} \qquad (21\text{–}28)$$

The $x$, $y$, $z$ axes in Fig. 21–16 represent *principal axes of inertia* of the body for *any* spin of the body about these axes. Hence, the moments of inertia are constant and will be represented as $I_{xx} = I_{yy} = I$ and $I_{zz} = I_z$. Since $\boldsymbol{\Omega} \neq \boldsymbol{\omega}$, Eqs. 21–26 are used to establish the rotational equations of motion. Substituting into these equations the respective angular-velocity components defined by Eqs. 21–27 and 21–28, their corresponding time derivatives, and the moment of inertia components yields

$$\Sigma M_x = I(\ddot{\theta} - \dot{\phi}^2 \sin\theta\cos\theta) + I_z\dot{\phi}\sin\theta(\dot{\phi}\cos\theta + \dot{\psi})$$
$$\Sigma M_y = I(\ddot{\phi}\sin\theta + 2\dot{\phi}\dot{\theta}\cos\theta) - I_z\dot{\theta}(\dot{\phi}\cos\theta + \dot{\psi}) \qquad (21\text{–}29)$$
$$\Sigma M_z = I_z(\ddot{\psi} + \ddot{\phi}\cos\theta - \dot{\phi}\dot{\theta}\sin\theta)$$

Each moment summation applies only at the fixed point $O$ or the center of mass $G$ of the body. Since the equations represent a coupled set of nonlinear second-order differential equations, in general a closed-form solution may not be obtained. Instead, the Euler angles $\phi$, $\theta$, and $\psi$ may be obtained graphically as functions of time using numerical analysis and computer techniques.

A special case, however, does exist for which simplification of Eqs. 21–29 is possible. Commonly referred to as *steady precession*, it occurs when the nutation angle $\theta$, precession $\dot{\phi}$, and spin $\dot{\psi}$ all remain *constant*. Equations 21–29 then reduce to the form

$$\boxed{\Sigma M_x = -I\dot{\phi}^2 \sin\theta\cos\theta + I_z\dot{\phi}\sin\theta(\dot{\phi}\cos\theta + \dot{\psi})} \qquad (21\text{–}30)$$

$$\Sigma M_y = 0$$
$$\Sigma M_z = 0$$

Equation 21–30 may be further simplified by noting that, from Eq. 21–27, $\omega_z = \dot{\phi} \cos \theta + \dot{\psi}$, so that

$$\Sigma M_x = -I \dot{\phi}^2 \sin \theta \cos \theta + I_z \dot{\phi} \sin \theta \omega_z$$

or

$$\boxed{\Sigma M_x = \dot{\phi} \sin \theta (I_z \omega_z - I \dot{\phi} \cos \theta)} \qquad (21\text{–}31)$$

It is interesting to note what effects the spin $\dot{\psi}$ has on the moment about the $x$ axis. In this regard consider the spinning rotor shown in Fig. 21–17. Here $\theta = 90°$, in which case Eq. 21–30 reduces to the form

$$\Sigma M_x = I_z \dot{\phi} \dot{\psi}$$

or

$$\boxed{\Sigma M_x = I_z \Omega_y \omega_z} \qquad (21\text{–}32)$$

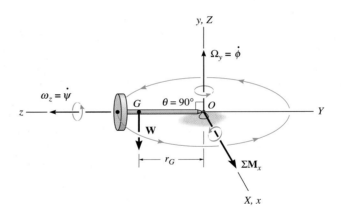

Fig. 21–17

From the figure it is seen that vectors $\Sigma \mathbf{M}_x$, $\mathbf{\Omega}_y$, and $\boldsymbol{\omega}_z$ all act along their respective *positive axes* and therefore are mutually perpendicular. Instinctively, one would expect the rotor to fall down under the influence of gravity! However, this is not the case at all, provided the product $I_z \Omega_y \omega_z$ is correctly chosen to counterbalance the moment $\Sigma M_x = W r_G$ of the rotor's weight about $O$. This unusual phenomenon of rigid-body motion is often referred to as the *gyroscopic effect*.

Perhaps a more intriguing demonstration of the gyroscopic effect comes from studying the action of a *gyroscope*, frequently referred to as a *gyro*. A gyro is a rotor which spins at a very high rate about its axis of symmetry. This rate of spin is considerably greater than its precessional rate of rotation about the vertical axis. Hence, for all practical purposes, the angular momentum of the gyro can be assumed directed among its axis of spin. Thus, for the gyro rotor shown in Fig. 21–18, $\omega_z \gg \Omega_y$, and the magnitude of the angular momentum about point $O$, as determined from Eqs. 21–11, reduces to the form $H_O = I_z \omega_z$. Since both the magnitude and direction of $\mathbf{H}_O$ are constant as observed from $x$, $y$, $z$, direct application of Eq. 21–22 yields

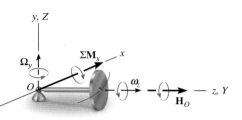

**Fig. 21–18**

$$\boxed{\Sigma \mathbf{M}_x = \boldsymbol{\Omega}_y \times \mathbf{H}_O} \tag{21–33}$$

Using the right-hand rule applied to the cross product, it is seen that $\boldsymbol{\Omega}_y$ always swings $\mathbf{H}_O$ (or $\boldsymbol{\omega}_z$) toward the sense of $\Sigma \mathbf{M}_x$. In effect, the *change in direction* of the gyro's angular momentum, $d\mathbf{H}_O$, is equivalent to the angular impulse caused by the gyro's weight about $O$, i.e., $d\mathbf{H}_O = \Sigma \mathbf{M}_x \, dt$, Eq. 21–20. Also, since $H_O = I_z \omega_z$ and $\Sigma M_x$, $\Omega_y$, and $H_O$ are mutually perpendicular, Eq. 21–33 reduces to Eq. 21–32.

When a gyro is mounted in gimbal rings, Fig. 21–19, it becomes *free* of external moments applied to its base. Thus, in theory, its angular momentum $\mathbf{H}$ will never precess but, instead, maintain its same fixed orientation along the axis of spin when the base is rotated. This type of gyroscope is called a *free gyro* and is useful as a gyrocompass when the spin axis of the gyro is directed north. In reality, the gimbal mechanism is never completely free of friction, so such a device is useful only for the local navigation of ships and aircraft. The gyroscopic effect is also useful as a means of stabilizing both the rolling motion of ships at sea and the trajectories of missiles and projectiles. Furthermore, this effect is of significant importance in the design of shafts and bearings for rotors which are subjected to forced precessions.

**Fig. 21–19**

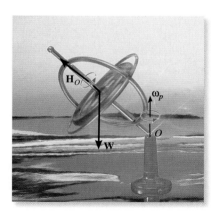

The spinning of the gyro within the frame of this toy gyroscope produces angular momentum $\mathbf{H}_O$ which is changing direction as the frame precesses $\boldsymbol{\omega}_p$ about the vertical axis. The gyroscope will not fall down since the moment of its weight $\mathbf{W}$ about the support is balanced by the change in the direction of $\mathbf{H}_O$.

# EXAMPLE 21.7

$\omega_s = 100$ rad/s

$G$   60°

$\omega_p = \dot{\phi}$

$O$

50 mm

(a)

Fig. 21–20

The top shown in Fig. 21–20*a* has a mass of 0.5 kg and is precessing about the vertical axis at a constant angle of $\theta = 60°$. If it spins with an angular velocity $\omega_s = 100$ rad/s, determine the precessional velocity $\omega_p$. Assume that the axial and transverse moments of inertia of the top are $0.45(10^{-3})$ kg·m² and $1.20(10^{-3})$ kg·m², respectively, measured with respect to the fixed point $O$.

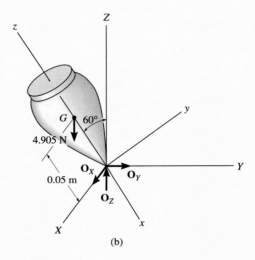

(b)

## Solution

Equation 21–30 will be used for the solution since the motion is *steady precession*. As shown on the free-body diagram, Fig. 21–20*b*, the coordinate axes are established in the usual manner, that is, with the positive $z$ axis in the direction of spin, the positive $Z$ axis in the direction of precession, and the positive $x$ axis in the direction of the moment $\Sigma M_x$ (refer to Fig. 21–16). Thus,

$$\Sigma M_x = -I\dot{\phi}^2 \sin\theta\cos\theta + I_z\dot{\phi}\sin\theta(\dot{\phi}\cos\theta + \dot{\psi})$$

$$4.905\,\text{N}(0.05\,\text{m})\sin 60° = -[1.20(10^{-3})\,\text{kg}\cdot\text{m}^2\,\dot{\phi}^2]\sin 60°\cos 60°$$
$$+ [0.45(10^{-3})\,\text{kg}\cdot\text{m}^2]\,\dot{\phi}\sin 60°(\dot{\phi}\cos 60° + 100\,\text{rad/s})$$

or

$$\dot{\phi}^2 - 120.0\dot{\phi} + 654.0 = 0 \tag{1}$$

Solving this quadratic equation for the precession gives

$$\dot{\phi} = 114\,\text{rad/s} \qquad \text{(high precession)} \qquad \qquad Ans.$$

and

$$\dot{\phi} = 5.72\,\text{rad/s} \qquad \text{(low precession)} \qquad \qquad Ans.$$

In reality, low precession of the top would generally be observed, since high precession would require a larger kinetic energy.

E X A M P L E  **21.8**

The 1-kg disk shown in Fig. 21–21a is spinning about its axis with a constant angular velocity $\omega_D = 70$ rad/s. The block at $B$ has a mass of 2 kg, and by adjusting its position $s$ one can change the precession of the disk about its supporting pivot at $O$. Determine the position $s$ which will enable the disk to have a constant precessional velocity $\omega_p = 0.5$ rad/s about the pivot. Neglect the weight of the shaft.

(a)

(b)

(c)

Fig. 21–21

**Solution**

The free-body diagram of the disk is shown in Fig. 21–21b, where **F** represents the force reaction of the shaft on the disk. The origin for both the $x$, $y$, $z$ and $X$, $Y$, $Z$ coordinate systems is located at point $O$, which represents a *fixed point* for the disk. (Although point $O$ does not lie on the disk, imagine a massless extension of the disk to this point.) In the conventional sense, the $Z$ axis is chosen along the axis of precession, and the $z$ axis is along the axis of spin, so that $\theta = 90°$. Since the precession is *steady*, Eq. 21–31 may be used for the solution. This equation reduces to

$$\Sigma M_x = \dot{\phi} I_z \omega_z$$

which is the same as Eq. 21–32. Substituting the required data gives

$$9.81 \text{ N}(0.2 \text{ m}) - F(0.2 \text{ m}) = 0.5 \text{ rad/s}[\tfrac{1}{2}(1 \text{ kg})(0.05 \text{ m})^2](-70 \text{ rad/s})$$
$$F = 10.0 \text{ N}$$

As shown on the free-body diagram of the shaft and block $B$, Fig. 21–21c, summing moments about the $x$ axis requires

$$(19.62 \text{ N})s = (10.0 \text{ N})(0.2 \text{ m})$$
$$= 0.102 \text{ m} = 102 \text{ mm} \qquad \qquad Ans.$$

## *21.6 Torque-Free Motion

When the only external force acting on a body is caused by gravitation, the general motion of the body is referred to as *torque-free motion*. This type of motion is characteristic of planets, artificial satellites, and projectiles—provided the effects of air friction are neglected.

In order to describe the characteristics of this motion, the distribution of the body's mass will be assumed *axisymmetric*. The satellite shown in Fig. 21–22 is an example of such a body, where the $z$ axis represents an axis of symmetry. The origin of the $x$, $y$, $z$ coordinates is located at the mass center $G$, such that $I_{zz} = I_z$ and $I_{xx} = I_{yy} = I$ for the body. Since gravitation is the only external force present, the summation of moments about the mass center is zero. From Eq. 21–21, this requires the angular momentum of the body to be constant, i.e.,

$$\mathbf{H}_G = \text{constant}$$

At the instant considered, it will be assumed that the inertial frame of reference is oriented so that the positive $Z$ axis is directed along $\mathbf{H}_G$ and the $y$ axis lies in the plane formed by the $z$ and $Z$ axes, Fig. 21–22. The Euler angle formed between $Z$ and $z$ is $\theta$, and therefore, with this choice of axes the angular momentum may be expressed as

$$\mathbf{H}_G = H_G \sin \theta \mathbf{j} + H_G \cos \theta \mathbf{k}$$

Furthermore, using Eqs. 21–11, we have

$$\mathbf{H}_G = I\omega_x \mathbf{i} + I\omega_y \mathbf{j} + I_z \omega_z \mathbf{k}$$

where $\omega_x$, $\omega_y$, $\omega_z$ represent the $x$, $y$, $z$ components of the body's angular velocity. Equating the respective $\mathbf{i}$, $\mathbf{j}$, and $\mathbf{k}$ components of the above two equations yields

$$\omega_x = 0 \qquad \omega_y = \frac{H_G \sin \theta}{I} \qquad \omega_z = \frac{H_G \cos \theta}{I_z} \qquad (21\text{–}34)$$

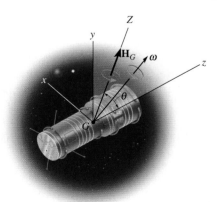

Fig. 21–22

or

$$\boldsymbol{\omega} = \frac{H_G \sin \theta}{I}\mathbf{j} + \frac{H_G \cos \theta}{I_z}\mathbf{k} \qquad (21\text{--}35)$$

In a similar manner, equating the respective $\mathbf{i}$, $\mathbf{j}$, $\mathbf{k}$ components of Eq. 21–27 to those of Eq. 21–34, we obtain

$$\dot{\theta} = 0$$

$$\dot{\phi} \sin \theta = \frac{H_G \sin \theta}{I}$$

$$\dot{\phi} \cos \theta + \dot{\psi} = \frac{H_G \cos \theta}{I_z}$$

Solving, we get

$$\theta = \text{const}$$

$$\dot{\phi} = \frac{H_G}{I}$$

$$\dot{\psi} = \frac{I - I_z}{I I_z} H_G \cos \theta \qquad (21\text{--}36)$$

Thus, for torque-free motion of an axisymmetrical body, the angle $\theta$ formed between the angular-momentum vector and the spin of the body remains constant. Furthermore, the angular momentum $\mathbf{H}_G$, precession $\dot{\phi}$, and spin $\dot{\psi}$ for the body remain constant at all times during the motion. Eliminating $H_G$ from the second and third of Eqs. 21–36 yields the following relationship between the spin and precession:

$$\dot{\psi} = \frac{I - I_z}{I_z} \dot{\phi} \cos \theta \qquad (21\text{--}37)$$

(a)

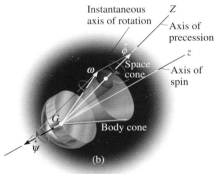

(b)

**Fig. 21–23**

As shown in Fig. 21–23a, the body precesses about the $Z$ axis, which is fixed in direction, while it spins about the $z$ axis. These two components of angular motion may be studied by using a simple cone model, introduced in Sec. 20.1. The *space cone* defining the precession is fixed from rotating, since the precession has a fixed direction, while the *body cone* rotates around the space cone's outer surface without slipping. On this basis, an attempt should be made to imagine the motion. The interior angle of each cone is chosen such that the resultant angular velocity of the body is directed along the line of contact of the two cones. This line of contact represents the instantaneous axis of rotation for the body cone, and hence the angular velocity of both the body cone and the body must be directed along this line. Since the spin is a function of the moments of inertia $I$ and $I_z$ of the body, Eq. 21–36, the cone model in Fig. 21–23a is satisfactory for describing the motion, provided $I > I_z$. Torque-free motion which meets these requirements is called *regular precession*. If $I < I_z$, the spin is negative and the precession positive. This motion is represented by the satellite motion shown in Fig. 21–23b ($I < I_z$). The cone model may again be used to represent the motion; however, to preserve the correct vector addition of spin and precession to obtain the angular velocity $\boldsymbol{\omega}$, the inside surface of the body cone must roll on the outside surface of the (fixed) space cone. This motion is referred to as *retrograde precession*.

Satellites are often given a spin before they are launched. If their angular momentum is not collinear with the axis of spin they will exhibit precession. In the photo on the left regular precession will occur since $I > I_z$, and in the photo on the right, retrograde precession will occur since $I < I_z$.

# EXAMPLE 21.9

The motion of a football is observed using a slow-motion projector. From the film, the spin of the football is seen to be directed 30° from the horizontal, as shown in Fig. 21–24a. Also, the football is precessing about the vertical axis at a rate $\dot{\phi} = 3$ rad/s. If the ratio of the axial to transverse moments of inertia of the football is $\frac{1}{3}$, measured with respect to the center of mass, determine the magnitude of the football's spin and its angular velocity. Neglect the effect of air resistance.

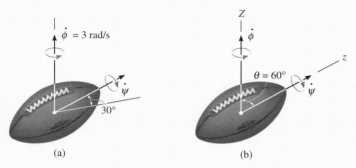

(a)                                    (b)

**Fig. 21–24**

## Solution

Since the weight of the football is the only force acting, the motion is torque-free. In the conventional sense, if the $z$ axis is established along the axis of spin and the $Z$ axis along the precession axis, as shown in Fig. 21–24b, then the angle $\theta = 60°$. Applying Eq. 21–37, the spin is

$$\dot{\psi} = \frac{I - I_z}{I_z}\dot{\phi}\cos\theta = \frac{I - \frac{1}{3}I}{\frac{1}{3}I}(3)\cos 60°$$

$$= 3 \text{ rad/s} \qquad \qquad Ans.$$

Using Eqs. 21–34, where $H_G = \dot{\phi}I$ (Eq. 21–36), we have

$$\omega_x = 0$$

$$\omega_y = \frac{H_G \sin\theta}{I} = \frac{3I \sin 60°}{I} = 2.60 \text{ rad/s}$$

$$\omega_z = \frac{H_G \cos\theta}{I_z} = \frac{3I \cos 60°}{\frac{1}{3}I} = 4.50 \text{ rad/s}$$

Thus,

$$\omega = \sqrt{(\omega_x)^2 + (\omega_y)^2 + (\omega_z)^2}$$

$$= \sqrt{(0)^2 + (2.60)^2 + (4.50)^2}$$

$$= 5.20 \text{ rad/s} \qquad \qquad Ans.$$

# PROBLEMS

**21-61.** Show that the angular velocity of a body, in terms of Euler angles $\phi$, $\theta$, and $\psi$, may be expressed as $\omega = (\dot{\phi} \sin \theta \sin \psi + \dot{\theta} \cos \psi)\mathbf{i} + (\dot{\phi} \sin \theta \cos \psi - \dot{\theta} \sin \psi)\mathbf{j} + (\dot{\phi} \cos \theta + \dot{\psi})\mathbf{k}$, where $\mathbf{i}$, $\mathbf{j}$, and $\mathbf{k}$ are directed along the $x$, $y$, $z$ axes as shown in Fig. 21–15d.

**21-62.** A thin rod is initially coincident with the $Z$ axis when it is given three rotations defined by the Euler angles $\phi = 30°$, $\theta = 45°$, and $\psi = 60°$. If these rotations are given in the order stated, determine the coordinate direction angles $\alpha$, $\beta$, $\gamma$ of the axis of the rod with respect to the $X$, $Y$, and $Z$ axes. Are these directions the same for any order of the rotations? Why?

**21-63.** The turbine on a ship has a mass of 400 kg and is mounted on bearings $A$ and $B$ as shown. Its center of mass is at $G$, its radius of gyration is $k_z = 0.3$ m, and $k_x = k_y = 0.5$ m. If it is spinning at 200 rad/s, determine the vertical reactions at the bearings when the ship undergoes each of the following motions: (a) rolling, $\omega_1 = 0.2$ rad/s, (b) turning, $\omega_2 = 0.8$ rad/s, (c) pitching, $\omega_3 = 1.4$ rad/s.

**\*21-64.** The 30-kg wheel rolls without slipping. If it has a radius of gyration $k_{AB} = 1.2$ m about its axle $AB$, and the vertical drive shaft is turning at 8 rad/s, determine the normal reaction the wheel exerts on the ground at $C$.

**21-65.** The 30-kg wheel rolls without slipping. If it has a radius of gyration $k_{AB} = 1.2$ m about its axle $AB$, determine its angular velocity $\omega$ so that the normal reaction at $C$ becomes 600 N.

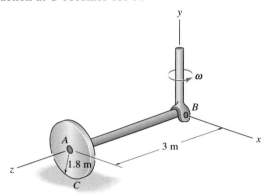

**Probs. 21–64/65**

**21-66.** The 20-kg disk is spinning about its center at $\omega_s = 20$ rad/s while the supporting axle is rotating at $\omega_y = 6$ rad/s. Determine the gyroscopic moment caused by the force reactions which the pin $A$ exerts on the disk due to the motion.

**Prob. 21–63**

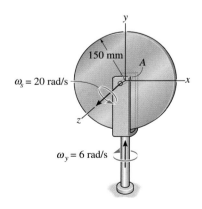

**Prob. 21–66**

**21-67.** The motor weighs 50 kN ($\approx$ 5000 kg) and has a radius of gyration of 0.2 m about the $z$ axis. The shaft of the motor is supported by bearings at $A$ and $B$, and is turning at a constant rate of $\boldsymbol{\omega}_s = \{100\mathbf{k}\}$ rad/s, while the frame has an angular velocity of $\boldsymbol{\omega}_y = \{2\mathbf{j}\}$ rad/s. Determine the moment which the bearing forces at $A$ and $B$ exert on the shaft due to this motion.

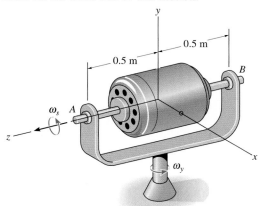

Prob. 21–67

**21-69.** A wheel of mass $m$ and radius $r$ rolls with constant spin $\boldsymbol{\omega}$ about a circular path having a radius $a$. If the angle of inclination is $\theta$, determine the rate of precession. Treat the wheel as a thin ring. No slipping occurs.

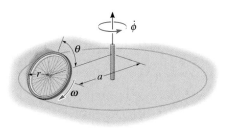

Prob. 21–69

***21-68.** The conical top has a mass of 0.8 kg, and the moments of inertia are $I_x = I_y = 3.5(10^{-3})$ kg·m² and $I_z = 0.8(10^{-3})$ kg·m². If it spins freely in the ball-and-socket joint at $A$ with an angular velocity $\omega_s = 750$ rad/s, compute the precession of the top about the axis of the shaft $AB$.

Prob. 21–68

**21-70.** The top consists of a thin disk that has a weight of 8 N and a radius of 0.3 m. The rod has a negligible mass and a length of 0.5 m. If the top is spinning with an angular velocity $\omega_s = 300$ rad/s, determine the steady-state precessional angular velocity $\omega_p$ of the rod when $\theta = 40°$.

**21-71.** Solve Prob. 21–70 when $\theta = 90°$.

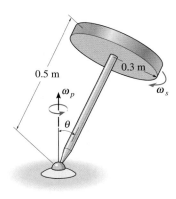

Probs. 21–70/71

**\*21-72.** The top has a mass of 30 kg and can be considered as a solid cone. If it is observed to precess about the vertical axis at a constant rate of 5 rad/s, determine its spin.

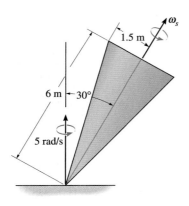

**Prob. 21–72**

**21-73.** The toy gyroscope consists of a rotor $R$ which is attached to the frame of negligible mass. If it is observed that the frame is precessing about the pivot point $O$ at $\omega_p = 2$ rad/s, determine the angular velocity $\omega_R$ of the rotor. The stem $OA$ moves in the horizontal plane. The rotor has a mass of 200 g and a radius of gyration $k_{OA} = 20$ mm about $OA$.

**Prob. 21–73**

**21-74.** The car is traveling at $v_C = 100$ km/h around the horizontal curve having a radius of 80 m. If each wheel has a mass of 16 kg, a radius of gyration $k_G = 300$ mm about its spinning axis, and a radius of 400 mm, determine the difference between the normal forces of the rear wheels, caused by the gyroscopic effect. The distance between the wheels is 1.30 m.

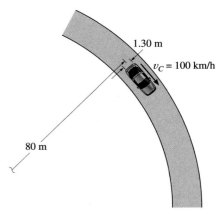

**Prob. 21–74**

**21-75.** The projectile shown is subjected to torque-free motion. The transverse and axial moments of inertia are $I$ and $I_z$, respectively. If $\theta$ represents the angle between the precessional axis $Z$ and the axis of symmetry $z$, and $\beta$ is the angle between the angular velocity $\omega$ and the $z$ axis, show that $\beta$ and $\theta$ are related by the equation $\tan \theta = (I/I_z) \tan \beta$.

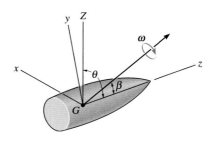

**Prob. 21–75**

**\*21-76.** While the rocket is in free flight, it has a spin of 3 rad/s and precesses about an axis measured 10° from the axis of spin. If the ratio of the axial to transverse moments of inertia of the rocket is 1/15, computed about axes which pass through the mass center $G$, determine the angle which the resultant angular velocity makes with the spin axis. Construct the body and space cones used to describe the motion. Is the precession regular or retrograde?

Prob. 21–76

**21-77.** The 0.2-kg football is thrown with a spin $\omega_z = 35$ rad/s. If the angle $\theta$ is measured as 60°, determine the precession about the $Z$ axis.

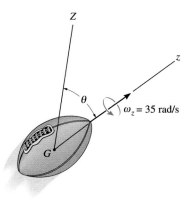

Prob. 21–77

**21-78.** The space capsule has a mass of 3.2 Mg, and about axes passing through the mass center $G$ the axial and transverse radii of gyration are $k_z = 0.90$ m and $k_t = 1.85$ m, respectively. If it is spinning at $\omega_s = 0.8$ rev/s, determine its angular momentum. Precession occurs about the $Z$ axis.

Prob. 21–78

**21-79.** The 4-kg disk is thrown with a spin $\omega_z = 6$ rad/s. If the angle $\theta$ is measured as 160°, determine the precision about the $Z$ axis.

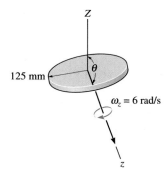

Prob. 21–79

**\*21-80.** The rocket has a mass of 4 Mg and radii of gyration $k_z = 0.85$ m and $k_y = 2.3$ m. It is initially spinning about the $z$ axis at $\omega_z = 0.05$ rad/s when a meteoroid $M$ strikes it at $A$ and creates an impulse $\mathbf{I} = \{300\mathbf{i}\}$ N·s. Determine the axis of precession after the impact.

Prob. 21–80

## CHAPTER REVIEW

- *Moments and Products of Inertia.* A body has six components of inertia for any specified $x, y, z$ axes. Three of these are moments of inertia about each of the axes, $I_x, I_y, I_z$, and three are products of inertia, each defined from two orthogonal planes, $I_{xy}, I_{yz}, I_{xz}$. If either one or both of the planes are planes of symmetry, then the product of inertia with respect to these planes will be zero.

  The moments and products of inertia can be determined by direct integration, or by using tabulated values. If these quantities are to be determined with respect to axes or planes that do not pass through the mass center, then parallel-axis and parallel-plane theorems must be used.

  Provided the six components of inertia are known, then the moment of inertia about any axis can be determined using the transformation equation

$$I_{Oa} = I_{xx}u_x^2 + I_{yy}u_y^2 + I_{zz}u_z^2 - 2I_{xy}u_xu_y - 2I_{yz}u_yu_z - 2I_{zx}u_zu_x$$

- *Principal Moments of Inertia.* At any point on or off the body, the $x, y, z$ axes can be oriented so that the products of inertia will be zero. The resulting moments of inertia are called the principal moments of inertia, one of which will be a maximum and the other a minimum moment of inertia for the body.

- *Principle of Impulse and Momentum.* The angular momentum for a body can be determined about any point $A$ using the equation

$$\mathbf{H}_A = \boldsymbol{\rho}_{G/A} \times m\mathbf{v}_G + \mathbf{H}_G$$

If it is to be determined using principal axes of inertia, with origin located at the body's mass center or at a fixed point, then the components of momentum become

$$H_x = I_{xx}\omega_x - I_{xy}\omega_y - I_{xz}\omega_z$$
$$H_y = -I_{yx}\omega_x + I_{yy}\omega_y - I_{yz}\omega_z$$
$$H_z = -I_{zx}\omega_x - I_{zy}\omega_y + I_{zz}\omega_z$$

Once the linear and angular momentum for the body have been formulated, then the principle of impulse and momentum can be used to solve problems that involve force, velocity, and time. These equations are

$$m(\mathbf{v}_G)_1 + \Sigma \int_{t_1}^{t_2} \mathbf{F}\, dt = m(\mathbf{v}_G)_2$$

$$(\mathbf{H}_O)_1 + \Sigma \int_{t_1}^{t_2} \mathbf{M}_O\, dt = (\mathbf{H}_O)_2$$

- *Principle of Work and Energy.* The kinetic energy for a body is usually determined relative to a fixed point or the body's mass center. Provided the axes are principal axes of inertia, then for a fixed point,

$$T = \tfrac{1}{2}I_x\omega_x^2 + \tfrac{1}{2}I_y\omega_y^2 + \tfrac{1}{2}I_z\omega_z^2$$

And relative to the mass center,

$$T = \tfrac{1}{2}mv_G^2 + \tfrac{1}{2}I_x\omega_x^2 + \tfrac{1}{2}I_y\omega_y^2 + \tfrac{1}{2}I_z\omega_z^2$$

These formulations can be used with the principle of work and energy to solve problems that involve force, velocity, and displacement. This equation is

$$T_1 + \Sigma U_{1-2} = T_2$$

- **Equations of Motion.** There are three scalar equations of translational motion for a rigid body that moves in three dimensions. They are

$$\Sigma F_x = m(a_G)_x$$
$$\Sigma F_y = m(a_G)_y$$
$$\Sigma F_z = m(a_G)_z$$

The three scalar equations of rotational motion depend upon the location of the $x$, $y$, $z$ reference. Most often, these axes are oriented so that the axes are principal axes of inertia. If the axes are fixed in and move with the rotation $\boldsymbol{\omega}$ of the body, then the equations are referred to as the Euler equations of motion. They are

$$\Sigma M_x = I_x \dot{\omega}_x - (I_y - I_z)\omega_y\omega_z$$
$$\Sigma M_y = I_y \dot{\omega}_y - (I_z - I_x)\omega_z\omega_x$$
$$\Sigma M_z = I_z \dot{\omega}_z - (I_x - I_y)\omega_x\omega_y$$

If the axes have a rotation $\Omega \neq \omega$, then the equations become

$$\Sigma M_x = I_x \dot{\omega}_x - I_y \Omega_z \omega_y + I_z \Omega_y \omega_z$$
$$\Sigma M_y = I_y \dot{\omega}_y - I_z \Omega_x \omega_z + I_x \Omega_z \omega_x$$
$$\Sigma M_z = I_z \dot{\omega}_z - I_x \Omega_y \omega_x + I_y \Omega_x \omega_y$$

A free-body diagram should always accompany the application of these equations.

- **Gyroscopic Motion.** The angular motion of a gyroscope is best described using the changes in motion of the three Euler angles. These angular velocity components are the precession $\dot{\phi}$, the nutation $\dot{\theta}$, and the spin $\dot{\psi}$. If $\ddot{\psi} = 0$ and $\dot{\phi}$ and $\theta$ are constant, then the motion is referred to as steady precession. In this case, the equations of rotational motion become

$$\Sigma M_x = -I\dot{\phi}^2\sin\theta\cos\theta + I_z\dot{\phi}\sin\theta(\dot{\phi}\cos\theta + \dot{\psi})$$
$$\Sigma M_y = 0$$
$$\Sigma M_z = 0$$

It is the spin of a gyro rotor that is responsible for holding the rotor from falling downward, and instead causing it to precess about a vertical axis. This phenomenon is called the gyroscopic effect.

- **Torque-Free Motion.** A body that is only subjected to a gravitational force will have no moments on it about its mass center, and so the motion is described as torque-free motion. The angular momentum for the body will remain constant. This causes the body to have both a spin and a precession. The behavior depends upon the size of the moment of inertia of a symmetric body about the spin axis $I_z$ versus that about a perpendicular axis $I$. If $I > I_z$, then regular precession occurs. If $I < I_z$ then the motion is referred to as retrograde precession.

The analysis of vibrations plays an important role in the study of
the behavior of structures subjected to earthquakes.

# CHAPTER
# 22

# Vibrations

- To discuss undamped one-degree-of-freedom vibration of a rigid body using the equation of motion and energy methods.
- To study the analysis of undamped forced vibration and viscous damped forced vibration.
- To introduce the concept of electrical circuit analogs to study vibrational motion.

## *22.1   Undamped Free Vibration

A *vibration* is the periodic motion of a body or system of connected bodies displaced from a position of equilibrium. In general, there are two types of vibration, free and forced. *Free vibration* occurs when the motion is maintained by gravitational or elastic restoring forces, such as the swinging motion of a pendulum or the vibration of an elastic rod. *Forced vibration* is caused by an external periodic or intermittent force applied to the system. Both of these types of vibration may be either damped or undamped. *Undamped* vibrations can continue indefinitely because frictional effects are neglected in the analysis. Since in reality both internal and external frictional forces are present, the motion of all vibrating bodies is actually *damped*.

Equilibrium position

$x$

$k$

(a)

$W = mg$

$F = kx$

$N_B$

(b)

The simplest type of vibrating motion is undamped free vibration, represented by the model shown in Fig. 22–1a. The block has a mass $m$ and is attached to a spring having a stiffness $k$. Vibrating motion occurs when the block is released from a displaced position $x$ so that the spring pulls on the block. The block will attain a velocity such that it will proceed to move out of equilibrium when $x = 0$, and provided the supporting surface is smooth, oscillation will continue indefinitely.

The time-dependent path of motion of the block may be determined by applying the equation of motion to the block when it is in the displaced position $x$. The free-body diagram is shown in Fig. 22–1b. The elastic restoring force $F = kx$ is always directed toward the equilibrium position, whereas the acceleration $\mathbf{a}$ is assumed to act in the direction of *positive displacement*. Noting that $a = d^2x/dt^2 = \ddot{x}$, we have

$$\xrightarrow{+} \Sigma F_x = ma_x; \qquad\qquad -kx = m\ddot{x}$$

Note that the acceleration is proportional to the block's displacement. Motion described in this manner is called *simple harmonic motion*. Rearranging the terms into a "standard form" gives

$$\ddot{x} + \omega_n^2 x = 0 \qquad\qquad (22\text{–}1)$$

The constant $\omega_n$ is called the *circular frequency* or *natural frequency*, expressed in rad/s, and in this case

$$\boxed{\omega_n = \sqrt{\frac{k}{m}}} \qquad\qquad (22\text{–}2)$$

$k$

Equilibrium position

$y$

(a)

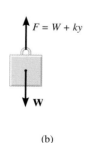

$F = W + ky$

$\mathbf{W}$

(b)

Equation 22–1 may also be obtained by considering the block to be suspended and measuring the displacement $y$ from the block's *equilibrium position*, Fig. 22–2a. When the block is in equilibrium, the spring exerts an upward force of $F = W = mg$ on the block. Hence, when the block is displaced a distance $y$ downward from this position, the magnitude of the spring force is $F = W + ky$, Fig. 22–2b. Applying the equation of motion gives

$$+\downarrow \Sigma F_y = ma_y; \qquad\qquad -W - ky + W = m\ddot{y}$$

or

$$\ddot{y} + \omega_n^2 y = 0$$

**Fig. 22–2**

which is the same form as Eq. 22–1, where $\omega_n$ is defined by Eq. 22–2.

Equation 22–1 is a homogeneous, second-order, linear, differential equation with constant coefficients. It can be shown, using the methods of differential equations, that the general solution is

$$x = A \sin \omega_n t + B \cos \omega_n t \qquad (22\text{–}3)$$

where $A$ and $B$ represent two constants of integration. The block's velocity and acceleration are determined by taking successive time derivatives, which yields

$$v = \dot{x} = A\omega_n \cos \omega_n t - B\omega_n \sin \omega_n t \qquad (22\text{–}4)$$

$$a = \ddot{x} = -A\omega_n^2 \sin \omega_n t - B\omega_n^2 \cos \omega_n t \qquad (22\text{–}5)$$

When Eqs. 22–3 and 22–5 are substituted into Eq. 22–1, the differential equation is indeed satisfied, showing that Eq. 22–3 is the solution to Eq. 22–1.

The integration constants $A$ and $B$ in Eq. 22–3 are generally determined from the initial conditions of the problem. For example, suppose that the block in Fig. 22–1a has been displaced a distance $x_1$ to the right from its equilibrium position and given an initial (positive) velocity $\mathbf{v}_1$ directed to the right. Substituting $x = x_1$ at $t = 0$ into Eq. 22–3 yields $B = x_1$. Since $v = v_1$ at $t = 0$, using Eq. 22–4 we obtain $A = v_1/\omega_n$. If these values are substituted into Eq. 22–3, the equation describing the motion becomes

$$x = \frac{v_1}{\omega_n} \sin \omega_n t + x_1 \cos \omega_n t \qquad (22\text{–}6)$$

Equation 22–3 may also be expressed in terms of simple sinusoidal motion. Let

$$A = C \cos \phi \qquad (22\text{–}7)$$

and

$$B = C \sin \phi \qquad (22\text{–}8)$$

where $C$ and $\phi$ are new constants to be determined in place of $A$ and $B$. Substituting into Eq. 22–3 yields

$$x = C \cos \phi \sin \omega_n t + C \sin \phi \cos \omega_n t$$

Since $\sin(\theta + \phi) = \sin \theta \cos \phi + \cos \theta \sin \phi$, then

$$x = C \sin(\omega_n t + \phi) \qquad (22\text{–}9)$$

If this equation is plotted on an $x$-versus-$\omega_n t$ axis, the graph shown in Fig. 22–3 is obtained. The maximum displacement of the block from its

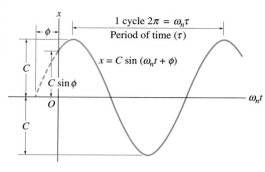

**Fig. 22–3**

equilibrium position is defined as the *amplitude* of vibration. From either the figure or Eq. 22–9 the amplitude is $C$. The angle $\phi$ is called the *phase angle* since it represents the amount by which the curve is displaced from the origin when $t = 0$. The constants $C$ and $\phi$ are related to $A$ and $B$ by Eqs. 22–7 and 22–8. Squaring and adding these two equations, the amplitude becomes

$$C = \sqrt{A^2 + B^2} \tag{22–10}$$

If Eq. 22–8 is divided by Eq. 22–7, the phase angle is

$$\phi = \tan^{-1}\frac{B}{A} \tag{22–11}$$

Note that the sine curve, Eq. 22–9, completes one *cycle* in time $t = \tau$ (tau) when $\omega_n\tau = 2\pi$, or

$$\tau = \frac{2\pi}{\omega_n} \tag{22–12}$$

This length of time is called a *period*, Fig. 22–3. Using Eq. 22–2, the period may also be represented as

$$\tau = 2\pi\sqrt{\frac{m}{k}} \tag{22–13}$$

The *frequency* $f$ is defined as the number of cycles completed per unit of time, which is the reciprocal of the period:

$$f = \frac{1}{\tau} = \frac{\omega_n}{2\pi} \tag{22–14}$$

or

$$f = \frac{1}{2\pi}\sqrt{\frac{k}{m}} \tag{22–15}$$

The frequency is expressed in cycles/s. This ratio of units is called a *hertz* (Hz), where 1 Hz = 1 cycle/s = $2\pi$ rad/s.

When a body or system of connected bodies is given an initial displacement from its equilibrium position and released, it will vibrate with the *natural frequency*, $\omega_n$. Provided the body has a single degree of freedom, that is, it requires only one coordinate to specify completely the position of the system at any time, then the vibrating motion of the body will have the same characteristics as the simple harmonic motion of the block and spring just presented. Consequently, the body's motion is described by a differential equation of the same "standard form" as Eq. 22–1, i.e.,

$$\ddot{x} + \omega_n^2 x = 0 \tag{22–16}$$

Hence, if the natural frequency $\omega_n$ of the body is known, the period of vibration $\tau$, natural frequency $f$, and other vibrating characteristics of the body can be established using Eqs. 22–3 through 22–15.

## IMPORTANT POINTS

- Free vibration occurs when the motion is maintained by gravitational or elastic restoring forces.
- The amplitude is the maximum displacement of the body.
- The period is the time required to complete one cycle.
- The frequency is the number of cycles completed per unit of time, where 1 Hz = 1 cycle/s.
- Only one position-coordinate system is needed to describe the location of a one-degree-of-freedom system.

## PROCEDURE FOR ANALYSIS

As in the case of the block and spring, the natural frequency $\omega_n$ of a rigid body or system of connected rigid bodies having a single degree of freedom can be determined using the following procedure:

*Free-Body Diagram.*

- Draw the free-body diagram of the body when the body is displaced by a *small amount* from its equilibrium position.
- Locate the body with respect to its equilibrium position by using an appropriate *inertial coordinate q.* The acceleration of the body's mass center $\mathbf{a}_G$ or the body's angular acceleration $\boldsymbol{\alpha}$ should have a sense which is in the *positive direction* of the position coordinate.
- If the rotational equation of motion $\Sigma M_P = \Sigma(\mathcal{M}_k)_P$ is to be used, then it may be beneficial to also draw the kinetic diagram since it graphically accounts for the components $m(\mathbf{a}_G)_x, m(\mathbf{a}_G)_y,$ and $I_G\boldsymbol{\alpha},$ and thereby makes it convenient for visualizing the terms needed in the moment sum $\Sigma(\mathcal{M}_k)_P.$

*Equation of Motion.*

- Apply the equation of motion to relate the elastic or gravitational *restoring* forces and couple moments acting on the body to the body's accelerated motion.

*Kinematics.*

- Using kinematics, express the body's accelerated motion in terms of the second time derivative of the position coordinate, $\ddot{q}.$
- Substitute the result into the equation of motion and determine $\omega_n$ by rearranging the terms so that the resulting equation is of the "standard form," $\ddot{q} + \omega_n^2 q = 0.$

E X A M P L E **22.1**

(a)

(b)

Determine the period of vibration for the simple pendulum shown in Fig. 22–4a. The bob has a mass $m$ and is attached to a cord of length $l$. Neglect the size of the bob.

### Solution

*Free-Body Diagram.* Motion of the system will be related to the position coordinate $(q =) \theta$, Fig. 22–4b. When the bob is displaced by an angle $\theta$, the *restoring force* acting on the bob is created by the weight component $mg \sin \theta$. Furthermore, $\mathbf{a}_t$ acts in the direction of *increasing $s$* (or $\theta$).

*Equation of Motion.* Applying the equation of motion in the *tangential direction*, since it involves the restoring force, yields

$$+\nearrow \Sigma F_t = ma_t; \qquad -mg \sin \theta = ma_t \qquad (1)$$

*Kinematics.* $a_t = d^2s/dt^2 = \ddot{s}$. Furthermore, $s$ may be related to $\theta$ by the equation $s = l\theta$, so that $a_t = l\ddot{\theta}$. Hence, Eq. 1 reduces to

$$\ddot{\theta} + \frac{g}{l} \sin \theta = 0 \qquad (2)$$

The solution of this equation involves the use of an elliptic integral. For *small displacements*, however, $\sin \theta \approx \theta$, in which case

$$\ddot{\theta} + \frac{g}{l} \theta = 0 \qquad (3)$$

Comparing this equation with Eq. 22–16 ($\ddot{x} + \omega_n^2 x = 0$), it is seen that $\omega_n = \sqrt{g/l}$. From Eq. 22–12, the period of time required for the bob to make one complete swing is therefore

$$\tau = \frac{2\pi}{\omega_n} = 2\pi \sqrt{\frac{l}{g}} \qquad \qquad Ans.$$

This interesting result, originally discovered by Galileo Galilei through experiment, indicates that the period depends only on the length of the cord and not on the mass of the pendulum bob or the angle $\theta$.

The solution of Eq. 3 is given by Eq. 22–3, where $\omega_n = \sqrt{g/l}$ and $\theta$ is substituted for $x$. Like the block and spring, the constants $A$ and $B$ in this problem may be determined if, for example, one knows the displacement and velocity of the bob at a given instant.

# E X A M P L E 22.2

The 10-kg rectangular plate shown in Fig. 22–5a is suspended at its center from a rod having a torsional stiffness $k = 1.5\ \text{N} \cdot \text{m/rad}$. Determine the natural period of vibration of the plate when it is given a small angular displacement $\theta$ in the plane of the plate.

(a)

(b)

**Fig. 22–5**

## Solution

*Free-Body Diagram.* Fig. 22–5b. Since the plate is displaced in its own plane, the torsional *restoring* moment created by the rod is $M = k\theta$. This moment acts in the direction opposite to the angular displacement $\theta$. The angular acceleration $\ddot{\theta}$ acts in the direction of *positive* $\theta$.

*Equation of Motion.*

$$\Sigma M_O = I_O\alpha; \qquad -k\theta = I_O\ddot{\theta}$$

or

$$\ddot{\theta} + \frac{k}{I_O}\theta = 0$$

Since this equation is in the "standard form," the natural frequency is $\omega_n = \sqrt{k/I_O}$.

From the table on the inside back cover, the moment of inertia of the plate about an axis coincident with the rod is $I_O = \frac{1}{12}m(a^2 + b^2)$. Hence,

$$I_O = \frac{1}{12}(10\ \text{kg})[(0.2\ \text{m})^2 + (0.3\ \text{m})^2] = 0.108\ \text{kg} \cdot \text{m}^2$$

The natural period of vibration is therefore,

$$\tau = \frac{2\pi}{\omega_n} = 2\pi\sqrt{\frac{I_O}{k}} = 2\pi\sqrt{\frac{0.108}{1.5}} = 1.69\ \text{s} \qquad \textit{Ans.}$$

E X A M P L E  22.3

(a)

||

(b)

(c)

The bent rod shown in Fig. 22–6a has a negligible mass and supports a 5-kg collar at its end. Determine the natural period of vibration for the system.

## Solution

*Free-Body and Kinetic Diagrams.* Fig. 22–6b. Here the rod is displaced by a small amount $\theta$ from the equilibrium position. Since the spring is subjected to an initial compression of $x_{st}$ for equilibrium, then when the displacement $x > x_{st}$ the spring exerts a force of $F_s = kx - kx_{st}$ on the rod. To obtain the "standard form," Eq. 22–16, $5a_y$ acts *upward*, which is in accordance with positive $\theta$ displacement.

*Equation of Motion.* Moments will be summed about point $B$ to eliminate the unknown reaction at this point. Since $\theta$ is small,

$$\zeta + \Sigma M_B = \Sigma(\mathcal{M}_k)_B;$$
$$kx(0.1 \text{ m}) - kx_{st}(0.1 \text{ m}) + 49.05 \text{ N}(0.2 \text{ m}) = -(5 \text{ kg})a_y(0.2 \text{ m})$$

The second term on the left side, $-kx_{st}(0.1 \text{ m})$, represents the moment created by the spring force which is necessary to hold the collar in *equilibrium*, i.e., at $x = 0$. Since this moment is equal and opposite to the moment 49.05(0.2) created by the weight of the collar, these two terms cancel in the above equation, so that

$$kx(0.1) = -5a_y(0.2) \quad (1)$$

*Kinematics.* The positions of the spring and the collar may be related to the angle $\theta$, Fig. 22–6c. Since $\theta$ is small, $x = (0.1 \text{ m})\theta$ and $y = (0.2 \text{ m})\theta$. Therefore, $a_y = \ddot{y} = 0.2\ddot{\theta}$. Substituting into Eq. 1 yields

$$400(0.1\theta)0.1 = -5(0.2\ddot{\theta})0.2$$

Rewriting this equation in the "standard form" gives

$$\ddot{\theta} + 20\theta = 0$$

Compared with $\ddot{x} + \omega_n^2 x = 0$ (Eq. 22–16), we have

$$\omega_n^2 = 20 \qquad \omega_n = 4.47 \text{ rad/s}$$

The natural period of vibration is therefore

$$\tau = \frac{2\pi}{\omega_n} = \frac{2\pi}{4.47} = 1.40 \text{ s} \qquad \textit{Ans.}$$

EXAMPLE **22.4**

A 5-kg block is suspended from a cord that passes over a 7.5-kg disk, as shown in Fig. 22–7a. The spring has a stiffness $k = 3500$ N/m. Determine the natural period of vibration for the system.

(a)                                       (b)

**Solution**

*Free-Body and Kinetic Diagrams.* Fig. 22–7b. The *system* consists of the disk, which undergoes a rotation defined by the angle $\theta$, and the block, which translates by an amount $s$. The vector $I_O\ddot{\theta}$ acts in the direction of *positive* $\theta$, and consequently $m_B\mathbf{a}_s$ acts downward in the direction of *positive* $s$.

*Equation of Motion.* Summing moments about point $O$ to eliminate the reactions $\mathbf{O}_x$ and $\mathbf{O}_y$, realizing that $I_O = \frac{1}{2}mr^2$, yields

$$\zeta+\Sigma M_O = \Sigma(\mathcal{M}_k)_O;$$
$$[5(9.81)\text{ N}](0.25\text{ m}) - F_s(0.25\text{ m})$$
$$= \frac{1}{2}(7.5\text{ kg})(0.25\text{ m})^2\ddot{\theta} + (5\text{ kg})a_s(0.25\text{ m}) \quad (1)$$

*Kinematics.* As shown on the kinematic diagram in Fig. 22–7c, a small positive displacement $\theta$ of the disk causes the block to lower by an amount $s = 0.25\theta$; hence, $a_s = \ddot{s} = 0.25\ddot{\theta}$. When $\theta = 0°$, the spring force required for *equilibrium* of the disk is 5(9.81) N, acting to the right. For position $\theta$, the spring force is $F_s = (3500\text{ N/m})(0.25\theta\text{ m}) + 5(9.81)$ N. Substituting these results into Eq. 1 and simplifying yields

$$\ddot{\theta} + 400\theta = 0$$

Hence,

$$\omega_n^2 = 400 \quad \omega_n = 20\text{ rad/s}$$

Therefore, the natural period of vibration is

$$T = \frac{2\pi}{\omega_n} = \frac{2\pi}{20} = 0.314\text{ s} \qquad\qquad Ans.$$

(c)

# PROBLEMS

**22-1.** When a 2-kg weight is suspended from a spring, the spring is stretched a distance of 40 mm. Determine the natural frequency and the period of vibration for a 0.5-kg weight attached to the same spring.

**22-2.** A spring has a stiffness of 600 N/m. If a 4-kg block is attached to the spring, pushed 50 mm above its equilibrium position, and released from rest, determine the equation which describes the block's motion. Assume that positive displacement is measured downward.

**22-3.** When a 3-kg block is suspended from a spring, the spring is stretched a distance of 60 mm. Determine the natural frequency and the period of vibration for a 0.2-kg block attached to the same spring.

**\*22-4.** An 8-kg block is suspended from a spring having a stiffness $k = 80$ N/m. If the block is given an upward velocity of 0.4 m/s when it is 90 mm above its equilibrium position, determine the equation which describes the motion and the maximum upward displacement of the block measured from the equilibrium position. Assume that positive displacement is measured downward.

**22-5.** A 2-kg weight is suspended from a spring having a stiffness $k = 800$ N/m. If the weight is pushed 25 mm upward from its equilibrium position and then released from rest, determine the equation which describes the motion. What is the amplitude and the natural frequency of the vibration?

**22-6.** A 6-kg weight is suspended from a spring having a stiffness $k = 1200$ N/m. If the weight is given an upward velocity of 6 m/s when it is 50 mm above its equilibrium position, determine the equation which describes the motion and the maximum upward displacement of the weight, measured from the equilibrium position. Assume positive displacement is downward.

**22-7.** A 6-kg block is suspended from a spring having a stiffness of $k = 200$ N/m. If the block is given an upward velocity of 0.4 m/s when it is 75 mm above its equilibrium position, determine the equation which describes the motion and the maximum upward displacement of the block measured from the equilibrium position. Assume that positive displacement is downward.

**\*22-8.** A 3-kg block is suspended from a spring having a stiffness of $k = 200$ N/m. If the block is pushed 50 mm upward from its equilibrium position and then released from rest, determine the equation that describes the motion. What are the amplitude and the natural frequency of the vibration? Assume that positive displacement is downward.

**22-9.** Determine the frequency of vibration for the block. The springs are originally compressed $\Delta$.

**22-10.** A pendulum has a 0.4-m-long cord and is given a tangential velocity of 0.2 m/s toward the vertical from a position $\theta = 0.3$ rad. Determine the equation which describes the angular motion.

**22-11.** A cable is used to suspend the 800-kg safe. If the safe is being lowered at 6 m/s when the motor controlling the cable suddenly jams (stops), determine the maximum tension in the cable and the frequency of vibration of the safe. Neglect the mass of the cable and assume it is elastic such that it stretches 20 mm when subjected to a tension of 4 kN.

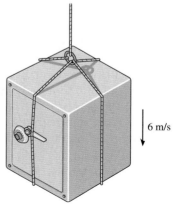

6 m/s

**Prob. 22–11**

***22-12.** The uniform beam is supported at its ends by two springs $A$ and $B$, each having the same stiffness $k$. When nothing is supported on the beam, it has a period of vertical vibration of 0.83 s. If a 50-kg mass is placed at its center, the period of vertical vibration is 1.52 s. Compute the stiffness of each spring and the mass of the beam.

**Prob. 22–12**

**22-13.** The body of arbitrary shape has a mass $m$, mass center at $G$, and a radius of gyration about $G$ of $k_G$. If it is displaced a slight amount $\theta$ from its equilibrium position and released, determine the natural period of vibration.

**22-14.** The thin hoop of mass $m$ is supported by a knife-edge. Determine the natural period of vibration for small amplitudes of swing.

**22-15.** The semicircular disk weighs 200 N ($\approx$ 20 kg). Determine the natural period of vibration if it is displaced a small amount and released.

***22-16.** The square plate has a mass $m$ and is suspended at its corner by the pin $O$. Determine the natural period of vibration if it is displaced a small amount and released.

**22-17.** The disk has a mass of 10 kg and rolls without slipping on the horizontal surface as it oscillates about its equilibrium position. If the disk is displaced, by rolling it counterclockwise 0.4 rad, determine the equation which describes its oscillatory motion when it is released.

$k = 1000$ N/m

1 m

**Prob. 22–17**

**22-18.** The pointer on a metronome supports a 0.2-kg slider $A$, which is positioned at a fixed distance from the pivot $O$ of the pointer. When the pointer is displaced, a torsional spring at $O$ exerts a restoring torque on the pointer having a magnitude $M = (1.8\theta)$ N · m, where $\theta$ represents the angle of displacement from the vertical, measured in radians. Determine the natural period of vibration when the pointer is displaced a small amount $\theta$ and released. Neglect the mass of the pointer.

$A$

75 mm

$O$

$k = 1.8$ N · m/rad

**Prob. 22–18**

**22-19.** The connecting rod is supported by a knife edge at $A$ and the period of vibration is measured as $\tau_A = 3.38$ s. It is then removed and rotated 180° so that it is supported by the knife edge at $B$. In this case the perod of vibration is measured as $\tau_B = 3.96$ s. Determine the location $d$ of the center of gravity $G$, and compute the radius of gyration $k_G$.

$A$

$d$

$G$  250 mm

$B$

**Prob. 22–19**

**\*22-20.** The disk, having a weight of 15 kN ($\approx 1.5$ tonnes), is pinned at its center $O$ and supports the block $A$ that has a weight of 3 kN ($\approx 300$ kg). If the belt which passes over the disk is not allowed to slip at its contacting surface, determine the natural period of vibration of the system.

0.75 m

$O$

$k = 80$ kN/m

$A$

**22-21.** While standing in an elevator, the man holds a pendulum which consists of an 0.45-m cord and a 0.25-kg bob. If the elevator is descending with an acceleration $a = 1.2$ m/s², determine the natural period of vibration for small amplitudes of swing.

**22-22.** The 50-kg spool is attached to two springs. If the spool is displaced a small amount and released, determine the natural period of vibration. The radius of gyration of the spool is $k_G = 1.5$ m. The spool rolls without slipping.

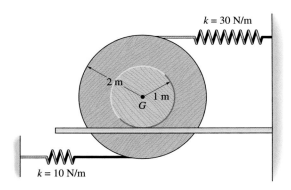

**22-23.** The platform $AB$ when empty has a mass of 400 kg, center of mass at $G_1$, and natural period of oscillation $\tau_1 = 2.38$ s. If a car, having a mass of 1.2 Mg and center of mass at $G_2$, is placed on the platform, the natural period of oscillation becomes $\tau_2 = 3.16$ s. Determine the moment of inertia of the car about an axis passing through $G_2$.

***22-24.** The uniform rod has a mass $m$ and is supported by the pin $O$. If the rod is given a small displacement and released, determine the natural period of vibration. The springs are unstretched when the rod is in the position shown.

**22-25.** The 50-kg wheel has a radius of gyration about its mass center $G$ of $k_G = 0.7$ m. Determine the frequency of vibration if it is displaced slightly from the equilibrium position and released. Assume no slipping.

## *22.2 Energy Methods

The simple harmonic motion of a body, discussed in the previous section, is due only to gravitational and elastic restoring forces acting on the body. Since these types of forces are *conservative*, it is also possible to use the conservation of energy equation to obtain the body's natural frequency or period of vibration. To show how to do this, consider again the block and spring in Fig. 22–8. When the block is displaced an arbitrary amount $x$ from the equilibrium position, the kinetic energy is $T = \frac{1}{2}mv^2 = \frac{1}{2}m\dot{x}^2$ and the potential energy is $V = \frac{1}{2}kx^2$. By the conservation of energy equation, Eq. 14–21, it is necessary that

$$T + V = \text{constant}$$
$$\tfrac{1}{2}m\dot{x}^2 + \tfrac{1}{2}kx^2 = \text{constant} \tag{22–17}$$

The differential equation describing the *accelerated motion* of the block can be obtained by *differentiating* this equation with respect to time; i.e.,

$$m\dot{x}\ddot{x} + kx\dot{x} = 0$$
$$\dot{x}(m\ddot{x} + kx) = 0$$

Since the velocity $\dot{x}$ is not *always* zero in a vibrating system,

$$\ddot{x} + \omega_n{}^2 x = 0 \qquad \omega_n = \sqrt{k/m}$$

which is the same as Eq. 22–1.

If the energy equation is written for a *system of connected bodies*, the natural frequency or the equation of motion can also be determined by time differentiation. Here it is *not necessary* to dismember the system to account for reactive and connective forces which do no work.

Equilibrium
position

$x$

$k$

The suspension of a railroad car consists of a set of springs which are mounted between the frame of the car and the wheel truck. This will give the car a natural frequency of vibration which can be determined.

## PROCEDURE FOR ANALYSIS

The circular or natural frequency $\omega_n$ of a body or system of connected bodies can be determined by applying the conservation of energy equation using the following procedure.

### Energy Equation.

- Draw the body when it is displaced by a *small amount* from its equilibrium position and define the location of the body from its equilibrium position by an appropriate position coordinate $q$.
- Formulate the equation of energy for the body, $T + V = $ constant, in terms of the position coordinate.
- In general, the kinetic energy must account for both the body's translational and rotational motion, $T = \frac{1}{2}mv_G^2 + \frac{1}{2}I_G\omega_n^2$, Eq. 18–2.
- The potential energy is the sum of the gravitational and elastic potential energies of the body, $V = V_g + V_e$, Eq. 18–16. In particular, $V_g$ should be measured from a datum for which $q = 0$ (equilibrium position).

### Time Derivative.

- Take the time derivative of the energy equation using the chain rule of calculus and factor out the common terms. The resultant differential equation represents the equation of motion for the system. The value of $\omega_n$ is obtained after rearranging the terms in the "standard form," $\ddot{q} + \omega_n^2 q = 0$.

**E X A M P L E 22.5**

(a)

(b)

The thin hoop shown in Fig. 22–9a is supported by a peg at O. Determine the natural period of oscillation for small amplitudes of swing. The hoop has a mass $m$.

**Solution**

*Energy Equation.* A diagram of the hoop when it is displaced a small amount $(q =) \theta$ from the equilibrium position is shown in Fig. 22–9b. Using the table on the inside back cover and the parallel-axis theorem to determine $I_O$, we can express the kinetic energy as

$$T = \tfrac{1}{2} I_O \omega_n^2 = \tfrac{1}{2}[mr^2 + mr^2]\dot{\theta}^2 = mr^2\dot{\theta}^2$$

If a horizontal datum is placed through the center of gravity of the hoop when $\theta = 0$, then the center of gravity moves upward $r(1 - \cos\theta)$ in the displaced position. For *small angles*, $\cos\theta$ may be replaced by the first two terms of its power series expansion, $\cos\theta = 1 - \theta^2/2 + \cdots$. Therefore, the potential energy is

$$V = mgr\left[1 - \left(1 - \frac{\theta^2}{2}\right)\right] = mgr\frac{\theta^2}{2}$$

The total energy in the system is

$$T + V = mr^2\dot{\theta}^2 + mgr\frac{\theta^2}{2}$$

*Time Derivative.*

$$mr^2 2\dot{\theta}\ddot{\theta} + mgr\theta\dot{\theta} = 0$$

$$mr\dot{\theta}(2r\ddot{\theta} + g\theta) = 0$$

Since $\dot{\theta}$ is not always equal to zero, from the terms in parentheses,

$$\ddot{\theta} + \frac{g}{2r}\theta = 0$$

Hence,

$$\omega_n = \sqrt{\frac{g}{2r}}$$

so that

$$\tau = \frac{2\pi}{\omega_n} = 2\pi\sqrt{\frac{2r}{g}} \qquad\qquad Ans.$$

# EXAMPLE 22.6

A 10-kg block is suspended from a cord wrapped around a 5-kg disk, as shown in Fig. 22–10a. If the spring has a stiffness $k = 200$ N/m, determine the natural period of vibration for the system.

$k = 200$ N/m

0.15 m

O

(a)

## Solution

*Energy Equation.*  A diagram of the block and disk when they are displaced by respective amounts $s$ and $\theta$ from the equilibrium position is shown in Fig. 22–10b. Since $s = (0.15 \text{ m})\theta$, the kinetic energy of the system is

$$T = \tfrac{1}{2}m_b v_b^2 + \tfrac{1}{2}I_O\omega_d^2$$
$$= \tfrac{1}{2}(10 \text{ kg})[(0.15 \text{ m})\dot{\theta}]^2 + \tfrac{1}{2}[\tfrac{1}{2}(5 \text{ kg})(0.15 \text{ m})^2](\dot{\theta})^2$$
$$= 0.141(\dot{\theta})^2$$

Establishing the datum at the equilibrium position of the block and realizing that the spring stretches $s_{st}$ for equilibrium, we can write the potential energy as

$$V = \tfrac{1}{2}k(s_{st} + s)^2 - Ws$$
$$= \tfrac{1}{2}(200 \text{ N/m})[s_{st} + (0.15 \text{ m})\theta]^2 - 98.1 \text{ N}[(0.15 \text{ m})\theta]$$

The total energy for the system is, therefore,

$$T + V = 0.141(\dot{\theta})^2 + 100(s_{st} + 0.15\theta)^2 - 14.72\theta$$

$\theta$

$s_{st} + s$

0.15 m

$0.15\,\theta$

$\theta$

O

Datum

$s = 0.15\ \theta$

98.1 N

(b)

**Fig. 22–10**

*Time Derivative.*

$$0.281(\dot{\theta})\ddot{\theta} + 200(s_{st} + 0.15\theta)0.15\dot{\theta} - 14.72\dot{\theta} = 0$$

Since $s_{st} = 98.1/200 = 0.4905$ m, the above equation reduces to the "standard form"

$$\ddot{\theta} + 16\theta = 0$$

so that

$$\omega_n = \sqrt{16} = 4 \text{ rad/s}$$

Thus,

$$\tau = \frac{2\pi}{\omega_n} = \frac{2\pi}{4} = 1.57 \text{ s} \qquad \qquad Ans.$$

# PROBLEMS

**22-26.** Solve Prob. 22–13 using energy methods.

**22-27.** Solve Prob. 22–15 using energy methods.

**\*22-28.** Solve Prob. 22–16 using energy methods.

**22-29.** Solve Prob. 22–20 using energy methods.

**22-30.** The uniform rod of mass $m$ is supported by a pin at $A$ and a spring at $B$. If the end $B$ is given a small downward displacement and released, determine the natural period of vibration.

**22-31.** Determine the differential equation of motion of the 3-kg block when it is displaced slightly and released. The surface is smooth and the springs are originally unstretched.

Prob. 22–31

**\*22-32.** The machine has a mass $m$ and is uniformly supported by *four* springs, each having a stiffness $k$. Determine the natural period of vertical vibration.

**22-33.** The 7-kg disk is pin-connected at its midpoint. Determine the natural period of vibration of the disk if the springs have sufficient tension in them to prevent the cord from slipping on the disk as it oscillates. *Hint:* Assume that the initial stretch in each spring is $\delta_O$. This term will cancel out after taking the time derivative of the energy equation.

Prob. 22–33

**22-34.** Determine the natural period of vibration of the pendulum. Consider the two rods to be slender, each having a weight of 8 N/m ($\approx 0.8$ kg/m).

Prob. 22–34

**22-35.** Determine the natural period of vibration of the disk having a mass $m$ and radius $r$. Assume the disk does not slip on the surface of contact as it oscillates.

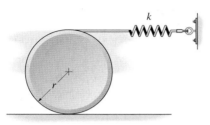

***22-36.** Determine the natural period of vibration of the 3-kg sphere. Neglect the mass of the rod and the size of the sphere.

**22-37.** The slender rod has a mass $m$ and is pinned at its end $O$. When it is vertical, the springs are unstretched. Determine the natural period of vibration.

Prob. 22–37

**22-38.** Determine the natural frequency of vibration of the 20-kg disk. Assume the disk does not slip on the inclined surface.

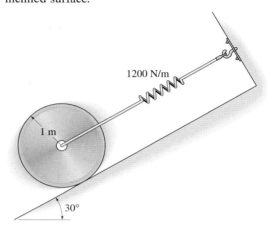

Prob. 22–38

**22-39.** If the disk has a mass of 8 kg, determine the natural frequency of vibration. The springs are originally unstretched.

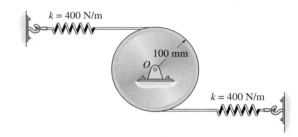

***22-40.** Determine the differential equation of motion of the 3-kg spool. Assume that it does not slip at the surface of contact as it oscillates. The radius of gyration of the spool about its center of mass is $k_G = 125$ mm.

# *22.3 Undamped Forced Vibration

Equilibrium position

(a)

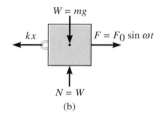

$W = mg$

$kx$

$F = F_0 \sin \omega t$

$N = W$

(b)

**Fig. 22–11**

Undamped forced vibration is considered to be one of the most important types of vibrating motion in engineering work. The principles which describe the nature of this motion may be used to analyze the forces which cause vibration in many types of machines and structures.

**Periodic Force.** The block and spring shown in Fig. 22–11a provide a convenient model which represents the vibrational characteristics of a system subjected to a periodic force $F = F_0 \sin \omega_0 t$. This force has an amplitude of $F_0$ and a *forcing frequency* $\omega_0$. The free-body diagram for the block when it is displaced a distance $x$ is shown in Fig. 22–11b. Applying the equation of motion yields

$$\stackrel{+}{\rightarrow} \Sigma F_x = ma_x; \qquad F_0 \sin \omega t - kx = m\ddot{x}$$

or

$$\ddot{x} + \frac{k}{m}x = \frac{F_0}{m}\sin \omega_0 t \qquad (22\text{–}18)$$

This equation is referred to as a nonhomogeneous second-order differential equation. The general solution consists of a complementary solution, $x_c$, *plus* a particular solution, $x_p$.

The *complementary solution* is determined by setting the term on the right side of Eq. 22–18 equal to zero and solving the resulting homogeneous equation, which is equivalent to Eq. 22–1. The solution is defined by Eq. 22–3, i.e.,

$$x_c = A \sin \omega_n t + B \cos \omega_n t \qquad (22\text{–}19)$$

where $\omega_n$ is the natural frequency, $\omega_n = \sqrt{k/m}$, Eq. 22–2.

Since the motion is periodic, the *particular solution* of Eq. 22–18 may be determined by assuming a solution of the form

$$x_p = C \sin \omega_0 t \qquad (22\text{–}20)$$

where $C$ is a constant. Taking the second time derivative and substituting into Eq. 22–18 yields

$$-C\omega^2 \sin \omega_0 t + \frac{k}{m}(C \sin \omega_0 t) = \frac{F_0}{m}\sin \omega_0 t$$

Factoring out $\sin \omega t$ and solving for $C$ gives

$$C = \frac{F_0/m}{(k/m) - \omega^2} = \frac{F_0/k}{1 - (\omega/\omega_n)^2} \qquad (22\text{–}21)$$

Substituting into Eq. 22–20, we obtain the particular solution

$$\boxed{x_p = \frac{F_0/k}{1 - (\omega_0/\omega_n)^2}\sin \omega_0 t} \qquad (22\text{–}22)$$

Shaker tables provide forced vibration and are used to separate out granular materials.

(a)

(b)

(c)

(d)

The *general solution* is therefore

$$x = x_c + x_p = A \sin \omega_n + B \cos \omega_n + \frac{F_0/k}{1 - (\omega/\omega_n)^2} \sin \omega t \quad (22\text{--}23)$$

Here $x$ describes two types of vibrating motion of the block. The *complementary solution* $x_c$ defines the *free vibration*, which depends on the circular frequency $\omega_n = \sqrt{k/m}$ and the constants $A$ and $B$, Fig. 22–12a. Specific values for $A$ and $B$ are obtained by evaluating Eq. 22–23 at a given instant when the displacement and velocity are known. The *particular solution* $x_p$ describes the *forced vibration* of the block caused by the applied force $F = F_0 \sin \omega t$, Fig. 22–12b. The resultant vibration $x$ is shown in Fig. 22–12c. Since all vibrating systems are subject to *friction*, the free vibration, $x_c$, will in time dampen out. For this reason the free vibration is referred to as *transient*, and the forced vibration is called *steady-state*, since it is the only vibration that remains, Fig. 22–12d.

From Eq. 22–21 it is seen that the *amplitude* of forced vibration depends on the *frequency ratio* $\omega/\omega_n$. If the *magnification factor* MF is defined as the ratio of the amplitude of steady-state vibration, $(x_p)_{\max}$, to the static deflection $F_0/k$, which would be produced by the amplitude of the periodic force $F_0$, then, from Eq. 22–22,

The soil compactor operates by forced vibration developed by an internal motor. It is important that the forcing frequency not be close to the natural frequency of vibration, which is determined when the motor is turned off; otherwise resonance will occur and the machine will become uncontrollable.

MF

**Fig. 22–13**

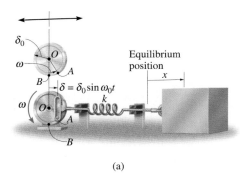

Equilibrium position

$\delta = \delta_0 \sin \omega_0 t$

$k$

(a)

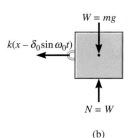

$W = mg$

$k(x - \delta_0 \sin \omega_0 t)$

$N = W$

(b)

**Fig. 22–14**

$$\mathrm{MF} = \frac{(x_p)_{\max}}{F_0/k} = \frac{1}{1 - (\omega/\omega_n)^2} \qquad (22\text{–}24)$$

This equation is graphed in Fig. 22–13. Note that for $\omega_0 \approx 0$, the MF $\approx 1$. In this case, because of the very low frequency $\omega \ll \omega_n$, the magnitude of the force **F** changes slowly and so the vibration of the block will be in phase with the applied force **F**. If the force or displacement is applied with a frequency close to the natural frequency of the system, i.e., $\omega/\omega \approx 1$, the amplitude of vibration of the block becomes extremely large. This occurs because the force **F** is applied to the block so that it always follows the motion of the block. This condition is called *resonance*, and in practice, resonating vibrations can cause tremendous stress and rapid failure of parts.* When the cyclic force $F_0 \sin \omega t$ is applied at high frequencies $(\omega > \omega_n)$, the value of the MF becomes negative, indicating that the motion of the block is out of phase with the force. Under these conditions, as the block is displaced to the right, the force acts to the left, and vice versa. For extremely high frequencies $(\omega \gg \omega_n)$ the block remains almost stationary, and hence the MF is approximately zero.

**Periodic Support Displacement.** Forced vibrations can also arise from the periodic excitation of the support of a system. The model shown in Fig. 22–14a represents the periodic vibration of a block which is caused by harmonic movement $\delta = \delta_0 \sin \omega_0 t$ of the support. The free-body diagram for the block in this case is shown in Fig. 22–14b. The coordinate $x$ is measured from the point of zero displacement of the support, i.e., when the radial line $OA$ coincides with $OB$, Fig. 22–14a. Therefore, general displacement of the spring is $(x - \delta_0 \sin \omega t)$. Applying the equation of motion yields

$$\xrightarrow{+} F_x = ma_x; \qquad -k(x - \delta_0 \sin \omega t) = m\ddot{x}$$

or

$$\ddot{x} + \frac{k}{m}x = \frac{k\delta_0}{m}\sin \omega t \qquad (22\text{–}25)$$

By comparison, this equation is identical to the form of Eq. 22–18, *provided* $F_0$ is *replaced* by $k\delta_0$. If this substitution is made into the solutions defined by Eqs. 22–21 to 22–23, the results are appropriate for describing the motion of the block when subjected to the support displacement $\delta = \delta_0 \sin \omega t$.

*A swing has a natural period of vibration, as determined in Example 22.1. If someone pushes on the swing only when it reaches its highest point, neglecting drag or wind resistance, resonance will occur since the natural and forcing frequencies will be equal.

# E X A M P L E  22.7

The instrument shown in Fig. 22–15 is rigidly attached to a platform $P$, which in turn is supported by *four* springs, each having a stiffness $k = 800$ N/m. Initially the platform is at rest when the floor is subjected to a displacement $\delta = 10\sin(8t)$ mm, where $t$ is in seconds. If the instrument is constrained to move vertically and the total mass of the instrument and platform is 20 kg, determine the vertical displacement $y$ of the platform as a function of time, measured from the equilibrium position. What floor vibration is required to cause resonance?

### Solution
Since the induced vibration is caused by the displacement of the supports, the motion is described by Eq. 22–23, with $F_0$ replaced by $k\delta_0$, i.e.,

$$y = A\sin\omega_n t + B\cos\omega_n t + \frac{\delta_0}{1 - (\omega/\omega_n)^2}\sin\omega t \qquad (1)$$

Here $\delta = \delta_0\sin\omega t = 10\sin(8t)$ mm, so that

$$\delta_0 = 10 \text{ mm} \qquad \omega_0 = 8 \text{ rad/s}$$

$$\omega_n = \sqrt{\frac{k}{m}} = \sqrt{\frac{4(800 \text{ N/m})}{20 \text{ kg}}} = 12.6 \text{ rad/s}$$

From Eq. 22–22, with $k\delta_0$ replacing $F_0$, the amplitude of vibration caused by the floor displacement is

$$(y_{\omega_n})_{\max} = \frac{\delta_0}{1 - (\omega_0/\omega_n)^2} = \frac{10}{1 - [(8 \text{ rad/s})/(12.6 \text{ rad/s})]^2} = 16.7 \text{ mm} \quad (2)$$

Hence, Eq. 1 and its time derivative become

$$y = A\sin(12.6t) + B\cos(12.6t) + 16.7\sin(8t)$$
$$\dot{y} = A(12.6)\cos(12.6t) - B(12.6)\sin(12.6t) + 133.3\cos(8t)$$

The constants $A$ and $B$ are evaluated from these equations. Since $y = 0$ and $\dot{y} = 0$ at $t = 0$, then

$$0 = 0 + B + 0 \qquad\qquad B = 0$$
$$0 = A(12.6) - 0 + 133.3 \quad A = -10.5$$

The vibrating motion is therefore described by the equation

$$y = -10.5\sin(12.6t) + 16.7\sin(8t) \qquad\qquad \textit{Ans.}$$

Resonance will occur when the amplitude of vibration caused by the floor displacement approaches infinity. From Eq. 2, this requires

$$\omega = \omega_n = 12.6 \text{ rad/s} \qquad\qquad \textit{Ans.}$$

## *22.4   Viscous Damped Free Vibration

The vibration analysis considered thus far has not included the effects of friction or damping in the system, and as a result, the solutions obtained are only in close agreement with the actual motion. Since all vibrations die out in time, the presence of damping forces should be included in the analysis.

In many cases damping is attributed to the resistance created by the substance, such as water, oil, or air, in which the system vibrates. Provided the body moves slowly through this substance, the resistance to motion is directly proportional to the body's speed. The type of force developed under these conditions is called a *viscous damping force*. The magnitude of this force is expressed by an equation of the form

$$F = c\dot{x} \tag{22–26}$$

where the constant $c$ is called the *coefficient of viscous damping* and has units of N · s/m or lb · s/ft.

The vibrating motion of a body or system having viscous damping may be characterized by the block and spring shown in Fig. 22–16a. The effect of damping is provided by the *dashpot* connected to the block on the right side. Damping occurs when the piston $P$ moves to the right or left within the enclosed cylinder. The cylinder contains a fluid, and the motion of the piston is retarded since the fluid must flow around or through a small hole in the piston. The dashpot is assumed to have a coefficient of viscous damping $c$.

Equilibrium position

(a)

If the block is displaced a distance $x$ from its equilibrium position, the resulting free-body diagram is shown in Fig. 22–16b. Both the spring force $kx$ and the damping force $c\dot{x}$ oppose the forward motion of the block, so that applying the equation of motion yields

$$\xrightarrow{+} \Sigma F_x = ma_x; \qquad -kx - c\dot{x} = m\ddot{x}$$

or

$$m\ddot{x} + c\dot{x} + kx = 0 \tag{22–27}$$

This linear, second-order, homogeneous, differential equation has solutions of the form

$$x = e^{\lambda t}$$

where $e$ is the base of the natural logarithm and $\lambda$ (lambda) is a constant. The value of $\lambda$ may be obtained by substituting this solution into Eq. 22–27, which yields

$$m\lambda^2 e^{\lambda t} + c\lambda e^{\lambda t} + ke^{\lambda t} = 0$$

or

$$e^{\lambda t}(m\lambda^2 + c\lambda + k) = 0$$

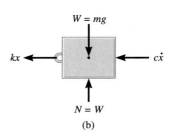

(b)

**Fig. 22–16**

Since $e^{\lambda t}$ is never zero, a solution is possible provided

$$m\lambda^2 + c\lambda + k = 0$$

Hence, by the quadratic formula, the two values of $\lambda$ are

$$\lambda_1 = -\frac{c}{2m} + \sqrt{\left(\frac{c}{2m}\right)^2 - \frac{k}{m}}$$

$$\lambda_2 = -\frac{c}{2m} - \sqrt{\left(\frac{c}{2m}\right)^2 - \frac{k}{m}}$$

(22–28)

The general solution of Eq. 22–27 is therefore a linear combination of exponentials which involves both of these roots. There are three possible combinations of $\lambda_1$ and $\lambda_2$ which must be considered. Before discussing these combinations, however, we will first define the *critical damping coefficient* $c_c$ as the value of $c$ which makes the radical in Eqs. 22–28 equal to zero; i.e.,

$$\left(\frac{c_c}{2m}\right)^2 - \frac{k}{m} = 0$$

or

$$c_c = 2m\sqrt{\frac{k}{m}} = 2m\omega_n$$

(22–29)

Here the value of $\omega_n$ is the natural frequency $\omega_n = \sqrt{k/m}$, Eq. 22–2.

**Overdamped System.**   When $c > c_c$, the roots $\lambda_1$ and $\lambda_2$ are both real. The general solution of Eq. 22–27 may then be written as

$$x = Ae^{\lambda_1 t} + Be^{\lambda_2 t}$$

(22–30)

Motion corresponding to this solution is *nonvibrating*. The effect of damping is so strong that when the block is displaced and released, it simply creeps back to its original position without oscillating. The system is said to be *overdamped*.

**Critically Damped System.**   If $c = c_c$, then $\lambda_1 = \lambda_2 = -c_c/2m = -\omega_n$. This situation is known as *critical damping*, since it represents a condition where $c$ has the smallest value necessary to cause the system to be nonvibrating. Using the methods of differential equations, it may be shown that the solution to Eq. 22–27 for critical damping is

$$x = (A + Bt)e^{-\omega_n t}$$

(22–31)

**Underdamped System.** Most often $c < c_c$, in which case the system is referred to as *underdamped*. In this case the roots $\lambda_1$ and $\lambda_2$ are complex numbers, and it may be shown that the general solution of Eq. 22–27 can be written as

$$x = D[e^{-(c/2m)t} \sin(\omega_d t + \phi)] \qquad (22\text{–}32)$$

where $D$ and $\phi$ are constants generally determined from the initial conditions of the problem. The constant $\omega_d$ is called the *damped natural frequency* of the system. It has a value of

$$\omega_d = \sqrt{\frac{k}{m} - \left(\frac{c}{2m}\right)^2} = \omega_n \sqrt{1 - \left(\frac{c}{c_c}\right)^2} \qquad (22\text{–}33)$$

where the ratio $c/c_c$ is called the *damping factor*.

The graph of Eq. 22–32 is shown in Fig. 22–17. The initial limit of motion, $D$, diminishes with each cycle of vibration, since motion is confined within the bounds of the exponential curve. Using the damped natural frequency $\omega_d$, the period of damped vibration may be written as

$$\tau_d = \frac{2\pi}{\omega_d} \qquad (22\text{–}34)$$

Since $\omega_d < \omega_n$, Eq. 22–33, the period of damped vibration, $\tau_d$, will be greater than that of free vibration, $\tau = 2\pi/\omega_n$.

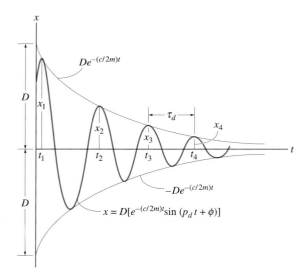

**Fig. 22–17**

# *22.5  Viscous Damped Forced Vibration

The most general case of single-degree-of-freedom vibrating motion occurs when the system includes the effects of forced motion and induced damping. The analysis of this particular type of vibration is of practical value when applied to systems having significant damping characteristics.

If a dashpot is attached to the block and spring shown in Fig. 22–11a, the differential equation which describes the motion becomes

$$m\ddot{x} + c\dot{x} + kx = F_0 \sin \omega t \qquad (22\text{–}35)$$

A similar equation may be written for a block and spring having a periodic support displacement, Fig. 22–14a, which includes the effects of damping. In that case, however, $F_0$ is replaced by $k\delta_0$. Since Eq. 22–35 is nonhomogeneous, the general solution is the sum of a complementary solution, $x_c$, and a particular solution, $x_p$. The complementary solution is determined by setting the right side of Eq. 22–35 equal to zero and solving the homogeneous equation, which is equivalent to Eq. 22–27. The solution is therefore given by Eq. 22–30, 22–31, or 22–32, depending on the values of $\lambda_1$ and $\lambda_2$. Because all systems contain friction, however, this solution will dampen out with time. Only the particular solution, which describes the *steady-state vibration* of the system, will remain. Since the applied forcing function is harmonic, the steady-state motion will also be harmonic. Consequently, the particular solution will be of the form

$$x_p = A' \sin \omega t + B' \cos \omega t \qquad (22\text{–}36)$$

The constants $A'$ and $B'$ are determined by taking the necessary time derivatives and substituting them into Eq. 22–35, which after simplification yields

$$(-A'm\omega^2 - cB'\omega + kA') \sin \omega t +$$

$$(-B'm\omega^2 + cA'\omega + kB') \cos \omega t = F_0 \sin \omega t$$

Since this equation holds for all time, the constant coefficients of $\sin \omega t$ and $\cos \omega t$ may be equated; i.e.,

$$-A'm\omega^2 - cB'\omega + kA' = F_0$$

$$-B'm\omega^2 + cA'\omega + kB' = 0$$

Solving for $A'$ and $B'$, realizing that $\omega_n{}^2 = k/m$, yields

$$A' = \frac{(F_0/m)(\omega_n{}^2 - \omega^2)}{(\omega_n{}^2 - \omega^2)^2 + (c\omega/m)^2}$$

$$B' = \frac{-F_0(c\omega/m^2)}{(\omega_n{}^2 - \omega^2)^2 + (c\omega/m)^2} \qquad (22\text{-}37)$$

It is also possible to express Eq. 22–36 in a form similar to Eq. 22–9,

$$x_p = C' \sin(\omega t - \phi') \qquad (22\text{-}38)$$

in which case the constants $C'$ and $\phi'$ are

$$C' = \frac{F_0/k}{\sqrt{[1 - (\omega/\omega_n)^2]^2 + [2(c/c_c)(\omega/\omega_n)]^2}}$$

$$(22\text{-}39)$$

$$\phi' = \tan^{-1}\left[\frac{2(c/c_c)(\omega/\omega_n)}{1 - (\omega/\omega_n)^2}\right]$$

The angle $\phi'$ represents the phase difference between the applied force and the resulting steady-state vibration of the damped system.

The *magnification factor* MF has been defined in Sec. 22.3 as the ratio of the amplitude of deflection caused by the forced vibration to the deflection caused by a static force $\mathbf{F}_0$. From Eq. 22–38, the forced vibration has an amplitude of $C'$; thus,

$$\text{MF} = \frac{C'}{F_0/k} = \frac{1}{\sqrt{[1 - (\omega/\omega_n)^2]^2 + [2(c/c_c)(\omega/\omega_n)]^2}} \qquad (22\text{-}40)$$

The MF is plotted in Fig. 22–18 versus the frequency ratio $\omega/\omega_n$ for various values of the damping factor $c/c_c$. It can be seen from this graph that the magnification of the amplitude increases as the damping factor decreases. Resonance obviously occurs only when the damping factor is zero and the frequency ratio equals 1.

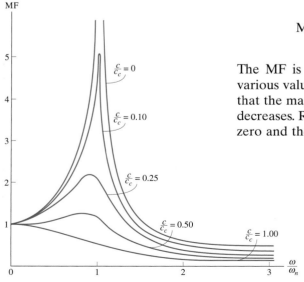

Fig. 22–18

**E X A M P L E   22.8**

The 30-kg electric motor shown in Fig. 22–19 is supported by *four* springs, each spring having a stiffness of 200 N/m. If the rotor $R$ is unbalanced such that its effect is equivalent to a 4-kg mass located 60 mm from the axis of rotation, determine the amplitude of vibration when the rotor is turning at $\omega = 10$ rad/s. The damping factor is $c/c_c = 0.15$.

**Solution**

The periodic force which causes the motor to vibrate is the centrifugal force due to the unbalanced rotor. This force has a constant magnitude of

$$F_0 = ma_n = mr\omega^2 = 4 \text{ kg}(0.06 \text{ m})(10 \text{ rad/s})^2 = 24 \text{ N}$$

Since $F = F_0 \sin \omega t$, where $\omega = 10$ rad/s, then

$$F = 24 \sin 10t$$

The stiffness of the entire system of four springs is $k = 4(200 \text{ N/m}) = 800$ N/m. Therefore, the natural frequency of vibration is

$$\omega_n = \sqrt{\frac{k}{m}} = \sqrt{\frac{800 \text{ N/m}}{30 \text{ kg}}} = 5.16 \text{ rad/s}$$

Since the damping factor is known, the steady-state amplitude may be determined from the first of Eqs. 22–39, i.e.,

$$
\begin{aligned}
C' &= \frac{F_0/k}{\sqrt{[1 - (\omega/\omega_n)^2]^2 + [2(c/c_c)(\omega/\omega_n)]^2}} \\[2mm]
&= \frac{24/800}{\sqrt{[1 - (10/5.16)^2]^2 + [2(0.15)(10/5.16)]^2}} \\[2mm]
&= 0.0107 \text{ m} = 10.7 \text{ mm} \qquad\qquad \textit{Ans.}
\end{aligned}
$$

# *22.6 Electrical Circuit Analogs

(a)

(b)

**Fig. 22–20**

The characteristics of a vibrating mechanical system may be represented by an electric circuit. Consider the circuit shown in Fig. 22–20a, which consists of an inductor $L$, a resistor $R$, and a capacitor $C$. When a voltage $E(t)$ is applied, it causes a current of magnitude $i$ to flow through the circuit. As the current flows past the inductor the voltage drop is $L(di/dt)$, when it flows across the resistor the drop is $Ri$, and when it arrives at the capacitor the drop is $(1/C)\int i\, dt$. Since current cannot flow past a capacitor, it is only possible to measure the charge $q$ acting on the capacitor. The charge may, however, be related to the current by the equation $i = dq/dt$. Thus, the voltage drops which occur across the inductor, resistor, and capacitor may be written as $L\, d^2q/dt^2$, $R\, dq/dt$, and $q/C$, respectively. According to Kirchhoff's voltage law, the applied voltage balances the sum of the voltage drops around the circuit. Therefore,

$$L\frac{d^2q}{dt^2} + R\frac{dq}{dt} + \frac{1}{C}q = E(t) \qquad (22–41)$$

Consider now the model of a single-degree-of-freedom mechanical system, Fig. 22–20b, which is subjected to both a general forcing function $F(t)$ and damping. The equation of motion for this system was established in the previous section and can be written as

$$m\frac{d^2x}{dt^2} + c\frac{dx}{dt} + kx = F(t) \qquad (22–42)$$

By comparison, it is seen that Eqs. 22–41 and 22–42 have the same form, and hence mathematically the problem of analyzing an electric circuit is the same as that of analyzing a vibrating mechanical system. The analogs between the two equations are given in Table 22–1.

This analogy has important application to experimental work, for it is much easier to simulate the vibration of a complex mechanical system using an electric circuit, which can be constructed on an analog computer, than to make an equivalent mechanical spring-and-dashpot model.

### TABLE 22–1 • Electrical–Mechanical Analogs

| Electrical | | Mechanical | |
|---|---|---|---|
| Electric charge | $q$ | Displacement | $x$ |
| Electric current | $i$ | Velocity | $dx/dt$ |
| Voltage | $E(t)$ | Applied force | $F(t)$ |
| Inductance | $L$ | Mass | $m$ |
| Resistance | $R$ | Viscous damping coefficient | $c$ |
| Reciprocal of capacitance | $1/C$ | Spring stiffness | $k$ |

# PROBLEMS

**22-41.** The block shown in Fig. 22–16 has a mass of 20 kg, and the spring has a stiffness $k = 600$ N/m. When the block is displaced and released, two successive amplitudes are measured as $x_1 = 150$ mm and $x_2 = 87$ mm. Determine the coefficient of viscous damping, $c$.

**22-42.** The 20-kg block is attached to a spring having a stiffness of 200 N/m. A force $F = (60 \cos 2t)$ N. where $t$ is in seconds, is applied to the block. Determine the maximum speed of the block after frictional forces cause the free vibrations to dampen out.

**22-43.** A 4-kg block is suspended from a spring that has a stiffness of $k = 600$ N/m. The block is drawn downward 50 mm from the equilibrium position and released from rest when $t = 0$. If the support moves with an impressed displacement of $\delta = (10 \sin 4t)$ mm, where $t$ is in seconds, determine the equation that describes the vertical motion of the block. Assume positive displacement is downward.

**\*22-44.** If the block is subjected to the impressed force $F = F_0 \cos \omega t$, show that the differential equation of motion is $\ddot{y} + (k/m)y = (F_0/m) \cos \omega t$, where $y$ is measured from the equilibrium position of the block. What is the general solution of this equation?

$F = F_0 \cos \omega t$

**Prob. 22–44**

**22-45.** The light elastic rod supports a 4-kg sphere. When an 18-N vertical force is applied to the sphere, the rod deflects 14 mm. If the wall oscillates with harmonic frequency of 2 Hz and has an amplitude of 15 mm, determine the amplitude of vibration for the sphere.

**Prob. 22–45**

**22-46.** A block having a mass of 0.8 kg is suspended from a spring having a stiffness of 120 N/m. If a dashpot provides a damping force of 2.5 N when the speed of the block is 0.2 m/s, determine the period of free vibration.

**22-47.** A 5-kg block is suspended from a spring having a stiffness of 300 N/m. If the block is acted upon by a vertical force $F = (7 \sin 8t)$ N, where $t$ is in seconds, determine the equation which describes the motion of the block when it is pulled down 100 mm from the equilibrium position and released from rest at $t = 0$. Assume that positive displacement is downward.

$k = 300$ N/m

$F = 7 \sin 8t$

**Prob. 22–47**

**\*22-48.** The electric motor has a mass of 50 kg and is supported by *four springs*, each spring having a stiffness of 100 N/m. If the motor turns a disk $D$ which is mounted eccentrically, 20 mm from the disk's center, determine the angular rotation $\omega$ at which resonance occurs. Assume that the motor only vibrates in the vertical direction.

**22-49.** The instrument is centered uniformly on a platform $P$, which in turn is supported by *four* springs, each spring having a stiffness $k = 130$ N/m. If the floor is subjected to a vibration $\omega = 7$ Hz, having a vertical displacement amplitude $\delta_0 = 0.17$ m, determine the vertical displacement amplitude of the platform and instrument. The instrument and the platform have a total weight of 1.8 kg.

**22-50.** The fan has a mass of 25 kg and is fixed to the end of a horizontal beam that has a negligible mass. The fan blade is mounted eccentrically on the shaft such that it is equivalent to an unbalanced 3.5-kg mass located 100 mm from the axis of rotation. If the static deflection of the beam is 50 mm as a result of the weight of the fan, determine the amplitude of steady-state vibration of the fan when the angular velocity of the fan is 10 rad/s. *Hint:* See the first part of Example 22.8.

**22-51.** What will be the amplitude of steady-state vibration of the fan in Prob. 22–50 if the angular velocity of the fan is 18 rad/s? *Hint:* See the first part of Example 22.8.

Probs. 22–50/51

**\*22-52.** The electric motor turns an eccentric flywheel which is equivalent to an unbalanced 1-N ($\approx 0.1$-kg) weight located 0.2 m from the axis of rotation. If the static deflection of the beam is 0.02 m because of the weight of the motor, determine the angular velocity of the flywheel at which resonance will occur. The motor weighs 600 N ($\approx 60$ kg). Neglect the mass of the beam.

**22-53.** What will be the amplitude of steady-state vibration of the motor in Prob. 22–52 if the angular velocity of the flywheel is 20 rad/s?

**22-54.** Determine the angular velocity of the flywheel in Prob. 22–52 which will produce an amplitude of vibration of 0.005 m.

**22-55.** The engine is mounted on a foundation block which is spring-supported. Describe the steady-state vibration of the system if the block and engine have a total weight of 7500 N ($\approx$ 750 kg) and the engine, when running, creates an impressed force $F = (250 \sin 2t)$ N, where $t$ is in seconds. Assume that the system vibrates only in the vertical direction, with the positive displacement measured downward, and that the total stiffness of the springs can be represented as $k = 30$ kN/m.

*****22-56.** Determine the rotational speed $\omega$ of the engine in Prob. 22–55 which will cause resonance.

Prob. 22–57

**22-58.** A 7-kg block is suspended from a spring having a stiffness of $k = 225$ N/m. The support to which the spring is attached is given simple harmonic motion which may be expressed as $\delta = (0.45 \sin 2t)$ m, where $t$ is in seconds. If the damping factor is $c/c_c = 0.8$, determine the phase angle $\phi$ of forced vibration.

**22-59.** Determine the magnification factor of the block, spring, and dashpot combination in Prob. 22–58.

*****22-60.** The 15-kg block is attached to two springs having a stiffness of 150 N/m. A force $F = (40 \cos 3t)$ N, where $t$ is in seconds, is applied to the block. Determine the maximum speed of the block after frictional forces cause the free vibrations to dampen out.

Probs. 22–55/56

**22-57.** The block, having a weight of 15 N ($\approx$ 1.5 kg) is immersed in a liquid such that the damping force acting on the block has a magnitude of $F = (0.8|v|)$ N, where $v$ is in m/s. If the block is pulled down 0.8 m and released from rest, determine the position of the block as a function of time. The spring has a stiffness of $k = 40$ N/m. Assume that positive displacement is downward.

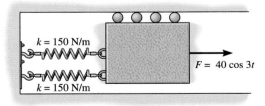

**22-61.** A block having a mass of 7 kg is suspended from a spring that has a stiffness $k = 600$ N/m. If the block is given an upward velocity of 0.6 m/s from its equilibrium position at $t = 0$, determine its position as a function of time. Assume that positive displacement of the block is downward and that motion takes place in a medium which furnishes a damping force $F = (50|v|)$ N, where $v$ is in m/s.

**22-62.** The damping factor, $c/c_c$, may be determined experimentally by measuring the successive amplitudes of vibrating motion of a system. If two of these maximum displacements can be approximated by $x_1$ and $x_2$, as shown in Fig. 22–17, show that the ratio $\ln x_1/x_2 = 2\pi(c/c_c)/\sqrt{1-(c/c_c)^2}$. The quantity $\ln x_1/x_2$ is called the *logarithmic decrement*.

**22-63.** Draw the electrical circuit that is equivalent to the mechanical system shown. Determine the differential equation which describes the charge $q$ in the circuit.

**Prob. 22–63**

**\*22-64.** The 20-kg block is subjected to the action of the harmonic force $F = (90 \cos 6t)$ N, where $t$ is in seconds. Write the equation which describes the steady-state motion.

**22-65.** Determine the differential equation of motion for the damped vibratory system shown. What type of motion occurs? Take $k = 100$ N/m, $c = 200$ N·s/m, $m = 25$ kg.

**Prob. 22–65**

**22-66.** The 10-kg block-spring-damper system is continually damped. If the block is displaced to $x = 50$ mm and released from rest, determine the time required for it to return to the position $x = 2$ mm.

# CHAPTER REVIEW

- *Undamped Free Vibration.*   A body has free vibration provided gravitational or elastic restoring forces cause the motion. This motion is undamped when friction forces are neglected. The periodic motion of an undamped, freely vibrating body can be studied by displacing the body from the equilibrium position and then applying the equation of motion along the path. For a one-degree-of-freedom system, the resulting differential equation can be written in the form $\ddot{x} + \omega_n^2 x = 0$. Here $\omega_n$ is the circular or natural frequency. If it is known, then the cycle time is $\tau = 2\pi/\omega_n$. Also, the frequency, or number of cycles completed per unit of time, is

$$f = \omega_n/2\pi$$

- *Energy Methods.*   Provided the restoring forces acting on the body are gravitational and elastic, then conservation of energy can also be used to determine its simple harmonic motion. To do this, the body is displaced a small amount from its equilibrium position, and an expression for its kinetic and potential energy is written. The time derivative of this equation can then be rearranged in the standard form $\ddot{x} + \omega_n^2 x = 0$. Knowing $\omega_n$, the other properties of the motion can then be obtained.

- *Undamped Forced Vibration.*   When the equation of motion is applied to a body, which is subjected to a periodic force or a periodic support displacement having a frequency $\omega$, then the displacement consists of a complementary solution and a particular solution. The complementary solution is caused by the free vibration and can be neglected. The particular solution is caused by the forced vibration. Resonance will occur if the natural period of vibration, $\omega_n$, is equal to the forcing frequency, $\omega$. This should be avoided, since the motion will become unbounded.

- *Viscous Damped Free Vibration.*   A viscous damping force is caused by a fluid drag on the system as it vibrates. If the motion is slow, this drag force is then proportional to the velocity, that is $F = c\dot{x}$. Here $c$ is the coefficient of viscous damping. By comparing its value to the critical damping coefficient $c_c = 2m\omega_n$, we can specify the type of vibration that occurs. If $c > c_c$, it is an overdamped system; if $c = c_c$, it is a critically damped system; if $c < c_c$, it is an underdamped system.

- *Viscous Damped Forced Vibration.*   The most general type of vibration for a one-degree-of-freedom system occurs when the system is damped and subjected to periodic forced motion. The solution provides insight as to how the damping factor, $c/c_c$, and the frequency ratio, $\omega/\omega_n$, influence the vibration. Resonance is avoided provided $c/c_c \neq 0$ and $\omega/\omega_n \neq 1$.

- *Electrical Circuit Analogs.*   The vibrating motion of a complex system can be studied by modeling it as an electrical circuit. This is possible since the differential equations that govern the behavior of each system are the same.

# Mathematical Expressions

## Quadratic Formula

If $ax^2 + bx + c = 0$, then $x = \dfrac{-b \pm \sqrt{b^2 - 4ac}}{2a}$

## Hyperbolic Functions

$$\sinh x = \frac{e^x - e^{-x}}{2}, \qquad \cosh x = \frac{e^x + e^{-x}}{2}, \qquad \tanh x = \frac{\sinh x}{\cosh x}$$

## Trigonometric Identities

$$\sin \theta = \frac{A}{C}, \quad \csc \theta = \frac{C}{A}$$

$$\cos \theta = \frac{B}{C}, \quad \sec \theta = \frac{C}{B}$$

$$\tan \theta = \frac{A}{B}, \quad \cot \theta = \frac{B}{A}$$

$$\sin^2 \theta + \cos^2 \theta = 1$$

$$\sin(\theta \pm \phi) = \sin \theta \cos \phi \pm \cos \theta \sin \phi$$

$$\sin 2\theta = 2 \sin \theta \cos \theta$$

$$\cos(\theta \pm \phi) = \cos \theta \cos \phi \mp \sin \theta \sin \phi$$

$$\cos 2\theta = \cos^2 \theta - \sin^2 \theta$$

$$\cos \theta = \pm\sqrt{\frac{1 + \cos 2\theta}{2}}, \quad \sin \theta = \pm\sqrt{\frac{1 - \cos 2\theta}{2}}$$

$$\tan \theta = \frac{\sin \theta}{\cos \theta}$$

$$1 + \tan^2 \theta = \sec^2 \theta \qquad\qquad 1 + \cot^2 \theta = \csc^2 \theta$$

## Power-Series Expansions

$$\sin x = x - \frac{x^3}{3!} + \cdots \qquad\qquad \sinh x = x + \frac{x^3}{3!} + \cdots$$

$$\cos x = 1 - \frac{x^2}{2!} + \cdots \qquad\qquad \cosh x = 1 + \frac{x^2}{2!} + \cdots$$

## Derivatives

$$\frac{d}{dx}(u^n) = nu^{n-1}\frac{du}{dx}$$

$$\frac{d}{dx}(uv) = u\frac{dv}{dx} + v\frac{du}{dx}$$

$$\frac{d}{dx}\left(\frac{u}{v}\right) = \frac{v\dfrac{du}{dx} - u\dfrac{dv}{dx}}{v^2}$$

$$\frac{d}{dx}(\cot u) = -\csc^2 u\frac{du}{dx}$$

$$\frac{d}{dx}(\sec u) = \tan u \sec u\frac{du}{dx}$$

$$\frac{d}{dx}(\csc u) = -\csc u \cot u\frac{du}{dx}$$

$$\frac{d}{dx}(\sin u) = \cos u\frac{du}{dx}$$

$$\frac{d}{dx}(\cos u) = -\sin u\frac{du}{dx}$$

$$\frac{d}{dx}(\tan u) = \sec^2 u\frac{du}{dx}$$

$$\frac{d}{dx}(\sinh u) = \cosh u\frac{du}{dx}$$

$$\frac{d}{dx}(\cosh u) = \sinh u\frac{du}{dx}$$

## Integrals

$$\int x^n \, dx = \frac{x^{n+1}}{n+1} + C, \ n \neq -1$$

$$\int \frac{dx}{a+bx} = \frac{1}{b}\ln(a+bx) + C$$

$$\int \frac{dx}{a+bx^2} = \frac{1}{2\sqrt{-ba}}\ln\left[\frac{a+x\sqrt{-ab}}{a-x\sqrt{-ab}}\right] + C, \ ab < 0$$

$$\int \frac{x \, dx}{a+bx^2} = \frac{1}{2b}\ln(bx^2+a) + C,$$

$$\int \frac{x^2 \, dx}{a+bx^2} = \frac{x}{b} - \frac{a}{b\sqrt{ab}}\tan^{-1}\frac{x\sqrt{ab}}{a} + C, \ ab > 0$$

$$\int \frac{dx}{a^2-x^2} = \frac{1}{2a}\ln\left[\frac{a+x}{a-x}\right] + C, \ a^2 > x^2$$

$$\int \sqrt{a+bx} \, dx = \frac{2}{3b}\sqrt{(a+bx)^3} + C$$

$$\int x\sqrt{a+bx} \, dx = \frac{-2(2a-3bx)\sqrt{(a+bx)^3}}{15b^2} + C$$

$$\int x^2\sqrt{a+bx} \, dx = \frac{2(8a^2-12abx+15b^2x^2)\sqrt{(a+bx)^3}}{105b^3} + C$$

$$\int \sqrt{a^2-x^2} \, dx = \frac{1}{2}\left[x\sqrt{a^2-x^2} + a^2\sin^{-1}\frac{x}{a}\right] + C, \ a > 0$$

$$\int x\sqrt{a^2-x^2} \, dx = -\frac{1}{3}\sqrt{(a^2-x^2)^3} + C$$

$$\int x^2\sqrt{a^2-x^2} \, dx = -\frac{x}{4}\sqrt{(a^2-x^2)^3}$$
$$+ \frac{a^2}{8}\left(x\sqrt{a^2-x^2} + a^2\sin^{-1}\frac{x}{a}\right) + C, a > 0$$

$$\int \sqrt{x^2 \pm a^2} \, dx = \frac{1}{2}\left[x\sqrt{x^2 \pm a^2} \pm a^2\ln(x+\sqrt{x^2 \pm a^2})\right] + C$$

$$\int x\sqrt{x^2 \pm a^2} \, dx = \frac{1}{3}\sqrt{(x^2 \pm a^2)^3} + C$$

$$\int x^2\sqrt{x^2 \pm a^2} \, dx = \frac{x}{4}\sqrt{(x^2 \pm a^2)^3} \mp \frac{a^2}{8}x\sqrt{x^2 \pm a^2}$$
$$- \frac{a^4}{8}\ln(x+\sqrt{x^2 \pm a^2}) + C$$

$$\int \frac{dx}{\sqrt{a+bx}} = \frac{2\sqrt{a+bx}}{b} + C$$

$$\int \frac{x \, dx}{\sqrt{x^2 \pm a^2}} = \sqrt{x^2 \pm a^2} + C$$

$$\int \frac{dx}{\sqrt{a+bx+cx^2}} = \frac{1}{\sqrt{c}}\ln\left[\sqrt{a+bx+cx^2}\right.$$
$$\left. + x\sqrt{c} + \frac{b}{2\sqrt{c}}\right] + C, c > 0$$

$$= \frac{1}{\sqrt{-c}}\sin^{-1}\left(\frac{-2cx-b}{\sqrt{b^2-4ac}}\right) + C, c > 0$$

$$\int \sin x \, dx = -\cos x + C$$

$$\int \cos x \, dx = \sin x + C$$

$$\int x\cos(ax) \, dx = \frac{1}{a^2}\cos(ax) + \frac{x}{a}\sin(ax) + C$$

$$\int x^2\cos(ax) \, dx = \frac{2x}{a^2}\cos(ax)$$
$$+ \frac{a^2x^2-2}{a^3}\sin(ax) + C$$

$$\int e^{ax} \, dx = \frac{1}{a}e^{ax} + C$$

$$\int xe^{ax} \, dx = \frac{e^{ax}}{a^2}(ax-1) + C$$

$$\int \sinh x \, dx = \cosh x + C$$

$$\int \cosh x \, dx = \sinh x + C$$

# APPENDIX B

# Numerical and Computer Analysis

Occasionally the application of the laws of mechanics will lead to a system of equations for which a closed-form solution is difficult or impossible to obtain. When confronted with this situation, engineers will often use a numerical method which in most cases can be programmed on a microcomputer or "programmable" pocket calculator. Here we will briefly present a computer program for solving a set of linear algebraic equations, and three numerical methods which can be used to solve an algebraic or transcendental equation, evaluate a definite integral, and solve an ordinary differential equation. Application of each method will be explained by example, and an associated computer program written in Microsoft BASIC, which is designed to run on most personal computers, is provided.* A text on numerical analysis should be consulted for further discussion regarding a check of the accuracy of each method and the inherent errors that can develop from the methods.

## B.1  Linear Algebraic Equations

Application of the equations of static equilibrium or the equations of motion sometimes requires solving a set of linear algebraic equations. The computer program listed in Fig. B–1 can be used for this purpose. It is based on the method of a Gaussian elimination and can solve at

---

*Similar types of programs can be written or purchased for programmable pocket calculators.

```
 1 PRINT"Linear system of equations":PRINT    20 PRINT"Unknowns"                   39 NEXT I
 2 DIM A(10,11)                               21 FOR I = 1 TO N                    40 FOR I = M+1 TO N
 3 INPUT"Input number of equations : ",N      22 PRINT "X(";I;")=";A(I,N+1)        41 FC=A(I,M)/A(M,M)
 4 PRINT                                       23 NEXT I                            42 FOR J = M+1 TO N+1
 5 PRINT"A  coefficients"                      24 END                               43 A(I,J)=A(I,J)-FC*A(M,J)
 6 FOR I = 1 TO N                              25 REM Subroutine Guassian           44 NEXT J
 7 FOR J = 1 TO N                              26 FOR M=1 TO N                       45 NEXT I
 8 PRINT "A(";I;",";J;                         27 NP=M                              46 NEXT M
 9 INPUT")=",A(I,J)                            28 BG=ABS(A(M,M))                    47 A(N,N+1)=A(N,N+1)/A(N,N)
10 NEXT J                                      29 FOR I = M TO N                    48 FOR I = N-1 TO 1 STEP -1
11 NEXT I                                      30 IF ABS(A(I,M))<=BG THEN 33        49 SM=0
12 PRINT                                       31 BG=ABS(A(I,M))                    50 FOR J=I+1 TO N
13 PRINT"B  coefficients"                      32 NP=I                              51 SM=SM+A(I,J)*A(J,N+1)
14 FOR I = 1 TO N                              33 NEXT I                            52 NEXT J
15 PRINT "B(";I;                               34 IF NP=M THEN 40                   53 A(I,N+1)=(A(I,N+1)-SM)/A(I,I)
16 INPUT")=",A(I,N+1)                          35 FOR I = M TO N+1                  54 NEXT I
17 NEXT I                                      36 TE=A(M,I)                         55 RETURN
18 GOSUB 25                                    37 A(M,I)=A(NP,I)
19 PRINT                                       38 A(NP,I)=TE
```

Fig. B–1

most 10 equations with 10 unknowns. To do so, the equations should first be written in the following general format:

$$A_{11}x_1 + A_{12}x_2 + \cdots + A_{1n}x_n = B_1$$
$$A_{21}x_1 + A_{22}x_2 + \cdots + A_{2n}x_n = B_2$$
$$\vdots$$
$$A_{n1}x_1 + A_{n2}x_2 + \cdots + A_{nn}x_n = B_n$$

The "$A$" and "$B$" coefficients are "called" for when running the program. The output presents the unknowns $x_1, \ldots, x_n$.

---

## EXAMPLE B.1

Solve the two equations

$$3x_1 + x_2 = 4$$
$$2x_1 - x_2 = 10$$

### Solution

When the program begins to run, it first calls for the number of equations (2); then the $A$ coefficients in the sequence $A_{11} = 3$, $A_{12} = 1$, $A_{21} = 2$, $A_{22} = -1$; and finally the $B$ coefficients $B_1 = 4$, $B_2 = 10$. The output appears as

Unknowns
$X(1) = 2.8$       *Ans.*
$X(2) = -4.4$       *Ans.*

## B.2 Simpson's Rule

Simpson's rule is a numerical method that can be used to determine the area under a curve given as a graph or as an explicit function $y = f(x)$. Likewise, it can be used to find the value of a definite integral which involves the function $y = f(x)$. To do so, the area must be subdivided into an *even number* of strips or intervals having a width $h$. The curve between three consecutive ordinates is approximated by a parabola, and the entire area or definite integral is then determined from the formula

$$\int_{x_0}^{x_n} f(x)\, dx \approx \frac{h}{3}[y_0 + 4(y_1 + y_3 + \cdots + y_{n-1})$$
$$+ 2(y_2 + y_4 + \cdots + y_{n-2}) + y_n] \qquad \text{(B–1)}$$

The computer program for this equation is given in Fig. B–2. For its use, we must first specify the function (on line 6 of the program). The upper and lower limits of the integral and the number of intervals are called for when the program is executed. The value of the integral is then given as the output.

```
1 PRINT"Simpson's rule":PRINT
2 PRINT" To execute this program :":PRINT
3 PRINT"    1- Modify right-hand side of the equation given below,
4 PRINT"       then press RETURN key"
5 PRINT"    2- Type  RUN 6":PRINT:EDIT 6
6 DEF FNF(X)=LOG(X)
7 PRINT:INPUT" Enter Lower Limit = ",A
8 INPUT" Enter Upper Limit = ",B
9 INPUT" Enter Number (even) of Intervals = ",N%
10 H=(B-A)/N%:AR=FNF(A):X=A+H
11 FOR J%=2 TO N%
12 K=2*(2-J%+2*INT(J%/2))
13 AR=AR+K*FNF(X)
14 X=X+H:NEXT J%
15 AR=H*(AR+FNF(B))/3
16 PRINT" Integral = ",AR
17 END
```

Fig. B–2

# EXAMPLE B.2

Evaluate the definite integral

$$\int_2^5 \ln x \, dx$$

**Solution**

The interval $x_0 = 2$ to $x_6 = 5$ will be divided into six equal parts $(n = 6)$, each having a width $h = (5 - 2)/6 = 0.5$. We then compute $y = f(x) = \ln x$ at each point of subdivision.

| $n$ | $x_n$ | $y_n$ |
|---|---|---|
| 0 | 2 | 0.693 |
| 1 | 2.5 | 0.916 |
| 2 | 3 | 1.099 |
| 3 | 3.5 | 1.253 |
| 4 | 4 | 1.386 |
| 5 | 4.5 | 1.504 |
| 6 | 5 | 1.609 |

Thus, Eq. B–1 becomes

$$\int_2^5 \ln x \, dx \approx \frac{0.5}{3}[0.693 + 4(0.916 + 1.253 + 1.504)$$
$$+ 2(1.099 + 1.386) + 1.609]$$
$$\approx 3.66 \qquad\qquad Ans.$$

This answer is equivalent to the exact answer to three significant figures. Obviously, accuracy to a greater number of significant figures can be improved by selecting a smaller interval $h$ (or larger $n$).

Using the computer program, we first specify the function $\ln x$, line 6 in Fig. B–2. During execution, the program input requires the upper and lower limits 2 and 5 and the number of intervals $n = 6$. The output appears as

$$\text{Integral} = 3.66082 \qquad\qquad Ans.$$

# B.3 The Secant Method

The secant method is used to find the real roots of an algebraic or transcendental equation $f(x) = 0$. The method derives its name from the fact that the formula used is established from the slope of the secant line to the graph $y = f(x)$. This slope is $[f(x_n) - f(x_{n-1})]/(x_n - x_{n-1})$, and the secant formula is

$$x_{n+1} = x_n - f(x_n)\left[\frac{x_n - x_{n-1}}{f(x_n) - f(x_{n-1})}\right] \tag{B-2}$$

For application it is necessary to provide two initial guesses, $x_0$ and $x_1$, and thereby evaluate $x_2$ from Eq. B–2 ($n = 1$). One then proceeds to reapply Eq. B–2 with $x_1$ and the calculated value of $x_2$ and obtain $x_3$ ($n = 2$), etc., until the value $x_{n+1} \approx x_n$. One can see this will occur if $x_n$ is approaching the root of the function $f(x) = 0$, since the correction term on the right of Eq. B–2 will tend toward zero. In particular, the larger the slope, the smaller the correction to $x_n$, and the faster the root will be found. On the other hand, if the slope is very small in the neighborhood of the root, the method leads to large corrections for $x_n$, and convergence to the root is slow and may even lead to a failure to find it. In such cases other numerical techniques must be used for solution.

A computer program based on Eq. B–2 is listed in Fig. B–3. We must first specify the function on line 7 of the program. When the program is executed, two initial guesses, $x_0$ and $x_1$, must be entered in order to approximate the solution. The output specifies the value of the root. If it cannot be determined, this is so stated.

```
1 PRINT"Secant method":PRINT
2 PRINT" To execute this program :":PRINT
3 PRINT"    1) Modify right hand side of the equation given below,"
4 PRINT"       then press RETURN key."
5 PRINT"    2) Type   RUN 7"
6 PRINT:EDIT 7
7 DEF FNF(X)=.5*SIN(X)-2*COS(X)+1.3
8 INPUT"Enter point #1 =",X
9 INPUT"Enter point #2 =",X1
10 IF X=X1 THEN 14
11 EP=.00001:TL=2E-20
12 FP=(FNF(X1)-FNF(X))/(X1-X)
13 IF ABS(FP)>TL THEN 15
14 PRINT"Root can not be found.":END
15 DX=FNF(X1)/FP
16 IF ABS(DX)>EP THEN 19
17 PRINT "Root = ";X1;"          Function evaluated at this root = ";FNF(X1)
18 END
19 X=X1:X1=X1-DX
20 GOTO 12
```

**Fig. B–3**

## E X A M P L E  B.3

Determine the root of the equation

$$f(x) = 0.5 \sin x - 2 \cos x + 1.30 = 0$$

**Solution**

Guesses of the initial roots will be $x_0 = 45°$ and $x_1 = 30°$. Applying Eq. B–2,

$$x_2 = 30° - (-0.1821)\frac{(30° - 45°)}{(-0.1821 - 0.2393)} = 36.48°$$

Using this value in Eq. B–2, along with $x_1 = 30°$, we have

$$x_3 = 36.48° - (-0.0108)\frac{36.48° - 30°}{(-0.0108 + 0.1821)} = 36.89°$$

Repeating the process with this value and $x_2 = 36.48°$ yields

$$x_4 = 36.89° - (0.0005)\left[\frac{36.89° - 36.48°}{(0.0005 + 0.0108)}\right] = 36.87°$$

Thus $x = 36.9°$ is appropriate to three significant figures.

   If the problem is solved using the computer program, first we specify the function, line 7 in Fig. B–3. During execution, the first and second guesses must be entered in radians. Choosing these to be 0.8 rad and 0.5 rad, the result appears as

Root = 0.6435022

Function evaluated at this root = 1.66893E-06

This result converted from radians to degrees is therefore

$$x = 36.9° \qquad\qquad \textit{Ans.}$$

# B.4 Runge-Kutta Method

The Runge-Kutta method is used to solve an ordinary differential equation. It consists of applying a set of formulas which are used to find specific values of $y$ for corresponding incremental values $h$ in $x$. The formulas given in general form are as follows:

**First-Order Equation.** To integrate $\dot{x} = f(t, x)$ step by step, use

$$x_{i+1} = x_i + \frac{1}{6}(k_1 + 2k_2 + 2k_3 + k_4) \tag{B-3}$$

where

$$
\begin{aligned}
k_1 &= hf(t_i, x_i) \\
k_2 &= hf\left(t_i + \frac{h}{2}, x_i + \frac{k_1}{2}\right) \\
k_3 &= hf\left(t_i + \frac{h}{2}, x_i + \frac{k_2}{2}\right) \\
k_4 &= hf(t_i + h, x_i + k_3)
\end{aligned}
\tag{B-4}
$$

**Second-Order Equation.** To integrate $\ddot{x} = f(t, x, \dot{x})$, use

$$
\begin{aligned}
x_{i+1} &= x_i + h\left[\dot{x}_i + \frac{1}{6}(k_1 + k_2 + k_3)\right] \\
\dot{x}_{i+1} &= \dot{x}_i + \frac{1}{6}(k_1 + 2k_2 + 2k_3 + k_4)
\end{aligned}
\tag{B-5}
$$

where

$$
\begin{aligned}
k_1 &= hf(t_i, x_i, \dot{x}_i) \\
k_2 &= hf\left(t_i + \frac{h}{2}, x_i + \frac{h}{2}\dot{x}_i, \dot{x}_i + \frac{k_1}{2}\right) \\
k_3 &= hf\left(t_i + \frac{h}{2}, x_i + \frac{h}{2}\dot{x}_i + \frac{h}{4}k_1, \dot{x}_i + \frac{k_2}{2}\right) \\
k_4 &= hf\left(t_i + h, x_i + h\dot{x}_i + \frac{h}{2}k_2, \dot{x}_i + k_3\right)
\end{aligned}
\tag{B-6}
$$

To apply these equations, one starts with initial values $t_i = t_0$, $x_i = x_0$ and $\dot{x}_i = \dot{x}_0$ (for the second-order equation). Choosing an increment $h$ for $t_0$, the four constants $k$ are computed, and these results are substituted into Eq. B–3 or B–5 in order to compute $x_{i+1} = x_1$, $\dot{x}_{i+1} = x_1$, corresponding to $t_{i+1} = t_1 = t_0 + h$. Repeating this process using $t_1$, $x_1$, $\dot{x}_1$ and $h$, values for $x_2$, $\dot{x}_2$ and $t_2 = t_1 + h$ are then computed, etc.

Computer programs which solve first- and second-order differential equations by this method are listed in Figs. B–4 and B–4, respectively. In order to use these programs, the operator specifies the function $\dot{x} = f(t, x)$ or $\ddot{x} = f(t, x, \dot{x})$ (line 7), the initial values $t_0$, $x_0$, $\dot{x}_0$ (for second-order equation), the final time $t_n$, and the step size $h$. The output gives the values of $t$, $x$, and $\dot{x}$ for each time increment until $t_n$ is reached.

```
1 PRINT"Runge-Kutta Method for 1-st order Differential Equation":PRINT
2 PRINT" To execute this program :":PRINT
3 PRINT"    1) Modify right hand side of the equation given below,"
4 PRINT"       then Press RETURN key"
5 PRINT"    2) Type  RUN 7"
6 PRINT:EDIT 7
7 DEF FNF(T,X)=5*T+X
8 CLS:PRINT" Initial Conditions":PRINT
9 INPUT"Input  t    = ",T
10 INPUT"       x    = ",X
11 INPUT"Final  t    = ",T1
12 INPUT"step size   = ",H:PRINT
13 PRINT"       t              x"
14 IF T>=T1+H THEN 23
15 PRINT USING"######.#####";T;X
16 K1=H*FNF(T,X)
17 K2=H*FNF(T+.5*H,X+.5*K1)
18 K3=H*FNF(T+.5*H,X+.5*K2)
19 K4=H*FNF(T+H,X+K3)
20 T=T+H
21 X=X+(K1+K2+K2+K3+K3+K4)/6
22 GOTO 14
23 END
```

Fig. B–4

```
1 PRINT"Runge-Kutta Method for 2-nd order Differential Equation":PRINT
2 PRINT" To execute this program :":PRINT
3 PRINT"    1) Modify right hand side of the equation given below,"
4 PRINT"       then Press RETURN key"
5 PRINT"    2) Type  RUN 7"
6 PRINT:EDIT 7
7 DEF FNF(T,X,XD)=
8 INPUT"Input  t    = ",T
9 INPUT"       x    = ",X
10 INPUT"       dx/dt = ",XD
11 INPUT"Final  t    = ",T1
12 INPUT"step size   = ",H:PRINT
13 PRINT"       t              x           dx/dt"
14 IF T>=T1+H THEN 24
15 PRINT USING"######.#####";T;X;XD
16 K1=H*FNF(T,X,XD)
17 K2=H*FNF(T+.5*H,X+.5*H*XD,XD+.5*K1)
18 K3=H*FNF(T+.5*H,X+(.5*H)*(XD+.5*K1),XD+.5*K2)
19 K4=H*FNF(T+H,X+H*XD+.5*H*K2,XD+K3)
20 T=T+H
21 X=X+H*XD+H*(K1+K2+K3)/6
22 XD=XD+(K1+K2+K2+K3+K3+K4)/6
23 GOTO 14
24 END
```

Fig. B–5

E X A M P L E  B.4

Solve the differential equations $\dot{x} = 5t + x$. Obtain the results for two steps using time increments of $h = 0.02$ s. At $t_0 = 0$, $x_0 = 0$.

Solution

This is a first-order equation, so Eqs. B–3 and B–4 apply. Thus, for $t_0 = 0$, $x_0 = 0$, $h = 0.02$, we have

$$k_1 = 0.02(0 + 0) = 0$$
$$k_2 = 0.02[5(0.01) + 0] = 0.001$$
$$k_3 = 0.02[5(0.01) + 0.0005] = 0.00101$$
$$k_4 = 0.02[5(0.02) + 0.00101] = 0.00202$$
$$x_1 = 0 + \tfrac{1}{6}[0 + 2(0.001) + 2(0.00101) + 0.00202] = 0.00101$$

Using the values $t_1 = 0 + 0.02 = 0.02$ and $x_1 = 0.00101$ with $h = 0.02$, the value for $x_2$ is now computed from Eqs. B–3 and B–4.

$$k_1 = 0.02[5(0.02) + 0.00101] = 0.00202$$
$$k_2 = 0.02[5(0.03) + 0.00202] = 0.00304$$
$$k_3 = 0.02[5(0.03) + 0.00253] = 0.00305$$
$$k_4 = 0.02[5(0.04) + 0.00406] = 0.00408$$
$$x_2 = 0.00101 + \tfrac{1}{6}[0.00202 + 2(0.00304) + 2(0.00305) + 0.00408]$$
$$= 0.00405 \qquad\qquad\qquad Ans.$$

To solve this problem using the computer program in Fig. B–4, the function is first entered on line 7, then the data $t_0 = 0$, $x_0 = 0$, $t_n = 0.04$, and $h = 0.02$ is specified. The results appear as

| $t$ | $x$ |
|---|---|
| 0.00000 | 0.00000 |
| 0.02000 | 0.00101 |
| 0.04000 | 0.00405 |

*Ans.*

# Vector Analysis

The following discussion provides a brief review of vector analysis. A more detailed treatment of these topics is given in *Engineering Mechanics: Statics*.

**Vector.**　A vector, **A**, is a quantity which has magnitude and direction, and adds according to the parallelogram law. As shown in Fig. C–1, **A** = **B** + **C**, where **A** is the *resultant vector* and **B** and **C** are *component vectors*.

**Unit Vector.**　A unit vector, $\mathbf{u}_A$, has a magnitude of one "dimensionless" unit and acts in the same direction as **A**. It is determined by dividing **A** by its magnitude $A$, i.e,

$$\mathbf{u}_A = \frac{\mathbf{A}}{A} \tag{C–1}$$

Fig. C–1

Fig. C–2

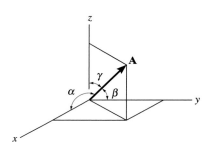

Fig. C–3

## Cartesian Vector Notation.
The directions of the positive $x, y, z$ axes are defined by the Cartesian unit vectors $\mathbf{i}, \mathbf{j}, \mathbf{k}$, respectively.

As shown in Fig. C–2, vector $\mathbf{A}$ is formulated by the addition of its $x, y, z$ components as

$$\mathbf{A} = A_x\mathbf{i} + A_y\mathbf{j} + A_z\mathbf{k} \qquad (C–2)$$

The *magnitude* of $\mathbf{A}$ is determined from

$$A = \sqrt{A_x^2 + A_y^2 + A_z^2} \qquad (C–3)$$

The *direction* of $\mathbf{A}$ is defined in terms of its *coordinate direction angles*, $\alpha, \beta, \gamma$, measured from the *tail* of $\mathbf{A}$ to the *positive x, y, z* axes, Fig. C–3. These angles are determined from the *direction cosines* which represent the $\mathbf{i}, \mathbf{j}, \mathbf{k}$ components of the unit vector $\mathbf{u}_A$; i.e., from Eqs. C–1 and C–2.

$$\mathbf{u}_A = \frac{A_x}{A}\mathbf{i} + \frac{A_y}{A}\mathbf{j} + \frac{A_z}{A}\mathbf{k} \qquad (C–4)$$

so that the direction cosines are

$$\cos\alpha = \frac{A_x}{A} \qquad \cos\beta = \frac{A_y}{A} \qquad \cos\gamma = \frac{A_z}{A} \qquad (C–5)$$

Hence, $\mathbf{u}_A = \cos\alpha\mathbf{i} + \cos\beta\mathbf{j} + \cos\gamma\mathbf{k}$, and using Eq. C–3, it is seen that

$$\cos^2\alpha + \cos^2\beta + \cos^2\gamma = 1 \qquad (C–6)$$

## The Cross Product.
The cross product of two vectors $\mathbf{A}$ and $\mathbf{B}$, which yields the resultant vector $\mathbf{C}$, is written as

$$\mathbf{C} = \mathbf{A} \times \mathbf{B} \qquad (C–7)$$

and reads $\mathbf{C}$ equals $\mathbf{A}$ "cross" $\mathbf{B}$. The *magnitude* of $\mathbf{C}$ is

$$C = AB\sin\theta \qquad (C–8)$$

where $\theta$ is the angle made between the *tails* of $\mathbf{A}$ and $\mathbf{B}$ ($0° \leq \theta \leq 180°$). The *direction* of $\mathbf{C}$ is determined by the right-hand rule, whereby the fingers of the right hand are curled *from $\mathbf{A}$ to $\mathbf{B}$* and the thumb points in the direction of $\mathbf{C}$, Fig. C–4. This vector is perpendicular to the plane containing vectors $\mathbf{A}$ and $\mathbf{B}$.

The vector cross product is *not* commutative, i.e., $\mathbf{A} \times \mathbf{B} \neq \mathbf{B} \times \mathbf{A}$. Rather,

$$\mathbf{A} \times \mathbf{B} = -\mathbf{B} \times \mathbf{A} \qquad (C–9)$$

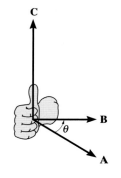

Fig. C–4

The distributive law is valid; i.e.,

$$\mathbf{A} \times (\mathbf{B} + \mathbf{D}) = \mathbf{A} \times \mathbf{B} + \mathbf{A} \times \mathbf{D} \tag{C–10}$$

And the cross product may be multiplied by a scalar $m$ in any manner; i.e.,

$$m(\mathbf{A} \times \mathbf{B}) = (m\mathbf{A}) \times \mathbf{B} = \mathbf{A} \times (m\mathbf{B}) = (\mathbf{A} \times \mathbf{B})m \tag{C–11}$$

Equation C–7 can be used to find the cross product of any pair of Cartesian unit vectors. For example, to find $\mathbf{i} \times \mathbf{j}$, the magnitude is $(i)(j) \sin 90° = (1)(1)(1) = 1$, and its direction $+\mathbf{k}$ is determined from the right-hand rule, applied to $\mathbf{i} \times \mathbf{j}$, Fig. C–2. A simple scheme shown in Fig. C–5 may be helpful in obtaining this and other results when the need arises. If the circle is constructed as shown, then "crossing" two of the unit vectors in a *counterclockwise* fashion around the circle yields a *positive* third unit vector, e.g., $\mathbf{k} \times \mathbf{i} = \mathbf{j}$. Moving *clockwise*, a *negative* unit vector is obtained, e.g., $\mathbf{i} \times \mathbf{k} = -\mathbf{j}$.

If $\mathbf{A}$ and $\mathbf{B}$ are expressed in Cartesian component form, then the cross product, Eq. C–7, may be evaluated by expanding the determinant

$$\mathbf{C} = \mathbf{A} \times \mathbf{B} = \begin{vmatrix} \mathbf{i} & \mathbf{j} & \mathbf{k} \\ A_x & A_y & A_z \\ B_x & B_y & B_z \end{vmatrix} \tag{C–12}$$

which yields

$$\mathbf{C} = (A_y B_z - A_z B_y)\mathbf{i} - (A_x B_z - A_z B_x)\mathbf{j} + (A_x B_y - A_y B_x)\mathbf{k}$$

Recall that the cross product is used in statics to define the moment of a force $\mathbf{F}$ about point $O$, in which case

$$\mathbf{M}_O = \mathbf{r} \times \mathbf{F} \tag{C–13}$$

where $\mathbf{r}$ is a position vector directed from point $O$ to *any point* on the line of action of $\mathbf{F}$.

**The Dot Product.** The dot product of two vectors $\mathbf{A}$ and $\mathbf{B}$, which yields a scalar, is defined as

$$\mathbf{A} \cdot \mathbf{B} = AB \cos \theta \tag{C–14}$$

and reads $\mathbf{A}$ "dot" $\mathbf{B}$. The angle $\theta$ is formed between the *tails* of $\mathbf{A}$ and $\mathbf{B}$ ($0° \le \theta \le 180°$).

The dot product is commutative; i.e.,

$$\mathbf{A} \cdot \mathbf{B} = \mathbf{B} \cdot \mathbf{A} \tag{C–15}$$

The distributive law is valid; i.e.,

$$\mathbf{A} \cdot (\mathbf{B} + \mathbf{D}) = \mathbf{A} \cdot \mathbf{B} + \mathbf{A} \cdot \mathbf{D} \tag{C–16}$$

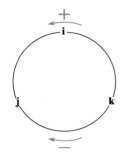

Fig. C–5

And scalar multiplication can be performed in any manner, i.e.,

$$m(\mathbf{A} \cdot \mathbf{B}) = (m\mathbf{A}) \cdot \mathbf{B} = \mathbf{A} \cdot (m\mathbf{B}) = (\mathbf{A} \cdot \mathbf{B})m \qquad \text{(C–17)}$$

Using Eq. C–14, the dot product between any two Cartesian vectors can be determined. For example, $\mathbf{i} \cdot \mathbf{i} = (1)(1)\cos 0° = 1$ and $\mathbf{i} \cdot \mathbf{j} = (1)(1)\cos 90° = 0$.

If $\mathbf{A}$ and $\mathbf{B}$ are expressed in Cartesian component form, then the dot product, Eq. C–14, can be determined from

$$\boxed{\mathbf{A} \cdot \mathbf{B} = A_x B_x + A_y B_y + A_z B_z} \qquad \text{(C–18)}$$

The dot product may be used to determine the *angle θ formed between two vectors*. From Eq. C–14,

$$\theta = \cos^{-1}\left(\frac{\mathbf{A} \cdot \mathbf{B}}{AB}\right) \qquad \text{(C–19)}$$

It is also possible to find the *component of a vector in a given direction* using the dot product. For example, the magnitude of the component (or projection) of vector $\mathbf{A}$ in the direction of $\mathbf{B}$, Fig. C–6, is defined by $A \cos \theta$. From Eq. C–14, this magnitude is

$$A \cos \theta = \mathbf{A} \cdot \frac{\mathbf{B}}{B} = \mathbf{A} \cdot \mathbf{u}_B \qquad \text{(C–20)}$$

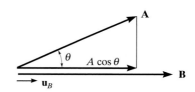

Fig. C–6

where $\mathbf{u}_B$ represents a unit vector acting in the direction of $\mathbf{B}$, Fig. C–6.

**Differentiation and Integration of Vector Functions.** The rules for differentiation and integration of the sums and products of scalar functions also apply to vector functions. Consider, for example, the two vector functions $\mathbf{A}(s)$ and $\mathbf{B}(s)$. Provided these functions are smooth and continuous for all $s$, then

$$\frac{d}{ds}(\mathbf{A} + \mathbf{B}) = \frac{d\mathbf{A}}{ds} + \frac{d\mathbf{B}}{ds} \qquad \text{(C–21)}$$

$$\int (\mathbf{A} + \mathbf{B})\, ds = \int \mathbf{A}\, ds + \int \mathbf{B}\, ds \qquad \text{(C–22)}$$

For the cross product,

$$\frac{d}{ds}(\mathbf{A} \times \mathbf{B}) = \left(\frac{d\mathbf{A}}{ds} \times \mathbf{B}\right) + \left(\mathbf{A} \times \frac{d\mathbf{B}}{ds}\right) \qquad \text{(C–23)}$$

Similarly, for the dot product,

$$\frac{d}{ds}(\mathbf{A} \cdot \mathbf{B}) = \frac{d\mathbf{A}}{ds} \cdot \mathbf{B} + \mathbf{A} \cdot \frac{d\mathbf{B}}{ds} \qquad \text{(C–24)}$$

# Review for the Fundamentals of Engineering Examination

The Fundamentals of Engineering (FE) exam is given semiannually by the National Council of Engineering Examiners (NCEE) and is one of the requirements for obtaining a Professional Engineering License. A portion of this exam contains problems in dynamics, and this appendix provides a review of the subject matter most often asked on this exam. Before solving any of the problems, you should review the sections indicated in each chapter in order to become familiar with the boldfaced definitions and the procedures used to solve the various types of problems. Also, review the example problems in these sections.

The following problems are arranged in the same sequence as the topics in each chapter. Besides helping as preparation for the FE exam, these problems also provide additional examples for general practice of the subject matter. Partial solutions and answers to *all the problems* are given at the back of this appendix.

### Chapter 12—Review Sections 12.1, 12.4–12.6, 12.8–12.9

**D-1.** The position of a particle is $s = (0.5t^3 + 4t)$ m, where $t$ is in seconds. Determine the velocity and the acceleration of the particle when $t = 3$ s.

**D-2.** After traveling a distance of 100 m, a particle reaches a velocity of 30 m/s, starting from rest. Determine its constant acceleration.

**D-3.** A particle moves in a straight line such that $s = (12t^3 + 2t^2 + 3t)$ m, where $t$ is in seconds. Determine the velocity and acceleration of the particle when $t = 2$ s.

**D-4.** A particle moves along a straight line such that $a = (4t^2 - 2)$ m/s$^2$, where $t$ is in seconds. When $t = 0$, the particle is located 2 m to the left of the origin, and when $t = 2$ s, it is 20 m to the left of the origin. Determine the position of the particle when $t = 4$ s.

**D-5.** Determine the speed at which the basketball at $A$ must be thrown at the angle of 30° so that it makes it to the basket at $B$.

**Prob. D–5**

**D-6.** A particle moves with curvilinear motion in the $x$–$y$ plane such that the $y$ component of motion is described by the equation $y = (7t^3)$ m, where $t$ is in seconds. If the particle starts from rest at the origin when $t = 0$, and maintains a *constant* acceleration in the $x$ direction of 12 m/s$^2$, determine the particle's speed when $t = 2$ s.

**D-7.** Water is sprayed at an angle of 90° from the slope at 20 m/s. Determine the range $R$.

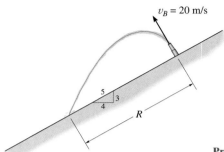

**Prob. D–7**

**D-8.** An automobile is traveling with a *constant speed* along a horizontal circular curve that has a radius of $\rho = 250$ m. If the magnitude of acceleration is $a = 1.5$ m/s$^2$, determine the speed at which the automobile is traveling.

**D-9.** A boat is traveling along a circular path having a radius of 30 m. Determine the magnitude of the boat's acceleration if at a given instant the boat's speed is $v = 6$ m/s and the rate of increase in speed is $\dot{v} = 2$ m/s$^2$.

**D-10.** A train travels along a horizontal circular curve that has a radius of 600 m. If the speed of the train is uniformly increased from 40 km/h to 60 km/h in 5 s, determine the magnitude of the acceleration at the instant the speed of the train is 50 km/h.

**D-11.** At a given instant, the automobile has a speed of 25 m/s and an acceleration of 3 m/s$^2$ acting in the direction shown. Determine the radius of curvature of the path and the rate of increase of the automobile's speed.

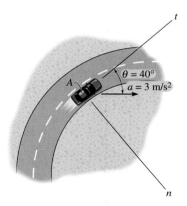

**Prob. D–11**

**D-12.** At the instant shown, cars $A$ and $B$ are traveling at the speeds shown. If $B$ is accelerating at 1200 km/h$^2$ while $A$ maintains a constant speed, determine the velocity and acceleration of $A$ with respect to $B$.

20 km/h
45°
100 m
$A$
$B$
65 km/h

Prob. D–12

**D-13.** Determine the speed of point $P$ on the cable in order to lift the platform at 2 m/s.

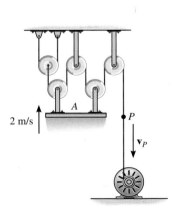

2 m/s
$A$
$P$
$\mathbf{v}_P$

Prob. D–13

## Chapter 13—Review Sections 13.1–13.5

**D-14.** The effective weight of a man in an elevator varies between 650 N and 850 N while he is riding in the elevator. When the elevator is at rest the man weighs 765 N. Determine how fast the elevator car can accelerate, going up and going down.

**D-15.** Neglecting friction and the mass of the pulley and cord, determine the acceleration at which the 4-kg block $B$ will descend. What is the tension in the cord? Block $A$ has a mass of 2 kg.

$A$
$B$

Prob. D–15

**D-16.** The blocks are suspended over a pulley by a rope. Neglecting the mass of the rope and the pulley, determine the acceleration of both blocks and the tension in the rope.

$B$  25 kg
$B$
$A$  15 kg

Prob. D–16

**D-17.** Block $B$ rests upon a smooth surface. If the coefficients of static and kinetic friction between $A$ and $B$ are $\mu_s = 0.4$ and $\mu_k = 0.3$, respectively, determine the acceleration of each block if $P = 63$ N.

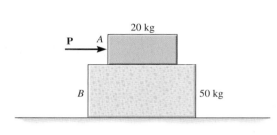

Prob. D–17

**D-18.** The block rests at a distance of 2 m from the center of the platform. If the coefficient of static friction between the block and the platform is $\mu_s = 0.3$, determine the maximum speed which the block can attain before it begins to slip. Assume the angular motion of the disk is slowly increasing.

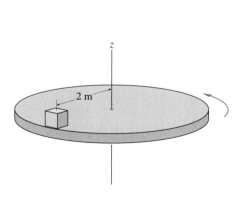

Prob. D–18

**D-19.** Determine the maximum speed that the jeep can travel over the crest of the hill and not lose contact with the road.

Prob. D–19

**D-20.** A pilot weighs 750 N ($\approx$ 75 kg) and is traveling at a constant speed of 36 m/s. Determine the normal force he exerts on the seat of the plane when he is upside down at $A$. The loop has a radius of curvature of 120 m.

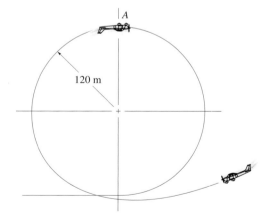

Prob. D–20

**D-21.** The sports car is traveling along a 30° banked road having a radius of curvature of $\rho = 150$ m. If the coefficient of static friction between the tires and the road is $\mu_s = 0.2$, determine the maximum safe speed for travel so no slipping occurs. Neglect the size of the car.

Prob. D–21

**D-22.** The 5-kg pendulum bob $B$ is released from rest when $\theta = 0°$. Determine the tension in string $BC$ immediately after it is released and when the pendulum reaches point $D$, where $\theta = 90°$.

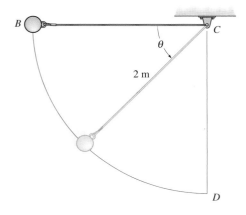

Prob. D–22

## Chapter 14—Review All Sections

**D-23.** A 7500-kg freight car is pulled along a horizontal track. If the car starts from rest and attains a velocity of 12 m/s after traveling a distance of 90 m, determine the total work done on the car by the towing force in this distance if the rolling frictional force between the car and track is 400 N.

**D-24.** The 20-kg block resting on the 30° inclined plane is acted upon by a 40-N force. If the block's initial velocity is 5 m/s down the plane, determine its velocity after it has traveled 10 m down the plane. The coefficient of kinetic friction between the block and the plane is $\mu_k = 0.2$.

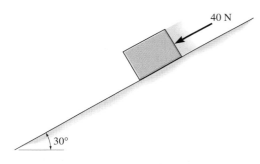

Prob. D–24

**D-25.** The 3-kg block is subjected to the action of the two forces shown. If the block starts from rest, determine the distance it has moved when it attains a velocity of 10 m/s. The coefficient of kinetic friction between the block and the surface is $\mu_k = 0.2$.

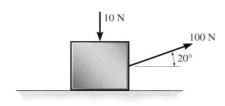

Prob. D–25

**D-26.** The 3-kg ball is to be fired from rest using a spring having a stiffness of $k = 600$ N/m. Determine how far the spring must be compressed so that when the ball reaches a height of 2.4 m it has a velocity of 1.8 m/s.

$v = 1.8$ m/s

2.4 m

$k = 600$ N/m

Prob. D–26

**D-27.** The 2-kg pendulum bob is released from rest when it is at $A$. Determine the speed of the bob and the tension in the cord when the bob passes through its lowest position, $B$.

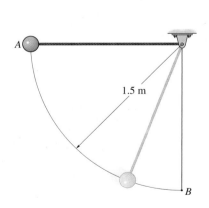

$A$

1.5 m

$B$

Prob. D–27

**D-28.** The 5-kg collar is released from rest at $A$ and travels along the frictionless guide. Determine the speed of the collar when it strikes the stop $B$. The spring has an unstretched length of 0.5 m.

$A$

1 m

$k = 40$ N/m

1.5 m

$B$

Prob. D–28

**D-29.** The 2-kg collar is given a downward velocity of 4 m/s when it is at $A$. If the spring has an unstretched length of 1 m and a stiffness of $k = 30$ N/m, determine the velocity of the collar at $s = 1$ m.

2 m

4 m/s

$A$

$B$

$s$

$k = 30$ N/m

$C$

Prob. D–29

## Chapter 15—Review Sections 15.1–15.4

**D-30.** A 30-tonne engine exerts a constant horizontal force of 200 kN on a train having three cars that have a total weight of 250 tonnes. If the rolling resistance is 50 N per tonne for both the engine and cars, determine how long it takes to increase the speed of the train from 6 m/s to 9 m/s. What is the driving force exerted by the engine wheels on the tracks?

**D-31.** A 5-kg block is moving up a 30° inclined plane with an initial velocity of 3 m/s. If the coefficient of kinetic friction between the block and the plane is $\mu_k = 0.3$, determine how long a 100-N horizontal force must act on the block in order to increase the velocity of the block to 10 m/s up the plane.

**D-32.** The 10-kg block $A$ attains a velocity of 1 m/s in 5 seconds, starting from rest. Determine the tension in the cord and the coefficient of kinetic friction between block $A$ and the horizontal plane. Neglect the weight of the pulley. Block $B$ has a mass of 8 kg.

**Prob. D–32**

**D-33.** Determine the velocity of each block 10 seconds after the blocks are released from rest. Neglect the mass of the pulleys.

**Prob. D–33**

**D-34.** The two blocks have a coefficient of restitution of $e = 0.5$. If the surface is smooth, determine the velocity of each block after impact.

**Prob. D–34**

**D-35.** A 6-kg disk $A$ has an initial velocity of $(v_A)_1 = 20$ m/s and strikes head-on disk $B$ that has a mass of 24 kg and is originally at rest. If the collision is perfectly elastic, determine the speed of each disk after the collision and the impulse which disk $A$ imparts to disk $B$.

**D-36.** Blocks $A$ and $B$ have masses of 5 kg and 10 kg, respectively. After striking block $B$, $A$ slides 0.2 m to the right, and $B$ slides 0.3 m to the right. If the coefficient of kinetic friction between the blocks and the surface is $\mu_k = 0.2$, determine the coefficient of restitution between the blocks. Block $B$ is originally at rest.

**Prob. D–36**

**D-37.** Disk $A$ weighs 2 N and is sliding on the smooth horizontal plane with a velocity of 3 m/s. Disk $B$ weighs 11 N and is initially at rest. If after the impact $A$ has a velocity of 1 m/s, directed along the positive $x$ axis, determine the speed of disk $B$ after impact.

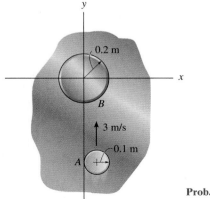

**Prob. D–37**

## Chapter 16—Review Sections 16.3, 16.5–16.7

**D-38.**   If gear $A$ is rotating clockwise with an angular velocity of $\omega_A = 3$ rad/s, determine the angular velocities of gears $B$ and $C$. Gear $B$ is one unit, having radii of 2 cm and 5 cm.

**Prob. D–38**

**D-39.**   The spin drier of a washing machine has a constant angular acceleration of 2 rev/s², starting from rest. Determine how many turns it makes in 10 seconds and its angular velocity when $t = 5$ s.

**D-40.**   Starting from rest, point $P$ on the cord has a constant acceleration of 20 m/s². Determine the angular acceleration and angular velocity of the disk after it has completed 10 revolutions. How many revolutions will the disk turn after it has completed 10 revolutions and $P$ continues to move downward for 4 seconds longer?

**D-41.**   The center of the wheel has a velocity of 3 m/s. At the same time, it is slipping and has a clockwise angular velocity of $\omega = 2$ rad/s. Determine the velocity of point $A$ at the instant shown.

**Prob. D–41**

**D-42.**   A cord is wrapped around the inner core of the gear and it is pulled with a constant velocity of 2 m/s. Determine the velocity of the center of the gear, $C$.

**Prob. D–40**

**Prob. D–42**

**D-43.** The center of the wheel is moving to the right with a speed of 2 m/s. If no slipping occurs at the ground, $A$, determine the velocity of point $B$ at the instant shown.

Prob. D–43

**D-44.** If the velocity of the slider block at $B$ is 2 m/s to the left, compute the velocity of the block at $A$ and the angular velocity of the rod at the instant shown.

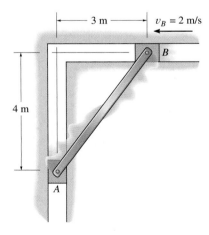

Prob. D–44

**D-45.** Determine the angular velocity of link $AB$ at the instant shown.

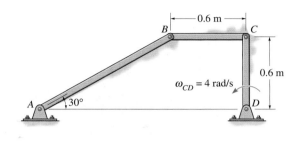

Prob. D–45

**D-46.** When the slider block $C$ is in the position shown, the link $AB$ has a clockwise angular velocity of 2 rad/s. Determine the velocity of block $C$ at this instant.

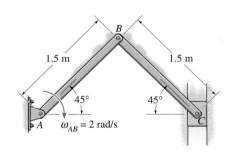

Prob. D–46

**D-47.** The center of the pulley is being lifted vertically with an acceleration of 3 m/s², and at the instant shown its velocity is 2 m/s. Determine the accelerations of points $A$ and $B$. Assume that the rope does not slip on the pulley's surface.

Prob. D–47

**D-48.** At a given instant, the slider block $A$ has the velocity and deceleration shown. Determine the acceleration of block $B$ and the angular acceleration of the link at this instant.

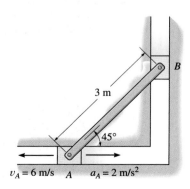

Prob. D–48

## Chapter 17—Review All Sections

**D-49.** The 1750-kg car has a center of mass located at $G$. Determine the normal reactions of both front and both rear wheels on the road and the acceleration of the car if it is rolling freely down the incline. Neglect the weight of the wheels.

Prob. D–49

**D-50.** The 20-kg link $AB$ is pinned to a moving frame at $A$ and held in a vertical position by means of a string $BC$ which can support a maximum tension of 100 N. Determine the maximum acceleration of the link without breaking the string. What are the corresponding components of reaction at the pin $A$?

Prob. D–50

**D-51.** The 50-kg triangular plate is released from rest. Determine the initial angular acceleration of the plate and the horizontal and vertical components of reaction at $B$. The moment of inertia of the plate about the pinned axis $B$ is $I_B = 20.0$ kg · m$^2$.

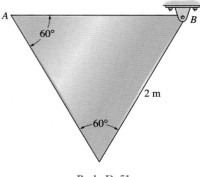

**Prob. D–51**

**D-52.** The 20-kg slender rod is pinned at $O$. Determine the reaction at $O$ just after the cable is cut.

**Prob. D–52**

**D-53.** The 20-kg wheel has a radius of gyration of $K_G = 0.8$ m. Determine the angular acceleration of the wheel if no slipping occurs.

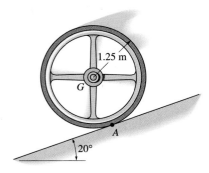

**Prob. D–53**

**D-54.** The 15-kg wheel has a wire wrapped around its inner hub and is released from rest on the inclined plane, for which the coefficient of kinetic friction is $\mu_k = 0.1$. If the centroidal radius of gyration of the wheel is $k_G = 0.8$ m, determine the angular acceleration of the wheel.

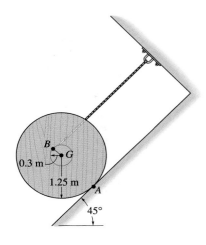

**Prob. D–54**

**D-55.** The 2-kg gear is at rest on the surface of a gear rack. If the rack is suddenly given an acceleration of 5 m/s$^2$, determine the initial angular acceleration of the gear. The radius of gyration of the gear is $k_G = 0.3$ m.

**Prob. D–55**

## Solutions and Answers

**D-1.** $v = \dfrac{ds}{dt} = 1.5t^2 + 4|_{t=3} = 17.5$ m/s   *Ans.*

$a = \dfrac{dv}{dt} = 3t|_{t=3} = 9$ m/s$^2$   *Ans.*

**D-2.** $(30)^2 = (0)^2 + 2a(100 - 0)$
$a = 4.5$ m/s$^2$   *Ans.*

**D-3.** $v = \dfrac{ds}{dt} = 36t^2 + 4t + 3|_{t=2} = 155$ m/s   *Ans.*

$a = \dfrac{dv}{dt} = 72t + 4|_{t=2} = 148$ m/s$^2$   *Ans.*

**D-4.** $v = \int (4t^2 - 2)\, dt$

$v = \dfrac{4}{3}t^3 - 2t + C_1$

$s = \int \left( \dfrac{4}{3}t^3 - 2t + C_1 \right) dt$

$s = \dfrac{1}{3}t^4 - t^2 + C_1 t + C_2$

$t = 0,\ s = -2,\ C_2 = -2$
$t = 2,\ s = -20,\ C_1 = -9.67$
$t = 4,\ s = 28.7$ m   *Ans.*

**D-5.** $\xrightarrow{+}\ s = s_0 + v_0 t$
$10 = 0 + v_A \cos 30° \, t$

$+\uparrow\ s = s_0 + v_0 t + \dfrac{1}{2}a_c t^2$

$3 = 1.5 + v_A \sin 30° \, t + \dfrac{1}{2}(-9.81)t^2$

$t = 0.933,\ v_A = 12.4$ m/s   *Ans.*

**D-6.** $v = v_0 + a_c t$
$v_x = 0 + 12(2) = 24$ m/s

$v_y = \dfrac{dy}{dt} = 21t^2|_{t=2} = 84$ m/s

$v = \sqrt{(24)^2 + (84)^2} = 87.4$ m/s   *Ans.*

**D-7.** $(\xrightarrow{+})\ s = s_0 + v_0 t$
$R\left(\dfrac{4}{5}\right) = 0 + 20\left(\dfrac{3}{5}\right)t$

$(+\uparrow)\ s = s_0 + v_0 t + \dfrac{1}{2}a_c t^2$

$-R\left(\dfrac{3}{5}\right) = 0 + 20\left(\dfrac{4}{5}\right)t + \dfrac{1}{2}(-9.81)t^2$

$t = 5.10$ s
$R = 76.5$ m   *Ans.*

**D-8.** $a_t = 0$

$a_n = a = 1.5 = \dfrac{v^2}{250};\ v = 19.4$ m/s   *Ans.*

**D-9.** $a_t = 2$ m/s$^2$

$a_n = \dfrac{v^2}{\rho} = \dfrac{(6)^2}{30} = 1.20$ m/s$^2$

$a = \sqrt{(2)^2 + (1.20)^2} = 2.33$ m/s$^2$   *Ans.*

**D-10.** $a_t = \dfrac{\Delta v}{\Delta t} = \dfrac{60 - 40}{[(5 - 0)/3600]} = 14\,400$ km/h$^2$

$a_n = \dfrac{v^2}{\rho} = \dfrac{(50)^2}{0.6} = 4167$ km/h$^2$

$a = \sqrt{(14.4)^2 + (4.167)^2}\ 10^3 = 15.0(10^3)$ km/h$^2$
   *Ans.*

**D-11.** $a_t = 3 \cos 40° = 2.30$ m/s$^2$   *Ans.*

$a_n = \dfrac{v^2}{\rho};\ 3 \sin 40° = \dfrac{(25)^2}{\rho},\ \rho = 324$ m   *Ans.*

**D-12.** $\mathbf{v}_A = \mathbf{v}_B + \mathbf{v}_{A/B}$
$-20 \cos 45°\, \mathbf{i} + 20 \sin 45°\, \mathbf{j} = 65\mathbf{i} + \mathbf{v}_{A/B}$
$\mathbf{v}_{A/B} = -79.14\mathbf{i} + 14.14\mathbf{j}$

$v_{A/B} = \sqrt{(-79.14)^2 + (14.14)^2} = 80.4$ km/h   *Ans.*
$\mathbf{a}_A = \mathbf{a}_B + \mathbf{a}_{A/B}$
$\dfrac{(20)^2}{0.1}\cos 45°\, \mathbf{i} + \dfrac{(20)^2}{0.1}\sin 45°\, \mathbf{j} = 1200\mathbf{i} + \mathbf{a}_{A/B}$
$\mathbf{a}_{A/B} = 1628\mathbf{i} + 2828\mathbf{j}$
$a_{A/B} = \sqrt{(1628)^2 + (2828)^2} = 3.26(10^3)$ km/h$^2$ *Ans.*

**D-13.** $4s_A + s_P = l$
$v_P = -4v_A = -4(-2) = 8$ m/s   *Ans.*

**D-14.** $+\uparrow\ \Sigma F_y = ma_y;\quad 850 - 765 = \dfrac{765}{9.81}a$
$a = 1.09$ m/s$^2$ ↑   *Ans.*

$+\downarrow \Sigma F_y = ma_y;\quad 765 - 650 = \dfrac{765}{9.81}a'$

$a' = 1.47$ m/s$^2$ ↓   *Ans.*

**D-15.** Block $B$:
$+\downarrow\ \Sigma F_y = ma_y;\ 4(9.81) - T = 4a$
Block $A$:
$\xrightarrow{+}\ \Sigma F_x = ma_x;\ T = 2a$
$T = 13.1$ N,$\quad a = 6.54$ m/s$^2$   *Ans.*

**D-16.** Block $A$:

$+\downarrow \Sigma F_y = ma_y;\ 15(9.81) - T = -15a$

Block $B$:

$+\downarrow \Sigma F_y = ma_y;\ 25(9.81) - T = 25a$

$a = 2.45 \text{ m/s}^2,\ T = 184 \text{ N}$   *Ans.*

**D-17.** Blocks $A$ and $B$:

$\xrightarrow{+} \Sigma F_x = ma_x;\ 63 = (70)a;\ a = 0.9 \text{ m/s}^2$

Check if slipping occurs between $A$ and $B$.

$\xrightarrow{+} \Sigma F_x = ma_x;\ 63 - F = (20)(0.9)$

$F = 45 \text{ N} < 0.4(20)(9.81) = 78.5 \text{ N}$

$a_A = a_B = 0.9 \text{ m/s}^2$   *Ans.*

**D-18.** $\Sigma F_n = m\dfrac{v^2}{\rho};\ (0.3)m(9.81) = m\dfrac{v^2}{2}$

$v = 2.43 \text{ m/s}$   *Ans.*

**D-19.** $+\downarrow \Sigma F_n = ma_n;\ m(9.81) = m\left(\dfrac{v^2}{250}\right)$

$v = 49.5 \text{ m/s}$   *Ans.*

**D-20.** $+\downarrow \Sigma F_n = ma_n;\ 750 + N_p = \dfrac{750}{9.81}\left(\dfrac{36^2}{120}\right)$

$N_p = 76.69 \text{ N}$   *Ans*

**D-21.** $\xrightarrow{+} \Sigma F_n = ma_n;\ N_c \sin 30° + 0.2\ N_c \cos 30° = m\dfrac{v^2}{150}$

$+\uparrow \Sigma F_b = 0;$

$\qquad N_c \cos 30° - 0.2\ N_c \sin 30° - m(9.81) = 0$

$v = 35.96 \text{ m/s}$   *Ans.*

**D-22.** At $B$:

$\xrightarrow{+} \Sigma F_n = ma_n,\ T = (5)\left(\dfrac{(0)^2}{2}\right) = 0$   *Ans.*

In the general position,

$+\nearrow \Sigma F_n = ma_n;\ T - 5(9.81)\sin\theta = (5)\left(\dfrac{v^2}{2}\right)$

$\searrow + \Sigma F_t = ma_t;\ 5(9.81)\cos\theta = (5)\left(\dfrac{v\,dv}{2\,d\theta}\right)$

$\displaystyle\int_0^{90°} 19.62\cos\theta\,d\theta = \int_0^v v\,dv$

$v = 6.26 \text{ m/s},$

When $\theta = 90°$;

$T = 147.2 \text{ N}$   *Ans.*

**D-23.** $T_1 + \Sigma U_{1-2} = T_2$

$0 + U_{1-2} - 400(90) = \dfrac{1}{2}(7500)(12)^2$

$U_{1-2} = 576 \text{ kJ}$   *Ans.*

**D-24.** $T_1 + \Sigma U_{1-2} = T_2$

$\dfrac{1}{2}(20)(5)^2 + 40(10) - (0.2)(20)(9.81\cos 30°)(10)$

$\quad + 20(9.81)(10\sin 30°) = \dfrac{1}{2}(20)v^2$

$v = 11.4 \text{ m/s}$   *Ans.*

**D-25.** $+\uparrow \Sigma F_y = ma_y;\ N_b + 100\sin 20° - 10 - 3(9.81) = 0$

$N_b = 5.23 \text{ N}$

$T_1 + \Sigma U_{1-2} = T_2$

$0 + (100\cos 20°)d - 0.2(5.23)d = \dfrac{1}{2}(3)(10)^2$

$d = 1.61 \text{ m}$   *Ans.*

**D-26.** $T_1 + V_1 = T_2 + V_2$

$0 + \dfrac{1}{2}(600)(x)^2 = \dfrac{1}{2}(3)(1.8)^2 + 3(9.81)(2.4)$

$x = 0.502 \text{ m}$   *Ans.*

**D-27.** $T_A + V_A = T_B + V_B$

$0 + 2(9.81)(1.5) = \dfrac{1}{2}(2)(v_B)^2 + 0$

$v_B = 5.42 \text{ m/s}$   *Ans.*

$+\uparrow \Sigma F_n = ma_n;\ T - 2(9.81) = 2\left(\dfrac{(5.42)^2}{1.5}\right)$

$T = 58.9 \text{ N}$   *Ans.*

**D-28.** $T_A + V_A = T_B + V_B$

$0 + \dfrac{1}{2}(40)(2.5 - 0.5)^2 + 5(9.81)(2.5)$

$\quad = \dfrac{1}{2}(5)v_B^2 + \dfrac{1}{2}(40)(1 - 0.5)^2$

$v_B = 8.89 \text{ m/s}$   *Ans.*

**D-29.** $T_1 + V_1 = T_2 + V_2$

$\dfrac{1}{2}(2)(4)^2 + \dfrac{1}{2}(30)(2 - 1)^2$

$\quad = \dfrac{1}{2}(2)(v)^2 - 2(9.81)(1) + \dfrac{1}{2}(30)(\sqrt{5} - 1)^2$

$v = 5.26 \text{ m/s}$   *Ans.*

**D-30.** Three cars:

$$\xrightarrow{+} mv_1 + \Sigma \int F \, dt = mv_2$$

$$250(6) + (200)(t) - \left(\frac{50}{1000}\right)(250)t = (250)(9)$$

$t = 4.0$ s   *Ans.*

Engine:

$$\xrightarrow{+} mv_1 + \Sigma \int F \, dt = mv_2$$

$$30(6) + F(4) - \left(\frac{50}{1000}\right)(30)(4) = (30)(9)$$

$F = 24$ kN   *Ans.*

**D-31.**  $+\nwarrow \Sigma F_y = 0;$

$N_b - 5(9.81)\cos 30° - 100 \sin 30° = 0$

$N_b = 92.48$ N

$+\nearrow mv_1 + \Sigma \int F \, dt = mv_2$

$5(3) + (100 \cos 30°)t - 5(9.81)\sin 30°(t) -$
$$\qquad\qquad\qquad 0.3(92.48)t = 5(10)$$

$t = 1.02$ s   *Ans.*

**D-32.** Block $B$:

$$(+\downarrow)\ mv_1 + \int F \, dt = mv_2$$

$$0 + 8(9.81)(5) - T(5) = (8)(1)$$

$T = 76.88$   *Ans.*

Block $A$:

$$(\xrightarrow{+})\ mv_1 + \int F \, dt = mv_2$$

$$0 + (76.88)(5) - \mu_k(10)(9.81)(5) = (10)(1)$$

$\mu_k = 0.763$   *Ans.*

**D-33.**  $2s_A + s_B = l$

$2v_A = -v_B$

$+\downarrow m(v_A)_1 + \int F \, dt = m(v_A)_2$

$0 + 10(9.81)(10) - 2T(10) = 10(v_A)_2$

$+\downarrow m(v_B)_1 + \int F \, dt = m(v_B)_2$

$0 + 50(9.81)(10) - T(10) = 50(v_B)_2$

$T = 70.1$ N

$(v_A)_2 = -42.0$ m/s $= 42.0$ m/s $\uparrow$   *Ans.*

$(v_B)_2 = 84.1$ m/s $\downarrow$   *Ans.*

**D-34.**  $\xrightarrow{+} \Sigma mv_1 = \Sigma mv_2;\ 5(2) - 2(5) = 5(v_A)_2 + 2(v_B)_2$

$$\xrightarrow{+} e = \frac{(v_B)_2 - (v_A)_2}{(v_A)_1 - (v_B)_1};\ 0.5 = \frac{(v_B)_2 - (v_A)_2}{2 - (-5)}$$

$(v_A)_2 = -1$ m/s $= 1$ m/s $\leftarrow$   *Ans.*

$(v_B)_2 = 2.5$ m/s $\rightarrow$   *Ans.*

**D-35.**  $\xrightarrow{+} \Sigma mv_1 = \Sigma mv_2;\ 6(20) + 0 = 6(v_A)_2 + 24(v_B)_2$

$$\xrightarrow{+} e = \frac{(v_B)_2 - (v_A)_2}{(v_A)_1 - (v_B)_1};\ 1 = \frac{(v_B)_2 - (v_A)_2}{20 - 0}$$

$(v_A)_2 = -12$ m/s $= 12$ m/s $\leftarrow$   *Ans.*

$(v_B)_2 = 8$ m/s $\rightarrow$   *Ans.*

Disk $A$:

$mv_1 + \int F \, dt = mv_2;$

$6(20) - \int F \, dt = -6(12)$

$\int F \, dt = 192$ N·s   *Ans.*

**D-36.** After collision: $T_1 + \Sigma U_{1-2} = T_2$

$$\frac{1}{2}(5)(v_A)_2^2 - 0.2(5)(9.81)\left(\frac{2}{10}\right) = 0$$

$(v_A)_2 = 0.886$ m/s

$$\frac{1}{2}(10)(v_B)_2^2 - 0.2(10)(9.81)\left(\frac{3}{10}\right) = 0$$

$(v_B)_2 = 1.085$ m/s

$\Sigma mv_1 = \Sigma mv_2$

$5(v_A)_1 + 0 = 5(0.886) + 10(1.085)$

$(v_A)_1 = 3.056$ m/s

$$e = \frac{(v_B)_2 - (v_A)_2}{(v_B)_1 - (v_A)_1} = \frac{1.085 - 0.886}{3.056 - 0} = 0.0651 \ \textit{Ans.}$$

**D-37.**  $\Sigma m(v_x)_1 = \Sigma m(v_x)_2$

$$0 + 0 = \frac{2}{9.81}(1) + \frac{11}{9.81}(v_{Bx})_2$$

$(v_{Bx})_2 = -0.1818$ m/s

$\Sigma m(v_y)_1 = \Sigma m(v_y)_2$

$$\frac{2}{9.81}(3) + 0 = 0 + \frac{11}{9.81}(v_{By})_2$$

$(v_{By})_2 = 0.545$ m/s

$$(v_B)_2 = \sqrt{(-0.1818)^2 + (0.545)^2} = 0.575 \text{ m/s } \textit{Ans.}$$

**D-38.**  $\omega_B(5) = 3(4)$

$\omega_B = 2.40$ rad/s $\gamma$   *Ans.*

$\omega_C(3) = 2.40(2)$

$\omega_C = 1.60$ rad/s $\downarrow$   *Ans.*

**D-39.**  $\theta = \theta_0 + \omega_0 t + \frac{1}{2}\alpha_c t^2$

$$\theta = 0 + 0 + \frac{1}{2}(2)(10)^2 = 100 \text{ rev} \qquad \textit{Ans.}$$

$\omega = \omega_0 + \alpha_c t$

$\omega = 0 + 2(5) = 10$ rev/s   *Ans.*

**D-40.** $\alpha = \dfrac{a_t}{r} = \dfrac{20}{2} = 10$ rad/s$^2$  *Ans.*

$10$ rev $= 20\pi$ rad

$\omega^2 = \omega_0^2 + 2\,\alpha_c(\theta - \theta_0)$

$\omega^2 = 0 + 2(10)(20\pi - 0)$

$\omega = 35.4$ rad/s  Ans.

$\theta = \theta_0 + \omega_0 t + \dfrac{1}{2}\alpha_c t^2$

$\theta = 0 + 35.4(4) + \dfrac{1}{2}(10)(4)^2 = 222$ rad

$\theta = \dfrac{222}{2\pi} = 35.3$ rev.  *Ans.*

**D-41.** $\mathbf{v}_A = \mathbf{v}_C + \boldsymbol{\omega} \times \mathbf{r}_{A/C}$

$v_A\mathbf{i} = 3\mathbf{i} + (-2\mathbf{k}) \times (-0.5\mathbf{j})$

$v_A = 2$ m/s $\rightarrow$  *Ans.*

**D-42.** $\mathbf{v}_A = \mathbf{v}_B + \boldsymbol{\omega} \times \mathbf{r}_{A/B}$

$2\mathbf{i} = 0 + (-\omega\mathbf{k}) \times (1.5\mathbf{j})$

$\omega = 1.33$ rad/s $\downarrow$

$\mathbf{v}_C = \mathbf{v}_B + \boldsymbol{\omega} \times \mathbf{r}_{C/B}$

$v_C\mathbf{i} = 0 + (-1.33\mathbf{k}) \times (1\mathbf{j})$

$v_C = 1.33$ m/s $\rightarrow$  *Ans.*

**D-43.** $\mathbf{v}_O = \mathbf{v}_A + \boldsymbol{\omega} \times \mathbf{r}_{O/A}$

$2\mathbf{i} = 0 + (-\omega\mathbf{k}) \times 1.5\mathbf{j}$

$\omega = 1.33$ rad/s $\downarrow$

$\mathbf{v}_B = \mathbf{v}_O + \boldsymbol{\omega} \times \mathbf{r}_{B/O}$

$\mathbf{v}_B = 2\mathbf{i} + (-1.33\mathbf{k}) \times (1.5 \cos 30°\,\mathbf{i} + 1.5 \sin 30°\,\mathbf{j})$

$\mathbf{v}_B = \{3\mathbf{i} - 1.73\mathbf{j}\}$ m/s  *Ans.*

**D-44.** $\mathbf{v}_A = \mathbf{v}_B + \boldsymbol{\omega} \times \mathbf{r}_{A/B}$

$-v_A\mathbf{j} = -2\mathbf{i} + \omega\mathbf{k} \times (-3\mathbf{i} - 4\mathbf{j})$

$v_A = 1.5$ m/s $\downarrow$  *Ans.*

$\omega = 0.5$ rad/s $\uparrow$  *Ans.*

**D-45.** $v_C = 4(0.6) = 2.4$ m/s $\leftarrow$

$\mathbf{v}_B = \mathbf{v}_C + \boldsymbol{\omega} \times \mathbf{r}_{B/C}$

$-v_B \sin 30°\,\mathbf{i} + v_B \cos 30°\,\mathbf{j}$

$\qquad\qquad = -2.4\mathbf{i} + (\omega_{BC}\mathbf{k}) \times (-0.6\mathbf{i})$

$v_B = 4.80$ m/s $\nwarrow$  $\omega_{BC} = 6.93$ rad/s $\downarrow$

$\omega_{AB} = \dfrac{4.80}{0.6/\sin 30°} = 4$ rad/s $\uparrow$  *Ans.*

**D-46.** $v_B = 2(1.5) = 3$ m/s $\searrow$

$\mathbf{v}_C = \mathbf{v}_B + \boldsymbol{\omega} \times \mathbf{r}_{C/B}$

$-v_C\mathbf{j} = 3 \cos 45°\,\mathbf{i} - 3 \sin 45°\,\mathbf{j}$

$\qquad\quad + (\omega\mathbf{k}) \times (1.5 \cos 45°\,\mathbf{i} - 1.5 \sin 45°\,\mathbf{j})$

$v_C = 4.24$ m/s $\downarrow$  *Ans.*

$\omega = 2$ rad/s $\downarrow$

**D-47.** $\omega = \dfrac{v_B}{r_{B/C}} = \dfrac{2}{0.4} = 5$ rad/s $\downarrow$

$\alpha = \dfrac{a_B}{r_{B/C}} = \dfrac{3}{0.4} = 7.5$ rad/s$^2$ $\downarrow$

$\mathbf{a}_A = \mathbf{a}_B + \boldsymbol{\alpha} \times \mathbf{r}_{A/B} - \omega^2 \mathbf{r}_{A/B}$

$\mathbf{a}_A = 3\mathbf{j} + (-7.5\mathbf{k}) \times (-0.4\mathbf{j}) - (5)^2(-0.4\mathbf{j})$

$\mathbf{a}_A = \{-3\mathbf{i} + 13\mathbf{j}\}$ m/s$^2$  *Ans.*

$a_B = 3$ m/s$^2$  *Ans.*

**D-48.** $\mathbf{v}_B = \mathbf{v}_A + \boldsymbol{\omega} \times \mathbf{r}_{B/A}$

$-v_B\mathbf{j} = -6\mathbf{i} + \omega\mathbf{k} \times (3 \cos 45°\,\mathbf{i} + 3 \sin 45°\,\mathbf{j})$

$\omega = 2.828$ rad/s $\downarrow$, $v_B = 6$ m/s $\downarrow$

$\mathbf{a}_B = \mathbf{a}_A + \boldsymbol{\alpha} \times \mathbf{r}_{B/A} - \omega^2 \mathbf{r}_{B/A}$

$-a_B\mathbf{j} = 2\mathbf{i} + (\alpha\mathbf{k}) \times (3 \cos 45°\,\mathbf{i} + 3 \sin 45°\,\mathbf{j})$

$\qquad\qquad\quad - (2.828)^2 (3 \cos 45°\,\mathbf{i} + 3 \sin 45°\,\mathbf{j})$

$a_B = 31.9$ m/s$^2$ $\downarrow$  *Ans.*

$\alpha = 7.06$ rad/s$^2$ $\downarrow$  *Ans.*

**D-49.** $+\swarrow \Sigma F_x = m(a_G)_x;\ (1750)(9.81) \sin 20° = 1750a_G$

$a_G = 3.355$ m/s$^2$  *Ans.*

$+\nwarrow \Sigma F_y = m(a_G)_y;$

$N_A + N_B - (1750)(9.81) \cos 20° = 0$

$\downarrow + \Sigma M_G = 0;\ N_B(1.2) - N_A(0.9) = 0$

$N_A = 9.218$ kN  *Ans.*

$N_B = 6.914$ kN  *Ans.*

**D-50.** $\downarrow + \Sigma M_A = \Sigma(M_k)_A;\ 100\left(\dfrac{3}{5}\right)(7) = (20)a(3.5)$

$a = 6.0$ m/s$^2$  *Ans.*

$\xrightarrow{+} \Sigma F_x = m(a_G)_x;\ A_x + 100\left(\dfrac{3}{5}\right) = (20)(6.0)$

$A_x = 60$ N  *Ans.*

$+\uparrow \Sigma F_y = m(a_G)_y;\ A_y - 20(9.81) + 100\left(\dfrac{4}{5}\right) = 0$

$A_y = 116.2$ N  *Ans.*

**D-51.** $\zeta + \Sigma M_B = I_B \alpha;\ 50(9.81)(1) = 2.0\alpha$

$\alpha = 24.5\ \text{rad/s}^2$ *Ans.*

$a_G = \left(\dfrac{1}{\cos 30°}\right)(24.5) = 28.3\ \text{m/s}$

$\xrightarrow{+} \Sigma F_x = m(a_G)_x;$

$B_x = (50)(28.3)\sin 30° = 707.5\ \text{N}$ *Ans.*

$+\uparrow \Sigma F_y = m(a_G)_y;$

$B_y - (50)(9.81) = -(50)(28.3)\cos 30°$

$B_y = -734.9\ \text{N}$ *Ans.*

**D-52.** $\zeta + \Sigma M_O = I_O \alpha;$

$20(9.81)(0.5) = \left[\dfrac{1}{12}(20)(3)^2 + 20(0.5)^2\right]\alpha$

$\alpha = 4.90\ \text{rad/s}^2$ *Ans.*

**D-53.** No slipping, so that

$a_G = 1.25\alpha$

$\zeta + \Sigma M_A = \Sigma(M_k)_A;\ 20(9.81)\sin 20°(1.25)$

$\qquad\qquad = 20(0.8)^2\alpha + (20a_G)(1.25)$

$\alpha = 1.90\ \text{rad/s}^2$ *Ans.*

$a_G = 2.38\ \text{m/s}^2$

**D-54.** $+\nwarrow \Sigma F_y = 0;\ N_A - 15(9.81)\cos 45° = 0;$

$N_A = 104.1\ \text{N}$

$a_G = \alpha(0.3)$

$\zeta + \Sigma M_B = \Sigma(M_k)_B;\ (0.1)(104.1)(1.55) -$

$\qquad 15(9.81)\sin 45°(0.3) = -15(0.8)^2\alpha - 15(a_G)(0.3)$

$a_G = 0.413\ \text{m/s}^2$

$\alpha = 1.38\ \text{rad/s}^2$ *Ans.*

**D-55.** $\xrightarrow{+} \Sigma F_x = m(a_G)_x;\ F_A = 2a_G$

$\zeta + \Sigma M_G = I_G \alpha;\ F_A(0.4) = 2(0.3)^2\alpha$

$\mathbf{a}_A = \mathbf{a}_G + \boldsymbol{\alpha} \times \mathbf{r}_{A/G} - \omega^2 r_{A/G}$

$5\mathbf{i} = a_G\mathbf{i} + (\alpha\mathbf{k}) \times (-0.4\mathbf{j}) - \mathbf{0}$

$5 = a_G + 0.4\alpha$

$F_A = 3.60\ \text{N}$

$a_G = 1.80\ \text{m/s}^2$

$\alpha = 8\ \text{rad/s}^2$ *Ans.*

# Answers to Selected Problems

## Chapter 12

**12–1.** $a_c = 1.74 \text{ m/s}^2, \ t = 4.80 \text{ s}$

**12–2.** $a_c = 1.6 \text{ m/s}^2, \ t = 12.5 \text{ s}$

**12–3.** $v_2 = 16.3 \text{ m/s}^2, \ t = 1.20 \text{ s}$

**12–5.** $t = 30 \text{ s}, \ s = 792 \text{ m}$

**12–6.** $s = 41.0 \text{ m}, \ a = 1.00 \text{ m/s}^2$

**12–7.** $a_{\max} = 12.6 \text{ m/s}^2, \ v_{\max} = 40.5 \text{ m/s}$

**12–9.** $t = 21.9 \text{ s}$

**12–10.** $a = 0.554 \text{ m/s}^2$

**12–11.** $v = 32 \text{ m/s}, \ s = 67 \text{ m}, \ d = 66 \text{ m}$

**12–13.** $s|_{t=6} = -5.4 \text{ m}, \ s_{\text{tot}} = 13.8 \text{ m}$

**12–14.** $s|_{t=6} = -18 \text{ m}, \ s_{\text{tot}} = 46 \text{ m}$

**12–15.** $s = 7.87 \text{ m}$

**12–17.** $d_A = 41.0 \text{ m}, \ d_B = 200 \text{ m}$
$\Delta sa_{AB} = 152 \text{ m}$

**12–18.** $a|_{t=4} = 1.06 \text{ m/s}^2$

**12–19.** $\Delta s = 48.3 \text{ m}$

**12–21.** $k = -10.2 \text{ s}^{-2}, \ s = 1.56 \text{ m}$

**12–22.** $v = 322 \text{ m/s}, \ t = 19.3 \text{ s}$

**12–23.** $t = 5.62 \text{ s}$

**12–25.** $v = 1.29 \text{ m/s}$

**12–26.** $v_B = 8.974 \text{ m/s}$

**12–29.** $\Delta s = 3.56 \text{ m}$

**12–30.** $v = 1.29 \text{ m/s}$

**12–31.** $t = 48.3 \text{ s}$

**12–33.** **a)** $v = 45.5 \text{ m/s}$, **b)** $v = 100 \text{ m/s}$

**12–34.** $v = 11.2 \text{ km/s}$

**12–35.** $v = 3.02 \text{ km/s} \downarrow$

**12–38.** $t = 7.48 \text{ s}$

**12–39.** $t' = 27.3 \text{ s}$

**12–41.** $v_{\max} = 0.89442 \text{ m/s}, \ t' = 0.44721 \text{ s}$

**12–45.** $t' = 33.3 \text{ s}$

**12–46.** $s = 114 \text{ m}$

**12–47.** $s = 1080 \text{ m}, \ (v_{\text{sp}})_{\text{avg}} = 9 \text{ m/s}$

**12–49.** $a_{\max} = 2.4 \text{ m/s}^2$

**12–50.** $(v_{\text{sp}})_{\text{avg}} = 11.3 \text{ m/s}, \ s_T = 340 \text{ m}$

**12–51.** $s = 144 \text{ m}$

**12–53.** $\Delta s = 87.5 \text{ m}$

**12–55.** At $s = 75 \text{ m}, \ v = 27.4 \text{ m/s}$;
at $s = 100 \text{ m}, \ v = 31.62 \text{ m/s}$;
at $s = 125 \text{ m}, \ v = 82.3 \text{ m/s}$

**12–58.** $t = 9.88 \text{ s}$

**12–59.** At $s = 50 \text{ m}, \ a = 0.32 \text{ m/s}^2$;
at $s = 150 \text{ m}, \ a = -0.32 \text{ m/s}^2$

**12–62.** At $s = 100 \text{ m}, \ a = 16 \text{ m/s}^2$;
at $s = 150 \text{ m}, \ a = 4.5 \text{ m/s}^2$

**12–63.** For $s = 40 \text{ m}, \ v = 12.7 \text{ m/s}$;
for $s = 90 \text{ m}, \ v = 22.8 \text{ m/s}$;
for $s = 200 \text{ m}, \ v = 36.1 \text{ m/s}$

**12–65.** At $s = 15 \text{ m}, \ v = 6.7 \text{ m/s}$;
at $s = 45 \text{ m}, \ v = 11.6 \text{ m/s}$;
at $s = 60 \text{ m}, \ v = 14.2 \text{ m/s}$

**12–66.** $(4, 2, 6) \text{ m}$

**12–67.** $a = 80.2 \text{ m/s}^2, \ (42.7, 16.0, 14.0) \text{ m}$

**12–69.** $v = 9.68 \text{ m/s}, \ a = 16.8 \text{ m/s}^2$

**12–70.** $\Delta r = 3.61 \text{ km}, \ d = 5 \text{ km}$

**12–71.** $(v_{sp})_{\text{avg}} = 4.28 \text{ m/s}$

**12–73.** $a_{AB} = \{0.404 \text{ i} + 7.07 \text{ j}\} \text{ m/s}^2,$
$a_{AC} = \{2.50 \text{ i}\} \text{ m/s}^2$

**12–74.** $v_x = 0.398 \text{ m/s}, \ v_y = 3.98 \text{ m/s}$

**12–75.** $a_y = c, \ a_x = \dfrac{c}{2k}(y + ct^2)$

**12–77.** $v_x = v_0 \left[1 + \left(\dfrac{\pi}{L}c\right)^2 \cos^2\left(\dfrac{\pi}{L}x\right)\right]^{-\frac{1}{2}},$
$v_y = \dfrac{v_0 \pi c}{L}\left(\cos\dfrac{\pi}{L}x\right)$
$\left[1 + \left(\dfrac{\pi}{L}c\right)^2 \cos^2\left(\dfrac{\pi}{L}x\right)\right]^{-\frac{1}{2}}$

**12–78.** $d = 4.00 \text{ m}, \ a = 37.8 \text{ m/s}^2$

**12–79.** $v = 201 \text{ m/s}, \ a = 405 \text{ m/s}^2$

**12–81.** $h = 2.87 \text{ m}, \ s_x = 19.9 \text{ m}$

**12–82.** $t = 3.55 \text{ s}, \ v = 32.0 \text{ m/s}$

**12–83.** $h = 3.33 \text{ m}$

**12–85.** $v_0 = 21.16 \text{ m/s}, \ \theta = 56.5°$

**12–86.** $v_A = 8.24 \text{ m/s}$

**12–87.** $v_A = 11.1 \text{ m/s}, \ h = 3.45 \text{ m}$

**12–89.** $a = g = -9.81 \text{ m/s}^2,$
$v_B = 19.5 \text{ m/s}$

**12–90.** $d = 49.11 \text{ m}$

**12–91.** $v_A = 19.4 \text{ m/s}, \ t_{AB} = 4.54 \text{ s}$

**12–93.** $x = 4.0 \text{ m}, \ y = -2.13 \text{ m}$

**12–94.** $v_A = 5.0 \text{ m/s}, \ v_B = 8.825 \text{ m/s}$

**12–95.** $v_A = 13.1 \text{ m/s}, \ s = 2.38 \text{ m}$

**12–97.** The two roots are $\theta_D = 14.7°$,
$\theta_c = 75.3°$; $\ \Delta t = 1.45 \text{ s}$

**12–98.** $x = 9.62 \text{ m}, \ y = 1.806 \text{ m}, \ v = 21.7 \text{ m/s}$

**12–99.** $d = 8.21 \text{ m}, \ v_B = 6.0 \text{ m/s}$

**12–101.** $a = 6.49 \text{ m/s}^2, \ \Delta s = 12.15 \text{ m}$

**12–102.** $a_t = 10.5 \text{ m/s}^2, \ \rho = 791.8 \text{ m}$

**12–103.** $a = 2.23 \text{ m/s}^2$

**12–105.** $v = 1.96 \text{ m/s}, \ a = 0.930 \text{ m/s}^2$

**12–106.** $a = 0.921 \text{ m/s}^2$

**12–107.** $v = 5.66 \text{ m/s}, \ a = 1.02 \text{ m/s}^2$

**12–109.** $a = 4.52 \text{ m/s}^2, \ \Delta s = 4.2 \text{ m}$

**12–110.** $v = 19.9 \text{ m/s}, \ a = 24.2 \text{ m/s}^2$

**12–111.** $a_t = 3.62 \text{ m/s}^2, \ \rho = 29.6 \text{ m}$

**12–113.** $v = 29.2 \text{ m/s}, \ a = 12.8 \text{ m/s}^2$

**12–114.** $v = 34.6 \text{ m/s}, \ a = 17.5 \text{ m/s}^2$

**12–115.** $v = 4.58 \text{ m/s}, \ a = 0.653 \text{ m/s}^2$

**12–117.** $a_n = 5.02 \text{ m/s}^2$

**12–118.** $v = 17.0 \text{ m/s}, \ a = 3.44 \text{ m/s}^2$

**12–119.** $v_B = 3.68 \text{ m/s}, \ a_B = 4.98 \text{ m/s}^2$

**12–121.** $a = 8.61 \text{ m/s}^2$

**12–122.** $y = -0.0766x^2, \ v = 8.37 \text{ m/s},$
$a_n = 9.38 \text{ m/s}^2, \ a_t = 2.88 \text{ m/s}^2$

**12–123.** $v_n = 0, \ v_t = 7.21 \text{ m/s},$
$a_n = 0.555 \text{ m/s}^2,$
$a_t = 2.77 \text{ m/s}^2$

**12–125.** **a)** $s_A = 1.40 \text{ m}, \ s_B = 3 \text{ m},$
**b)** $r_A = \{1.38 \text{ i} + 0.195 \text{ j}\} \text{ m},$
$r_B = \{-2.82 \text{ i} + 0.873 \text{ j}\} \text{ m},$
**c)** $\Delta r = 4.26 \text{ m}$

**12–126.** $t = 14.3 \text{ s}, \ a_B = 0.45 \text{ m/s}^2$

**12–127.** $t = 1.21 \text{ s}$

**12–129.** $v_x = \dfrac{v_0}{\sqrt{1 + b^2}}, \ v_y = \dfrac{v_0 b}{\sqrt{1 + b^2}},$
$a_n = \dfrac{2c \, v_0^2}{(1 + b^2)^{3/2}}$

**12–130.** $y = \{0.839x - 0.131x^2\} \text{ m},$
$a_t = 3.94 \text{ m/s}^2, \ a_n = 8.98 \text{ m/s}^2$

**12–131.** $d = 17.0 \text{ m}, \ a_A = 190 \text{ m/s}^2,$
$a_B = 12.8 \text{ m/s}^2$

**12–133.** $v = 4.58 \text{ m/s}, \ a = 0.653 \text{ m/s}^2$

**12–134.** $a = 10.5 \text{ m/s}^2, \ s = 20.1 \text{ m}$

**12–135.** $\alpha = 52.5°, \ \beta = 142°, \ \gamma = 85.1°$
or $\alpha = 128°, \ \beta = 37.9°, \ \gamma = 94.9°$

**12–137.** $v_r = -1.66 \text{ m/s}, \ v_\theta = -2.07 \text{ m/s},$
$a_r = -4.20 \text{ m/s}^2, \ a_\theta = 2.97 \text{ m/s}^2$

**12–138.** $a = 14.3 \text{ m/s}^2$

**12–139.** $v = 40$ m/s, $a = 25.6$ m/s$^2$

**12–141.** $v_r = -2.33$ m/s, $v_\theta = 7.91$ m/s,
$a_r = -158$ m/s$^2$, $a_\theta = -18.6$ m/s$^2$

**12–142.** $a = 2.32$ m/s$^2$

**12–143.** $v_r = 16.0$ m/s, $v_\theta = 1.94$ m/s
$a_r = 7.76$ m/s$^2$, $a_\theta = 1.94$ m/s$^2$

**12–145.** $a_r = -6.67$ m/s$^2$, $a_\theta = 3$ m/s$^2$

**12–146.** $a = 48.3$ cm/s$^2$

**12–147.** $v_r = 1.20$ m/s, $v_\theta = 1.26$ m/s,
$a_r = -3.77$ m/s$^2$, $a_\theta = 7.20$ m/s$^2$

**12–149.** $v_r = 1.20$ m/s, $v_\theta = 1.50$ m/s,
$a_r = -4.50$ m/s$^2$, $a_\theta = 7.20$ m/s$^2$

**12–150.** $v = 12.6$ m/s, $a = 83.2$ m/s$^2$

**12–151.** $\mathbf{v} = \{-116\mathbf{u}_r - 163\mathbf{u}_z\}$ mm/s,
$\mathbf{a} = \{-5.81\mathbf{u}_r - 8.14\mathbf{u}_z\}$ mm/s$^2$

**12–153.** $a = 0.217$ m/s$^2$

**12–154.** $v_r = -0.212$ m/s, $v_\theta = 0.812$ m/s,
$a_r = -0.703$ m/s$^2$, $a_\theta = 0.0838$ m/s$^2$

**12–155.** $v_r = -2.80$ m/s, $v_\theta = 19.8$ m/s

**12–157.** $v = 1.98$ m/s, $a = 1.15$ m/s$^2$

**12–158.** $v = 7.23$ m/s, $a = 2.45$ m/s$^2$

**12–160.** $v = 164$ mm/s, $a = 668$ mm/s$^2$

**12–161.** $\dot{\theta} = 0.0178$ rad/s

**12–162.** $\ddot{\theta} = 0.00404$ rad/s$^2$

**12–163.** $v_r = -\dfrac{6}{\sqrt{1 + \theta^2}}$, $v_\theta = \dfrac{6\theta}{\sqrt{1 + \theta^2}}$
When $\theta = 1$ rad, $v_r = -4.24$ m/s
$v_\theta = 4.24$ m/s

**12–165.** $v_r = 0.242$ m/s, $v_\theta = 0.943$ m/s,
$a_r = -2.32$ m/s$^2$, $a_\theta = 1.74$ m/s$^2$

**12–166.** $a = 6.54$ m/s$^2$

**12–167.** $\dot{\theta} = 0.75$ rad/s

**12–169.** $v = 7.83$ m/s, $a = 2.27$ m/s$^2$

**12–170.** $v = 0.242$ m/s, $a = 0.169$ m/s$^2$,
$v_x = 0.162$ m/s, $v_y = 0.180$ m/s

**12–171.** $v = 6.0$ m/s, $a = 22.4$ m/s$^2$

**12–173.** $v_B = 0.5$ m/s ↑

**12–174.** $v_A = 4$ m/s →

**12–175.** $t = 160$ s

**12–177.** $v_P = 3.6$ m/s

**12–178.** $\Delta s_B = 0.5$ m ↑

**12–179.** $v_A = 0.3$ m/s ↑, $a_A = 0.15$ m/s$^2$ ↓

**12–181.** $v_B = 0.3$ m/s ↑

**12–182.** $v_{B/C} = 10$ m/s ↑

**12–183.** $v_E = 0.250$ m/s ↑

**12–185.** $v_C = 0.45$ m/s ↑

**12–186.** $v_C = 0.667$ m/s ↑

**12–187.** $\dot{s}_B = 0.36$ m/s ↓, $\ddot{s}_B = 0.334$ m/s$^2$ ↑

**12–189.** $v_C = 1.2$ m/s ↑, $a_C = 0.512$ m/s$^2$ ↑

**12–190.** $\dot{x}_B = 1.82$ m/s

**12–191.** $v_B = 1.41$ m/s ↑

**12–193.** $v_A = -v_B\left(1 + \left(\dfrac{h}{s_A}\right)^2\right)^{1/2}$,
$a_A = -a_B\left(1 + \left(\dfrac{h}{s_B}\right)^2\right)^{1/2} + \dfrac{v_A v_B h^2}{s_A^3}\left(1 + \left(\dfrac{h}{s_A}\right)^2\right)^{-1/2}$

**12–194.** $\Delta s_C = 0.6$ m

**12–195.** $v_{A/C} = 2.40$ m/s, $\theta = 50.3°$ ↗

**12–197.** $v_{B/A} = 42.3$ km/h, $\theta = 40.9°$ ↙
$a_{B/A} = 2.87(10^3)$ km/h$^2$, $\theta = 72.0°$ ↙

**12–198.** $a_{B/A} = 3128$ km/h$^2$, $\theta = 0.767°$ ↘

**12–199.** $v_{A/B} = 6.51$ m/s, $\theta = 18.0°$ ↗
$t = 36.9$ s

**12–201.** $v_{A/B} = 6.69$ m/s, $\theta = 53.3°$ ↗,
$a_{A/B} = 1.52$ m/s$^2$, $\theta = 41.9°$ ↗

**12–202.** $v_{B/A} = 45.6$ km/h, $\theta = 44.5°$ ↙
$a_{B/A} = 5469$ km/h$^2$, $\theta = 80.6°$ ↙

**12–203.** $v_{A/B} = 29.5$ m/s, $\theta = 67.6°$ ↗
$a_{A/B} = 5.94$ m/s$^2$, $\theta = 57.4°$ ↙

**12–205.** $v_b = 6.21$ m/s, $t = 11.4$ s

**12–206.** $v_r = 34.6$ km/h

**12–207.** $v_{C/B} = 17.8$ m/s, $\theta = 76.2°$ ↘,
$a_{C/B} = 9.81$ m/s$^2$ ↓

## Chapter 13

**13–1.** $F = 199(10^{18})$N

**13–2.** $v = 13.0$ m/s, $s = 17.1$ m

**13–3.** $t_B = 1.09$ s, $t_C = 1.54$ s, $t_D = 2.32$ s

**13–5.** $a = 0.19$ m/s$^2$ ↑

**13–6.** $a = 0.343$ m/s$^2$, $a = 0.436$ m/s$^2$

**13–7.** $T = 3.01$ kN

**13–9.** $a = 1.66$ m/s$^2$

**13–10.** $a = 1.75$ m/s$^2$

**13–11.** $v_2 = 19.226$ m/s

**13–13.** $s = 227.8$ m

**13–14.** $a_A = \dfrac{P}{2m} - 2\mu g$

**13–15.** $a = 1.04$ m/s

**13–17.** For $0 \le t < 10$ s: $F = 3211$ N
for $10 < t \le 30$ s: $F = 535$ N

**13–18.** $a = 4.50$ m/s$^2$

**13–19.** $R = 1.33$ m, $t = 1.65$ s

**13–21.** $T = 4.92$ kN

**13–22.** $v = 4.68$ m/s

**13–23.** $s = 19.6$ m

**13–25.** $m_A = 13.7$ kg

**13–26.** $a_E = 0.75$ m/s$^2$ ↑, $T = 1.32$ kN

**13–27.** $a_B = 0.7$ m/s$^2$ ↑

**13–29.** $s = 5.43$ m

**13–30.** $a_A = 1.51$ m/s$^2$ ↑, $T_A = 90.6$ N,
$a_B = 6.04$ m/s$^2$ ↓, $T_B = 22.6$ N

**13–31.** $v = 30$ m/s

**13–33.** $a_C = 7.49$ m/s$^2$, $\theta = 22.8°$ ↗

**13–34.** **a)** $T = 200$ N **b)** $T = 297.9$ N

**13–35.** $A_x = 361.2$ N, $A_y = 2361$ N
$M_A = 2722$ N

**13–37.** $t = 2.04$ s

**13–38.** $v = 11.1$ m/s

**13–39.** $v_B = 4.52$ m/s

**13–41.** $a_B = 2.36$ m/s$^2$

**13–42.** $P = 2mg \tan\theta$

**13–43.** $P = 2mg\left(\dfrac{\sin\theta + \mu_s \cos\theta}{\cos\theta - \mu_s \sin\theta}\right)$

**13–45.** $x = \dfrac{mv_0}{k}\cos\theta_0(1 - e^{-(k/m)t})$,
$y = -\dfrac{mgt}{k} + \dfrac{m}{k}\left(v_0 \sin\theta_0 + \dfrac{mg}{k}\right)(1 - e^{-(k/m)t})$,
$x_{\max} = \dfrac{mv_0 \cos\theta_0}{k}$

**13–46.** $T = 1.63$ kN

**13–47.** $T = 1.80$ kN

**13–49.** $x = d$, $v = \sqrt{\dfrac{kd^2}{(m_A + m_B)}}$

**13–50.** $x = d$

**13–51.** $d = \dfrac{(m_A + m_B)g}{k}$

**13–53.** $v_{max} = 24.4$ m/s

**13–54.** $v_{min} = 12.2$ m/s

**13–55.** $3.13$ m/s

**13–57.** $T = 9.09$ kN, $\theta = 43.3°$

**13–59.** $a_t = 4.905$ m/s$^2$, $T = 175.8$ N

**13–61.** $\theta = 72.2°$

**13–62.** $\theta = 69.2°$

**13–63.** $v = 31.3$ m/s

**13–65.** $N = 1170$ N, $F = 191$ N

**13–66.** $\theta = 47.0°$

**13–67.** $v = 6.30$ m/s, $F_n = 283$ N, $F_t = 0$,
$F_b = 490$ N

**13–69.** $a_t = 3.36$ m/s$^2$ ↙, $T = 361$ N

**13–70.** $v_C = 5.42$ m/s, $N_C = 78.24$ N
$v_B = 5.72$ m/s

**13–71.** $\rho = 9.32$ m

**13–73.** $F_f = 3.51$ kN, $N = 6.73$ kN

**13–74.** $v = 2.10$ m/s

**13–75.** $N = 57.64$ N, $a_t = 7.0$ m/s$^2$

**13–77.** $v = 1.48$ m/s

**13–78.** $t = 7.39$ s

**13–79.** $N = 1.02$ kN

**13–81.** $a_t = 8.9$ m/s$^2$, $N = 347.3$ N

**13–82.** $a = 7.32$ m/s$^2$, $N = 59.2$ N

**13–83.** $F_r = -240$ N, $F_\theta = 66$ N,
$F_z = -3.28$ N

**13–85.** $F_A = 42.50$ N

**13–86.** $(F_A)_{max} = 42.50$ N,
$(F_A)_{min} = 29.50$ N

**13–87.** $(F_z)_{min} = 15.6$ N, $(F_z)_{max} = 23.6$ N

**13–89.** $N = 30.34$ N

**13–90.** $F = 4.71$ N

**13–91.** $N = 5.79$ N, $F = 1.78$ N

**13–93.** $N = 59.3$ N, $P = 17.8$ N

**13–94.** $F = -0.509$ N

**13–95.** $F = -0.353$ N

**13–97.** $F = 7.67$ N

**13–98.** $F = 7.82$ N

**13–99.** $F_r = -20.0$ N, $F_\theta = 0$, $F_z = 2.45$ kN

**13–101.** $\dot{\theta} = 4.00$ rad/s, $T = 8$ N

**13–102.** $N = 24.8$ N, $F = 24.8$ N

**13–103.** $N = 54.4$ N, $F = 54.4$ N

**13–105.** $T = 3340$ N

**13–106.** $a_t = 12$ m/s$^2$, $5.71°$↘

**13–107.** $a_t = 11.0$ m/s$^2$, $5.71°$↘

**13–109.** $P = 206.8$ N, $N = 69.3$ N

**13–110.** $N = 597.1$ N

**13–111.** $r = 0.198$ m

**13–114.** $v_B = 7.71$ km/s, $v_A = 4.63$ km/s

**13–115.** $v_p = 7.31$ km/s

**13–117.** **a)** $r = 317(10^3)$ km,
**b)** $r = 640(10^3)$ km,
**c)** $317(10^3)$ km $< r < 640(10^3)$ km
**d)** $r > 640(10^3)$ km

**13–118.** $v_{r/s} = 1.68$ km/s

**13–119.** $v_0 = 7.45$ km/s

**13–121.** $v_p = 7.47$ km/s

**13–122.** $v_a = 3.94$ km/s, $t = 46.1$ min

**13–123.** $\Delta v_A = -466$ m/s,
$\Delta v_B = -2.27$ km/s

**13–125.** $v_A = 6.11$ km/s, $\Delta v_B = -2.37$ km/s

**13–126.** $v_B = 1.20$ km/s, $\Delta v_A = -2.17$ km/s

**13–127.** $t = 2.90$ hr, $v = 4.42$ km/s,
$\Delta v = 578$ m/s

## Chapter 14

**14–1.** $U_W = 4.12$ kJ, $U_{N_P} = -2.44$ kJ;
The difference accounts for a change
in kinetic energy.

**14–2.** $s = 59.7$ m

**14–3.** $v = 12.6$ m/s

**14–5.** $v = 0.090$ m/s

**14–6.** $v_2 = 2.12$ km/s (approx.)

**14–7.** $k = 15.0$ MN/m$^2$

**14–9.** $d = 12$ m

**14–10.** $s = 179$ mm

**14–11.** $s = 3.41$ m

**14–13.** $v_2 = 6.08$ m/s in $A$'s frame,
$v_2 = 4.08$ m/s in $B$'s frame

**14–14.** $v = 2.64$ m/s, $T = 115$ N

**14–15.** $v_A = 1.77$ m/s

**14–17.** $v_C = 1.37$ m/s

**14–18.** $h = 47.5$ m

**14–19.** $v_2 = 15.4$ m/s

**14–21.** $s = 2.29$ m

**14–22.** $v_A = 1.12$ m/s

**14–23.** $v_B = 2.18$ m/s, $N_B = 135.8$ N,
$v_C = 5.13$ m/s
$N_C = 664$ N, $v_D = 5.50$ m/s

**14–25.** $k_B = 11.1$ kN/m

**14–26.** $s = 0.510$ m, $T_A = 360$ N

**14–27.** $s_{Tot} = 3.185$ m

**14–29.** $\rho = 17.64$ m

**14–30.** $v_A = 28.3$ m/s

**14–31.** $s = 0.730$ m

**14–33.** $y = 0.815$ m, $N_b = 568$ N,
$a = 6.23$ m/s$^2$

**14–34.** $s = 1.67$ m

**14–35.** $v_D = 17.7$ m/s, $R = 33.0$ m

**14–37.** $s = 0.572$ m

**14–38.** $v_A = 3.82$ m/s

**14–39.** $v_C = 2.36$ m/s

**14–41.** $P_{avg} = 200$ kW

**14–42.** power input $= 9.23$ kW

**14–43.** $\Delta t = 5.10$ s

**14–45.** power input $= 102$ kW

**14–46.** $P_{max} = 118$ kW

**14–47.** $s = 34.0$ m

**14–49.** $P_{min} = 531.2$ W

**14–50.** $s = \dfrac{mv^3}{3P}$

**14–51.** $t = 63.4$ min

**14–53.** $P_O = 35.4$ kW

**14–54.** $P_O = 1.12$ kW

**14–55.** $P_i = 22.2$ kW

**14–57.** $P_i = 483$ kW

**14–58.** $P_i = 622$ kW

**14–59.** $P_i = 1.35$ kW

**14–61.** $P = 0.174$ kW

**14–62.** For $0 \le t \le 0.2$: $P = 53.3t$ kW;
for $0.2 \le t \le 0.3$:
$P = (160t - 533t^2)$ kW;
$U = 1.69$ kJ

**14–63.** $P_{max} = 10.7$ kW

**14–65.** $v_A = 1.17$ m/s

**14–66.** $v = 1.37$ m/s

**14–67.** $s = 0.730$ m

**14–69.** $v_B = 2.18$ m/s, $N_B = 135.8$ N

$v_C = 5.13$ m/s,

$N_C = 664$ N, $v_D = 5.50$ m/s

**14–70.** $k_B = 287$ N/m

**14–71.** $v_B = 8.86$ m/s

**14–73.** $v_2 = 8.43$ m/s

**14–74.** $v_2 = 4.53$ m/s

**14–75.** $v_A = 2.45$ m/s

**14–77.** $v = 3.796$ m/s, $N_C = 94.6$ N

**14–78.** $v_C = 9.8$ m/s

**14–79.** $h = 24.5$ m, $N_B = 0$, $N_C = 16.8$ kN

**14–81.** $v_C = 7.58$ m/s,

just before striking $B$: $T = 1.56$ kN,

just after striking $B$: $T = 2.90$ kN

**14–82.** $v_B = 10.6$ m/s

**14–83.** $l = 30$ m, $h = 73.0$ m, $a = 147.2$ m/s$^2$

**14–85.** $v = 31.32$ m/s, $N_G = 4758$ N

**14–86.** $\theta = 22.3°$, $s = 0.587$ m

**14–87.** $x = 8.86$ m, $y = 4.43$ m

**14–89.** $d = 8.53$ m, $v_D = 10$ m/s

**14–90.** $\theta = 48.2°$

**14–91.** $v = 9.78$ m/s

**14–93.** Only one spring compresses, by

$s = 0.063$ m

**14–94.** $s_A = 1.515$ m

# Chapter 15

**15–1.** $v = 10.3$ m/s

**15–2.** $t = 0.306$ s, $v_B = 5.20$ m/s

**15–3.** $t = 0.432$ s

**15–5.** $I = 450$ N·s

**15–6.** $I = 0.706$ N·s, $40°\measuredangle$

**15–7.** $I = 1.02$ N·s

**15–9.** $I = 63.4$ N·s

**15–10.** $I = 2.61$ N·s, $30°\measuredangle$

**15–11.** $t = 8.85$ m/s

**15–13.** $F_0 = 2.67$ kN

**15–14.** $v = 7.40$ m/s in $A$'s frame,

$v = 5.40$ m/s in $B$'s frame

**15–15.** $t = 8.77$ s

**15–17.** $F = 24$ kN, $T = 24$ kN

**15–18.** $F_{avg} = 19.9$ kN

**15–19.** $I = 63.4$ N·s

**15–21.** $(v_x)_2 = 20.8$ m/s $\leftarrow$

**15–22.** $v = 20.4$ m/s

**15–23.** $I = 8.49$ N·s

**15–25.** $v_A = 6.54$ m/s $\uparrow$, $v_B = 6.54$ m/s

**15–26.** $t = 5.47$ s

**15–27.** $(v_A)_2 = 3.22$ m/s $\rightarrow$

**15–29.** $v_2 = 21.8$ m/s

**15–30.** $v_2 = 3.44$ m/s $\downarrow$

**15–31.** $v_2 = 7.65$ m/s

**15–33.** $v_2 = 0.200$ m/s $\leftarrow$

**15–34.** $v = 1.75$ m/s $\rightarrow$

**15–35.** $\theta = \phi\ 9.52°$

**15–37.** $v_M = 0.178$ m/s, $N = 771$ N

**15–38.** $v_C = 0.0577$ m/s, $t = 3.06$ s

**15–39.** $s_b = 9.09$ m

**15–41.** $t_{tot} = 0.510$ s, $d_{tot} = 0.0510$ m

**15–42.** $(v_B)_2 = 1.64$ m/s

**15–43.** $W_B = 375$ N

**15–45.** $R = 29.8$ m

**15–46.** a) $v_c = 0.390$ m/s $\leftarrow$

b) $v_c = 0.390$ m/s $\leftarrow$

**15–47.** $d = 6.87$ mm

**15–49.** $v = 1$ m/s, $t = 0.510$ s

**15–50.** $t = 0.510$ s, $s = 0.255$ m

**15–51.** $v_B = 1.10$ m/s, $v_C = 5.43$ m/s, $35.8°\measuredangle$

**15–53.** $v_{b/c} = 0.632$ m/s $\rightarrow$

**15–54.** $v_A = 3.29$ m/s, $v_B = 2.19$ m/s

**15–55.** $e = 0.901$

**15–57.** $(v_A)_2 = 1.53$ m/s $\leftarrow$,

$(v_B)_2 = 1.27$ m/s $\rightarrow$

**15–58.** $(v_A)_2 = 0.3322$ m/s, $(v_B)_3 = 0.307$ m/s

$(v_C)_3 = 3.79$ m/s

**15–61.** a) $v_{p2} = 7.46$ m/s, $v_{m2} = 3.70$ m/s

b) $x = 0.652$ m

**15–62.** $h = 1.204$ m

**15–63.** $(v_C)_2 = \dfrac{v(1 + e)^2}{4}$

**15–65.** $d = 6.915$ m

**15–66.** $e = 0.394$, $d = 2.62$ m

**15–67.** $h = 21.8$ mm

**15–69.** $e = \dfrac{\sin\phi}{\sin\theta}\left(\dfrac{\cos\theta - \mu\sin\theta}{\mu\sin\phi + \cos\phi}\right)$

**15–70.** $\mu = 0.25$

**15–71.** a) $(v_A)_2 = 0.600$ m/s $\leftarrow$,

$(v_B)_2 = 3.40$ m/s $\leftarrow$,

b) $s = 304$ mm

**15–73.** $v_A = 8.859$ m/s, $v_{B2} = 10.0$ m/s,

$\theta = 27.7°$

**15–74.** $v_A = 8.859$ m/s, $v_{B2} = 10.23$ m/s

$e = 0.770$

**15–75.** $h = 0.390$ m

**15–77.** $v_{B3} = 3.24$ m/s, $\theta = 43.9°$

**15–78.** $s = 0.426$ m

**15–79.** $v_b = \left(\dfrac{1 + e}{7}\right)v$

**15–81.** $d = 0.328$ m, $h = 0.220$ m

**15–82.** $(v_B)_2 = \dfrac{\sqrt{3}}{4}(1 + e)v$,

$\Delta U_k = \dfrac{3mv^2}{16}(1 - e^2)$

**15–83.** $(v_B)_2 = 0.298$ m/s, $(v_A)_2 = 0.766$ m/s,

**15–85.** $v_A = 1.35$ m/s $\rightarrow$, $v_B = 5.89$ m/s,

$32.9°\measuredangle$

**15–86.** $e = 0.0113$

**15–87.** $v_B = 3.50$ m/s, $v_A = 6.47$ m/s

**15–89.** $\theta = 90°$

**15–90.** $(H_A)_0 = \{-58.9\mathbf{i} - 29.4\mathbf{k}\}$ kg·m$^2$/s

**15–91.** $\mathbf{H}_O = \{42\mathbf{i} + 21\mathbf{k}\}$ kg·m$^2$/s

**15–93.** $(H_A)_P = -57.6$ kg·m$^2$/s,

$(H_B)_P = 94.4$ kg·m$^2$/s,

$(H_C)_P = -41.2$ kg·m$^2$/s

**15–94.** $\mathbf{H}_O = \{-541\mathbf{i} + 480\mathbf{j} - 760\mathbf{k}\}$ kg·m$^2$/s

**15–95.** $\mathbf{H}_P = \{-460\mathbf{i} - 300\mathbf{j} - 1120\mathbf{k}\}$ kg·m$^2$/s

**15–97.** $(H_A)_0 = 72.0$ kg·m$^2$/s$\downarrow$,

$(H_B)_0 = 59.5$ kg·m$^2$/s$\downarrow$

**15–98.** $(H_A)_P = 66.0$ kg·m$^2$/s$\downarrow$,

$(H_B)_P = 73.9$ kg·m$^2$/s$\downarrow$

**15–99.** $v = 3.47$ m/s

**15–101.** $v = 13.4$ m/s

**15–102.** $v_2 = 0.6$ m/s

**15–103.** $v_B = 10.2$ km/s, $r_B = 13.8$ Mm

**15–105.** $v_2 = 4.6$ m/s, $\Sigma U_{1-2} = 24.5$ J

**15–106.** $r_2 = 0.761$ m, $t = 0.739$ s

**15–107.** $v_2 = 2.30$ m/s

**15–109.** $v = 6.17$ m/s, $h = 1.94$ m

**15–110.** $h = 196$ mm, $\theta = 75.0°$

**15–111.** $F_f = 103.2$ N, $N = 864$ N

**15–113.** $A_x = 3.98$ kN, $A_y = 3.81$ kN,
$M = 1.99$ kN·m

**15–114.** $F_s = 51.9$ N, $F_y = 26.0$ N

**15–115.** $T = 3.914$ N

**15–117.** $F_x = 409$ N ←, $F_y = 8.334$ N ↑

**15–118.** $a = 0.528$ m/s²

**15–119.** $p = 452$ Pa

**15–121.** $F = v^2 \rho A$ in each case

**15–122.** $F = 163$ N

**15–123.** 9.72 N

**15–125.** $v_{max} = 165.3$ m/s

**15–126.** $F = 3.49$ kN

**15–127.** $a = 0.0476$ m/s²

**15–129.** $\dfrac{dm}{dt} = m_0\left(\dfrac{(a_0 + g)}{v_{e/r}}\right)e[(a_0 + g)/v_{e/r}]t$

**15–130.** $F_D = 11.5$ kN

**15–131.** $a = 10.9$ m/s²

**15–133.** $F = m'v^2$

**15–134.** $F = (7.85t + 0.320)$ N

**Chapter 16**

**16–1.** $\theta = 3.32$ rev, $t = 1.67$ s

**16–2.** $a_t = 0.169$ m/s², $a_n = 1080$ m/s²

**16–3.** $v_A = 2.60$ m/s, $a_A = 9.35$ m/s²

**16–5.** $\omega_B = 22.3$ rad/s

**16–6.** $\alpha = 10.0$ rad/s², $\omega = 35.4$ rad/s,
$\theta = 35.3$ rev

**16–7.** $\theta = 5443$ rev, $\omega = 740$ rad/s,
$\alpha = 8$ rad/s²

**16–9.** $v_P = 12.60$ cm/s, $a_P = 20.0$ cm/s²
$(v_{Pmax}) = 32$ cm/s

**16–10.** $a_n = 242$ m/s², $a_t = 12$ m/s²

**16–11.** $a_n = 322$ m/s², $a_t = 9$ m/s²

**16–13.** $v_B = 1.37$ m/s, $a_B = 0.472$ m/s²

**16–14.** $v = 52.0$ cm/s, $a_t = 12.0$ cm/s²,
$a_n = 1.35(10^3)$ cm/s²,

**16–15.** $t = 100$ s

**16–17.** $v_P = 390$ cm/s, $a_P = 25.3(10^3)$ cm/s²

**16–18.** $v_B = 14.7$ m/s

**16–19.** $v_B = 1.34$ m/s

**16–21.** $v_F = 0.318$ mm/s

**16–22.** $\omega_B = 465$ rad/s

**16–23.** $\omega_B = 12$ rad/s

**16–25.** $(a_P)_n = 4267$ m/s², $(a_P)_t = 20.7$ m/s²

**16–26.** $v_A = v_B = 0.72$ m/s, $a_A = 0.12$ m/s²,
$a_B = 5.185$ m/s²

**16–27.** $\omega_H = 126$ rad/s

**16–29.** $(\omega_B)_{max} = 8.49$ rad/s, $v_C = 0.6$ m/s

**16–30.** $(\omega_B)_2 = 10.6$ rad/s

**16–31.** $a = \dfrac{\omega^2}{2\pi}\left(\dfrac{r_2 - r_1}{L}\right)d$

**16–33.** $v_{AB} = \omega l\cos\theta$, $a_{AB} = -\omega^2 l\sin\theta$

**16–34.** $\dot{y} = 0.6\cot\theta$

**16–35.** $v_{CD} = -\omega l\sin\theta$, $a_{CD} = -\omega^2 l\cos\theta$

**16–37.** $v = -\left(\dfrac{r_1^2\,\omega\sin 2\theta}{2\sqrt{r_1^2\cos^2\theta + r_2^2 + 2r_1 r_2}}\right.$
$\left. + r_1\,\omega\sin\theta\right)$

**16–38.** $v_P = 18.5$ m/s ←

**16–39.** $\omega = 8.70$ rad/s, $\alpha = -50.5$ rad/s²

**16–41.** $\omega' = -\dfrac{(R - r)\omega}{r}$, $\alpha' = -\dfrac{(R - r)\alpha}{r}$

**16–42.** $\omega = \dfrac{-v(\sin\phi)}{l\cos(\phi - \theta)}$,
$\alpha = \dfrac{-v^2\sin^2\phi\sin(\phi - \theta)}{l^2\cos^3(\phi - \theta)}$

**16–43.** $\omega = -\left(\dfrac{r}{x\sqrt{x^2 - r^2}}\right)v_A$,
$\alpha = \left[\dfrac{r(2x^2 - r^2)}{x^2(x^2 - r^2)^{3/2}}\right]v_A^2$

**16–45.** $v_C = L\omega\!\uparrow$, $a_C = 0.577\,L\omega^2\!\uparrow$

**16–46.** $\omega = 1.08$ rad/s, $v_B = 4.39$ m/s

**16–47.** $v_B = \dfrac{15\omega\sin\theta}{(34 - 30\cos\theta)^{\frac{1}{2}}}$,
$a_B = \dfrac{15(\omega^2\cos\theta + \alpha\sin\theta)}{(34 - 30\cos\theta)^{\frac{1}{2}}} - \dfrac{225\omega^2\sin^2\theta}{(34 - 30\cos\theta)^{\frac{3}{2}}}$

**16–49.** $\omega_A = 2\left(\dfrac{\sqrt{2}\cos\theta - 1}{3 - 2\sqrt{2}\cos\theta}\right)$

**16–50.** $v_B = 25.2$ cm/s, 65.7° ⬊

**16–51.** $v_C = 50$ m/s

**16–53.** $\omega = 20$ rad/s, $v_A = 1$ m/s →

**16–54.** $v_C = 1.64$ m/s

**16–55.** $v_C = 1.70$ m/s

**16–57.** $\omega_{AB} = 2.00$ rad/s

**16–58.** $\omega_{CD} = 4.03$ rad/s

**16–59.** $\omega_A = 32.0$ rad/s

**16–61.** $v_G = 9$ m/s ←

**16–62.** $\omega = 5.33$ rad/s

**16–63.** $\omega_P = 5$ rad/s, $\omega_A = 1.67$ rad/s

**16–65.** $\omega_A = 0$

**16–66.** $v_A = 0.95$ m/s ←

**16–67.** $\omega_{CB} = 2.45$ rad/s ↺,
$v_C = 2.20$ m/s ←

**16–69.** $v_G = 5t$ m/s →

**16–70.** $\omega = 6$ rad/s ↺

**16–71.** $v_A = -0.173$ m/s

**16–73.** $v_D = 7.07$ m/s

**16–74.** $\omega_R = 11.4$ rad/s↓

**16–75.** $v_C = 0.776$ m/s↙, $v_D = 1.06$ m/s ↖

**16–77.** $v_E = 8.84$ cm/s

**16–78.** $v_C = 50$ m/s

**16–79.** $v_C = 1.64$ m/s

**16–81.** $v_G = 9$ m/s ←

**16–82.** $\omega = 5.33$ rad/s

**16–83.** $\omega_P = 5$ rad/s, $\omega_A = 1.67$ rad/s

**16–85.** $v_A = 0.95$ m/s ←

**16–87.** $\omega_{BC} = 6.79$ rad/s

**16–89.** $v_B = 2.2$ m/s →, $v_A = 0.849$ m/s,
45° ⬋

**16–90.** $\omega_{AB} = 6$ rad/s ↺, $v_E = 4.76$ m/s,
40.9° ⬊

**16–91.** $\omega_{BC} = 5.77$ rad/s, $\omega_{CD} = 2.17$ rad/s

**16–93.** $v_A = 18$ m/s →,
$v_C = 66$ m/s ←,
$v_B = 48.37$ m/s →, 60.3° ⬊

**16–94.** $\omega_{CB} = 7.81$ rad/s, $v_C = 2.45$ m/s

**16–95.** $\omega_{AB} = 13.1$ rad/s

**16–97.** $v_C = 2.50$ m/s, $v_E = 7.91$ m/s

**16–98.** $v_C = 0.897$ m/s ↗

**16–99.** $v_D = 0.518$ m/s ↘

**16–101.** $v_D = 5.72$ m/s, 36.2° ⬊

**16–102.** $\omega_C = 26.7$ rad/s, $\omega_B = 28.75$ rad/s,
$\omega_A = 14.0$ rad/s

**16–103.** $\omega_{AB} = 7.17$ rad/s

**16–105.** $\alpha = 1.47$ rad/s², $a_B = 12.5$ m/s² ↓

**16–106.** $\alpha = 0.0962$ rad/s²,
$a_A = 0.193$ m/s →

**16–107.** $\alpha = 0.332$ rad/s², $a_B = 7.88$ cm/s² ←

**16–109.** $a_B = 3.84$ m/s², 8.80° ⬋

**16–110.** $a_A = 12.5$ m/s² ←

**16–111.** $\alpha_{AB} = 0.75$ rad/s² ↺,
$\alpha_{BC} = 3.94$ rad/s² ↺

**16–113.** $a_B = 2.25$ m/s², 32.6°⤺

**16–114.** $a_D = 10.0$ m/s², 2.02°⤴

**16–115.** $a_A = 5.94$ m/s², 53.9°⤴

**16–117.** $\alpha_{BC} = 5.21$ rad/s² ⤹

**16–118.** $\alpha_W = 0.231$ rad/s²

**16–119.** $\omega = 2$ rad/s, $\alpha = 7.68$ rad/s² ↓,

**16–121.** $v_C = 9.38$ cm/s ↙, $a_C = 54.7$ cm/s² ↙,

**16–122.** $\alpha = 10.67$ rad/s² ⤹, $a_D = 14.1$ cm/s²

**16–123.** $\omega_F = 10.7$ rad/s, $\omega_{AC} = 0$,

$\alpha_{AC} = 28.7$ rad/s² ↓

**16–125.** $v_B = 1.58\,\omega\,a$,

$a_B = 1.58\alpha\,a - 1.77\omega^2\,a$

**16–126.** $a_A = 73.0$ cm/s², 80.5° ⤺

$a_B = 113$ cm/s² →,

$\alpha_{AB} = 18$ rad/s² ↓

**16–127.** $\alpha_{AB} = 36$ rad/s²↓

**16–129.** $\omega = 4.73$ rad/s ⤹, $\alpha = 131$ rad/s² ↓

**16–130.** $\omega = 0.25$ rad/s ↓, $v_B = 5.00$ m/s ↓,

$\alpha = 0.875$ rad/s² ⤹, $a_B = 1.51$ cm/s²,

85.2° ⤺

**16–131.** $\mathbf{a}_A = \{-5.60\mathbf{i} - 16\mathbf{j}\}$ m/s²

**16–133.** $\mathbf{v}_A = \{-2.50\mathbf{i} + 2.00\mathbf{j}\}$ m/s,

$\mathbf{a}_A = \{-3.00\mathbf{i} + 1.75\mathbf{j}\}$ m/s²

**16–134.** $\mathbf{v}_B = \{-12.0\mathbf{i} + 5.77\mathbf{j}\}$ m/s,

$\mathbf{a}_B = \{-28.9\mathbf{i} - 70.0\mathbf{j}\}$ m/s²

**16–135.** $\mathbf{v}_m = \{2\mathbf{i} - 2\mathbf{j}\}$ m/s,

$\mathbf{a}_m = \{2\mathbf{i} + 0.2\mathbf{j}\}$ m/s²,

**16–137.** a) $\mathbf{a}_B = \{-1\mathbf{i}\}$ m/s²,

b) $\mathbf{a}_B = \{-1.69\mathbf{i}\}$ m/s²

**16–138.** a) $\mathbf{a}_B = \{-1\mathbf{i} + 0.2\mathbf{j}\}$ m/s²,

b) $\mathbf{a}_B = \{-1.69\mathbf{i} + 0.6\mathbf{j}\}$ m/s²

**16–139.** $v_C = 2.40$ m/s ←,

$a_C = \{-14.4\mathbf{j}\}$ m/s²

**16–141.** $\omega_{CD} = 0.750$ rad/s,

$\alpha_{CD} = 1.95$ rad/s²

**16–142.** $\mathbf{v}_C = \{-0.944\mathbf{i} + 2.20\mathbf{j}\}$ m/s,

$\mathbf{a}_C = \{-11.2\mathbf{i} - 4.15\mathbf{j}\}$ m/s²

**16–143.** $\omega_{DC} = 3.22$ rad/s ↓,

$\alpha_{DC} = 7.26$ rad/s² ↓

**16–145.** $\omega_{BC} = 0.720$ rad/s ⤹,

$\alpha_{BC} = 2.02$ rad/s² ⤹,

**16–146.** $\omega_{CD} = 1.73$ rad/s, $\alpha_{CD} = 3.46$ rad/s²

**16–147.** $\mathbf{v}_C = \{-3.5\mathbf{i} + 8.66\mathbf{j}\}$ m/s,

$\mathbf{a}_C = \{-17.32\mathbf{i} - 7.55\mathbf{j}\}$ m/s²

**16–149.** $\mathbf{v}_C = \{-3.75\mathbf{i} - 18.5\mathbf{j}\}$ m/s,

$\mathbf{a}_C = \{42.5\mathbf{i} - 3.75\mathbf{j}\}$ m/s²

**16–150.** $\mathbf{v}_D = \{-15.75\mathbf{i} - 6.50\mathbf{j}\}$ m/s,

$\mathbf{a}_D = \{6.5\mathbf{i} - 39.75\mathbf{j}\}$ m/s²

## Chapter 17

**17–1.** $I_y = \dfrac{1}{3}m\,l^2$

**17–2.** $I_z = m\,R^2$

**17–3.** $I_x = \dfrac{3}{10}m\,r^2$

**17–5.** $k_y = 1.56$ cm

**17–6.** $I_x = \dfrac{2}{5}m\,r^2$

**17–7.** $I_z = m\left(R^2 + \dfrac{3}{4}a^2\right)$

**17–9.** $I_y = 0.0294$ kg·m²

**17–10.** $I_x = \dfrac{93}{70}mb^2$

**17–11.** $I_y = \dfrac{m}{6}(a^2 + h^2)$

**17–13.** $L = 6.39$ m, $I_o = 53.2$ kg·m²

**17–14.** $I_o = 6.99$ kg·m²

**17–15.** $I_A = 7.67$ kg·m²

**17–17.** $I_O = \dfrac{1}{2}ma^2$

**17–18.** $I_A = 106.65$ kg·m²

**17–19.** $k_O = 3.15$ m

**17–21.** $I_O = 13.4$ kg·m²

**17–22.** $I_X = 2947$ kg·m²

**17–23.** $I_O = 6.23$ kg·m²

**17–25.** $a_{max} = 4.73$ m/s²

**17–26.** $a_G = 1.84$ m/s²

**17–27.** $F_{CD} = 289$ kN

**17–29.** $N_A = 568$ N, $N_B = 544$ N

**17–30.** $a = 3.96$ m/s²

**17–31.** $N_B = 475$ N, $N_A = 525$ N

$s = 2.94$ m

**17–33.** $M_A = 78.8(10^3)$ N·m

**17–34.** $T = 1.52$ kN, $\theta = 18.6°$

**17–35.** $T = 2.38$ kN, $a = 1.33$ m/s²

**17–37.** $T = 15.7$ kN, $C_x = 8.92$ kN,

$C_y = 16.3$ kN

**17–38.** For rear-wheel drive: $t = 17.5$ s,

for 4-wheel drive: $t = 11.3$ s

**17–39.** $N_A = 6969$ N, $N_B = 4281$ N

$t = 2.68$ s

**17–41.** $a_G = 0.327$ m/s², $N_B = 433.3$ N

$N_A = 1066.7$ N

**17–43.** $a = 29.4$ m/s²

**17–45.** $s = 24.5$ m loaded or empty

**17–46.** $a = 2.01$ m/s² The crate will slide.

**17–47.** $N_A' = 383$ N, $N_B' = 620$ N

**17–49.** $N_B = 402$ N, $N_A = 391$ N

**17–50.** $\alpha = 5.95$ rad/s²

**17–51.** $\alpha = 9.82$ rad/s²

**17–53.** $A_x = 0$, $A_y = 262$ N

**17–54.** $\omega = 56.2$ rad/s, $A_x = 0$, $A_y = 98.1$ N

**17–55.** $\omega = 20.8$ rad/s

**17–57.** $P = 39.6$ N, $N_A = N_B = 325$ N

**17–58.** $\omega = 8.35$ rad/s

**17–59.** $\omega = 6.03$ rad/s

**17–61.** $\alpha = 7.28$ rad/s²

**17–62.** $t = 6.71$ s

**17–63.** $\omega = 2.71$ rad/s

**17–66.** $r_P = 2.67$ m, $A_x = 0$

**17–67.** $\alpha = 7.36$ rad/s², $a_G = 7.36$ m/s²

**17–69.** $\omega = 150$ rad/s

**17–70.** $A_x = 11.25$ kN, $A_y = 18.75$ kN

**17–71.** $8.82$ m/s²

**17–73.** $F_{CB} = 193$ N, $t = 3.11$ s

**17–74.** $\alpha = \dfrac{2mg}{R(M + 2m)}$, $v = \sqrt{\dfrac{8mgR}{M + 2m}}$

**17–75.** $a = \dfrac{g(M_B - M_A)}{\frac{1}{2}M + M_B + M_A}$

**17–77.** $M = 0.3gml$

**17–78.** $v = 0.548$ m/s

**17–79.** $A_x = 89.2$ N, $A_y = 66.9$ N, $t = 1.26$ s

**17–81.** $\theta = 29.8°$

**17–82.** $t = 3.57$ s

**17–83.** $N = \omega x\left[\dfrac{\omega^2}{g}\left(L - \tfrac{x}{2}\right) + \cos\theta\right]$,

$V = \omega x \sin\theta$, $M = \tfrac{1}{2}\omega x^2 \sin\theta$

**17–85.** $\omega = 800$ rad/s

**17–86.** $\omega = 9.72$ rad/s

**17–89.** does not slip

**17–90.** $\alpha = 0.250$ rad/s², $a_B = 14.93$ m/s²

80.3° ⤺,

**17–91.** $a_G = 3.924$ m/s², $\alpha = 2.35$ rad/s²

**17–93.** $\alpha = 1.25$ rad/s, $T = 2.32$ kN

**17–94.** $T = 3.13$ kN, $\alpha = 1.684$ rad/s,

$a_C = 1.35$ m/s²

**17–95.** $\alpha = 1.30 \text{ rad/s}^2$

**17–97.** $\alpha = 15.6 \text{ rad/s}^2$

**17–98.** $\omega = 5.22 \text{ rad/s}$

**17–99.** $T = 5.61 \text{ N}, \ \alpha = 28.0 \text{ rad/s}^2$

**17–101.** $a_A = 51 \text{ m/s}^2$

**17–102.** $\alpha = 5.01 \text{ rad/s}^2$

**17–103.** $B_x = 166.7 \text{ N}, B_y = 187.5 \text{ N},$
$C_y = 312.5 \text{ N}$

**17–105.** $\alpha = \dfrac{6P}{mL}, \ a_B = \dfrac{2P}{m} \rightarrow$

**17–106.** $\alpha = \dfrac{3g}{2l} \cos\theta$

**17–107.** $s = 1.19 \text{ m}$

**17–109.** $A_y = 150 \text{ N}, A_x = 15.29 \text{ N},$
$a_G = 1.00 \text{ m/s}^2$

**17–110.** $A_y = 118 \text{ N}$

**17–111.** $\alpha = 13.4 \text{ rad/s}^2$

**17–113.** $B_y = 97.86 \text{ N}, \alpha = 7.13 \text{ rad/s}^2$

## Chapter 18

**18–2.** $\omega = 14.1 \text{ rad/s}$

**18–3.** $T = 1687.5 \text{ N} \cdot \text{m}$

**18–5.** $T = 0.0087 \text{ N} \cdot \text{m}$

**18–6.** $\omega = 8.35 \text{ rad/s}$

**18–7.** $\omega = 6.03 \text{ rad/s}$

**18–9.** $\omega = 2.02 \text{ rad/s}$

**18–10.** $\omega = 5.65 \text{ rad/s}$

**18–11.** $s = 0.250 \text{ m}$

**18–13.** $\omega_2 = 2.83 \text{ rad/s}$

**18–14.** $v_A = 13.5 \text{ m/s}$

**18–15.** $U = 237 \text{ J}$

**18–17.** $\omega = 11.2 \text{ rad/s}$

**18–18.** $v = 4.97 \text{ m/s}$

**18–19.** $v = 5.34 \text{ m/s}$

**18–21.** $v = 2.10 \text{ m/s}$

**18–22.** $\omega = 11.0 \text{ rad/s}$

**18–23.** $s = 2.00 \text{ m}$

**18–25.** $\omega_{AB} = 3.70 \text{ rad/s}$

**18–26.** $\omega = 0.731 \text{ rad/s}$

**18–27.** $\theta = 8.53°$

**18–29.** $\theta = 0.891 \text{ rad/s} \text{ regardless of orientation}$

**18–30.** $\omega_{AB} = 2.36 \text{ rad/s}$

**18–31.** $\theta_0 = 1.66 \text{ rad}$

**18–33.** $v_G = 3\sqrt{\dfrac{3}{7}gR}$

**18–34.** $v_A = 4.29 \text{ m/s}$

**18–35.** $\omega = 2.83 \text{ rad/s}$

**18–37.** $\omega_{AB} = 2.36 \text{ rad/s}$

**18–38.** $s = 0.250 \text{ m}$

**18–39.** $v_G = v_A = 4.29 \text{ m/s}$

**18–41.** $s = 0.301 \text{ m}, \ T = 163 \text{ N}$

**18–42.** $k = 42.8 \text{ N/m}$

**18–43.** $\omega = 1.01 \text{ rad/s}$

**18–45.** $\omega_{AB} = \omega_{BC} = \sqrt{\dfrac{3g}{L}\sin\theta}$

**18–46.** $\omega = 19.8 \text{ rad/s}$

**18–47.** $v_A = 1.40 \text{ m/s}$

**18–49.** $\omega = 0.962 \text{ rad/s}$

**18–50.** $v = 1.52 \text{ m/s}$

**18–51.** $\theta = 70.5°$

**18–53.** $\omega = 5.02 \text{ rad/s}$

**18–54.** $\omega = 41.8 \text{ rad/s}$

**18–55.** $\omega = 39.3 \text{ rad/s}$

**18–57.** $\omega = 2.17 \text{ rad/s}$

**18–58.** $\theta = 32.3°$

**18–59.** $k = 1668 \text{ N/m}$

## Chapter 19

**19–5.** $\omega = 20.8 \text{ rad/s}$

**19–6.** $\omega = 56.2 \text{ rad/s}, \ A_x = 0, \ A_y = 98.1 \text{ N}$

**19–7.** $\omega = 150 \text{ rad/s}$

**19–9.** $T_{BC} = 193 \text{ N}, \ t = 3.11 \text{ s}$

**19–10.** $\omega = 18.7 \text{ rad/s}$

**19–11.** $\omega = 2.32 \text{ rad/s}, (v_G)_2 = 377 \text{ m/s}$

**19–13.** $\omega = 6.13 \text{ rad/s}$

**19–14.** $\omega_B = 3.56 \text{ rad/s}, \ t = 5.12 \text{ s}$

**19–15.** $\int M \, dt = 0.833 \text{ kg} \cdot \text{m}^2/\text{s}$

**19–17.** $\omega = 27.9 \text{ rad/s}$

**19–18.** $v_A = 24.1 \text{ m/s}$

**19–19.** $\omega = 3.88 \text{ rad/s}$

**19–21.** $t = 5.08 \text{ s}$

**19–22.** $\omega_2 = 16.35 \text{ rad/s}$

**19–23.** $v_B = 10.25 \text{ m/s}$

**19–25.** $\omega = 119 \text{ rad/s}, v_G = 20.2 \text{ m/s}, 22.5° \, \measuredangle$

**19–26.** $\theta = \tan^{-1}(3.5\mu)$

**19–27.** $v_B = 1.30 \text{ m/s}$

**19–29.** $\omega_0 = 2.5\left(\dfrac{v_0}{r}\right)$

**19–30.** $y = \dfrac{\sqrt{2}}{3}a$

**19–31.** $\int F \, dt = 15.2 \text{ kN} \cdot \text{s}$

**19–33.** $v_0 = \sqrt{\dfrac{2gd m_s}{m}\sin\theta}$

**19–34.** $\omega = \dfrac{m_A k_A^2 \omega_A + m_B k_B^2 \omega_B}{m_A k_A^2 + m_B k_B^2}$

**19–35.** $\omega = 0.175 \text{ rad/s}$

**19–37.** $\omega' = \dfrac{11}{3}\omega_1$

**19–38.** $(\omega_z)_2 = 6.75 \text{ rad/s}$

**19–39.** a) $\omega_M = 0$, b) $\omega_M = \dfrac{I}{I_z}\omega$, c) $\omega_M = \dfrac{2I}{I_z}\omega$

**19–41.** $\omega = 0.0906 \text{ rad/s}$

**19–42.** $\omega = 0.0708 \text{ rad/s}$

**19–43.** $\omega_2 = \dfrac{1}{3}\omega_1$

**19–45.** $\omega_1 = 7.37 \text{ rad/s}$

**19–46.** $h = \dfrac{7}{5}r$

**19–47.** $\theta = 17.9°$

**19–49.** $\omega = 3.23 \text{ rad/s}, \theta = 32.8°$

**19–50.** $\theta = 22.4°$

**19–51.** $(v_b)_2 = 3.36 \text{ m/s} \rightarrow$

**19–53.** $\omega_2 = 7.73 \text{ rad/s}$

**19–54.** $\omega_1 = 1.02\sqrt{\dfrac{g}{r}}$

**19–55.** $\theta = \tan^{-1}\left(\sqrt{\dfrac{7}{5}e}\right)$

## Chapter 20

**20–1.** $\mathbf{v}_A = \{-1.56\mathbf{i} - 3.6\mathbf{j} + 6.24\mathbf{k}\} \text{ m/s},$
$\mathbf{a}_A = \{-7.23\mathbf{i} - 4.0\mathbf{j} - 2.16\mathbf{k}\} \text{ m/s}^2$

**20–2.** $\mathbf{v}_A = \{-1.56\mathbf{i} - 3.6\mathbf{j} + 6.24\mathbf{k}\} \text{ m/s},$
$\mathbf{a}_A = \{-1.0\mathbf{i} - 6.40\mathbf{j} + 2.0\mathbf{k}\} \text{ m/s}^2$

**20–3.** $\omega = \{5.66\mathbf{j} + 6.26\mathbf{k}\} \text{ rad/s},$
$\alpha = \{-3.39\mathbf{i}\} \text{ rad/s}^2$

**20–5.** $\mathbf{v}_C = \{-0.800\mathbf{i} + 0.400\mathbf{j} + 0.800\mathbf{k}\} \text{ m/s},$
$\mathbf{a}_C = \{-10.3\mathbf{i} - 3.84\mathbf{j} + 0.320\mathbf{k}\} \text{ m/s}^2$

**20–6.** $\omega = 41.2 \text{ rad/s}, v_P = 4.00 \text{ m/s},$
$\alpha = 400 \text{ rad/s}^2, \ a_P = 100 \text{ m/s}^2$

**20–7.** $\mathbf{v}_A = \{-2.60\mathbf{i} - 0.75\mathbf{j} + 1.30\mathbf{k}\} \text{ m/s},$
$\mathbf{a}_A = \{2.77\mathbf{i} - 11.7\mathbf{j} + 2.34\mathbf{k}\} \text{ m/s}^2$

**20–9.** $\mathbf{v}_B = \{-7.06\mathbf{i} - 7.52\mathbf{k}\}$ m/s,
$\mathbf{a}_B = \{77.3\mathbf{i} - 28.3\mathbf{j} + 0.657\mathbf{k}\}$ m/s$^2$

**20–10.**
$$\boldsymbol{\omega}_A = \left(\frac{r_C}{h_1}\right)\left(\frac{r_B h_1 \omega}{r_C h_2 + r_B h_1}\right)\mathbf{j} + \left(\frac{r_B h_1 \omega}{r_C h_2 + r_B h_1}\right)\mathbf{k}$$

**20–11.** $\boldsymbol{\omega}_P = \{-40\mathbf{j}\}$ rad/s,
$\boldsymbol{\alpha} = \{-6400\mathbf{i}\}$ rad/s$^2$

**20–13.** $\boldsymbol{\omega} = \{4.35\mathbf{i} + 12.7\mathbf{j}\}$ rad/s,
$\boldsymbol{\alpha} = \{-26.1\mathbf{k}\}$ rad/s$^2$

**20–14.** $\mathbf{v}_A = \{-1.80\mathbf{i}\}$ m/s,
$\mathbf{a}_A = \{-0.720\mathbf{i} - 0.831\mathbf{k}\}$ m/s$^2$

**20–15.** $\mathbf{v}_A = \{-2.60\mathbf{i} + 2.40\mathbf{j} - 4.17\mathbf{k}\}$ m/s,
$\mathbf{a}_A = \{-7.44\mathbf{i} + 2.49\mathbf{j} - 9.27\mathbf{k}\}$ m/s$^2$

**20–17.** $\omega_A = 47.8$ rad/s, $\omega_B = 7.78$ rad/s

**20–18.** $\boldsymbol{\omega}_{BD} = \{-2.00\mathbf{i}\}$ rad/s

**20–19.** $\boldsymbol{\omega}_{BD} = \{-2.00\mathbf{i}\}$ rad/s,
$\boldsymbol{\alpha}_{BD} = \{34.5\mathbf{i}\}$ rad/s$^2$

**20–21.** $\mathbf{a}_B = \{-96.5\mathbf{i}\}$ cm/s$^2$

**20–22.** $v_B = 1.875$ m/s

**20–23.** $a_B = -6.57$ m/s$^2$

**20–25.** $\boldsymbol{\omega}_{BC} = \{0.769\mathbf{i} - 2.31\mathbf{j} + 0.513\mathbf{k}\}$ rad/s,
$\mathbf{v}_B = \{-0.333\mathbf{j}\}$ m/s

**20–26.** $\mathbf{v}_A = \{-2.50\mathbf{k}\}$ cm/s
$\mathbf{v}_C = \{4.33\mathbf{i} + 2.17\mathbf{j} - 2.50\mathbf{k}\}$ cm/s

**20–27.** $v_B = 4.71$ cm/s,
$\boldsymbol{\omega}_{AB} = \{1.17\mathbf{i} + 1.27\mathbf{j} - 0.779\mathbf{k}\}$ rad/s

**20–29.** $\boldsymbol{\omega} = \{1.50\mathbf{i} + 2.60\mathbf{j} + 2.00\mathbf{k}\}$ rad/s,
$\mathbf{v}_C = \{10.4\mathbf{i} - 7.79\mathbf{k}\}$ m/s

**20–30.** $\mathbf{a}_C = \{99.6\mathbf{i} - 117\mathbf{k}\}$ m/s$^2$,
$\boldsymbol{\alpha} = \{10.4\mathbf{i} + 30.0\mathbf{j} + 3\mathbf{k}\}$ rad/s$^2$

**20–31.** $\mathbf{v}_C = \{-1.00\mathbf{i} + 5.00\mathbf{j} + 0.800\mathbf{k}\}$ m/s,
$\mathbf{a}_C = \{-28.8\mathbf{i} - 5.45\mathbf{j} + 32.3\mathbf{k}\}$ m/s$^2$

**20–33.** $\mathbf{v}_A = \{5.20\mathbf{i} - 5.20\mathbf{j} - 3.00\mathbf{k}\}$ m/s,
$\mathbf{a}_A = \{25\mathbf{i} - 26.8\mathbf{j} + 8.78\mathbf{k}\}$ m/s$^2$

**20–34.** $\mathbf{v}_C = \{-6.75\mathbf{i} - 6.25\mathbf{j}\}$ m/s,
$\mathbf{a}_A = \{28.75\mathbf{i} - 26.25\mathbf{j} - 4\mathbf{k}\}$ m/s$^2$

**20–35.** $\mathbf{v}_B = \{-5.20\mathbf{i} + 5.64\mathbf{j} + 3\mathbf{k}\}$ m/s,
$\mathbf{a}_B = \{-5.73\mathbf{i} + 7.2\mathbf{j} - 2.6\mathbf{k}\}$ m/s$^2$

**20–37.** $\mathbf{v}_P = \{2\mathbf{i} + 20\mathbf{j}\}$ m/s,
$\mathbf{a}_P = \{-101\mathbf{i} - 14.8\mathbf{j}\}$ m/s$^2$

**20–38.** $\mathbf{v}_B = \{-10.2\mathbf{i} - 30\mathbf{j} + 52.0\mathbf{k}\}$ m/s,
$\mathbf{a}_B = \{-31.0\mathbf{i} - 161\mathbf{j} - 90\mathbf{k}\}$ m/s$^2$

**20–39.** $\mathbf{v}_B = \{-10.2\mathbf{i} - 28\mathbf{j} + 52.0\mathbf{k}\}$ m/s,
$\mathbf{a}_B = \{-33.0\mathbf{i} - 159\mathbf{j} - 90\mathbf{k}\}$ m/s$^2$

**20–41.** $\mathbf{v}_P = \{-25.5\mathbf{i} - 13.4\mathbf{j} + 20.5\mathbf{k}\}$ m/s,
$\mathbf{a}_P = \{161\mathbf{i} - 249\mathbf{j} - 39.6\mathbf{k}\}$ m/s$^2$

**20–42.** $\mathbf{v}_P = \{-25.5\mathbf{i} - 13.4\mathbf{j} + 20.5\mathbf{k}\}$ m/s,
$\mathbf{a}_P = \{161\mathbf{i} - 243\mathbf{j} - 33.9\mathbf{k}\}$ m/s$^2$

**20–43.** $\mathbf{v}_P = \{-0.849\mathbf{i} + 0.849\mathbf{j} + 0.566\mathbf{k}\}$ m/s,
$\mathbf{a}_P = \{-5.09\mathbf{i} - 7.35\mathbf{j} + 6.79\mathbf{k}\}$ m/s$^2$

**20–45.** $\mathbf{v}_C = \{2.80\mathbf{j} - 5.60\mathbf{k}\}$ m/s,
$\mathbf{a}_C = \{-56\mathbf{i} + 2.1\mathbf{j}\}$ m/s$^2$

**20–46.** $\mathbf{v}_C = \{2.80\mathbf{j} - 5.60\mathbf{k}\}$ m/s
$\mathbf{a}_C = \{-56\mathbf{i} + 2.1\mathbf{j} - 1.40\mathbf{k}\}$ m/s$^2$

**20–47.** $\mathbf{v}_A = \{-8.66\mathbf{i} + 2.26\mathbf{j} + 2.26\mathbf{k}\}$ m/s,
$\mathbf{a}_A = \{-22.6\mathbf{i} - 47.8\mathbf{j} + 4.53\mathbf{k}\}$ m/s$^2$

## Chapter 21

**21–2.** $I_{zz} = \dfrac{m}{12}(3a^2 + 4h^2)$

**21–3.** $I_y = 1\,089\,033$ kg·m$^2$

**21–5.** $I_y = 4.48(10^3)\rho$

**21–6.** $I_{yz} = \dfrac{m}{6}ah$

**21–7.** $I_{xy} = \dfrac{m}{12}a^2$

**21–9.** $I_{x'} = \dfrac{m}{12}(a^2 + h^2)$

**21–10.** $\begin{pmatrix} \frac{2}{3}ma^2 & \frac{1}{4}ma^2 & \frac{1}{4}ma^2 \\ \frac{1}{4}ma^2 & \frac{2}{3}ma^2 & -\frac{1}{4}ma^2 \\ \frac{1}{4}ma^2 & -\frac{1}{4}ma^2 & \frac{2}{3}ma^2 \end{pmatrix}$

**21–11.** $I_x = 4.50$ kg·m$^2$, $I_y = 4.38$ kg·m$^2$,
$I_z = 0.125$ kg·m$^2$

**21–13.** $\bar{y} = 0.15$ m, $\bar{x} = -0.20$ m
$I_{x'} = 0.134$ kg·m$^2$,
$I_{y'} = 0.0765$ kg·m$^2$,
$I_{z'} = 0.210$ kg·m$^2$

**21–14.** $I_{z'} = 0.0595$ kg·m$^2$

**21–15.** $I_x = 4.71$ kg·m$^2$

**21–17.** $I_{aa} = 7405$ kg·m$^2$

**21–18.** $I_z = 0.429$ kg·m$^2$

**21–19.** $I_z = 5248.6$ kg·m$^2$,
$I_x = I_y = 6504.4$ kg·m$^2$

**21–23.** $\omega_{OB} = 15.1$ rad/s

**21–25.** $T_2 = 0.904$ J

**21–26.** $T = \dfrac{9mh^2}{20}\left[1 + \dfrac{r^2}{6h^2}\right]\omega^2$

**21–27.** $h = 0.612$ m

**21–29.** $H_A = 26.9$ kg·m$^2$/s

**21–30.** $v_G = \{-5.6\mathbf{k}\}$ m/s

**21–31.** $\omega_y = 26.2$ rad/s

**21–33.** $\omega_2 = 9.67$ rad/s

**21–34.** $\omega_2 = 10.46$ rad/s

**21–35.** $\omega_{AB} = 21.4$ rad/s, the same

**21–37.** $\omega = 32.5$ rad/s

**21–38.** $\boldsymbol{\omega} = \{0.0536\mathbf{i} + 0.0536\mathbf{k}\}$ rad/s

**21–39.** For the **i** component:
$$\Sigma M_x = \frac{d}{dt}(I_x\omega_x - I_{xy}\omega_y - I_{xz}\omega_z) -$$
$$\Omega_z(I_y\omega_y - I_{yz}\omega_z - I_{yx}\omega_x) +$$
$$\Omega_y(I_z\omega_z - I_{zx}\omega_x - I_{zy}\omega_y)$$

**21–42.** $F_A = 277$ N, $F_B = 166$ N

**21–43.** $F_A = 213$ N, $F_B = 128$ N

**21–45.** $A_x = -19.62$ N, $A_y = -2.16$ N
$B_x = 19.62$ N,
$B_y = -21.81$ N

**21–46.** $\theta = \cos^{-1}\left(\dfrac{3g}{2L\omega^2}\right)$

**21–47.** $F_A = 41.7$ N, $F_B = 154.5$ N

**21–49.** $D_y = -12.9$ N, $\dot{\omega}_z = 200$ rad/s$^2$,
$D_x = -37.5$ N, $C_x = -37.5$ N,
$C_y = -11.1$ N, $C_z = 36.8$ N

**21–50.** $\dot{\omega}_y = 25.9$ rad/s$^2$, $B_x = -0.0791$ N,
$B_z = 12.3$ N, $A_x = -1.17$ N,
$A_z = 12.3$ N

**21–51.** $B_y = -133.3$ N, $B_x = -12.5$ N
$A_x = -15.6$ N, $A_y = -1966.7$ N
$A_z = 490.5$ N

**21–53.** $T = 7550$ N·m

**21–54.** $\Sigma M_x = 0$,
$\Sigma M_y = (-0.036 \sin\theta)$ N·m,
$\Sigma M_z = (0.003 \sin 2\theta)$ N·m

**21–55.** $M_z = -0.9\omega^2$ mN·m

**21–57.** $\dot{\omega}_y = -102$ rad/s$^2$, $A_x = B_x = 0$,
$A_y = 0$,
$A_z = 297$ N, $B_z = -143$ N

**21–58.** $A_x = 0$, $A_y = 23.63$ N, $A_z = 26.78$ N
$M_x = -12.39$ N·m, $M_y = 0$, $M_z = 0$

**21–59.** $\theta_D = 139°$, $m_D = 0.661$ kg, $\theta_F = 40.9°$,
$m_F = 1.32$ kg

**21–62.** $\alpha = 90°$, $\beta = 135°$, $\gamma = 45°$; no

**21–63.** a) $A_y = 1.49$ kN, $B_y = 2.43$ kN,
b) $A_y = -1.24$ kN, $B_y = 5.17$ kN,

**c)** $A_y = 1.49$ kN, $B_y = 2.43$ kN

**21–65.** $\omega = 3.57$ rad/s

**21–66.** $M_x = 27.0$ N·m

**21–67.** $M_x = 400$ N·m, $M_y = 0$, $M_z = 0$

**21–69.** $\dot{\phi} = \left(\dfrac{2g \cot \theta}{a + r \cos \theta}\right)^{1/2}$

**21–70.** $\omega_p = 0.365$ rad/s (low precession),
$\omega_p = 77.1$ rad/s (high precession)

**21–71.** $\omega_p = 0.363$ rad/s

**21–73.** $\omega_R = 368$ rad/s

**21–74.** $\Delta F = 53.4$ N

**21–77.** $\dot{\phi} = 23.3$ rad/s

**21–78.** $H_G = 17.2$ Mg·m²/s

**21–79.** $\dot{\phi} = 12.8$ rad/s

**Chapter 22**

**22–1.** $\tau = 0.201$ rad/s, $f = 4.985$ Hz

**22–2.** $x = -0.05 \cos(12.2t)$ m

**22–3.** $f = 7.88$ Hz, $\tau = 0.127$ s

**22–5.** $f = 3.18$ Hz, $C = 25$ mm
$y = (0.025 \cos 19.7t)$ m

**22–6.** $y = (-0.424 \sin (14.14t) -$
$0.050 \cos (14.14t))$ m,
$C = 0.427$ m

**22–7.** $x = -0.0693 \sin(5.77t) - 0.075 \cos(5.77t)$,
$C = 0.102$ m

**22–9.** $f = \dfrac{1}{\pi}\sqrt{\dfrac{k}{m}}$

**22–10.** $\theta = -0.101 \sin(4.95t) + 0.3 \cos(4.95t)$

**22–11.** $f = 2.52$ Hz, $T_{\max} = 83.7$ kN

**22–13.** $\tau = 2\pi\sqrt{\dfrac{k_G^2 + d^2}{gd}}$

**22–14.** $\tau = 2\pi\sqrt{\dfrac{2r}{g}}$

**22–15.** $\tau = 2.13$ s

**22–17.** $\theta = 0.4 \cos(11.55t)$

**22–18.** $\tau = 0.164$ s

**22–19.** $k_G = 0.627$ m, $d = 146$ mm

**22–21.** $\tau = 1.27$ s

**22–22.** $\tau = 4.79$ s

**22–23.** $(I_{G_z})_C = 2.50(10^3)$ kg·m²

**22–25.** $f = 0.367$ Hz

**22–26.** $\tau = 2\pi\sqrt{\dfrac{k_G^2 + d^2}{gd}}$

**22–27.** $\tau = 2.13$ s

**22–29.** $\tau = 0.727$ s

**22–30.** $\tau = 2\pi\sqrt{\dfrac{m}{3k}}$

**22–31.** $\ddot{x} + 333x = 0$

**22–33.** $\tau = 0.339$ s

**22–34.** $\tau = 2.757$ s

**22–35.** $\tau = 3.85\sqrt{\dfrac{m}{k}}$

**22–37.** $\tau = \dfrac{4\pi}{\sqrt{3}}\left(\dfrac{ma}{5ka + mg}\right)^{\frac{1}{2}}$

**22–38.** $f = 1.01$ Hz

**22–39.** $f = 2.25$ Hz

**22–41.** $c = 18.9$ N·s/m

**22–42.** $v_{max} = 1.0$ m/s

**22–43.** $y = (-3.66 \sin 12.25t$
$+ 50 \cos 12.25t + 11.2 \sin 4t)$ mm

**22–45.** $(x_P)_{\max} = 29.5$ mm

**22–46.** $\tau_d = 0.666$ s

**22–47.** $y = (361 \sin 7.75t$
$+ 100 \cos 7.75t - 350 \sin 8t)$ mm

**22–49.** $(x_p)_{\max} = 29.86$ mm

**22–50.** $(x_p)_{\max} = 14.6$ mm

**22–51.** $(x_p)_{\max} = 35.5$ mm

**22–53.** $C = 1.47$ m

**22–54.** $\omega = 21.44$ rad/s

**22–55.** $x_p = (0.00928 \sin 2t)$ m

**22–57.** $y = 0.801 \,|e^{-0.262t} \sin(5.108t + 1.52)|$ m

**22–58.** $\phi' = 32.81°$

**22–59.** MF $= 0.960$

**22–61.** $y = (-0.0702e^{-3.57t} \sin 8.54t)$ m

**22–63.** $L\ddot{q} + R\dot{q} + \dfrac{1}{C}q = 0$

**22–65.** $\ddot{y} + 16\dot{y} + 12y = 0$
is overdamped.

**22–66.** $t = 3.99$ s

**Review Problems 1**

**R1–1.** $t_{min} = 23.8$ s
**R1–2.** $y = 0.0208x^2 + 0.333x$
**R1–3.** $v_B = 16.8$ m/s, $v_A = 8.4$ m/s
**R1–5.** $v = 13.4$ m/s
**R1–6.** **a)** $t = 1.07$ s, **b)** $v_{A/B} = 5.93$ m/s $\rightarrow$
**R1–7.** $t = 5$ s

**R1–9.** $a = 0.343$ m/s², $a = 0.436$ m/s²

**R1–10.** $y = 3 \ln\left(\dfrac{\sqrt{x^2 + 4} + x}{2}\right)$

**R1–11.** $v_B = 1$ m/s $\uparrow$, $v_{B/C} = 4$ m/s $\uparrow$

**R1–13.** $s = 1.84$ m

**R1–14.** $s = 980$ m

**R1–15.** $P = 946$ kW

**R1–17.** $v = 4.38$ m/s

**R1–18.** $x = 25.9$ cm

**R1–19.** $v_B = 10.4$ m/s

**R1–21.** $(v_B)_2 = 0.575$ m/s, $71.5° \searrow$,
$\Delta T = -6.18$ J

**R1–22.** $a = 29.0$ m/s²

**R1–23.** $v_B = 0.5$ m/s $\uparrow$

**R1–25.** $(v_A)_{min} = 0.838$ m/s,
$(v_A)_{max} = 1.76$ m/s

**R1–26.** $v = 1.04$ m/s

**R1–27.** $v = 9.29$ m/s

**R1–29.** $a = 322$ m/s², $26.6° \measuredangle$

**R1–30.** $F = 38.5$ N

**R1–31.** $s = 20.2$ m

**R1–33.** $N_s = 1199$ N

**R1–34.** $v_B = 15.2$ m/s

**R1–35.** $e = 0.901$

**R1–37.** $v_2 = 7.63$ m/s

**R1–38.** $T = 158$ N

**R1–39.** $s = 20.0$ m

**R1–41.** $v_A = 8.34$ m/s $\downarrow$

**R1–42.** $t' = 27.3$ s

**R1–43.** $P_i = 45$ kW

**R1–45.** **a)** $a_B = a_A = 0.857$ m/s²
**b)** $a_A = 2.94$ m/s², $a_B = 1.18$ m/s²

**R1–46.** $s = 0.933$ m

**R1–47.** $v_2 = 31.7$ m/s

**R1–49.** $v_2 = 6.86$ m/s

**R1–50.** $a_A = 0.755$ m/s², $a_B = 1.51$ m/s²,
$T_A = 90.6$ N,
$T_B = 45.3$ N

**R1–51.** $v = 2.10$ m/s

**Review Problems 2**

**R2–1.** $\alpha_A = 12.5$ m/s² $\leftarrow$

**R2–2.** $v_W = 7.13$ m/s, $a_W = 0.13$ m/s²

**R2–3.** $\omega = 28.6$ rad/s, $\theta = 24.1$ rad,
$v_P = 7.16$ m/s,
$a_P = 205$ m/s$^2$

**R2–5.** $h = 1.80$ m

**R2–6.** $\omega = 0.275$ rad/s, $\alpha = 0.0922$ rad/s$^2$

**R2–7.** **a)** $C_y = 7.22$ N, $B_y = 7.22$ N,
**b)** $C_y = 14.7$ N, $B_y = 14.7$ N

**R2–9.** $v_C = 25.3$ cm/s, 63.4° ∠,
$a_C = 73.8$ cm/s$^2$, 32.5° ⬎

**R2–10.** $\alpha = 8.89$ rad/s$^2$

**R2–11.** $\omega = 25.0$ rad/s

**R2–13.** $v = -r\omega \sin \theta$, $a = -r\omega^2 \cos \theta$

**R2–14.** $a_A = 17.86$ m/s$^2$

**R2–15.** $a = \dfrac{s}{2\pi}\omega^2$

**R2–17.** $v = 4.78$ m/s

**R2–18.** $\theta = \tan^{-1}\left[\dfrac{\mu(k_O^2 + r^2)}{k_O^2}\right]$

**R2–19.** $d = 7.92$ m

**R2–21.** $T = 218$ N, $\alpha = 21.0$ rad/s$^2$

**R2–22.**
$$v = -r_1\omega \sin \theta - \frac{r_1^2\omega \sin 2\theta}{2\sqrt{(r_1 + r_2)^2 - (r_1 \sin \theta)^2}}$$

**R2–23.** $L = 7111$ kg·m$^2$

**R2–25.** $v_B = 0.860$ m/s

**R2–26.** $a_B = 8.00$ m/s$^2$ ↑

**R2–27.** $\alpha = 8$ rad/s$^2$, $F = 150$ N

**R2–29.** $\omega = 656$ rad/s

**R2–30.** $\omega = 120.2$ rad/s

**R2–31.** $P = 240$ N, $a_G = 0.981$ m/s$^2$
$N_B = 146.7$ N,
$N_A = 653.3$ N

**R2–33.** $B_y = 180$ N, $A_y = 252$ N, $A_x = 139$ N

**R2–34.** $B_y = 143$ N, $A_y = 200$ N, $A_x = 34.3$ N

**R2–35.** 14.2 rad/s$^2$

**R2–37.** $F_C = 61.2$ N, $N_B' = 15.4$ kN
$N_A' = 6.57$ kN, $F_A' = 336.4$ N

**R2–38.** $\omega_A = 3.47$ rad/s, $\omega_B = 10.4$ rad/s

**R2–39.** $E_x = 3177$ N, $E_y = 2908$ N
$M_E = 4362$ N·m

**R2–41.** $F_B' = 4.50$ kN, $N_A' = 1.78$ kN,
$N_B' = 5.58$ kN

**R2–42.** 1.41 m/s$^2$, 1.38 m/s$^2$

**R2–43.** $N_A' = 383$ N, $N_B' = 620$ N

**R2–45.** $\alpha_A = 17.81$ m/s$^2$ ↓, $\alpha_B = 12.66$ m/s$^2$
50.8° ⬈

**R2–46.** 39.2°

**R2–47.** 2.26 m/s$^2$, $N_B = 226$ N, $N_A = 559$ N,
$N_B = 454$ N

**R2–49.** 0.661 m

**R2–50.** 0.859 m

**R2–51.** 3.46 m/s

# Index

# Geometric Properties of Line and Area Elements

| Centroid Location | Centroid Location | Area Moment of Inertia |
|---|---|---|

### Centroid Location

$$L = 2\theta r$$

$$\frac{r \sin \theta}{\theta}$$

Circular arc segment

### Centroid Location

$$A = \theta r^2$$

$$\frac{2}{3} \frac{r \sin \theta}{\theta}$$

Circular sector area

### Area Moment of Inertia

$$I_x = \tfrac{1}{4} r^4 (\theta - \tfrac{1}{2} \sin 2\theta)$$

$$I_x = \tfrac{1}{4} r^4 (\theta + \tfrac{1}{2} \sin 2\theta)$$

---

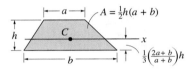

$$L = \tfrac{\pi}{2} r \qquad \frac{2r}{\pi} \qquad L = \pi r$$

Quarter and semicircle arcs

$$A = \tfrac{1}{4} \pi r^2$$

$$\frac{4r}{3\pi}$$

$$\frac{4r}{3\pi}$$

Quarter circle area

$$I_x = \tfrac{1}{16} \pi r^4$$

$$I_y = \tfrac{1}{16} \pi r^4$$

---

$$A = \tfrac{1}{2} h(a + b)$$

$$\tfrac{1}{3}\left(\frac{2a + b}{a + b}\right) h$$

Trapezoidal area

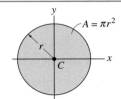

$$A = \frac{\pi r^2}{2}$$

$$\frac{4r}{3\pi}$$

Semicircular area

$$I_x = \tfrac{1}{8} \pi r^4$$

$$I_y = \tfrac{1}{8} \pi r^4$$

---

$$\tfrac{2}{5} a$$

$$A = \tfrac{2}{3} ab$$

$$\tfrac{3}{8} b$$

Semiparabolic area

$$A = \pi r^2$$

Circular area

$$I_x = \tfrac{1}{4} \pi r^4$$

$$I_y = \tfrac{1}{4} \pi r^4$$

---

$$A = \tfrac{1}{3} ab$$

$$\tfrac{3}{10} b$$

$$\tfrac{3}{4} a$$

Exparabolic area

$$A = bh$$

$$I_x = \tfrac{1}{12} bh^3$$

$$I_y = \tfrac{1}{12} hb^3$$

Rectangular area

---

$$A = \tfrac{4}{3} ab$$

$$\tfrac{2}{5} a$$

Parabolic area

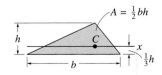

$$A = \tfrac{1}{2} bh$$

$$\tfrac{1}{3} h$$

$$I_x = \tfrac{1}{36} bh^3$$

Triangular area

# Center of Gravity and Mass Moment of Inertia of Homogeneous Solids

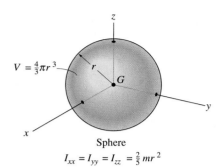

$V = \frac{4}{3}\pi r^3$

Sphere

$I_{xx} = I_{yy} = I_{zz} = \frac{2}{5}mr^2$

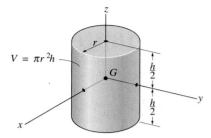

$V = \pi r^2 h$

Cylinder

$I_{xx} = I_{yy} = \frac{1}{12}m(3r^2 + h^2) \quad I_{zz} = \frac{1}{2}mr^2$

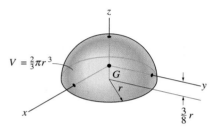

$V = \frac{2}{3}\pi r^3$

Hemisphere

$I_{xx} = I_{yy} = 0.259mr^2 \quad I_{zz} = \frac{2}{5}mr^2$

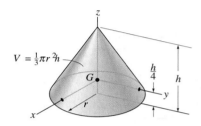

$V = \frac{1}{3}\pi r^2 h$

Cone

$I_{xx} = I_{yy} = \frac{3}{80}m(4r^2 + h^2) \quad I_{zz} = \frac{3}{10}mr^2$

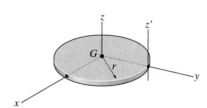

Thin Circular disk

$I_{xx} = I_{yy} = \frac{1}{4}mr^2 \quad I_{zz} = \frac{1}{2}mr^2 \quad I_{z'z'} = \frac{3}{2}mr^2$

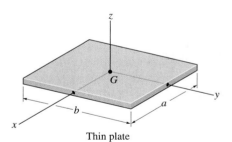

Thin plate

$I_{xx} = \frac{1}{12}mb^2 \quad I_{yy} = \frac{1}{12}ma^2 \quad I_{zz} = \frac{1}{12}m(a^2 + b^2)$

Thin ring

$I_{xx} = I_{yy} = \frac{1}{2}mr^2 \quad I_{zz} = mr^2$

Slender Rod

$I_{xx} = I_{yy} = \frac{1}{12}m\ell^2 \quad I_{x'x'} = I_{y'y'} = \frac{1}{3}m\ell^2 \quad I_{z'z'} = 0$